Jousting in Medieval and Renaissance Iberia

Jousting was for some 500 years the major spectator sport in western Europe. And yet, despite its enormous popularity in the Middle Ages and the Renaissance, very little is known about its practicalities. How was the score determined and kept? How and why did jousting armour evolve, how effective was it, and how did it differ from the field armour worn by knights in battle? What constituted technical virtuosity in the lists? And why did jousting die out?

This book uses previously untapped Iberian source material to provide answers to such questions. It focuses on three jousting manuals, written by practising champions at the time: Ponç de Menaguerra's *Lo Cavaller* ('The Knight', 1493); Juan Quijada de Reayo's *Doctrina del arte de la cavalleria* ('Doctrine of the Art of Chivalry', 1548); and Luis Zapata's *Del Justador* ('On the Jouster', c. 1589–93). As well as editions, with the first English translation, of these important texts, it includes introductions and an analytical study; there are also chapters on the arms and armour of the joust. Nearly 200 colour and black-and-white illustrations, many never previously published, illuminate the sometimes complex technical terminology of these authors, and provide further evidence of how weapons and armour were actually used.

NOEL FALLOWS is Professor of Spanish and Associate Dean, University of Georgia.

Armour and Weapons

ISSN 1746-9449

Series Editors

Kelly DeVries
Robert W. Jones
Robert C. Woosnam-Savage

Throughout history armour and weapons have been not merely the preserve of the warrior in battles and warfare, but potent symbols in their own right (the sword of chivalry, the heraldic shield) representing the hunt and hall as well as the battlefield. This series aims to provide a forum for critical studies of all aspects of arms and armour and their technologies, from the end of the Roman Empire to the dawn of the modern world; both new research and works of synthesis are encouraged.

New proposals for the series are welcomed; they should be sent to the publisher at the address below.

Boydell & Brewer Limited
PO Box 9
Woodbridge, Suffolk, IP12 3DF
editorial@boydell.co.uk

Previously published titles in the series
are listed at the back of this volume

Noel Fallows

Jousting in Medieval and Renaissance Iberia

THE BOYDELL PRESS

First published 2010
The Boydell Press, Woodbridge
Paperback edition 2024

ISBN 978-1-84383-594-3 hardback
ISBN 978-1-83765-159-7 paperback

The Boydell Press is an imprint of Boydell & Brewer Ltd
PO Box 9, Woodbridge, Suffolk IP12 3DF, UK
and of Boydell & Brewer Inc.
668 Mt Hope Avenue, Rochester, NY 14620–2731, USA
website: www.boydellandbrewer.com

The publisher has no responsibility for the continued existence or accuracy
of URLs for external or third-party internet websites referred to in this book,
and does not guarantee that any content on such websites is,
or will remain, accurate or appropriate

A CIP catalogue record for this book is available
from the British Library

Designed and typeset in Adobe Jenson Pro by
David Roberts, Pershore, Worcestershire

Contents

Illustrations

Maps

Figures

Facsimile

Woodcut decorations

To Sydney Anglo

Preface

T HIS book is aimed as much at the general reading community as it is at the specialist academic community. I hope that it will also be of use to practising jousting enthusiasts. Given that I myself have never jousted and the most I could probably hope for in a re-enactment would be to play the role of a nefarious chicken thief, I only hope that I do the sport and the technical manuals the justice that is their due, and that die-hard jousting enthusiasts enjoy the read as much as the general reader and my colleagues in the sedentary world of academe. Reviews submitted to internet sites and scholarly journals will be the judge of my success in accommodating these different audiences.

For the general reader's benefit, quotations are translated into English in the body of the text and for the specialist's interest the original language is provided in a footnote. Whenever possible I have used published translations; if none is indicated in the notes, this means that the translation is my own. In some instances, even when a published translation is available, I have translated the quotation myself, usually in order to capture some technical nuance or other. In order to avoid redundancy I have not included the original language in a footnote when quoting from the texts edited and translated in Part II. In the case of book titles, when applicable I translate the title into English the first time it is mentioned; I subsequently cite the title in the original language only.

When possible I have provided available details from published catalogues about the weights and measurements of original artefacts. This issue is complicated by the fact that some items have been weighed and measured by judicious curators during the cataloguing process and others have not. Those that have not are often inaccessible in that they are displayed under glass and can only be taken out at great cost or inconvenience to the museum. In a similar vein, regarding the illustrations, the Real Armería in Madrid generously responded to my steady stream of requests for images, but for various reasons could not authorise reproduction of any of the garnitures in the collection belonging to Charles V or Philip II. This situation has not adversely affected the illustration of this particular book for two reasons: firstly, taking into account that Charles, Philip and other wealthy noblemen of the time who could afford high-quality armour were global citizens, chronological precision is of much more importance than the national origin of the wearer; and secondly, it has meant that I have been quite felicitously compelled to seek out lesser-known but equally

important armours in other museums, images of which in some cases have never been published before.

Finally, following the lead of other scholars of arms and armour, throughout this book I have avoided a term coined by nineteenth-century collectors: 'suit of armour'. Since practising knights in the Middle Ages and the Renaissance described their kit as an 'armour', a 'harness' or a 'garniture', these are the terms I have preferred to use in my own descriptions.

Acknowledgements

COMPLETION of this book would have been impossible without the unfailing kindness and generosity of family, friends, colleagues and institutions.

Over the past fifteen years or so I have benefited from the counsel and inspiration of the person to whom this book is dedicated, Professor Emeritus Sydney Anglo. We first discussed the treatises of Ponç de Menaguerra and Juan Quijada de Reayo in letters and telephone conversations in the early 1990s. More recently Professor Anglo read a draft of my translation of *Lo Cavaller* and sent via e-mail detailed comments and suggestions for improvement. I feel fortunate to consider him a colleague, a mentor and a friend.

A gargantuan debt of gratitude is owed to Dr Tobias Capwell, formerly Curator of Arms and Armour at Glasgow Museums and currently Curator of Arms and Armour at The Wallace Collection in London, who allowed me open access to the vast collections of armour and books in the R. L. Scott Collection and The Wallace Collection, respectively. Toby then went above and beyond the call of duty not only by agreeing to read and critique drafts of my translations and various chapters of the introductory study, but also by patiently answering my many technical questions, openly sharing his encyclopaedic, unrivalled theoretical and practical knowledge about arms, armour and the joust, and arranging photography of numerous items of importance for my project. Over the years we have enjoyed talking for hours about armour and sharing information via e-mail, on the telephone and in person in Glasgow, London and Athens, GA. May our friendship and collaborations continue long into the future.

I am also indebted to Mr Donald J. LaRocca, Curator of Arms and Armour at The Metropolitan Museum of Art in New York, Ms Karen Watts, Senior Curator of Armour and Art at The Royal Armouries in Leeds and Dr Álvaro Soler del Campo, Director of the Real Armería in Madrid. It was a true thrill when, during my visits to The Metropolitan Museum, Don LaRocca would wheel out what looked suspiciously like a dessert trolley except for the fact that it was garnished with weapons and pieces of armour for inspection and discussion. He also agreed to read some excerpts of my work, offering insightful comments and clarifications. Similarly Karen Watts and I had the pleasure of exchanging ideas at the International Medieval Congress held in Leeds in July, 2008, at the session entitled 'Practice, Print, and Performance: Interpreting Jousts and Chivalric Spectacle in the Late Middle Ages', in which we both participated.

After the conference, during a visit to the Royal Armouries, Karen single-handedly opened up an enormous display case and allowed me to examine some extremely rare fifteenth-century pieces in the collection. Handling such items can best be described as akin to travelling in time, and is one of the great luxuries of being a medievalist. And finally, Álvaro Soler gave me a personal tour of the Real Armería and provided helpful suggestions in the early days of the project. As well as being hospitable all of these curators took the time to arrange special photography of items for my book.

For input and advice on a variety of issues I wish to thank the following family members, friends and colleagues: Ms Meghan Boenig (Head Coach, University of Georgia Women's Equestrian Team), Ms Allison Callaway (CC Farms, Winterville, Georgia), Dr Rafael Beltrán Llavador (University of Valencia), Dr Ivy Corfis (University of Wisconsin), Dr Steven Dworkin (University of Michigan), Mrs. Pat Fallows (Liverpool, UK), Dr Jeffrey L. Forgeng (Higgins Armory Museum), Dr José Manuel Fradejas Rueda (University of Valladolid), Dr Francisco Gago-Jover (College of the Holy Cross), Dr Marc Gener Moret (CSIC, Madrid), Mr Stephen Hick (Falls Church, Virginia), Dr Alexander Ibarz (University of Sheffield), Dr David Mackenzie (University College Cork), Dr Francisco Marcos Marín (University of Texas at San Antonio), Mr Ralph Moffat (Glasgow Museums), Dr John O'Neill (Hispanic Society of America, New York), Mr Keith Pope (Lapeer, Michigan), Dr Jesús Rodríguez-Velasco (Columbia University), Dr Joseph T. Snow (Michigan State University), Cr. Juan Martín Soria (Córdoba, Argentina), Dr Max Wheeler (University of Sussex) and Dr Roger Wright (University of Liverpool). For constructive comments and suggestions about the translations I must also thank my colleagues and students at the University of Georgia, Ms Nicole Babcock, Dr Dana Bultman, Dr Amélia Hutchinson, Dr Martin Kagel, Dr María Mizzi, Dr Jan Pendergrass, Dr Tom Peterson, Dr Max Reinhart, Dr Alexander Sager and Dr Elizabeth Wright. María Mizzi in particular played a key role in the early days of the Menaguerra translation. Mr Jeff Clippard, IT specialist in the Department of Romance Languages, responded to all of my computer-related questions with characteristic patience and good cheer.

I have received much assistance from a number of libraries and museums in the United States and Europe. As ever, I am grateful to the Interlibrary Loan Office at The University of Georgia, in particular to Ms Virginia Feher, for promptly fulfilling my requests for books and articles. I have been made to feel most welcome by the staff of the Biblioteca Nacional (Madrid), the Biblioteca de Palacio (Madrid), The British Library (London), The Hispanic Society of America (New York), the Instituto de Valencia de Don Juan (Madrid), The Kelvingrove Museum (Glasgow), The Metropolitan Museum of Art (New York), the Real Academia de la

Historia (Madrid), the Real Biblioteca de San Lorenzo de El Escorial and The Society of Antiquaries (London).

Research for this book was funded in part by a Junior Faculty Research Grant awarded by The Renaissance Society of America in 1997. This grant allowed me to lay the groundwork for the book by studying in various libraries in Madrid during the summer of that year. I have since then become a senior faculty member, my progress on the book having been delayed because I was elected Head of the Department of Romance Languages at The University of Georgia in 1998 and, in the midst of my third elected term, was appointed Associate Dean in UGA's Franklin College of Arts and Sciences in October, 2007. In both of these positions I have benefited enormously from a research account provided by Dr Wyatt W. Anderson and Dr Garnett S. Stokes, former and current Deans, respectively, of the Franklin College of Arts and Sciences.

Last but not least I would like to thank my wife, Kristin M. Pope – who verily outshines in beauty, intellect and dress-sense all of the comely damsels of the *Passo Honroso* and the tournament at Binche combined – for her constant support and encouragement during this lengthy process.

It goes without saying that I alone am responsible for any remaining mistakes and misunderstandings in this book.

MAP I The Iberian Peninsula *c.* 1434

MAP 2 The Iberian Peninsula in the sixteenth century

~: PART I :~

Introductory Study

Introduction

THE joust appealed throughout its long history to knights across Western Europe and is one of the first tangible manifestations of what today would be called preparation to compete in a global society. Thus the overarching subject of this book is of necessity the joust in medieval and renaissance Europe, but, as the title indicates, the perspective from which the subject is approached is Iberian. The late fourteenth century, when the lance-rest was introduced, through the late sixteenth century, when jousting gradually went out of fashion in the Iberian Peninsula, will be my approximate chronological boundaries.

One of the advantages of studying the joust from the Iberian perspective is that a number of informative treatises focus exclusively or partially on theories and techniques of the sport. They are as follows: King Alfonso XI of Castile and Leon, *Libro de la Orden de la Banda* (Book of the Order of the Band), 1330;[1] King Duarte I of Portugal, *Livro da ensinança de bem cavalgar toda sella* (Book of Instruction for Riding Well on All Saddles), c. 1434;[2] Ponç de Menaguerra, *Lo Cavaller* (The Knight), 1493; Juan Quijada de Reayo, *Doctrina del arte de la cavallería* (Doctrine of the Art of Chivalry), 1548; and Luis Zapata de Chaves, 'Del Justador' (On the Jouster), a chapter which forms part of a much larger work called *Miscelánea, o Varia historia* (Miscellany, or Varied History), composed between the years 1589 and 1593.

As stated by Ponç de Menaguerra, an issue that had to be taken into account when royals jousted against non-royals was that no matter how poorly the royals performed they always had to win.[3] With this bias in

---

[1] The Order of the Band was a monarchical order of knighthood, the statutes of which are said to have been composed by King Alfonso XI in 1330. The last two statutes of the Order are about tourneys and jousts, respectively. The statutes were subsequently incorporated verbatim into Alonso de Cartagena's *Doctrinal de los caballeros* (c. 1444). The most accessible editions are those of Ceballos-Escalera y Gila, *La orden y divisa de la Banda Real de Castilla*, and Cartagena, *Doctrinal de los caballeros*, in *Tratados Militares*, ed. Fallows, pp. 311–22.

[2] The standard edition in Portuguese is as follows: Duarte I, King of Portugal, *Livro da ensinança de bem cavalgar toda sela que fez El-Rey Dom Eduarte de Portogal e do Algarve e Senhor de Ceuta*, ed. Piel. A complete English translation is now available: *The Royal Book of Horsemanship, Jousting and Knightly Combat*, trans. Preto and Preto. A partial translation by Dr Amélia Hutchinson is included in Barber and Barker, *Tournaments*, pp. 197–205.

[3] See below, Part II, Ponç de Menaguerra, *Lo Cavaller*, ch. 14.

mind, and without disrespecting or entirely discounting the contributions of King Duarte I of Portugal and King Alfonso XI of Castile and Leon to our understanding of the joust, the primary emphasis in this book will be on the treatises written by and ostensibly for non-royals, that is, the treatises written by three practising jousters who were masters of the lance but amateurs of the pen: *Lo Cavaller* by Menaguerra; *Doctrina del arte de la cavallería* by Quijada de Reayo; and 'Del Justador' by Zapata. Critical editions of these three texts, with translations into English, are included in Part II.

In a book about jousting it is important not to use terms such as 'joust', 'tourney' and 'tournament' indiscriminately, since each was a distinct activity with its own history and evolution.[4] They are best clarified here in reverse order, beginning with the tournament. The mêlée tournament is defined by Tobias Capwell as follows:

> Today we think of a tournament as a competitive event with several groups and stages, but originally it had a much more specific meaning. The original tournaments were fought between teams of mounted knights. Each participant was armed with a sword or club, and the idea was simply to fight the other team until a halt was called.[5]

The mêlée tournament flourished in the twelfth century and eventually went out of style around the middle of the fourteenth century.[6] In a mêlée tournament, which would have taken place over a vast surface area, it would have been impossible to gauge accurately the performance of each and every contestant; hence *post facto* written accounts of the details could easily be manipulated and distorted without being impugned, especially in the case of high-ranking, wealthy contestants who had the wherewithal to pay for – and pay off – chroniclers and biographers who may not even have seen the event as it was taking place. The mêlée tournament has been described as a political arena, where at a basic level political agendas could be pushed and old scores could be settled, often by targeting a particular individual for a sound thrashing.[7] Because of the opportunities for being victimised by a gang of murderous knights, it would be wrong to assume

---

4 Other equestrian activities, such as the quintain and tilting at the ring, are beyond the scope of this book. These sports – in particular in France and Spain – are discussed at length by Clare, *La Quintaine, la course de bague et le jeu des têtes*, esp. pp. 11–167.

5 Capwell, *The Real Fighting Stuff*, p. 36.

6 Barber, *The Knight and Chivalry*, pp. 159–82; Barber and Barker, *Tournaments*, pp. 13–44; Barker, *The Tournament in England, 1100–1400*, pp. 4 and 13–16; Crouch, *Tournament*, p. 1; Norman, 'The Tournament', pp. 304–10.

7 On the tournament as political event, see especially Barber, *The Knight and Chivalry*, pp. 183–92, Barker, *The Tournament in England, 1100–1400*, pp. 45–69, and Barker and Keen, 'The Medieval English Kings and the Tournament'.

that every participant thoroughly enjoyed the mêlée tournament, and it seems reasonable to assume that at least some participated not because they wanted to but because they felt that they had to for social or political reasons. For these men, the bigger the tournament the better, since they could loiter at the periphery looking as though they were doing something, eschewing the violence whilst still maintaining a presence.

Even at their apogee in north-west Europe the mêlée tournaments were governed at best by rudimentary customary rules. An early set of rules allegedly dating to 938 for a tournament held at Magdeburg, for example, focuses exclusively on protocol, with emphasis on proof of lineage and protection of private property.[8] Centuries later, issues concerning planning, protocol and structure are discussed by René of Anjou, titular king of Jerusalem and Aragon, in his *Traicté de la forme et devis d'ung tournoy* (Treatise on the Form and Organisation of a Tournament), written *c.* 1460. In the wake of the preliminary histrionics the only rule of combat mentioned by King René is that: 'My lords the judges pray and require that none of you gentlemen tourneyers beat another with the point or back of the sword, nor below the belt, as you have promised, nor strike nor draw unless it is permitted; and also that none of you attack anyone whose helm falls off until he has put it on again.'[9] In the absence of standardised methods for quantification of performance or of clearly delineated opportunities for scoring, a typical large-scale mêlée tournament might consist of passive clusters of men who were there to be seen rather than to participate, counterbalanced by more sinister groups of men who desultorily pursued, ambushed, thwacked and cudgelled their victims.

The principal difference between the mêlée tournament and the tourney was one of spatial and numerical scale. Some confusion about the nomenclature of the tourney arises in medieval Castile which requires clarification. In *Las Siete Partidas* (The Seven Divisions), an extensive law code compiled during the reign of King Alfonso X of Castile (1221–84; ruled 1252–84), the term 'torneo' is used to refer to a real skirmish on the battlefield and the Alphonsine neologism 'torneamiento' is used to refer to the tourney with swords or

---

[8] These rules are translated into English by Nickel, 'The Tournament: An Historical Sketch', pp. 251–3. Cátedra, 'Fiestas caballerescas en tiempos de Carlos V', p. 96, has suggested that they are apocryphal.

[9] 'Messeigneurs les juges prient et requièrent entre vous messeigneurs les tournoyeurs, que nul ne frappe autre d'estoc ne de revers, ne depuis la sainture en bas, comme promis l'avez, ne ne boute ne tire, s'il n'est recommandé; et aussi que se d'aventure le heaulme cheoit à aucun de la teste, qu'on ne lui touche jusques ad ce qu'on le lui ait remis' (Anjou, *A Treatise on the Form and Organization of a Tournament*, ed. and trans. Bennett, pp. 18 and 17). On the evolution of tournament rules, see Barker, *The Tournament in England, 1100–1400*, pp. 140–5.

clubs.[10] As is so often the case with Alphonsine neologisms, however, the term 'torneamiento' did not take root beyond *Las Siete Partidas* and by the fourteenth and fifteenth centuries in Castile the noun 'torneo' was the standard term used to refer to both the tourney and the tournament.[11]

Documentary evidence concerning the rules of the tourney is rare. In the wake of *Las Siete Partidas*, not so much the rules *per se* as a series of questions about the types of issue that can arise are posed by Geoffroi de Charny in his *Demandes pour la joute, les tournois et la guerre* (Questions Concerning the Joust, Tournaments and War), composed *c.* 1350.[12] The most detailed set of practical rules for the medieval tourney is that contained in the statutes of the Order of the Band, which pre-date Charny by some twenty years. Since the *Libro de la Orden de la Banda* has never been translated into English the section on the rules of the tourney is worth quoting in full, as follows:

> We declare that the first thing that judges must do when knights should wish to begin a tourney, is to check that the swords they are carrying are not too sharp along the cutting edge or at the point, but rather that they are blunt. And they should likewise check that they have not sharpened the vervelles of the cervellieres.[13] Furthermore they should make all the knights swear an oath that they will under no circumstance strike with them in the face with the point or the flat of the blade. And furthermore, if anyone's cervelliere or helm should fall off, that he not be struck until he has put it back on. And furthermore, if anyone falls to the ground, that he not be trampled.
>
> Furthermore, the judges should tell them to begin the tourney at the sound of the trumpets and kettledrums, and when they hear the trumpet sound, they should step out and take their places. And

---

10 Alfonso X, *Las Siete Partidas*, II.xxvi.18, ed. Sánchez-Arcilla, p. 335. See also Barber and Barker, *Tournaments*, p. 91.

11 Such is the case, for example, in the fourteenth-century *Libro de la Orden de la Banda* and the fifteenth-century *Doctrinal de los caballeros*. See Cartagena, *Doctrinal de los caballeros*, in *Tratados Militares*, ed. Fallows, pp. 266 and 321. The plural noun 'fiestas' was also sometimes used to describe the tournament of this epoch.

12 This work is available in a bilingual edition. See Muhlberger, *Jousts and Tournaments: Charny and the Rules for Chivalric Sport in Fourteenth-Century France*. For Charny's questions about the tourney, see pp. 116–37.

13 In the 1330s the helmet used for tourneys would typically be a cervelliere with curved surfaces in order to deflect blows with swords or clubs. A mail aventail could be attached to the cervelliere by means of a series of staples, called vervelles, that were riveted down the sides of the face-opening and along the lower edge. Over the cervelliere a helm could also be worn. The fact that legislation was drafted in order to curb cheating indicates that the tactic of sharpening the vervelles with a view to puncturing or lacerating the opponent's hands was not uncommon.

furthermore, we declare that, if the tourney were large, with many knights, in which each side carries its own standards, and they have to grapple with each other in order to knock each other off their horses, the horses captured by the knights on each team should be led to the area where the standards are kept, and they should not be returned to the knights who lost them until the tourney is over.

And furthermore we declare that after the tourney is over, the judges must assemble and declare, in the name of the truth that they are sworn as judges to uphold, which knights in their opinion won the tourney, one from each side, so that they can give the prizes to the knights who performed the best on each side.

And if the tourney should involve thirty knights or less, we declare that there be four judges for one side and another four for the other side. And if it should involve fifty knights or more, let there be eight noble judges for one side and another eight for the other. And if the tourney should involve a hundred knights or more, let there be twelve judges for one side and another twelve for the other.[14]

As evinced from the rules above the tourney could take place between two contestants or between two teams of contestants and the rules that regulated the combat were quite basic, having hardly changed at all from Alfonso's rules of 1330 through René's large-scale tournament rules of 1460.

---

[14] 'Decimos que la primera cosa que deben los fieles hacer cuando los caballeros quisieren comenzar el torneo, que han a catar las espadas que no las traigan muy agudas en el tajo ni en la punta, sino que sean romas. Y eso mismo caten, que no traigan agudos los aros de las capellinas. Otrosí, que tomen jura a todos los caballeros que no den con ellas de puntas en ninguna guisa, ni de revés, a rostro. Y otrosí, si a alguno cayere la capellina o el yelmo, que no le den hasta que la ponga. Y otrosí, si alguno cayere en tierra, que no le atropellen. ❴ Otrosí, les han de dezir los fieles que comiencen el torneo cuando dieren las trompetas y los atabales, y cuando oyeren el añafil tañer, que se quiten afuera y se recojan cada uno a su parte. Y otrosí, decimos que, si el torneo fuere grande, de muchos caballeros, en que haya pendones de cada parte, y se hubieren a trabar los unos a los otros para derribarse de los caballos, que los [caballos] de los caballeros que fueren ganados de la una parte y de la otra que sean llevados a donde estuvieren los pendones, y que no sean dados a los caballeros que los perdieren hasta el torneo pasado. ❴ Y otrosí, decimos que desque fuere pasado el torneo, que se deben ayuntar todos los fieles y decir, por la verdad que son tenidos de decir como fieles, según su entendimiento, cuál caballero tuvo la mejoría del torneo, también de los de la una parte como de los de la otra, por que den prez a un caballero de la una y a otro de la otra que hallaren que anduvo allí mejor. ❴ Y si fuere el torneo de treinta caballeros ayuso, decimos que haya ahí cuatro fieles de la una parte y otros cuatro de la otra. Y si fuere de cincuenta caballeros, o dende arriba, que sean ocho caballeros fieles de la una parte y otros ocho de [la] otra. Y si fuere el torneo de cien caballeros o más, que sean doce fieles de la una parte y otros doce de la otra' (Cartagena, *Doctrinal de los caballeros*, in *Tratados militares*, ed. Fallows, p. 321).

1 *Tapisserie du Tournoi*, full view (see figs. 48 and 63 for details). Late 15th century. 497 × 579 cm (16 ft 4in × 19 ft)

Fig. 1 is a detailed depiction of a fifteenth-century tourney in progress in a tapestry known as the *Tapisserie du Tournoi* (Tapestry of the Tourney). This tapestry was ordered by Friedrich, Elector of Saxony in 1494 to celebrate a tournament organised in Antwerp during the establishment of Philip The Handsome (1478–1506; *jure uxoris* King of Castile, 1504–6) as governor.[15] It is a well-conceived snap-shot of knights scuffling in the haphazard manner that characterised the tourney.

Unlike the large-scale mêlée tournament and the smaller-scale tourney, the joust was limited to lance combat. It has been defined as follows by Capwell:

[15] On the history of this tapestry, see Hénault, 'La Tapisserie du "Tournoi" au Musée de Valenciennes', and *Chefs-d'œuvre de la tapisserie*, ed. Salet et al., pp. 72–5.

In a joust two mounted knights charged at each other with lances and attempted to strike each other as accurately and with as much force as possible. That was the game – a controlled way of experiencing armoured lance combat on horseback.[16]

Until the thirteenth century jousts with lances between two contestants served as preludes to or, in the words of one scholar, 'sideshows',[17] at the main event of the mêlée tournament. The thirteenth century marks the rise of the joust, for it is at this time that many knights disengaged from the madness that was the mêlée, preferring instead to compete with each other one on one. In the long term, jousting superseded the mêlée tournament in popularity, with the result that beyond the fourteenth century the tournament no longer focused primarily on the wide-ranging mêlée but was more of a 'happening' consisting of a variety of contained chivalric martial arts. In this new context, jousting, along with various types of foot combats, became a central sporting activity instead of a peripheral one. This was partly because jousts could be confined to much smaller sites than tournaments between teams, and they were much less disruptive to local communities than mêlée tournaments.[18] Also, developments in armour allowed for greater technical virtuosity with the lance. Mêlée tournaments were never as frequent in the Iberian Peninsula as they were elsewhere in Europe, and the enduring popularity of the joust in the region may perhaps be explained, on the one hand, by the opportunities for fighting in real battle throughout the Reconquest and, on the other, by the logistical difficulties of staging and publicising large-scale events within the amorphous and permeable political frontiers of the Christian kingdoms at the time of the Reconquest.

In the case of jousts, individual performance was paramount and every action and manoeuvre was closely scrutinised with a view to awarding points to each jouster. Attempts at cheating were seldom successful;[19] loss of composure at the crucial moment of impact was always embarrassingly obvious. Indeed, it was because all actions and manoeuvres were so visible – even more so in one-on-one jousts than in team events – that in order to accommodate protocol the special overtly biased rules had to be invented

---

[16] Capwell, *The Real Fighting Stuff*, pp. 33–4.

[17] Crouch, *Tournament*, p. 116. Similarly Barber, *The Knight and Chivalry*, p. 184, describes the joust at this time as an 'appendage' of the tournament, and Cripps-Day, *The History of the Tournament in England and in France*, p. 46, describes it as 'practice for the great mêlée'.

[18] Barber and Barker, *Tournaments*, p. 23; Crouch, *Tournament*, p. 119; Vale, 'Violence and the Tournament'.

[19] For example, see below, Part II, *Passo Honroso* Selections 10, 11 and 18, where certain knights in the jousts of the Pass of Honour of Suero de Quiñones are caught cheating.

for royal contestants, stating simply that they always had to win, no matter what. As we shall see, despite the deferential treatment of royalty, in so far as martial expertise was concerned, jousts simply had much more to offer than mêlée tournaments, for contestants and spectators alike.

From both a physical and a symbolic point of view jousts offered tangible evidence of a man's prowess, of the meaningful role that he played in the masculine active life and of his rejection of a life of sloth or recreance. The French poet Chrétien de Troyes (d. *c.* 1185) summarises this ethos in the following lapidary statement: 'No man can win fame by inactivity.'[20] At the highest political level, that of the monarchy, the masculine active life asserted itself during times of peace not only in the form of participation in tournaments, but also in the construction of buildings such as churches, monasteries and palaces, in the ability to play musical instruments and even in arduous — and not necessarily monogamous — love-making. In what has to be the most erotic jousting metaphor ever conceived, the fictitious knight Tirant lo Blanc's prowess in the enclosure is compared to his prowess in the bedroom as follows:

> The queen bade goodnight to all of her damsels and led the valorous Tirant to the side of his lady, who received him far more eagerly than on the previous night. Having placed them in the lists together, where they prepared to wage delightful battle, the queen went to bed, trusting that the combat would never stop. Tirant, like a valiant knight, did not sleep the whole night long, since whoever is constant in battle should be equally constant in bed.[21]

Tirant lo Blanc was composed *c.* 1460 by Joanot Martorell (1410–65) and published in Valencia in 1490, some twenty-five years after the author's death.[22] The ruling monarchs in Spain in the year 1490 were the self-styled 'Catholic Monarchs', Ferdinand of Aragon and Isabella of Castile.

---

20 'N'ai soing, fet il, de reposer; / ne s'en puet nus hom aloser'. See Chrétien de Troyes, *Yvain ou Le Chevalier au Lion*, ed. Nelson *et al.*, p. 206 lines 5097–8. For the translation, see *Yvain (The Knight with the Lion)*, in *Arthurian Romances*, trans. Owen, p. 349.

21 'La reyna donà comiat a totes les donzelles e féu lo valerós Tirant posar al costat de sa senyora, lo qual fon rebut ab major amor que la passada nit. E la reyna, aprés que·ls hagué posats dins la liça, concordes de la delitosa batalla, se n'anà a dormir, confiant que·s concordarien que jamés la batalla no vendria a fi'. See Martorell, *Tirant lo Blanch*, ed. Hauf, ch. 445, p. 1434. For the translation, see *Tirant lo Blanc*, trans. LaFontaine, p. 755.

22 Throughout this book I identify Martorell as the one and only author of *Tirant lo Blanc*. Due to a reference in the colophon of the first printed edition of *Tirant lo Blanc* scholars had assumed for well over a century that the book was begun by Joanot Martorell and finished by a certain Martí Joan de Galba. Recent scholarship, however, indicates that Galba was a loan shark to whom Martorell was forced,

Despite the sanctimonious sobriquet, King Ferdinand's sexual prowess with multiple partners, just like Tirant's, is duly affirmed by Hernando del Pulgar, the official chronicler of their reign: he is described in the same paragraph as a highly accomplished jouster, a loving husband and a man with many lovers.[23]

The fact that the technical lexicon of jousting lends itself to schoolboyish double-entendre with the result that it has been syntactically and symbolically affiliated with sexual proclivity is great fun, but it also dumbs down the complexities of this chivalric martial art.[24] When this dumbing down is conjoined with the fact that the theoretical manuals on jousting have received so little critical attention, it should come as no surprise that this activity tends to be largely misunderstood. Indeed, the extent of the scholarship which deals with the systematic analysis of European jousting manuals consists of one groundbreaking article and one groundbreaking book, both by Sydney Anglo.[25] One of the reasons why the scholarship in this emerging field of enquiry is so exiguous has been given by Anglo, who notes that: 'Renaissance Spanish texts on the martial arts pose technical problems which have scarcely been addressed by modern scholars.'[26] Similarly, in the case of the treatise composed in the Valencian dialect of medieval Catalan edited and translated in Part II below – Ponç de Menaguerra's *Lo Cavaller* – the Catalonian scholar Martín de Riquer, at the same time as he recognises the importance of this text, metaphorically throws up his hands in despair, lamenting the fact that: 'Unfortunately the Valencian Ponç de Menaguerra writes very shabbily, and much effort is required in order to be able to understand what he is trying to say.'[27] Both Anglo and Riquer are alluding primarily to the lack of unified technical vocabularies

tragically, to pawn his manuscript in order to pay off debts. See Beltrán, *Tirant lo Blanc, de Joanot Martorell*, pp. 15–24. For Martorell's birth and death dates, see also Beltrán, p. 15.

[23] 'Justaba sueltamente e con tanta destreza, que ninguno en todos sus Reynos lo facía mejor ... E comoquiera que amaba mucho a la Reyna su muger, pero dábase a otras mugeres' ('He jousted agilely and with such skill, that no-one in all his Kingdoms could do it better ... And even though he loved the Queen, his wife, a lot, he still surrendered himself to other women'). See Pulgar, *Crónica de los señores reyes católicos don Fernando y doña Isabel de Castilla y de Aragón*, ed. Rosell, p. 256b.

[24] The lexicon as it relates to sexual innuendo is discussed by Clare, *La Quintaine, la course de bague et le jeu des têtes*, pp. 158–63, and Macpherson and MacKay, 'Textiles and Tournaments'.

[25] See Anglo, 'Jousting – the earliest treatises' and Anglo, *The Martial Arts of Renaissance Europe*, esp. pp. 202–52.

[26] Anglo, *The Martial Arts of Renaissance Europe*, p. 5.

[27] 'Dissortadament el valencià Ponç de Menaguerra escriu de manera molt roïna, i cal fer esforços per a arribar a comprendre què vol dir'. See Riquer, *L'Arnès del cavaller*, p. 168. In fairness to Ponç de Menaguerra, other critics do praise the 'gentils

and the often circumstantial or elliptic descriptions that characterise the martial arts treatises of the time.

On a more optimistic note, while there is as yet no systematic treatment of jousting in Iberia, major contributions have been made to the various facets of chivalric culture which can provide the background to facilitate a more judicious comprehension of the Iberian jousting manuals. The first half of the twentieth century witnessed a particularly active period for the study of armour and tournaments spearheaded by a remarkable 'brother-hood' of gentlemen scholars who between them would lay the groundwork for subsequent research in these areas.[28] Mention must also be made of the post-war classic general study of armour that has yet to be surpassed: Claude Blair's *European Armour*. No other systematic treatments of Spanish arms and armour would be published until the early 1970s, when Ada Bruhn de Hoffmeyer published the first volume of her meticulous study of the evolution of arms and armour in medieval Iberia up to and including the fourteenth century. Her work has been followed by that of Álvaro Soler del Campo, whose 1993 book on the subject of Iberian arms and armour up to and including the fourteenth century is comple-mented by a shorter article published in 2006 which also touches upon the fifteenth century.[29] Similarly, Enrique de Leguina's indispensible *Glosario de voces de Armería* (1912) is now complemented by Francisco Gago-Jover's

paraules' ('elegant words') of the prologue. See Menaguerra, *Lo Cavaller*, ed. Janer et al., fol. IIIr.

[28] On arms and armour in general, see ffoulkes, *The Armourer and his Craft*, and ffoulkes, *Armour and Weapons*. On Spain, see Calvert, *Spanish Arms and Armour*, Cripps-Day, *Fragmenta Armamentaria*, vol. II: *Miscellanea*, part V: *An Inventory of the Armour of Charles V*, and Mann, 'Notes on the Armour worn in Spain from the tenth to the fifteenth Century'. On tournaments, see Clephan, *The Medieval Tournament*, and Cripps-Day, *The History of the Tournament in England and in France*. The group is referred to as a brotherhood by ffoulkes in his preface to Clephan, *The Medieval Tournament*, p. v. It must be borne in mind that passionate political views sometimes intrude into these early works of scholarship. Writing at the end of World War I, Cripps-Day manages to work into his discussion of the tournament a condemnation of a certain nameless nation which would 'desire … to steal the wealth of another' and which, he says, 'misleads democracy by an absolutely false use of the lofty ideal of patriotism'. This in contrast to another nation which succeeds 'by superior intelligence and industry in penetrating into the domain of the less intelligent, acquiring wealth and power … at the same time as it spreads nobler ideas and a higher culture'. See Cripps-Day, *The History of the Tournament in England and in France*, pp. 124–5. Writing in 1919 Clephan more openly states that: 'The Germans have always been wont to borrow the inventions and processes of other nations, and then often to cheapen them'. See Clephan, *The Medieval Tournament*, p. 38.

[29] Hoffmeyer, *Arms and Armour in Spain: A Short Survey*; Soler del Campo, *La evolución del armamento en el reino castellano-leonés y al-Andalus (siglos XII–XIV)*;

Vocabulario Militar Castellano (siglos XIII–XV) (2002).[30] And thanks to the admirable efforts of the Valencian based publishing house Librerías París-Valencia we now have easy access to a facsimile edition of the catalogue of the Spanish Royal Armoury prepared by the Conde viudo de Valencia de Don Juan in 1898.[31] Not to be outdone, the evolution of arms and armour in Catalonia has received extensive treatment in a study published by Martín de Riquer in 1968. Under Riquer's direction Victoria Cirlot wrote a doctoral dissertation on the same subject, parts of which have been published in journals and edited volumes.[32] In addition to these works on arms and armour, the vast corpus of medieval Castilian chivalric manuals has received the treatment it richly deserves in articles by Ángel Gómez Moreno and José Luis Martín and Luis Serrano-Piedecasas, as well as several comprehensive studies by Jesús D. Rodríguez Velasco.[33] Selections from much of the literature discussed in these analytical studies have been edited in anthologies by José María Viña Liste and Rodríguez Velasco and Carlos Heusch.[34]

Joachim K. Rühl and Évelyne van den Neste both lamented the 'considerable blanks in regard to the history of the tournament in Spain',[35] as reflected in *Das ritterliche Turnier im Mittelalter*, the collection of essays on the tournament in medieval Europe edited by Josef Fleckenstein in 1985. Some of these blanks have since been filled by a number of studies which address the socio-historical, political-propagandistic and cultural

and Soler del Campo, 'El armamento medieval hispano'. For the fifteenth and sixteenth centuries, see Blair, *European Armour*, pp. 77–142.

[30] The standard reference for armorial terms in English is Stone, *A Glossary of the Construction, Decoration and Use of Arms and Armour in All Countries and in All Times*. The *Glossarium Armorum*, ed. Gamber, also includes definitions in English and five other languages, but not Spanish.

[31] Valencia de Don Juan, *Catálogo Histórico-Descriptivo de la Real Armería de Madrid*.

[32] Riquer, *L'Arnès del cavaller*. Riquer also published a host of subsequent articles on arms and armour in medieval France and Iberia, many of which are now available in the following volume of his collected works on the subject: Riquer, *Caballeros medievales y sus armas*. Cirlot's unpublished doctoral dissertation is entitled *El armamento catalán de los siglos XI al XIV*. I cite some of the publications that resulted from this dissertation elsewhere in the present volume.

[33] Gómez Moreno, 'La caballería como tema en la literatura medieval española: tratados teóricos', Martín and Serrano-Piedecasas, 'Tratados de Caballería. Desafíos, justas y torneos', Rodríguez Velasco, *El debate sobre la caballería en el siglo XV*, and Rodríguez Velasco, 'Invención y consecuencias de la caballería'.

[34] Viña Liste, ed., *Textos medievales de caballerías*, and Heusch and Rodríguez Velasco, *La caballería castellana de la baja edad media: Textos y Contexos*.

[35] Rühl, 'German Tournament Regulations of the 15th Century', p. 167; Neste, *Tournois, joutes, pas d'armes dans les villes de Flandre à la fin du Moyen Âge (1300–1486)*, p. 3.

significance of tournaments in medieval and renaissance Spain.[36] Heavily armed with this substantial body of scholarship, my own task in this book is much less daunting than it would have been twenty or thirty years ago.

As far as my own theoretical approach is concerned, although *Lo Cavaller*, *Doctrina del arte de la cavallería* and 'Del Justador' are the central focus of my analysis, these texts must also be viewed simultaneously as a point of departure, for any discussion of a sport that is no longer officially sanctioned or practised[37] must necessarily rely on a wide variety of interdisciplinary supporting materials – literary, artistic and archaeological – in order to unlock the mysteries of both the joust and the Iberian masters' take on it.

In the fourteenth century, Don Juan Manuel – author, knight, politician and noble patron of the Dominican Order – listed a hierarchy of the most reliable texts for transmitting knowledge to future generations, from the Bible, the Decretum and Decretals, vernacular legal codes, scientific treatises, and books that describe 'great deeds and things that happened, which are called chronicles'.[38] With these words in mind, as far as literary materials are concerned, as a counterpoint to Menaguerra's, Quijada de Reayo's and Zapata's theoretical discussions of jousting I shall refer frequently in this book to one of the most detailed chronicles of jousting ever composed in medieval Europe, which just happens to be Iberian; Castilian, to be exact. Most chronicles stress the tabloid aspects of the jousts, such as accident, injury and death, as opposed to detailed explanations of rules, regulations and technique – with one notable exception, that is. This is a chronicle entitled *El Passo Honroso de Suero de Quiñones* (The Pass of Honour of Suero de Quiñones). The jousts and other events at this passage of arms were recorded in exquisite detail by Pero Rodríguez de Lena, who was both an eye-witness and the official chronicler of the

---

[36] See especially: Andrés Díaz, 'Las fiestas de caballería en la Castilla de los Trastámara'; Barber and Barker, *Tournaments*, pp. 91–102; Cátedra, *El sueño caballeresco*, esp. pp. 81–126; Cátedra, 'Fiestas caballerescas en tiempos de Carlos V'; Cátedra, 'Fiestas caballerescas: ideología y literatura en tiempos de Carlos V'; Flores Arroyuelo, 'El torneo caballeresco: De la preparación militar a la fiesta y representación teatral'; Ladero Quesada, *Las fiestas en la cultura medieval*, pp. 129–40; Ruiz, 'Fiestas, Torneos y Símbolos de realeza en la Castilla del siglo XV. Las fiestas de Valladolid de 1428'; and Ruiz-Domènech, 'El torneo como espectáculo en la España de los siglos XV–XVI'.

[37] It should be noted here that there are enthusiasts who still practise and study the joust, but not, of course, on the same scale as this sport was practised in the Middle Ages and the Renaissance.

[38] 'Los grandes fechos et cosas que pasaron a que llaman crónicas'. Juan Manuel, *Crónica abreviada*, ed. Blecua, p. 575.

event, which took place at the Orbigo Bridge in Leon from Saturday, 10 July, through Monday, 9 August 1434.[39]

Rodríguez de Lena was one of the more gifted chroniclers of his epoch. The reader is always conscious of his presence in his own chronicle, in which he performs two quite different tasks. On the one hand, he writes as the official chronicler. In this capacity his task is to 'retail' – as Anglo would put it[40] – the Pass of Honour of Suero de Quiñones, presenting a notarial reconstruction of the actual events that were judged by the two elected judges, Pero Barba and Gómez Arias de Quiñones, in accordance with the twenty-two Articles by which the passage of arms was regulated. On the other hand, as an eye-witness and one who was often standing at the judges' side when they conferred about official outcomes, he includes many details that are not mentioned in the official Articles and that had no effect whatsoever on the official outcome or judgement of the jousts, but that were of great interest to participants, spectators and fans. To cite but one example, Menaguerra notes that after making a successful encounter that shatters the lance, the length of the broken lance stave 'counts neither more nor less'.[41] This was a standard rule of the joust in medieval Iberia and the Pass of Honour of Suero de Quiñones was no exception. Rodríguez de Lena obviously knew this, and yet he persists in mentioning time and again the length of the broken shafts, undoubtedly because this detail was taken into account by many an enthusiastic participant and fan.

In rhetorical terms the technique of narrating in minute detail is known as hypotyposis. This technique serves three distinct purposes, all of which interact with each other simultaneously throughout the narrative. First and foremost, the details serve as a mechanism for enabling the chronicler, affording Rodríguez de Lena the opportunity to establish himself as a 'cultivator of the truth',[42] for he who wrote in such detail must certainly have been there and seen everything – this is certainly not a narrative twice-removed. It should be noted that some of the participants in the Pass of Honour of Suero de Quiñones exchanged letters with each other about their own performance and the performance of other competitors in the jousts at this event. These letters have been analysed by Martín de Riquer as a means of elucidating the political motivations of certain Catalonian challengers. In his analysis Riquer demonstrates that the letters complement and lend further credence to the official account by Rodríguez de

[39] For the location of the Orbigo Bridge, see Map I.

[40] Anglo, *The Martial Arts of Renaissance Europe*, p. 224.

[41] See below, Part II, Ponç de Menaguerra, *Lo Cavaller*, ch. 23.

[42] I borrow the term 'cultivator of the truth' ('cultorem ueritatis') from the fifteenth-century Castilian chronicler Alfonso de Palencia. See Palencia, *Gesta Hispaniensia ex annalibus suorum dierum collecta*, ed. and trans. Tate and Lawrance, p. 2.

Lena as to the events that actually took place.[43] Thus we can have confidence in the chronicler's veracity in this case.

Secondly, the technique of hypotyposis serves to facilitate Rodríguez de Lena's task of bridging the gaps from stage to page and between viewer and do-er, of cultivating the truth at the same time as he is presenting in written form what was at its core a fiction, but one in which jousting played a central role. The passage of arms witnessed by Rodríguez de Lena was, like many other medieval passages of arms, inspired by an emprise, a term that has been defined as follows: 'The word emprise literally means "enterprise, undertaking", but ... it has the connotation of "challenge". Emprise also referred to a specific set of commitments and rules.'[44] In the case of Suero de Quiñones, he and the nine other defenders of the passage of arms formally presented themselves at the court of King John II of Castile (1405–54; ruled 1406–54)[45] on New Year's Day, 1434, with a view to explaining the emprise which would take place six months later. It has been said that the medieval passage of arms provided knights with an opportunity to dramatise life,[46] and Suero was doing just that. He vowed to wear a large iron ring around his neck every Thursday, a gesture that was intended to represent a topos of the medieval sentimental romance, namely, that he was symbolically imprisoned by love. The only way he could be freed from captivity was by breaking 300 lances with fellow team-members against all comers. And let it be said that these jousts, in which seasoned jousters risked life and limb in the lists at the same time that they were acting out an amorous emprise invented by Suero de Quiñones, took place long before the exercise of jousting had 'degenerated into a ceremonial breaking of fragile lances'.[47]

Thirdly, since the people most likely to read Rodríguez de Lena's chronicle were the participants in the Pass of Honour of Suero de Quiñones, and since they did not have the luxury of being able to take a step back and watch themselves as they were actually jousting, the anatomical detail of the chronicler's narrative would allow them to perform a *post facto* dissection or autopsy of each and every joust. Thus in hypotyposis the chronicler is

---

[43] Riquer, ed., *Lletres de batalla*, vol. II, pp. 107–210; also Riquer, *Caballeros andantes españoles*, pp. 52–99, and Riquer, *Caballeros catalanes y valencianos en el Passo Honroso*, pp. 7–8 and 32–53.

[44] Muhlberger, *Jousts and Tournaments: Charny and the Rules of Chivalric Sport in Fourteenth-Century France*, p. 22. See also Andrés Díaz, 'Las fiestas de caballería en la Castilla de los Trastámara', pp. 98–100, Gaier, 'Technique des combats singuliers d'après les auteurs "bourguignons" du XVe siècle', p. 429, n. 39, and Jourdan, 'Le thème du Pas et de l'Emprise', pp. 176–8.

[45] A regency was in place until John II reached his majority in 1419.

[46] Flores Arroyuelo, 'El torneo caballeresco: De la preparación militar a la fiesta y representación teatral', p. 274.

[47] Anglo, *The Martial Arts of Renaissance Europe*, p. 250.

using writing practices as a means of shaping subjectivity. To the untrained eye, the descriptions may seem repetitive, even boring. To the experienced jouster, however, each contest was unique in its details. Leaving aside the fictional *raison d'être* that underpinned the events of the Pass of Honour of Suero de Quiñones, these exquisite details constituted the medieval rhetorical equivalent of a slow-motion action replay. An added boon – fortunately for modern scholars – is that Rodríguez de Lena obviously was not only conversant with the subject matter, but also a die-hard jousting enthusiast who had an unrivalled technical knowledge of the event he was commissioned to chronicle. Indeed, it is possible that chronicling martial events was one of Rodríguez de Lena's specialties, which may be why he was chosen to narrate this passage of arms in the first place. Thus, unlike other medieval accounts of jousting, such as Jean Froissart's description of the jousts at St Inglevert in the spring of 1390,[48] which has been described appropriately as 'a novelette of the perfect joust',[49] the Pass of Honour of Suero de Quiñones might best be termed a 'hard-core' narrative written by a chronicler-cum-fan, and a very knowledgeable fan at that. Part II of this book includes a selection of chapters from *El Passo Honroso de Suero de Quiñones* that are intended to serve as test case scenarios to buttress the observations about jousting technique made by the authors of the later theoretical manuals.

In my discussion of the joust and of the technical treatises by Menaguerra, Quijada de Reayo and Zapata, in addition to the selections edited and translated from *El Passo Honroso de Suero de Quiñones*, a few words must be said about theoretical approaches to the chivalric culture of the late Middle Ages and early Renaissance. The birth of modern chivalric theory can be traced to the year 1924, when the Dutch historian Johan Huizinga published his germinal book *The Autumn of the Middle Ages*. As its title suggests, this book approaches later medieval civilisation as a time of decadence and decay. Huizinga sees in the fifteenth century a veritable obsession with images, symbols and the development of form at the expense of the idea:

> Literature and art of the fifteenth century possess both parts of that general characteristic that we have already spoken of as being essential for the medieval mind: the full elaboration of all details, the tendency not to leave any thought unexpressed, no matter what idea urges itself on the mind, so that eventually everything could

---

[48] Froissart states that the jousts took place in May, but in fact the St Inglevert jousts began on Monday, 21 March 1390. See Froissart, *Chroniques*, ed. Ainsworth and Varvaro, p. 446, n. 2.

[49] Muhlberger, *Deeds of Arms*, p. 198 (and pp. 205–15 for further comments on the St Inglevert jousts).

be turned into images as distinctly visible and conceptualized as possible.[50]

Huizinga argues that chivalry itself is an expression of a waning mode of thought and the conventions of chivalry in this period – the tournaments, the military orders, the models of courtly behaviour – were little more than surface decoration. For him: 'The whole aristocratic life of the later Middle Ages ... is an attempt to play out a dream.'[51] The main charge against Huizinga is that his thesis rejects social realities in favour of an examination of literature and art, which in turn leads to the conclusion that the nobility of the late fifteenth century hardly lived in a real world at all, but rather in a fantasy world of their own creation.

So compelling was Huizinga's argument that it remained essentially unchallenged for almost sixty years. In the case of early modern Hispanic studies, where the spectre of Cervantes looms so large, the chivalric culture that I shall be studying in this book, using local knowledge, has all too often been caricatured through the prism of Don Quixote, conceived of as always, already obsolete practices linked to the mad dreams of hidalgo knights and to the decay of a spent medieval culture. Jousting, in particular, paid a high price in Cervantes' masterpiece, being reduced in the English language to a stock quixotic metaphor of delusion, of fighting unwinnable battles against imaginary foes, or 'tilting at windmills'.

In 1981 and 1984 respectively, in large part as a reaction to Huizinga's theories on the development of form at the expense of the idea, Malcolm Vale and Maurice Keen set out to demonstrate that chivalry in the late Middle Ages was in fact an active ideal, one that played an important, functional role in society in the fourteenth and fifteenth centuries. For Vale and Keen the notion of a decline of chivalry in the later Middle Ages is a distortion. Instead of devoting his attention exclusively to art or imaginative literature, in his own analysis Vale focuses above all on military organisation whilst Keen approaches the subject primarily from social, political, and religious perspectives.[52] Keen in particular emphasises the secular origins of chivalry, holding them to be equally as important as the religious origins; he takes issue with Huizinga's representation of late-medieval society as essentially a cultural phenomenon and argues that chivalry 'was at once a cultural and a social phenomenon, which retained its vigour because it remained relevant to the social and political realities of the time'.[53] Vale and Keen each arrive at a similar and convincing conclusion: that chivalry was an active ideal closely adhered to by aristocrats of a

---

[50] Huizinga, *The Autumn of the Middle Ages*, trans. Payton and Mammitzsch, p. 333.

[51] Huizinga, *The Autumn of the Middle Ages*, trans. Payton and Mammitzsch, p. 42.

[52] Vale, *War and Chivalry*, esp. pp. 1–12; Keen, *Chivalry*, esp. pp. 219–20.

[53] Keen, *Chivalry*, p. 219.

knightly caste, and that it played an important, functional role in society in the fourteenth and fifteenth centuries.

As diametrically opposed as the theoretical approaches of Huizinga and Vale and Keen seem, however, they are not necessarily incompatible. Riquer, for example, describes the complex interplay between the social reality of chivalry and representations of chivalry in art and literature in the Middle Ages as a kind of osmosis.[54] Other scholars have advocated in favour of reconciliation by underscoring that written primary sources, be they chronicles, legal codes, biographies, technical manuals or works of imaginative literature, must be considered holistically if the institution of chivalry and the chivalric *mentalité* is to be properly understood.[55] The Spanish critic Pedro Cátedra reconciles the myriad types of chivalric discourse in terms of what he cleverly calls 'paper chivalry'.[56] Fernando Bouza goes one step further in the push to break with empirical systems of rigid generic classification in the early modern period by arguing in favour of a 'communicative trinity' based on the interplay of oral, visual and written expression as a means of understanding the communication of ideas at that time.[57] With the theories postulated by Kaeuper, Cátedra and Bouza in mind I shall also argue that chivalry is best understood when its inherent tensions, paradoxes and contradictions are celebrated and embraced. Thus in the present study I shall not discount the many works of imaginative literature and art in the Middle Ages, in Iberia and elsewhere, that include pertinent references to jousting or representations thereof at the same time as I endeavour to shed new light on the practical manuals on the subject.

When researching royal military and legal codes such as the *Libro de la Orden de la Banda*, one is immediately struck by the luxurious quality and the enormous physical dimensions of the extant manuscripts. Rodríguez Velasco refers to the 'non-transportability' of these precious codices, making the pertinent observation that the reader physically had to go to the texts in order to read them, since these were codices that were never intended for removal from their designated location.[58] The notion of the

---

[54] Riquer, *Caballeros andantes españoles*, esp. p. 12, Riquer, *Cavalleria fra Realtà e Letteratura nel Quattrocento*, pp. 5–6, and Riquer, *Caballeros catalanes y valencianos en el Passo Honroso*, pp. 25–6.

[55] See especially Kaeuper, *Chivalry and Violence in Medieval Europe*, p. 29, and Kaeuper, 'Literature as Essential Evidence for Understanding Chivalry'. Also Scaglione, *Knights at Court*, pp. 78–83, and Strohm, *Hochon's Arrow: The Social Imagination of Fourteenth-Century Texts*, pp. 3–9.

[56] 'caballería de papel'. See Cátedra, *El sueño caballeresco*, esp. pp. 13–39.

[57] Bouza, *Communication, Knowledge, and Memory in Early Modern Spain*, trans. López and Agnew, p. 11.

[58] Rodríguez Velasco, 'Invención y consecuencias de la caballería', p. xxix. Professor Rodríguez Velasco explores this issue in great detail in his forthcoming book,

non-transportability of the book and the secrecy of its contents is high-lighted in statute 23 of the Order of the Band, which reads as follows:

> And furthermore, we declare that any knight of the Band who
> discloses to another knight who is not a member of the Order of
> the Band any of the things that are contained in this book, let his
> punishment be that he not wear the band for three months. And if
> another knight of the Band were to see or discover him doing this,
> let him immediately tell the grand master. And if he were not to
> disclose this to the grand master, let him have that same punishment
> as the person who actually commits the crime. And this punish-
> ment shall be for the first time, but if he lapses for the second time,
> let the punishment be doubled.[59]

In a similar vein, the sole surviving manuscript copy of King Duarte
of Portugal's *Livro da ensinança de bem cavalgar toda sela* is but one text
in a large volume, measuring 282 × 405 mm (11¹¹⁄₁₆ in × 1 ft 3¾ in), which
contains a variety of other texts such as Duarte's own *Leal Conselheiro*
(Loyal Counsellor), and Portuguese translations of Pseudo-Aristotle's
Secretum Secretorum (Secret of Secrets) and Cicero's *De Officiis* (On Duties),
to name but a few.[60] It is apparent that this codex, considered holistically,
constitutes one man's personal 'mirror of princes'. In the case of these royal
books the actual codex was as valuable as the knowledge contained within.
The stipulation about the secrecy of King Alfonso's book of statutes of
the Order of the Band – which is also hinted at via the inclusion of the
Secretum Secretorum in Duarte's book – when considered in conjunction
with the size, weight and quality of the books themselves, underscores the
fact that these were works of inside knowledge; the exclusive domain of
a privileged few. In short, the very codices proclaim themselves as royal
books composed strictly for private consumption.

On the other hand, jousting manuals such as Menaguerra's *Lo Cavaller*
and Quijada de Reayo's *Doctrina del arte de la cavallería*, like many other
military treatises written by amateurs of the pen and dilettantes, were

---

Citizenship, Monarchical Sovereignty, and Chivalry. My thanks to prof. Rodríguez
Velasco for kindly sharing the unpublished manuscript with me.

59 'Y otrosí, decimos que cualquier caballero de la Banda que descubriere a otro
caballero, que no sea de la Banda, alguna de las cosas que en este libro se contienen,
que le den por pena que no traiga la banda en esos tres meses. Y si otro caballero
de la Banda se lo viere o se lo supiere, que se lo diga luego al maestre. Y si no se lo
descubriere, que haya esa misma pena que ha de haber el que hace el yerro. Y esta
pena será por la primera vez, pero si la segunda vez cayere, que la pena sea doblada'
(Cartagena, *Doctrinal de los caballeros*, in *Tratados Militares*, ed. Fallows, p. 321).

60 Paris, Bibliothèque Nationale, MS Fonds Portugais 5. For a bibliographic
description, see *Bibliografia de Textos Antigos Galegos e Portugueses* (BITAGAP),
Manid. 1154.

never reproduced in manuscript copies, being produced instead by the early printers. I should add a clarification: Zapata's *Miscelánea* was not printed until the nineteenth century, and the only surviving copy from the sixteenth century is a manuscript in the Biblioteca Nacional in Madrid. But the fact is that this work, like all of Zapata's literary output, was originally intended for dissemination in printed form. Like the vast majority of late medieval and renaissance vernacular scientific treatises, it is important to take into account that the Iberian jousting manuals under discussion in this book were – or were intended to be – circulated and disseminated with the help of the printing press.

The first printing press in the Iberian Peninsula is believed to have been established in 1471 or 1472 in Segovia. Subsequently in the fifteenth century presses were established throughout the peninsula in cities such as Burgos, Barcelona, Seville, Valencia and Lisbon.[61] Working in collusion with the first- and second-generation printers, men such as Menaguerra and Quijada de Reayo, who today would be called early adapters, eschewed manuscript culture and oversized codices in favour of slim, light-weight printed editions that could be carried in a purse or valise and consulted with ease. To cite but a few examples of the physical dimensions of books written by amateurs of the pen about jousting, equestrian technique and warfare, Quijada de Reayo's *Doctrina del arte de la cavallería* (1548) measures 130 × 180 mm (5⅛ × 7 in), as does Pedro de Aguilar's *Tratado de la caballería de la gineta* (Treatise on Jennet Cavalry, 1600), and Luis Gutiérrez de la Vega's *Nuevo tratado y compendio de re militari* (New Treatise and Compendium on Matters Military, 1569) measures in at a compact 90 × 140 mm (3½ × 5½ in). Jennifer Goodman has shown that the printed editions of chivalric romances also underwent a metamorphosis around this same time, decreasing in size until the 'tightly packed pocket edition on comparatively flimsy paper'[62] had been achieved by the end of the sixteenth century. This concurrent metamorphosis in the physical presentation of romance fiction and vernacular technical literature further accentuates the osmotic relationship between genres.

Much knowledge that had traditionally been passed down from one generation to another by word of mouth would have been lost forever were it not for the collusion between theorists and printers and the fact that the early printers were entrepreneurs who embraced the works written by amateurs of the pen as much as those written by *bona fide* scholars. By the 1490s in Spain, with the rise of empire there was a market for technical literature of all sorts; and as well as being innovative this literature was always portable. In the public domain, the first readers of the manuals

---

[61] On the spread of printing in Iberia, see Abad, *Los primeros tiempos de la imprenta en España (c. 1471–1520)*, esp. pp. 45–114.

[62] Goodman, *Chivalry and Exploration, 1298–1630*, p. 37.

C Doctrina del arte dela caua-
lleria, ordenado por Juan quixada de reayo vezino dela villa de Olmedo hombre de armas dela capitania del muy Il
lustrissimo señor el duque de Alburquerque a fin ð dar cóse
jo a vn hijo suyo como mas viejo ē las guardas delos reyes
passados de gloriosa memoria. So correction de otros caua
lleros que lo saben mejor hazer y dezir.

2 Title page of Juan Quijada de Reayo, *Doctrina del arte de la cavallería*
(Medina del Campo: Pedro de Castro, 1548)

were the printers themselves. As entrepreneurs they did not publish books for the fun of it; their goal was to make money. So what was the appeal of jousting manuals? The answer in part may be teased out of the woodcuts that grace the title pages – the first page a prospective book-buyer would turn to – of these and other technical manuals.[63] In the case of Quijada de Reayo's treatise, for example, the frontispiece depicts a mounted knight leaping in a curvet, carrying a shield and wielding a sword overhead. A city rises in the background and broken lances are scattered in the foreground. The image is anachronistic in that the equipment and armour depicted belong to an earlier epoch (fig. 2). In fact, as José Manuel Lucía Megías has demonstrated, it is fashioned after the frontispiece of the first printed edition of the greatest Spanish chivalry novel of all time, *Amadís de Gaula* (Amadis of Gaul), published in Saragossa by Georg Koch in 1508 (fig. 3).[64] Why dress up the title page of a technical manual with a woodcut taken from a best-selling novel? The typological connection exemplifies Bouza's notion of 'the powerful image whose contemplation was propitiatory'.[65] That is to say, in addition to serving as a means of drawing in readers of varied social classes whose recollection of *Amadís de Gaula* would ensure that Quijada de Reayo's book would sell as well as its illustrious predecessor, this image suggests that the printer, Pedro de Castro, in his role as reader also considered the book not just a jousting manual *per se*, but a key, or a reader's or an aspiring author's guide, to the technical aspects of combat as they were described in the enormously popular chivalry novels of the time.

Unlike the non-transportable manuscripts of the fourteenth and fifteenth centuries, in the case of the printed jousting treatises only the knowledge contained within the book was what mattered; the book itself was intended to be consulted vigorously, until it quite literally fell apart. It has been estimated that an average print run in the fifteenth century consisted of no more than 200 copies.[66] Assuming this to be the case with *Lo Cavaller* and *Doctrina del arte de la cavallería*, it is a fortunate circumstance indeed that at least one original copy of each text has survived the vicissitudes of time.[67] Riquer, as noted above, dwells exclusively on the osmotic relationship between chivalric culture and imaginative literature, but printed jousting law was osmotic in other ways as well, transcending geographic, linguistic and even temporal frontiers. In the case of the sole

[63] The title page was one of the great innovations of print culture. See Steinberg, *Five hundred Years of Printing*, pp. 145–53.

[64] Lucía Megías, *Imprenta y Libros de caballerías*, pp. 191–4, fig. 48 and p. 248, fig. 84.

[65] Bouza, *Communication, Knowledge, and Memory in Early Modern Spain*, trans. López and Agnew, p. 38; also p. 26.

[66] Steinberg, *Five Hundred Years of Printing*, p. 140.

[67] On the extant copies, see Part II.

3 Title page of Garci Rodríguez de Montalvo, *Amadís de Gaula*
(Saragossa: Georg Koch, 1508)

surviving copy of the 1493 edition of *Lo Cavaller*, for example, this is a Catalan treatise with coetaneous hand-written annotations in Spanish, underscoring the international nature of jousting and the universal applicability of the rules. It is also significant that the sole surviving copies of the 1493 and 1532 editions of *Lo Cavaller*, as well as that of *Doctrina del arte de la cavallería* are all in poor condition. The 1493 edition of *Lo Cavaller* is missing its frontispiece and both the 1532 edition and the copy of Quijada de Reayo's *Doctrina del arte de la cavallería* have at one time had every page repaired along the inner seam. These books were never meant to be preserved as treasured artefacts. Quite the opposite: they were meant to be used, to be consulted frequently, to be annotated by jousters, judges, spectators and perhaps also the occasional reader of chivalry novels.

Part II below includes a facsimile of the 1493 edition of Ponç de Menaguerra's *Lo Cavaller*. As celebratory functions, medieval and renaissance tournaments attracted a wide social spectrum who orbited around the élite jousters. Unlike expensive jousting armour, which was accessible to the privileged few at the epicentre of these events, inexpensive jousting treatises were pieces of ephemera that were accessible to the many. This incunable in and of itself thus constitutes a concrete, tangible artefact of the joust, one that was meant to be carried, consulted and annotated (and not necessarily in Catalan) by the competitors and their aiders,[68] the judges or the spectators. Indeed, I reiterate that excessive use is surely one of the main reasons why only one well-used copy of each edition of this text has survived the vicissitudes of history. In short, in addition to their literary value I consider the treatises – of which Menaguerra's book is a fine, representative example – to be as much a pertinent archaeological remnant of the joust as surviving examples of arms and armour.

Jennifer Goodman approaches the institution of chivalry from the point of view of geographic exploration. I would also argue that chivalric pioneers such as Ponç de Menaguerra, Juan Quijada de Reayo and Luis Zapata pursued an agenda of linguistic and technical exploration. Each author attempted to articulate, contextualise and codify in writing – in that newfangled technical innovation known as the printed book – rules, systems and techniques which hitherto had either been passed down by word of mouth or hastily scribbled in annotated form on cartels which were discarded immediately or soon after the event had taken place. In the late fifteenth and early sixteenth centuries, with the growth of lay literacy and, moreover, of a literacy no longer inextricably linked to the use of Latin, the vernacular came of age for technical literature, more people knew how to read and write, and more men of Menaguerra's, Quijada de Reayo's and

---

[68] The aiders were experienced knights who served as personal tutors, assistants, advisors and advocates to the aspiring jouster. See also below, Part II, Quijada de Reayo, *Doctrina del arte de la cavallería*, ch. 2.

Zapata's ilk felt confident enough to read for themselves and even to put pen to paper and have a go at writing.[69]

As more writers opted for the vernacular, it logically followed that fewer books were imported and more were published in Iberia or in colonial possessions. Those who wrote about military strategy and organisation, however, had an important advantage over those who would attempt to write about jousting. The military strategists were able to modify or plagiarise in the vernacular the ideas of the classical strategists like Vegetius and Frontinus, but since jousting in its medieval and renaissance iterations did not exist in classical Rome or Greece those who wrote about this subject were compelled to complete their tasks without the crutch of a Latin or Greek antecedent. Furthermore, despite the wonders of the printing press, the early writers did not have easy access to each other's work, nor did they have a unified technical vocabulary, nor did they even define much of their own unique terminology. Their challenge was not to make their own work obsolete a short while after it had appeared in print.

In 1509 Pietro Monte published a book about armour and the martial arts entitled *Exercitiorum Atque Artis Militaris Collectanea* (Collected Works on Military Training and the Art of War). Monte had made a valiant attempt to write in Latin, but he was forced by circumstances to invent so many words that this book is now, and probably was then, extremely difficult to follow. To cite but one simple example, the Roman helmet called either 'Cassis' or 'Galea' bore no resemblance whatsoever to the frog-mouthed jousting helm used in Monte's day, so he invents his own term: 'Elmus'.[70] While I agree with Anglo that Monte's book is a remarkable accomplishment, having worked with it I am also convinced that if one holds it close to the ear it is possible to hear the sound of Cicero rolling in his grave. Interestingly, there is a paraphrased version of Monte's *Exercitiorum Atque Artis Militaris Collectanea* written in Spanish and entitled *Libro del exercicio de las armas*, which is currently held in the library of the Escorial Monastery in Spain. Anglo has argued convincingly that Monte was indeed a Spaniard.[71] Thus, although the Spanish paraphrased version may have been composed after the Latin version had already been published, it is just as tempting to speculate that this codex could be a partial set of notes written by Monte himself before or as he prepared the longer Latin version, in which case the author would have debated which

[69] On the early vernacular scientific treatises in Spain, see Lawrance, 'The spread of lay literacy in late medieval Castile', and Lawrance, 'Las lecturas científicas de los castellanos en la Baja Edad Media'.

[70] On Monte's 'Elmus', see ch. 3 below.

[71] Anglo, *The Martial Arts of Renaissance Europe*, pp. 1 and 214. See also Monte, *Libro del exercicio de las armas*, Escorial, Real Biblioteca del Monasterio, MS a-IV-23, fols. 1r–52v.

of the two languages would work best for the printed version. As the case may be, this text attests to the importance of the vernacular when writing about the new martial arts of the Middle Ages and Renaissance. Most other writers on the subject would choose to write exclusively in the vernacular and, despite their shortcomings, the early jousting manuals are among the first examples of technical writing as we have come to know it today.

To go back to Anglo's remark about the problems posed by the jousting manuals, one expectation of the authors – as opposed to the printers – of the early printed treatises on jousting and other military and chivalric matters was that their readers would already be somewhat knowledgeable about or familiar with the subject matter. These were jousters writing primarily for jousters, who together formed 'une sorte de club', as Georges Duby appropriately calls the knights.[72] This club had infinite subsidiaries across Europe. Each subsidiary of 'the club' knew exactly what 'their' author was talking about, so it did not occur to the authors to include diagrams, for example – they simply were not necessary, just as it was not absolutely necessary to explain every little detail to seasoned or aspiring practitioners and readers. And if I may be so bold as to share what in this case is a moment of philological and hastiludial angst with a famous former Prince of Denmark: 'Ay, there's the rub.' For in order to be able to decipher the technical terms used by each author, the modern scholar must analyse each text paradoxically as a very distinct, individual artefact at the same time that this text belongs to a larger corpus. In our own times the practitioners of a discipline often use different language and terminology than the academics who study that same discipline, though comprehension of competing terminologies is easily acquired via dictionaries or the Internet. In the case of the early jousting manuals the authors were also the principal practitioners, whose arduous task was to create from scratch the discipline-specific terminology that would define both the practice and study of jousting. Although the technical terminology used by each author tends to be consistent throughout that particular text, in the days before instant dissemination via the Internet it does not always follow that these same terms would be used or have the same meanings imputed to them by other authors, not even by those who were writing within the same orbit at around the same time on the same subject.

The notion of members of a club striving to communicate in writing the sophisticated rules of their sport prompts me at this point to refer to another important study by Johan Huizinga. In his book *Homo Ludens*,

---

[72] 'a sort of club'. See Duby, *Guillaume le Maréshal, ou le meilleur chevalier du monde*, p. 113. They have also been called 'une sorte de vaste confrérie' ('a sort of vast brotherhood'). See Heers, *Fêtes, jeux et joutes dans les sociétés d'Occident à la fin du Moyen Âge*, p. 33.

composed in 1938, Huizinga develops a theory of what he calls the 'play-element' in culture. A number of his salient ideas about play are germane to the evolution of jousting. Firstly, Huizinga argues that all play takes place within a 'play-ground' defined by its physical or symbolic boundaries. These play-grounds represent 'forbidden spots, isolated, hedged round, hallowed, within which special rules obtain. All are temporary worlds within the ordinary world, dedicated to the performance of an act apart.'[73] By 'temporary worlds' Huizinga means that play is often a finite concept with well-defined temporal as well as spatial boundaries. Secondly, the most sophisticated play is strictly regulated and the players are bound by rules which apply inside the play-ground, thereby creating a sense of order and fairness. The rules are the glue that holds this 'temporary world within the ordinary world' together. The integrity of this world can only be maintained if there is a willingness among the players to follow the rules. Deviation from the rules, argues Huizinga, 'spoils the game, robs it of its character and makes it worthless.' He makes a distinction between the cheat, whose actions are predicated upon the implicit recognition of the rules and who therefore 'pretends to be playing the game and, on the face of it, still acknowledges the magic circle'; and the spoil-sport, who 'trespasses against the rules or ignores them', and thereby 'shatters the play-world itself', robbing it of its illusion.[74] Thirdly, in addition to boundaries and a specially defined enclosure, play is often informed by exclusivity and secrecy, where the players are members of a club who use their own technical terminology, follow customs or etiquette known only to initiates and dress in a distinctive manner. Thus play may require a special kit, for example, which allows the players to express what Huizinga calls their 'differentness', and either to play a role or even to become someone else the moment they don the kit.[75] These theoretical suppositions will become more evident as my own discussion of the joust progresses.

   With the kit firmly in mind, I feel compelled in this study to go one audacious step further than Cátedra's notion of paper chivalry, taking into account Michel Stanesco's philosophy that chivalric spectacle is above all an 'emprise du visuel'.[76] Of course it could be said that the printed word is nothing if not visual, but in the case of jousting there is much more to this important facet of the institution of chivalry than the written word in whatever form of paper chivalry it may manifest itself. Recalling Huizinga's theories of play, as an 'emprise du visuel' jousting was a chromatic spectacle defined in large part by its specially designed, iconographic kit. Thus, in addition to analysing medieval and renaissance texts about jousting in

[73] Huizinga, *Homo Ludens*, p. 10.

[74] Huizinga, *Homo Ludens*, p. 11.

[75] Huizinga, *Homo Ludens*, pp. 12–13.

[76] Stanesco, *Jeux d'errance du chevalier médiéval*, esp. pp. 173–82.

Part I of the present study and editing and translating those texts in Part II, I have included illustrations as a means of elucidating what might best be termed 'metal chivalry'.

In the case of jousting, the language of academic discourse alone is an inadequate tool for explaining the subject at hand, since even with the aid of detailed and clear descriptions specialist readers may not be entirely familiar with, or able to visualise accurately, the technical terms that jousters would have bandied about with impunity, such as 'flaon bolt', 'stop-rib' and 'barricading the lance'. With Stanesco's philosophy in mind, I shall contend in this book that chivalry must be seen in order to be properly understood. After all, in the world of jousting, before they were ever described in words new innovations were worn, their meaning and function to be interpreted by wearer and beholder. I include photographs of complete harnesses and pertinent pieces of armour, as well as illuminations and woodcuts from manuscripts and early printed books. Furthermore, in order to facilitate maximum comprehension I have endeavoured to maintain a healthy balance between colour and black and white images of arms and armour. Then as now, with its infinite hues, polished steel has its place in the world of art appreciation as much as painted canvas,[77] and the medieval and renaissance joust will continue to be misrepresented and misunderstood so long as images of jousting armour continue to be reproduced primarily or exclusively in black and white.

This synergistic interface of paper and metal that celebrates and embraces inherent tensions, paradoxes and contradictions will, I hope, give the reader a more complete understanding and appreciation of the joust and the full materiality of medieval and renaissance chivalric culture.

---

[77] On the importance of armour as art and in art, see especially Capwell, 'Introduction', in *A Celebration of Arms and Armour at Hertford House*, pp. 21–9.

The Three Jousters

Ponç de Menaguerra

WHILST *Lo Cavaller* is the only medieval Catalan treatise that deals exclusively with jousting, in so far as the vast corpus of paper chivalry is concerned the text did not emerge from a vacuum and has affinities with other types of chivalric discourse produced in medieval Catalonia.[1] For instance, one could hardly begin to understand knighthood in the Middle Ages without reading Ramon Llull's influential *Llibre de l'Orde de cavalleria* (Book of the Order of Chivalry, c. 1275). Llull imparts his wisdom through the *mise-en-fiction* of the retired-knight-cum-hermit-teacher. His book focuses above all on the religious aspects of chivalry, dwelling on such matters as the symbolic significance of arms and armour and the relationship between traditional biblical virtues and vices (charity, loyalty, justice and truth versus animosity, disloyalty, injustice and falsehood, etc.) and knighthood. Less well known, and standing at an intersection between Llull and Menaguerra, is the allegoric poem about the knight and his armour by Pere March (1336/7–1413), known today as 'L'arnès del cavaller' (The Knight's Harness, composed c. 1370–80), which imputes symbolic values to every piece of the knight's harness, from head to toe. So, for example, the bascinet symbolises humility, since it protects the head from pride, the gauntlets symbolise largesse, for they protect the hands from avarice, and the spurs symbolise the knight's perseverance on the road to paradise.[2] Still other lesser-known Catalan treatises in the English-speaking world include *De batalla* (Of Battle), a procedural manual for judges of single combats composed sometime between 1251 and 1255, and the late-fourteenth-century *Tractat de cavalleria* (Treatise on Chivalry), a translation by King Peter III of Catalonia (1319–87; ruled 1336–87) of the sections of King Alfonso X of Castile's

---

[1] On Catalan chivalric manuals, see Frattale, 'Trattati di cavalleria e norme sul torneo nella Catalogna medievale'.

[2] See March, 'L'arnès del cavaller', in *Obra completa*, ed. Cabré, p. 205 lines 106–7 (bascinet), p. 214 lines 446–9 (gauntlets), p. 225 lines 890–4 (spurs). On the symbolic significance of the pieces of the harness and the knight's arsenal, see also Llull, *Llibre de l'Orde de Cavalleria*, ed. Gustà, part V, pp. 69–73. Numerous allegorical works of this kind are known in England and France as well as Catalonia. See March, *Obra completa*, ed. Cabré, pp. 78–82, and Crouch, *Tournament*, pp. 137–8. Riquer, *L'Arnès del cavaller*, pp. 27–48 and 74–91, provides an excellent discussion of arms and armour in Llull and March, respectively.

second *Partida* that focus on the law of arms for kings and their noble vassals.[3]

In addition to having one foot firmly planted in the tradition of vernacular chivalric manuals *Lo Cavaller* boasts what I believe is a conscious typological connection with the world of chivalric fiction. The first sentence of the work reads as follows: 'The members of the military estate in the noble city of Valencia beseech Lord Ponç de Menaguerra with words of the following tenor'. The turn of phrase at the end of this sentence, 'with words of the following tenor', sounds just as flowery in medieval Catalan: 'ab estil de semblants paraules'. This is none other than the peculiar formula for introducing speeches that is peppered throughout Martorell's best-selling masterpiece *Tirant lo Blanc*, which as I stated in the Introduction was first published in Valencia in 1490. Since Ponç de Menaguerra published the first edition of *Lo Cavaller* in Valencia in 1493, this stylistic tribute to the White Knight would have been instantly recognisable to most readers. From the printer's point of view this would have been a cunning marketing strategy to boost the sales of this little treatise.

The first edition of *Lo Cavaller* consists of just eight folios and the second edition consists of nine, so it really is a little treatise. I feel confident, however, making the assertion that it is paradoxically the least known yet the most important jousting treatise ever written in medieval Europe, let alone Catalonia. *Lo Cavaller* is an ideal complement to the most cryptic and frustrating jousting treatise ever written in medieval Europe: Charny's *Demandes pour la joute, les tournois et la guerre*.[4] While Charny's questions were undoubtedly meant to stimulate debate, and in some cases it is possible to arrive at plausible answers through logical deduction, no concrete written answers have survived. Without entering explicitly into dialogue with Charny (or anyone else, for that matter), Menaguerra's treatise consists of a series of compact chapters which, incidentally, provide answers to some of the questions asked by the French author.

Despite the importance of *Lo Cavaller*, as is unfortunately the case with other Iberian jousting treatises written by noble amateurs of the pen, very little is known about the book's author, Ponç de Menaguerra. He was from Valencia, that much is certain. This city, located on the south-east coast of Spain, is described in *Tirant lo Blanc* as follows:

> This is a magnificent city, founded in prosperous fortune and blessed with many valiant knights; and except in spices, it is fertile and abundant in all things, by which means it exports more commodities than

---

[3] Both these treatises – along with several others – have been edited by Bohigas, ed., *Tractats de cavalleria*, pp. 79–96 (*De Batalla*) and 97–154 (*Tractat de cavalleria*).

[4] Muhlberger, *Jousts and Tournaments: Charny and the Rules for Chivalric Sport in Fourteenth-Century France*, pp. 95–141.

any other city. The natives of this city are good and peaceful people, and excellent in conversation.[5]

As the principal Mediterranean port in the Iberian Peninsula, Valencia was a major European centre for the import and export of arms and armour,[6] so Menaguerra was living in the perfect location for the acquisition of state-of-the-art pieces. He certainly seems to have taken pride in his Valencian heritage, about which linguistic hints are provided throughout the text. Firstly and most obviously, he wrote in Catalan. Secondly and less obviously, Ponç de Menaguerra and his patrons betray their Valencian heritage by consistently using forms such as 'per gentilea' ('gracefully'), 'bellea' ('beauty'), 'destrea' ('skill') and 'naturalea' ('nature'), as opposed to 'per gentilesa', 'bellesa', 'destresa' and 'naturalesa'. The forms they use (ending in -ea instead of -esa) are an accurate reflection of actual pronunciation, one that even today is peculiar to Valencia and does not occur anywhere else in the Western Catalan dialect, where valencià is normally included. As noted by Antonio Badía Margarit, such forms were censured in the late fifteenth century in the Catalan grammatical treatise entitled Regles de esquivar vocables o mots grossers o pagesívols (Rules for Avoiding Crude or Rustic Terms or Words), which implies that among literary men, at least, they were considered grammatically incorrect; even quite vulgar.[7]

Despite what for some was a questionable diction it can be deduced from the prologue of Lo Cavaller, where Ponç de Menaguerra is addressed as 'Mossèn', that he was of noble stock. This is an honorific title used in Aragon-Catalonia and to a much lesser extent in Castile in the Middle Ages. Possibly a calque on the French word 'Monseigneur', it is a close equivalent to the English title of Lord. The title 'Mossèn' was a sign of respect reserved for knights and members of the clergy.[8] It was doubtless because of his reputation as a valiant and noble knight that Menaguerra's anonymous patrons – the members of the military estate in the city of Valencia – commissioned him to write this definitive guide to jousting. The text itself is cast in the form of a written request to the author to

---

5 'La qual ciutat fon edificada en pròspera fortuna de ésser molt pomposa e de molt valentíssims cavallers poblada, e de tots béns fructífera. Exceptat spècies, de totes les altres coses molt abundosa, de hon se trahen més mercaderies que de ciutat que en tot lo món sia. La gent qui és de allí natural, molt bona e pacífica e de bona conversació'. See Martorell, Tirant lo Blanch, ed. Hauf, ch. 330, p. 1183. For the translation, see Tirant lo Blanc, trans. LaFontaine, p. 625.

6 See Riquer, L'Arnès del cavaller, pp. 95–7.

7 Badía Margarit, Gramática histórica catalana, p. 203, §87.II; also Moll, Gramática histórica catalana, p. 288, §414.

8 For further information about this term, see Rodríguez Velasco, El debate sobre la caballería en el siglo XV, pp. 216–17.

explain the intricacies of the joust, to which he then responds in writing. This premise places the narrative squarely within the rhetorical boundaries of epistolary discourse, which in turn allows for the conversational and uniquely Valencian discursive style that permeates the text. If the quotation from *Tirant lo Blanc* about Valencia is anything to go by this was the appropriate style for a native son of the city whose residents excelled in the art of conversation.

Ponç de Menaguerra has been identified as one of the captains of the Valencian cavalry who accompanied the future King Ferdinand of Aragon-Catalonia on his expedition to relieve the city of Perpignan when it was besieged by the French in 1473.[9] Ferdinand, who ascended the throne in 1479, is referred to as the ruling monarch in chapter 20 of *Lo Cavaller*. This reference establishes the year 1479 as a *terminus a quo* for the date of composition of the work, whence it has been conjectured that *Lo Cavaller* is associated with the royal entry of King Ferdinand and Queen Isabella into Valencia in December of 1481.[10] According to the Catholic Monarchs' official chronicle:

> They came to the city of Valencia, where they were received very merrily, with lavish and very sumptuous festivals, the expenses footed as much by the entire city as by many individual knights who staged jousts and tourneys in all the principal squares and streets with grand finery.[11]

It is not unreasonable to postulate that Menaguerra either participated in or adjudicated at these very jousts, where according to *Lo Cavaller* a debate apparently took place over blows to the shield in the wake of which the following rule would have been clarified in a Criee:[12] 'Losing the shield because of an attaint or a full hit is worth three lances to the knight who delivers the stroke, plus one for the encounter itself makes four, and the knight is out of the lists, as is determined by our lord King Ferdinand.'

Other inferences about the life of the author can be made from the text. Thus, for example, there are references in chapters 15 and 31 to certain rules

---

[9] See Menaguerra, *Lo Cavaller*, ed. Janer *et al.*, fol. IIIr; Menaguerra, *Lo Cavaller*, in *Tractats de cavalleria*, ed. Bohigas, p. 34; and Anglo, *The Martial Arts of Renaissance Europe*, p. 234.

[10] Ruiz-Domènech, 'El torneo como espectáculo en la España de los siglos XV–XVI', p. 188.

[11] 'Vinieron para la cibdad de Valencia, en la qual fueron recibidos muy alegremente, con grandes e muy sumptuosas fiestas, ansí de gastos generales de la cibdad como particulares de muchos caballeros que ficieron justas e torneos en todas las plazas e calles principales con grandes arreos'. See Pulgar, *Crónica de los señores reyes católicos don Fernando y doña Isabel de Castilla y de Aragón*, ed. Rosell, p. 362a.

[12] The Criee was a formal announcement which often constituted an amendment to the tournament articles. See below, Part II, *Passo Honroso* Selection 14.

of the joust in Germany and Hungary. It is highly unlikely that Menaguerra knew of the jousting regulations in these two countries through
reading about them in books. With respect to Germany, Rühl observes
that: 'Regulations in Germany did not obey a central code. They were in
the hands of the well-off nobility, issued randomly, proclaimed in public for
just one single event, and therefore rather short-lived and soon forgotten.'[13]
The most logical explanation for Menaguerra's knowledge of the regulations of the joust in Germany and Hungary is that he had witnessed or
actually participated in a 'Gestech' or 'Scharfrennen', two types of joust
that were staged primarily in Germany and certain neighbouring states in
the late fifteenth and early sixteenth centuries.

The Germans did practise their own version of the type of joust with
tilt to which Menaguerra was accustomed in Iberia, which they called
the 'Italian Joust over the Tilt' ('Welschgestech über die Planken') and
which is now a term often used by scholars to describe jousts with a tilt.[14]
Menaguerra, however, is referring to the peculiarities of the Gestech and
the Scharfrennen. These jousts were run at large with unusually long,
thick and heavy lances secured in place by a special bar fitted under the
jouster's arm known as the queue ('Rasthaken').[15] The kit for the Gestech
consisted of a heavy frog-mouthed helm and a small shield, and the lance
was fitted with a rebated coronel. The armour for the Scharfrennen was
distinguished by a sallet and bevor complemented by a large, protective
shield called a 'Renntartsche', and large leg-defences, the purpose of which
was to protect the otherwise unarmoured thighs and knees. These leg-
defences had two variant designs: the 'Dilgen', sometimes referred to in
English as 'tilting sockets',[16] were closely shaped around the jouster's leg;
and the 'Streiftarschen' (literally, 'swipe-shields') were flatter and designed
to protect the riders if they knocked into each other at the knee when
passing close together without being separated by a tilt.[17] The lances for
this class of joust were fitted with single-pointed heads.[18] The impacts in

---

[13] Rühl, 'German Tournament Regulations of the 15th Century', p. 163.

[14] This type of joust is also sometimes called the 'Plankengestech' in German.

[15] On this device, see Blair, *European Armour*, p. 223; also Capwell, *The Real Fighting
Stuff*, p. 34.

[16] Although this term is widely used in English, it is perhaps not the best, since no tilt
was used in this class of joust.

[17] The two types of leg defence are illustrated and discussed by Capwell, *The Real
Fighting Stuff*, pp. 34–5.

[18] See Buttin, 'La lance et l'arrêt de cuirasse', pp. 153–4. Within the two main classes
of German joust there were various nuanced sub-classes, each with slight variants
in the type of armour worn. For a list of sixteen permutations of German armoured
combats, see Nickel, 'The Tournament: An Historical Sketch', p. 250. See also
Clephan, *The Medieval Tournament*, pp. 92–110.

4–5 Stechzeug for the German Gestech. Nuremberg, late 15th century. Weight 27,357 g (60 lb 5 oz)

these jousts were often so violent and torturous that they could knock both horse and rider to the ground and, as Menaguerra observes, special points were awarded just for being able to withstand the force of the blow. Figs. 4–5 show two views of a composite German Stechzeug, the special armour for the Gestech. Made in Nuremberg in the late fifteenth century, in its current configuration this kit weighs 27,357 g (60 lb 5 oz). This weight would have been spread evenly over the wearer's body.[19] Of particular note are the deep scratches on the helm, indicating that this armour was actually used and direct hits were scored upon it. Figs. 6–7 show two views of a Hungarian saddle for the Scharfrennen of this period. The saddle is believed to have been presented by King Sigismund of Hungary (1368–1437; ruled 1387–1437) to King Henry V of England (1386–1422; ruled 1413–22) when the two monarchs met in London in the year 1416. It has a low bow and no cantle, thereby making it more difficult to withstand a blow from a

---

[19] On this armour, see Grancsay, *Catalogue of Armor: The John Woodman Higgins Armory*, pp. 56–9, and Karcheski, 'The Nuremburg *Stechzeuge* Armours'. The shield for this armour is missing.

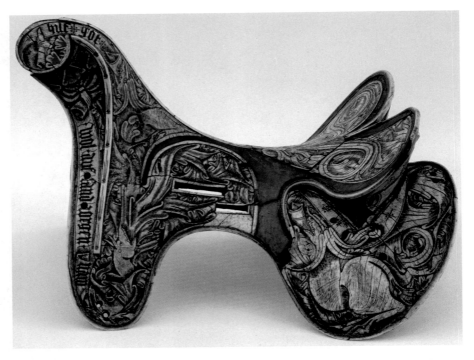

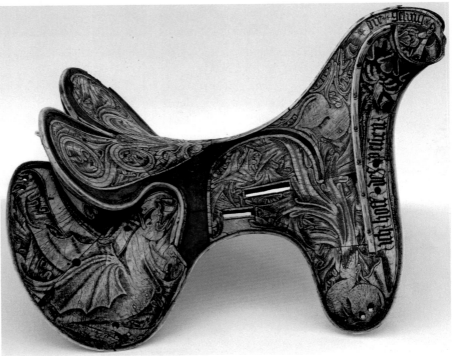

6–7 Hungarian saddle for the Scharfrennen, *c.* 1410–40, left and right views

lance without falling. Karen Watts has argued persuasively that saddles of this type were designed specifically for the Scharfrennen.[20]

Though it is safe to assume that being knocked out of the saddle in the German and Hungarian jousts would have been painful, it is also true that no special assistance would have been required for mounting or dismounting. As noted in *Las Siete Partidas*, an ethos of the armoured knight was that he not be hindered by his kit. Thus, of armoured knights, we are told:

> Moreover, they should be well informed, so that they can direct the arms, as well as the armor which they bear, to be made strong, light, and elegant; for the strength of the armor protects them better, and they are then enabled to endure more; and with strong weapons they can inflict greater damage, and do it sooner. Elegance gives those who use them a finer appearance, and causes them to be more feared by their enemies. Lightness renders them easier to handle, and enables them to make a better use of them, and this includes both those that are defensive and those that are offensive; for it would seem very absurd if he who wears armor or carries arms to defend himself from death or imprisonment by another, should be killed or taken prisoner by reason of his being hindered by them. Wherefore it is not only suitable for knights to know how to wear such armor, and use their arms as we have stated but they should also understand how to arm themselves with them, and do this early, so that they may be masters of their weapons and not their weapons masters of them.[21]

---

[20] Watts, 'Une selle médiévale d'Europe centrale au Royal Armouries Museum', esp. p. 56. I am grateful to Ms Watts for supplying me with a copy of this article while it was still in press. On this saddle, see also ffoulkes, *Inventory and Survey of The Armouries of the Tower of London*, vol. I, p. 208.

[21] *Las Siete Partidas*, II.xxiii.8: 'E otrosí deben ser sabidores que, tanto las armas como las armaduras, que las sepan mandar hacer fuertes, e ligeras, e apuestas, pues la fortaleza de las armaduras los ampara mejor e podrán sufrir más; con las armas que fueren fuertes podrán hacer mayor daño, e más aína. E el apostura les hará parecer mejor con ellas, e ser temidos de sus enemigos; e la ligereza, que las pueden más sufrir e ayudarse, tanto de las que traen para amparanza como de las que han de herir. Pues semeja cosa de mala casta mucho el que trae armaduras o armas, para defenderse de muerte o de prisión de otro, que él sea muerto o preso por embargamiento de ellas. E, por esto, no tan solamente conviene a los caudillos de ser sabidores para traer tales armaduras e armas como dicho habemos, mas aún, que sepan armarse de ellas bien, e aína, de guisa que ellos se apoderen de las armas, e no sean ellas apoderadas de ellos' (*Las Siete Partidas*, ed. Sánchez-Arcilla, p. 306ab. For the translation, see *Las Siete Partidas*, trans. Scott and Burns, vol. II, p. 444).

8 Gestech between William IV of Bavaria and Graf Christoph von Ortenburg.

Fig. 8 shows a German Gestech in progress between Duke William IV of Bavaria, on the viewer's left, and Graf Christoph von Ortenburg. Both men are wearing crested helms and charging with large, heavy lances fitted with coronels and Duke William's lance is decorated with tinsel for added effect. Fig. 9 illustrates a Scharfrennen between Duke William and Johann von der Leiter. In this instance they wear sallets and bevors and charge with single-pointed lances, Duke William with contrasting key decorations to his opponent's locks and with characteristic tinsel on lance. In both of these jousting competitions Duke William's supporting queue is clearly visible, as are the leg-defences and large shields in the Scharfrennen.[22] In the year 1437 the Cordovan nobleman and traveller Pero

[22] There is a facsimile edition of this tournament book with black and white plates. See Leidinger, *Miniaturen aus Handschriften der Kgl. Hof- und Staatsbibliothek in München*, Heft 3: *Turnierbuch Herzog Wilhelms IV von Bayern*, plates III.1– III.2 and III.19–III.20. The German tournament books constitute a unique and

From the *Turnierbuch* (1510–45) of Duke William IV of Bavaria, illuminated by the court painter Hans Ostendorfer II

Tafur witnessed a Scharfrennen in Breslau and was struck in particular by the sheer skill involved. In his own words: 'It is seldom that a day passes at this court without a contest, the parties having sharpened lances and steel helmets and shields, but they are all so used to the practice and so skilful that there is no more danger than in a contest with jousting lances.'[23]

largely unexplored genre. For a synopsis of the books and relative scholarship, see Watanabe-O'Kelly, 'Literature and the Court, 1450–1720', pp. 641–4; also Jackson, 'The Tournament and Chivalry in German Tournament Books of the Sixteenth Century and in the Literary Works of Emperor Maximilian I'.

[23] 'Pocos eran los días en que en esta corte non se corrían puntas con fierros agudos e sombreros de açero e escudos de açero, pero en tal manera lo an acostumbrado e tan diestramente lo fazen que es mucho menos peligro que justar con roquetes'. See Tafur, *Andanças e viajes de un hidalgo español*, ed. Jiménez de la Espada, p. 146. For the translation, see Tafur, *Travels and Adventures*, trans. Letts, p. 217.

9 Scharfrennen between William IV of Bavaria and Johann von der Leiter.

Figs. 10–11 are extant examples of the types of lance-head that were used in each competition.[24]

In addition to the German tournament, a cryptic reference to the Lombard tournament is made in chapter 31 of the treatise, as follows:

> Thus it was declared in Lombardy that if the knight, entering the lists to tourney, fell to the ground whilst spurring on his horse, whether it was his fault or not, he would be disqualified from winning the jewel that day, because by meeting with such a disaster he spoiled the festival.

A detail of some importance is that up to this point in the text Menaguerra always uses the term 'prize' ('pris') to describe the reward granted to

[24] See Valencia de Don Juan, *Catálogo histórico-descriptivo de la Real Armería de Madrid*, pp. 276–7.

From the *Turnierbuch* (1510–45) of Duke William IV of Bavaria, illuminated by the court painter Hans Ostendorfer II

the winner of the tournament,[25] which he suddenly changes in this chapter to the more specific term 'jewel' ('joia'). It is known that jewels – in particular diamonds and rubies – and jewellery were often the top prize in tournaments organised by dukes,[26] and we are fortunate that a complete set of rules for a fifteenth-century Lombard ducal tournament has survived. This was the tournament hosted in Milan in 1465 by the Duke of Milan, Francesco Sforza Visconti, on the occasion of the marriage of his daughter, Ippolita Maria Sforza, to Alfonso of Aragon, Duke of Calabria, the son of Ferdinand I, King of Naples. The Duke of Milan drew up a *Regolamento delle giostre* (Regulation of the jousts) to be shared amongst the combatants, one of the statutes of which reads as follows:

[25] For example, see below, Part II, Menaguerra, *Lo Cavaller*, chapters 2, 10 and 25.

[26] See Neste, *Tournois, joutes, pas d'armes dans les villes de Flandre à la fin du Moyen Âge (1300–1486)*, p. 92.

10 (*left*) Coronel for the German Gestech. 16th century

11 (*above*) Lance-head for the German Scharfrennen. 16th century

Item, if one of the jousters falls, he may not joust again, except if he falls through a collision, or if his horse is injured or maimed by an opponent, or if he falls by himself without being struck, in such cases he may continue jousting, and change horses.[27]

In addition to this written rule a pictorial record of the tournament as it was practised in Lombardy around the time Menaguerra was writing has been left to us by the artist Floriano Ferramola (1480–1528). Fig. 12 is Ferramola's fresco of *The Piazza Maggiore at Brescia with a Tournament*, the largest and finest of a set of frescoes that he painted of the Piazza Maggiore in about 1511. This fresco is believed to commemorate a jousting competition held in honour of Caterina Cornaro, Queen of Cyprus, during her stay in Brescia in 1495, just two years after publication of the first edition of *Lo Cavaller*. The viewer is afforded a spectator's view of the event that is highly unusual in that we are watching the jousters as they ride out, before the encounter takes place. They are seated on high saddles so that each rider is elevated about 12–15 cm (or 5–6 in) off the horses back, and they are wearing jousting armour which would have been compatible with that worn by Menaguerra.[28] A tilt consisting of ten planks separates the combatants. This high tilt would have protected the horses entirely. Alongside it is an early depiction of counter-tilts, the height of which is parallel with the fourth plank from the bottom of the tilt barrier. Since these knights are not wearing legharness a fall from the horse onto the counter-tilt would have been particularly injurious and would have 'spoiled

27 Rühl, 'Regulations for the Joust in Fifteenth-Century Europe: Francesco Sforza Visconti (1465) and John Tiptoft (1466)', p. 196.

28 The issue of compatibility is discussed more fully in the next chapter.

12 Floriano Ferramola (1480–1528),
fresco of *The Piazza Maggiore at Brescia with a Tournament, c.* 1511

the festival', as Menaguerra would say. As with the reference to Germany and Hungary, although there is no concrete proof that Menaguerra participated in this class of joust, it is safe to assume that he had travelled at some point in his life to Lombardy, perhaps in a diplomatic or military capacity, where he became directly familiar with the nuances of the Lombard rules.

In sum, in the absence of concrete birth and death dates it is reasonable to postulate that Ponç de Menaguerra flourished *c.* 1460–1500. Based on the inferences and deductions made above, his life may be summarised by the wise words of the thirteenth-century French poet Jean Renart: 'Noblemen have a hard task, travelling / from one place to another in search of glory.'[29] These words rang equally as true in fifteenth-century Iberia. For medieval knights, acquiring a reputation was not at all easy, given the fact that even the most sedentary international travel – let alone fighting in sieges and competing in tournaments – involved a high risk of death, injury or disease. Ponç de Menaguerra was clearly a distinguished veteran of European wars and tournaments, a true knight errant who had acquired the kind of solid reputation for his successes on the battlefield and in the lists that was admired and coveted. In short, this renowned son of Valencia was, in every personal and professional sense, qualified to write *Lo Cavaller.*

Juan Quijada de Reayo

LIKE Menaguerra's treatise, *Doctrina del arte de la cavallería* is unique with regard to the amount of detail it provides about jousting, though it too forms part of a long-established, rich tradition of chivalric manuals in Spain.[30] Quijada de Reayo's book is a compendium of use to all jousters, and the work represents the sum total of the author's personal experiences in the lists and on the field of battle. *Doctrina del arte de la cavallería* is characteristic of the types of chivalric treatise that were being published in the sixteenth century in Spain in that it is written not by a prelate or a professional scholar, but by an experienced jouster and combat veteran. Conscious of his own limitations as a writer, the author admits with genuine modesty in the first paragraph that he writes 'under the correction of other knights who know better than I what to do and say'.

Unlike Menaguerra's treatise, which was commissioned by an anonymous group of patrons, Quijada de Reayo's book was commissioned by a specific individual: Don Beltrán de la Cueva (1478?–1559). Don Beltrán

---

[29] 'a grant paine quierent lor pris / prodome de pais en autre'. See Renart, *The Romance of the Rose or of Guillaume de Dole (Roman de la Rose ou de Guillaume de Dole)*, ed. and trans. Psaki, p. 134 lines 2938–9.

[30] On the medieval treatises, see the exhaustive study by Rodríguez Velasco, *El debate sobre la caballería en el siglo XV*, pp. 383–420.

was the third duke of Alburquerque, son of Don Francisco Fernández de la Cueva, the second duke. Both Beltrán and Francisco Fernández were renowned warriors from an established noble family. Don Beltrán also married into a powerful noble family. His wife, Doña Isabel Girón, was the daughter of the Count and Countess of Ureña, Don Juan Téllez Girón and Doña Leonor de Velasco. Over the course of their marriage she bore him five children: two daughters, Doña Francisca and Doña Leonor; and three sons, Don Gabriel, Don Juan and Don Francisco.[31]

Beltrán de la Cueva typified the new generation of what could be termed vernacular warriors of sixteenth-century Spain. On the one hand he was a family man. On the other hand he was a man who stood at the intersection of what traditionally were two quite different forms of institutional expression: the profession of soldiering and the profession of writing, with special emphasis on the contextualisation of soldiering in printed books. Although he was not a writer himself, Beltrán de la Cueva was the patron of more than one military author. A multifaceted warrior, strategist and diplomatist, he commissioned Diego Montes to compose a treatise on infantry tactics entitled *Instruçión y regimiento de guerra* (Training and Organisation for War), which was published in Saragossa in 1537 by the publisher of *Amadís de Gaula*, Georg Koch.[32] Eleven years later, in 1548, he commissioned Juan Quijada de Reayo to write *Doctrina del arte de la cavallería*, the treatise on jousting and heavy cavalry tactics edited and translated in the present book. As Viceroy of Navarre, the third duke of Alburquerque was the official representative of Charles V in that region. It was in this capacity that he commissioned an official parliamentary record of Navarrese laws and ordinances. In keeping with the duke's affinity for print culture, this compilation of laws was published in Estella in 1553 and has the distinction of being the first known printed edition of parliamentary records in Spain.[33] Finally, a treatise entitled *Libro de linajes* (Book of Lineages) was dedicated to the duke in the 1550s. The extant manuscript copy of this text contains genealogical information on the most powerful families in Spain and the emerging empire at the time, including Beltrán de la Cueva's own family.[34]

---

[31] See López de Haro, *Nobiliario Genealógico de los Reyes y Títulos de España*, vol. I, p. 350a.

[32] For the dedication see Montes, *Instruçión y regimiento de guerra*, fol. 1r.

[33] The book has been reproduced in facsimile with a modern transcription and scholarly introduction. See *Quaderno de Leyes, Ordenanças, y Provisiones, hechas a suplicación de los tres Estados del Reyno de Navarra, por su Magestad o en su nombre*, ed. Sánchez Martínez.

[34] *Libro de los linajes dirigido a Don Beltrán de la Cueva, Duque de Alburquerque*, Madrid, Monasterio de las Descalzas Reales, MS F/30. A copy of this MS is available on microfilm at Madrid, Biblioteca de Palacio, MC/MD/3193.

The duke's performance on the battlefield and his reputation in the European military arena is indicative of Spain's military strength and political influence in the early modern period. By the 1530s he had accompanied Charles V on numerous European campaigns and he had distinguished himself in battle as both a fearless leader and a prudent strategist. His military career does not seem to have taken off until he was in his early forties, as it is not until this time that his martial accomplishments are documented in contemporary chronicles. His earlier life is well documented, but the emphasis here is usually placed on the bizarre 'Kind Hearts and Coronets' sequence of events that led to his inheritance of the dukedom. Although he never engaged in any wrongdoing, his extended family was plagued by a strange series of disasters and untimely deaths that catapulted him from the lowest to the highest rung of the inheritance ladder. None other than Luis Zapata, in fact, included a chapter in his *Miscelánea* entitled 'On extraordinary inheritances' in which he describes the various deaths and disasters that befell this unfortunate family and that led to Beltrán's inheritance of the dukedom in the year 1525.[35]

Beltrán de la Cueva's obstinate valour was confirmed during the campaign in Navarre in 1521 when, at the risk of being captured himself, he pursued a group of French knights in full flight from the city of Pamplona, and took them all prisoner. This incident so impressed Charles V that he promoted him to the rank of general and gave him command of the heavy cavalry for the duration of the campaign. Shortly thereafter Beltrán de la Cueva proved his abilities as a shrewd tactician when he orchestrated and commanded the sack of Saint Jean de Luz in 1522.[36] He acquitted himself well in 1525 at the battle of Pavia becoming, some ten years after that, the dedicatee of a poem of twenty-eight stanzas about the battle composed by Vasco Díaz Tanco.[37] Two years after the rout at Pavia Beltrán de la Cueva can be placed at the tournament held in Valladolid to commemorate the birth of Charles V's son and heir, where he captained a team consisting entirely of family members. In keeping with the festivities he adopted the persona of 'The Knight of the Serpent' for the duration of the

---

35 Zapata, *Miscelánea*, ed. Carrasco González, ch. 57, pp. 73–4, 'De herencias extraordinarias'. See also Fallows, *Un texto inédito sobre la caballería del Renacimiento español: 'Doctrina del arte de la cauallería', de Juan Quijada de Reayo*, pp. 5–8 and 61–4.

36 Mexía, *Historia del Emperador Carlos V*, ed. Mata Carriazo, p. 271, and Sandoval, *Historia de la vida y hechos del Emperador Carlos V*, ed. Seco Serrano, vol. I, p. 464b, and vol. II, p. 8a. The Pamplona incident is also immortalised by Zapata, *Carlo Famoso*, facsimile, ed. Terrón Albarrán, fol. 46rb.

37 Díaz Tanco, *Triumpho béllico notable sobre la gloriosa victoria de España contra Francia quando su Rey fue en prisión*, facsimile, ed. Sancho Rayón.

tournament.[38] Subsequently, in 1534 the Emperor himself inducted Don Beltrán into the élite Order of the Golden Fleece in a special ceremony held in the former Castilian capital of Toledo.[39]

His renown as a cavalry officer reached its apogee four years before he commissioned *Doctrina del arte de la cavallería*, that is, in 1544, when a combined force of Spanish and English troops reclaimed the city of Boulogne from King Francis I of France. The duke played an instrumental role in planning the siege of the city. Indeed, his reputation preceded him as far as the shores of England with the result that King Henry VIII requested that Charles V grant Henry permission to give Beltrán de la Cueva command of an English platoon in this campaign. Thus Beltrán de la Cueva had the singular distinction of being one of the few Spaniards in history to lead an English army.[40] By the mid-sixteenth century he had proven his mettle as well as his leadership abilities. In short, he was the personification of the renaissance Spanish ideal of the 'Perfect Captain': a family man, a competent administrator and tactician, a seasoned warrior and an enlightened patron and dedicatee of militaristic treatises.[41]

If the salient details of the military career of Beltrán de la Cueva are well documented, the same cannot be said about the man he commissioned to write *Doctrina del arte de la cavallería*. As is the case with Ponç de Menaguerra, but for the details the author supplies in the treatise, very little is known about Juan Quijada de Reayo. He is, he tells us in the paragraph dedicatory, a 'man-at-arms', a term generally used to denote 'men who fought as knights whatever their precise social status'.[42] By 1548, the date of publication of his treatise, Quijada de Reayo informs the reader that he is the oldest surviving member of the personal bodyguard of the Catholic Monarchs, King Ferdinand and Queen Isabella. This statement hints at the kind of man he must have been, since the qualities required for royal bodyguards are described in some detail in the following law of *Las Siete Partidas*:

> Men of this kind should possess six qualities. They should be of good ancestry, loyal, intelligent, prudent, vigilant, and strong. For if they

---

[38] Beltrán's device consisted of a serpent emerging from a cave (Spanish 'cueva'). See Ruiz García and Valverde Ogallar, 'Relación de las fiestas caballerescas de Valladolid de 1527: un documento inédito', pp. 157–8.

[39] López de Haro, *Nobiliario Genealógico de los Reyes y Títulos de España*, vol. I, p. 348b.

[40] For the details of the siege of Boulogne, see Sandoval, *Historia de la vida y hechos del Emperador Carlos V*, ed. Seco Serrano, vol. III, p. 206a.

[41] The notion of the 'perfect captain' is expounded upon at great length by Diego de Alava y Viamont in his 1590 treatise *El Perfecto Capitán instruido en la Disciplina Militar y nueva ciencia de la Artillería*.

[42] Williams, *The Knight and the Blast Furnace*, p. 903.

are not of good descent, it might happen that they, sometime, would not be ashamed to do something unbecoming to them. Where they are not loyal, they cannot love the king, or protect him as they ought. If they are not intelligent, they may fail greatly in the service and protection which they are required to render. When they are not prudent, they do not know how to appreciate or respect the benefits which are conferred upon them. If they are not vigilant, they will not know how to avert, or face dangers which may suddenly arise. If they are lacking in strength, they will not venture to defend or attack, when the king orders them to do so. And, leaving out of consideration all that we have said, they should be of good habits, quiet, neat, and civil in speech: for it is proper that those who constantly have to guard the body of the king, should be persons of this description.[43]

The only other clue from the text which sheds light on the author's life is a reference in chapter 3 where he states that he has seen four people killed from blows through the visor of the helmet: 'First, the son of the Count of Oñate, at the Queen's palace; Don Luis Osorio, at Tafalla in Navarre; and in Saragossa, Don Gaspar, son of the Count of Sástago; and Hieronymus Dansa.' Although these references place the author in certain locations at certain points in history, the exact dates of some of the deaths are difficult to pinpoint. Thanks to a reference in a chronicle the death of the first victim, Don Pedro Vélez de Guevara, eldest son of the second Count of Oñate, can be traced to an exact date. It is known that he was killed at a tournament on 23 February 1533, when a splinter from a lance pierced his visor.[44] As for Don Luis Osorio, it is known that he participated successfully in the tournament at Valladolid in 1527, where he adopted the persona of 'The Knight of the Gorgeous Mistress', which means that he must have been killed sometime between 1527 and

---

[43] 'E estos tales deben haber en sí seis cosas: que sean de buen linaje, e leales, e entendidos, e de buen seso, e apercibidos, e esforzados. Pues si de buen linaje no fuesen, podrían ser que algunas veces no hubiesen vergüenza de hacer cosa que les estuviese mal; e no siendo leales no sabrían amar al rey, ni le guardarían en aquellas cosas que debiesen; e si no fuesen bien entendidos podrían mucho menguar en el servicio, en la guarda que hubiesen de hacer; e cuando no hubiesen buen seso no sabrían conocer ni guardar el bien que les ficiesen. E si apercibidos no fuesen, no sabrían desviar ni acorrer a los peligros que a so hora podrían acaecer; e si les menguase el esfuerzo, no se atreverían a amparar ni acometer las cosas que el rey mandase. E sin todo esto que dijimos, ha menester que sean bien acostumbrados, e mansos, e apuestos, e de buena palabra, pues derecho es que los que todavía han de guardar el cuerpo del rey que tales sean'. See Las Siete Partidas, II.ix.9, ed. Sánchez-Arcilla, pp. 217b–218a. For the translation, see Las Siete Partidas, trans. Scott and Burns, vol. II, p. 317.

[44] Girón, Crónica del Emperador Carlos V, ed. Sánchez Montes, p. 24.

1548.[45] Despite years of searching, I have yet to find any other concrete references than those in Quijada de Reayo's treatise to the death of Don Gaspar, son of the Count of Sástago. The last victim, Hieronymus Dansa, was a notorious Renaissance scrapper, though the precise date of his death is obscure. He had the dubious distinction of fighting in the last public duel in Spain, which was presided over by Charles V in Valladolid on 29 December 1522 and subsequently immortalised in a play by Calderón de la Barca called *El postrer duelo de España* (The Last Duel in Spain). The duel was a foot combat, in which he and his opponent, Don Pedro Torrellas, beat each other to a pulp, but survived.[46] Since Quijada de Reayo states that he saw him get killed in a joust, this must have happened between 1522 and 1548. Perhaps of more importance than the specific dates is the fact that Quijada de Reayo was obviously an active spectator, and probably also a participant, in the Iberian jousting circuit.

In addition to the assumption that Quijada de Reayo was at his master's side in Beltrán de la Cueva's various military campaigns and tournaments, contemporary chronicles offer documentary evidence that Quijada de Reayo was a renowned fighter in his own right. On 18 July 1549, for example, almost a year after publication of *Doctrina del arte de la cavallería*, we find a description of some cane games staged in Ghent, consisting of two teams of three quadrilles per team. The first team, captained by Don Juan Pimentel, consisted of quadrilles captained by Pimentel himself, as well as Don Diego de Acevedo and Don Luis de Ávila y Zúñiga. Significantly, we find one 'Juan Quijada' in Pimentel's quadrille and none other than Don Gabriel de la Cueva, the youngest son of Don Beltrán de la Cueva, in Acevedo's quadrille.[47]

In August of that year the same Juan Quijada participated in the tournaments at the lavish festival of Binche in Flanders. In the first tourney at Binche, staged in the courtyard of the palace on 23 or 24 August, we are informed that Juan Quijada was picked to form part of an international team which consisted of ten knights from France, Italy and Spain captained by the Prince of Piedmont (and first cousin of the future King Philip II of Spain), Emmanuel Philibert of Savoy (1528–80). The team offered to take on all comers from ten o'clock in the morning until

---

45 'El Caballero de la Linda Amiga'. See Ruiz García and Valverde Ogallar, 'Relación de las fiestas caballerescas de Valladolid de 1527: un documento inédito', p. 159.

46 On this duel, see Fallows, *Un texto inédito sobre la caballería del Renacimiento español: 'Doctrina del arte de la cauallería', de Juan Quijada de Reayo*, pp. 65–73, and Riquer, *L'Arnés del cavaller*, pp. 94 and 206.

47 Calvete de Estrella, *El felicíssimo viaje del muy alto y muy poderoso Príncipe don Phelippe*, ed. Cuenca, p. 203. The members of each quadrille are also listed by Frieder, *Chivalry and The Perfect Prince*, pp. 196–8. I discuss the cane game more fully in chapter 7.

sundown. The articles of this tourney required that the teams engage in foot combats. Each pair of combatants was expected to do the following: deliver three blows with the pike; five strokes with the sword; three blows each with the head and shaft of the lance; cast one spear; deliver seven strokes with the two-handed sword; and nine blows with the axe.[48] At the banquet hosted after the tourney at which the prizes were awarded to the victorious knights, two members of Emmanuel Philibert's team – both from Spain – were honoured in the presence of the Emperor Charles V and his court for their skill with weaponry: Don Gaspar de Robles was awarded a diamond, the top prize for axe combat; and Juan Quijada was awarded a golden sword, the top prize for sword combat.[49] This was one of the most coveted prizes in an age when the art of fencing was of paramount importance in the chivalric arena.

On 25 August 1549, a fantastic tournament was staged, inspired by the chivalry novel *Amadís de Gaula*, and called The Adventure of the Enchanted Sword.[50] Recalling Huizinga's play-element, the *mise-en-fiction* hinged upon the rhetorical exercise of prosopopoeia, whereby each participant assumed the identity of an appropriate counterpart in the novel. Juan Quijada was now Don Guilán the Pensive, known variously as 'the good knight' and 'the most obliging and the most gentle and kind to his friends'.[51] The idea was that the contestants had to undergo a series of progressively more difficult trials by combat in order to reach the Dark Castle and then secure the release of fellow knights who were being held prisoner there by

[48] See Cabanillas, *Relación verdadera de las grandes fiestas que la serenísima Reina doña María ha hecho al Príncipe nuestro señor en Flandes, en un lugar que se dice Vince*, ed. Huarte, vol. II, p. 211; Calvete de Estrella, *El felicíssimo viaje del muy alto y muy poderoso Príncipe don Phelippe*, ed. Cuenca, p. 321; Santa Cruz, *Crónica del Emperador Carlos V*, ed. Blázquez y Delgado-Aguilera and Beltrán y Rózpide, vol. V, p. 267.

[49] Calvete de Estrella, *El felicíssimo viaje del muy alto y muy poderoso Príncipe don Phelippe*, ed. Cuenca, p. 325.

[50] For a detailed contemporary account of this tournament, see especially Calvete de Estrella, *El felicíssimo viaje del muy alto y muy poderoso Príncipe don Phelippe*, ed. Cuenca, pp. 325–42. For summaries in English, see Barber and Barker, *Tournaments*, pp. 134–5, Strong, *Art and Power: Renaissance Festivals, 1450–1650*, pp. 91–5, and, especially, Frieder, *Chivalry and The Perfect Prince*, pp. 135–58.

[51] The name in Spanish is Don Guilán el Cuidador. See Calvete de Estrella, *El felicíssimo viaje del muy alto y muy poderoso Príncipe don Phelippe*, ed. Cuenca, p. 336. Frieder, *Chivalry and The Perfect Prince*, p. 147, translates the name as Don Guilán the Watchful, but the verb 'cuidar' in Old Spanish and in this context means 'to think'. Don Guilán is described as 'el buen cauallero' and 'más comedido y más manso y humano … con sus amigos' by Rodríguez de Montalvo, *Amadís de Gaula*, ed. Place, bk I, ch. 36 (vol. I, p. 291a) and bk IV, ch. 24 (vol. IV, p. 1226b), respectively. For the translation, see Rodríguez de Montalvo, *Amadis of Gaul*, trans. Place and Behm, bk I, ch. 36 (vol. I, p. 345) and bk IV, ch. 24 (vol. II, p. 613).

a wizard called Norabroch. Next to the castle was the Fortunate Isle, the focal point of which was a cliff or crag surmounted by a red pillar, which in turn was reminiscent of an earlier Flemish passage of arms known as the *Pas du Perron Fée* (Passage of Arms of the Enchanted Pillar) staged at Bruges in 1463.[52] Through this pillar the enchanted sword had been thrust, to be removed by the victor of the tournament. Thus, after reaching the Dark Castle and securing the release of the prisoners, the contestants in this tournament had to continue pursuing their quest to the Fortunate Isle in search of the enchanted sword, all the while fighting against defenders whose task it was to protect the weapon.

The first knight who managed to overcome all the obstacles, releasing the prisoners from the Dark Castle and reaching the pillar, was Don Guilán the Pensive, a testimony to Juan Quijada's chivalric mettle and verve.[53] For his labours he was awarded a special coronet known as a crance-lin.[54] It should be noted, however, that construction of the elaborate sets for The Adventure of the Enchanted Sword was overseen directly by Charles V's sister, Queen Mary of Hungary (1505–58). This was a detail of some importance since she had had a prophecy inscribed upon the pillar that only a prince would be entitled to pull out the sword. Perhaps frustratingly for Quijada, then, Queen Mary had rigged the tournament so that no-one except Charles' son and heir, prince Philip, could possibly win. Since Philip's victory was pre-arranged, in his case we can safely assume that the defenders offered deliberately feeble resistance to his cuts and thrusts in order to allow him to make it through to the final stage of the tournament, whilst in Quijada's case, these same sycophants did their utmost to prevent him from making any progress; hence the fact that he made it to the end is further testimony to this man's prowess.

We find one final reference to Juan Quijada from this period, this time at the jousts staged at The Brussels Park on the first Sunday of Lent, 1550. At this joust he fought in a team of six with fellow jousting champion Don Luis Zapata.[55]

If the author of *Doctrina del arte de la cavallería* were a member of the personal body guard of the Catholic Monarchs late in their reign – perhaps

---

[52] On the *Pas du Perron Fée*, see Barber and Barker, *Tournaments*, pp. 120–1, and Neste, *Tournois, joutes, pas d'armes dans les villes de Flandre à la fin du Moyen Âge (1300–1486)*, p. 326.

[53] Don Guilán the Pensive in *Amadís de Gaula* also releases a group of imprisoned knights and maidens from the dungeon of Gandinos the Good-for-nothing (Sp. 'Gandinos el Follón'). See Rodríguez de Montalvo, *Amadis of Gaul*, trans. Place and Behm, bk II, ch. 48 (vol. I, p. 468).

[54] Calvete de Estrella, *El felicíssimo viaje del muy alto y muy poderoso Príncipe don Phelippe*, ed. Cuenca, p. 336.

[55] Calvete de Estrella, *El felicíssimo viaje del muy alto y muy poderoso Príncipe don Phelippe*, ed. Cuenca, p. 544; also Frieder, *Chivalry and The Perfect Prince*, p. 208.

in the early 1500s – it is by no means unreasonable to conjecture that he would still have been old enough to have performed well in the martial arena in the late 1540s. There were certainly precedents for seasoned Castilian warriors participating in wars and tournaments in their fifties and sixties. Thus, for example, the Castilian nobleman Don Diego Gómez de Sandoval fought in the battle of Olmedo (19 May 1445) at the age of fifty-nine; and Don Pero Niño acquitted himself well in the tournament at Valladolid in 1428 when he was fifty.[56] Perhaps not coincidentally, of the character Juan Quijada chose from *Amadís de Gaula* in the tournament at Binche we are informed that 'Don Guilán, although he was older, was more valiant and skilled in arms'; the ideal role for an older man to play.[57]

The Juan Quijada at Ghent, Binche and Brussels shared the same name and first surname as Juan Quijada de Reayo and neither one of them was accorded the honorific title of 'Don'. The fact that Juan Quijada and Don Gabriel de la Cueva were on the cane game teams at Ghent is also suggestive, since Don Gabriel was Beltrán de la Cueva's son and we know from the prologue of *Doctrina del arte de la cavallería* that Quijada de Reayo was commissioned to write the book for one of the duke's sons.

There are, in my view, too many coincidences for the two Quijadas to be aught but the same man. Juan Quijada de Reayo's outstanding performance at the tournaments in Flanders reveals exactly why the Duke of Alburquerque would have entrusted his son Don Gabriel's martial education to this man-at-arms. It makes sense that a powerful duke such as Don Beltrán de la Cueva would have taken advantage of the royal tour of Italy and the Low Countries to dispatch master and pupil as a means of guaranteeing representation from the ducal house of Alburquerque and, more importantly, as a means of introducing his son and heir into the international courtly, political and martial arena.[58] Here were opulent international festivals informed by martial activity that took place just one year after the publication of Quijada de Reayo's instructional treatise. Indeed, the Spanish fleet had set sail from Barcelona to northern Italy in November 1548, and we know from the colophon of *Doctrina del arte de la cavallería* that the book was published on 22 October of that year. Thus the royal tour would have been an ideal opportunity for putting fresh

---

56 For Sandoval, see Pérez de Guzmán, *Generaciones y semblanzas*, ed. Tate, p. 28; for Pero Niño, see Díaz de Games, *El victorial*, ed. Beltrán Llavador, p. 719.

57 'Don Guilán, ahunque de más días fuesse, era más valiente y vsado en armas'. See Rodríguez de Montalvo, *Amadís de Gaula*, ed. Place, bk II, ch. 50 (vol. II, p. 405b). For the translation, see Rodríguez de Montalvo, *Amadis of Gaul*, trans. Place and Behm, bk II, ch. 50 (vol. I, p. 475).

58 The dukedom was initially inherited by Gabriel's brother Francisco, who became the fourth Duke of Alburquerque. He was then succeeded by Gabriel, who became the fifth Duke. See López de Haro, *Nobiliario Genealógico de los Reyes y Títulos de España*, vol. I, p. 350ab.

Thurnier/Kampff/
Vom Thournier vber die Schrancken/
Vnd außrüffung der Preiß.

ALs solchs alles geschehen/ hat mann alle Ritter gleich zu bayden theylen ab
gethaylt/vnd vber Schrancken erstlich mit langen Spiessen/ volgendes mit
Kürißschwertern/ allzumal lassen Thournieren/ So sehr lustig zu sehen ge
west/vnd schier einer Schlacht gleich geschehen/ Inn welchen jr Fürstlich Durch
leuchtigkeyt/sich mit dem Schwerdt sehr wol gehalten/vnd den Preiß so ein Ru
bin gewest/ erlanget. Vnd ist also solcher Thournier/nach dem ein Rott nach der
andern wie sie kommen gewest/abtretten/geendet worden.

Nach dem nacht essen seind schöne Tentz gehalten/ vnnd die Preiß außgethaylt
worden/wie volget:

Nemlich dem Don Johan Guirada/ der Preiß im langen Spieß.

Dem Herrn von Quirinaim/ der preiß im Kürißschwert.

Dem

13 Portrait purportedly of Juan Quijada de Reayo.
From *Thournier Kampff unnd Ritterspiel* (Frankfurt am Main: Christian Egenolff, 1550), unnumbered fol.

Thournier/Kmpff/

Er erst ſo über das waſſer kame/ war Don Johann Guixada ein Spanier/
ſo ſich Don Wilhelm den hochmütigen nennet/ vnd mit braun Samet mit
goldt belegt gekleydt war/ Welcher ſich dermaſſen ann allen dreien paſſen
hielte/ daß jm über das waſſer zufaren erlaubt/ vnnd wurde von dem Herrenn vom
Buſſu/ der Key: May: groſſenn ſtalmeyſter hinüber geleytet .   Inn dem Schiff
darinn er überfarenn ſolte/ war ein ſchöner ſeſſel mit Carmoſin atlas bedecket/
darein ſich der Ritter ſetzte/ Vnnd die ſo rüderten/ weiß vnnd rot atlas wammes
vnd hoſſen an hetten/ Als er nun ann das land kame/ ward er von des Schiffs Patron auff den Felſen geführet/ vnd alda zuckt er ein mal das Schwerdt/ Als er es a-
ber nicht gewinnen kundte/ ſchanckte jm gemelter Patron von wegen der Königin
mit danckſagung ein ſchön krentzlin/ vnnd zoge alſo wider über das waſſer/ vnnd zu
roſs hinder durch alle päſs.

Ein Brüder Luis/ Guixada erzeygt ſich nach jhm gleicher weiſe überal ſo
wol/ daß er über das waſſer kommen vnnd auch ein krentzlin dauon bracht
hat.

Nach

14 Another portrait purportedly of Juan Quijada de Reayo.
From *Thournier Kampff unnd Ritterspiel* (Frankfurt am Main: Christian Egenolff, 1550), unnumbered fol.

theory into practice and quite probably was the reason why this book was commissioned: a passport to a smooth rite of passage.

Figs. 13–14 offer some fascinating insights into the tournament at Binche whilst underscoring at the same time the inherent tensions and paradoxes of paper chivalry. Both are folios from a lavishly illustrated German account of the tournament published in 1550, entitled *Thournier Kampff unnd Ritterspiel* (Tournament Battle and Knightly Games). The woodcut in fig. 13 purports to show Juan Quijada on the far side of the tilt barrier defeating his opponent on the near side for the viewer's pleasure. The caption reads as follows:

> *Concerning the tournament over the barriers*
> *and the calling out of the prizes.*

When all had been arranged, all the knights were divided into two groups, and first they had them tourney over the barriers with long spears, then following that all together with cuirass-swords.[59] This was very amusing to see and came off almost like a battle, in which His Princely Majesty acquitted himself very well with the sword and gained the prize, which was a ruby. And thus did such a tournament, after each group had departed one after the other in the order they had arrived, come to an end.

After the evening meal, lovely dances were held, and the prizes were given out as follows:

Namely, to Don Johan Guixada the prize in the long spear;

To the Herr von Quirinaim the prize in the cuirass-sword.[60]

The woodcut in fig. 14 shows Quijada being presented with his crancelin in the wake of The Adventure of the Enchanted Sword. The text surrounding this woodcut reads as follows:

---

[59] The long spear is the lance; the cuirass-sword is a peculiarly German way of referring to the arming sword for cutting and thrusting. The arming sword was worn on the body in battle, strapped around the cuirass. It was considered as essential a part of the basic armour as the cuirass; hence its nomenclature in German texts of this epoch.

[60] 'Als solchs alles geschehen hat mann alle Ritter gleich zu bayden theylen ab gethaylt und uber Schrancken erstlich mit langen Spiessen, volgendes mit Kürißschwertern allzumal lassen Thournieren. So sehr lustig zu sehen gewest und schier einer Schlacht gleich geschehen; Inn welchen ir fürstlich Durchleuchtigkeyt sich mit dem Schwerdt sehr wol gehalten und den Preiß, so ein Rubin gewest, erlanget. Und ist also solcher Thournier, nach dem ein Rott nach der andern, wie sie kommen gewest, abtretten, geendet worden. ℂ Nach dem nacht essen seind schöne Tenz gehalten unnd die Preiß außgethaylt worden wie volget: ℂ Nemlich dem Don Johan Guixada der Preiß im langen Spieß; ℂ Dem Herrn von Quirinaim der preiß im Kürißschwert'. See *Thournier Kampff unnd Ritterspiel*, unnumbered fol.

The first thus to come across the sea was Don Johann Guixada, a Spaniard, also called Don Wilhelm the High Spirited, who came laden with brown samite inlaid with gold. He had sojourned at all three of the passes, as necessitated by his journey across the sea, accompanied by Herr von Bussu, who was in charge of His Majesty's livery. In the ship in which he sailed was a handsome chair covered with carmine atlas,[61] and the knight sat in it. The rowers were clothed in gambesons and hose of white and red atlas. When he had come to land he was led by the ship's patron to the rock, where he pulled once on the sword. But when he was unable to draw it out, the same patron, on behalf of the Queen, presented him with a handsome crancelin as a token of their gratitude. Then he set out again across the sea and, on horseback, over all of the passes.

His brother Luis Guixada afterwards acquitted himself equally well, also crossing the sea and taking away a crancelin from there.[62]

As texts were copied and translated it was not uncommon for the protagonists' names to be butchered in varying degrees of severity; hence in this German version Juan Quijada becomes Johann Guixada and his pseudonym is quite far removed from the one he actually chose for himself. Assignation of the honorific title 'Don' to Juan Quijada is forgivable, given that the German chronicler may not have been familiar with the nuances of Spanish titles. However, when looking at these woodcuts the reader is left wondering why a prominent martial arts expert like Quijada de Reayo would have jousted in an outdated, early-sixteenth-century-style German Stechzeug in 1549 and what magic elixir he must have been taking in order to maintain such boyish good looks so late in life. The answer is that these woodcuts are plagiarised from *Theuerdank* (Precious

---

[61] Atlas is a kind of satin; carmine (a shade of crimson) is a heraldic colour associated with Castile.

[62] 'Der erste so über das Wasser kame war Don Johann Guixada, ein Spanier, so sich Don Wilhelm den hochmütigen nennet und mit braun Samet mit goldt belegt gekleydt war. Welcher sich dermassen ann allen dreien passen hielte, daß jm über das wasser zufaren erlaubt, unnd wurde von dem Herren vonn Bussu, der Keyserlichen Meyestät grossenn stalmeyster hinüber geleytet. Inn dem Schiff darinn er überfarenn sollte, war ein schöner sessel mit Carmosin attlas bedecket, darein sich der Ritter setzte. Unnd die so rüderten, weiß unnd rot atlas wammes und hossen an hetten. Als er nun ann das land kame, ward er von des Schiffes Patron auf den Felsen gefüret, und alda zuckt er ein mal das Schwerdt. Als er es aber nicht gewinne kundte, schanckte jm gemelter Patron von wegen der Königinn mit dancksagung ein schön krentzlin, unnd zoge also wider über das wasser, unnd zu ross hinder durch alle päss. ℭ Sein Bruoder Luis Guixada erzeygt sich nach ihm gleicher weise überal so wol, daß er über das wasser kommen unnd auch ein krentzlin dauon bracht hat'. See *Thournier Kampff unnd Ritterspiel*, unnumbered fol.

Thanks), a poem published in 1517 to celebrate the life and deeds of the
Emperor Maximilian I (1459–1519; ruled 1493–1519).[63] Christian Egenolff,
the printer of *Thournier Kampff unnd Ritterspiel*, had acquired the blocks
used for the first edition of *Theuerdank* with a view to reusing them in his
own edition of this book. In order to illustrate *Thournier Kampff unnd
Ritterspiel* he used a selection of the same blocks. Thus my initial elation at
a unique discovery was dampened by the fact that the man in the woodcuts is not Juan Quijada de Reayo at all. On a superficial level, and in
fairness to Egenolff, recycling the same blocks would have enabled him
to save money in production costs. Paradoxically, however, even though
the blocks are plagiarised from another work the resemblance between
the images in the woodcuts and the events they are supposed to depict
is uncanny. In other words, the layout and selection are quite deliberate.
As far as the layout is concerned each block is framed by text at the top
and bottom, thus creating an interplay between text and image. When
conjoined with the deliberate selection of certain blocks the overall effect
is twofold: firstly, a typological connection is forged between Queen Mary
of Hungary and her paternal grandmother Mary of Burgundy, the first
wife of Maximilian I, whom he woos in *Theuerdank*; secondly, humble
Quijada de Reayo is elevated in stature based on his skill with weaponry
with the result that he is portrayed as nothing less than a latter-day
Maximilian.

At home in Cuéllar young Gabriel de la Cueva would have trained with
other boys of his own age. The visit to the Low Countries was the occasion of his initiation into the world of adult combat. At first Gabriel was
allowed to participate in the most innocuous of the chivalric activities, a
cane game, under the watchful eye of his personal tutor who was riding
close by. After that, the pupil was allowed only to witness his master in
action, until almost one year later, on 11 May 1550 he finally participated
in a tourney of forty against forty in The Brussels Park.[64] This was perhaps
the final practical lesson for this son and heir in an apprenticeship that
would lead him to emulate his master and mentor Juan Quijada de Reayo:
equally at home in a cane game, a foot combat or a joust; able to perform
well on his own or as part of a team; an accomplished, multifaceted fighter
with an international reputation for excellence.

[63] The standard critical edition in German, with a complete facsimile, is that of
   Laschitzer, ed. *Der Theuerdank*. See p. 493, woodcut 103 (joust) and p. 509, woodcut
   107 (crancelin). A magnificent colour facsimile with accompanying introduction in
   English is also now available: *The Adventures of the Knight Theuerdank*, facsimile,
   ed. Füssel, woodcuts 103 and 107. Both blocks were designed by Leonhard Beck
   (fl. 1512–18).

[64] Calvete de Estrella, *El felicíssimo viaje del muy alto y muy poderoso Príncipe don
   Phelippe*, ed. Cuenca, p. 549; also Frieder, *Chivalry and The Perfect Prince*, p. 210.

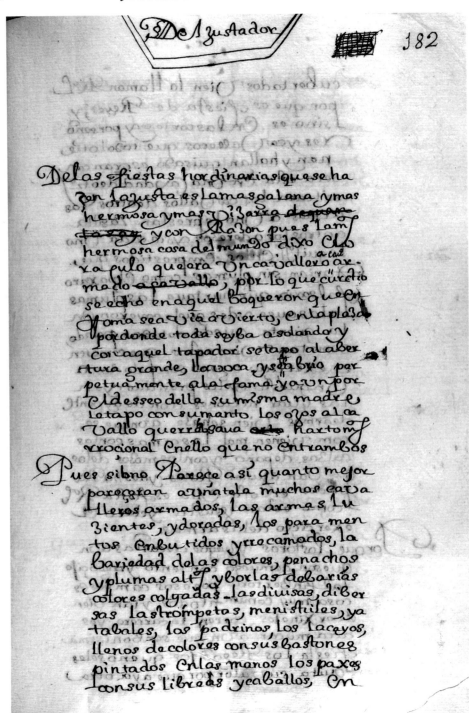

¶ Del Iustador

182

Delas fiestas hordinarias quese ha
zen la iusta es la mas galana y mas
hermosa y mas bizarra ~~de que~~
~~fazer~~ y con Razon pues la mas
hermosa cosa del mundo dixo Cipi
a Lelio que era Un cavallero ar
mado ~~a cavallo~~ por lo que cierto
se echo en aquel boqueron que en
Roma sea via avierto, en la plaça
por donde toda sey ba asolando y
con aquel tapador setapo al aber
tura grande, llarroca y seabrio per
petuamente a la fama y aun por
el desseo della su misma madre
le tapo con su manto los ojos al ca
vallo guerra ~~agua esto~~ hartom̄
rrocional en ello que no entrambos

¶ Pues si bien Parece asi quanto mejor
pareçeran a una tela muchos cava
lleros armados, las armas lu
zientes, y doradas, los para men
tos enbutidos y rrecamados, la
bariedad delas colores, penachos
y plumas altiss̄ y borlas debarias
colores colgadas —las diuisas, diber
sas las trompetas, menistriles, y a
tabales, los padrinos, los lacayos,
llenos de colores consus bastones
pintados en las manos los paxes
consus libreas y caballos, en

Luis Zapata de Chaves (1526–95)

UNLIKE Mossèn Ponç de Menaguerra and Juan Quijada de Reayo, Don Luis Zapata de Chaves rather helpfully delighted in talking about himself. Also unlike his predecessors, he was a multifaceted author who wrote about every conceivable aspect of sixteenth-century mores and culture, and not just jousting. What I am referring to in this book as Zapata's treatise on jousting, 'Del Justador', is actually one of 255 chapters or disquisitions in a much larger work entitled *Miscelánea, o Varia historia*, an eclectic compendium of anecdotes and personal memories, all of which, according to the author, are absolutely true.[65] The overarching purpose of the book, he says with characteristic flair and panache, is 'to remind, inform, entertain and delight'.[66]

The *Miscelánea* has survived in just one manuscript copy that was not made available in print until 1859.[67] Unfortunately this printed edition contains some serious errors in transcription which have been repeated by subsequent editors who have based their own editions on the 1859 edition instead of checking the original manuscript. This manuscript was most likely dictated by Zapata and it has been written by at least four different hands, one of which is Zapata's own. In the case of 'Del Justador' one amanuensis is responsible for the bulk of the text, a second amanuensis has reviewed the work of the first, making corrections, additions, deletions and stylistic changes to the text, and finally, Luis Zapata himself makes accretions, some of which are immodest in the extreme. A fourth interlocutor who makes a comment regarding the authorship of the treatise is obviously a later hand and not a part of the original team. Fig. 15 shows the first folio of 'Del Justador'.

The question arises: what exactly *is* this sole surviving manuscript of the *Miscelánea*? It begins and ends abruptly and is devoid of both prologue and epilogue, which is unusual for works written in the sixteenth century. Personal inspection of the manuscript indicates that these sections have not been torn out, but that they were most likely never written. Furthermore, Zapata states on two occasions that it is his intention to divide the book into twelve parts, but there is no indication in the extant manuscript where the twelve divisions are to be made.[68] It would appear, then, that this manuscript copy is a working draft of the master copy that Zapata was

---

[65] Zapata, *Miscelánea*, ed. Carrasco González, ch. 197, p. 304: 'esto certifico, que ninguna cosa escribo sin haber antes averiguádola con gran diligencia que es cierta'.

[66] Zapata, *Miscelánea*, ed. Carrasco González, ch. 155, p. 210: 'acordar, avisar, recrear y deleitar'.

[67] Zapata, *Miscelánea*, ed. Gayangos.

[68] Zapata, *Miscelánea*, ed. Carrasco González, ch. 51, pp. 66 and 68: 'quise repartir este mi libro en doce partes' and 'serán doce las partes de esta mi *Varia historia*'.

preparing for the printer. That it was never submitted for publication can be explained by the simple fact that the author died and the draft itself was never completed. A further complication may have been that neither Zapata nor the executors of his estate were able (or, in the case of the executors, willing) to finance publication of such a lengthy work, since he does complain in the *Miscelánea* that a previous publication, his epic poem devoted to the reign of Charles V some 290 printed folios long, cost the huge sum of 400,000 maravedís to publish.[69] It does seem clear, however, that the author's ultimate goal was to publish the *Miscelánea* in printed form with the result that, as an historical artefact, this codex provides fascinating insight into the creative process at the same time as it reveals what preliminary manuscript drafts looked like before being polished for eventual submission for publication.

Ever the loquacious raconteur, it is Zapata himself who provides clues as to the date of composition of this, his last literary work, as well as his age at the time of writing. The most important clue provided by the text is in chapter 130, where the author states that he will turn sixty-seven on 16 November 1593. Thus we can deduce from the *Miscelánea* that he was born on 16 November 1526.[70] In his epic poem *Carlo Famoso*, Zapata confirms this date, adding that he was born just after midday.[71] In chapter 50 of the *Miscelánea* Zapata states that he is writing in the year 1589, when he would have been sixty-three years old. In so far as the date of composition is concerned, this year constitutes the *terminus a quo*. In chapters 57 and 64 he states that the year is now 1592, by which time he would have reached the age of sixty-six. In chapter 47 of the text he makes the point that he would never have made it to the ripe old age of sixty-six had he not eaten temperately, and he declares once again that he is sixty-six in chapter 241 of the book. The latest date mentioned occurs in chapters 85, 130, 180 and 197, when Zapata states that the current year is 1593. This year thus constitutes the *terminus ad quem* for this work. The date of composition of 'Del Justador', and, indeed, of the *Miscelánea* itself, can reasonably be set between 1589 and 1593. The fact that the references to the author's age are so scattered indicates that the extant manuscript does not constitute a linear narrative. These are sporadic musings assembled piecemeal over a period of five years.

Don Luis Zapata had a chequered career. As he tells us in the *Miscelánea*, he was of noble stock, born and bred in the town of Llerena in Extremadura, that sun-drenched, arid yet stunningly beautiful region

---

[69] Zapata, *Miscelánea*, ed. Carrasco González, ch. 164, p. 224.

[70] In his 1859 edition Gayangos transcribed Zapata's age as 61 instead of 67 based on his misreading of Biblioteca Nacional MS 2790, fol. 198r, and he thus set Zapata's birth date erroneously at 1532.

[71] Zapata, *Carlo Famoso*, facsimile, ed. Terrón Albarrán, fol. 162rb.

of Spain that had produced so many famous conquistadors.[72] He was named Luis in memory of his paternal grandfather.[73] His mother, the daughter of the Count of Medellín, died shortly after giving birth to him and after just one year of marriage to Luis' father Francisco Zapata de Chaves.[74] As a boy he was introduced at court, where by nine years of age he had become one of the thirty or so pages in attendance to Isabella of Portugal, wife of the Emperor Charles V.[75] During his early court career he would be assigned as a page to Charles and Isabella's son, the future King Philip II of Spain. At the tender age of thirteen, on 24 October 1539, Zapata had his first personal taste of the code of chivalry, as like his father before him he was inducted into the military Order of St James. The conferral of this honour required a period as a noviciate in the convent of Uclés, during which time the young knight learned the rules of the Order, professing his allegiance on 2 June 1541. He would now be entitled to an annual stipend of 12,000 maravedís.[76] An incurable profligate, Zapata would spend this allowance and, after the death of his father in 1544, his other inherited sources of income in Extremadura and Granada, with glee. He would enjoy the pleasures of life to the full, including, if 'Del Justador' is anything to go by, the very best jousting armour that money could buy.

As Philip's page Luis Zapata travelled extensively with the royal retinue throughout Spain and Europe. He can be placed as a spectator at the Valladolid jousts of 1537[77] and he is known to have accompanied the prince on the royal visit to Italy, Germany and the Low Countries from 1548–51. Like Quijada de Reayo, Zapata visited Brussels and participated in the festivities at Binche. Without being aided and abetted by sycophants like his master, he acquitted himself particularly well at jousting. Don Luis participated in a joust held in the square in Brussels on 5 May 1549.[78] He rode on the same team as Quijada de Reayo in the Ghent cane game, though as a member of Don Luis de Ávila y Zúñiga's quadrille, and he fought in the same foot combats as Quijada de Reayo in the courtyard of the palace at Binche in August 1549, though once again on Ávila y Zúñiga's

---

[72] For the location of Llerena, see Map II.

[73] See Menéndez Pidal, 'Discurso de Don Juan Menéndez Pidal', p. 10.

[74] Zapata, *Miscelánea*, ed. Carrasco González, ch. 58, p. 77.

[75] Zapata, *Miscelánea*, ed. Carrasco González, ch. 141, p. 188.

[76] See Menéndez Pidal, 'Discurso de Don Juan Menéndez Pidal', p. 15.

[77] Zapata, *Miscelánea*, ed. Carrasco González, ch. 141, p. 188 and ch. 250, p. 350.

[78] Calvete de Estrella, *El felicíssimo viaje del muy alto y muy poderoso Príncipe don Phelippe*, ed. Cuenca, p. 140. For the lists of teams for this competition, see Frieder, *Chivalry and The Perfect Prince*, p. 194.

team.[79] He also participated in The Adventure of the Enchanted Sword, where he adopted the persona of dangerously handsome swashbuckler Don Gavarte of The Fearful Valley.[80] On 30 August he was active again in a five-man team at a joust staged in the town square of Binche.[81] Zapata can subsequently be placed in Antwerp at a joust royal staged on 15 September 1549 with his team-mate Prince Philip and other high-ranking nobles.[82] As he states in 'Del Justador', he always preferred team events over one-on-one competitions since in his view the pace was much more rapid and exciting. None the less it was in a one-on-one joust in that city against jousting champion Ruy Gómez de Silva, who had just beaten Juan Quijada de Reayo, that Zapata took the prize of a gold cup and gold chain.[83] After Antwerp, and as he mentions in 'Del Justador', Don Luis participated vigorously in the 1550 jousts at The Brussels Park. Although we know for certain that his team-mate at this event was Juan Quijada de Reayo, we can only speculate as to how the twenty-four year old snob and dandy[84] from the imperial retinue may have interacted with the pragmatic, seasoned combat veteran from Cuéllar.

Zapata had been trained at court, along with Prince Philip and other pages, by the martial arts master Gaspar de Orihuela, whom he remembers with fondness in the pages of the *Miscelánea*.[85] His younger years were very much informed by jousting and physical fitness, even to the point of

---

[79] Calvete de Estrella, *El felicíssimo viaje del muy alto y muy poderoso Príncipe don Phelippe*, ed. Cuenca, pp. 203 and 322; also Frieder, *Chivalry and The Perfect Prince*, pp. 197 and 199.

[80] In Spanish: Don Gabarte de Valtemeroso. See Calvete de Estrella, *El felicíssimo viaje del muy alto y muy poderoso Príncipe don Phelippe*, ed. Cuenca, pp. 337–8. For the lists of teams for each competition, see Frieder, *Chivalry and The Perfect Prince*, p. 201. Don Gabarte makes his first appearance in *Amadís de Gaula*, bk II, ch. 63. He received his name after slaying a serpent in the valley of that name (*Amadís de Gaula*, bk III, ch. 67).

[81] Calvete de Estrella, *El felicíssimo viaje del muy alto y muy poderoso Príncipe don Phelippe*, ed. Cuenca, p. 351; also Frieder, *Chivalry and The Perfect Prince*, p. 204.

[82] Calvete de Estrella, *El felicíssimo viaje del muy alto y muy poderoso Príncipe don Phelippe*, ed. Cuenca, p. 436; also Frieder, *Chivalry and The Perfect Prince*, p. 206.

[83] Calvete de Estrella, *El felicíssimo viaje del muy alto y muy poderoso Príncipe don Phelippe*, ed. Cuenca, p. 544. See also Segura Covarsí, 'La *Miscelánea* de D. Luis Zapata', p. 423.

[84] He is called a dandy by Márquez Villanueva, *Fuentes literarias cervantinas*, pp. 127–32.

[85] Zapata, *Miscelánea*, ed. Carrasco González, ch. 104, pp. 135–7. What little is known about Master Gaspar is documented by Gonzalo Sánchez-Molero, *El aprendizaje cortesano de Felipe II (1527–1546)*, pp. 97–8. He was contracted by Charles V in 1536 and appears to have died around 1550, at which time he was succeeded by Master Juan de Nápoles.

bodily abuse. For example, in order to stay in shape, as a lad Zapata paid careful attention to his diet, eating just one meal a day, avoiding alcohol and even sleeping in his greaves to keep his legs straight and thin.[86] Zapata would state in the prologue of one of the surviving manuscript copies of his *Libro de cetrería* (Book on Falconry) that in his youth he had three aspirations:

> Plato used to praise his gods for three things: that they had made him a man as opposed to a beast; a male as opposed to a female; a Greek as opposed to a barbarian. In the age of my youth I found myself praising those same things, and bettering the last one by being a Spaniard, I wished for three more: to be a great courtier and a great poet and a great jouster.[87]

As he strove to fulfil his ambitions, his techniques for physical fitness seem to have paid off, for as Zapata immodestly but quite correctly points out in the manuscript copy of 'Del Justador': 'I myself ... have been one of the most consummate and successful jousters in Spain.' Unlike Menaguerra and Quijada de Reayo, Zapata devoted himself entirely to jousting and never once set foot on a battlefield. Even at court he was able to expend all his energy on sport and spectacle, as he never once held an official position. Thus, until the late 1550s his life was very much that of the carefree *bon viveur*, with emphasis on the noble pursuits of hunting and jousting. Just as the great hero of chivalric fiction Amadis of Gaul was instantly recognisable whenever he jousted in disguise because of his peerless technique, so Zapata, without making an explicit comparison but doubtless with the allusion in mind, states that when he jousted in disguise he would betray his true identity the moment he placed the lance in the rest, such was his unique style.[88] He would have jousting on his mind to the very end. With the exception of the facsimile edition of the *Miscelánea*,[89] all the modern editions of this work fail to include one of its most endearing aspects, that is, the doodles in the margins, drawn by the author himself. One such doodle shows an ink sketch of a joust and a bull-run complete

[86] Zapata, *Miscelánea*, ed. Carrasco González, ch. 47, p. 59.

[87] 'Por tres cosas alabava Platón a sus dioses: que le avían hecho honbre y no bestia; varón y no hembra; griego y no bárbaro. Yo en la juvenil edad que me hallé con aquellas mismas, y mejor la postrera que es ser español, deseé otras tres: ser gran cortesano y gran poeta y gran justador'. Madrid, Biblioteca Nacional, MS 7844, fol. 2v. The prologue is reproduced in Zapata, *Libro de cetrería*, facsimile, ed. Terrón Albarrán, pp. cxii–cxviii (at p. cxiv). This particular passage is also quoted by Menéndez Pidal, 'Discurso de Don Juan Menéndez Pidal', p. 16, n. 5.

[88] Zapata, *Miscelánea*, ed. Carrasco González, ch. 37, p. 47. On Amadis, see Rodríguez de Montalvo, *Amadis of Gaul*, trans. Place and Behm, bk I, ch. 8 (vol. I, p. 91).

[89] Zapata, *Miscelánea*, facsimile, ed. Terrón Albarrán.

16 Zapata's jousting and bull-run doodles in the *Miscelánea*, 1589–93

with spectators, reflecting the distracted musings of an elderly man on his halcyon days (fig. 16).

It was after returning to Spain from northern Europe in 1551 that Zapata turned his hand to writing. In 1552 he started work on his first book, a lengthy epic poem entitled *Carlo Famoso*, dedicated to the life and times of the Emperor Charles V. His interest in epic poetry is clearly reflected in the *Miscelánea*, which includes several references to the Italian master of the genre, Ludovico Ariosto, the author of *Orlando Furioso* (1516).[90] He also mentions *La Araucana*, the Spanish masterpiece of the genre composed by Alonso Ercilla y Zúñiga, a soldier who recounted through the medium of verse his experiences in the Arauco Wars, the first of which took place in the 1530s.[91] Years in the making, it would not be until 1569, 1578 and 1589 that *La Araucana* was published in three instalments, which makes *Carlo Famoso* its precursor and a possible influence. Like Ercilla, Zapata

---

90 Zapata, *Miscelánea*, ed. Carrasco González, ch. 134, p. 175 and ch. 184, pp. 250–1.

91 Zapata, *Miscelánea*, ed. Carrasco González, ch. 46, p. 58 and ch. 125, pp. 164–5.

spent some fourteen years working on his own epic poem, and he did not actually publish *Carlo Famoso* until 1566. Although this was not his only literary work, it would be one of just two that would find their way into print in Zapata's lifetime.

In 1556, after serving Philip for twenty-one years, Don Luis Zapata was formally and abruptly dismissed from the royal court. This dismissal, as Francisco Márquez Villanueva points out, was one of Philip's first acts as king.[92] It would not be forgotten by Zapata, who would in subsequent years petulantly – perhaps also foolishly – seek vengeance through the medium of print. A year after this political and personal slight Zapata married Doña Leonor Puertocarrero, daughter of the third Count of Medellín, his mother's niece and, therefore, Zapata's own first cousin. In late 1557 Doña Leonor gave birth to a son, christened Francisco after his grandfather. Like his own father before him, the boy would never get to know his mother, for she suffered the same fate as her aunt, dying some two days after the birth, in January 1558. Doña Leonor's death had a profound impact on Zapata, which he openly expresses in the pages of *Carlo Famoso*.[93] Later in life, for all his garrulousness, he would mention this traumatic event only in passing in the *Miscelánea*.[94]

Zapata's grief manifested itself in the form of some 'lost years', from 1558–63. This phase in his life was mostly spent in a drunken stupor, travelling with a group of noble male friends between Llerena and Seville, hunting, drinking heavily, womanising and sinking ever further into debt.[95] It was during this most dissolute period, in the year 1561, that lesser-known poet Baltasar del Hierro published his epic poem about the life and deeds of seafarer Álvaro de Bazán (1526–88), which is, ironically, preceded by two panegyric sonnets about Zapata, one written by Hierro, the other by Gregorio Silvestre, as follows:

> To the most illustrious lord Don Luis Zapata.
> A Sonnet.
>
> Heroic, illustrious, great and generous,
> Extreme of charm and gallantry,
> Paragon of herculean manliness
> And abundant river of virtues,

---

[92] Márquez Villanueva, *Fuentes literarias cervantinas*, pp. 156–7.

[93] For the stanzas in question, see Zapata, *Libro de cetrería*, facsimile, ed. Terrón Albarrán, pp. xxix–xxx.

[94] Zapata, *Miscelánea*, ed. Carrasco González, ch. 58, p. 77.

[95] On this phase of Zapata's life, see Segura Covarsí, 'La *Miscelánea* de D. Luis Zapata', pp. 427–8. On the enormous extent of his debts, see especially Maldonado Fernández, 'Don Luis Zapata de Chaves, III Señor del Estado de Çehel de las Alpujarras y de las Villas de Jubrecelada (Llerena), Ulela y Ulula'.

I implore you to have mercy
By forgiving my boldness,
For if they were worthy, who would not
Protect themselves with the most precious shield?

For what the poets did not achieve
Whose names are now in heaven
Written among constellations and planets,

Fortune concedes to me, for from the ground
I hold my trumpets much higher,
For they are borne aloft by your outstretched wings.[96]

∿ ✦ ∿

To the most illustrious lord Don Luis Zapata.
Gregorio Silvestre.
A Sonnet.

If the equanimity and justice of Trajan,
That courageous heart
And that great and generous spirit of Caesar,
The valour and great courage of Alexander

Could come together in one human being
He would still be defective,
Wishing in vain to compare himself to the valiant,
Illustrious Don Luis Zapata.

His spirit and valour and his greatness
Are very well known, for everywhere
Fame publishes it and proclaims it.

Nature finished her work with him;
Minerva polished him. All that was left was Mars,
And Belona is always there to suckle him.[97]

---

[96] 'Al muy yllustre señor Don Luys Çapata. / Soneto. / Eroyco, yllustre, magno y generoso, / Extremo en gentileza y gallardía, / Dechado de la hercúlea varonía / Y río de virtudes caudaloso, / Suplico que te muestres piadoso / En otorgar perdón de mi osadía, / Porque por merecer, ¿Quién dexaría / Cubrirse del escudo más preciosso? / Que lo que no alcançaron los poetas / Que tienen ya sus nombres en el cielo, / Escriptos entre signos y planetas, / Fortuna me concede, pues del suelo / Pongo muy más arriba mis trompetas, / Que suben con las alas de tu buelo'. See Hierro, *Libro y primera parte de los victoriosos hechos del muy valeroso cavallero don Álvaro de Baçán*, fol. Aiʳ.

[97] 'Al muy yllustre señor Don Luys Çapata. / Gregorio Silvestre. / Soneto. / Si el peso y la justicia de Trajano; / De César aquel pecho animoso / Y aquel ánimo grande y generoso; / De Alexandre el valor y esfuerço mano / Pudieran verse en

In the wake of this hollow rhetoric, and some four years after the death of Leonor, on 27 April 1562, Zapata was granted licence to remarry. He did so in February of 1563, taking as his wife Doña Leonor de Ribera. Within another three years, in 1566, the strength of the second marriage would be tested to the full. The bulk of that year was spent as happily as ever, enjoying much marital and some financial stability thanks to Doña Leonor and her dowry, and putting the finishing touches to the epic poem that had taken almost fifteen years to write. On the one hand Zapata fulfilled his ambition to be a poet by publishing *Carlo Famoso* in Valencia on 20 June 1566. On the other hand, he was arrested in the wake of the book's publication, accused of committing unspecified 'crimes and excesses'. In a royal decree dated 30 August 1566 he was formally stripped of his insignia of the Order of St James at the fortress of Segura de la Sierra. This ceremony, in which the naturally gregarious knight was forced to stand alone in sombre silence whilst the distinctive insignia of the Order, a red cross, was literally and violently ripped off his cape, was designed to humiliate as well as to punish.[98] Now aged forty, Zapata had spent enough time in the world of court festival and ceremony to understand the meaning of this monumental event. He must have felt as if they were ripping out his heart.

Though initially harsh, the sentence was attenuated somewhat in 1569 when Zapata was allowed to move with his wife and child to Hornachos and thence to the fortress of Valencia de la Torre near his home town of Llerena. He would remain under house arrest for a staggering twenty-six years, when he was officially pardoned and freed by royal decree in 1592.[99] Doña Leonor coped as best as she could with the strain and shame of her husband's imprisonment and with the massive debts that had been incurred through years of extravagant living. She finally succumbed in 1570, leaving Zapata a widower for the second time. As with other traumatic moments in Zapata's life, the memory of his ignominious arrest

---

un subjecto humano / Viniera quasi a ser defectuoso, / Queriendo compararse al valeroso, / Yllustre don Luys Çapata en vano. / Su ánimo y valor y su grandeza / Muy conoscidos son, qu'en toda parte / La Fama lo divulga y lo pregona. / Su punto acabó en él Naturaleza; / Minerva lo esmeró. Restósse Marte, / Y vale a mamantar siempre Belona'. See Hierro, *Libro y primera parte de los victoriosos hechos del muy valeroso cavallero don Álvaro de Baçán*, fol. Aii^v; also cited by Segura Covarsí, 'La Miscelánea de D. Luis Zapata', pp. 420–1.

[98] The royal decree refers to 'delitos y ecesos'. See Menéndez Pidal, 'Discurso de Don Juan Menéndez Pidal', p. 62. The entire procedure is described in a document entitled *Traslado autorizado de lo que se hizo con Don Luis Zapata, caballero de Santiago, preso en la fortaleza de Segura de la Sierra* (Madrid, Biblioteca Nacional, MS 10475). This MS is edited in Zapata, *Libro de cetrería*, facsimile, ed. Terrón Albarrán, pp. xlvi–liii.

[99] Márquez Villanueva, *Fuentes literarias cervantinas*, p. 155.

and imprisonment seems to have been so painful that he could not bring himself to discuss it openly in the pages of his *Miscelánea*.

The key to Zapata's arrest and imprisonment is provided by Márquez Villanueva, who demonstrates convincingly that *Carlo Famoso* was a subtly reactionary, subversive work in which the author promoted an Erasmian-influenced pacifist agenda whilst at the same time he condemned what he perceived as the absolutism and imperialist warmongering of the Hapsburg dynasty, all sprinkled with a liberal dose of irony. Whether or not Philip, to whom the poem is dedicated, really could be considered an imperialist at this stage in his reign is a matter open to debate. Henry Kamen, for example, states categorically that Philip's court, 'except in the triumphalist years of the early 1580s, was not imperialist', while Geoffrey Parker has argued a brilliant case in favour of what he calls the 'messianic imperialism' that underpinned the king's political philosophy throughout his reign.[100] Zapata was a keen observer and saw himself as a teller of truths, albeit an outspoken and sometimes imprudent one, and he may well have seen the writing on the wall as early as the 1560s. One other reason why Márquez Villanueva imputes the arrest to the epic poem is that although Zapata had been leading a dissolute life, so had many other noblemen of the time and they were not sentenced to imprisonment.[101] To this observation I would add that Zapata was really a parenthetical rather than a habitual libertine, sent over the edge for a short time in the wake of his first wife's premature death. With the exception of his spending habits, he seems to have pulled his personal life back together by the time of his second marriage. What seems likely, then, is that *Carlo Famoso* was read by the dedicatee, who himself was a devoted bibliophile quite capable of reading between the lines. Offence was duly taken, and Philip II set in motion draconian steps to muzzle his former page. Indeed, it is tempting to speculate that incipient anti-imperialist opinions, a propensity for profligacy and a pathological incapacity for political discretion led to Zapata's original 1556 dismissal from court, his larger-than-life personality slowly but surely having grated on his taciturn master's every last nerve.[102]

Towards the end of his life Zapata would not forget what he perceived as Philip's betrayals, and even in 'Del Justador' he cannot resist an ironic snipe bordering on *Schadenfreude* about the king's questionable abilities in the lists that would have made Erasmus proud. After forcing home the point that jousting is above all a royal activity, Zapata notes that 'where posture in the saddle is concerned no man ever outclassed my master, King

---

[100] Kamen, *Philip of Spain*, p. 236; Parker, *The Grand Strategy of Philip II*, esp. pp. 93–102.

[101] Márquez Villanueva, *Fuentes literarias cervantinas*, pp. 109–82.

[102] The two major biographies of King Philip II in English offer diametrically opposed interpretations of this complex individual. Both do agree, however, on Philip's taciturnity. See Kamen, *Philip of Spain*, p. 223, and Parker, *Philip II*, p. 92.

Philip. He never used to break many lances, for this is not just the truth, it is a known fact.' Despite Philip's efforts, muzzled Zapata never would be, and he was writing the *Miscelánea* even while he was still technically imprisoned. Thus, in the end it could be said that Zapata had the last word in an epic battle of wits fuelled by an epic poem. The sole surviving manuscript copy of the *Miscelánea* means that his delightful, subversive irony can be appreciated to this day.

Unfortunately for Zapata, after his death *Carlo Famoso* was targeted for criticism in the book-burning scene in Miguel de Cervantes' *Don Quixote*, part I, chapter 7.[103] Though *Carlo Famoso* was torched with some regret, having one's work consigned to the flames in one of the most famous chapters of one of the most famous novels of all time was the kiss of death. *Carlo Famoso* has been published in its entirety only once since 1566, in a facsimile edition.[104] The *Miscelánea*, on the other hand, is believed to have circulated quite widely in manuscript form after Zapata's death and to have had an influence on Cervantes, which is an indication of Zapata's ultimate literary triumph, though as a writer of prose rather than poetry. Circulation in manuscript form in an age of print hints at the subversive content embedded in the *Miscelánea* and could indicate that, given Zapata's well-known fate after he forged ahead with publication of *Carlo Famoso*, no-one really dared publish this work, despite its literary merits, for fear of the consequences.

In addition to *Carlo Famoso* and the *Miscelánea*, on 30 November 1583 Zapata completed work on his *Libro de cetrería*, a lengthy book about falconry dedicated to his friend Don Diego de Córdoba, whom he mentions by name in 'Del Justador'. This book is unusual in that it is a technical treatise written in hendecasyllabic poetic verse. Only an eccentric like Zapata would have attempted such an undertaking. He never did find a publisher, though three manuscript copies are known to exist.[105] Whilst in prison he also completed a verse translation into Spanish of Horace's *Epistola ad Pisones*. Consisting of just twenty-six folios, this short work did reach the presses and was published in Lisbon by Alexandre de Syqueira in 1592 shortly after Zapata's release. Senectitude had done nothing to temper Zapata's hubris, however, which in this work set him up for failure. He

---

[103] See Márquez Villanueva, *Fuentes literarias cervantinas*, pp. 158–82.

[104] Zapata, *Carlo Famoso*, facsimile, ed. Terrón Albarrán. Portions of the poem have been edited and annotated by Toribio Medina and Reynolds, *El Primer Poema que trata del Descubrimiento y Conquista del Nuevo Mundo*, pp. 21–138. In addition, Canto XXVII has been edited by Sánchez Jiménez, *El Sansón de Extremadura: Diego García de Paredes en la literatura española del siglo XVI*, pp. 89–166.

[105] Madrid, Biblioteca Nacional, MSS 3336, 4219 and 7844. See Zapata, *Libro de cetrería*, facsimile, ed. Terrón Albarrán, which reproduces MS 4219. As noted by Terrón Albarrán, p. cxii, Zapata provides the date of completion of the original text in a note at the end of MS 7844.

made the terrible mistake of prefacing the book with a disquisition about bad translators and bad poets which he then immediately followed with his own dreadful verse translation of Horace. Although there were some apologists, the book was widely criticised by Zapata's contemporaries for his audacity when compared to the overall poor quality of the poetry, and it rapidly fell into oblivion.[106]

Zapata would live just another three years, his exact death date unknown, but estimated, on the basis of documents about his insurmountable debts currently held in the municipal archive of Llerena, to have fallen at some point between July and October of the year 1595.[107] Sadly, by the end of his life he was something of a caricature, for the master of subversive irony had become the quintessential impoverished Spanish nobleman, the very target of ironic satire in the masterpiece by Cervantes that had in turn been influenced by the *Miscelánea*.

To end this chapter on a positive note, the short disquisition on jousting edited and translated in this book does show Luis Zapata de Chaves at his very best, which is remarkable considering that he was writing in his late sixties, physically exhausted after having spent so many years in prison. In his clauses he pays rhetorical tribute to the Attic style, often suppressing the verb in favour of an accumulation of nouns complemented by well-placed adjectives, similes and puns. In consequence, the pace is brisk and the wit is sharp. With the expression 'you can't keep a good man down' firmly in mind it is quite telling that Zapata does not say, 'I myself *was* one of the most consummate and successful jousters in Spain.' On the contrary, what he scribbles in the margin of his manuscript, making the point that this was omitted and has to be inserted into the final draft, is: 'I myself *have been* one of the most consummate and successful jousters in Spain.' The sentence is predicated upon a perfect tense verb which uses the present, the here and now, as the reference point for reflection upon the past, the implicit meaning being that he always has been and still is one of the most consummate jousters in Spain. In sum, of his three youthful ambitions, Zapata failed as both a courtier and a poet, but there was and is no question whatsoever that he triumphed as a jouster.

---

[106] See Segura Covarsí, 'La *Miscelánea* de D. Luis Zapata', pp. 436–9. The book has been reproduced in facsimile. See Zapata, *El arte poética de Horacio*, facsimile, ed. Amezúa.

[107] See Carrasco, 'Documentos de 1584 a 1595, relativos a Don Luis Zapata de Chaves, existentes en el Archivo municipal de Llerena', p. 366; also Zapata, *Libro de cetrería*, facsimile, ed. Terrón Albarrán, p. lx.

~: 2 :~

Arms and Armour of the Joust I:
The Fifteenth Century

I T is fitting in the context of the present volume to look to the documentary evidence as a point of departure for the discussion of arms and
armour. Castilian knights had long since been enjoined to be knowledgeable about armour and weaponry, as evinced from the thirteenth-century
law code *Las Siete Partidas*, II.xxi.10:

> They should also know how to form a judgment of armor, in three
> different ways; first, be able to determine whether the iron, wood,
> leather, or other material of which it is composed, is good; second,
> be able to ascertain whether it is strong; and third, whether it is
> light. This also applies to offensive arms, which should be well-made,
> strong, and light. For, the better knights are acquainted with these
> things and are skilled in their use, the more and the better can they
> be aided by them, and employ them for their advantage.[1]

What this law does not make absolutely clear (or does not anticipate)
is that armour and weaponry would evolve with unprecedented rapidity
throughout the Middle Ages and the Renaissance, a rapidity that did
not go unnoticed by contemporaries, even by those who were not practising knights themselves. In the late fourteenth century Chaucer in 'The
Knight's Tale' would remark of armour that 'There's never a new fashion
but it's old.'[2] And around the year 1444 Alonso de Cartagena would
remonstrate against Castilian knights as follows:

> But what shall we say, when we see the kingdom full of cuirasses
> and pauldrons, and those people in Granada living in peace, and the
> refined practice of arms is spent on gathering armies against kinsmen

---

[1] 'Otrosí, deben haber sabiduría en tres maneras: la primera, si es bueno de hierro, o
el fuste, o el cuero, o la otra cosa de que les hacen; la segunda, para conocer si son
fuertes; la tercera, que sean ligeros. Eso mismo es de las armas para herir, que han
de ser bien hechas, e fuertes, e ligeras. Pues cuanto más los caballeros conocieren
estas cosas, e las usaren, tanto más, e mejor, se ayudarán de ellas, e las tornarán a
su pro' (*Las Siete Partidas*, ed. Sánchez-Arcilla, p. 290b. For the translation, see *Las
Siete Partidas*, trans. Scott and Burns, vol. II, p. 422).

[2] 'Ther is no newe gyse that is nas old'. Chaucer, 'The Knight's Tale', in *The Riverside
Chaucer*, ed. Benson, p. 54a line 2125. For the translation, see Chaucer, *The
Canterbury Tales*, trans. Coghill, p. 76.

and against those who should be friends, or in jousts or tourneys, of which one is abhorrent and abominable and a thing that brings dishonour and destruction, the other a game or a test of strength, but not the principal act of chivalry? Whence The Philosopher says that in tourneys and trials of arms the strongest man is not revealed, for true fortitude is understood to be the terrible and dangerous deeds to the death that are done on behalf of the Republic. And they say that it is an ancient proverb that on occasion the good tourneyer is a timorous and cowardly warrior.[3] And jousts were prohibited for a time in France, because they devoted themselves so much to them that the war in the Holy Land was hindered.

And thus, taking the two extremes, that is to say, either playing with arms or threatening those whom we call friends with them, we abandon the purpose for which they were made, which is to humble the pride of enemies. And I would greatly wish that chivalry's valiant and powerful should pay heed to the fact that the knights' acclaim does not lie in having many arms or in changing the conformation of them and devoting one's energy to discovering new pieces of armour and giving them new names so that if our ancestors arose from the dead they would not understand them, but rather in exalting the holy faith with them and expanding the kingdom's frontiers. And therefore, to be sure, the arms are honoured when, this having been done, they return in triumph and glory. And it should please God that in pourpoints and bascinets we were to do what some of the previous generations did, for greater honour would follow from that than from entering courts and cities overly accompanied by pages and wearing armets and panaches, arriving by a secure and short road. And who cannot see that this is more a demonstration and display of wealth than of virtue?[4]

---

[3] 'The Philosopher' is Aristotle. In this case Cartagena is imposing an interpretation upon Aristotle, *Nicomachean Ethics*, III.viii.8–9.

[4] 'Mas, ¿qué diremos nosotros, que vemos el reino lleno de platas y de guardabrazos, y estar en paz los de Granada, y el hermoso meneo de las armas ejercitarse en ayuntar huestes contra los parientes y contra los que debían ser amigos, o en justas o en torneos, de lo cual, lo uno es aborrecible y abominable, y cosa que trae deshonra y destruición, lo otro un juego o ensaye, mas no principal acto de la caballería? Onde, el Filósofo dice que en los torneos y en las pruebas de las armas no se parece cuál es el fuerte, ca la fortaleza verdadera en los hechos terribles y peligrosos de muerte que por la república se hacen se conoce. Y proverbio antiguo dicen que es, que a las veces el buen torneador es temeroso y cobarde batallador. Y vedadas fueron en un tiempo las justas en Francia, porque tanto se daban a ellas que se destorbaba la guerra de Ultramar. ℭ Y así, tomando los dos extremos, es a saber, o jugando con las armas o amenazando con ellas a los que llamamos amigos, dejamos el medio para que se hicieron, que es para abajar la soberbia de los enemigos. Y

Despite the bishop's frustration with armour- and tournament-crazed Castilian knights, for the purposes of this chapter his inflammatory remarks do underscore the fact that armour was never static for too long. Indeed, from the twelfth through the fourteenth centuries Álvaro Soler del Campo has been able to divide the evolutionary stages of Iberian field armour into fairly consistent fifty-year increments.[5] Jousting armour was defined by its own, almost constant, process of evolution, which in turn is a reflection of the frequency with which tournaments were staged throughout Europe. Because there were many more tournaments than battles, in the case of armour designed specifically for the joust, as of the fifteenth century, Soler del Campo's fifty-year increments could probably even be reduced to decades. Taking into account the perennial mysteries of personal preference and minor yet compatible variations in design, to a certain extent the armour for the joust did allow for some uniformity in development, since the jousters themselves tended to be peripatetic, interacting with each other on national and international circuits. They would have talked plenty of shop, discussed new innovations and, in collusion with the major European armourers, prompted many a universal change in design. Their relationship with the armourers was symbiotic, for the major medieval and renaissance armourers boasted an international clientele and they, too, could have made itinerant jousters from the Christian kingdoms of Iberia aware of new innovations being used by German, French, English and Italian customers. Certainly Soler del Campo has forced home the point that evolutionary trends in Castilian armour developed and progressed in congruence with major trends in other European countries, and he too mentions tournaments as an international point of contact.[6] On this note, and in order to give some idea of the evolution of

mucho querría que parasen mientes los valientes y poderosos en la caballería, que no consiste el loor de los caballeros en tener muchas armas ni en mudar el tajo de ellas y poner su trabajo en hallar nuevas formas de armaduras y poner nombres nuevos, que si nuestros antecesores se levantasen no los entenderían, mas en exalzar con ellas la santa fe y ensanchar los términos del reino. Y entonces, por cierto, vienen ellas honradas cuando, esto hecho, tornan con triunfo y gloria. Y pluguiese a Dios que con perpuntes y capellinas hiciésemos lo que algunos de los pasados hicieron, ca se seguiría de ello mayor honra que entrar en las cortes y en las ciudades muy acompañados de pajes y con almetes y penachos, viniendo de seguro y breve camino. ¿Y quién no ve que esto es más muestra de ostentación de riqueza que de virtud?' See Cartagena, *Doctrinal de los caballeros*, in *Tratados militares*, ed. Fallows, pp. 265–6.

[5] Soler del Campo, *La evolución del armamento medieval en el reino castellano-leonés y al-Andalus (siglos XII–XIV)*, pp. 173–200, and Soler del Campo, 'El armamento en el Medievo hispano', p. 125.

[6] Soler del Campo, *La evolución del armamento medieval en el reino castellano-leonés y al-Andalus (siglos XII–XIV)*, pp. 28, 132–3, 194, 205.

jousting armour, I shall consider the arms and armour mentioned in each of the texts edited in Part II in chronological order, starting with *El Passo Honroso de Suero de Quiñones*.

El Passo Honroso de Suero de Quiñones (1434)

GIVEN the amount of intrepid border-crossing participants at this passage of arms – seventy-seven total, from Aragon-Catalonia, Brittany, Castile, Germany, Italy and Portugal – the armour worn by the contestants is best considered holistically. The first point to be made is that, in keeping with the rules of passages of arms in general, the combatants were wearing field armour – in this case primarily of Italian manufacture or design – over which at this event in particular one reinforcing piece could be worn. Plate armour for the field tiptoes tentatively into the chronicles with one isolated reference by Giraldus Cambrensis in 1171, and is mentioned with much greater frequency after 1250.[7] By the time of the Pass of Honour of Suero de Quiñones, the sustained evolution of defensive plate armour was well under way.

While fakes and reproductions abound, original, homogeneous Italian-made armours from the mid-1430s are non-existent. There are but two composite examples that come chronologically close to the Pass of Honour of Suero de Quiñones: Churburg Castle armour CH 18; and the Avant armour in the R. L. Scott Collection in Glasgow, so called because the word 'Avant' ('Forward!') is inscribed repeatedly in *pointillé*, or pointwork, around the edge of the breastplate.[8] Fig. 17 shows the Avant armour, which was made *c.* 1440–5 for a member of the Matsch family of Churburg Castle, located in what is now the extreme north of Italy. This armour is virtually complete and original to the period, with some exceptions that should be noted: the right gauntlet is original to the period but does not match; the left gauntlet is a modern reproduction; the right gardbrace and the tassets are missing;[9] and it is currently displayed with a type of helmet

---

7 Blair, *European Armour*, pp. 37–52; Soler del Campo, *La evolución del armamento medieval en el reino castellano-leonés y al-Andalus (siglos XII–XIV)*, p. 127.

8 On the Churburg armour, see Trapp and Mann, *The Armoury of the Castle of Churburg*, pp. 35–41; Boccia and Coelho, *L'Arte dell'Armatura in Italia*, fig. 52 and p. 119; Boccia *et al.*, *Armi e Armature Lombarde*, p. 52; and Scalini *et al.*, *L'Armeria Trapp di Castel Coira*, pp. 69–73, 258–9. On the Avant armour (formerly Churburg CH 20; now Glasgow Museums E.1939.65.e), see especially Joubert, *Catalogue of the Collection of European Arms and Armour Formed at Greenock by R. L. Scott*, ed. Woosnam-Savage and Capwell, pp. 9–11, and Capwell, *The Real Fighting Stuff*, pp. 26–9.

9 The reason for the missing tassets is unknown. After closely examining the right shoulder Capwell suggests that the right gardbrace may have been prised off in combat. See Capwell, *The Real Fighting Stuff*, p. 28.

17 The Avant armour. Italian, made by the Corio family of Milan, *c.* 1440–45.
Weight 26,000 g (57 lb 5 oz)

18 Paolo Uccello, *Niccolò Mauruzi da Tolentino at the Battle of San Romano, c.* 1435.
Egg tempera with walnut oil and linseed oil on poplar. 181.6 × 320 cm (5 ft 11½ in × 10 ft 6 in)

sometimes called a barbute, though as Capwell observes, it would originally
have been worn with an armet, a type of headpiece that I discuss more fully
below.[10] These nugatory details are far outweighed by the armour's overall
completeness, splendour and pristine condition. In its current configuration the armour weighs 26,000 g (57 lb 5 oz).[11] Made in Milan by the Corio
family of armourers this was at the time of its manufacture a state-of-the-
art, high-quality field armour which allows us to contextualise the type of
full harness that would have been worn at this passage of arms.

Various individual pieces of armour from the same period have also
survived intact. In addition, there are some contextual images from this
period that accurately depict the variations of full Italianate field harnesses
close to the time of the Pass of Honour of Suero de Quiñones. Amongst
the most significant are the battle of San Romano panels by Paolo Uccello
(fig. 18), which on the basis of the armour worn by the combatants have
been dated to *c.* 1435,[12] and the illustrations of 'Uomini illustri' (Famous
men) in the *Libro di Giusto* (fig. 19). Attributed to an anonymous Tuscan
artist, these illustrations also date from *c.* 1435.[13]

As far as headpieces are concerned, by the mid-fifteenth century the
man-at-arms could choose from a variety of different yet compatible

[10] Capwell, *The Real Fighting Stuff*, p. 28.
[11] Churburg CH18 weighs a comparable amount: 26,670 g (58 lb 13 oz).
[12] Boccia, 'Le armature di Paolo Uccello'; Borsi, *Paolo Uccello*, pp. 212–31.
[13] Boccia and Coelho, *L'Arte dell'Armatura in Italia*, fig. 60 and pp. 135–6.

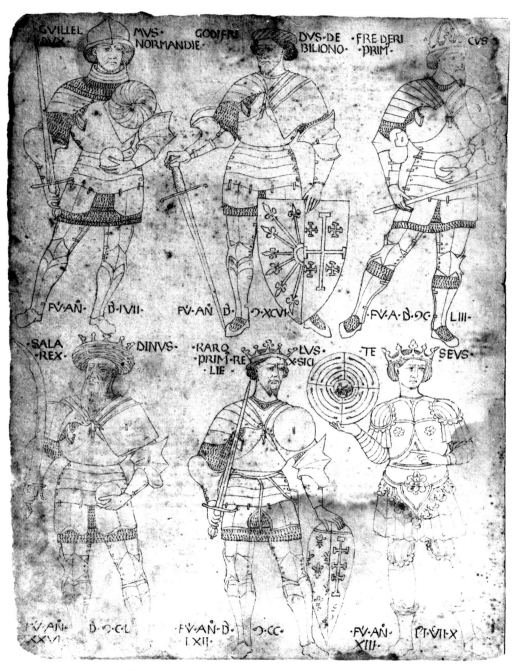

19 Portraits of armoured knights in the *Libro di Giusto*, c. 1435

20 The King of Hungary in Council. From Jean Froissart, *Chroniques*, 15th century

alternatives. There are unfortunately no contemporary contextual images of the Pass of Honour of Suero de Quiñones; fig. 20, however, shows a cluster of men-at-arms in an illumination from a mid-fifteenth-century copy of Froissart's chronicles who demonstrate the kind of variation in headpieces that could exist at any given moment, including in the case of this particular illustration helms, armets and sallets. Like the men in this illumination the knights at the Pass of Honour of Suero de Quiñones for the most part were wearing either a sallet and bevor combination or an armet with wrapper. In one case a helm was worn, since there is a reference to this knight being struck on the charnel, a device for attaching the helm to the breastplate that I shall describe more fully below. Sallets and armets are field helmets, so both would have been equally appropriate for a passage of arms, and even topping off a war harness with a helm would not have been entirely inappropriate at such an event in the 1430s.[14]

The sallets and armets worn by the combatants were equipped with a brow reinforce and a moveable visor, to be raised ostensibly after breaking the requisite three lances so as to promote the idea of the knights jousting incognito until the final dramatic anagnorisis, followed by the customary

---

[14] On the wearing of helms at passages of arms, see Riquer, *L'Arnès del cavaller*, pp. 119–20.

invitation to dinner. Fig. 21 shows a sallet with matching bevor made c. 1430–40.[15] On this example the brow reinforce and the visor are two separate pieces, but examples are also known where the brow reinforce is integral to the visor.[16]

Figs. 22–5 show three armets from the same period. The armet in fig. 22 dates to c. 1435. For many years this armet was displayed with a genuine but associated visor and a restored rondel. Because it is such a rare and important type it has been shown since 1991 with no visor rather than with one that did not originally belong to it, and without the rondel. In its current configuration the armet weighs 4,288 g (9 lb 7¼ oz).[17] Because the armet is missing its visor the cheek pieces are clearly visible, as is the projecting lip at the front designed to maximise protection for the face and deflect the lance. The cheek pieces on this style of armet are hinged at the sides on the inside so that they can be splayed open in order to place the armet on the head; they then fasten together at the front with a spring-pin. As is also the case with armets of the period the base is fitted with a row of copper alloy vervelles and holes to which a mail aventail would have been attached. This particular armet is fitted with a brow reinforce, secured in place by two rivets. The armet illustrated in figs. 23–4

21 Sallet and matching bevor, c. 1430–40

[15] On this sallet and bevor, see Reverseau, 'L'Habit de guerre des français en 1446: Le manuscrit anonyme fr. 1997 de la Bibliothèque Nationale', pp. 183–4.

[16] See, for example, Blair, *European Armour*, p. 200, figs 103 and 105.

[17] On this armet, see Boccia, *Le Armature di S. Maria delle Grazie di Curtatone di Mantova e l'Armatura Lombarda del '400*, fig. 44, and Williams, *The Knight and the Blast Furnace*, pp. 172–3 (shown in both cases with the associated visor and restored rondel).

22 Armet. Italian, c. 1435.
Weight 4,288 g (9 lb 7¼ oz)

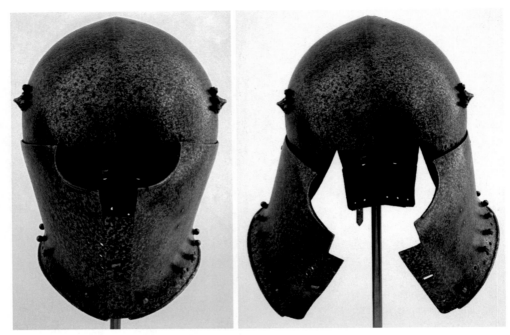

23, 24 Armet, *c.* 1435, shown closed shut *(left)* and splayed open *(right).*
Italian, made by Benedetto da Molteno of Milan, *c.* 1435. Weight 4,300 g (9 lb 8 oz)

is originally from Rhodes. It also dates to *c.* 1435 and is attributed to the
Italian armourer Benedetto da Molteno of Milan.[18] In its current configuration this armet weighs 4,300 g (9 lb 8 oz). Like the armet in fig. 22 it is
missing its visor. Also like the same armet, when shown from the front,
the distinctive light-bulb shape with shallow medial ridge is clearly visible.
There are, however, some differences between this armet and the one in
fig. 22. For example, the Rhodes armet has no brow reinforce; as well as
the vervelles and holes along the lower edge there is an alignment of holes
punched into the brow of this armet to accommodate a lining; and it is
equipped with six ventilation holes set in the shape of a triangle on the
right cheek piece.

The armet in fig. 25 dates to *c.* 1440 and was made by an Italian armourer
known as Lionardo. This is a magnificent and rare specimen. Not only has
the armet survived over five hundred years of history virtually free of dents
and with its original visor and rondel intact, but the steel from which it
is made has miraculously retained much of its original lustre, unaffected

---

[18] See Karcheski and Richardson, *The Medieval Armour from Rhodes,* pp. 1–2, and
Williams, *The Knight and the Blast Furnace,* p. 75.

by rust, corrosion or pitting.[19] The armet measures 26.34 cm (10⅜ in) high and 20.32 cm (8 in) wide and weighs 4,196 g (9 lb 4 oz). As is the case with armets of this type the eye-slit is not cut directly into the visor but is formed instead by a small space between the upper edge of the visor and the folded lower edge of the brow reinforce. Like the armets described above it has a slight medial ridge on the top, and as far as the evolutionary process is concerned, it can be determined from this armet that by 1440 the shallow brow reinforce of 1435 has evolved on this example into a much larger, cusped reinforce that sweeps back over the brow.

As can be seen from the Avant armour (fig. 17), breastplates with shallow plackarts, and backplates, were worn by all combatants. Evidence from Rodríguez de Lena's chronicle suggests that those who did opt for extra protection in the jousts of the Pass of Honour of Suero de Quiñones typically wore a rudimentary reinforcing breastplate over the principal breastplate, which would have been secured in place by two turning-clasps aligned vertically at the top and bottom. A surviving example of this type of breastplate reinforce is in the collection of the Real Armería in Madrid, inv. E59. It dates from the mid-fifteenth century (fig. 26).[20] The breastplate has one set of staples aligned vertically on the

25 Armet. Italian, made by Lionardo, c. 1440.
Weight 4,196 g (9 lb 4 oz)

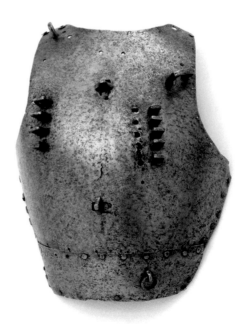

26 Reinforced breastplate for the joust.
Castile, mid-15th century

[19] On this armet, see Blair, *European Armour*, p. 87; De Cosson and Burges, *Ancient Helmets and Examples of Mail*, p. 54, no. 36, fig. 32; and Williams, *The Knight and the Blast Furnace*, p. 174.

[20] Valencia de Don Juan, *Catálogo histórico-descriptivo de la Real Armería de Madrid*, pp. 166–7 and fig. 96; also Riquer, *L'Arnès del cavaller*, p. 107 and fig. 153 (shown in both cases with an associated rest which has since been removed).

right-hand side to accommodate the lance-rest and another set on the left
to accommodate the shield. A small ring can be seen on the bottom left.
Various theories have been postulated as to the purpose of these rings that
are sometimes found on Iberian armours of the period. From the least to
the most plausible they are that they were intended for: securing weapons;
tightening the shield; or connecting the breastplate by means of a cord
or string to the bridle hand.[21] Securing weapons that would clatter onto
the abdomen and that would not in fact be used in a joust seems coun-
terintuitive. The shield theory would make sense only if the rings were
much smaller and more closely set in order to allow for faster tightening.
The bridle hand theory strikes me as the most plausible because the rings
would enable the rider to tie up his bridle arm when clad in heavy armour
that could not be supported for extended periods by the strength of the
arm alone, whilst also allowing for some flexibility of movement.

From the chronicle it is apparent that the reinforcing breastplates
differed in quality: in some instances they offered adequate protection; in
others they were unmercifully skewered. Most participants at the Pass of
Honour of Suero de Quiñones were wearing an arming-doublet and a soft
linen chemise beneath their armour.[22] Some wore jupons or surcoats over
their breastplates embroidered with a symbolic device; others wore white
armour, which is best described as 'armour of plain, polished steel, without
a permanently-attached covering'.[23]

As clarified by *Amadís de Gaula*, in medieval Castile white armour
denoted a certain level of skill since it was typically worn by novice knights.[24]

---

[21] The three theories are postulated respectively by: Domínguez Ortiz et al.,
*Resplendence of the Spanish Monarchy: Renaissance Tapestries and Armor from the
Patrimonio Nacional*, p. 110; Viollet-le-Duc, *Dictionnaire raisonné du mobilier français
de l'époque carlovingienne à la renaissance*, vol. VI, pp. 239–40; and Cripps-Day, *The
History of the Tournament in England and in France*, p. 100.

[22] On the arming doublets of the 1430s, see Capwell, 'A Depiction of an Italian
Arming Doublet, *c*. 1435–45'.

[23] Blair, *European Armour*, p. 58. See also DeVries, *Medieval military technology*,
pp. 80–1, and Riquer, *L'Arnès del cavaller*, pp. 97–100.

[24] Cp. the following passages: (1) 'Y yo ge lo toue en merced, y le dixe que tomaría
el cauallo, porque era muy bueno, y la loriga y el yelmo; mas que las otras armas
hauían de ser blancas, como a cauallero nouel conuenían'; (2) 'Pues a esta hora
llegaron Gandalín y Lasindo, escudero de don Bruneo, armados de armas blancas
como conuenía a caualleros noueles'; (3) 'Los passados que la orden de la cauallería
establescieron touieron por bueno que a la nueua alegría nueuas armas y blancas
se diessen'. ('And I considered it as a boon and I told him I would take the horse,
because it was very good, and the cuirass and the helmet; but that the other arms
were to be white as is fitting for a novice knight'; 'Then at this hour there arrived
Gandalin and Lasindo, squire of Don Bruneo, both wearing white armour, as
befitted novice knights'; 'The men of the past who established the order of chivalry
considered it good that for the new joy, new, white arms be given.') Rodríguez

The clarification is borne out by the Pass of Honour of Suero de Quiñones where the longest joust, consisting of twenty-seven courses, nineteen of which are complete misses, is fought by two of the least skilled knights, who are pointedly described as wearing white armour.[25] White, polished armour would still have been expensive and of high quality, and on an aesthetic note it would have reflected the sun with the result that on those long July and August days in 1434 with each awkward movement a myriad hues would have glistened and shimmered hypnotically from dawn until dusk. It would be up to the pragmatic ecclesiastic Alonso de Cartagena – in the quotation cited at the beginning of this chapter – to question whether or not armour with more lavish decoration really did connote a high level of virtue and skill or if it merely drew undue attention to obscene wealth. His remarks suggest that he is challenging a belief that the white armour worn by the novices was akin rhetorically to the modesty topos so typical of the exordium in medieval and renaissance literary works,[26] and the reader, as it were, would watch the novices' career unfold from exordium to conclusion as if each tournament were a new chapter in which their progress could be followed with interest. The confluence of paper chivalry and what I have called 'metal chivalry' shows that if extant harnesses and dating techniques allow scholars to determine when certain pieces went in and out of style, contemporary written sources explain what the harnesses meant and why pieces came in or went out of style. It is in and through the written sources that the armour itself is considered a type of text, but metal chivalry is an inherently paradoxical text. At an intellectual level, an act of collusion between armourer, wearer and beholder was required in order to impute meaning to the text. As we have seen, the purest example at this level was the plain, polished steel plate commissioned and worn by novices who were recognised as such by informed viewers. The act of collusion at this level could be entirely passive: novices did not have to joust or engage in any

---

de Montalvo, *Amadís de Gaula*, ed. Place, bk IV, ch. 109 (vol. IV, pp. 1087a and 1090b) and bk IV, ch. 133 (vol. IV, p. 1336ab). For the translation, see Rodríguez de Montalvo, *Amadis of Gaul*, trans. Place and Behm, bk IV, ch. 109 (vol. II, pp. 454 and 458) and bk IV, ch. 133 (vol. II, p. 737).

[25] See below, Part II, *Passo Honroso* Selection 5.

[26] On the modesty topos, see the prologues in Part II of Menaguerra, *Lo Cavaller*, and Quijada de Reayo, *Doctrina del arte de la cavallería*. Menaguerra addresses his patrons as follows: 'Since you wish, however, ordering me to do so, that I unfurl the bales of my inferior cloth into the hands of your superior intelligence, obeying you as lords and masters, I submit to your corrections, so that you can emend the grammar and poor style of the chapters that I narrate, protesting so that I not be called presumptuous; for I know well that beseeching and learning pertain to me, whilst correcting is your own craft'. Quijada de Reayo states less eloquently that he writes: 'Under the correction of other knights who know better than I what to do and say'.

27 Armour of Graf Moritz von Oldenburg
(d. 1420) with stop-rib

activity at all, for the armour alone betrayed their status and level of skill. But this plain-looking armour – this text – was in fact technologically complex, and in order to move beyond the status of a novice it was necessary to become fully engaged with it. Technological advancement required practical implementation. Thus the type of meaning that underpinned the evolution of armour was a paradox that hinged upon construction and destruction: in order to be able to extrapolate or construct meaning from and thereby understand the text – its strengths, its weaknesses, its vulnerabilities – the text's concomitant and inexorable destruction was essential.

Some of the breastplates worn at the Pass of Honour of Suero de Quiñones had a bar riveted just below the neck, known as a 'lisière d'arrêt' or stop-rib. Stop-ribs made their first appearance c. 1380–90. The earliest examples were distinctly Y-shaped, as for example on the breastplate of the effigy of Graf Moritz von Oldenburg (d. 1420) in St Ulrich's Church in Rastede (fig. 27) and in the sketch by Jacopo Bellini known as 'An Equestrian Knight and Messenger at an Open Grave', which has been dated to around 1420–40 (fig. 28).[27] Over time they shrank to a distinct V-shape as on Churburg armour CH 18, c. 1435–40 (fig. 29), and then tended to disappear altogether c. 1455.[28] As is evident from this passage of arms, one reason they became obsolete was because, although their intended purpose was to deflect the spearhead and prevent injury to the neck, stop-ribs actually often had the opposite effect, guiding the spearhead into the armpit or up into the neck in a most dangerous manner.

[27] On Graf Moritz von Oldenburg, see Mann, 'Notes on the Evolution of Plate Armour in Germany in the Fourteenth and Fifteenth Century', fig. 2; on the approximate date of the Bellini sketch, see Eisler, *The Genius of Jacopo Bellini*, pp. 99–104.

[28] Blair, *European Armour*, pp. 61 and 82.

28 Jacopo Bellini, *An Equestrian Knight and Messenger at an Open Grave*. 15th century.
Pen on paper. 38 × 25 cm (1 ft 3 in × 9⅞ in)

29 Field armour: detail of the stop-rib, arrêt à vervelles and ursus-style spaulders,
c. 1435–40

They also tended to get ripped off by powerful blows, ultimately leading armourers to address the issue of skating lances by simply enlarging the turned edges of the neck and arm scyes of the cuirass.[29]

Without exception, all participants at the Pass of Honour of Suero de Quiñones were not only required to joust with lance-rests, but they were also cautioned by the judges not to set off down the lists until their spears had been placed in the rest. The lance-rest was probably introduced by the French in the last decade of the fourteenth century. Blair and Buttin state that it did not become common in Europe until after c. 1420, though Riquer provides compelling documentary evidence that its use was already wide-spread in the Valencia region by 1403.[30] The rests used at the Pass of Honour of Suero de Quiñones are of an early type known as the 'arrêt à vervelles'. The vervelles, or staples, were arranged vertically on the right-hand side of the breastplate as can clearly be seen on Real Armería reinforcing breast-plate E59 and the Avant armour (figs. 26 and 17); the bracket of the lance-

---

[29] The technical term used to describe the stop-rib in medieval Spanish is 'el borde'. See below, Part II, *Passo Honroso* Selection 27, course 5, and Selection 33, course 1.

[30] Blair, *European Armour*, p. 61; Buttin, 'La lance et l'arrêt de cuirasse', pp. 101–2; Riquer, *L'Arnès del cavaller*, pp. 79–80. On the usage of the lance prior to the invention of the rest, see Cirlot, 'Techniques guerrières en Catalogne féodale: le maniement de la lance'.

rest was then secured to the vervelles with a retaining pin. By the 1430s this type of rest was associated primarily with Italianate armour.[31] An example is shown on the breastplate of Churburg armour CH 18 in fig. 29. Some of the participants in the Pass of Honour of Suero de Quiñones may have purchased their harnesses directly from Italy, though Italianate armour would certainly also have been produced in the principal Iberian centres of armour-making such as Burgos, Calatayud, Castejón de las Armas and Seville.[32] As with all accoutrements attached by rivets and staples, however, a powerful blow, either given or received, could cause irreparable damage to the accoutrement in question, and the arrêt à vervelles was no exception.[33] They are ripped off time and again in this passage of arms, often precipitating hand injuries into the bargain. In the case of the lance-rest, however, the freedom of movement that it allowed was indisputable and probably saved this little piece from extinction;[34] hence, instead of disappearing like the clumsy stop-rib, the lance-rest survived to become a standard piece of the jouster's equipment and would continue to be refined and perfected through many years of trial and error.

Moving from the body to the extremities, pauldrons offered protection for the shoulders, vambraces were worn on the arms and gauntlets covered the hands. As regards the gauntlets worn in the Pass of Honour of Suero de Quiñones, the chronicler refers in particular to a piece called the 'guarda de la manopla', which is susceptible to damage or to being ripped off. This is a reference to a single-plate gauntlet reinforce with which knights and armourers were experimenting in Western Europe during the 1430s and 1440s. Examples of this reinforce are known on effigies of the period that show Italian export armour of the type that was being worn by the participants in the Pass of Honour of Suero de Quiñones. Fig. 30 shows the effigy of John Fitzalan, 7th Earl of Arundel (d. 1435), in the Fitzalan Chapel of Arundel Castle in West Sussex. This effigy dates to c. 1435–40. The detail in fig. 31 shows Fitzalan's left hand with distinctive single-plate gauntlet reinforce. It is secured in place with a staple and pin, and what

[31] Blair, *European Armour*, p. 93.

[32] On these centres, see Blair, *European Armour*, p. 108; Soler del Campo, 'La producción de armas personales: 1500–1700', pp. 854–60; and Williams, *The Knight and the Blast Furnace*, pp. 815–21. See also Map I. Toledo would not become a major centre for the armourer's craft until the sixteenth century. See Fraxno and Bouligny, *Memoria sobre la teoría y fabricación del acero en general y de su aplicación a las armas blancas*, pp. 117–24.

[33] The fragility of the arrêt à vervelles is discussed by Buttin, 'La lance et l'arrêt de cuirasse', pp. 103, 118, 149–50, and Cirlot, 'El juego de la muerte. La elección de las armas en las fiestas caballerescas de la España del siglo XV', pp. 63–4. See also below, Part II, *Passo Honroso* Selection 3, course 1, and Selection 6, course 1.

[34] Freedom of movement and lance-play is discussed in chapter 4 below. On freedom of movement, see also Buttin, 'La lance et l'arrêt de cuirasse', p. 162.

30 (*above*) Effigy (*c.* 1435–40) of John Fitzalan, 7th Earl of Arundel (d. 1435), in the Fitzalan Chapel of Arundel Castle in West Sussex

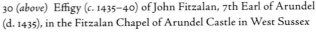

31 (*left*) Detail of fig. 30: Fitzalan's single-plate gauntlet reinforce

looks like a thin leather strap. The reinforce is worn over Fitzalan's left gauntlet only, doubtless because the right hand was not as vulnerable to injury and needed to be more flexible for carrying sword or lance. This concurs with the descriptions in the Pass of Honour of Suero de Quiñones, which always mention the gauntlet reinforce in the context of the left hand. Not unlike stopribs, because these gauntlet reinforces were held in place with a staple and pin they were prone to being ripped off; hence in the context of tournaments they rapidly went out of style.[35] One contestant at the Pass of Honour of Suero de Quiñones, the Castilian knight Juan de Soto, was wearing a mitten gauntlet on his left hand to which was attached a rondel on a short stem for added protection. This is an early documented reference to a feature that would be retained for jousting use until the early sixteenth century. A fine example of such a

[35] See below, Part II, *Passo Honroso* Selection 2, course 10, Selection 11, course 8, Selection 18, course 1, and Selection 24, course 5. Other examples of effigies with the experimental single-plate gauntlet reinforce include: John Beaufort, Earl of Somerset (d. 1410), Canterbury Cathedral, Kent (*c.* 1439); and Thomas, Duke of Clarence (killed in 1421 at Bauge), Canterbury Cathedral, Kent (*c.* 1439). I am grateful to Dr Tobias Capwell for the references to these effigies. For other types of gauntlet in use at this time, see Blair, *European Armour*, pp. 80 and 99.

32 Jousting gauntlet with rondel for the left hand. Lombardy, c. 1500

gauntlet, made in Lombardy c. 1500, is shown in fig. 32.[36] Riquer has shown
that in the context of the fifteenth-century Iberian Christian kingdoms
this particular feature met with mixed reactions from the jousting community and was regarded by some as a gimmick.[37]

In a similar vein to the gauntlets, different types of shoulder defence
were being worn at the Pass of Honour of Suero de Quiñones. Indeed, in
so far as jousting was concerned, of the myriad pieces of the harness, the
shoulder defence, especially on the left-hand side, was subject to the most
amounts of variation and change because, as correctly stated in *Tirant lo
Blanc*, the left pauldron was the area most frequently struck in jousting.[38]
By far the most common type in use at this passage of arms were pauldrons
reinforced with gardbraces and with a slightly flanged or winged haute-
piece, or pauldrons reinforced with large rondels. Such shoulder defences
are clearly illustrated in the San Romano panels (fig. 18). Similarly in the
Libro di Giusto (fig. 19) three men (top row left and right; bottom row centre)
are wearing large rondels over their left pauldron and two (top row centre;
bottom left) are wearing fitted gardbraces similar to the left gardbrace on
the Avant armour (fig. 17). One contestant at the Pass of Honour of Suero

[36] See Boccia *et al.*, *Armi e Armature Lombarde*, p. 104. On Juan de Soto's gauntlet, see
Part II below, *Passo Honroso* Selection 7, course 21.

[37] Riquer, *L'Arnès del cavaller*, pp. 111–12.

[38] See Martorell, *Tirant lo Blanch*, ed. Hauf, ch. 71, p. 291: 'E stà en veritat que Tirant
havia fet dos encontres en lo guardabraç squerre e havia'l un poch desmarchat
allí hon vénen quasi los més encontres' ('And it is true that Tirant had made two
attaints on the left pauldron and he had mangled it somewhat in the spot where
almost all blows strike').

33 Left pauldron with stop-rib. Italian, c. 1430–40

de Quiñones, Pedro de los Ríos, is described as having a stop-rib on his left pauldron, which is not an uncommon feature on Italianate armour of the period.[39] A surviving example of such a pauldron, dating to 1430–40, is illustrated in fig. 33.[40] The upper lame of this piece is a modern restoration; otherwise all the lames are original and they are affixed with sliding rivets to facilitate smooth articulation. In addition to these variations some men may have been wearing 'Ursus'-type spaulders, which consisted of an integral besagew made in one piece with the pauldron, as shown on Churburg armour CH 18 (fig. 29).[41] And finally, all contestants wore legharness in the jousts at this passage of arms.

Although it was agreed by theorists that armour should always be bespoke, harnesses were available on loan at the Pass of Honour of Suero de Quiñones. On the one hand, when Suero de Quiñones jousted against the German knight Arnold von Rottenwald, both men – who owned their own custom-fitted armour – made much display of arming and disarming in public.[42] This in turn was a rare exception to one of the key theatrical features of the passage of arms: that the knights joust incognito, recognising each other only in the final anagnorisis upon completion of the joust. Customised, bespoke armour would have made a knight instantly recognisable. Loaning armour therefore made some sense in the context of this particular passage of arms, since the contestants would not have been immediately recognisable and the hosts would have had greater control over a crucial jousting principle that I shall discuss in chapter 4: the Principle of Equality. It is also fair to say that even though the one man who was killed at this passage of arms, Asbert de Claramunt, was wearing a borrowed harness, he was killed not because his armour was an improper fit, but by a chance blow through the eye-slit. The official chronicler belabours this very point in his description of this particular joust.

---

[39] See Mann, 'Six Armours of the Fifteenth Century', pp. 131–2. For the reference to Pedro's pauldron, see below, Part II, *Passo Honroso* Selection 2, course 15.

[40] On this pauldron, see Karcheski and Richardson, *The Medieval Armour from Rhodes*, pp. 94–5.

[41] See below, Part II, *Passo Honroso* Selection 7, course 1. On the ursus spaulder, see also Blair, *European Armour*, p. 211, fig. 181, and Norman, 'The Effigy of Alexander Stewart Earl of Buchan and Lord of Badenoch (1343?–1405?)', pp. 106–9.

[42] On this incident, see also chapter 4 below.

The Pass of Honour of Suero de Quiñones is fairly straightforward as far as weaponry is concerned. Technically, since the jousts at this passage of arms were jousts of war I prefer to describe the lance in this case as a spear, to which single-pointed heads were attached. 'Speare' is also the preferred nomenclature of Sir John Bourchier when describing jousts of war in his 1523–5 English translation of the chronicles of Froissart, so there is a reputable precedent for this choice of words.[43] Single-pointed spearheads would have a socket of metal at the base, called the eye, into which the shaft of the spear would slot. Opposing nails would then be driven at an angle into each side of the eye in order to secure the head to the spear. This method for affixing the spearhead to the spear is encountered on a wide variety of hafted weapons in the Middle Ages.[44] As the terminology in the chronicle makes clear, the spearheads used in these jousts of war were made of iron, and they were in fact referred to synecdochically as 'irons' ('fierros') in medieval Castilian. The iron spearheads were specially forged in Milan for this passage of arms. Two examples of Castilian spearheads for the joust of war from around this time, though made of steel as opposed to iron, are shown in figs. 34 and 35.[45] The makers of lances and spearheads were specialists in their own right who worked independently of the armourers, as clarified by Pero Tafur, who describes his vivid impressions of Milan during a visit to the city in the late 1430s as follows:

> It is a grander sight and more interesting to see the city on a work-day than on a holiday. The streets and the houses of the armourers are most remarkable, as well as those of the spear-makers, the saddlers and tailors who make the uniforms and materials for war. They know how many rulers and leaders of armies there are in Italy, and their devices, and they and the other craftsmen are so well provided that they can supply them with everything they need, though it be for the greatest lord in Italy. All the craftsmen are marvellously skilful and do their work with great regularity.[46]

[43] Froissart, *The Chronicle of Froissart*, trans. Sir John Bourchier, passim.

[44] See the detailed treatment by Waldman, *Hafted Weapons in Medieval and Renaissance Europe*, pp. 87–98. On the Spanish terminology –'el ojo', see Leguina, *Glosario de voces de Armería*, p. 670.

[45] See Stone, *A Glossary of the Construction, Decoration and Use of Arms and Armour in All Countries and in All Times*, p. 408.

[46] 'E aquí más arreada está e mejor de ver la çibdat en día de lavor que de fiestas; las calles e casas de los armeros es una singular cosa de ver, e ansimesmo asteros e sylleros e xastres, que fazen avillaviço de guerra, e saben quántos Señores traen conducta de gente por Italia, e sus devisas; e ansí estos como los otros oficiales están tan proveydos, que de golpe fallan recabdo de todo lo que an menester, e aunque sea el mayor Señor de Italia; e ansí de los otros atavíos maravillosamente e con grant orden tienen sus ofiçios'. See Tafur, *Andanças e viajes de un hidalgo*

34, 35 Steel spearheads for the joust of war. Castilian, 15th century.
(left) 11 × 6.3 cm (4⁵⁄₁₆ × 2½ in); (right) 14.6 × 5.1 cm (5¾ × 2 in)

Three types of spear were available for the combatants, as follows: 'Some were very thick, and others medium, and others thin, but they were very stout and strong, so that with each one of the three types described every good knight or gentleman could do his deeds of arms without fear that they would break from a light blow.'[47] It was standard practice both at jousts of war and jousts of peace for the contestants to be offered a selection of lances from which they could choose.[48]

      español, ed. Jiménez de la Espada, pp. 122–3. For the translation, see Tafur, *Travels and Adventures*, trans. Letts, p. 179. On the Milanese foundries, see Williams, *The Knight and the Blast Furnace*, pp. 894–5.

[47] 'Unas muy gruesas, e otras medianas, y otras delgadas, pero que asaz eran de recias e fuertes, para con cada una de las tres maneras aclaradas poder fiziese sus armas todo buen cavallero o gentilhome sin temor que del ligero golpe quebrasen'. See Rodríguez de Lena, *El Passo Honroso de Suero de Quiñones*, ed. Labandeira Fernández, p. 115.

[48] Buttin, 'La lance et l'arrêt de cuirasse', p. 124.

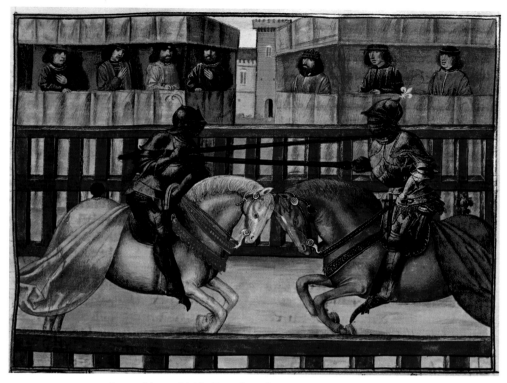

36 Joust without shields. From Jean de Wavrin, Seigneur de Forestel,
Les Chroniques d'Angleterre, late 15th century

The men at this passage of arms fought without shields, which was rare
though not unprecedented, as demonstrated in jousts illustrated in various
fifteenth-century texts (figs. 36–8). Since no shields were allowed, certain
concessions were made in the name of safety. So, for example, despite the
fact that vamplates were generally not used on war spears,[49] all the spears
at this passage of arms were equipped with small vamplates to protect the
jousters' right hands.[50] The Pass of Honour of Suero de Quiñones took
place in the open countryside adjacent to the Orbigo bridge, the idea being
to imitate the impromptu jousts of chivalric fiction staged within make-
shift enclosures.[51] However, in the case of this passage of arms, within the
enclosure there was also an apparatus designed to prevent swerving and

[49] Buttin, 'La lance et l'arrêt de cuirasse', p. 109.

[50] See below, Part II, *Passo Honroso* Selection 6, course 1.

[51] For an example from Spanish chivalric fiction, see Rodríguez de Montalvo, *The
Labors of the Very Brave Knight Esplandián*, trans. Little, p. 446. The first known
edition of this work (now lost) was printed in Seville in 1510. The work is generally
dated *c.* 1510, since there may have been earlier editions that have been lost.

37 Joust without shields.
From the *Livre du très chevalereux comte d'Artois et de sa femme fille du comte de Boulloigne, c.* 1476

collisions and to ensure fruitful encounters: a tilt. Scholars generally agree
that the tilt was first used either in Iberia or Italy in the 1420s.[52] To this
assertion I would add that its appearance coincides with the widespread
use of the lance-rest in these regions. The earliest documentary reference
to the tilt that I have found dates to 6 March 1419, in a detailed eyewitness

[52] Barber and Barker, *Tournaments*, pp. 194–5, suggest Spain or Portugal; Blair,
European Armour, p. 158, and Gravett, 'Tournament Courses', p. 335, suggest Italy;
Clephan, *The Medieval Tournament*, p. 102, suggests Portugal; Neste, *Tournois,
joutes, pas d'armes dans les villes de Flandre à la fin du Moyen Âge (1300–1486)*, p. 83,
cites Barber and Barker, but suggests only Portugal. Dillon and Contamine refer to
documentary evidence from 1429 of some jousts staged in France with a tilt 'in the
Portuguese fashion' ('à l'usage de Portingal'). See Dillon, 'Tilting in Tudor Times',
p. 297, and Contamine, 'Les tournois en France à la fin du moyen âge', p. 444, n. 65.

38 Joust without shields. From a Catalan translation of Diego de San Pedro,
Cárcel de Amor (Barcelona: J. Rosenbach, 1493)

account of a joust staged in Madrid during which the royal favourite of
King John II of Castile, Don Álvaro de Luna (1388?–1453), was injured in
the head.[53] Since this reference does not point to the tilt as a unique feature

[53] *Crónica de Don Álvaro de Luna*, ed. Mata Carriazo, p. 29. The date of the joust is
given on p. 28. The reference to the tilt reads as follows: 'E a la sazón estaba en el
rencle de la tela, de la otra parte, Gonçalo de Quadros, que era uno de los mayores
justadores e más valientes e punteros que por aquellos días avía en la corte del
Rey' ('And at that time Gonzalo de Cuadros was standing at the tilt, on the other
side, who was one of the greatest and bravest and most outstanding jousters there
was in those days at the King's court'). As Mata Carriazo points out, although
this chronicle was composed *c.* 1445–60 the anonymous author was clearly an
eyewitness to the events described and is therefore quite credible (pp. XLII and
XLVII).

or innovation and, likewise, since none of the contestants at the Pass of Honour of Suero de Quiñones is recorded as lodging a complaint about or raising an objection to the apparatus, it seems that by the 1420s and 1430s it was already a well-established feature of Iberian jousts, in which case it was probably introduced earlier in the century than has previously been thought. Conversely, despite this safety apparatus not a single piece of horse armour was worn at the Pass of Honour of Suero de Quiñones, though a few horses were covered by cloth caparisons.[54] The fact that some horses were struck in the neck and rump, and the fact that in one case a barricaded lance slides between the front arçon and the belly of the opposing knight, indicates that the height of the tilt in this case was about level with the contestants' saddles and not higher, as was the later practice.[55]

In sum, this passage of arms is a fine example of the medieval joust of war fought in field harness, with a few basic concessions made in the name of safety. Many men were skewered, battered and bruised, as could be expected in an extreme contact sport. Given, however, that only one man was killed out of well over 700 courses, we can conclude that as basic as the safety precautions were, the event was on the whole a resounding success and a testimony to the endurance and performance of the Italianate armour of the time.

Lo Cavaller (1493)

THE field armour worn in jousts of war and the jousting armour worn in jousts of peace – or jousts royal, as they are often called in contemporary texts – were quite different, a fact that is underscored by an analysis of the armour mentioned in Ponç de Menaguerra's Lo Cavaller. Hints from Menaguerra's text, as well as the publication date of the first edition (1493) enable us to envision the type of armour the author is talking about.

Firstly, the author makes it clear that there is but one appropriate headpiece for the joust: the helm, which is the term used throughout the text.[56] By the late fifteenth century the frog-mouthed helm was worn exclusively

---

54 On the evolution of horse armour, see Blair, European Armour, pp. 184–7, Pyhrr et al., The Armored Horse in Europe, 1480–1620, pp. 8–18, and Ruiz Alcón, 'Armaduras de caballos en la Real Armería de Madrid'.

55 On striking the horse in the head and neck, see Part II below, Passo Honroso Selection 10, course 1, Selection 11, course 8, Selection 19, course 3, and Selection 33, course 3. On the rump, see Selection 19, course 5. For the barricaded lance, see Selection 12, course 4.

56 Although Menaguerra uses the term 'lo elm' to refer specifically to the frog-mouthed jousting helm worn at the end of the fifteenth century, Catalan 'elm' and Castilian 'yelmo' were used to describe a variety of headgear worn by knights throughout the Middle Ages. For a synopsis, see Gago-Jover, 'Las voces militares en los diccionarios de español: el caso de yelmo'.

in jousts and never in battle.[57] Jousting helms were first held in place with leather straps, but when these proved not to be strong enough and susceptible to damage, charnels were introduced in the second half of the fifteenth century. These were hinged hasps riveted to the base of the helm that attached to pegs arranged vertically on the breastplate and backplate. A retaining pin would then be slotted through the pegs to secure the charnel firmly in place. The helm would sometimes also be fitted with a trap-door or cut-out on the wearer's right, which could be opened up after the course had been run for the purposes of ventilation.[58] These trap-doors or cut-outs are never found on the left-hand side of the helm, the area most likely to be struck by the opponent's lance. An example of this style of jousting helm is shown in fig. 39. It was made at the Negroli workshop in Milan *c.* 1500, probably for export to the Low Countries or Iberia. Made of steel, the helm weighs 6,747 g (14 lb 14 oz).[59] A deep indentation on the front left indicates that its wearer at one time endured a nasty knock.

39 Jousting helm and charnel. Negroli workshop, Milan, *c.* 1500. Weight 6,747 g (14 lb 14 oz)

Much is also made in Menaguerra's treatise of the crest that surmounted the helm. The crest was an important and popular part of the jouster's equipment, especially in the jousts of peace. Because they were worn on the head, crests were made up from light-weight materials such as moulded and hardened leather (known as 'cuir bouilli'), wood, parchment and feathers. Elaborately painted and sometimes silvered or gilded, crests could be derived from the wearer's heraldry, but might also represent some other allegory or chivalric symbol, often one of specific relevance to the theme of the particular tournament.

As regards the attachment of the crest to the jousting helm, it is likely that the knights of Menaguerra's time employed a similar method to that

---

[57] Blair, *European Armour*, pp. 73, 157–8.

[58] On the trap-door, see Blair, *European Armour*, p. 158.

[59] On this helm, see Pyhrr *et al.*, *Heroic Armor of the Italian Renaissance: Filippo Negroli and his Contemporaries*, p. 6 and p. 22, n. 16.

advocated by René of Anjou in his *Traicté de la forme et devis d'ung tournoy* (c. 1460), as follows:

> First the crest ought to be mounted on a piece of cuir bouilli, which ought to be well padded to a finger's thickness, or more on the inside; and the piece of leather ought to cover all the top of the helm, and be covered with a mantling, decorated with the arms of whoever carries it. And on the mantling above the top of the helm should be the crest, and around it should be a twisted roll of whatever colors the tourneyer wishes, about the thickness of an arm or more or less at his pleasure.[60]

In times of peace a single crest could define the prowess of a knight; in times of war a catalogue of crests could define the might and splendour of an entire army. Such was the case during what was quite possibly the most turbulent year of the fifteenth century in Iberia, when, on 19 May 1445, two enormous armies representing rival factions of noblemen met at Olmedo to settle the question of royal and political hegemony in Castile. The variety of crests worn on the sallets and armets of the troops of King John II of Castile, led by Don Álvaro de Luna, is described as follows in the official chronicle of Don Álvaro's life and deeds:

> Some were wearing timbres [*i.e. crests*] of wild beasts and others panaches of sundry colours, and there were others who were wearing some feathers as crests both on their sallets and on the shaffrons of their horses. Nor was there any lack of people there who had bunches of feathers flowing out like wings that were hanging down to their shoulders.[61]

Because they were made of perishable materials, very few crests have

---

[60] 'Tout premièrement le timbre doibt estre sur une pièce de cuir boully, laquelle doibt estre bien faultrée d'ung doy d'espez, ou plus par le dedens; et doibt contenir ladite pièce de cuir tout le sommet du heaulme, et sera couverte ladite pièce du lambequin, armoyé des armes de cellui qui le portera. Et sur ledit lambequin au plus hault du sommet sera assis ledit timbre, et autour d'icellui aura ung tortis des couleurs que vouldra ledit tournoyeur du gros du bras ou plus ou moins à son plaisir'. See René of Anjou, *A Treatise on the Form and Organization of a Tournament*, ed. and trans. Bennett, p. 6 (English) and p. 6 (French). On crests, see also Barber and Barker, *Tournaments*, pp. 152 and 161; Barker, *The Tournament in England, 1100–1400*, pp. 180–1; Blair, *European Armour*, pp. 30, 48, 74, 79 and 140; Crouch, *Tournament*, pp. 146–7; Edge and Paddock, *Arms and Armor of the Medieval Knight*, p. 54; and Riquer, *L'Arnès del cavaller*, pp. 119–22.

[61] 'Unos llebaban tinbles de bestias salvajes e otros penachos de diversos colores, e otros avía que llebaban algunas plumas así por çimeras de sus çeladas como de las testeras de sus caballos. Nin fallesçieron allí gentes que sacaron plumajes como alas que se tendían contra las espaldas'. *Crónica de Don Álvaro de Luna*, ed. Mata Carriazo, p. 166.

survived the vicissitudes of time. The most
famous surviving Iberian crest is of the
wild beast variety described in the quotation above: the fifteenth-century winged
dragon reputedly worn on the helm of
King Martin I of Aragon and Sicily
(1356–1410; King of Aragon, 1396–1410;
King of Sicily, 1409–10), currently in the
collection of the Real Armería in Madrid
(fig. 40).[62] This crest consists of a base made
of pasteboard reinforced on the inside with
cloth. The base is in turn surmounted by
an impressive, three-dimensional winged
dragon. From a distance the dragon looks
as though it is made of solid gold, but it is
in fact made of parchment covered with a
thin layer of gilded gesso. It is believed that
it once had claws which became detached
over time due to their fragility.[63]

Some well-preserved jousting armours
from the late fifteenth century have
survived. One of the finest examples of an
Iberian jousting armour from this period
is currently housed in the Real Armería,
Madrid. Harness A16 was worn by Philip
I The Handsome and was made in Menaguerra's home town of Valencia.[64] Fig. 41
is a reconstruction of what this harness

40 Winged dragon crest, reputedly worn on the
helm of King Martin I of Aragon and Sicily.
Early 15th century

would have looked like with the shield in place; fig. 42 shows the same
harness with the shield detached and the parts labelled. The frog-mouthed

[62] Modern Spanish and Catalan studies usually refer to this crest by its medieval
Aragonese nomenclature: 'drac pennat' or 'drac alat'. See Valencia de Don Juan,
Catálogo histórico-descriptivo de la Real Armería de Madrid, pp. 139–41, inv. DII; and
Riquer, *L'Arnès del cavaller*, p. 121 and fig. 185.

[63] Barón de las Cuatro-Torres, *El casco del Rey D. Jaime el Conquistador*, p. 13.
Published in 1894, this book erroneously attributes the crest to King James I of
Aragon (1208–76; ruled 1239–76). Despite this attribution, the author's physical
description of the crest is still useful.

[64] The Valencian maker's marks are discussed by Riquer, *L'Arnès del cavaller*, p. 168,
and Valencia de Don Juan, *Catálogo histórico-descriptivo de la Real Armería de
Madrid*, p. 13. On this harness, see also Domínguez Ortiz et al., *Resplendence of the
Spanish Monarchy: Renaissance Tapestries and Armor from the Patrimonio Nacional*,
pp. 110–13. It is attributed erroneously to King Philip II by ffoulkes, *The Armourer
and his Craft*, p. 111.

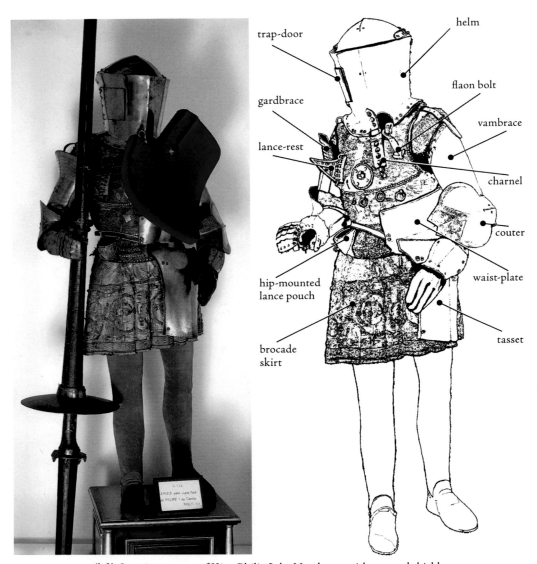

41 *(left)* Jousting armour of King Philip I the Handsome with restored shield

42 *(right)* Labelled line-drawing of the armour in fig. 41 with shield removed

helm of this armour is polished steel, which is in turn complemented by a globose breastplate. A reinforcing halter or bib fits over the shoulders with straps and is secured at the front by two gilded turning-clasps aligned vertically at the top and centre of the host breastplate, as well as the pegs for the charnel, which slot through corresponding holes in the reinforce. It is secured at the back by adjustable leather straps. Both breastplates are decorated with gilt brocade in a Morisco pattern, with a matching brocade skirt. Soler del Campo has pointed out that the primary influence of

43 The breastplate of Philip I's jousting armour

al-Andalus on the evolution of Castilian armour was decorative,[65] and this cuirass is a prime example of such influence. Figs. 43–7 are a study of the breastplates of harness A16. Of particular note is the corset-fastening at the back of the host breastplate, where a metal reinforce was not necessary due to the impossibility of being struck in the back. The host breastplate originally also had adjustable crotch straps riveted to the waist, though these have long since worn away.

Not unlike his father-in-law King Ferdinand, Philip's prowess is duly underscored in the official chronicle of his short reign, where in the same paragraph he is described as a very good jouster, a man who had many secret lovers, and a devoted husband.[66] Philip The Handsome would certainly have lived up to his flattering sobriquet in this armour; a three-dimensional embodiment of the knights who were woven into the elaborate tapestries that palliated the walls of his castles and palaces, the kind of tapestry mentioned by Menaguerra in his own finely crafted preamble to *Lo Cavaller*, and the kind of tapestry into which Philip and his wife the redoubtable Joanna the Mad are known to have been woven as enthusiastic

---

[65] Soler del Campo, *La evolución del armamento medieval en el reino castellano-leonés y al-Andalus (siglos XII–XIV)*, p. 127.

[66] 'Era muy buen justador … A mugeres dábase muy secretamente … Quiso mucho a la Reina'. See Padilla, *Crónica de Felipe I llamado el hermoso*, ed. Salvá and Sainz de Baranda, p. 149.

44–7 Further views of the breastplates of Philip I's jousting armour

48 *Tapisserie du Tournoi*: detail showing Philip the Handsome as a spectator, standing next to the pillar on the far right, wearing a carmine cap and doublet

spectators of tournaments (fig. 48, a detail of fig. 1).[67] The notable difference between this knight of flesh and blood and the knights of wool and silk was that, whereas the knights woven into the tapestries were appreciated in private by the king, the knight clad in this beautiful and unique harness was appreciated in public by spectators and fellow contestants alike.

The stop-ribs of Suero de Quiñones' day had long since disappeared from the breastplate by the 1490s. The distinguishing features of King Philip I's breastplate, as confirmed by Menaguerra's treatise, are the lance-rest, the

[67] See Hénault, 'La Tapisserie du "Tournoi" au Musée de Valenciennes', esp. pp. 152–4.

49 Jousting armour of King Philip I the
Handsome, or possibly Maximilian I,
made by the Flemish Master 'H'.
Late 15th century

charnel, and the flaon bolt, all of which are
gilded.[68] By the late fifteenth century the
flaon was a long socket that was attached
to the breastplate to hold the shield in
place. It was attached to the armour by
means of a thick steel loop at one end
that passed through a stout ring on the
breastplate. The other end of the flaon had
a long, threaded bolt running into it, the
bolt having a flanged head. The bolt was
unscrewed and an accoutrement known as
the poire was slipped on, the flaon cylinder
passing through a hole through the centre
of the poire. The shield inserted onto the
socket over the poire, the end of the flaon
cylinder protruding slightly through the
front surface of the shield. The bolt was
then screwed back into place and tightened, thereby holding the shield firmly in
place. Only the flanged head of the flaon
bolt would have been visible when the
shield was fixed into place. The original
shield which belonged to Real Armería
harness A16 is now lost, as is the poire
through which the cylinder of the flaon
slotted.[69]

Another example of a homogeneous
jousting harness from this period varies
very little from Real Armería A16. This
armour was made *c.* 1500 by the Flemish
Master 'H' probably for Philip The Handsome or possibly for his father the Emperor

68 Buttin, 'La lance et l'arrêt de cuirasse', p. 106,
notes that lance-rests were often gilded.
From an aesthetic point of view it makes
sense that the other accoutrements on
the cuirass were also gilded for the sake of
consistency.

69 In photographs of this armour taken in the
late nineteenth and early twentieth century
the poire is clearly visible. See Valencia de
Don Juan, *Catálogo histórico-descriptivo de
la Real Armería de Madrid*, p. 9, plate I, and
Calvert, *Spanish Arms and Armour*, plate 15.

Maximilian I (fig. 49).[70] The helm is secured in place with bolts rather than a charnel, but the breastplate is distinguished by the lance-rest and flaon bolt, which on this armour is removable.

In contemporary Spanish and Catalan texts, including *Lo Cavaller*, the flaon bolt is referred to cryptically as 'the snail' ('caracol' or 'caragol'), doubtless because of the spiral thread that characterises the bolt itself.[71] Torsion was a relatively new technological innovation in the 1490s, but it seems that Ponç de Menaguerra was familiar with the meaning that had recently been imputed to the word 'caragol' in order to describe this piece. Although rare, the noun appears in several armour inventories. In the 1461 inventory of the effects of Carlos of Aragon, Prince of Viana (1421–61), for example, part of one of his kits for the joust royal is described as follows: 'A Neapolitan jousting kit trimmed with white leather, with the bolt, with the burnished shield'.[72] A more detailed reference is included in the inventory of the contents of the castle of Cuéllar, the ancestral home of the dukes of Alburquerque. Written in Spanish, the inventory was compiled in 1560 upon the death of the duke who commissioned Quijada de Reayo's treatise, Don Beltrán de la Cueva. Part of one of his armours for the joust royal is described as follows: 'A helm and a kit, with the following pieces: a shield and a flaon with its spanner and bolt and screw'.[73] This type of jousting shield consisted of a wooden, shield-shaped wedge often covered in leather to help prevent the wood from splitting, over which was placed the steel shield proper, both of which were then attached to the breastplate by means of the flaon.

---

[70] See Thomas and Gamber, *Kunsthistorisches Museum, Wien: Waffensammlung: Katalog der Leibrüstkammer*, I: *Der Zeitraum von 500 bis 1530*, pp. 149–50, inv. S.11.

[71] Valencia de Don Juan, *Catálogo histórico-descriptivo de la Real Armería de Madrid*, p. 14, refers to this accoutrement simply as a bolt ('aldaba'). The same term is used to describe the flaon bolt on a late-fifteenth-century composite Spanish jousting armour in the Museo de Armería, Vitoria. See Cortés Echanove, *Museo Provincial de Alava: Armería (Vitoria)*, p. 22, inv. 3.

[72] 'Hun tacle de junyir de Napols guarnit en cuyro blanch, ab caragol, ab lo sobretacle febrit'. See Bofarull y de Sartorio, ed., 'Inventario de los bienes del Príncipe de Viana', p. 144. The term 'caragol'/'caracol' is not registered by Riquer, *L'Arnès del cavaller*, or by Leguina, *Glosario de voces de Armería*. The situation is further complicated by the fact that Alcover, *Diccionari català-valencià-balear*, vol. X, p. 98b, mistakenly defines the word 'tacle' in the Viana inventory as the lance used for tilting at the ring. Riquer, *L'Arnès del cavaller*, p. 236, comes closer when he suggests that 'tacle' could be a type of shield. In fact Catalan and Spanish 'tacle' most likely derives from the same etymological root as English 'tackle', referring in this context to the jousting rig or kit.

[73] 'Un yelmo y un tacle, con las piezas siguientes: un escudo y un fracón con su llave y caracol y tornillo'. See Rodríguez Villa, *Inventario del moviliario, alhajas, ropas, armería y otros efectos del Excmo. Sr. D. Beltrán de la Cueva*, p. 75.

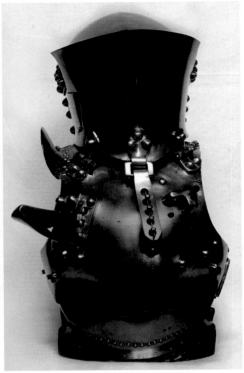

50, 51 Portions of two Italian armours for the joust royal,
made by Giovanni Angelo Missaglia of Milan, c. 1490

Extant examples of European jousting armour of the period suggest that
the flaon bolt is a uniquely Iberian or Ibero-Flemish method for securing
the shield to the breastplate. Examples of contemporary jousting armour
from Italy, for example, show a set of perpendicular staples in place of the
flaon bolt. Figs. 50–1 show portions of two armours for the joust royal,
both made by the Italian master armourer Giovanni Angelo Missaglia of
Milan, c. 1490. The armour in fig. 50 was made for Gasparo Fracasso and is
currently in the Kunsthistorisches Museum in Vienna. It would originally
have had a left vambrace, couter and gauntlet, a right gauntlet, a bouched
shield and a single left tasset.[74] The armour in fig. 51 is in the collection of
the Palazzo Ducale of Venice. It too would originally have had vambraces,

[74] See Thomas and Gamber, *Kunsthistorisches Museum, Wien: Waffensammlung:
Katalog der Leibrüstkammer*, I: *Der Zeitraum von 500 bis 1530*, pp. 184–5, inv. S.1 (B2);
also Williams, *The Knight and the Blast Furnace*, p. 216. Line drawings of the
missing portions of this armour are illustrated alongside a photograph of the
extant portions in Gamber, 'Der Italienische Harnisch im 16. Jahrhundert', p. 85,
fig. 65.

couters, gauntlets, shield and tasset. In its present assemblage this armour weighs 23,000 g (50 lb 11 oz).[75] A detail worthy of note is that the helm of this armour does not align tightly with the breastplate. It is impossible to say for certain if this is how the armour was originally made, but if it was – possibly to allow air to circulate inside the helm – the misalignment would have left a vulnerable and dangerous gap right at the wearer's neck. The arrangement of staples is a later evolution of an attachment consisting of a single staple set horizontally, as seen on jousting breastplate E59 of the Real Armería (see fig. 26). In the case of the Palazzo Ducale armour a second set of holes suggests that the staples can be set in two different positions on the breastplate. The shield was attached to the staples with cords that were knotted and then tightened with a pear-shaped toggle.[76]

These late-fifteenth-century Italian armours would have been compatible with their Iberian counterparts. The two styles of shield attachment – flaon bolt versus staples – point to different schools of jousting to which the men who wore them belonged. The Neapolitan rig owned by the Prince of Viana is highly suggestive of one particular school. The Aragonese monarchs had long since had close ties to Naples, and King Ferdinand the Catholic, as well as being King of Aragon (1479–1516) and of Castile and Leon (1474–1516) was also King of Naples (1504–16). The inventory of arms and armour of Lorenzo de' Medici compiled in 1492 and copied in 1512 contains numerous jousting cuirasses with a special accoutrement called in Italian 'la vite', or 'the bolt', which almost certainly refers to the flaon bolt. One entry reads as follows: 'Two cuirasses for the joust in the Neapolitan style, one covered with green velvet, the other with velvet from Alexandria, both with the bolt'.[77] The inventory likewise includes 'two

---

[75] See Boccia et al., Armi e Armature Lombarde, pp. 92–3, fig. 81, and Franzoi, L'Armeria del Palazzo Ducale a Venezia, pp. 69–70 and p. 159, fig. 12.

[76] This method of attachment is described in an anonymous 1446 French MS entitled Traité du costume militaire (Treatise on military costume). The treatise has been edited in French by Cripps-Day, The History of the Tournament, app. IX, pp. lxxxix–xciv, ffoulkes, The Armourer and his Craft, app. D, pp. 177–9, and Reverseau, 'L'Habit de guerre des français en 1446: Le manuscrit anonyme fr. 1997 de la Bibliothèque Nationale'. I refer to Reverseau's edition, in this case pp. 194–5.

[77] 'Dua chorazze da giostra alla napolitana coperta l'una di velluto verde, l'altra di velluto alexandrino, tutte con la vite'. See Scalini, 'The Weapons of Lorenzo de' Medici', p. 25, no. 44. I have taken the liberty of making some corrections to Scalini's punctuation and translation. Cp. also, in the same article, nos. 42, 43 and 45: 'A cuirass for the joust made for Lorenzo, covered with velvet from Alexandria, with the bolt and lance-rest and spaulders and straps'; 'A cuirass for the joust made for Giuliano di Piero, covered with white velvet, with the bolt and lance-rest and spaulders'; 'Three cuirasses for the joust covered with leather, as follows: two covered with white leather and one with red leather, all with the bolt' ('Una chorazza da giostra fatta per Lorenzo, coperta di velluto alexandrino, colla vite et resta et spalletti et cignetti'; 'Una chorazza da giostra fatta per Giuliano di Piero,

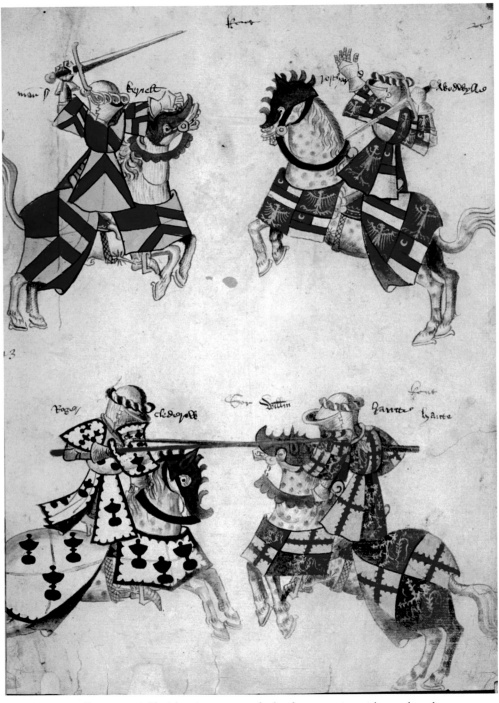

52 Four mounted knights, in armour and tabards, tourneying with swords and
jousting with bouched shields. From *Sir Thomas Holme's Book of Arms, c. 1448*

Neapolitan helms for the joust'.[78] On the understanding that Naples was at this time an Iberian territory, it is possible that this Neapolitan style represents the Iberian-style armour for the joust royal of the type worn by Philip The Handsome and inferred from the descriptions in *Lo Cavaller*. Menaguerra refers specifically to a School of Jousting at the end of his treatise, where he once again underscores the importance of the flaon bolt. The reference adds further fuel to the argument that competing schools and technologies were a natural part of the evolutionary process. One further detail of note is that the removable flaon bolt on the Vienna Master 'H' armour is attached to a triangular bracket that is screwed onto the cuirass at the same angle as the staples on the contemporaneous Italian jousting armours. Although there is no concrete proof, it is not unreasonable to speculate that bolts and staples may in some cases have been interchangeable depending on the occasion. In the case of flaon bolt versus staples, both of these compatible yet competing mechanisms would ultimately be superseded by the invention of the grandguard, which I shall discuss in the next chapter.

The shield itself, states Menaguerra, should have a bouche, or notch, cut into the right-hand top corner, ostensibly for supporting the lance when couched. The manuscript illumination in fig. 52 shows two knights tourneying with swords at the top of the folio and at the bottom another two knights jousting with bouched shields. The image, which dates to before 1448, shows clearly how the bouche helps support the lance. Ever aware of appearances Menaguerra notes that another use of the bouche is for resting the hand thereon in a nonchalant manner before actually setting off down the lists. In other words, armour was pulchritudinous as well as practical. The situation in *Lo Cavaller* is complicated somewhat by the fact that Menaguerra says that at one time the knight could also look nonchalant by clutching 'the buckle of the guige', that is, the long leather strap worn around the neck and used to adjust the height at which the shield would sit. In order to set the bouche of the shield in place it would be necessary to tighten or loosen the guige. The guige would pass down the right side of the neck in front of the body and could be grasped for stylistic reasons so as not to leave the arm dangling. The buckle could sit over the area of the right pectoral or close to the charnel, depending on the exact placement and size of the shield. In the fifteenth-century illumination in fig. 53 the guiges worn by the knights are conveniently shown from the front and back. The complication is that I have found no evidence to indicate that guiges were

coperta di velluto bianco, cola vite et resta et spalletti'; 'iii chorazze da giostra di quoio coperte così: dua coperte di quoio bianche et una di quoio rosso, tutte colla vite').

[78] 'ii elmi da giostra napoletani'. Scalini, 'The Weapons of Lorenzo de' Medici', p. 26, no. 71.

53 Joust between Sir John Holland and Regnault de Roye, with details of the guige.
From Jean de Wavrin, Seigneur de Forestel, *Les Chroniques d'Angleterre*,
late 15th century

ever used in conjunction with flaon bolts. On the contrary, guiges were
the standard method of shield suspension some twenty years before *Lo
Cavaller* was written, but at a time when Menaguerra was probably more
active than he was in 1493. In a similar vein, bouched shields were well on
their way out by the 1490s. Thus the reference to the guige in this instance
suggests the recollections of a man who had enjoyed a long jousting career
that had witnessed various changes in armour and accoutrements.

The lance-rest on Real Armería A16 consists of a gilded iron frame
constructed along similar principles to a modern-day shadow box. Into the
hollow recess a specially contoured block of wood has been fitted which is
covered with brocade and decorated with closely set gilded rivets so as to

match the design of the cuirass. As I shall explain more fully below, this type of rest was intended to engage the grapper of the lance as securely as possible.

Along with the specially accoutred cuirass, another defining piece of the harness as it is described by Menaguerra is the single tasset. According to chapter 1 of *Lo Cavaller*, the left tasset – in order to allow for ease of mounting – was the only piece of armour that did not have to be secured in place before the knight approached the tilt. Otherwise, he was expected to take his place at the head of the lists fully armoured. Since jousters would be struck on the left-hand side, the left tasset on jousting armours tended to be longer, broader and heavier than the tasset worn on the right. It was therefore less clumsy to mount the horse first, and then attach the left tasset. It is clear from the armour for the joust royal of King Philip I that the right tasset was sometimes omitted entirely from Iberian jousting armours of this period. The *Inventario iluminado* (Illuminated Inventory), a catalogue of the Real Armería of Madrid consisting of detailed water-colour images of the arms and armour in the collection around 1544, also shows this armour with its single tasset (fig. 54).[79] This is the reason why Menaguerra simply refers to 'the tasset' in this chapter without feeling a need to specify which one he is discussing. On harness A16 the tasset is made of a single piece and is riveted to a reinforcing waist-plate. This two-piece rig is attached to and suspended from a leather belt, which buttresses Menaguerra's opinion for it would not have been at all difficult or time-consuming to fasten on the rig after arriving at the head of the lists.

Various kinds of jousting saddle were being used in the 1490s, depending on the class of joust. Writing *c.* 1440–2 about the Castilian knight Don Pero Niño's experiences in Paris in 1405, the chronicler Gutierre Díaz de Games describes a popular kind of joust that attempts to mimic war in the sense that it takes place in the open field without a tilt. In every other sense it is a joust of peace that requires a special, high saddle with long leg guards, and leather horse armour, as follows:

The French joust after another fashion than that followed in Spain. They joust without lists,[80] and strike after the fashion of war. They

---

[79] Black and white facsimiles of the pages of the *Inventario iluminado* are included in the articles by Valencia de Don Juan, 'Bilderinventar der Waffen, Rüstungen, Gewänder und Standarten Karl V in der Armería Real zu Madrid' and 'Bilderinventar der Waffen, Rüstungen, Gewänder und Standarten Karl V in der Armería Real zu Madrid (Fortsetzung)'. For detailed descriptions in English of each page, see Cripps-Day, *Fragmenta Armamentaria*, vol. II: *Miscellanea*, part V: *An Inventory of the Armour of Charles V*, pp. 126–36.

[80] This is a frustratingly cryptic remark, which I feel comfortable discussing only in a footnote. Since Don Pero Niño states that the French joust without the tilt, does he mean that the Castilians joust with it? Because he uses a present-tense verb it is

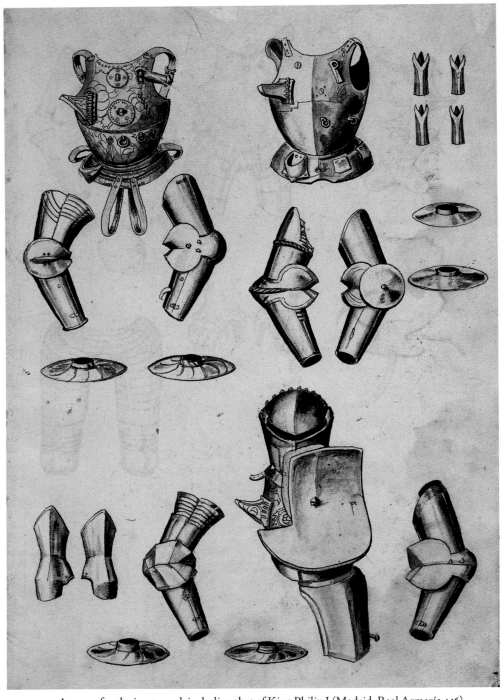

54 Armour for the joust royal, including that of King Philip I (Madrid, Real Armería A16),
as illustrated in the *Inventario iluminado*, c. 1544. 43 × 31.5 cm (17 × 12⅜ in)

arm the horses with head pieces and petrels, which are armour made
of very thick leather, and their saddles, likewise very strong, cover
their legs nearly to the feet. It often happens that one horse runs
against another, and one falls, or that they both fall. It is a most
perilous jousting and one that all men do not attempt, but only those
who are very skilful and very good horsemen. The staves are all of
the same length; there is in all the court only two or three craftsmen
who make them, with the permission of the governors of the lists,
and they are sworn masters. There is neither one that holds the lists,
nor joust of one man against another by champions assigned; but
each attacks whomsoever he will. All are assailants; ten, or twenty,
or thirty, or more, take their place on one side and as many on the
other. As soon as one takes his lance, the other at once grasps his;
and not only one goes out against him, but in their great ardour it
happens that two or three come forward together against him who
has stood forth, notwithstanding their courtesy; for if they see how
the matter is going, never against one man does more than one man
come forward. It is therefore needful that the knight who jousts
there should be practised therein, and should be a strong and most
skilful horseman.[81]

The terminology in this case refers to the high, tightly fitted saddle
used for jousts of peace throughout the fifteenth century on which the
rear arçon extends around to support the hips. This type of saddle helped
prevent the pelvis moving sideways out of its alignment with the horse's

unfortunately not clear if he means that this was the case in 1405 – in which case
this is an early, albeit insinuated, reference to the use of a tilt in Castile – or if he
is discussing a past event from the perspective of *c.* 1440–2, the approximate date
he wrote this section of his chronicle. Cp. also the French source cited above, n. 52,
where jousting with a tilt in France was considered to be a Portuguese custom.

[81] 'Los françeses justan por otra guisa que non fazen en España: justan sin tela, a
manera de guerra, por el topar. Arman los cavallos de testera e picheras, que son
unas armas de cuero muy fuertes; e las sillas muy fuertes, que cubren la pierna fasta
çerca del pie. Conteçe muchas vezes que topan un cavallo con otro, e caen amos e
dos: o cae el uno, o amos e dos. Es muy peligrosa justa; non la fazen todos honbres,
mas honbres diestros e muy cavalgadores. Las varas son todas medidas; non las
faze sino un maestro o dos en toda la corte: éste con liçençia de los governadores, e
aquél es el fiel. Non ay allí mantenedor, ni justa uno con otro señaladamente, sino
quien más se atiene. Todos son ventureros; pónense a la una parte diez, o veynte,
o treynta, o más; ál tantos de la otra. En tomando uno la vara, ya el otro tiene la
suya; e non solamente sale uno, mas con la grand cobdiçia conteçe que salen a él
dos, e aun tres, non enbargante que son corteses, que si se viesen no yría más de
uno. Ansí es menester que el cavallero que allí justare que lo aya bien usado, o
sea fuerte, o grand cavalgador' (Díaz de Games, *El victorial*, ed. Beltrán Llavador,
p. 577). For the translation, see Díaz de Gamez, *The Unconquered Knight*, trans.
Evans, pp. 142–3).

55 Saddle of wood covered with rawhide,
for the joust of peace. German, *c.* 1500.
Height 119.38 cm (3 ft 11 in); weight 15,676 g (35 lb)

spine and was thus of great help to the experienced rider in maintaining his seat upon and immediately after impact. Fig. 55 shows an extant example of this type of saddle. Standing 119.38 cm (3 ft 11 in) tall and weighing 15,676 g (35 lb), it is made of wood and is covered in rawhide which at one time was painted.[82] Fig. 56 is a fluid depiction of a tournament at Constantinople by the early-fifteenth-century Czech artist known as the Master of the Mandeville Travels, similar to the one described by Díaz de Games.[83] The knight on the viewer's left is in the process of raising his lance in order to place it in the rest, which is visible on the breastplate. The second knight from the left has dealt a praiseworthy blow to his opponent's helm that has shattered the lance. The force of the blow is indicated by the extent to which his opponent leans back in the saddle, which according to Menaguerra is a natural consequence of competent jousting and is therefore not worth any points;[84] his shield has also been dislodged from his left shoulder and has swung around behind the right, thus providing incidental evidence that shields knotted to staples were perhaps not as secure as those bolted on with a flaon. A knight on the viewer's right is receiving assistance from two aiders: one is putting on the crested helm; the other is tying on the shield, which the knight himself is adjusting as the knot is tightened. The long forks of the saddles are richly painted and the horses are armoured with matching shaffrons and peytrals attached by straps to the saddles, exactly as described in Díaz de Games' account. A herald in the centre of the illumination is leading a horse to the lists. It is unarmoured, which suggests that the peytral and shaffron were not attached until the joust was about to begin, in a similar vein to the tasset mentioned above. It should be noted that the Vienna Master 'H' armour illustrated in fig. 49 is accompanied by a matching shaffron for the horse, though this one is made of steel rather than leather.

The principal kind of joust discussed by Menaguerra, however, does

---

[82] See Blair, *European Armour*, p. 160; Dufty and Reid, *European Armour in the Tower of London*, plate CLIII; and ffoulkes, *Inventory and Survey of The Armouries of the Tower of London*, vol. I, p. 208.

[83] On the artist, see Krása, *The Travels of Sir John Mandeville: A Manuscript in the British Library*, trans. Kussi, pp. 15, 37 and plate 20.

[84] See below, Part II, Menaguerra, *Lo Cavaller*, ch. 29.

56 A tournament in Constantinople.
From a Czech translation of the *Travels* of Sir John Mandeville, early 15th century

have a tilt, and for the most part Menaguerra's jouster rides on a saddle that the author refers to variously as 'sella closa' and 'sella de la guisa'. This most likely refers to a bastard saddle, which is to say, a saddle that is similar to, or reminiscent of, the one illustrated in fig. 55, but with modifications for the joust with a tilt. This saddle would have looked much the same as that illustrated in the Ferramola fresco in fig. 12 (see above, chapter 1). It lifts the rider some 12–15 cm (5–6 in) off the horse's back, rather like the jousting saddle described above, though not quite as high and without the long leg guards, which would have been unnecessary because of the protection afforded by the tasset and the tilt itself. It has a high rear arçon that supports the lower back and hips. In this jousting saddle Menaguerra seems to think that there are no good excuses or justifications for being unhorsed, referring to such an accident as a 'disgrace'.[85]

As far as weaponry is concerned in Menaguerra's text, we are no longer in the same realm as the jousts of war at the Pass of Honour of Suero de Quiñones. As, for example, in chapter 10 of Menaguerra's treatise where the discussion focuses on 'combats with rebated arms', the author makes it clear that he is writing predominantly about the joust of peace, run in specially designed jousting armour, quite unlike war harness, using lances tipped with crown-shaped safety heads known as coronels as opposed to single-pointed war heads. Perhaps not coincidentally, the same term for the coronel used by Ponç de Menaguerra –'punta de billeta'– is used in chapter 46 of *Tirant lo Blanc*. Although we can only speculate as to whether or not Martorell discussed the technicalities of jousting with the most famous jouster in his home town of Valencia, the following quotation from *Tirant lo Blanc*, like the frontispieces I discussed in the Introduction, underscores the close typological ties between chivalric fiction and the jousting manuals:

> On Monday it was announced by the aforementioned kings-of-arms and heralds that anyone who wished to joust with arms royal (*armes reals*) or with arms of war (*armes de guerra*), should make the lance-head for the arms royal with four very waxed points on the rochet, with wax smeared on each point of the coronel. The other lances for the arms of war (*armes de seguir*) to have at the end of the lance a circular iron plate, upon which is attached five points of steel fashioned in the shape of a diamond, very finely sharpened, and this circular plate with the diamond lance-head should be joined onto the stave as one single lance-head.[86]

---

[85] See below, Part II, Menaguerra, *Lo Cavaller*, ch. 26.

[86] 'Lo diluns fon publicat per los desús dits reys d'armes e erauts, qualsevulla que volgués junyir ab armes reals o ab armes de guerra, fossen los ferros de les armes reals ab quatre punts en lo broquet molt encerades, ab cera gomada cascuna punta de la billeta. Les altres lances de les armes de seguir al cap de la lança una planxa

In this abstruse quotation the author is differentiating between the lance-head for the joust royal and that for two classes of joust of war, which he calls 'armes de guerra' and 'armes de seguir'. Cripps-Day translates the Spanish equivalent term 'de seguir', which is peppered throughout the 1558 inventory of Charles V's armour, as 'for the field'. Riquer notes with a keen eye that armour inventories tend to describe the armour designated for 'armes de seguir' as sumptuously decorated with silk, brocade and velvet. He thus speculates that while the term 'armes de guerra' refers to jousts of war in general, 'armes de seguir' quite possibly refers to more opulent versions thereof in which only royals and their retinues or suite (where 'de seguir' refers to 'those who follow') were allowed to participate, on the understanding that in both cases the basic design of the armour and weaponry would have been the same.[87] This line of argument, according to which the decoration defines a special class of joust, is not dissimilar to the claims made about white armour in *Amadís de Gaula*. There was certainly an incentive for royal-only sub-classes of jousts given the fact that Menaguerra points out in chapter 14 of *Lo Cavaller* that the performance of royal jousters could only truly be quantified when they fought against their social peers; otherwise it was understood that the royal jouster was forever doomed to win.

Tirant's lance-head for the joust of peace is a text-book description of a coronel. The type described has four blunted tines that spread out from the socket. The coronel was thus prevented from entering the sight in the case of blows to the head and helped the lance gain a purchase, lessening the possibility of the lance skating dangerously into the underarms or groin in the case of blows to the shield or body. Waxing the tines of the coronel would not only help them gain a purchase, but would also prevent sparks from flying, which Menaguerra disdains and which perhaps not coincidentally are never struck in the sundry jousts described in *Tirant lo Blanc*. The coronel also considerably or entirely reduced both the likelihood of the jouster's armour being pierced and the lethality of accidental blows to his horse. Both of these dangers were part and parcel of the joust of war and had been a particular problem at the Pass of Honour of Suero de Quiñones, although this much more dangerous style of jousting seems to have become less common by the second half of the fifteenth century. Unlike the spearheads used in jousts of war, which were virtually always made of iron, the coronels used in jousts of peace were most often made

de ferre redonda, hon si stigués V puntes de açer fetes a taill de diamà, molt ben smolades, e aquesta plancha redona ab los ferres de diamà se vénen encasar dins la lança de un ferro tot sol' (Martorell, *Tirant lo Blanch*, ed. Hauf, p. 213).

[87] Cripps-Day, *Fragmenta Armamentaria*, vol. II: *Miscellanea*, part V: *An Inventory of the Armour of Charles V*, p. 19, nos. 13 and 26, p. 36, no. 45, p. 40, no. 75, and p. 60, nos. 38–9; Riquer, *L'Arnès del cavaller*, pp. 174–6.

57 *(left)* Four-prong coronel ('punta de billeta') for the joust royal. German, early 16th century

58 *(centre)* Three-prong coronel for the joust royal. Spanish, *c.* 1500

59 *(right)* Diamond-faceted lance-head. Spanish, *c.* 1500

of tempered steel.[88] Fig. 57 shows the type of four-pronged coronel that would have been used by Menaguerra. This example measures 19.69 cm (7¾ in) high by 8.56 cm (3⅖ in) wide. Similarly, fig. 58 illustrates the more common three-pronged version of this lance-head; this particular example is associated with Real Armería jousting armour A16 made for Philip The Handsome.[89] Both of these coronels date to *c.* 1500.

The other type of lance-head mentioned by Martorell is described as being shaped like a diamond. Like Martorell, Menaguerra refers to other activities in his treatise that were more perilous than the jousts of peace and that would have required a different kind of lance-head. The first such activity is called 'running with sharp lances' ('passos de córrer puntes'). Riquer provides unimpeachable documentary evidence that this permutation of the joust of war involved running at large with lances, the heads of which were of the diamond type.[90] In the mid-fifteenth century this class of

---

[88] Buttin, 'La lance et l'arrêt de cuirasse', p. 134.

[89] Valencia de Don Juan, *Catálogo histórico-descriptivo de la Real Armería de Madrid*, pp. 276–8, inv. 1168.

[90] Riquer, *L'Arnès del cavaller*, p. 166.

joust of war seems to have originated in France, whence it spread to other parts of Europe, including the Iberian Christian kingdoms. In 1434, for example, Rodríguez de Lena emphasises Gonzalo de Castañeda's formidable skill with the lance by observing that 'he had travelled in France and jousted with sharp lances'.[91] Using the terminology at his disposal, it will be recalled that Pero Tafur had used the Spanish expression 'correr puntas' to describe the Scharfrennen, a class of German joust which in his eyes was not dissimilar to this French-Iberian iteration.[92]

As for the lance-head for this class of joust Riquer interprets the description of the diamond-head in *Tirant lo Blanc* to mean that it has metal tines that flare out from the socket and are bent at the middle in such a way that the tips of the tines point inward, thus resembling a setting of the type found on diamond rings. His theory is undermined by the fact that this hypothetical lance-head would resemble an impractical, bent safety coronel rather than a dangerous point. Not surprisingly he was unable to find an extant example of such a lance-head and instead provides an interpretive line drawing.[93] My own view is that Tirant's 'five points of steel fashioned in the shape of a diamond' are loosely analogous to the way in which a diamond is cut – in other words, a lance-head with facets. This lance-head is 'very finely sharpened' which leads me to envision an inverted diamond whereby the table face sits on the lance stave so that the pavilion and pointed culet are at the tip. Fig. 59 shows what I believe to be a late-fifteenth-century diamond-faceted head in the collection of the Real Armería in Madrid.[94] The alternate gilt and steel 'facets' are clearly visible, and the lance-head tapers to a point as one would expect in 'passos de córrer puntes'. The lavish gilding on this particular example connotes wealth and status and lends credence to Riquer's suggestion that in the interests of fair play special sub-classes of the jousts of war were open to royals and members of the royal suite only.

Menaguerra's treatise includes several references to one other permutation of the joust of war. Comments made in *Lo Cavaller* about jousts in which knights do not actually get killed but instead are 'counted as dead' (chapters 13 and 25) suggest mock jousts of war. The mock jousts of war of Menaguerra's time, at least as practised in the Iberian Peninsula, may very well have involved another type of lance-head, a form of safety coronel cunningly disguised as a war-point. This large leaf-bladed spearhead remained very thick at its point, where it was cut off flat and

---

[91] 'havía andado en França e fecho puntas'. Rodríguez de Lena, *El Passo Honroso de Suero de Quiñones*, ed. Labandeira Fernández, p. 238.

[92] See above, chapter 1, n. 23.

[93] Riquer, *L'Arnès del cavaller*, p. 169.

[94] Valencia de Don Juan, *Catálogo histórico-descriptivo de la Real Armería de Madrid*, p. 278, inv. 1173.

60 *(left)* Duck-billed ('ab bech d'àneda') steel
spearhead for the mock joust of war. Spanish
(possibly from Aragon-Catalonia), *c.* 1500

61 *(right)* Duck-billed ('ab bech d'àneda') steel
spearhead for the mock joust of war. Spanish
(possibly from Aragon-Catalonia), *c.* 1500

filed into a series of crown-like teeth,
thereby producing a lance that appeared,
from more than about ten feet away, to be
a weapon of war, but that was still much
safer to use than the genuine article. Four
late-fifteenth-century Iberian coronels
that look like leaf-bladed spearheads are
now in the Real Armería in Madrid, two
of which are illustrated in figs. 60 and 61.[95]
As far as the nomenclature of this type
of lance-head is concerned, Riquer edits
an intriguing group of cartels of defiance
that two Aragonese knights by the names
of Joan d'Íxer and Joan de Luna exchanged
between 7 January and 17 February 1434.
The two men debate whether or not
to fight 'like knights from France and
England' ('segons cavallers ... de Ffrança e
d'Anglaterra') or 'according to the custom
of Aragon' ('segons la ... costuma d'Aragó')
which involves jousting with the 'lance
with duck-billed spearhead' ('lança de
fferro ab bech d'àneda').[96] We know from
the *Passo Honroso* that 'fferro' here refers
to the leaf-bladed spearhead used in jousts
of war. We also know that the duels that
resulted from the cartels of defiance often
involved posturing rather than real fights to the death. Thus these two men
are debating whether or not to fight a real joust of war or a mock joust of
war, and although Riquer merely documents the duck-billed spearhead for
its intrinsic linguistic value, I would venture to suggest that it refers to the
special type of covert coronel described above, which never took off beyond
the kingdom of Aragon.

The other specific part of the lance mentioned by Menaguerra is the
grapper, which he also refers to in the plural as the grappers. The grapper
was a ring of metal or leather fitted around the lance at the point where it
either was gripped between the inside of the jouster's arm and his pectoral
area or was engaged with the lance-rest. Its function was to help the jouster
resist the shock of his impacting lance, thereby enabling him to strike with
greater force than the strength of his arm alone would allow. Grappers

95 Valencia de Don Juan, *Catálogo histórico-descriptivo de la Real Armería de Madrid,*
      p. 278, inv. 1179 and 1233. See also inv. 1176 and 1178.
96 Riquer, *L'Arnès del cavaller,* pp. 167, 177 and 195–6.

were first introduced in the early fourteenth century and became standard after the introduction of the lance-rest in the late 1300s. A description of the grapper as it was configured in 1446 is provided in an anonymous French manuscript as follows:

> Item, the said grappers are intentionally full of sharp little spikes like little diamonds, similar in size to little hazelnuts, which spikes engage the inside surface of the rest, which surface of the rest is filled with wood or lead in order that the said spikes cannot slip, because of which the said lance resists the blow; in such a way that it must break to bits, whether it be well aligned, or whether the jouster bends his spine so forcefully that he will really feel it.[97]

By Menaguerra's time the jousting grappers often still had cog-like teeth that assisted the fixed interaction with the rest, but by the 1490s the rest itself was usually fitted with a narrow over-hanging shelf for the teeth to lock onto. Such grappers are depicted in the unfinished *Beauchamp Pageant*, which was drawn in the mid-1480s (fig. 62), and the *Tapisserie du Tournoi* (fig. 63, a detail of fig. 1).[98] The 1492 Medici inventory of arms and armour indicates that grappers were removable, since we find a prodigious '107 lance grappers' stacked in the room off the terrace overlooking the street in the Medici-Riccardi Palace, which served as a storage space for the bulk of the family's jousting equipment, and another eight stacked in a guard-room.[99] Of note is that the *Beauchamp Pageant* grapper illustrated on the broken lance in fig. 62 is facing the wrong way. I chose this particular folio for the following reason: since the manuscript is characterised by outstanding draftsmanship, and since grappers were removable, this could be an accurate depiction of a grapper that was hastily and inadvertently fitted by a novice knight or a distracted aider; a subtle hint, perhaps, that things did not always go as smoothly as planned in jousting competitions.

---

[97] 'Item, lesdictes grappes sont voulentiers plaines de petittes pointes agues comme petiz dyamens, de grosseur comme petittes nouzilles, lesquelles pointes se viennent arrester dedans le creux de larrest, lequel creux de larrest plain de bois ou de plomb affin que lesdittes pointes ne puissent fouir, par quoy vient ladicte lance à tenir le cop; en faczon quil fault que elle se rompe en pièces, que len alligne bien ou que le jousteur ploye leschine si fort que bien le sente'. See Reverseau, 'L'Habit de guerre des français en 1446: Le manuscrit anonyme fr. 1997 de la Bibliothèque Nationale', p. 196.

[98] See Sinclair, *The Beauchamp Pageant*, pp. 61, 110 and 113, and Hénault, 'La Tapisserie du "Tournoi"', pp. 148–9. On the grapper, see also Anglo, *The Martial Arts of Renaissance Europe*, p. 211; Peine and Breiding, 'An Important Find of Late 14th and Early 15th Century Arms and Armour from Haus Herbede, Westphalia', pp. 16–18; and Riquer, *L'Arnès del cavaller*, pp. 168–9.

[99] Scalini, 'The Weapons of Lorenzo de' Medici', p. 28, no. 157: 'centosette ghorzetti da lancie'; also p. 29, no. 192.

62 Detail of a broken lance with grapper.
From John Rous, *Life and Acts of Richard Beauchamp, Earl of Warwick*, *c.* 1483

In chapter 18 of his treatise Menaguerra states that 'lacerations' caused either by the grapper or by the lance itself from the force of the blow delivered are not to be taken into any account by the judges, since such lacerations should not impede further performance in the lists. The jouster's hand might get injured by the grapper if it became caught between the lance and the breastplate as the lance was forced back by a particularly violent impact. As I shall discuss more fully in chapter 5, however, the Pass of Honour of Suero de Quiñones makes it clear that the most common grapper injuries were in fact dislocations more so than lacerations.

One final note about Menaguerra's jousting armour that can be inferred from *Lo Cavaller* is that it allowed for some interchanging components,

63 *Tapisserie du Tournoi*: detail showing a broken lance and grapper in the foreground.
Late 15th century

since he includes a tantalising allusion to the garniture ('guarnició') as opposed to the harness ('arnès') in his 'School of Jousting'. This is an early reference to a system that would evolve in complexity throughout the sixteenth century. As I shall discuss in chapter 5, garnitures with interchangeable pieces posed special problems for Menaguerra, as they complicated the issue of scoring. As for what, exactly, a garniture is, we must look to the sixteenth century for further enlightenment about this stage in the evolution of the jousting kit.

~: 3 :~

Arms and Armour of the Joust II:
The Sixteenth Century

T HE sixteenth century is particularly significant in relation to arms and armour in Spain. In the 1540s finely crafted Italian and German armours were simultaneously in vogue at the Hapsburg court. By the mid-sixteenth century, armour – whether it was made in Italy or Germany – was the highest form of male fashion and of masculine, artistic self-expression, from the point of view of both the wearer and the maker.

In the case of Italian armour, Mantua and Milan, both located in Lombardy, had since Suero de Quiñones' day been highly regarded centres for the manufacture of quality armour and accoutrements. By the sixteenth century the Mantuan master armourer Caremolo Modrone (1498–1543) and his School boasted an international reputation, and Caremolo himself was one of Charles V's favourite armourers, as was the Negroli family of armourers, who worked out of Milan.[1] Given the Emperor's patronage of the Italian master armourers, it follows that there was also a die-hard cohort of Spanish nobles who favoured custom, Italian-made armour.

As Holy Roman Emperor Charles V enjoyed luxuries that few others could ever hope to afford. One such luxury was the wherewithal to travel extensively and purchase expensive, bespoke harnesses from the most skilled craftsmen in Germany as well as those in Italy. And let us not forget that in the case of emperors, kings and princes, the armourers also had sound reasons for approaching them, as opposed to the other way around. In the case of German armour, ever since Charles V had appointed Kolman Helmschmied (1470–1532) his personal armourer Augsburg had been the centre to which yet another cohort of Spanish noblemen who favoured German-made armour and who could afford it gravitated for their harnesses. Upon Kolman's death in 1532, he was succeeded by his son Desiderius (1513–79) and Augsburg continued to flourish as the main German supplier of fine armour to the Spanish court.[2] Desiderius Helmschmied made several armours for Charles' son, the future King Philip II, between 1544 and 1552, including the 'Flowers' garniture, in which

---

[1] On the Italian master armourers, see Pyhrr et al., *Heroic Armor of the Italian Renaissance: Filippo Negroli and his Contemporaries*, esp. pp. 115–270.

[2] On the Helmschmieds, see Reitzenstein, 'Die Ordnung der Augsberger Plattner', and Williams, *The Knight and the Blast Furnace*, pp. 361–5.

Titian portrayed Philip in 1551.[3] However, by the late 1540s, around the time Quijada de Reayo published his little treatise, Philip's taste for Augsburg armour was waning, and in 1550 he shifted his patronage to Landshut. Philip was travelling through Germany at this time (his father introduced him to Titian in Augsburg in 1550) so it is not unreasonable to speculate that he visited the various armour workshops, either liked what he saw or was overwhelmed by the package he was offered at Landshut and, during these formative years when he was branching out into what one of his biographers has called 'a positive expression of his own preferences',[4] opted to break with the Augsburg style.

Landshut's master armourer Wolfgang Grosschedel (1517–62) was commissioned to make armour for both Philip and Philip's son Don Carlos.[5] Grosschedel, later in partnership with his son Franz, went on to forge a number of famous garnitures for Philip, including the 'Cloud Bands' and 'Burgundy Cross' garnitures.[6] Once Philip's personal taste in armour shifted to Landshut, so too did that of the fashion-conscious cohort of Spanish noblemen who favoured German-made armour. The Augsburg armour industry suffered accordingly: Soler del Campo notes that the number of active armour workshops in Augsburg decreased from twenty-seven to nine in just ten years, a downturn which reflects the vast extent to which they relied on Spanish patronage.[7] An extraordinary piece of documentary evidence records this dramatic shift in tastes: the pattern-book of the Augsburg etcher Jörg Sorg, which records his commissions from 1548–63. Between 1549 and 1551 the majority of the armours Sorg was decorating were commissions for Spanish noblemen. After 1551 only three Spanish commissions are recorded – one in 1553 and two in or around 1563.[8]

---

[3] On this garniture, see Valencia de Don Juan, *Catálogo histórico-descriptivo de la Real Armería de Madrid*, pp. 74–5, inv. A217–A230; also Frieder, *Chivalry and The Perfect Prince*, pp. 118–21.

[4] Kamen, *Philip of Spain*, p. 72.

[5] On the Grosschedel family, see Reitzenstein, 'Die Landshuter Plattner, ihre Ordnung und ihre Meister'; Williams, 'The Grosschedel Family of Armourers of Landshut and their Metallurgy'; and Williams, *The Knight and the Blast Furnace*, pp. 551–7.

[6] On the Cloud Bands and Burgundy Cross garnitures, see Valencia de Don Juan, *Catálogo histórico-descriptivo de la Real Armería de Madrid*, pp. 83–6, inv. A243–A262, and pp. 86–9, inv. A263–A273, respectively; also Frieder, *Chivalry and The Perfect Prince*, pp. 63–5 and 97–103. Although not stated by Frieder, the Cloud Bands garniture was a double garniture: one for Philip, and the other, identical in style, made to fit his teenage son Don Carlos.

[7] Soler del Campo, 'La producción de armas personales: 1500–1700', pp. 849–50.

[8] The original codex is located at Stuttgart, Wurttembergische Landesbibliothek, Cod. Milit. 2° 24. It is now available in a critical edition by Becher *et al.*, *Das Stuttgarter Harnisch-Musterbuch, 1548–1563*, pp. 48–91.

Without wishing to belabour the point, however, this decline in Spanish commissions in Augsburg reflects the tastes of the cohort of nobles who preferred German-made armour and not necessarily the tastes of the entire Spanish nobility. And it is worth clarifying here that this is not a book about Charles V and Philip II. It is a book about jousting. Thus, given the healthy competition between German and Italian armourers and their international clientele, all of whom were wealthy and many of whom could afford armour of the highest quality, when it comes to the practical implementation and the aesthetic evolution of jousting armour in sixteenth-century continental Europe the salient details for consideration are not so much the personalities for whom the armour was made as the date of manufacture of the kit and the type of joust for which it was intended. It is in this general context that the treatises of Juan Quijada de Reayo and Luis Zapata must necessarily be considered.

Doctrina del Arte de la Cavallería (1548)

I N chapter 1 of *Doctrina del arte de la cavallería* Quijada de Reayo notes his own preference for saddles made in Mantua. In addition to this reference the inventory of his patron's armoury at Cuéllar indicates the availability of numerous circular pageant shields made in Naples.[9] Thus it would appear that the ducal armoury was particularly well stocked with Italian armour and accoutrements. Such emphasis on Italian-made armour confirms the Duke of Alburquerque's (and by extension Quijada de Reayo's) personal preference for the Italian craftsmanship that coexisted and healthily competed with contemporary German craftsmanship. Beltrán de la Cueva had had more direct contact with Italy than with Germany during his distinguished military career, which may explain an ongoing relationship with one of the Italian armourers and a preference for his work. The ducal armoury is revealing in one other sense, however, in that it should not be assumed that all Spanish knights habitually travelled hither and yon for every single acquisition. In addition to his Italian pieces the duke did own some locally made armour. One of his helmets was made in Saragossa and one of his jousting harnesses was made by 'Master Jerónimo', a reference to Jerónimo García, the prestigious master armourer of Valladolid who made armours for high-ranking nobles such as the Duke of Nájera and the future King Philip II.[10] Saragossa boasted

---

[9] Rodríguez Villa, *Inventario del moviliario, alhajas, ropas, armería y otros efectos del Excmo. Sr. D. Beltrán de la Cueva*, pp. 75–6.

[10] Rodríguez Villa, *Inventario del moviliario, alhajas, ropas, armería y otros efectos del Excmo. Sr. D. Beltrán de la Cueva*, p. 74 (helmet) and p. 71 (jousting harness). On Jerónimo García, see Cortés Echanove, 'Armas y armeros en la época de Felipe II', p. 260.

an international reputation for high-quality helmets.[11] Thus a deduction that can be teased out of Don Beltrán's armoury is that in Iberian chivalric circles everyone who was anyone owned at least one custom-made helmet from Saragossa.

As well as reflecting an era in armour evolution characterised by a sense of high fashion dominated in continental Europe by Germany and Italy, *Doctrina del arte de la cavallería* reflects an era characterised by great practical changes in the use and manufacture of armour. By Quijada de Reayo's time knights were required to fight in several different capacities on the battlefield and in tournaments. Each of these ways of fighting required different armour. However, it was not feasible to own and maintain many different armours, and simple practicality led to the development of the garniture – a complete armour that was accompanied by a number of pieces of exchange or, as Quijada de Reayo calls them, 'double-pieces'.[12] As we have seen in the Pass of Honour of Suero de Quiñones and the cryptic allusion to the garniture in *Lo Cavaller*, although the occasional reinforcing piece was used in the fifteenth century, especially in jousts, it would not be until the early sixteenth century that the complex full garniture was systematised in the European centres of armour-making. These garnitures began to be produced around the same time by German and Italian armourers, with the result that it is difficult to pinpoint with accuracy which armourer was responsible for the invention of the new system.[13]

As far as the practicalities of the garniture are concerned, the additional plates could be integrated into the armour in several different combinations, allowing the one armour to be configured and reconfigured, depending on the particular type of harness required. While some small

---

[11] Riquer, *L'Arnès del cavaller*, pp. 36 and 69.

[12] On the complexities of the sixteenth-century garniture, see especially Gamber, 'Die Harnischgarnitur'; Capwell, *The Real Fighting Stuff*, pp. 52–5; and Capwell, *The Royal Armouries: Armour and Equipment for the Joust* (forthcoming). My thanks to Dr Capwell for sharing an early draft of this book with me.

[13] Boccia *et al.*, *Armi e Armature Lombarde*, pp. 18–19, impute the invention of the garniture to the armourers of Milan. On the other hand, Gravett, 'Tournament Courses', p. 336, opts for the German armourers. Soler del Campo, 'La batalla y la armadura de Mühlberg en el retrato ecuestre de Carlos V', p. 91, cites the German armourer Lorenz Helmschmied (*c*. 1445–1515/16). What can be stated with certainty is that most of the earliest known full-fledged garnitures are German, and Lorenz and Kolman Helmschmied were on the cutting edge of garniture development in the late 15th and early 16th centuries, as testified by the Thun Sketchbook. The original copy of this sketchbook has been missing since 1945, though before its disappearance photographs of the pages were taken by the Städtische Kunstsammlungen in Augsburg. See Gamber, 'Der Turnierharnisch zur Zeit König Maximilians I. und das Thunsche Skizzenbuch', and Gamber, 'Kolman Helmschmid, Ferdinand I, und das Thun'sche Skizzenbuch'.

64, 65, 66 (*above*) Garniture for the field, tourney and joust of Gaspar de Quiñones, Count of Luna, 1549, made by Matthaus Frauenpreiss of Augsburg. From the pattern-book of Jörg Sorg, *c.* 1548–63

67, 68 (*left*) Garniture of Don Alonso de Osorio, Count of Trastámara, 1551, made by Hans Lutzenberger of Augsburg. From the pattern-book of Jörg Sorg, *c.* 1548–63

garnitures were designed only for war, allowing the wearer to fight on foot or on horseback in light, medium and heavy cavalry roles, the larger garnitures included pieces for foot combat, tourney and joust. Figs. 64–6 show the elaborate garniture for the field, tourney and joust of the Spanish nobleman Gaspar de Quiñones, Count of Luna, made in 1549 by the Augsburg armourer Matthaus Frauenpreis, as illustrated in the Sorg pattern-book. Interchangeable pieces are arranged around the armours. Moving clockwise around Quiñones' field armour (fig. 64) we see a burgeonet peak and falling buffe, a shield and an open-face burgeonet. Extra pieces for tourney and joust include: a special reinforce worn in tourneys over the crown of the helmet, called a gupfe; an articulated reinforcing bevor for the tourney; a demi-shaffron for the horse; a right mitten gauntlet for the joust; and a solid reinforcing bevor for the joust. Figs. 67 and 68 show a

69 The 'Eagle Garniture' made for Archduke Ferdinand of Tyrol (1525–95)
by the Innsbruck armourer Jörg Seusenhofer and etched by Hans Perckhammer, 1547

somewhat less complex garniture made by the Augsburg armourer Hans
Lutzenberger for Don Alonso de Osorio, Count of Trastámara, in 1551.

As a complement to these images fig. 69 shows a complete extant garniture of the highest quality and of the type being ordered from German
armourers by the Spanish clients in the Sorg pattern-book. It is remarkable not only because it has survived intact, but also because details have
survived about the maker, the etcher and its cost. This is the 'Eagle Garniture', ordered in the winter of 1546 during the Schmalkaldic War by Ferdinand I for his seventeen-year-old son the Archduke Ferdinand of Tyrol
(1525–95). The garniture was made by the Innsbruck master armourer Jörg
Seusenhofer and etched by Hans Perckhammer. The surviving bills of sale
indicate that it was completed in the autumn of 1547 – just one year before
the publication of Quijada de Reayo's treatise – and that it was not used
until 1548 at a tournament in Prague.[14] These bills further indicate that the
cost of the garniture was 1,258 Gulden, plus another 463 Gulden for the

[14] Gamber and Beaufort, *Kunsthistorisches Museum, Wien: Hofjagd- und Rüstkammer
(edem. Waffensammlung): Katalog der Leibrüstkammer, II: Der Zeitraum von 1530–
1560*, pp. 90–2, inv. A638; also discussed by Gamber, 'Die Harnischgarnitur', and
Oakeshott, *European Weapons and Armour*, pp. 76 and 101.

etching. As a point of comparison Gamber and Beaufort provide data to the effect that the salary of a court employee at this time was 100 Gulden per annum.[15]

The Eagle Garniture is currently displayed on five mannequins. The mannequin on the far right in fig. 69 displays the exchange pieces for a type of German tourney called the 'Free Course' ('Freiturnier'), which consisted of a mass lance-charge run at large without a tilt, followed by a tourney with swords. Next to this armour is a complete harness for the mid-sixteenth-century iteration of the Welschgestech über die Planken, the German version of the Italian joust with tilt barrier; the extra grand-guard and the wrapper behind the grandguard at the foot of this manne-quin have the smooth contours that are more accurately Italian or Spanish. This set also includes a demi-shaffron for the horse's head. Thus the first two mannequins on the right include armour for three different types of joust. The armour in the centre is the Archduke's field armour. Next to this is a tonlet with its distinctive skirt, which would have been used for foot combat in the lists. Finally, on the far left there are more exchange pieces for the field armour in the centre. These pieces would have been used to make the field armour a three-quarter armour that would have been appropriate for leading men on foot or in a light cavalry role. Every feasible aspect of sixteenth-century chivalric combat is therefore covered by this one garniture. Quijada de Reayo in his own discussion of the garni-ture in chapter 3 of his treatise provides ample notes on war armour for heavy cavalry combat before moving on specifically to discuss the exchange pieces for the joust.

One of the most frustrating aspects of Quijada de Reayo's treatise from the perspective of the twenty-first century is that he tends not to explain, preferring instead simply to tell or inform. This is because his book is written for a boy who is being trained how to fight; hence, in the tradi-tion of the medieval and renaissance tutor, Quijada de Reayo lectures his pupil on what the various pieces of armour are and what the boy needs to do with them. If Quijada de Reayo ever did entertain questions from his protégé about arms and armour, he would have been able to answer them with hands-on demonstrations using items from the extensive armoury in the ducal palace at Cuéllar.[16] It would be up to Luis Zapata, whose miscel-laneous autobiographical musings allow, rhetorically, for much more flex-ibility and prolixity, to explain in more detail some of the salient points made by Quijada de Reayo.

---

[15] Gamber and Beaufort, *Kunsthistorisches Museum, Wien: Hofjagd- und Rüstkammer (edem. Waffensammlung): Katalog der Leibrüstkammer, II: Der Zeitraum von 1530–1560*, pp. 92.

[16] The armoury at Cuéllar was ransacked by the troops of Hugo and Wellington during the Peninsular War.

Unlike Menaguerra, Quijada de Reayo frames his own treatise with first and last chapters devoted to saddles and bits, respectively, thereby drawing attention to the fundamental importance of the horse and horse trappings. In war, knights throughout medieval Europe typically rode on a small saddle characterised by its retaining cantle that offered protection to the rider's lower abdomen and back, whilst allowing for limited movement. Fig. 70 shows a war saddle of this style made in Milan *c.* 1570–80. It weighs 10,024 g (22 lb 1 oz).[17] In order to stabilise the rider in the saddle it was necessary to use long stirrup leathers so that he would ride with the legs stretched out. The thighs

70 War saddle of wood, textile, iron, leather, steel, silver and gold. Italian (Milan), *c.* 1570–80

were secured firmly in place by cushioned bolsters built into the saddle between the pommel and cantle, and the bridle always had long reins. The stirrups, when used in conjunction with the saddle bows, provided the lateral support necessary to absorb the impact in case of collision. The renaissance theorists who endorsed this style of riding, such as the Italian Federico Grisone, stressed that 'you shall let your legs hang straight, in the same way as when you are walking'.[18] The detailed explanation of yet another theorist, Juan Suárez Peralta, provides further practical reasons for standing in the saddle:

> In olden days knights would ride long because the horses were covered and armoured, and so it was necessary to ride long and to wear long spurs in order to be able to put spurs to the belly of the horse, and these were one palm long, so that they were constrained of necessity to ride that way.[19]

With the rise of the joust and the increased usage of the lance-rest,

---

[17] On this saddle, see Pyhrr *et al.*, *The Armored Horse in Europe, 1480–1620*, pp. 60–2. Line drawings of the saddle's construction are included in Part II below, Quijada de Reayo, *Doctrine of the Art of Chivalry*, ch. 1.

[18] 'Dexareys caer las piernas derechas de la manera que las tenéys andando a pie' (Grisón, *Reglas de la Cavallería de la Brida*, trans. Flórez de Benavides, fol. 11v).

[19] 'Antiguamente se vsaua yr los caualleros largos por causa que los cauallos yuan encubertados y armados, y assí era necessario yr largos y lleuar las espuelas largas para poder picar en la barriga al cauallo, y estas eran de vn palmo, de manera que eran constreñidos de necesidad a caualgar en aquel modo' (Suárez Peralta, *Tractado de la cavallería de la Gineta y Brida*, fol. 42v. For a modern edition of this text, see Suárez Peralta, *Tratado de la jineta y brida*, ed. Álvarez del Villar, p. 69).

certain modifications were made to these war saddles so that they would meet the specific needs of the jousters. The principal difference between the war saddle and the jousting saddle was that the jousting saddle required careful use of the stirrups whilst at the same time maintaining a perfect balance in the saddle. Thus, according to Duarte of Portugal, success in the war saddle depends on 'keeping the body erect on the saddle and pressing the legs – extended and maintaining a straight line with the body – against the beast, not paying great attention to the stirrups';[20] and success in the jousting saddle involves 'riding firm on the stirrups with the legs extended and not being seated on the saddle, but having the body balance helped by the saddle bows'.[21]

Although Quijada de Reayo does not use a specific nomenclature like Menaguerra, he does describe the mid-sixteenth-century iteration of the jousting saddle in detail in chapter 1 of his treatise. Like Duarte, Grisone and Suárez Peralta, he states that 'you should stand as straight in the saddle as if you were standing at attention before the king'. The basic difference between the jousting saddle and the war saddle as stated by Quijada de Reayo is that the jousting saddle further restricts movement by making the rear arçon not only higher than the one at the front, but also canted slightly inwards. This permutation makes perfect sense, since a jouster, unlike a mounted soldier, would have had no reason to turn in the saddle and every reason to concentrate on what was happening directly in front of him. Echoing Duarte, the other fundamental difference between the jousting saddle and the war saddle according to Quijada de Reayo is that the jouster's backside does not actually sit on the saddle and instead hovers just above the seat. He could thus stand on the stirrups and, pushed forward by the canted rear arçon, lean into the saddle as he pressed home his attack on his opponent. Jousting champion Luis Zapata gives the following specific advice: 'The length of the stirrups should be such that there is a palm's breadth between the knight's seat and the saddle.' In order for jousters to be able to stand one palm's breadth, or approximately 10.16 cm (4 in) above the saddle for extended periods of time they were required to have strong thighs, akin in gracefulness to modern-day ballet dancers. I shall return to this issue in the next chapter.

[20] 'se teer dereito, e apertar as pernas, segundo for o tempo, seendo sempre dereito em ellas, nom fazendo grande conta das strebeiras' (Duarte I, King of Portugal, *Livro da ensinança de bem cavalgar toda sela que fez El-Rey Dom Eduarte de Portogal e do Algarve e Senhor de Ceuta*, ed. Piel, p. 16). For the translation, see *The Royal Book of Horsemanship, Jousting and Knightly Combat*, trans. Preto and Preto, p. 22.

[21] 'Andar firmado nas stribeiras e pernas direitas no seendo dentro na sella, mas recebendo algũa ajuda dos arções' (Duarte I, King of Portugal, *Livro da ensinança de bem cavalgar toda sela que fez El-Rey Dom Eduarte de Portogal e do Algarve e Senhor de Ceuta*, ed. Piel, p. 17). For the translation, see *The Royal Book of Horsemanship, Jousting and Knightly Combat*, trans. Preto and Preto, p. 23.

According to Quijada de Reayo the saddle was further stabilised by connecting the stirrup leathers to the cinches: 'And the breast strap should be slit on the right-hand side, and the slit trimmed with a piece of leather, and pass the stirrup through it.' Over a hundred years earlier, Duarte of Portugal had recommended a similar system, whereby the jouster should 'equip the horse in such a way that the stirrups stay fixed to the horse's body using an additional system of interlaced ropes (tying the stirrups together underneath the horse's belly)'.[22] Quijada de Reayo also places emphasis on the need for a double girth and a crupper. The double girths, which prevented the saddle from shifting backwards due to the force of the encounter, tended only to be used for jousting since they restricted the horse's breathing and therefore could not be used for extended or unlimited periods of time. They also prevented the saddle from rolling, which was an important factor to consider in the joust. If a jouster received a hard blow he would inevitably lean over to one side, and if the saddle rolled or slipped under the strain, he would inevitably part company with the horse and end up on the ground through no fault of his own. Just as the double girths prevented the saddle from slipping backwards, so the crupper stopped it from sliding forward.[23]

It should be noted that the salient differences between the war saddle and the jousting saddle were not immediately obvious, and could only be discerned upon close inspection. This is clear from the Pass of Honour of Suero de Quiñones, where the contestants were expected to joust on war saddles, but some men cheated by surreptitiously applying extra girths and ties to their war saddles. The ruse was routinely discovered not because the judges could see the advantage from the stands but because they were alerted to the cheating by the opposing contestant who was near enough to note the additional accoutrements.

A final note on the saddle concerns an innovation mentioned by Quijada de Reayo, namely, the cut-out in the right side of the front saddle steel, used to brace the lance when the butt rested in the saddle recess near the underside of the right thigh. Figs. 71–3 show two sixteenth-century Italian saddles of the type preferred by Quijada de Reayo with the cut-out for the lance.[24] The saddle illustrated in figs. 72 and 73 also has a canted

[22] 'ordenar em tal guisa que as estrebeiras sejam firmes pera troxamento ou correas forçadas' (Duarte I, King of Portugal, *Livro da ensinança de bem cavalgar toda sela que fez El-Rey Dom Eduarte de Portogal e do Algarve e Senhor de Ceuta*, ed. Piel, p. 17). For the translation, see *The Royal Book of Horsemanship, Jousting and Knightly Combat*, trans. Preto and Preto, p. 23.

[23] On the double girths and the crupper, see Barker, *The Tournament in England, 1100–1400*, pp. 173–5.

[24] Valencia de Don Juan, *Catálogo histórico-descriptivo de la Real Armería de Madrid*, F10 and F22, pp. 174 and 175.

71 Saddle with cut-out for the lance.
Italian, 16th century

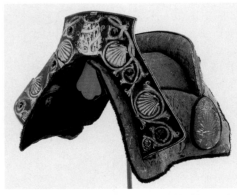

72, 73 Two views of a saddle owned by the Duke
of Mantua with cut-out for the lance and canted
rear arçon. Italian, 16th century, probably by
Caremolo Modrone of Mantua

rear arçon for jousting. This saddle was probably made by the Mantuan master armourer Caremolo Modrone and, as Quijada de Reayo points out: 'Mantuan saddles are better and more comfortable for riding and dismounting.'[25] It therefore represents what in his opinion was superlative saddlery.

With respect to the lance itself, since Quijada de Reayo was in the service of the Duke of Alburquerque and the ducal armoury contained examples of what Buttin calls the polygonal-shaped jousting lance, it can be inferred that this type of lance, which was thick and heavy, is the one with which master and pupil would have been most familiar.[26]

Quijada de Reayo makes a distinction throughout his treatise between two different types of lance-head, which he calls 'el borne' and 'la evilla'. As frustratingly as ever for the modern scholar, he does not explain the difference between the two, and, as lamented long ago by Valencia de Don Juan, no other contemporary Spanish author makes or explains this distinction.[27] Buttin has confirmed in some detail that Spanish 'borne' is the same lance-head as the French 'morne' and English 'mourne', that is, the type of lance-head with three or four tines used in jousts of peace as shown in the previous chapter, figs. 57 and 58. The

[25] On the attribution of Real Armería saddle F22 to Modrone, see Pyhrr et al., *Heroic Armor of the Italian Renaissance: Filippo Negroli and his Contemporaries*, p. 251.

[26] Rodríguez Villa, *Inventario del moviliario, alhajas, ropas, armería y otros efectos del Excmo. Sr. D. Beltrán de la Cueva*, p. 78; Buttin, 'La lance et l'arrêt de cuirasse', pp. 107 and 123.

[27] Valencia de Don Juan, *Catálogo histórico-descriptivo de la Real Armería de Madrid*, p. 278, n. 1. See also Anglo, *The Martial Arts of Renaissance Europe*, p. 239.

mourne was sometimes made of soft iron as opposed to tempered steel.[28] Since 'evilla' (modern Spanish 'hebilla') usually means 'buckle', and since buckles typically fasten with a prong, I infer that for Quijada de Reayo 'evilla' is a synecdoche referring to the single-pointed head used in jousts of war, though as we know from the variety of lance-heads in the collection of the Real Armería, even the descriptor 'single-pointed' is a loose categorisation since there was considerable variety among the single-pointed lance-heads. At the beginning of chapter 4 of his treatise Quijada de Reayo further states that:

> In the case of the single-pointed head (*evilla*), it behoves the lance-maker, on accoutring the lance, to place it tightly onto the seat of the stave so that it fits very snugly in place and so that the shaft of the lance-head is no more than half the length of the tip of the lance stave. This way, in the case of an encounter the single-pointed head will remain tightly in place, pressure will be exerted on the stave, and it will not penetrate.

The notion of the lance-head potentially being able to penetrate the opponent's armour lends credence to my belief that Quijada de Reayo's 'evilla' is a single-pointed tip used in jousts of war. If I am right, the terminology also constitutes unusual evidence that jousts of war, which had already fallen out of fashion in most of Europe by the second half of the fifteenth century, were still being practised in and around Cuéllar even at this late date.

In so far as armour is concerned, Quijada de Reayo offers a textbook description of the sixteenth-century garniture. His knight wears full harness, with emphasis on a custom-made, close fit. Starting with the armet, Quijada de Reayo recommends that it be fully lined and that there be five holes punched into the cheek pieces 'in the shape of a cross'. This recommendation is an example of the master imposing his personal tastes upon the boy under his tutelage, since extant armets and close-helmets from the period show different configurations of ear holes in the cheek pieces. The armet in fig. 74 has nine holes arranged in a circular pattern;[29] the close-helmet for field and tilt in fig. 75 has an arrangement of seven holes punched into the bevor;[30]

---

[28] Buttin, 'La lance et l'arrêt de cuirasse', pp. 34–7. Also Rodríguez Villa, *Inventario del moviliario, alhajas, ropas, armería y otros efectos del Excmo. Sr. D. Beltrán de la Cueva*, p. 75, where this type of lance-head forms part of a kit for the joust royal.

[29] Mann, *Wallace Collection Catalogues: European Arms and Armour*, vol. I, p. 15, inv. A22, and Norman, *Wallace Collection Catalogues: European Arms and Armour: Supplement*, p. 3, inv. A22.

[30] Mann, *Wallace Collection Catalogues: European Arms and Armour*, vol. I, p. 138, inv. A169, and Norman, *Wallace Collection Catalogues: European Arms and Armour: Supplement*, p. 63, inv. A169.

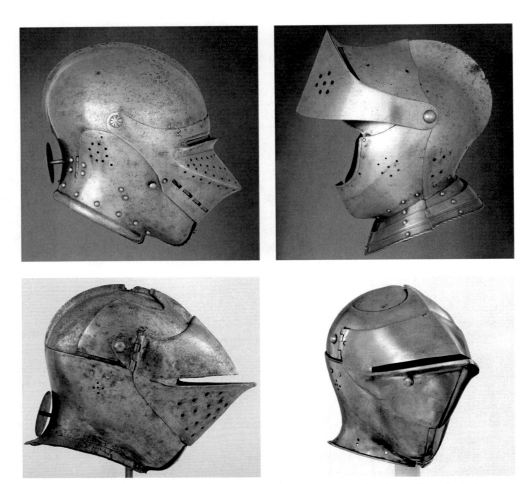

74 *(top left)* Armet with nine ear holes in a circular pattern. Note also the rondel at the back.
Possibly German, 16th century. Weight 2,825 g (6 lb 3½ oz)

75 *(top right)* Close-helmet for field and tilt with seven ear holes in a geometric pattern.
German, *c.* 1560. Weight 3,260 g (7 lb 3 oz)

76 *(bottom left)* Armet with five ear holes in the shape of a cross. Flemish, *c.* 1510

77 *(bottom right)* Armet for the tilt with five ear holes in the shape of a cross. Italian, *c.* 1520

and the armets in figs. 76 and 77 have the five-hole configuration preferred
by Quijada de Reayo.[31]

Unusually for Quijada de Reayo, he does explain the purpose of these
holes: 'so that you can hear clearly what is said to you'. Much more characteristically, he also mentions that the armet should be fitted with a rondel

[31] Leeds, Royal Armouries IV.1601 is originally from Witham church in Essex. On
Leeds, Royal Armouries IV.576, see Williams, *The Knight and the Blast Furnace*,
pp. 152–3.

at the back, but without explaining why. The purpose of the rondel is still not known for certain, though Blair has suggested that it was perhaps a reinforcement piece to protect the leather strap that supported the wrapper of the armet.[32]

The breastplate and backplate should be light and close fitting, the fauld set at a comfortable height, and the tassets, 'because they are more loose-fitting', should be lined with cloth. As usual Quijada de Reayo offers no explanation, though a cloth lining would prevent chafing on the rider's thigh and damage to the other pieces of armour with which the tassets came into contact.[33] In time Zapata would explain more fully why leather lining bands were an added boon on certain pieces.

By 1548, after constant trial and error, Quijada de Reayo forces home the point that the lance-rest should be bolted directly onto the breastplate, by which he means that it should not be secured in place with staples and a retaining pin. 'The pauldrons', he says, 'well made: the right one with its bars; and the left one somewhat thicker.' Of the thick left pauldron Matthias Pfaffenbichler has clarified that in the case of high-quality armour: 'Great care was taken to see that the metal was thickest over the most vulnerable parts. The thickness of the pieces varied, not only between different plates but in different parts of the same plate ... Also, the left side of good-quality armour was often made heavier than the right, because the left was the side turned towards an enemy.'[34] As far as the right pauldron is concerned, the meaning of 'bars' can only be inferred. Armours of the period reveal that the left pauldron is often heavier, more protective and less flexible than the right, which is more flexible and mobile, allowing the freer movement of the lance arm so that the knight can raise and position his lance correctly. Thus the most plausible explanation for the unique term 'bars' is that they denote the lames from which the main portion of the right pauldron is constructed. Beyond the asymmetric design of the pauldrons the upper body defence is completed by armour for the arms and hands in the form of vambraces and gauntlets with leather lining gloves.

For the legharness Quijada de Reayo recommends cuisses and demi-cuisses. As ever, he does not explain why the prospective jouster should use a cuisse and demi-cuisse combination – it will once again be up to Zapata to explain this nuance of the jousting harness. The cuisses should be complemented by long and elegant greaves with a vertical slit at the back to accommodate the arm of the rowel of the spur, and mail sabatons. The slit was a common feature on both field and jousting armour after

[32] Blair, *European Armour*, pp. 87–8; also Edge and Paddock, *Arms and Armor of the Medieval Knight*, p. 188.

[33] Chafing is discussed by ffoulkes, *The Armourer and his Craft*, pp. 91–2.

[34] Pfaffenbichler, *Medieval Craftsmen: Armourers*, p. 63. See also Williams, *The Knight and the Blast Furnace*, pp. 913–17.

c. 1500.[35] Judging by the words of Quijada de Reayo's contemporary, Gonzalo Fernández de Oviedo (1478–1557), it was an innovation worthy of some note. As a means of showing that he is on top of the latest developments in the world of arms and armour, Fernández de Oviedo's description of the process for arming and disarming an early sixteenth-century Spanish jouster reads as follows, with emphasis on the recently invented spur slit:

> The man-at-arms, or jouster, starts arming himself from the feet to the head, and when he disarms himself he starts from the head, and the first thing he does is to take off the helm. And thus when he started to arm himself he first of all put on the spurs, and when they are fastened in place the greaves are fitted and the arm of the spur projects through the heel of the greave through a certain slot or aperture that is made for this purpose in the heel of the greave. And then the rest of the armour follows, until he finally gets to the helm, and once that is strapped on, he rides on horseback or goes on foot, if the combat should be on foot, with the offensive weapons that are most appropriate for him to carry. This thing about the spurs is mentioned so that anyone who is not a courtier or who has not followed armour may know about it, thereby gaining an understanding of what is talked about in royal courts and the other kinds of thing that go on there.[36]

Fig. 78 shows the back of a German-made left greave and sabaton from the sixteenth century with the type of spur slit described by Quijada de Reayo and Fernández de Oviedo.

As a final note on basic required equipment for combat in the lists Quijada de Reayo adds that a shaffron should be placed on the horse's head when jousting. This is a sound recommendation given especially the many unfortunate accidents at the Pass of Honour of Suero de Quiñones

---

[35] Blair, *European Armour*, p. 102.

[36] 'El ombre darmas, o justador, se comiença a armar desde los pies hasta la cabeça, e quando se desarma comiença desde la cabeça, e lo primero que haze es quitarse el yelmo. E así quando se començó a armar se puso primero las espuelas, e después de calçadas asiéntanse las greuas e por el calcañar de la greua sale el asta de la espuela por çierta muesca o abertura que para ese efecto la greua tiene en el talón hecho. E después proçeden las armas rrestantes, hasta que al fin toma el yelmo, e aquél enlazado, caualga a cauallo o vase a pie, si el combate ha de ser a pie con las armas ofensiuas que más le conuiene lleuar. Esto ques dicho de las espuelas es para que el que no es cortesano, ni ha seguido las armas, lo sepa viendo lo ques dicho e otras cosas que en las cortes rreales se vsan' (Fernández de Oviedo, *Las Memorias de Gonzalo Fernández de Oviedo*, ed. Avalle-Arce, vol. I, p. 215). A reconstruction of the process for arming the knight is well illustrated in Capwell, *The Real Fighting Stuff*, pp. 38–9.

that could have been avoided by dint of this protective piece. Fig. 79 illustrates a high-quality shaffron made for a member of the powerful Rivera family of Seville c. 1550 and possibly etched by Jörg Sorg. It is said to come from the Rivera palace, the Casa de Pilatos in Seville. This example is typical of the Augsburg shaffrons that were being made for Spanish clients in Quijada de Reayo's time and it could have been used for both war and jousting.

The entire garniture can then be further reinforced for the joust with eight exchange pieces: plackart (now a complete reinforcing breastplate as opposed to the shallow plackarts of Suero de Quiñones' day); over-tasset; waist lame; grandguard; reinforcing bevor; reinforcing visor; pasguard; and manifer. The invention of these reinforcing pieces meant that the shield of Menaguerra's time was now obsolete, having been replaced by the pasguard, which protected the left arm, and the grandguard, which offered protection for the left shoulder. Sixteenth-century grandguards often had additional ridged trellis-work – either applied separately or embossed directly into the steel – so that the tines of the coronel of the opponent's lance could gain a purchase, engaging with the trellis-work without actually piercing through the targe. Furthermore, on the surface of many Spanish grandguards of this period it is not unusual to find fanciful and fashionable etchings of mythological figures such as satyrs and centaurs. Fig. 80 shows a sixteenth-century grandguard richly etched with satyr masks. This particular example was formerly in the armoury of the Dukes of Osuna.[37]

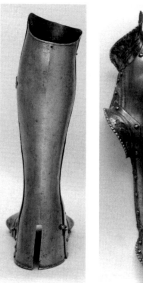

78 (*left*) Greave with spur slit at the heel. From a German armour made by Valentin Siebenbürger (c. 1510–64) of Nuremberg, c. 1520

79 (*right*) Shaffron for war or the joust made for a member of the Rivera family. Augsburg, c. 1550

80 Jousting targe with applied trellis-work. German, 16th century; from the armoury of the Dukes of Osuna

[37] Madrid, Real Armería, inv. D84. See Valencia de Don Juan, *Catálogo histórico-descriptivo de la Real Armería de Madrid*, p. 160, inv. D84.

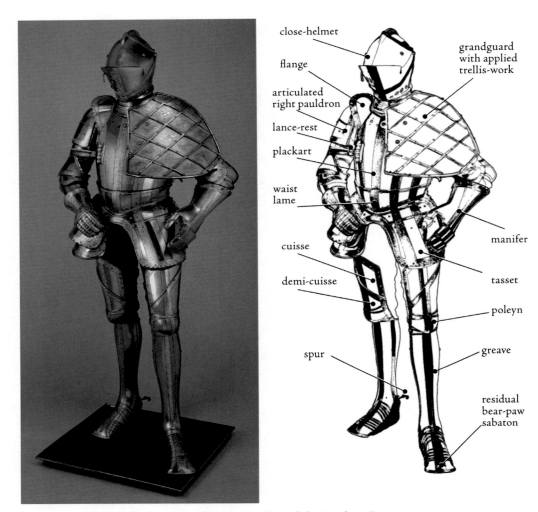

close-helmet

flange

articulated
right pauldron

lance-rest

plackart

waist
lame

cuisse

demi-cuisse

spur

grandguard
with applied
trellis-work

manifer

tasset

poleyn

greave

residual
bear-paw
sabaton

81 *(left)* Garniture of Maximilian II, made by Matthaus Frauenpreiss
of Augsburg and etched by Jörg Sorg, 1549

82 *(right)* Labelled line-drawing of the armour in fig. 81

Fig. 81 is an example of the top level of Augsburg armour that was being
worn throughout Europe at the time Quijada de Reayo published his treatise; fig. 82 shows this armour with the parts labelled. This stunning garniture was made in 1548–9 for Maximilian II by Matthaus Frauenpreiss and
etched by Jörg Sorg.[38] Of particular note are the grandguard with applied
trellis-work etched and gilt with centaurs, camels and elephants inside

---

[38] Gamber and Beaufort, *Kunsthistorisches Museum, Wien: Hofjagd- und Rüstkammer
(edem. Waffensammlung): Katalog der Leibrüstkammer, II: Der Zeitraum von 1530–
1560*, pp. 98–100, inv. A610, B73, B56, A2260, A2236, A641, A235.

each rhombus, the waist lame, the reinforcing breastplate or plackart, the cuisse and demi-cuisse leg armour and the long, elegant greaves that are cut with slits in the heels to accommodate the spurs, exactly as Quijada de Reayo recommends. The harness is completed by a pair of residual bear-paw sabatons. Bear-paw sabatons were a distinguishing characteristic of the Maximilian style which had been fashionable in the first three decades of the century. As noted by Blair, the Maximilian style bear-paws had 'broad toes, often splayed in an exaggerated manner'. The residual bear-paws of the mid-sixteenth century tended to have a more oblong shape with a slightly rounded toe, as is the case on this harness.[39]

Lessons learned the hard way about rivets meant that by Quijada de Reayo's time, as with the lance-rest, so too the exchange pieces for the joust were secured in place with stout bolts. In sixteenth-century garnitures these would either be screwed in from the outside or they would protrude from the host armour beneath the exchange pieces (as Quijada de Reayo seems to recommend) with the result that the exchange pieces would be fitted in place and nuts would then be screwed onto the protruding bolts to tighten the pieces. Lest the humble bolt ever be taken for granted, it should be noted that the thread of each bolt was meticulously crafted by hand, so they were not interchangeable. Each one would typically have a mark or number punched into the threaded stem. The same mark or number would then be punched into the corresponding holes into or out of which the bolts were screwed. Because each bolt was unique, the sets of bolts for individual harnesses were carefully stored in leather pouches.[40] Fig. 83 shows an Italian jousting armour made around 1560–70. Figs. 84–5 show details of the stout protruding bolts held in place with nuts on this armour and portions of another similar Italian jousting armour from the same period.[41] Note also that the armour portions in fig. 85 have three-piece tassets as recommended by Quijada de Reayo. On the other hand, figs. 86–7 show an armour produced probably in Augsburg c. 1550 for a member of the Hirnheim family of Swabia with a close-up view in fig. 88 of the exchange pieces for the Italian-style joust, the bolts of which screw in from the

[39] On the Maximilian style, see Blair, *European Armour*, pp. 115–16, and Klapsia and Thomas, 'Harnischstudien', pp. 147–55. On the sabatons, see Blair, *European Armour*, pp. 129–30.

[40] The storage pouch was commonly called a 'taleguilla' in Spanish. See Rodríguez Villa, *Inventario del moviliario, alhajas, ropas, armería y otros efectos del Excmo. Sr. D. Beltrán de la Cueva*, pp. 71–2.

[41] On Brescia, Museo Civico delle Armi Antiche Luigi Marzoli, B21, see Rossi and Carpegna, *Armi Antiche del Museo Civico L. Marzoli*, p. 16, no. 8, and Lanzardo, 'Il Convitato di ferro', p. 51, fig. 21, p. 52, fig. 22, p. 156, fig. 123. On London, Wallace Collection, A61, see Mann, *Wallace Collection Catalogues: European Arms and Armour*, vol. I, pp. 77–8, inv. A61, and Norman, *Wallace Collection Catalogues: European Arms and Armour: Supplement*, p. 33, inv. A61.

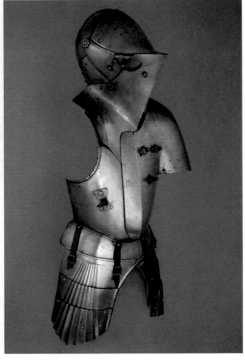

83 (*above*) Jousting armour. Italian, *c*. 1560–70

84 (*above right*) Detail of fig. 83, showing
protruding bolts for attaching the grandguard

85 (*right*) Detail of a different armour, showing
protruding bolts for attaching the grandguard

86, 87 Armour for the field and tilt made for a member of the Hirnheim family of
Swabia (shown with and without the exchange pieces). Augsburg, c. 1550

outside. The set-up consists of most of the pieces mentioned by Quijada
de Reayo: a reinforcing bevor; a plackart to cover the host breastplate with
a rectangular slit to accommodate the lance-rest; a waist lame with single
left tasset; a grandguard, which protects the left shoulder and chest; a
pasguard covering the elbow; and, instead of an independent manifer of
the type mentioned by Quijada de Reayo, a stout reinforce bolted over the
normal gauntlet beneath.[42] For maximum protection from lance thrusts

[42] See Mann, *Wallace Collection Catalogues: European Arms and Armour*, vol. I,
pp. 50–2, inv. A43; Norman, *Wallace Collection Catalogues: European Arms and*

88 Close-up of the exchange pieces
for the armour in figs. 86–7

the pasguard and gauntlet reinforce are faceted, a feature that also characterises the right couter on the armour of Philip I shown in figs. 41 and 54. Similarly, fig. 89 shows a reinforcing bevor and grandguard made in Augsburg in the mid-sixteenth century and attributed to the Spanish nobleman Don García Álvarez de Toledo, Marquis of Villafranca – this example also has bolts screwed in from the outside with domed, round heads.[43] It weighs 3,969 g (8 lb 12 oz). The numerous extant garnitures made for King Philip II on display in the Real Armería of Madrid suggest that this was a popular Spanish bolt set-up.

Ironically, after Quijada de Reayo outlines all the particulars in regard to the necessary exchange pieces for the joust, he abruptly observes that he does not think that they are really of much use, since, of the myriad injuries that can be sustained in the lists, the exchange pieces still cannot protect the wearer against the one injury that can prove fatal: a blow to the head from which splinters enter the sight and pierce the skull or eyes. The author's allusion to the 'Castilian style' in the last paragraph of chapter 3 of his treatise appears to mean that he prefers to joust in a kit that resembles field armour like the knights of the Pass of Honour of Suero de Quiñones. It is thus possible to draw two conclusions from the reference. On the one hand, if Quijada de Reayo really was jousting in a harness that resembled field armour in the 1540s, this reference adds further fuel to the argument that the joust of war was preserved much later than has previously been thought in a few conservative pockets. On the other hand, Quijada de Reayo, who was advanced in age at the time of writing *Doctrina del arte de la cavallería*, may be telling his protégé what he needs to know in order to be a successful jouster on the international circuit of the late 1540s – having himself kept abreast of all the latest trends in armour evolution – whilst at the same time he is voicing

Armour: Supplement, pp. 17–18, inv. A43; Dufty and Reid, *European Armour in the Tower of London*, p. 16 and plate XXXI.

43 Mann, *Wallace Collection Catalogues: European Arms and Armour*, vol. I, p. 176, inv. A250; Norman, *Wallace Collection Catalogues: European Arms and Armour: Supplement*, pp. 83–6, inv. A250.

an elderly disinterest in what he considers the newfangled fashions of the young, which were undoubtedly expensive and by no means guaranteed immunity to fatal wounds.

There is no explicit evidence in *Doctrina del arte de la cavallería* that the Castilian style equates to field armour *per se*, though the inference is clear on the point that this style is used in a more lightly armoured sort of joust than that which required exchange pieces. Although Quijada de Reayo's remarks are circumstantial, in the case of his Castilian style of jousting harness a combination of extant pictorial and physical evidence does allow for some speculation as to what it may have looked like. The last armour recorded in the Sorg pattern-book was commissioned by the Spanish nobleman Claudio Fernando de Quiñones, Count of Luna, around 1563. Made by Anton Peffenhauser this harness is specifically designated in the pattern-book as a jousting armour ('Stechküriss'),[44] yet it looks a lot like a field

89 Reinforcing bevor and grandguard of Don García Álvarez de Toledo, Marquis of Villafranca. Augsburg, mid-16th century. Weight: 3,969 g (8 lb 12 oz)

armour (fig. 90). Beyond the world of pictorial representation, a garniture made for Maximilian II c. 1550 either by Matthaus Frauenpreiss or Conrad Richter and etched by Jörg Sorg is typologically connected to the Quiñones armour (fig. 91) and is the kind of armour that was being made for Spanish clients at the time. This is a field armour with a breastplate for the joust attached. The full complement of exchange-pieces for this armour has not survived, but I would contend that this does not necessarily mean that the current set-up would have been incomplete or incompatible in a given situation. The harness has a short right tasset (shades of Menaguerra) and the left pauldron is articulated, as is the left pauldron on Quiñones' Stechküriss. In fact, the only difference between this harness and the one illustrated in the Sorg pattern-book is that the left pauldron does not have a haute-piece. The ubiquitous Claudio Fernando de Quiñones is depicted wearing a similar armour as he crushes his opponent at the Vienna tournament of 1560 in the 1566 edition of Hans von Francolin's *Thurnier Buch*

---

[44] The full caption for this sketch reads as follows: 'Ittem dissen stech kyris anthoni pfeffen hausser gehert dem graffen de luna' ('Item. This jousting armour by Anton Peffenhauser belongs to the Count of Luna'). See Becher *et al.*, *Das Stuttgarter Harnisch-Musterbuch, 1548–1563*, p. 90.

90 Jousting harness of Claudio Fernando
de Quiñones, Count of Luna,
c. 1563, by Anton Peffenhauser.
From the pattern-book of Jörg Sorg, c. 1548–63

91 Garniture of Maximilian II for the joust, by
Matthaus Frauenpreiss or Conrad Richter, and
etched by Jörg Sorg, Augsburg, c. 1550

(Tournament Book), printed by Georg Rabenof in Frankfurt am Main
(fig. 92).[45] Thus these jousting armours masquerading as war armours are
possible candidates for the Castilian style favoured by Quijada de Reayo
and other Spanish noblemen of the period.

[45] The woodcuts, which depict certain knights in close-up, were specially
made for the 1566 edition. A caption above the woodcut on fol. 45v reads as
follows: 'Rossz Thurnier. Folgt der vierdt Thurnier von dem Wolgebornen und
Hochberuempten Don Claudio Ferdinando de Quinones Graff von Luna deß
Durchleuchtigen Großmechtigsten und Catholischen Koenigs zu Hispanien und
zu dem unueberwindtlichsten Großmechtigsten Roemischen Keyser Ferdinand
und Bottschaft so zu Rossz gehalten worden ist vor der Statt Wien in dem
undern Werd jenthalben der Schlagbrucken underthalb dem Taeber in freyem
Feld' ('Horse Tourney. Here follows the fourth tourney of the High-Born and
Illustrious Don Claudio Fernando de Quiñones, Count of Luna, of His Most
Serene Highness, Most Powerful and Catholic King of Spain and also Most

92 Claudio Fernando de Quiñones in action at the Vienna tournament of 1560.
From Hans von Francolin, *Turnier Buch* (Frankfurt am Main: Georg Raben, 1566)

In addition to the exchange pieces Quijada de Reayo tells his protégé in chapter 4 of his treatise to 'place some bars on the stirrups, like a bridge, affixed to the inside of each stirrup and in such a way that you can fit the stirrup easily over the sabaton'. The description refers to a toe-cap that would be affixed to the stirrup with lugs and rivets. This accoutrement was designed to prevent the jouster from breaking his feet on the tilt or the counter-tilt. Most of the extant examples of these toe-caps are solid and many have a flanking ankle-plate for additional protection.

Invincible, Most Powerful Roman Emperor Ferdinand, and Justiciars, as was held on horsback before the city of Vienna, in the Lower Werd beyond the drawbridge below the fortification in an open field'). See Francolin, *Thurnier Buch*, fol. 45v. An earlier version of this tournament book was published in 1560, with the same text but cruder woodcuts. See Hans von Francolin, *Thurnier Buch* (Vienna: Raphael Hofhalter, 1560). Copies of this edition are located at Glasgow Museums, R. L. Scott Collection, call number E.1939.65.1180, and New York, Metropolitan Museum of Art, Thomas J. Watson Library, call number 959.4 F84. See fols. 58rv for the text. The illustration between fols. 57v and 58r of this edition is a large pull-out woodcut of an aerial view of a generic tournament scene with numerous types of combat taking place at the same time.

93, 94 Pair of toe-caps for the joust or tourney. Italian (probably Milanese), c. 1590

Figs. 93 and 94 illustrate a rare pair of decorated boot-stirrups for the joust
or tourney with large rounded toe-caps and side plates. Of Italian (probably Milanese) manufacture, they date to c. 1590 and may have belonged to
the Spanish nobleman Don Juan Alfonso de Pimentel, Duke of Benavente
(1533–1621).[46] The left and right weigh in at 1,260 g (2 lb 12 oz) and 1,200 g
(2 lb 10 oz), respectively. In addition to these boot-stirrups, open toe-caps
are known that consist of convex bars arranged at the front of the stirrup
so that they form a grill. An example of this type can be seen on an extant
bard probably made in Milan c. 1560 for a member of the Collalto family
(fig. 95).[47] These bars are not detachable now, though they may well have
been when they were originally made. As unusual as this type of toe-cap
is, it matches Quijada de Reayo's description more so than the solid type.
The bards with which these grilled toe-caps are associated were most often
used for war rather than jousting: further evidence of Quijada de Reayo's
apparent personal preference for wearing a permutation of field armour in
the lists.

Fig. 96 is a pen-and-ink drawing of a jousting competition executed
around the same time Quijada de Reayo was writing. The joust is taking
place within an octagonal enclosure in the middle of which is a high, sturdy
tilt. There is no counter-tilt. The knight on the left appears to be missing
his opponent as he himself is being struck in the visor. Other contestants
are awaiting their turn to joust on each side of the barrier. There appear
to have been no special lance-racks at this time as the lances – all of equal

46 Mann, *Wallace Collection Catalogues: European Arms and Armour*, vol. I, pp. 235–6,
   inv. A442–A443; Norman, *Wallace Collection Catalogues: European Arms and
   Armour: Supplement*, pp. 111–12, inv. A442–A443. As noted by Norman, plain boot-
   stirrups are quite common, but those that are decorated are very rare.
47 See Pyhrr *et al.*, *The Armored Horse in Europe, 1480–1620*, p. 26.

95 Stirrups with bars affixed, made in Milan *c.* 1560 for a member of the Collalto family

96 Pen-and-ink drawing of a joust. Mid-16th century

length – are loosely stacked at each end of the enclosure. Standing incon-
spicuously on some steps at the left of the tilt is a tiny armourer, hammer
in hand, whose job was to mend any damaged pieces of armour. Heralds
and trumpeters are carrying out their duties in the background. The
footman in the foreground with his baton may have the task of recording
the lance strokes or, given that he is looking in their direction, he may be
shepherding the successive competitors to the head of the tilt. One final,
extraordinary detail about this image which does not reflect the kind of
competency for which Quijada de Reayo was well known is that the two
jousters are riding in the wrong direction, right arm to right arm. Not
only that, one man holds his lance on the left, pointing right, and the
other holds his on the right, pointing right whilst at the same time being
blocked by his horse's head. The correct direction for jousting was always
left arm to left arm with the lance held on the right-hand side, pointing left.
Although this peculiarity may be due to poor draftsmanship, the words of
the professional jousters suggest that enthusiastic novices may occasionally have taken off in haste without paying attention to this fundamental
detail, not unlike the example of the hastily fitted grappers discussed in
chapter 2. In his role as tutor Quijada de Reayo offers a gentle reminder:
'When running with lances you should aim to the left.' Luis Zapata is
more forceful on this issue: 'Those who joust never encounter on the right-
hand side, but on the left, and this is not a superfluous matter; a knight is
obliged to know it.'[48]

The contextual images indicate that Quijada de Reayo knew what he
was talking about and that he advocated for safety measures even though
he may have felt experienced enough to eschew them himself. Given
Quijada de Reayo's experience, the intelligence and 'good habits' that led to
his selection as a royal bodyguard, there can be little doubt that the Duke
of Alburquerque's son was in capable hands with this man as his personal
tutor.

Del Justador (1589–93)

Zapata's treatise is a treasure-trove of information about jousting.
Thanks to the fact that he was detail-oriented and prolix, Zapata
explains much of what is left unsaid by Quijada de Reayo. From Zapata's
comments we learn above all the importance of style and the changing

---

[48] 'Los que justan nunca encuentran el lado derecho, sino el izquierdo, y esto no
es cosa superflua; está obligado a saberlo un caballero'. See Zapata, *Miscelánea*,
ed. Carrasco González, ch. 184, p. 251. The few known illustrations of jousters
charging incorrectly are listed by Anglo, *The Great Tournament Roll of Westminster*,
vol. I, p. 41, n. 4.

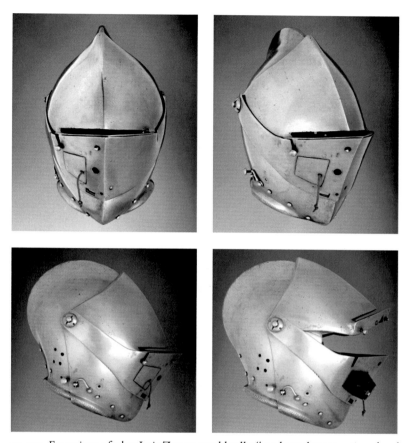

97–100 Four views of what Luis Zapata would call a 'handsomely proportioned and sized' close-helmet. German, c. 1590. Weight 5,670g (12 lb 8 oz)

nature of fashion in the sixteenth century. He describes the close-helmet, for example, as follows:

> The close-helmet not too pointed, for this looks like a rooster, nor too unsightly, nor too blunt, for this looks like an owl, but handsomely proportioned and sized … The visor secure and small and fitted close to the eyes.

Figs. 97–100 are a study of the type of close-helmet for the tilt favoured by Zapata. This example is of German manufacture and dates to c. 1590.[49] Weighing 5,670 g (12 lb 8 oz), it is well proportioned and characterised by graceful, smooth, clean lines, with a small, attractive visor that sits close

[49] Mann, *Wallace Collection Catalogues: European Arms and Armour*, vol. I, p. 152, inv. A190; Norman, *Wallace Collection Catalogues: European Arms and Armour: Supplement*, p. 72, inv. A190.

to the eyes. Figs. 101–8 constitute a chronological collage of close-helmets that span Zapata's adult life, c. 1540–87.[50] From a practical point of view this collage shows how the ear holes described by Quijada de Reayo gradually disappear around 1560. From an aesthetic point of view the reader must decide which ones are too pointed, which are too unsightly or blunt and which are just right!

Lest we forget, jousting headpieces always had padded linings for added protection. In the early years of the sixteenth century the martial arts theorist Pietro Monte had the following ingenious idea for a blunt trauma lining inside the characteristic frog-mouthed helm of his day:

> The helmet or headpiece for jousting, which we call in the mother tongue a frontally reinforced helm, must be broad so that it not only rests gently atop the head, but can also contain some kind of filling or lining inside to prevent the metal uppers from touching one's crown. Thus it can remain firmly in place. At the same time the helm must possess two transverse straps that intersect or form a cross so that it will remain more securely in place, since the iron itself cannot be seated upon the head. And for those who may be numbed by the shock of a blow, it is good to attach a thin bandage to the forehead, one that has been soaked in egg white and vinegar, or even to apply two bandages to the head, one in the front and the other in the back. Indeed, these things maintain the upright head in such a way that it cannot touch any part of the helmet, even if we receive a severe blow. Above all, one must apply wax especially to the front part of the helm, so that the clashing or the clamour which results from a blow cannot adversely affect the head. And to this end, a cloth generously coated in wax serves best. But the rear part of the helm, which is only half as thick, should receive some wax as well.[51]

[50] Mann, *Wallace Collection Catalogues: European Arms and Armour*, vol. I, pp. 134–5, inv. A163 (Nuremburg, circle of Valentine Siebenbürger, c. 1540), pp. 137–8, inv. A168 (Brunswick, c. 1550), pp. 54–6, inv. A46 (German, c. 1550–60), p. 138, inv. A169 (German, c. 1560), pp. 62–3, inv. A50 (Italian, c. 1560), pp. 142–3, inv. A176 (French, c. 1570), pp. 52–4, inv. A44 (Anton Peffenhauser of Augsburg, c. 1580), pp. 75–7, inv. A60 (Milan, made for Wolf Dietrich von Raitenau, c. 1587); Norman, *Wallace Collection Catalogues. European Arms and Armour: Supplement*, pp. 60–1, A163, pp. 62–3, inv. A168, pp. 19–20, inv. A46, p. 63, inv. A169, p. 26, inv. A50, p. 66, inv. A176, pp. 18–19, inv. A44, pp. 32–3, inv. A60.

[51] 'Cassis seu galea ad iustrandum quam materna lingua elmum dicimus anterius grossum et lata esse debet, et quod leviter in summitate capitis tangat, tamen quod aliquam saciatam vel foderam intus habeat, ne ferri sup[e]ra verticem capitis tangant; et taliter firma manere potest. Et similiter duas transversatas corrigias sive in cruce habere debet, ut tutius maneat, quod ferrum in summitate capitis sedere nequeat. Et pro illis, qui in percussione ictus soporantur, bonum est subtilem victam fronti alligare que in albumine ovi atque aceto madida fuerit,

101
Nuremburg,
circle of Valentin
Siebenbürger,
c. 1540. Weight
3,374 g (7 lb 7 oz)

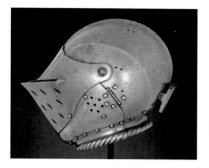

102
Brunswick,
c. 1550.
Weight 3,000 g
(6 lb 10 oz)

103
German,
c. 1550–60.
Weight 3,900 g
(8 lb 10 oz)

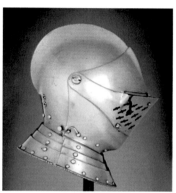

104
German, *c.* 1560.
Weight 3,260 g
(7 lb 3 oz)

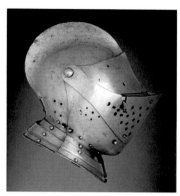

105
Italian, *c.* 1560.
Weight 3,130 g
(6 lb 14½ oz)

106
French, *c.* 1570.
Weight 5,220 g
(11 lb 8 oz)

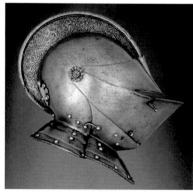

107
Anton Peffenhauser
of Augsburg, *c.* 1580.
Weight 3,860 g
(8 lb 8 oz)

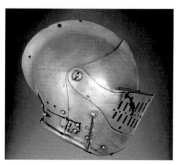

108
Milan, made for
Wolf Dietrich
von Raitenau,
c. 1587. Weight
4,480 g (9 lb 14 oz)

101–8 Collage of eight close-helmets, *c.* 1540–87

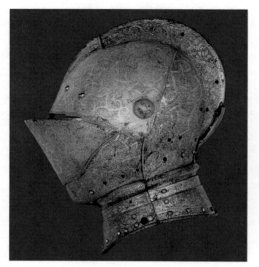

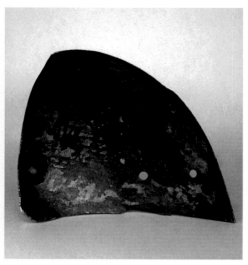

109   Close-helmet for the foot tournament, made in 1555 probably by Conrad Richter of Augsburg for the Emperor Ferdinand I

110   Close-up of the interior surface of the brow reinforce of the close-helmet in fig. 109, showing remnants of its beeswax coating

The treated bandages in this instance connote talismanic as well as practical protection – reminiscent of the magical restorative balsams of contemporary chivalry novels – given that the egg white and vinegar elixir was commonly believed to be a miracle cure for contusions and other superficial injuries. Because beeswax is a natural, perishable substance, few linings of this type have survived. The close-helmet for the foot tournament shown in fig. 109 was probably made by the Augsburg armourer Conrad Richter in 1555 for the Emperor Ferdinand I.[52] The interior surface of the brow reinforce of this helmet still retains traces of the original sixteenth-century beeswax coating like the one described by Monte (fig. 110).

Pragmatic as always, Quijada de Reayo simply yet sensibly points out to his young protégé that the armet must be big enough to accommodate a full lining. Zapata, like Monte, states that as well as being protected by

aut vero caput duabus victis alligare, quarum altera posterius et altera alterius attrahat. Hec siquidem directum caput manere faciunt adeo quod non potest in aliquo loco capsidis tangere, tametsi magnum ictum recipiamus. Et ante omnia per totum ipsum elmum ex parte anteriori ponenda est cera, eo quod fremitus seu clangor, qui ab ictu resultat, caput impedire nequeat; et ad hoc tela nimium incerata optima est; atque in anteriori parte elmi in dimidio grossitudinis aliquid de cera contineatur' (Monte, *Exercitiorum Atque Artis Militaris Collectanea*, bk II, ch. 96, sig. e6v). See also *Libro del exercicio de las armas*, fol. 45r.

[52] Mann, *Wallace Collection Catalogues: European Arms and Armour*, vol. I, pp. 150–1, inv. A188; Norman, *Wallace Collection Catalogues: European Arms and Armour: Supplement*, pp. 70–1, inv. A188.

111 Leather lining straps on the inside of
a close-helmet made by Anton Peffenhauser
of Augsburg, *c.* 1580

112 Leather lining straps on the inside of a
close-helmet. Augsburg, *c.* 1590

a silk or taffeta padded lining 'so that the blows do not resound', the head
should literally be bridled by means of internal leather suspension straps
fitted to the inside top of the skull. These straps acted as shock absorbers,
restraining the brow and holding the head tightly in place. Safety would
thus be ensured by floating the head between the padded brow band and
the pair of cross-straps that would prevent the head from slamming into
the back of the helmet and the face from striking the visor. Figs. 111 and
112 are examples of original close-helmet suspension straps of the type
described by Zapata.[53]

The Italian fencing master Giovanni Dall'Agocchie in his 1572 treatise
Dell'Arte di Scrimia (On the Art of Fencing), which includes a short section
on jousting, suggests that since it is so difficult to see anyway, the jouster
might as well plug or seal the left side of the sight in order to protect his
eyes from injury.[54] From around the mid 1560s numerous jousters were in
fact ordering helmets with a pronounced asymmetrical sight, whereby
the left-hand side of the eye-slit was narrowed or partially blocked out.
Two examples of left-side-blind close-helmets are shown in figs. 113 and 114.
Both were made in Germany, probably Augsburg, *c.* 1580, for the Italian-
style joust.[55]

[53] Mann, *Wallace Collection Catalogues: European Arms and Armour*, vol. I, p. 54,
inv. A45 (Anton Peffenhauser of Augsburg, *c.* 1580) and vol. I, pp. 138–9, inv. A170
(Augsburg, *c.* 1590); Norman, *Wallace Collection Catalogues: European Arms and
Armour: Supplement*, p. 19, inv. A45 and p. 63, inv. A170.

[54] Dall'Agocchie, *On the Art of Fencing*, trans. Swanger, fol. 64v.

[55] Blind horse shaffrons, where the apertures for the eyes are completely covered in
order to offer protection and to discourage the horse from stalling as the opposing
jouster makes his approach, are also known to have existed, though these were

113, 114 Two armets for the joust with pronounced asymmetrical eye-slits.
German, probably Augsburg, c. 1580

None of the aforementioned jousting theorists alludes to the possibility of additional protection over the helmet in the form of a metal skull
defence known as a gupfe, confirming that the gupfe was more a tourney
or battle accoutrement. Various types of gupfe are known: some cover
only the pate; others the area of the brow to about the midpoint; and
still others fit over the entire top bowl of the helmet. Some gupfes also
have tail-like appendages or lappets at the rear to help secure the gupfe
to the back of the helmet.[56] Fig. 115 shows a gupfe formed of eight steel
plates to which three long lappets are riveted at the back. This example
is believed to have been made c. 1550 by Sigismund Wolf of Landshut for
a Spanish client. It is a wonder of the armourer's craft, weighing a mere
1,067 g (2 lb 6 oz) and therefore ideal for placing directly on top of the head.
Judging by the sundry examples illustrated in the Sorg pattern-book (see
fig. 65, for example) these metal skull reinforces seem to have been widely
used throughout the sixteenth century in the context of tourneys and war.[57]

used exclusively in Germany in the late fifteenth through the sixteenth centuries.
See Blair, *European Armour*, pp. 187, and Pyhrr *et al.*, *The Armored Horse in Europe*,
1480–1620, pp. 34–5.

[56] Spanish authors refer to these tail-like appendages as 'strands' ('ramales'). See
Leguina, *Glosario de voces de Armería*, p. 348 (s.v. *escofia*).

[57] In addition to the Sorg illustration included in this volume, see Becher *et al.*, *Das
Stuttgarter Harnisch-Musterbuch, 1548–1563*, fols. 1v, 4v and 5v. See also *Glossarium
Armorum*, ed. Gamber, vol. I, p. 46, Stone, *A Glossary of the Construction, Decoration
and Use of Arms and Armour in All Countries and in All Times*, p. 222, fig. 272, and
Williams, *The Knight and the Blast Furnace*, pp. 407, 425 and 486.

The gupfe underscores the fact that in order to understand the larger puzzle of knightly martial arts it is imperative to take into consideration pictorial, documentary and physical evidence, since quite often what remains unsaid in one source is explained more fully by another.

Moving from one extreme of the harness to another, if Zapata rejects helmets whose visors are too blunt or too pointed, he also rejects the oblong, residual bear-paw sabatons that are found on armours of the 1540s and 1550s. The fact that he condemns bear-paw sabatons in the late 1580s suggests that a lot of outdated kit was continuing to be used thirty or so years after it was originally made, which in turn conflicted with some jousters' sense of high fashion. Certainly by the 1580s round boot-like toes were in vogue throughout Europe. In keeping with his taste for simple, clean lines, Zapata advocates for this very type of toe. Figs. 116 and 117 show a pair of well-shaped greaves and sabatons of German manufacture *c.* 1560 in this style. The left greave weighs 1,275 g (2 lb 13 oz) and the right 1,247 g (2 lb 12 oz).[58] Of particular note is the way in which the armourer has shaped the steel to the contour of the wearer's ankle bones and calves so that the greaves fit like a second steel skin. Similarly he has combined a sophisticated series of lames, four with a downwards overlap over the arch of the foot and four with an upwards overlap over the toes, the two sets of four joined in the middle by a ninth lame, thereby facilitating maximum articulation and fluid movement. Recalling

115 Steel and gold gupfe, made *c.* 1550 by Sigismund Wolf of Landshut for a Spanish client. Weight 1,067 g (2 lb 6 oz)

 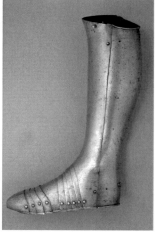

116, 117 Pair of greaves with rounded-toe sabatons. German, *c.* 1560

[58] Mann, *Wallace Collection Catalogues: European Arms and Armour*, vol. I, p. 189, inv. A298–A299; Norman, *Wallace Collection Catalogues: European Arms and Armour: Supplement*, p. 91, inv. A298– A299.

the words of Zapata, the man who wore these greaves would never have had his image tarnished by standing as stiff as a statue.

The smooth lines of helmet and sabaton are further reflected in Zapata's preference for the long-bellied, peascod breastplate which protrudes slightly in at the belly and has a central ridge sometimes referred to in English as a tapul. The breastplate is complemented by a small grandguard known as a targetta or manteau d'armes. As noted by Blair: 'A new piece apparently never made at Greenwich, was the so-called tilting-targe, manteau d'armes or targetta. This, which was used for the Italian tilt, was a steel shield, sometimes covered with applied trellis-work, screwed over the front of the left shoulder. It extended halfway down the left side of the breast and usually curved forward at the bottom';[59] hence Zapata states that it should be 'well shaped'. The difference between Quijada de Reayo's grandguard and Zapata's targetta is, as Zapata says, in the shape. Grandguards are shaped to the contour of the wearer's body and cover the lower face with an integral or companion reinforcing bevor, as shown in figs. 88 and 89, whereas targettas are steel shields, sometimes latticed, that bolted onto the armour without being as closely moulded to the body as the grandguard.

At the end of 'Del Justador' Zapata even defines the two types of joust by referring to them as 'jousts of war, and with the targetta and of peace'. Fig. 118 shows a complete and magnificent jousting harness which predates Zapata's treatise by around thirty years, but which is relevant to the present discussion because of its breastplate and targetta. It was made by Wolfgang Grosschedel of Landshut for King Philip II of Spain c. 1560.[60] The total weight of this armour is a comfortable 38,500 g (84 lb 14 oz). When confronted with a harness in this style the eye is immediately drawn to the distinctive peascod breastplate and the size, shape and beauty of the targetta; hence Zapata's synecdoche, where this one piece of jousting armour defines the entire harness and everything that this harness stands for: the jousts of peace. The targetta in this case is decorated with embossed trellis-work, though examples are also known with the trellis-work applied separately. Like the earlier stop-ribs of the Pass of Honour of Suero de Quiñones, applied trellis-work would have been prone to getting ripped off, which is a strong recommendation for the embossed variety. Just below the targetta, the pasguard is so perfectly shaped that it looks as if it has been poured over the elbow wing beneath, and this piece in turn is complemented by the manifer that protects the bridle hand. The tassets flare out from the breastplate, and the armour is completed by full legharness and residual bear-paw sabatons, reflecting the fashion of the time.

---

[59] Blair, *European Armour*, p. 167.

[60] See Prelle de la Nieppe and Van Malderghem, *Catalogue des armes et armures du Musée de la Porte de Hal*, pp. 75–6, fig. 34, and pp. 98–9, no. 41.

118 Jousting Armour of King Philip II of Spain by Wolfgang Grosschedel of Landshut, *c*. 1560.
Weight 38,500 g (84 lb 14 oz)

In so far as linings are concerned, Zapata reveals yet another secret about armour which is only hinted at by Quijada de Reayo. Thus, when Quijada de Reayo informs his pupil that the tassets must be lined on the inside, Zapata adds that the purpose of these lining bands is to ensure that the various pieces of the harness 'do not clatter or catch on each other', for 'it tarnishes a jouster's image if his armour clangs like kettles each time he moves'. On this note it is worth conjuring up an idea of what life must have been like in a typical renaissance Spanish town. On the one hand, the streets would have reeked of the smell of human and animal detritus, and rotting fruits and vegetables, to name but a few of the foulest odours. The men and women who walked those streets would have had an olfactory tolerance that would be inconceivable today. On the other hand, the noises to which most medieval and renaissance men and women were accustomed tended to be natural ones – there were no sirens or cell phones, there was no motorised traffic, no surround-sound, and even the great cathedrals were built to the rhythm of hammers and chisels chipping steadily away at stone as opposed to the relentless rattle of pneumatic drills on concrete and the deafening roar of fleets of bulldozers. It was a time when monks took vows of silence, monarchs were always 'serene', and even in the heat of battle, rhetoric dictated that knights must master the paradox of issuing strong, firm orders but in calm, deliberate tones.[61] Cult European chivalric arch-villains such as Robert the Devil were cacophony personified. Robert was not known for his body odour; rather, his sin was his din.[62] In this sense the leather noise-dampening strips on extant examples of armour from this period constitute a fascinating confluence of the

---

[61] See Alfonso X, *Las Siete Partidas*, II.xxiii.5: 'E aún dijeron los antiguos que los caudillos deben haber dos cosas, que semejan contrarias: la una, que fuesen habladores; e la otra, calladores. Pues bien razonados, e de buena palabra, deben ser para saber hablar con las gentes, e apercibirlas, e mostrarles lo que han de hacer antes que vengan al hecho; otrosí, deben haber buena palabra, e recia, para darles conhorte, e esfuerzo, cuando en el hecho fueren. Callado debe ser, de manera que no será cotidianamente hablador, porque hubiese su palabra a envilecer entre los hombres' ('The ancients also declared that commanders should possess two qualities which appear to be of a contradictory character; first, that they should be loquacious; second, that they should be silent. For they should be good reasoners and ready of speech, so as to know how to address their soldiers and instruct them and explain to them what they have to do, before they go into action. Their speech, moreover, should be agreeable and bold, in order to inspire them with comfort and valor, when they are engaged in battle. A general should be silent, so that he may not be continually talking on account of which his conversation will be despised by men'). *Las Siete Partidas*, ed. Sánchez-Arcilla, pp. 304b–305a. For the translation, see *Las Siete Partidas*, trans. Scott and Burns, vol. II, p. 442.

[62] Robert the Devil, the very inversion of everything a knight should be, was well known for never closing his mouth and always shouting. For the popular medieval Spanish version of the legend, see *La espantosa y maravillosa vida de Roberto el*

metallurgical and the rhetorical. Unlike knights in battle, for whom a silent, stealthy attack was strategically prudent, especially at night, jousters had no real practical reason for maintaining silence. And yet the jousters of the renaissance, whilst they enjoyed the smell of the 'aura seminalis', that proud mixture of stale semen and urine so carefully accumulated over a period of months in the depths of their codpieces – which stand proudly erect on folio after folio of the Sorg pattern-book[63] – they were at the same time repulsed by obnoxious clanking sounds made by armour. Zapata's treatise underscores above all the vital importance of form as well as function. Acquitting oneself well in the lists was but a fraction of a larger equation, for fine, bespoke armour was art

119 Leather noise-dampening strips on the inside right pauldron of a jousting armour made by Wolfgang Grosschedel of Landshut, c. 1560

incarnate, and the renaissance chivalric ideal could only be attained if, on the other side of the equation, its wearer did not clank as he made his way to and from the enclosure. Fig. 119 shows a leather lining band around the outer edge of the interior surface of a right pauldron belonging to a joust and tournament garniture made by Wolfgang Grosschedel of Landshut c. 1560.[64] Of particular interest is the fact that the leather has no stitch holes for securing a silk or cloth lining in place, for that was never its intended purpose. These were the integral noise-dampening strips described by Zapata that were designed to prevent acute embarrassment in the jousting enclosure.

Like Quijada de Reayo before him, Zapata also insists that the jouster wear full legharness which, he says, 'is fitting and proper so as not to hit the tilt or counter-tilt with your feet and break them and so as to enter safely

Diablo, ed. Blecua, esp. p. 201. The tale was translated into English and published by Wynkyn de Worde, *c.* 1500, with subsequent reprints.

[63] Metal codpieces were first introduced in the 1520s. See Blair, *European Armour*, p. 123. Sorg's tourneyers and jousters all sport cloth codpieces, the metal version being exclusively an infantry accoutrement.

[64] On this armour, see Mann, *Wallace Collection Catalogues: European Arms and Armour*, vol. I, pp. 39–42, inv. A34; Norman, *Wallace Collection Catalogues: European Arms and Armour: Supplement*, pp. 12–13, inv. A34. I have opted not to include a picture of the complete harness since it has been compromised by poorly executed nineteenth-century restorations. The right pauldron, however, is genuine. In its prime this armour was similar in style to that of King Philip II in the Musée Royal de l'Armée et d'Histoire Militaire in Brussels, as illustrated in fig. 118.

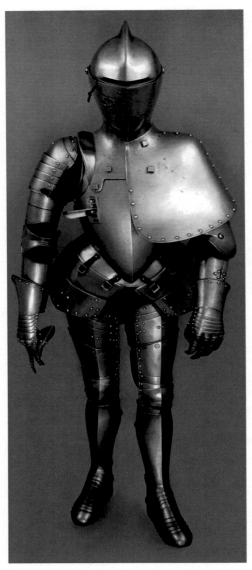

120 Jousting armour made by Anton Peffenhauser, c. 1590. Weight 33,470 g (73 lb 13 oz)

amidst the kicks of other horses'. The Sorg pattern-book shows that jousting without leg armour was still going on *c.* 1550.[65] By Zapata's time, however, the custom had for the most part died out, in which case this may be a reminiscence of an earlier epoch. It is common on German-made armours of the period for the cuisses on both legs to break down so that the legharness could be used for different functions, be it war, the joust, the tourney or foot combat. In the case of the joust, a full set of cuisses would typically be worn, whilst demi-cuisses would be for war or other more lightly armoured uses. Fig. 120 shows a state-of-the-art jousting harness made by the German master armourer Anton Peffen-hauser around 1590 for the Italian-style joust favoured by Zapata. The total weight of this armour is 33,470 g (73 lb 13 oz) which, it bears repeating, would have been spread evenly and comfortably over the wearer's body.[66] Figs. 121 and 122 show the cuisses and demi-cuisses from this harness in their assembled and disassembled configurations. When looking at the homogeneous harness it is impossible to appreciate that the cuisses, although a matching pair (both are marked with matching serial marks), are of unequal length. The detail confirms not only the appalling consequences of aristocratic inbreeding, but also the fact that the best armour was always bespoke and attuned to the peculiarities of one body only – as Zapata says: 'Where Nature should fail, let Art prevail.'

[65] See Becher *et al.*, *Das Stuttgarter Harnisch-Musterbuch, 1548–1563*, pp. 48–91, for sundry examples of jousting armours with no legharness.

[66] Mann, *Wallace Collection Catalogues: European Arms and Armour*, vol. I, pp. 61–2, inv. A49; Norman, *Wallace Collection Catalogues: European Arms and Armour: Supplement*, pp. 25–6, inv. A49.

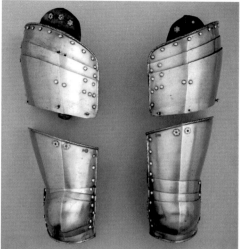

121, 122 Assembled and disassembled cuisses and demi-cuisses of the armour in fig. 120

It is in the area of legharness – the cuisses and demi-cuisses – that a unique detail emerges from the treatises of Quijada de Reayo, Zapata and other Spanish sources. Zapata addresses the issue succinctly as follows: 'On your right leg not an entire cuisse, but a demi-cuisse, in order to brace the lance well.' His remark can be supplemented by the inventory of the Duke of Infantado's armoury, where a jousting harness is described as having 'cuisses and greaves, except that the right one is a demi-cuisse for the joust'.[67] An example of a sixteenth-century jousting harness that explains this inference is illustrated in fig. 123; the same harness is illustrated in fig. 124 with the parts labelled. This harness was at one time in the armoury of the Dukes of Osuna.[68] The small, well-shaped targetta, in this case with applied trellis-work, and the peascod breastplate which protrudes slightly at the belly conform exactly to Zapata's descriptions. Furthermore, on this

[67] 'quijotes y grebas, salvo que el derecho es medio quijote para de justa'. See Rayón and Zabalburu, eds., 'Armería del Duque del Infantado en Guadalajara', p. 477. The inventory was compiled in 1643.

[68] See Florit y Arizcún and Sánchez Cantón, *Catálogo de las armas del Instituto de Valencia de Don Juan*, pp. 3–5, inv. 1. Sánchez Cantón finished this catalogue after Florit y Arizcún's untimely death. As Sánchez Cantón readily admits, he was not a specialist in armour. He suggests that the close-helmet, tassets and greaves may not belong. Having inspected this armour personally, however, my sense is that while it is possible that the close-helmet does not match, the tassets and greaves may in fact be original to this harness. Only by dismounting the harness and conducting a detailed analysis of the various pieces and their history would the issue be resolved definitively.

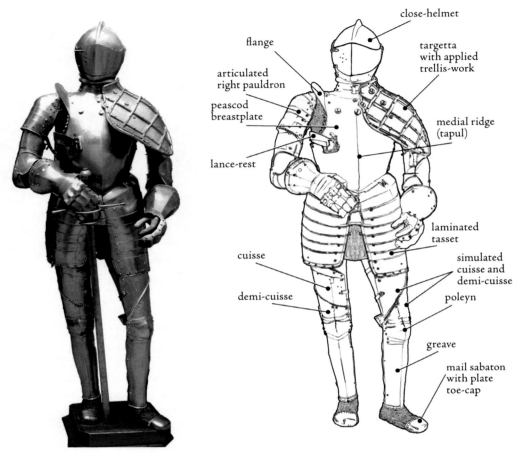

123 Spanish jousting armour. Late 16th century
124 Labelled line drawing of the armour in fig. 123

harness, as in the descriptions cited above, the right cuisse can be broken
down into two distinct parts in the usual manner, namely, the cuisse and
the demi-cuisse. The left cuisse, on the other hand, is unique in that it
cannot be broken down, as it has been more strongly built in a single piece
– this explains why Zapata uses the term 'entire cuisse' ('quixote entero') to
describe this piece. Symmetry with the right is provided by an embossed
ridge that mimics the top edge of the right demi-cuisse and two point-
holes that are decorative rather than functional. Figs. 125 and 126 show the
simulated left cuisse and demi-cuisse of this armour from the front and
back, illustrating the embossed ridge and imitation point-holes. Another
surviving example of a simulated left cuisse plate for the joust is illustrated
in fig. 127. Made in Augsburg, it dates to c. 1550. This cuisse plate is of
much higher quality than that illustrated in figs. 125–6, being decorated
with etched bands of foliage bordered with sprigs, possibly the work of

Jörg Sorg, but the overall construction is the same.[69] Although it is missing its poleyn at the knee, like the simulated cuisse illustrated in figs. 125–6 the top edge of the 'demi-cuisse' is in fact an embossed ridge. Unfortunately the client for whom this armour was made is unknown.

We know from Quijada de Reayo that garnitures had many uses, and thanks to exchange pieces each use in turn had many possible configurations and requirements. A fashion for jousts as they were practised in Spain and Spanish dominions implied in the theoretical works of Quijada de Reayo and Zapata was to opt for the strongest possible construction of the left cuisse of jousting armours whilst following the recommendation to break down the right. It could also well be that Spanish jousters who had these solid left cuisses never expected to use that particular armour for anything but the joust, an activity that did not require a two-part left cuisse.

125, 126 Front and back of a Spanish simulated cuisse and demi-cuisse for the left leg

Zapata's comments on the saddle not uncharacteristically concern form rather than function, as follows:

> The saddle not wide, because the knight would ride doing the splits; not placed too far back, for he will be slung backwards – very ugly and badly positioned and harnessed, with the result that he will be thrown –, but rather, the rider should sit straight in the saddle, as if he were standing on his feet. He shall walk with some room in the seat to rest, and without leaning on the front arçon, otherwise the rider will proceed looking like a travelling bag. In sum, the posture of the knight depends on the saddle; in a poorly fitted saddle there is no way that he will ever sit well.

In addition to this comment about the jousting saddle Zapata reveals information about a closely related saddle that is little

127 Simulated cuisse and demi-cuisse for the left leg. Augsburg, c. 1550, possibly etched by Jörg Sorg

[69] See Dufty and Reid, *European Armour in the Tower of London*, plate CXXXIII. On the various scattered pieces of armour associated with this cuisse plate, see Norman, *Wallace Collection Catalogues: European Arms and Armour: Supplement*, pp. 67–8, inv. A182.

known outside of Spain and that epitomises the notion of form, aesthetics and pure, unadulterated crowd pleasing. At the beginning of 'Del Justador' he alludes to a sixteenth-century phenomenon described by the Spanish verb 'ruar'. In Zapata's day this verb was loaded with meaning. It meant not only showing off on horseback, but also implied showing off on a city street (Spanish 'rúa'). It further implied riding in an ornate parade saddle called a 'silla de rúa', literally a 'saddle for showing off on city streets'. This type of saddle bore a resemblance to the jousting saddle, but it was impractical in the lists due to the fact that the rear arçon was not canted and both arçons were decorative rather than protective. The sole purpose of ambling around in these saddles seems to have been to let people know that the rider was a well-to-do, accomplished jouster even though he was not actually jousting at that moment: a distinctive sort of 'jouster's mufti'.[70] Fig. 128 shows a fine example of a sixteenth-century Spanish 'silla de rúa'. Beautifully painted in grisaille, this decoration is believed to be the work of the artist Diego de Arroyo (1498–1551).[71]

Zapata's principal contribution to our knowledge of weaponry is the clarification that the lances used in jousts should be pine and those used for war should be made of ash or beech. Scots pine, Austrian pine and Maritime pine, all of which are hard pines, were and still are the most common species in Western Europe, and all three could have a stem that could be used to make lances. Younger pine trees with more juvenile wood would most likely have been used for lances, since they would not be as heavy and strong as wood from mature trees. From a practical viewpoint, considering the tools of the time – the lance would most likely have been shaped using a draw knife – the best time to harvest a tree for manufacturing a lance would have been while it was still relatively young and had a small diameter. In addition, it would have been easy to make straight lances from pine, which has good form (relatively straight, small branches), especially if forest grown. This explains why authors such as Chrétien de Troyes (d. c. 1185) and Wolfram von Eschenbach (fl. c. 1195–1225) would often wax poetic about 'forests of lances' being shattered at tournaments.[72]

[70] A modern analogy to this phenomenon would be the off-duty soldiers of the prestigious Guards regiments who can sometimes be spotted in the vicinity of Wellington Barracks or St James's in London wearing their distinctive 'civvies' consisting of bowler hat, pinstripe suit and furled umbrella. For a contextual image of such a chap, see Roetzel, *Gentleman: A Timeless Fashion*, p. 263.

[71] The example shown is Madrid, Real Armería, inv. F52. See also Valencia de Don Juan, *Catálogo Histórico-Descriptivo de la Real Armería de Madrid*, pp. 177–8, inv. F56, F57, F59, F60 and F61. On Diego de Arroyo, see Ruiz Alcón, 'Real Armería. Sillas de montar de Diego de Arroyo'.

[72] Chrétien observes that the knights who prepare for one of his fictitious jousts, 'armé et desarmé asanblent; / les lances un grant bois resanblent' ('as they gather, some armed, some unarmed, the lances are like a great forest'). See Chrétien de

128 Parade saddle ('silla de rúa'). Spanish, 16th century

On the other hand, ash and beech are hard, resilient woods that would not be expected to shatter, compared to pine. Ash in particular was recognised for its flexibility and resistance and was used for bows and arrows in the Middle Ages.[73]

As a means of contextualising the joust as Zapata describes it, fig. 129 is a colourful and accurate depiction published in the year 1568 when he would have been forty-two. A long, high tilt separates the contestants, who are making an encounter near the middle section. The counter-tilts on each jouster's right are set at stirrup level. These are intended to prevent the horses from swerving, though at the same time it is easy to see that,

Troyes, *Le Chevalier de la Charrette (Lancelot)*, ed. Foulet and Uitti, p. 314 lines 5617–18. For the translation, see *Lancelot*, in *Arthurian Romances*, trans. Owen, p. 260. Similarly, Wolfram describes a fictitious joust in which 'dâ wart verswendet der walt / und manec ritter ab gevalt' ('a whole forest of lances were shattered and many knights were downed'). See Eschenbach, *Parzival*, ed. Lachmann, vol. I, p. 126. For the translation, see *Parzival*, trans. Hatto, p. 47 (also pp. 152 and 332). Certain tournaments were also referred to as 'forests'. See Barber and Barker, *Tournaments*, pp. 54, 125.

[73] Soler del Campo, *La evolución del armamento medieval en el reino castellano-leonés y al-Andalus (siglos XII–XIV)*, p. 64.

129　Jousting scene with tilt and counter-tilt, 1568. From Hans Wagner, *Kurtze doch gegründte Beschreibung des … Herren Wilhalmen, Pfaltzgraven bey Rhein, … und der selben geliebsten Gemahel, … gehalten hochzeitlichen Ehren Fests in … München 1568. Jahr.* Illustrated probably by Nicolas Solis

depending on what they are made of and where they are placed, they might also make the jousters' feet vulnerable to injury. By the 1560s the counter-tilts were also, as in this example, canted at each end in order to ensure that the jousters charged down the correct side of the tilt – the right side.

A remark made by Zapata about style in the type of joust illustrated serves as a fitting conclusion to this chapter. He makes the following observation about the ideal jouster:

> What looks really good is to turn the body slightly at the moment of impact, for better strokes are made this way and it looks graceful, for anything that stirs movement in an armoured man looks good, since it makes that fantastic figure seem like he is alive and not just a piece of iron. The distinguished knight Don Diego de Córdoba used to do this elegantly, for he used to acquit himself very gracefully with weapons, with the self-assurance with which a falcon acquits itself in the sky.

Armour has famously been described as 'sculpture in steel'. It has also been compared to the nude male form.[74] These analogies underscore the fact that the finest armour was perfectly contoured to the wearer's body. What Zapata's comment further underscores is that armour should not only be viewed – as, for example, when it is displayed on a mannequin in a museum – as a static object. It was made to be worn by men who were at the peak of physical fitness and who had been practising the art of jousting since childhood, just like Quijada de Reayo's protégé. Articulation, co-ordination, movement and function were equally as important as form. To add one more analogy to the mix – an analogy of dynamism and mobility – the jouster in the saddle, 'locked inside' his armour, can also be compared to the lone fighter ace in the cockpit of a high-performance aircraft, the myriad finely tuned components of which can be mastered, controlled and put through their paces only by the most consummate, skilled practitioners. Thus, jousting armour was indeed a form of sculpture, but it was one that was intended to be subjected to systematic abuse by the very person who had spent a fortune commissioning it, to be subjected to still more abuse by that person's opponents, to be deliberately exposed to the elements, damage and wanton destruction. Much like Cátedra's paper chivalry, with its inherent tensions and contradictions, we must not forget that metal chivalry – in this case jousting armour – was one of the most enduring paradoxes of the Middle Ages and the Renaissance. Beautiful to behold, it is a wonder that any has survived at all.

---

[74] The term 'sculpure in steel' was coined by Dr Bruno Thomas. On this term and the reference to the nude male form, see Blair, 'Foreward', in *The Churburg Armoury*, p. 19 and p. 302, n. 10.

~: 4 :~

The Quest for 'The Good Thrust'

IT was Wolfram's Parzival who long ago charged down the lists in search of what he called 'the good thrust' ('den guoten stich').[1] The fictitious hero's quest for martial perfection brings us to the principles of jousting. In 1918 Francis Henry Cripps-Day lamented 'how curious it is that we have no authority on how the tilt was run, no hint even in any mediaeval romance, and yet there must have been methods by means of which the expert could make his skill superior to weight and brute strength'.[2] Cripps-Day, however, never considered Iberian source material. On the basis of the Iberian sources, I shall argue in the present chapter that the medieval and renaissance joust was indeed constructed upon a theoretical framework that can be divided according to three distinct principles. I would label them as follows: The Principle of Pulchritude; The Principle of Equality; and The Principle of Transferability.

The Principle of Pulchritude

ALTHOUGH jousting always involved a certain amount of risk, it was never simply a matter of brute force or aimless thrill-seeking. Form always complemented function. The way a man carried himself on horseback in the lists and the way in which he wielded his lance were equally as important as his physical strength. That the joust was as much an intellectual as a physical exercise is underscored in *Tirant lo Blanc*:

> In former times the order of knighthood was so esteemed that none but the strong, courageous, prudent, and knowledgeable in the use of arms could reap knightly glory and honor. Bodily strength and valor should be exercised together with wisdom, for in battle it often happens that prudence and ingenuity will allow the few to defeat the

---

[1] Eschenbach, *Parzival*, ed. Lachmann, vol. I, p. 382, section 812 lines 9–16: 'Fünf stiche mac turnieren hân, / die sint mit mîner hant getân: / einer ist zem puneiz, / ze triviers ich den andern weiz, / der dritte ist zentmuoten; / ze rehter tjost den guoten / hurteclîch ich hân geriten, / und den zer volge ouch niht vermiten' ('The tournament knows five lance-strokes, and I have delivered them all! The first is straight ahead in massed charge; the second known to me is to the right obliquely; the third awaits the others' charge, selecting one's adversary; then I have ridden the good thrust at full tilt in regular joust, one to one; and I have not neglected the thrust in pursuit'). For the translation, see *Parzival*, trans. Hatto, p. 403.

[2] Cripps-Day, *The History of the Tournament in England and in France*, p. 137.

many; the wisdom and cunning of knights has sufficed to destroy the forces of their enemies. For this reason the ancients arranged jousts and tournaments, nurturing boys on the proper use of arms so that they would be strong and courageous in the face of the enemy.[3]

The level of skill required in order to joust successfully is apparent in particular from Menaguerra's treatise and is his greatest contribution to our understanding of the joust. The key to success in the lists is what Menaguerra calls restraint ('mesura'). As noted by Kaeuper: 'The frequent praise of *mesure*, restraint, balance, and reason in all forms of chivalric literature can surely be read as countering a tendency that was real, and dangerous.'[4] The tendency in this case refers to knights who were prone to being consumed by rage in the lists or on the battlefield. The quality of 'mesura' enabled them to keep blind fury in check. I would add, however, that as well as restraint, balance and reason, or a mechanism for controlling ire, 'mesura', as we shall see in *Lo Cavaller*, encapsulates other qualities, such as eloquence, wit and charisma. In his own description of the ideal knight, perhaps Ponç de Menaguerra had Rodrigo Díaz – El Cid – in mind, who is characterised in the *Poema del Cid* (Poem of the Cid, composed in or before 1207) by his 'mesura'. A detail of some significance in this regard is that although El Cid was Castilian by birth, he spent much of his life in the city of Valencia; hence the Valencians could claim him as their own as much as the Castilians could.

Because of 'mesura' the joust was as much a question of elegance, beauty and neatness as it was a question of splintering lances and drawing blood, though there was a fine line between bloodshed enhancing or spoiling the merriment of the chromatic spectacle. So long as the lance-stroke was not a foul, spilling an opponent's blood was often the only tangible evidence of a palpable hit and was probably also a guaranteed crowd-pleaser. The problem was that when making the best lance-strokes – to the head and torso – the lance-head was always in danger of skating off the armour and coming dangerously close to the eyes, groin and thighs, and it is to these three areas that the most devastating jousting injuries were sustained.

Stray blows through the sight were relatively uncommon, but invariably

---

[3] 'Antigament l'orde militar era tengut en tanta reverència, que no era decorat de honor de milícia sinó lo fort, animós, prudent e molt spert en lo exercici de les armes. Fortitud corporal e ardiment se vol exercir ab saviesa, com per la prudència e indústria dels batallants diverses vegades los pochs han obtesa victòria dels molts: la saviesa e astúcia dels cavallers ha bastat aterrar les forces dels enemichs. E per ço foren per los antichs ordenades justes e torneigs, nodrint los infants de pocha edat en lo exercici militar perquè en les batalles fossen forts e animosos e no hagassen terror de la vista dels enemichs'. See Martorell, *Tirant lo Blanch*, ed. Hauf, Pròlech, pp. 69–70. For the translation, see *Tirant lo Blanc*, trans. LaFontaine, p. 39.

[4] Kaeuper, *Chivalry and Violence in Medieval Europe*, p. 145.

fatal. According to Zapata it is virtually impossible to survive any injury caused by a splinter of more than one digit in length (approximately 1.9 cm [¾ in]) if the splinter penetrates the visor. He offers no solution to the problem, however. Nor does Duarte of Portugal in his *Livro da ensinança de bem cavalgar toda sela*, although Duarte does attempt to identify the cause. According to this authority, jousters run the risk of being struck in the visor because they instinctively close their eyes either at or just before the moment of impact.[5] Duarte merely offers a *post facto* solution, whereby the jouster's aiders ask him to reflect upon why he jousted poorly. Pietro Monte recommends that the jouster avoid looking at the tip of his own lance and concentrate instead on his opponent's head, paying particular attention to hand-to-eye co-ordination. He adds that it is easier to keep the eyes open if one keeps his mouth open as well:

> Some close their eyes when they see an adversary's lance coming. To remedy this, it will suffice to acquire the habit a few days in advance of keeping one's eyes open when a lance hits above the visor; and realising that no harm from the point of the lance can penetrate the helmet's visor, one should then take heart. And in this respect it is useful to open one's mouth so that the eyes will also remain open. We must, however, continually watch the opponent's head or wherever we wish to direct our lance; the hand must follow the eye, and not the eye the hand. Some maintain that the tip of our lance should be our focus of attention and that we should not worry about the opponent's spear. Certainly this can do no harm as far as piercing the shield or helmet is concerned. However it is always better to see one's adversary than the pointed end of the lance that we hold.[6]

Quijada de Reayo coincidentally concurs with Duarte about the cause

---

[5] Duarte I, King of Portugal, *Livro da ensinança de bem cavalgar toda sela que fez El-Rey Dom Eduarte de Portogal e do Algarve e Senhor de Ceuta*, ed. Piel, p. 82; translated in *The Royal Book of Horsemanship, Jousting and Knightly Combat*, trans. Preto and Preto, p. 82.

[6] 'Nonnulli oculos claudunt dum vident lanceam adversarii venire, pro quo satis prodest per aliquot dies ante in consuetudinem habere quod, cum aliqua lancea super viseram percutiatur, et ipse apertos oculos teneat; et videns non posse a ferro lancee aliquod detrimentum per viseram capsidis inferri animum assumat. Et ad huc bonum est os aperire ut etiam oculi apiantur. Assidue tamen caput alterius prospiciendum est aut ubi lanceam invertere volumus; et quod manus oculum insequatur, et non oculus manum. Nonnulli tenent quod semper sit respicienda puncta lancee, et quod de cuspide alterius nullam curam habeamus; non enim obesse potest quo ad transfigendum clypeum vel capsidem. Tandem melius est semper hostem aspicere quam cuspidem lancee nostre quam gestamus' (Monte, *Exercitiorum Atque Artis Militaris Collectanea*, bk II, ch. 96, sig. e6v). For a paraphrased version in Spanish, see *Libro del exercicio de las armas*, fol. 45r.

of closing the eyes. Like Monte he proposes a solution, though his is diametrically opposed to that described in the *Collectanea*. When charging, most jousters, Quijada de Reayo argues, focus their attention on the tip of their opponent's lance. They therefore erroneously believe that their opponent's lance is pointing at their own visor, which explains why they instinctively close their eyes in response. In his view the problem can be overcome if the prospective jouster does in fact focus his attention on the tip of his own lance as he charges towards his adversary. In a similar vein to Monte, Dall'Agocchie suggests that the jouster focus on the eye-slit of his opponent's helmet.[7] Rather than closing their eyes Menaguerra enjoins jousters not to shout inside their helms, advising them in his School of Jousting to focus on their opponent's right shoulder. Incidentally, all these methods for resolving the same problem allow for a better understanding of Quijada de Reayo's sage advice to his protégé in chapter 2 of his treatise that he be schooled by one master only lest he be confused by too many opposing points of view.

Forceful blows to the eyes often resulted in more than blindness because they penetrated deeply enough to cause trauma to the brain. Those who were struck in this area and survived were extremely lucky. One rare Castilian survivor of a serious eye injury is Diego de Bazán in the Pass of Honour of Suero de Quiñones. The estimated size of the shiver that penetrated his visor was four digits, that is, approximately 7.62 cm (3 in) in length. Given what Zapata says, it is therefore remarkable that he survived his horrific injury.[8] Equally remarkable is Bazán's public reaction: "'Tis nothing. 'Tis nothing', he declares, brushing off the injury as if it were little more than a mild irritation caused by an eyelash. Indifference in the face of miraculous escapes is not an uncommon public reaction among seasoned combat veterans. For example, at the height of the Battle of Britain, in World War II, fighter ace Geoffrey Page would refer irreverently to his daily brushes with death in the summer skies as 'Juggling with Jesus'.[9] In the context of the Middle Ages, Diego de Bazán's public fortitude makes some sense if we take into account what could be called the philosophy of chivalry, as outlined by Aristotle in *The Nicomachean Ethics*, III.ix.4, for example. This text was translated into Castilian in the Middle Ages and, as A. R. D. Pagden has observed, was often read as a manual

---

[7] Dall'Agocchie, *On the Art of Fencing*, trans. Swanger, fol. 61v.

[8] See below, Part II, *Passo Honroso* Selection 16, course 2. Cp. also Federico de Montefeltro, Duke of Urbino (1422–82), who lost his right eye and the bridge of his nose in a joust held in 1448. For the details, see Dennistoun, *Memoirs of the Dukes of Urbino, Illustrating the Arms, Arts and Literature of Italy, from 1440–1630*, vol. I, p. 95.

[9] Page, *Tale of a Guinea Pig*, p. 84.

of chivalric conduct.[10] According to Aristotle: 'The death or wounds that [Courage] may bring will be painful to the courageous man, and he will suffer them unwillingly; but he will endure them because it is noble to do so, or because it is base not to do so.'[11] This section of the *Ethics* was paraphrased by Alfonso de la Torre in the fifteenth century, as follows:

> And because courage is associated with terrible things, it is associated more with misery than delectation, for it is difficult in the extreme to endure misery and abstain from delectation, just as it is difficult to endure wounds to the flesh, for it requires great strength of will to endure them. And he also says that the death of the courageous man is more painful than the death of other men, for it was proper that such a man should live, and he is deprived of life.[12]

In particular at tournaments, Aristotelian chivalric philosophy was often expressed in impresas, the devices and mottoes with which knights decorated their shields and crests. The impresa of the English knight, Ambrose Dudley, Earl of Warwick, for example, was deciphered as follows: 'A noble mind digests even the most painful injuries.'[13] The same philosophy was espoused by the Order of the Band of Castile, one statute of which states that: 'No knight of the Band should ever say "Ow!" and as far as possible, he should avoid complaining about any wounds he has sustained.'[14]

Despite this philosophical ideal, by the fifteenth century in Castile, at a time when the bishops wielded a great deal of power within their own bishoprics, death in the lists could have serious spiritual ramifications, as

---

[10] Pagden, 'The Diffusion of Aristotle's Moral Philosophy in Spain, ca. 1400–ca. 1600'.

[11] Aristotle, *The Nicomachean Ethics*, III.ix.4, ed. and trans. Rackham, p. 173.

[12] 'E porque la fortaleza es cerca de las terribles cosas, es más cerca de la tristeza que de la delectación, car muy difícil es sostener las cosas tristes e abstener de la delectación, como sostener plagas en la carne, que es gran fortaleza de ánimo sostenerlas. E aún dize que en la muerte se duele el tal honbre más que otro porque era digno que un tal honbre biviera, e es privado de la vida' (Torre, *Compendio breve de los X libros de la Éthica de Aristótil*, fol. 29r).

[13] The impresa consisted of an ostrich with a key in its beak, above which was the Latin motto 'Spiritus durissima coquit'. See Young, *Tudor and Jacobean Tournaments*, p. 126.

[14] 'todo caballero de la Banda nunca debe decir "¡Ay!" y lo más que pudiere, excuse de quejarse por herida que haya' (Cartagena, *Doctrinal de los caballeros*, in *Tratados Militares*, ed. Fallows, p. 313). In the fifteenth century the Aristotelian theory of fortitude as it applies to jousting is also eloquently articulated by Duarte of Portugal, who had been introduced to Aristotle's works by his mentor Alonso de Cartagena during Cartagena's frequent diplomatic missions to Portugal. See *The Royal Book of Horsemanship, Jousting and Knightly Combat*, trans. Preto and Preto, pp. 43–53.

well as just 'spoiling the merriment of the jousts'.[15] This was the case with
Asbert de Claramunt, the Catalonian jouster who was fatally injured by
a lance-thrust through the eye-slit of his visor in the Pass of Honour of
Suero de Quiñones.[16] He was denied ecclesiastical burial not only by the
friars in attendance at the jousts, but also by Sancho de Rojas, Bishop of
Astorga (1423–40), in whose bishopric the passage of arms was staged.

Knights who were killed in tournaments had been denied ecclesiastical
burial from the Councils of Clermont (1130) and Rheims (1131) through
the Fourth Lateran Council (1215). These bans were subsequently lifted
by Pope John XXII (1316–34).[17] In Castile, however, certain high-ranking
prelates interpreted the law based on the Councils alone as opposed to the
subsequent decrees – known as 'extravagants' – made by individual popes.
As noted by the *Oxford English Dictionary*, these extravagants: '[seem] originally to have been applied casually to denote "stray" decrees not codified or
collected in the decretals. They were afterwards added to the decretals, but
retained their customary designation, to distinguish them from the older
portions of the collection.' Because of the 'stray' nature of these extravagants, it was felt by some that, whether they were intended to ratify or
to overturn decrees that had been approved at the international Councils,
they were inadmissible. Thus the Bishop of Burgos, Alonso de Cartagena,
made the following argument, *c.* 1444:

> Even though Civil Law appears to tolerate these trials of arms
> which take place so that men may demonstrate bodily strength
> and virtue, Canon Law, however, in one of the Lateran Councils,
> expressly forbids tourneys, denying Christian burial to those who
> die whilst tourneying. And a long time after that, Pope Clement V,

---

[15] See below, Part II, Menaguerra, *Lo Cavaller*, ch. 30.

[16] The incident as described by Pero Rodríguez de Lena is edited and translated in
Part II below, Selection 12. Riquer, *L'Arnès del cavaller*, p. 187, n. 4, confirms that
Asbert was from Catalonia and not Aragon.

[17] The Councils of Clermont and Rheims and the papal annulment are well
documented. See: Barber, *The Knight and Chivalry*, pp. 161 and 190–1; Barber
and Barker, *Tournaments*, p. 17; Barker, *The Tournament in England, 1100–1400*,
pp. 5 and 70–83; Carlson, 'Religious Writers and Church Councils on Chivalry';
Cripps-Day, *The History of the Tournament in England and in France*, pp. 39–45;
Crouch, *Tournament*, pp. 9–11; Keen, *Chivalry*, pp. 94–7; Neste, *Tournois, joutes,
pas d'armes dans les villes de Flandre à la fin du Moyen Âge (1300–1486)*, pp. 159–62.
For the wording of the prohibitions in the various Lateran Councils, see *Decrees
of the Ecumenical Councils*, ed. and trans. Alberigo *et al.* and Tanner, vol. I, pp. 200
(Lateran II, 1139), 221 (Lateran III, 1179) and 244 (Lateran IV, 1215), respectively.
For the annulments of John XXII, see *Extravagantes tum viginti D. Ioannis Papae
XXII tum communes suae integritati restitutae*, IX.i, in *Corpus Iuris Canonici*, ed.
Friedberg, vol. II, p. 1215, and Gregory IX, *Decretales*, V.xiii.1, in *Corpus Iuris
Canonici*, ed. Friedberg, vol. II, p. 804.

in an extravagant, prohibited jousts and tourneys in France and in England and in Germany and in certain other parts of the world, under threat of serious penalties, but his successor Pope John XXII, considering how many men were incurring the penalties, revoked the extravagant of his predecessor. To my mind, however, even though the penalties were once again annulled, the prohibition and the penalty stated in the Lateran Council were still in effect.[18]

Cartagena was reiterating here his own thoughts on the complex debate between papal monarchy and Conciliar sovereignty that had played itself out at the Council of Basle (1431–49), where Cartagena had led the Castilian delegation.[19] Even though the arch-diplomat Cartagena played both sides of the debate at the Council, in large part because the very delegation that he was leading was split on the matter, he was always a Conciliarist at heart, as is abundantly clear in the quotation above. Since the Castilian delegation had set out for the Council of Basle in May of 1434, the issue of Conciliar sovereignty would undoubtedly have been fresh in the Bishop of Astorga's mind in July of that year, when the fatal accident happened at the Pass of Honour of Suero de Quiñones. To complicate matters further, Alfonso V the Magnanimous (1396–1458; ruled 1416–58), the ruling monarch in Asbert de Claramunt's home kingdom of Aragon-Catalonia, was known at that time to be one of the principal opponents of Conciliarism. Furthermore, even setting aside the Council of Basle, Cartagena and a host of medieval European ecclesiastics shared the common belief that the Iberian knights' time would be better spent fighting against the natural enemies of Christendom – the Moslems of Granada – than fighting in what they perceived as mini civil wars, that is, martial contests that pitted Christian against Christian.[20] In short, beneath the glossy

---

[18] 'Comoquier que el derecho civil bien parece consentir estas pruebas de armas que por mostrar la fortaleza y virtud del cuerpo se hacen, pero el derecho canónico, en uno de los concilios que se hicieron en san Juan de Letrán, expresamente veda los torneos, privando de sepultura a quien torneando muere. Y luengos tiempos después, el papa Clemente V, en una extravagante, vedó las justas y torneos en Francia y en Inglaterra y en Alemania y en otras ciertas partes del mundo, so grandes penas. Mas el papa Juan XXII, su sucesor, considerando que muchos incurrían en ellas, revocó la extravagante de su antecesor. Mas, al mi cuidar, aunque las penas nuevamente puestas fueron quitadas, todavía quedó el vedamiento y la pena del Concilio de Letrán en vigor' (Cartagena, *Doctrinal de los caballeros*, in *Tratados Militares*, ed. Fallows, p. 311).

[19] On the Council of Basle and the debate between papal monarchy and Conciliar sovereignty, see Black, *Monarchy and Community*, pp. 7–52, and Fernández Gallardo, *Alonso de Cartagena: Una biografía política en la Castilla del siglo XV*, pp. 161–73.

[20] Ironically, tournaments, which often attracted an international crowd of competitors, were an ideal venue for clergy to recruit knights to participate

veneer of the Pass of Honour of Suero de Quiñones a viper's nest of political intrigue hissed and writhed. Poor Asbert de Claramunt could not have
been killed in a worse place at a worse time, for at this moment in history
the Bishop of Astorga could do nothing but deny him a church burial.

Crouch notes that in the twelfth and thirteenth centuries, astute tournament organisers often staged their events on the borders of principali-
ties because these fringe territories were the least vulnerable to official
censure from centralised authorities.[21] The Orbigo bridge was close enough
to what was at that time the border of the kingdom of Leon, but the Pass
of Honour of Suero de Quiñones was by no means a fringe event. It had
been widely publicised and was taking place in an area controlled by a
powerful bishop with strong political convictions who was informed about
the tragedy of Asbert de Claramunt's accidental death by messengers
dispatched by the prominent organiser of the event. Sancho de Rojas was
thus compelled through circumstances to make a decision. As drastic as
his decision was, it was also incontrovertible, which explains why Suero de
Quiñones did not attempt to challenge it.

In order for 'the elegance and disposition' of the jouster's 'majestic
beauty' to inspire 'joy and admiration',[22] as well as being technically and
intellectually gifted the jouster had to be athletic. Because of the physique
required in order to be able to spend long periods of time in the high,
wraparound jousting saddle, it is no coincidence that in the Middle Ages
a man's masculinity was often defined by his well-formed buttocks, thighs
and legs. Although this facet of the joust was a physical prerequisite for
success rather than an abstract theoretical concept it does, coincidentally,
have a Classical precedent, since Vegetius' ideal Tyro was also expected to
be 'slender in the buttocks, and have calves and feet that are not swollen by
surplus fat but firm with hard muscle'.[23]

Champion jouster Don Álvaro de Luna is described as having 'well-
made legs'; and in his prime King Henry VIII of England was renowned

---

in the various Christian crusades against Islam. Perhaps this is why there is
plenty of evidence to prove that Cartagena, as complex as ever, attended many a
tournament. For Cartagena's opinions on jousting and tourneying, see Fallows,
'Just Say No? Alfonso de Cartagena, the *Doctrinal de los caballeros*, and Spain's
Most Noble Pastime', and Morera, 'An Inherent Rivalry Between *Letrados* and
Caballeros? Alonso de Cartagena, the Knightly Estate, and an Historical Problem',
esp. pp. 85–7. See also Keen, *Chivalry*, pp. 97–101, and Neste, *Tournois, joutes, pas
d'armes dans les villes de Flandre à la fin du Moyen Âge (1300–1486)*, pp. 163–7.

[21] Crouch, *Tournament*, pp. 20–1 and 49–55.

[22] See below, Part II, Menaguerra, *Lo Cavaller*, School of Jousting.

[23] 'exilior clunibus, suris et pedibus non superflua carne distentis sed nervorum
duritia collectis'. See Vegetius, *Epitoma Rei Militaris*, ed. Reeve, I.6, pp. 10–11. For
the translation, see Vegetius, *Epitome of Military Science*, trans. Milner, p. 7.

for his ample thighs.[24] In the world of fiction, Guigemar in Marie de France's late-twelfth-century *lai* of the same name, as well as the anonymous survivor in her *lai* entitled *Chaitivel*, were both incapacitated by wounds to their thighs.[25] In a similar vein, the thirteenth-century German poet Gottfried von Strassburg notes of his callipygian hero, Tristan: 'His feet and legs (in which his beauty most appeared) deserved such praise as a man may give a man.' When Tristan rides we are informed that 'with thighs that beat like wings, with spurs and ankles, he took his horse by the flanks'.[26] It is in a joust to the death that Morold of Ireland strikes Tristan 'an ugly blow through the thigh, plunging almost to the very life of him, that his flesh and bone were laid bare through hauberk and jambs, and the blood spurted out and fell in a cloud on that island'.[27] And, what surely has to be the most painful fictional lance injury ever described – at least to a casual male observer such as myself – is that sustained by Wolfram von Eschenbach's King Anfortas. The king is reduced to a pathetic shadow of his former self when, after being struck through both thighs with a lance, the poisoned coronel and a length of bamboo shaft lodge permanently in his scrotum. Unable to walk or even to sit, the king can only recline, such is his agony.[28] In his own version of this legend Chrétien de Troyes clarifies that King Anfortas is known as the Fisher King because he is in such pain that he can no longer joust, and instead can only fish.[29] As if the image conjured by King Anfortas' flaccid fishing rod versus his erstwhile stout lance required explanation, D. D. R. Owen has none the less forced home the point that the many thigh wounds in medieval romance often symbolise infertility.[30] As stated in the previous chapter, the protective codpiece would not be introduced until the sixteenth century, and even

---

[24] On Don Álvaro de Luna, see *Crónica de Don Álvaro de Luna*, ed. Mata Carriazo, p. 207 ('las piernas bien fechas'); on Henry VIII see Anglo, *The Great Tournament Roll of Westminster*, vol. I, p. 6.

[25] France, *The Lais of Marie de France*, trans. Burgess and Busby, pp. 44 and 107–8.

[26] 'Sine vüze und siniu bein, / dar an sin schoene almeistic schein, / diu stuonden so ze prise wol, / als manz an manne prisen sol'... 'mit vliegenden schenkelen, / mit sporn und mit enkelen / nam er daz ors zen siten'. See Gottfried von Strassburg, *Tristan und Isold*, ed. Ranke, p. 42 lines 3341–4 and p. 86 lines 6839–41, respectively. For the translation, see Gottfried von Strassburg, *Tristan*, trans. Hatto, pp. 85 and 132, respectively.

[27] 'Biz er im durch daz diech sluoc / einen also hezlichen slac, / der vil nach hin zem tode wac, / daz ime daz vleisch und daz bein / durch hosen und durch halsperc schein / und daz daz bluot uf schraete / und after dem werde waete'. See Gottfried von Strassburg, *Tristan und Isold*, ed. Ranke, p. 87 lines 6924–30. For the translation, see Gottfried von Strassburg, *Tristan*, trans. Hatto, p. 133.

[28] Eschenbach, *Parzival*, trans. Hatto, pp. 243–55.

[29] Chrétien de Troyes, *Perceval*, in *Arturian Romances*, trans. Owen, p. 420.

[30] *Arthurian Romances*, trans. Owen, p. 521, note to line 436.

then it was worn exclusively with armour for foot combats. The codpiece is facetiously extolled as the most important piece of armour ever invented by Rabelais's wit Panurge, who, coincidentally, best summarises King Anfortas' misery when he states that: 'When a man loses his head, only the individual perishes; but if the balls were lost, the whole human race would die out.'[31] In the world of chivalric reality, survivors of thigh and groin wounds were lucky, for the femoral artery passes through the top of the thigh, near the groin, which is precisely why wounds in this region often proved fatal.

On a more (but only slightly) positive note, the French Neo-Latin poet Théodore de Bèze (1519–1605) had the bright idea of suggesting that no matter how ignominious the injury, the weapons themselves were ennobled the moment they pierced the flesh and inflicted disabling or mortal wounds upon men of noble stock. Such is his description of François Bourbon, Duke of Enghien (1519–46), who was killed when a friend – momentarily forgetting his 'mesura', no doubt – shot an arrow through his head during a particularly boisterous snowball fight:

> Although recently you escaped the swords and the brave enemy, you are lying here, François, yet you are not lying here by the sword. You were not able to meet your death in the enemies' camp, nor fall a brave man at the hands of a brave enemy. Rather it was at home, when you were engaged in a mock battle, that an arrow shot from an unlucky hand took your life – an arrow once fashioned, as I believe, from the Stygian cypress, an arrow, alas, ennobled by such a great slaying! An arrow, in which Mars himself had hidden Fate, when he had heard that your deeds rivaled his own. And so you fell, poor prince, and you were not long permitted to witness the trophies that your hand obtained. O Fortune, if you wish to toy with us, why mix grave death in with those games of yours?[32]

Wearing a full harness, especially in jousts of war, was the most sensible way of protecting the body from fatal injury. One wonders why it is, then,

---

[31] 'La teste perdue, ne perist que la personne; les couilles perdues, periroit toute humaine nature' (Rabelais, *Les Cinq Livres*, ed. Céard et al., p. 599). For the English translation, see Rabelais, *Gargantua and Pantagruel*, trans. Cohen, p. 309.

[32] 'Cum nuper gladios, et fortem evaseris hostem, / Hic, Francisce, iaces; nec tamen ense iaces. / Sed nec in hostili potuisti occumbere campo; / Nec fortis forti victus ab hoste cadis. / Sedibus at patriis, belli simulacra cientem / Missa infoelici sustulit arca manu: / Arca olim Stygia (credo) compacta cupressu, / Arca, eheu, quanta nobilitata nece! / Arca, in qua Parcam Mavors absconderat ipse, / Audiit ut factis aemula facta suis. / Sic igitur, miserande, cadis: nec cernere longum / Illa tua licuit parta trophaea manu. / At si nobiscum vis, o Fortuna, iocari, / Cur istis mors est seria mixta iocis?' (Bèze, *A View from the Palatine: The 'Iuvenalia' of Théodore de Bèze*, pp. 136–7).

that Suero de Quiñones approaches the judges in order to present the case that he be allowed to joust without the benefit of his visor, left pauldron and plackart. Had the judges allowed such madness he would almost certainly have been killed in the lists. Since the jousts at this passage of arms were for the most part pre-arranged, it is possible that Suero had made a secret pact with his opponent to strike lightly, or not to strike at all, in order to continue this rhetorical conceit. Or perhaps he banked on the judges standing firm in their resolve and disallowing the request, in which case he would make himself look dashing, daring and fearless in front of his lady-love and other (male and female) participants and spectators. From a purely theatrical point of view this incident is a perfect example of what has been called 'the current of aggression that runs throughout medieval visions of erotic relations'[33] and it serves to demonstrate that Suero de Quiñones is enthusiastically participating in his own emprise, the fiction of the man who is physically consumed and metaphorically imprisoned by love. After all, in the Middle Ages, love-sickness was considered to be a very real disease, with its own unique pathology and symptoms. It is therefore only right that Suero makes such a mad – and maddening – request, for, to quote one of the most eloquent of myriad examples, 'thus it happens that virtuous knights are deceived by the disorderly passions of love, which so often strip wise men of their understanding'.[34]

Although it is quite obvious from this incident that medieval and renaissance jousters were often heavily influenced by the topoi and leitmotivs of contemporary fiction, the authors of the jousting treatises tend not to engage or dialogue openly with chivalric fiction. Having said this, Menaguerra does touch tangentially upon a leitmotiv of chivalric romance in chapter 23 of his own treatise, where prospective jousters are advised that: 'Leaving a shard of the lance in the helm, in the shield or in any other part of the armour, is not worth any points, neither is making fire fly in an encounter, since, upon encountering and shattering, these disasters add no further value to a broken lance, and they are tied with any other knight who breaks his lance, even though a similar circumstance does not happen to him.' Making fire fly – that is, striking sparks – in the encounter was not an uncommon practice in the Middle Ages. Froissart, for example, mentions sparks repeatedly in his account of the St Inglevert jousts. According to him, the striking of sparks was a desirable accomplishment, as in the following instance in the joust between Sir John Holland and the Lord de Saimpi:

---

[33] Wack, *Lovesickness in the Middle Ages*, p. 161.

[34] 'E per semblant causa los virtuosos cavallers són decebuts per strema e desaforada amor, la qual acostuma moltes voltes tolre lo seny als hòmens savis'. See Martorell, *Tirant lo Blanch*, ed. Hauf, ch. 258, pp. 968–9. For the translation, see *Tirant lo Blanc*, trans. LaFontaine, p. 513.

Syr Johan Holande, who had great affection to do honorably, toke agayne his speare and spurred his horse; and whan the lorde of Saynt Pye sawe hym comyng, he dashed forth his horse to encountre hym; eche of them strake other on their helmes, that the fyre flasshed out: with that ataynt the lorde of Saynt Pye was unhelmed: and so they passed forthe and came agayne to their owne places. This course was greatly praysed.[35]

And why not? After all, the knights of medieval romance, especially those immortalised by Chrétien de Troyes, were forever 'making fire fly' when they struck each other's armour. Thus, for example, in the joust between Lancelot and Meleagant, we are alerted to the impressive fact that as the two men strike, 'the blazing sparks fly up towards the heavens from their helmets'.[36] In a similar vein, the tourney with swords between Cligès and the Duke of Saxony is described as follows:

With their swords they play such a tune on their clanging helmets that their supporters are astounded; and to the onlookers their helmets seem to catch fire and blaze; and as the swords rebound, bright sparks fly off as from the smoking iron that the smith hammers on the anvil after taking it from the forge.[37]

This leitmotiv was by no means limited to twelfth-century French romance. It would make its inevitable appearance in the Spanish chivalric

[35] 'Messire Jehan de Hollande, qui grant affection avoit de faire honnourablement ses armes, reprint sa lance et se joindy en sa targe et espouronna son cheval. Et quant le sire de Saintpy le vey venir, il ne refusa pas, mais s'en vint à l'encontre de luy au plus droit que il oncques pot; si se attaindirent les deux chevalliers de leurs lances de guerre sur les heaulmes d'achier, si dur et si roit que les estincelles toutes vermelles en vollerent. De cette attainte fu le sire de Saintpy desheaulmez et passerent les deux chevalliers moult frischement oultre et retourna chascun sur son lez. Ceste jouste fu moult grandement prisié' (Froissart, *Chroniques*, ed. Ainsworth and Varvaro, pp. 448–9). For the translation, see Froissart, *The Chronicle of Froissart*, trans. Bourchier, vol. V, p. 344. For more fiery smiting in the St Inglevert jousts, see also pp. 345, 348, 350, 352 and 354–7. For similar effects achieved at the tournament staged at Westminster in 1509 to celebrate the coronation of Henry VIII, see Anglo, *The Great Tournament Roll of Westminster*, vol. I, p. 49.

[36] 'Les estanceles vers les nues / Totes ardanz des hiaumes saillent'. See Chrétien de Troyes, *Le Chevalier de la Charrette (Lancelot)*, ed. Foulet and Uitti, p. 282 lines 5022–3. For the translation, see *Lancelot*, in *Arthurian Romances*, trans. Owen, p. 252.

[37] 'As espees notent un lai / sor les hiaumes qui retantissent / si que lor genz s'an esbaïssent. / Il sanble a ces qui les esgardent / que li hiaume espreignent et ardent, / car quant les espees resaillent, / estanceles ardanz an saillent / ausi come de fer qui fume / que li fevres bat sor l'anclume, / qant il le tret de la favarge'. See Chrétien de Troyes, *Cligès*, ed. Harf-Lancner, p. 278 lines 4052–61. For the translation, see *Cligès*, in *Arthurian Romances*, trans. Owen, p. 147.

romances as well. In Garci Rodríguez de Montalvo's *Amadís de Gaula*, for example, when Amadis fights Dardan, 'they were striking each other on their helmets, which were of fine steel, so that it seemed to all that their heads were flashing, because of the many sparks of fire emanating from them'.[38] Likewise in the sequel to this book entitled *Las sergas del muy esforzado caballero Esplandián* (The Labours of the Very Brave Knight Esplandián), in the foot combat between Esplandián and Furion the giant, we are informed that 'they struck such great blows on their helmets that great fire and flame flew from them'.[39]

Clearly Menaguerra was aware of the seductive allure of fiction, and in the case of this particular leitmotiv he remonstrates with knights who would attempt to emulate their romance heroes in an effort to impress the spectators. Menaguerra was having none of it. For him the artistry of the joust consisted of much more than recreating the noisy,[40] spark-filled world of fiction. In his own treatise Menaguerra is tacitly asserting himself as the jouster's jouster, a man for whom sparks are a trifling crowd-pleaser that detract from the true artistry of the joust as well as having a baleful influence on jousters who may lose sight of what they should be doing in order to satiate their desire to pander to the spectators.

For Menaguerra, if a crowd were to be wooed, the wooing was to be done through the jouster's own wit and charisma, with a flourish of the pen and a dash of poetic verve – through the application of his 'mesura' – as well as with flourishes of the lance. As he states in the School of Jousting:

> Let his shield, emblazoned or decorated with a sublime and elegant device, be girt in the centre as is customary. And above all, let him not forget to wear a beautiful crest, the motto for which, if it should be well conceived, shall be widely distributed in writing, at the first charge, to those who naturally wish to know the explanation of inventions.

The word 'invention' in this context has a double meaning, for it refers

---

[38] 'ellos se hirían por cima de los yelmos, que eran de fino azero, de manera que a todos pareçía que les ardían las cabeças, según el gran huego que dellos salía'. See Rodríguez de Montalvo, *Amadís de Gaula*, ed. Place, vol. I, p. 118a. For the translation, see Rodríguez de Montalvo, *Amadis of Gaul*, trans. Place and Behm, vol. I, p. 147 (also vol. I, p. 622 and vol. II, pp. 392, 468, 651 and 672 for more spark-filled fighting scenes).

[39] 'diéronse ... por encima de los yelmos tan grandes golpes, que el fuego salió en gran llama dellos'. See Rodríguez de Montalvo, *Las sergas del muy esforzado caballero Esplandián*, ed. Gayangos, p. 410b. For the translation, see Rodríguez de Montalvo, *The Labors of the Very Brave Knight Esplandián*, trans. Little, p. 92 (also p. 449).

[40] Although he never mentions sparks, Wolfram von Eschenbach does compare the clang of jousters colliding to a thunder storm. See Eschenbach, *Parzival*, trans. Hatto, p. 195.

broadly to the happening or event itself, and specifically to the impresa on the crest or the shield that would accompany the motto.[41] Impresas on crests and shields typically consisted of an ingenious motto, the meaning of which was elucidated by an equally ingenious and colourful device. It was up to the jousters to use their creative imagination to generate witty motto/impresa combinations and the spectators to decipher the hidden meaning of those combinations. As noted by Ian Macpherson these texts were made available in different forms:

> They decorated the lists as inscriptions on small boards (*rótulos*) erected at strategic points, or could be embroidered on the cloth hangings (*paramentos*) which decorated the lists; in some tournaments they were laid out with the decorated helms for inspection in the period immediately preceding the jousts, or passed round on small scraps of paper to participants and spectators during the course of the festivities.[42]

In the last two or three decades of the fifteenth century in Catalonia and Castile a unique literary genre developed when the jousters began writing and distributing among participants and spectators short poems of one to five octosyllabic verses in which they explained their impresas. One such collection of these poems is the *Jardinet de Orats*, which consists of the poems written about the crests of the Catalan and Castilian knights who participated in jousts at the tournament held in Barcelona on 22 April 1486. To cite but one representative example, the following poem was composed by the jouster Bernat Durall, whose crest took the form of a turret. The poem revolves around a common conceit, where Old Spanish 'penes' in the first verse refers to the poet's 'sorrows' whilst at the same time the noun is a neologism for the 'pen' (instead of the more usual noun 'pluma') that he uses to express his amorous imprisonment through the medium of poetry:

> To endure sorrows (*penes*) up here
> Two of us have climbed:
> Love, for mocking me;
> And I, for blaming you.[43]

---

[41] See Macpherson, *The 'Invenciones y Letras' of the 'Cancionero general'*, p. 11; Macpherson and MacKay, 'The Game of Courtly Love'; and MacKay, 'Signs Deciphered – The Language of Court Displays in Late Medieval Spain', pp. 288–9.

[42] Macpherson, *The 'Invenciones y Letras' of the 'Cancionero general'*, p. 12.

[43] 'A suffrir penes aqui / Hauemos sobido dos / Amor por burlar de mi / Y yo por culpar a vos'. The *Jardinet de Orats* has been edited by Dutton, *El Cancionero del siglo XV*, vol. I, pp. 38–48, and Cátedra, *Poemas castellanos de cancioneros bilingües y otros manuscritos barceloneses*, pp. 12–40. For the poem cited, see Dutton, vol. I, p. 40a, no. [ID4170] BUI-34-1, and Cátedra, p. 12. For further examples of this type of poetry, see also the poems collected under the general heading 'Invenciones y letras

Whether or not he participated in these jousts in his home territory, Menaguerra is clearly alluding to this poetic activity in his discussion of inventions. And as far as literary, geographical and even chronological transferability is concerned, this type of poetry subsequently became a standard, integral component of the sixteenth-century chivalry novels in Spain, underscoring once again the interplay between real and fictitious jousts.[44] Due to the international popularity and appeal of the Spanish chivalry novels, the art of writing poetry about impresas at jousts subsequently also became a standard practice in Elizabethan England.[45] One further detail of note that emerges from these poems is that in some cases the spectators were required to know personal details about their favourite jousters in order fully to comprehend the poet's wit. Recalling Huizinga's and Duby's club, while the top Iberian jousters did occasionally travel the international tournament circuit, they sparred with each other primarily within the boundaries of the Peninsula with the result that they formed a tightly knit community that came into regular contact and had a following of loyal fans who rooted for a particular jouster. Thus at the Valladolid tournament of 3 April 1475 nineteen-year-old champion jouster Pedro de Cartagena (1456–86) delivered a series of poetic responses to the mottoes of his colleagues in what might best be called a kind of medieval Roast, using his insight and rapier wit to outclass their own virtuosity with the pen and deflate their egos at the same time.[46] One of the amusing highlights of the event, this mock poetic rivalry reflects the close ties of kinship that bound the medieval and renaissance tournament community.

In the quotation by Menaguerra above, 'those who naturally wish to know the explanation of impresas' refers in large part to the spectators. Unlike at mêlée tournaments, where the spectators were expected to shout at and engage with the contestants,[47] there were certain spectatorial restrictions at jousts. Because of the presence of nobility and sometimes the presence of the ruling monarch, and because of the courtly and judicial nature of jousts, spectators were expected to watch the game in silence.

de justadores' ('Inventions and mottoes of jousters') in Castillo, *Cancionero General* (1511), accessible now in facsimile followed by a critical edition in Macpherson, *The 'Invenciones y Letras' of the 'Cancionero general'*, pp. 33–104. On the 'pena' = sorrow/pen conceit, see Rico, '*Un penacho de penas*: Sobre tres invenciones del *Cancionero general*'.

[44] See Del Río Nogueras, 'Libros de caballerías y poesía de cancionero: Invenciones y letras de justadores'; also Rico, 'Una torre por cimera'.

[45] See Young, *Tudor and Jacobean Tournaments*, pp. 123–43.

[46] Macpherson, *The 'Invenciones y Letras' of the 'Cancionero general'*, pp. 43–51, even-nos. 2–14. Poet, jouster and soldier, Pedro de Cartagena was killed at the siege of Loja on 22 May 1486. On his life and works, see Avalle-Arce, 'Tres poetas del *Cancionero General* (I): Cartagena'.

[47] See Crouch, *Tournament*, pp. 55–6, 74–6 and 95–6.

The tradition of solemn silence is repeated throughout the Middle Ages as much in technical manuals as in works of fiction. For example, the Catalan manual on judicial combat *De batalla* states that after the preliminary ceremonies, at the point when the combatants take the field: 'On each side of the field there rises up a cry, such a loud and repeated cry that no-one dares make while the battle is under way, neither by signal of word or deed, nor of hand nor of anything else; and he who should emit it, will right away be seized by the herald or by the armed men who guard the field with the herald, and will be punished as the judge sees fit.'[48] The point is reiterated in Diego de Valera's fifteenth-century *Tratado de las armas* (Treatise on Arms): 'And before the combatants commence the battle, the Constable, at the order of the King, shall have it proclaimed through the whole field that no-one dare make signals or say anything that may serve to warn or assist the combatants, on pain of death.'[49] The description in this case refers to the Castilian rules; the French rules on this issue as they are described by Valera in the same treatise concur exactly.[50] Similarly, in the world of medieval chivalric fiction, spectators at jousts described in *Curial e Güelfa* and *Tirant lo Blanc* are formally warned, on pain of death, not to speak, cough or make signals during the joust.[51] Noises and gestures from the wings could catch the knight's peripheral vision and distract his attention from what was already a dangerous sport, causing him to miss his opponent, make a foul stroke with the lance or collide with the tilt. In a similar vein, Ponç de Menaguerra in his School of Jousting urges prospective jousters not to shout out inside their helms upon or after making the encounter. And as we have seen in the previous chapter, the armoured knights themselves were expected to make the least amount of noise possible.

If not quite death, rowdy spectators did suffer dire consequences for their behaviour. Pero Rodríguez de Lena notes that during the joust between Johan Febra and Lope de Stúñiga at the Pass of Honour of Suero de Quiñones, one of Stúñiga's retainers shouted 'Charge, Sire!' in a

---

[48] 'A cada cantó del camp estia una crida, qui fortment e sovén crit que negú no gos fer, mentre la batayla·s farà, nengun senyal de paraula ne de fet, ne ab mà ne ab res; e qui ho farà, aquí matex sia pres per lo veger e per los armats qui guarden lo camp ab lo veguer, e sie punit a coneguda dells prohòmens' (*De batalla*, in *Tractats de cavalleria*, ed. Bohigas, p. 90).

[49] 'E ante que los conbatientes comenzen la batalla, el condestable, por mandado del rey, haze pregonar por todo el canpo que no sea osado de facer ninguno señas ni fablar cosa por que ninguno de los conbatientes pueda aver avisamiento o ayuda, so pena de la vida' (Valera, *Tratado de las armas*, ed. Penna, p. 126b).

[50] Valera, *Tratado de las armas*, ed. Penna, p. 121a.

[51] See *Curial e Güelfa*, ed. Aramoni i Serra, vol. I, p. 76, and Martorell, *Tirant lo Blanch*, ed. Hauf, ch. 81, p. 325.

moment of enthusiasm as both knights were in mid-charge.[52] At this point the joust was called to a halt and the anonymous retainer was seized and taken before the judges, who ordered that his tongue be cut out on the spot. Only through the intervention of some noble participants were the judges persuaded to mete out a slightly less gruesome punishment: the unfortunate retainer was sentenced to thirty blows with a stick on the back, arms and head, after which he was clapped in irons and removed from the field – harsh punishment indeed for a vociferous fan.

There was, however, a certain amount of complicity between jousters and spectators in this 'narrative of performance and display', to borrow an expression from Seth Lerer, especially in the festive moments before the jousts officially got under way.[53] Zapata notes – not without some disapproval – that jesters would sometimes be there to work the commonest element of the crowd and get them in a good mood.[54] In the wake of their merry japes the knight himself would make his grand entrance. In the School of Jousting Menaguerra notes that it is essential that the knight make as dramatic an entrance as possible so that 'the elegance and disposition of his majestic beauty inspires joy and admiration', always making sure that his horse's rump does not touch the tilt lest he look like a fool. A century later Luis Zapata was in full agreement. As noted by Zapata, prior to jousting before the hushed crowd, the knights themselves had to approach the head of the lists clad in all their defensive armour, neatly balanced and fitted in place. He further notes: 'Clothes and horse trappings elegant, fine-quality and splendid. Heraldic devices impressive, tasteful, original, and well suited to people and occasions.' As immodest as Zapata himself tends to be, in 'Del Justador' he places emphasis for everyone else on the rhetorical topos of 'aurea mediocritas', or seeking the golden mean. Thus, as elegant and impressive as the knight may be when he comes to the head of the lists, elsewhere Zapata strongly urges him not to be deceived into becoming overconfident about his abilities, for 'he who tilts with arrogance / shall never get to break a lance'.[55]

Even before the jouster approaches the head of the lists Menaguerra makes the following suggestion: 'taking care over his proper deportment, let him ride the customary lap around the lists'. The lists would often be erected in the middle of a courtyard or public plaza, two spaces that would typically be flanked on all four sides by apartments. In this overt act of

---

[52] '¡Señor, a él!' (Rodríguez de Lena, *El Passo Honroso de Suero de Quiñones*, ed. Labandeira Fernández, p. 164).

[53] Lerer, '"Represented now in yewer syght": The Culture of Spectatorship in Late Fifteenth-Century England', pp. 39–40.

[54] Zapata, *Carlo Famoso*, facsimile, ed. Terrón Albarrán, fol. 179vb.

[55] 'El que a la tela va con confiança / Entonces nunca acierta a quebrar lança'. Zapata, *Carlo Famoso*, facsimile, ed. Terrón Albarrán, fol. 189ra.

complicity between jouster and spectator, according to Menaguerra, each jouster should make his entrance by riding a preliminary lap around the lists. This was the time – before he entered the lists to demonstrate his technical virtuosity – when the knight was expected to survey and work the crowd, the time when the eyes of comely damsels and other spectators in the doorways, on the balconies and on the rooftops would be firmly fixed on him. This particular facet of the Principle of Pulchritude might well be called knightly nonchalance, and it is not unique to Menaguerra. Of the knight, statute §6 of the fourteenth-century *Libro de la Orden de la Banda* states that 'his bearing should be the gravest possible'.[56] And the hero of *Tirant lo Blanc* is advised that he should aspire to the following: 'in sitting, elegance; in walking, gravity'.[57] It is while he is riding this lap that the jouster is reminded by Menaguerra not to let his right arm dangle, but to rest his hand nonchalantly on the bouche of the shield, just as in the past he would have grasped the buckle of the guige. In his influential *Book of the Courtier* (1528) Baldasar Castiglione would christen this nonchalant style *sprezzatura*, the idea being to 'conceal design and show that what is done and said is done without effort and almost without thought'.[58]

After coming to the head of the lists, the knight must take up the lance, which he must be certain not to drop. The butt of the lance should then be placed in its special pouch. Made of iron or leather, this pouch would typically be mounted on the stirrup or the saddle. Another uniquely Iberian way of mounting the pouch was at the hip of the cuirass.[59] Duarte of Portugal is the first Iberian authority to refer to the alternative methods for carrying the lance, as follows:

> The lance is supported on the leg when wearing jousting armour in a pouch mounted on the cuirass, or on the arçon of the saddle or at the leg,[60] as each person prefers; and it seems like a good and comfortable way to me.[61]

[56] 'el su andar que sea el más sosegado que pudiere'. Cartagena, *Doctrinal de los caballeros*, in *Tratados Militares*, ed. Fallows, p. 314.

[57] 'en lo seure, manera; en lo anar, gravitat'. See Martorell, *Tirant lo Blanch*, ed. Hauf, ch. 143, p. 607. For reasons unknown, this passage is not translated by LaFontaine, so the translation in this instance is my own.

[58] 'nasconda l'arte e dimostri ciò che si fa e dice venir fatto senza fatica e quasi senza pensarvi' (Castiglione, *Il Libro del Cortegiano*, ed. Maier, pp. 127–8). For the translation, see Castiglione, *The Book of the Courtier*, trans. Opdycke, p. 30.

[59] Buttin, 'La lance et l'arrêt de cuirasse', pp. 151 and 177, and Hoffmeyer, *Arms and Armour in Spain*, vol. II, pp. 207 and 226.

[60] That is to say, on the stirrup.

[61] 'A lança se traz na perna em armas de justa em bolssa posta nas pratas, ou no arçom da sella ou sobre a perna, como cada hūu mais tem geito; e pareceme boa e folgada maneira'. (Duarte I, King of Portugal, *Livro da ensinança de bem cavalgar toda sela*

Duarte's explanation attests to the fact that the hip-mounted pouch on the cuirass was in use in Iberia as early as the 1430s and the syntax of the medieval Portuguese in the first clause indicates that at this time it was specific to jousting armour; the saddle- and stirrup-mounted pouches on the other hand could be used with field armour as well as the special jousting kit. In addition to these three alternatives, says Duarte, there are some particularly athletic men who are able to rest the butt of the lance on the top of their thigh and still others who carry it braced between their inner thigh and the saddle. Because they are able to carry the heavy jousting lance without any pouch at all, these men, he concludes, 'show greater strength and agility'.[62] Writing over a century later, Dall'Agocchie would confirm that the pouch was indeed invented to accommodate the heavy lance and it was going out of style in Italy by the 1570s in favour of resting the lance, which was by then a much lighter version than its medieval counterpart, directly on the thigh.[63] Reflecting current trends, Luis Zapata initially states that resting the lance – which he describes as short, sturdy, rigid, and light – on the thigh is his preferred method of supporting the weapon when setting out. He then, however, writes a rather confusing description that mixes one technique with another, as follows:

> So, setting out on the stirrups, after seeing that the opponent is preparing to set off, putting spurs to his horse, let him sally forth standing perfectly straight, the lance in the pouch, leaning the body slightly over the lance – and without revealing any emotion –, with as much force as possible on it that, like I used to have through long experience, the butt makes a permanent bruise on the thigh. And carrying the lance for a while in the pouch, as the horse gets ready to run the course, lift it out.

In this instance Zapata seems to have been inspired by what in his own day

---

que fez El-Rey Dom Eduarte de Portogal e do Algarve e Senhor de Ceuta, ed. Piel, p. 75). The translation in this instance is my own, since the published translation is defective, missing the nuance about jousting armour (medieval Portuguese 'armas de justa') and omitting the reference to the cuirass (medieval Portuguese 'pratas'). See The Royal Book of Horsemanship, Jousting and Knightly Combat, trans. Preto and Preto, p. 73.

[62] Duarte's exact wording is as follows: 'E outros sollamente na perna, e antre ella e o arçom; e os que a bem trazem sem outra vantagem, mostram mayor força ou soltura' ('And others support it on the leg alone, and between the leg and the arçon; and those who carry it well without any other advantage show greater strength and agility') See Duarte I, King of Portugal, Livro da ensinança de bem cavalgar toda sela que fez El-Rey Dom Eduarte de Portogal e do Algarve e Senhor de Ceuta, ed. Piel, p. 75. The translation is once again my own since the published translation strays too far from the original.

[63] Dall'Agocchie, On the Art of Fencing, trans. Swanger, fols. 60rv.

might well have been called the quixotic Muse, and today would be called a senior moment, commingling his theoretical musings about supporting the lance at one and the same time in the pouch and on the thigh.

As can be seen from chapter 2, figs. 41–7 and 54, the pouch was quite small and would have been impossible to see whilst wearing the jousting helm or an armet with the visor lowered. Placing the butt of the lance into the pouch had to be done through touch alone, and it was not uncommon for the jouster to have difficulty placing and keeping the lance in the pouch at the beginning of a course and likewise returning it to the pouch at the end. After successfully running the course, for example, Zapata states that the jouster 'should return the stub of the lance to the pouch, and subsequently discard it and without injuring any spectators'. Because placing the butt of the lance in the pouch after having encountered and run the length of the course was so difficult to do, Quijada de Reayo and Menaguerra are equally as sympathetic on the issue of missing the pouch at this point. In the words of Quijada de Reayo: 'If, when your horse comes to a halt, the lance should fall out of the pouch by accident, or should there be some mishap when placing the lance in the lance-rest, it is nothing to worry about, for this happens to many a good man-at-arms.'

In addition to agreeing about issues concerning the pouch both Menaguerra and Quijada de Reayo agree that the charge down the course consists of three distinct stages, though frustratingly, neither one states what those stages are. In chapter 2 of his treatise Quijada de Reayo says simply that 'you shall run the course in three parts'. Menaguerra is just as cryptic, stating in chapter 4 of his treatise that: 'If he loses the lance, the three stages having been passed, because it slips out of the pouch, or likewise before the three stages, the lance cannot be judged lost, according to our rules.' Not unlike a medieval triptych, in the context of jousting the three stages most likely refer to a central defining moment flanked on either side by the moments that lead to and from the centre, in which case the stages can be defined as follows: (1) the take-off and approach; (2) the impact; and (3) the ride-out and halt. Losing the lance during the second stage – the impact or encounter – would be a sign of a palpable and praiseworthy hit as opposed to poor technique. Doubtless because of the drama of the encounter this centre panel of the triptych was by far the preferred method of illustrating the joust in the Middle Ages and Renaissance, as shown in fig. 130 for example. Thus it can be inferred that Menaguerra's statement concerns poor handling of the lance after reaching the third stage (i.e. bad handling post-impact) or, most importantly, during the first stage (i.e. bad handling on the approach). As an incidental means of underscoring these three stages King Duarte of Portugal recommends that jousters be accompanied by three footmen, placed at what he calls the three principal points of the tilt ('pontas da tea'): two at opposite ends and one in the middle. Each footman was delegated specific responsibilities

130 Jousting scene. From *Oliveros de Castilla y Artus de Algarbe* (Burgos: Friedrich Biel, 1499)

such as placing the jouster's feet in and out of the stirrups, leading him into and out of the lists, and providing any necessary assistance immediately after the moment of impact.[64]

What, then, constituted bad handling of the lance? On this issue we are fortunate that Menaguerra, Quijada de Reayo and Zapata do all provide detailed information on how *not* to handle the lance. There were four main errors or fouls that could be made when managing the lance whilst charging: 'swooping', 'making the sign of the Cross', 'barricading' and 'fishing'.

The most common mistake seems to have been what these authors call swooping. That swooping was common is underscored by the fact that the terminology used is the same across all three treatises: 'fer calades' in medieval Catalan; 'hacer calada' in Spanish. The word 'calada' is a technical term most commonly used in falconry and hawking to describe the high-speed flight of falcons and hawks as they descend upon their prey; hence my own translation into English: 'swooping'. Quijada de Reayo graciously, and unusually, provides a definition in chapter 4 of his treatise: 'Swooping means that the lance does nothing but waver up and down when you are charging.' In the context of jousts, then, the term refers specifically to dropping the lance-head. This in turn would mean missing the

[64] *Livro da ensinança de bem cavalgar toda sela que fez El-Rey Dom Eduarte de Portogal e do Algarve e Senhor de Ceuta*, ed. Piel, pp. 100–1; *The Royal Book of Horsemanship, Jousting and Knightly Combat*, trans. Preto and Preto, pp. 99–100.

ideal targets of the opponent's head and torso and instead committing a foul, such as hitting his saddle, his thigh, his horse or the tilt. Swooping is tantamount to losing control of one's lance and misjudging the amount of movement that can happen at the tip through slight mishandling at the grapper. Quijada de Reayo notes that 'a movement of one digit at the lance-rest equates to two palms at the lance-head'. Being able to charge with the lance in the rest, but without swooping, was at the core of the technical virtuosity of the joust. Quijada de Reayo always recommends placing the lance in the rest sooner rather than later and, in order to avoid dropping the lance-head, he urges his protégé to lower the lance gradually whilst charging:

> Thus it is better, in accordance with others who are of the same opinion, to place the lance in the lance-rest right from the start and couch it and lower it little by little, like the weight of a clock, so that you are lowering and striking at the same time. In my opinion it is better to place the lance in the lance-rest sooner because if a setback with the lance occurs during the course, such as losing your grip on it or something else, you will have time to compensate for it and you will be able to make the encounter, and if you place the lance in the lance-rest later, you will not have time to compensate for it, and if you lose your grip on it because the opponent reaches you too quickly, there will be no time for you to recover it.

The point was important, since the author repeats his advice that 'when you are charging at a gallop you should not point the lance downwards or hold it in rest underarm, and raising the lance upwards and placing it in the lance-rest, couch it, and lower it little by little, like the weight of a clock'. Menaguerra had also recommended lowering little by little in his School of Jousting. Zapata gives the same advice in 'Del Justador', adding elsewhere with his customary lack of modesty that in his long jousting career he never once swooped a lance.[65]

Quijada de Reayo's corrective measures for avoiding the most common and dangerous fouls articulate in writing what had been known to jousters since widespread usage of that small, inconspicuous armorial accoutrement known as the lance-rest. A properly fitted lance-rest held the lance approximately at a 45-degree angle. When lowering the lance, the jouster would carefully lower it the first 45 degrees by hand, at the end of which movement the lance would be seated down onto the rest. Once fixed, the jouster would continue to lower the lance into the final striking position by leaning forward from the waist, being careful to keep his back straight and his eyes on his target. Both movements would need to be run smoothly together so that the lance would move down gracefully, 'little by little', or

[65] Zapata, *Miscelánea*, ed. Carrasco González, ch. 211, p. 319.

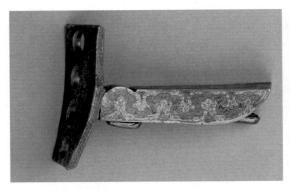

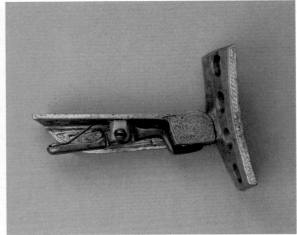

131–4 Study of the lance-rest belonging to the Cloud Bands garniture made by
Wolfgang Grosschedel of Landshut for Prince Don Carlos of Spain, 1554

as Quijada de Reayo says, like the weight of a clock. Figs. 131–4 are a study
of a lance-rest as it would have looked in Quijada de Reayo's day, at the
apogee of its technical and artistic perfection. It has been suggested that
this example was originally a part of the 'Cloud Bands' garniture made by
master armourer Wolfgang Grosschedel of Landshut for King Philip II of
Spain on the occasion of his visit to England after his marriage by proxy
to Queen Mary I in 1554. Because of its relatively small size, however, it
could actually have been a part of the matching garniture that Philip had
made for his son Don Carlos when Carlos was thirteen or fourteen years
old.[66] It is hinged and equipped with a spring-loaded lever placed discreetly

[66] On the attribution to Philip II, see Mann, *Wallace Collection Catalogues: European
Arms and Armour*, vol. I, p. 168, inv. A228; and Norman, *Wallace Collection
Catalogues: European Arms and Armour: Supplement*, p. 79, inv. A228. On the
Cloud Bands garniture, see chapter 3, n. 6 above. On the matching Cloud Bands

on the underside that enables the rest to lock into place. The innovation of the lance-rest allowed for unprecedented technical virtuosity in the lists. Judging both by extant armours and illustrations of jousters in action, the lance-rest was always set quite high in the early days after its invention, gradually moving further down the breastplate over time; hence in the fifteenth century lance carriage was high, as shown in figs. 36, 37, 38, 52, 53, 56, 62 and 130, whereas by the mid-sixteenth century lances were generally couched low, almost on the hip, as shown in figs. 92 and 96, for example. This gradual change in lance carriage can be inferred from Zapata's 'Del Justador', where, as a traditionalist, he urges that the lance-rest be affixed higher rather than lower.

In the Pass of Honour of Suero de Quiñones, where the jousting took place with sharp lance-heads and without shields and was therefore particularly dangerous, fouls were to be avoided at all costs. This explains the following tense exchange between Suero de Quiñones and the judges of the passage of arms, whose opinions are similar to those of Quijada de Reayo. Though somewhat lengthy, the passage is worth quoting in full, as follows:

> When the judges, wise knights, saw that the valiant knight Suero de Quiñones, the senior captain, was now inside the lists, with the lance on his thigh, they descended the stand and approached him and told him that they found that it was the law of arms that any knight who was to perform similar deeds of arms should set out with the lance in the rest, so as to avert the dangers which could be increased by losing the lance; thus they ordered him, as well as all the other knights and gentlemen, Answerers as well as Defenders, to set out with the lance in the rest whenever they performed deeds of arms, if on that day, as well as in the coming days, his rescue was ever to be accomplished.
>
> The order that the above-mentioned judges made having been heard by the senior captain of the field, Suero de Quiñones, he protested against it, saying that it was not fair, because in accordance with every good knight's good inclination and agility, it was ugly in the extreme to set out like that with the lance in the rest, which by his authority he would not permit.
>
> When the judges heard Suero's reply, they then told him that, since he well knew that he had sworn and promised to be subject to them and obey their orders, that on that oath which he had sworn to them, they ordered him for the second time to obey their order without giving another excuse, assuring him that until he made

garniture made for Don Carlos, see Valencia de Don Juan, *Catálogo histórico-descriptivo de la Real Armería de Madrid*, pp. 89–90, inv. A274–A276.

this promise to them they would not allow him to perform deeds of arms.[67]

Suero de Quiñones was outraged at what he perceived as a restriction because he wished to imitate real war. On the battlefield it was standard procedure to place the lance in the rest at the last minute before lowering it and striking the enemy.[68] But jousts that were staged within an enclosure were very different from real war fought on an open battlefield, and because of the constrictions imposed by the length of the lists, jousts had to be controlled if the jousters were to make the encounter.

Specific information has survived about the typical length of the lists. In the case of the Pass of Honour of Suero de Quiñones, Rodríguez de Lena states that the lists were 146 paces long, and more or less equal in width to the length of a lance, with a tilt running down the middle. Zapata's description of the length of the lists is remarkably similar, at a recommended 150 paces. These two figures average out to 148 paces, or approximately 225.5 m (244 yd 10½ in). As noted by Zapata, this space would be sufficient to enable the good man-at-arms to make 'a thousand elegant strokes with the lance and the bad one a thousand foul strokes'. Fig. 135 is an illustration of the enclosure included in a fifteenth-century Catalan manuscript. Of particular interest are the gates on opposite sides through which the opposing jousters would enter and exit. Next to each gate, inside the enclosure, are pavilions in which each man could prepare for combat or to which each could repair in the event he was wounded. The judges'

[67] 'Desque los juezes, cavalleros discretos, vieron como estava ya dentro en la liça el esforçado cavallero Suero de Quiñones, capitán mayor, con la lança en el muslo, descendieron del cadahalso y fueron luego a él y dixéronle que ellos falla[va]n que de derecho de armas era que qualquier cavallero que las semejantes armas fiziese, que devía de salir enristrado, por quitar los peligros que en perder de la lança se podría recrecer, que mandavan assí a él como a todos los otros cavalleros e gentileshomes, assí conquistadores como deffensores, que cada uno saliese enristrado sus lanças quando las armas fiziesse, si aquel día, como todos los otros días siguientes venideros en que su rescate avía de acavar. ⸿ Oýdo por el capitán mayor del campo, Suero de Quiñones, el mandamiento [que] los juezes desuso les fizieron, reclamó contra él, diziendo no ser justo, porque según vondad e soltura de todo buen cavallero, era gran fealdad salir assí enristrados, lo qual de su poder él no consintía. ⸿ Quando los juezes oyeron lo que Suero respondió, luego le dixeron que, pues él bien sabía cómo jurado e prometido tenía de estar a su obediencia e cumplir su mandamiento, que so aquella fee que prometido les avía, le mandavan por segunda vegada que su mandamiento cumpliesen sin otra scusa dar, certificándole que fasta se lo prometer que armas ningunas no le dexarían fazer' (Rodríguez de Lena, *El Passo Honroso de Suero de Quiñones*, ed. Labandeira Fernández, p. 149; Escorial MS f.II.19, fol. 49r).

[68] See Buttin, 'La lance et l'arrêt de cuirasse', pp. 112–14, and Soler del Campo, *La evolución del armamento medieval en el reino castellano-leonés y al-Andalus (siglos XII–XIV)*, pp. 51–2.

stand and an altar have been erected just outside the enclosure. The artist has also attempted to render the double fence in the middle of which the jousters' aiders would stand and observe.[69] The caption that accompanies the illustration describes appropriate dimensions for the tourney on foot and on horseback: 'The lists for foot combat should measure 40 paces square; those for combat on horseback, 80; those for a tourney of four against four should measure 120 paces; those of eight against eight or ten against ten, 150.'[70] According to this document, then, the enclosure for the one-to-one tourney on horseback was virtually half the size as that recommended for the joust.

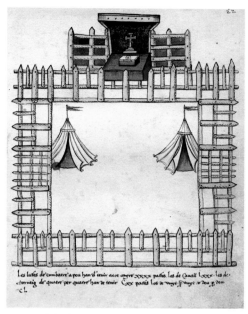

135 The lists. From *Linatges de Catalunya*, 15th century

As the judges of the Pass of Honour of Suero de Quiñones knew – anticipating Juan Quijada de Reayo's written comments by just over a hundred years – because of the relatively short distance to be run in the confined space of the lists it was appropriate to place the lance in the rest as early in the course as possible, and it did not behove the knights to court danger in the name of a fictional emprise. If Suero de Quiñones thought that it looked ugly to set off down the course with the lance already in the rest, Luis Zapata, ever conscious of the power of pulchritude, suggests in 'Del Justador' that since the lance must be removed from the pouch and lifted up from its vertical position in order to be placed in the rest, the knight ought as far as possible to try executing this manœuvre with a stylish twist of the wrist. As he puts it: 'And carrying the lance for a while in the pouch, as the horse gets ready to run the course, lift it out, raising it high with a twist of the hand, and place it, with a lunge and twisting your hand higher with proper gracefulness, into the lance-rest, and with another lunge couch it, and little by little the lance will incline, lowering without swooping .' As I mentioned in chapter 1, Zapata states elsewhere

[69] On the double fence, see also Barber and Barker, *Tournaments*, p. 193.

[70] 'Les lisses de combatre a peu han de tenir a tot cayre XXXX passos; les de cavall, LXXX; les de torneig de quatre per quatre han de tenir CXX passes; los de vuyt per vuyt o deu per deu, CL'. See *Linatges de Catalunya*, Salamanca, Biblioteca General Histórica, MS 2490, fol. 22. 40 paces = approx. 60.4 m (65 yd 1 ft 2⅖ in); 80 paces = approx. 120.8 m (130 yd 2 ft 8⅖ in); 120 paces = approx. 181.2 m (196 yd 11 in); 150 paces = approx. 226.5 m (245 yd 1 ft 1½ in). See also Riquer, *L'Arnès del cavaller*, fig. 251.

that even when he jousted in disguise he would betray his true identity the moment he placed the lance in the rest, such was his unique wrist action.[71]

Related to swooping is what Quijada de Reayo calls making the sign of the Cross. This term is defined as follows: 'Making the sign of the Cross means that the lance wavers from side to side, from right to left.' Although the specific terminology in this case is not mentioned by Menaguerra or Zapata, the type of foul that would occur as a result of moving the lance from side to side would primarily be missing one's opponent and striking the tilt. This in turn would lead to loss of points, an issue that I shall discuss in more depth in the next chapter.

The third kind of foul that can result from poor handling of the lance is known as barricading the lance. The same verb for describing this foul is used by Rodríguez de Lena in 1434, Quijada de Reayo in 1548 and Zapata in the 1590s: 'barrear'. Just over one hundred years before *El Passo Honroso de Suero de Quiñones* and well over two hundred years before *Doctrina del arte de la cavallería*, in 1330, the *Libro de la Orden de la Banda* refers to this same foul with its own distinct terminology – 'crossed lances' ('varas atravesadas') – as follows: 'Furthermore, we declare that the broken lances shall not be judged properly broken by breaking them crossed, but only by breaking them from a direct blow.'[72] Fortunately for modern scholars, Quijada de Reayo once again provides a concrete definition: 'Barricading the lance means crossing it too far sideways so that it does not strike and breaks poorly.' This was a particularly ugly foul. The lance, held on the right-hand side, was supposed to point ahead of the rider and then gradually be lowered at the same time as it was gently crossed over towards the left so that a direct hit could be scored upon the opponent's head or torso. Barricading meant that the rider crossed his lance too violently, a full 90 degrees, with the result that his opponent would run into a horizontal lance, snapping it without ever being hit with the point. The lance would break off at or near its weakest lower point: the grip (the butt being locked under the jouster's arm by the lance-rest, thus preventing the lance from being spun out of the jouster's hand without breaking). As ever, averting this foul would require patient lowering, gentle crossing and much practice. A barricaded lance is visible on the viewer's extreme right in the San Romano Battle Panel illustrated in chapter 1, fig. 18, whereby the lance skates in between the victim's left pauldron and rondel but without piercing

---

[71] Zapata, *Miscelánea*, ed. Carrasco González, ch. 37, p. 47.

[72] 'Otrosí, decimos que ninguna de las varas quebradas, que no sean juzgadas por quebrantadas, quebrándolas atravesadas, salvo quebrándolas de golpe'. See Cartagena, *Doctrinal de los caballeros*, in *Tratados Militares*, ed. Fallows, p. 322. Quijada de Reayo uses the term 'lanças atravessadas' just once, when he defines barricading. See below, Part II, Quijada de Reayo, *Doctrina del arte de la cavallería*, ch. 4.

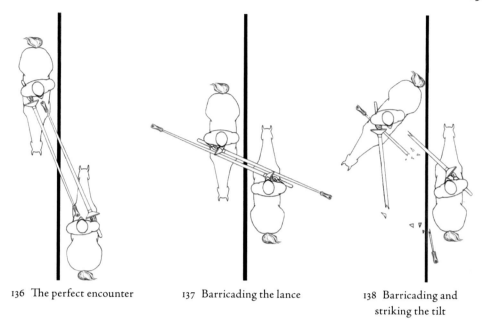

136 The perfect encounter   137 Barricading the lance   138 Barricading and
                                                                              striking the tilt

his armour. Figs. 136–8 depict overhead views of an ideal encounter, along
with the fouls of barricading the lance and striking the tilt.[73]

Last but not least, the fourth type of lance-stroke was apparently a
matter of some debate, since it was not a foul *per se*, though it was so difficult to accomplish that it more often than not led to serious fouls. This
lance-stroke is mentioned by both Quijada de Reayo and Zapata, though
only Zapata calls it by its proper name. It is a stroke known as fishing.
Quijada de Reayo defines this manœuvre as follows: 'Some jousters hold
the lance upright until the moment of the encounter and they lower it in
one sudden motion and it can drop low and lead to a foul stroke.' Zapata is
more forceful, expressing his own disapproval as follows: 'There are those
who lower the lance in one sudden motion, which is called fishing; I do not
approve of this, because the encounter goes awry a thousand times over
and the opponent and the tilt get struck with lance staves, and the tilt and
the horse get hit, and other foul and very unfortunate strokes are made.'
Like striking sparks, fishing was yet another stylish crowd-pleaser, since
lowering the lance in one sudden movement at the very last moment and
shattering it upon a bewildered opponent would doubtless have had the
spectators on the edge of their seats as they waited for the knight to deliver
his spectacular *coup-de-grâce*. This is the battle manœuvre that Suero de
Quiñones wanted to be allowed to perform in order to show off his own
skill with the lance. The problem was that in the relatively confined space

---

[73] These overhead views are inspired by a line drawing in Dillon, 'Tilting in Tudor
Times', p. 302, with further input from Dr Tobias Capwell and Mr Keith Pope.

of the lists only the most accomplished jouster could hope to pull off this move, and most often it resulted at best in an embarrassing and ugly foul or at worst in a dangerous accident. In sum, within the enclosure and lists, negotiating the complex relationship between lance and lance-rest required the greatest of skill: place the lance in the rest too early and it might swoop or make the sign of the Cross; place it in the rest too late and it would almost certainly fish. Perhaps the best advice on this and other jousting techniques is that of Zapata, who always recommends seeking the golden mean.

One final note about pulchritude. Courses did not end at the encounter, for as stated above, a course consisted of three stages, the third of which was the ride-out and halt. Ideally by the final stage the knight would be left with a broken lance stub. What to do with the stub whilst, as ever, not looking like a fool? It is Menaguerra who provides the most eloquent solution: 'After having encountered, let him raise his lance and slide his hand toward the vamplate, passing what is left of the lance back over the tilt to his footmen so that they can take it. And then, riding at a gentle pace, let him come to a halt at the end of the lists.' We know that this is sound practical advice, for King Henry II of France was injured when splinters from a lance entered his right orbit during a joust at a tournament held on 30 June 1559, subsequently causing intracranial infection and lingering, agonising death, all because his opponent the Constable de Montgomery (who would be executed some fifteen years later) failed to slow down and raise his broken lance stub in time.[74] Although it is not overtly stated in Menaguerra's text, the gentle pace of the final ride-out would, from a psychological point of view, have a pleasantly soothing effect on horse, rider and spectator alike; a fitting – and, of course, pulchritudinous – end to this competitive exercise and demonstration of showmanship, athleticism and sheer skill.

The Principle of Equality

THE Principle of Equality applies to the following issues: rank; arms and armour; and scoring opportunities.

The issue of rank is discussed in chapter 14 of *Lo Cavaller*. This chapter focuses on royalty versus everyone else. The author states that members of the royal family are on equal terms only when jousting against fellow family members, but when members of royalty joust against noblemen of lesser rank, it is understood that the royals – primarily for reasons of protocol – must always win. Since medieval society adhered rigidly to a system of estates, Menaguerra in this instance is reiterating a facet of

---

[74] On this incident, see Barber, *The Knight and Chivalry*, p. 188, and Martin, 'The Death of Henry II of France: A Sporting Death and Post-Mortem'.

chivalric culture of which all noble jousters would have been keenly aware: that the Principle of Equality applied as much to rank as it did to scoring and weaponry.

The Principle of Equality as it applies to armour is underscored in *El Passo Honroso de Suero de Quiñones*. At the beginning of Rodríguez de Lena's chronicle we are told of the preparations for the first joust of the passage of arms, between Suero de Quiñones and the German knight Arnold von Rottenwald, as follows:[75]

> The honourable judges, the knights Pero Barba and Gómez Arias, and the king-of-arms and the herald having been called into the pavilion, as you have heard, where the noble senior captain Suero de Quiñones was standing, his harness thoroughly inspected[76] and examined by them as is stated above, the famous captain Suero then said that he implored and besought the honourable judges and the king-of-arms and heralds, since they had thoroughly examined and inspected his armour, to go next to the pavilion where the German was standing and about to arm himself, and that they examine the armour chosen and brought by him, all of which he was using for the passage of arms, in such a way and means that steadfast and true equality among the armour of both men was maintained, so that neither man had an advantage, so that everything which was contained in the chapters was upheld and maintained; beseeching them always that equality truly be maintained, all of which he entrusted them in good conscience to do as best they could beyond their assurance and the promise made and granted by them.[77]

[75] Since this knight's name lends itself to literal, and quite poetic, translation into Castilian, he is known throughout the chronicle as Arnaldo de la Floresta Bermeja. He is identified as Arnold von Rottenwald by Riquer, *Caballeros andantes españoles*, p. 100, and Salicrú i Lluch, 'Caballeros cristianos en el Occidente europeo e islámico', p. 249, n. 115 and p. 285. There are two Rottenwalds: one up near Hamburg and another near Stuttgart, in southwest Germany. In the table of contents the chronicle states that he hails from the Marquesate of Brandenburg, which means that Arnold was from Rottenwald near Stuttgart. See Rodríguez de Lena, *El Passo Honroso de Suero de Quiñones*, ed. Labandeira Fernández, p. 64 (Escorial MS f.II.19, fol. 5r).

[76] Labandeira Fernández's edition has the gerund, *catando*, which is a mistake in transcription for *catado* (Escorial MS f.II.19, fol. 44v).

[77] 'Llamados los honrrados juezes cavalleros Pero Barba e Gómez Arias, e rey de armas, e faraute, según que oýdo avedes, dentro de la tienda, donde el noble capitán mayor, Suero de Quiñones estava; catado bien por ellos e visto su arnés como desuso es contado; luego el famoso Suero, capitán, dixo que rogava e pedía a los honorables juezes e rey de armas e farautes que, pues sus armas avían vien vistas e acatadas, que fuesen luego a la tienda do el alemán estava e armarse avía, e que viesen las armas por él escogidas e tomadas, en todas las quales en el paso

A similar exercise formed part of the conclusion of this particular joust, as follows:

> Then, since the famous senior captain of the passage of arms Suero de Quiñones had finished performing deeds of arms with the German, as you have been told, the honourable knights the Fabras brothers, the above named Lord Johan and Lord Pere, went after him. And as Suero de Quiñones was dismounting his horse outside of the enclosure, in front of his pavilion, the judges called the king-of-arms and herald who were coming from there; Suero took off his armour in public in front of everyone, so that they could see and witness that he had no artifice or advantage either with his armour or his horse, which he had made use of this day with the German knight, and everything having thus been seen by the judges, the king-of-arms and the herald, they stated and declared that he had no advantage, as they stated above, as is stated to you.[78]

In the interests of safety and equality the knights of the Pass of Honour of Suero de Quiñones were checked regularly for missing pieces of armour and severely reprimanded by the judges if the full harness were not worn.[79] For purely practical reasons, any gaps in a badly fitted harness would be a liability for the wearer, since all exposed flesh was vulnerable to injury. Even the jousters' horses were assessed before each joust

---

tenía, en tal manera e vía que firme e verdadera ygualdad sobrellas a ambos fuesen guardada, sin que ventaja a alguno dellos obiesen, porque tenido e bien guardado fuese todo lo que en sus capítulos era contenido; todavía les rogando que ygualdad verdaderamente fuese guardada, lo qual todo a sus conçiençias como mejor podían encargava allende de su fee e promesa fecha e por ellos otorgada' (Rodríguez de Lena, *El Passo Honroso de Suero de Quiñones*, ed. Labandeira Fernández, p. 144; Escorial MS f.II.19, fols. 44v–45r). On securing an advantage through reinforcement of the armour, see Buttin, 'La lance et l'arrêt de cuirasse', p. 161.

[78] 'Luego, como el famoso capitán mayor del passo Suero de Quiñones ovo acavado de fazer las armas con el alemán, según vos es contado, fueron en pos dél los honrrados cavalleros hermanos Fablas, mossén Johan e mossén Per que desuso son nombrados. E en Suero de Quiñones descavalgando de su cavallo fuera de la liça, delante de su tienda, llamaron los juezes al rey de armas e faraute que de allí venidos eran; Suero se desarmó en plaza ante todos, por que viessen e testiguasen que encubierta ni vantaja non avía ninguna en las armas ni cavallo que tenía, a con que fecho avía este día con el cavallero alemán, e todo assí luego visto por los juezes, rey de armas y faraute, dixeron e declararon que avantaja ninguna non avía, según que desuso dixeron, como a vos es dicho' (Rodríguez de Lena, *El Passo Honroso de Suero de Quiñones*, ed. Labandeira Fernández, p. 153; Escorial MS f.II.19, fols. 52rv).

[79] See below, Part II, *Passo Honroso* Selection 14, where Gómez de Villacorta and Bueso de Solís mutually agree to joust without gardbraces and are duly reprimanded by the judges.

139 Title page of *Corónica del noble cavallero Guarino Mesquino*
(Seville: Juan Varela de Salamanca, 1527)

in order to ensure, as far as possible, equality between steeds as well as
riders.[80]

The only defiance of this principle tends to be encountered in the fictitious jousts of the period. Fig. 139, for example, is the title page of the 1527
edition of the Spanish chivalry novel entitled *Corónica del noble cavallero*

[80] Rodríguez de Lena, *El Passo Honroso de Suero de Quiñones*, ed. Labandeira
Fernández, p. 146 and pp. 162–3.

Guarino Mesquino (Chronicle of the Noble Knight Guarino Mesquino).
The hero of this novel, Guarino Mesquino, is the son of the Duke of
Burgundy. As a child he is kidnapped by pirates and finally freed by the
Prince of Constantinople. He falls madly in love with Elisena, the daughter
of the Emperor of Constantinople and there is a jousting competition early
in Book I to win Elisena's hand in marriage. The title page depicts a scene
from this competition. Guarino's opponent is clearly an 'infidel' who is
riding in the traditional Arabic style with his legs bent at the knee and
wielding a falchion-like sword. He wears a fantasy harness, forged by the
imagination of the artist. In the novel Guarino does not know at this point
that he is Christian born, though his technique and accoutrements betray
his heritage. He is riding in the traditional north-west European style with
his legs stretched out, wielding a lance and wearing a full harness topped
by a helmet for the tourney. The idea is that he may be ignorant of his
true identity, but if he rides like a Christian and jousts like a Christian he
truly is a Christian. The woodcut is a striking image that underscores the
simultaneous and complex differentiation and intersection of opposing
cultures and identities in Iberia as manifested by riding techniques, arms
and armour. It also constitutes a fanciful xylographic deconstruction of
the Principle of Equality.

In all sports, the largest amounts of points are usually awarded for the
most difficult manœuvres, and, as the rules were honed through years of
constant practice, jousting was no exception. As I shall discuss in the next
chapter, large amounts of points could be earned in jousting by drawing
blood, but only if the lance-stroke that inflicted the damage were a legitimate, praiseworthy one and not a foul. Though they were by no means
easy to make, such strokes do underscore yet again that jousting was never
meant to be a jarring gore-fest so much as a slick display of athleticism and
skill.

In so far as weaponry is concerned, in order to help competitors avoid
coming a cropper in the lists, Article 19 of the twenty-two articles that
regulated the Pass of Honour of Suero de Quiñones stipulates that no-one
shall be allowed to use his own spear or spearhead, as these will be supplied
to everyone by the organisers in order to ensure equality in length, width
and weight. This point is reiterated by Quijada de Reayo as follows: 'It
behoves the judges to assure that the lance-maker provide lances of equal
length so that one is not longer than another, for if one is one digit longer
than another, the one that strikes first will splinter, and the other may or
may not break at all.'[81]

In determining equality it was essential, as is evident from Article 21 of
the regulations for the Pass of Honour of Suero de Quiñones as well as the

---

[81] For French sources on this same issue, see Buttin, 'La lance et l'arrêt de cuirasse',
pp. 125–32; also Clephan, *The Medieval Tournament*, p. 80.

treatises by Menaguerra, Quijada de Reayo and Zapata, to select honest, judicious and temperate judges. Throughout his book Menaguerra defers to the judges' knowledge and integrity on knotty issues of equality and advantage, and on the decision about which knight shall win the prize. As noted by Rühl, although ladies and damsels may have been the ones who presented the prize to the knight who jousted the best, the actual decisions made about scoring and winning or losing were always made by judges or heralds.[82]

The best judges were expected to be, or to have once been, accomplished jousters themselves. As noted in *El Passo Honroso de Suero de Quiñones*, the qualities a man must have in order to be a good judge are 'prudence and fortitude and restraint and justice'.[83] That the judges were expected to be accomplished jousters themselves is underscored in *Tirant lo Blanc*, where we are informed that: 'Good seed makes good fruit, and a virtuous knight an honest judge.'[84] These men were typically elected by their peers to judge the joust.[85] Their word was final, although in the days before action replays this did not prevent some contumacious knights from engaging in arguments with them. As we have seen, it was not uncommon for some jousters to approach the judges with a view to defying the rules that they themselves had set even before setting off down the lists. Albeit sometimes in the name of Eros, the excuses made for removing key pieces of body armour in order to impress male peers and comely damsels would be buttressed by the kind of logic and argumentation that these unfortunate judges must have dreaded, expected as they often were to participate in the fiction. Unfortunately this meant that they were required to call upon all of their fortitude and restraint as they listened to temperamental, obtuse and prolix jousters who had the audacity to question their decisions, challenging these reasonable men to rhetorical duels in which the judges were compelled to emulate Alice's White Queen and believe 'as many as six

---

[82] Rühl, 'Behind the Scenes of Popular Spectacle and Courtly Tradition: The Ascertainment of the Best Jouster'. Though not mentioned by Rühl, see also King Henry VIII's *Challenge for the Tournament* of February, 1511: 'Item, it is the pleasure of the King our moost dradde souuerain lord, that the quenes grace and the ladies, *with the aduice of the noble and discrete Juges*, to gyve prises after their deseruynges vnto both the parties' (Anglo, *The Great Tournament Roll of Westminster*, vol. I, p. 110, italics mine).

[83] 'cordura y fortaleza y mesura e justicia' (Rodríguez de Lena, *El Passo Honroso de Suero de Quiñones*, ed. Labandeira Fernández, p. 147; Escorial MS f.II.19, fol. 47v).

[84] 'De bon fruyt ix bon fruyter, e de virtuós cavaller juhí verdader'. See Martorell, *Tirant lo Blanch*, ed. Hauf, ch. 186, p. 779. For the translation, see *Tirant lo Blanc*, trans. LaFontaine, p. 421.

[85] Such was the case at the Pass of Honour of Suero de Quiñones. See Rodríguez de Lena, *El Passo Honroso de Suero de Quiñones*, ed. Labandeira Fernández, p. 81 and pp.117–22.

impossible things before breakfast'.[86] In the end, however, one thing was certain: where the sacred issue of equality was concerned, no matter how theatrical the bombast of the petitioner, no matter how persuasive the rhetoric, the judges always won.

The Principle of Transferability

What I call The Principle of Transferability concerns scoring opportunities and quantification of performance, which differed very little across Europe, or even across the centuries. Scoring is linked to equality. Thus Ponç de Menaguerra states unequivocally in chapter 21 of his treatise that 'in jousts much heed is paid to equality', by which he means that both combatants must be afforded the exact same opportunities for scoring points. In the case described in chapter 21 he is referring specifically to a lance-thrust to the helm which is so powerful that it dislodges the helm from the wearer's head. Such a stroke is worth the same as ten broken lances. This high score increases to the equivalent of twenty broken lances if, in addition to losing his helm, the opponent loses a tooth or receives an injury that bloodies his nose or mouth. In jousting competitions that consisted of a limited or set number of courses, the point on equality is that 'it is worth the same as if it happened in the first course or any of the others'. In other words, dislodging an opponent's helmet and injuring him into the bargain would not be worth more points if this happened in the first course rather than the second or third.

As far as quantification of performance was concerned, there were two main options for structuring jousts. Menaguerra places emphasis on set numbers of courses to be run. Whoever scores the most points in the set number of courses wins. This type of joust was popular throughout Europe and would eventually become the standard, as it meant that solid performance was the key to victory. So, for example, as early as 1330 it is recommended that when the knights of the Order of the Band of Castile stage a joust, 'they should run four courses, and no more'.[87] Similarly, King Henry VIII of England staged a joust on 12 February 1511 in which each knight was required to ride six courses. The rules for this joust further state that it is acceptable to complete the six courses over a period of two days.[88] Suero de Quiñones, on the other hand, stipulates a much more difficult option: jousts of war with a set number of spears to be broken – rather than courses run – in each match. When jousting with war spears, Duke Theseus in Chaucer's 'The Knight's Tale' states that 'No pair of combatants

---

[86] Carroll, *Through the Looking-Glass and What Alice Found There*, ed. Green, p. 177.

[87] 'que hagan cuatro venidas, y no más' (Cartagena, *Doctrinal de los caballeros*, in *Tratados Militares*, ed. Fallows, p. 322).

[88] See Anglo, *The Great Tournament Roll of Westminster*, vol. I, p. 110.

shall ride more than one course with spears.'[89] Suero's option was serious
business, as it often meant that hapless and exhausted competitors and
horses would run seemingly endless amounts of courses until such time
as the set amount of lances or spears was broken. A consequence of this
type of joust was that levels of skill were immediately obvious, for the best
jousters would break their three lances in three to five courses whilst the
least accomplished contestants would run course after course, sometimes
missing each other entirely as many as four or five times in a row. Repeated
misses are, according to Zapata, 'the stuff of laughter'. No matter which
option was chosen, the issue of identical scoring opportunities in jousts
was of paramount importance. It is to scoring options and the ubiquitous
applicability of those options that I shall turn in the next chapter.

---

[89] 'Ne no man shal unto his felawe ryde / But o cours with a sharpe ygrounde spere'.
Chaucer, 'The Knight's Tale', in *The Riverside Chaucer*, ed. Benson, p. 59b lines
2548–9. For the translation, see Chaucer, *The Canterbury Tales*, trans. Coghill,
p. 87.

Keeping the Score

B Y 1493 – the date of publication of the first edition of Menaguerra's treatise – jousts of war in field armour had all but disappeared, having been supplanted by much less dangerous jousts royal, or jousts of peace as they are also called. The types of lance-thrusts delivered in the jousts of peace were exactly the same as those delivered in the jousts of war. What had changed were the arms and armour. As we saw in chapter 2, each contestant now wore a special jousting kit, the distant cousin of field armour, and fought with specially designed rebated lances.

Chapter 19 of Menaguerra's treatise is an appropriate point of departure for the issue of scoring as it demonstrates that even with the new kit points were not as easy to quantify as it may seem. In this chapter of the treatise the author uses the guard of the vambrace, or couter reinforce, as a reference point for describing different possible scoring scenarios. So, for example, if the internal leather straps holding the piece in place burst (the couters on Real Armería A16 shown in chapter 2, figs. 41 and 54, are attached to the upper and lower cannons of the vambrace by means of such straps), the piece flies off and the jouster has to stop for a moment to strap it back in place, this equals 1 point for his opponent. If the entire piece is smashed to pieces and the jouster has to go off field to mend it, this equals four points for his opponent. Thus if an armour such as Real Armería A16 were struck on the left couter, the internal leathers burst and the entire set-up covering the arm fell apart, this would require that the jouster visit the workshop, remove the armour, have the rivets pulled and then have the entire set-up releathered. Such a repair could take days or possibly weeks to carry out.[1] These four points, then, are awarded for inflicting irreparable damage in the moment that the opposing jouster's squire or aider(s) cannot fix on the field in a reasonable amount of time. On the other hand, in the case of pieces held in place with leather straps that are repeatedly struck, the straps will inevitably work loose with the result that the piece they are securing will slip out of place and have to be tightened; hence Menaguerra's final note about scoring in this chapter is that if the piece is

---

[1] For detailed and pertinent information about the maintenance of armour and the great care required for the successful removal of creases and dents and the replacement of rivets, see Price, *Techniques of Medieval Armour Reproduction: The 14th Century*, pp. 341–6. On specific case studies based on fifteenth-century Burgundian sources, see Gaier, 'Technique des combats singuliers d'après les auteurs "bourguignons" du XVe siècle', pp. 449–50.

worked loose but the problem is fixed simply by tightening the straps, this is of no account.

As we have seen in chapter 2, however, the problem is that surviving armours for this class of joust from around the same period of Menaguerra's treatise show enough variation to complicate the issue of this rule applying exclusively to the guard of the vambrace. For example, it is unlikely that the right couter could be damaged or that it could be hit at all if the jouster had a large protective vamplate in place on his lance, though by the same token the folio of the *Inventario iluminado* on which Real Armería harness A16 is illustrated (chapter 2, fig. 54) includes six vamplates of varying shapes and sizes for the joust royal so there is no guarantee that such capacious vamplates were used in each and every joust. In the case of the left couter, the original shield for Real Armería A16 depicted in the *Inventario iluminado*, which is accurately replicated in chapter 2, fig. 41, covers most of the left side, but a low blow could still clip the left couter. Sometimes – but again, by no means always – armours of the period do have reinforces on the left couter as Menaguerra says, and this is another area of breakage that would be relevant. From a linguistic point of view, given that in medieval Catalan (and medieval Castilian) the term 'guarda', used throughout chapter 19, could refer to the guard of the vambrace or to the gardbrace, Menaguerra's discussion of the rules as they apply to the guard of the vambrace could just as easily be applied to the right gardbrace, which was another vulnerable area. Compatible jousting armours from this period at the Kunsthistorisches Museum in Vienna and the Palazzo Ducale in Venice (see chapter 2, figs. 50 and 51)[2] have a deep flange on the right side of the breastplate to help prevent the right shoulder being struck. In the case of both Real Armería A16 and Kunsthistorisches Museum HJRK S1 the right pauldron has a gardbrace that could conceivably get ripped off, especially if the coronel of the opponent's lance caught the leading edge. Another joust royal element associated with Real Armería harness A16 as it is illustrated in the *Inventario iluminado* is a left vambrace with a disk-shaped reinforce or rondel riveted over the left couter, and as we know from the Pass of Honour of Suero de Quiñones this is the sort of plate that could also be bent or removed by a particularly powerful blow.

Thus, although in chapter 19 of his treatise Menaguerra is talking about how to judge damage to the armour worn on the arms, he may also be inferring damage to the shoulders on the understanding that such damage is much rarer and therefore not worth discussing explicitly. He lists the most likely types of damage, thus alerting the judges to what they should be looking out for, his comments to be used as a guide for armour in general. As an experienced jouster who had witnessed many changes to the jousting

[2] Vienna, HJRK S1 and HJRK S11; Venice, inv. E22.

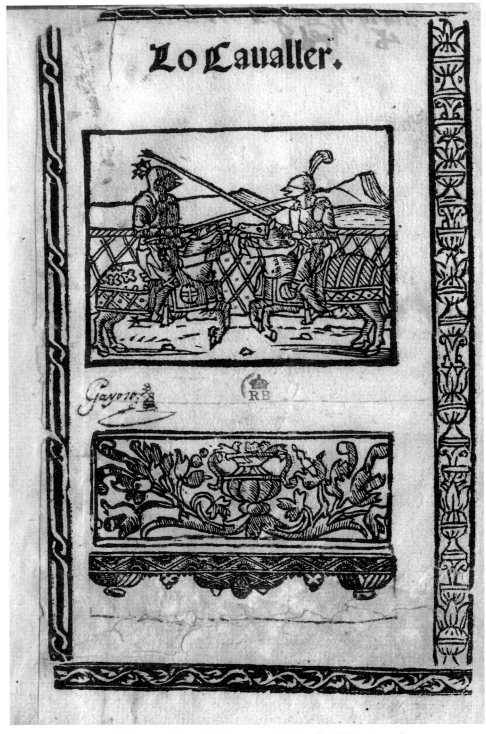

140 Title page of Ponç de Menaguerra, *Lo Cavaller* (Valencia, 1532)

kit in his own lifetime, he would have known that the exact set-up of the kit always varied. Even without anticipating future developments, at the time of writing Menaguerra would have been aware that Italians using his rules might be wearing one version of the harness for the joust royal; Catalonians and Castilians something slightly different. Indeed, it can be inferred from the *Inventario iluminado* that the armour acceptable for the joust royal could vary between individuals from the same area and even within armours produced by the same workshop. So at best Menaguerra is providing in his treatise enough guidance to work out the scoring for any situation, however unusual or kit-specific. To my mind this means that Ponç de Menaguerra is not as shoddy a writer as has previously been thought. If he is sometimes vague or elliptic it is because he has to be – any ambiguity or elasticity about armour and lance-play in *Lo Cavaller* is quite deliberate since both are always viewed by the author through the prism of Transferability.

Over the thirty-nine year period between publication of the first and second editions of *Lo Cavaller*, that is, from 1493 through 1532, great changes took place in jousting armour. Frustratingly, the frontispiece of the 1493 edition of *Lo Cavaller* has been lost to time and, although it was probably decorated with a woodcut of some sort, there is no bibliographical record or description of what this may have looked like. However, the woodcut on the frontispiece of the 1532 edition has survived intact (fig. 140). It depicts two knights jousting in full harness, holding their lances at hip level and sporting armets with visors lowered as opposed to the frog-mouthed helms that would have been worn in the 1490s. That is to say, as crudely wrought as this frontispiece is, it reflects the changes in equipment and lance carriage that had taken place by the early 1530s. And yet these changes are not reflected in the body of the text, which but for some minor textual variants remains unchanged. The explanation for this goes back to the Principle of Transferability discussed in chapter 4 of this book, for Menaguerra's treatise was above all a guide to the rules of conduct in the lists and the rules for quantification of performance. The frontispiece of the 1532 edition of *Lo Cavaller* underscores one of the paradoxes of the joust: from a chronological point of view the rules of the joust resisted change at the same time as the armour of the joust embraced change. Menaguerra's triumph is that he wrote a nuanced and well-balanced scoring manual that defied this paradox and stood the test of time.

Prior to the publication of Ponç de Menaguerra's treatise very little information at all on scoring and quantification of performance in the joust was written down. The result is that our knowledge of scoring before 1493 is rather sketchy. It is known that in England in the sixteenth century the rules of the joust were often codified in diagrammatic score cheques, the extant examples of which have been deciphered and analysed in detail by

141 Jousting Cheque for a contest at the Field of Cloth of Gold, 1520. Bodycolour on vellum. 36.5 × 27.3 cm (1 ft 2¼ in × 10⅝ in)

ffoulkes and Anglo.[3] As well as articulating the rules, these score cheques offer some insight into what actually took place in specific jousts. Fig. 141 shows the score cheque for a jousting competition that took place during the tournament to celebrate the meeting of kings Francis I of France and Henry VIII of England at the Field of Cloth of Gold in June, 1520. In

[3] ffoulkes, 'Jousting Cheques of the Sixteenth Century'; Anglo, 'Archives of the English Tournament: Score Cheques and Lists'.

bodycolour on vellum, the folio is richly decorated with the arms of the two kings and their respective collars of the Order of St Michael (Francis) and the Order of the Garter (Henry) along with the crests of other nobles in attendance. Amidst the two royal crests a scribe has penned in the score cheques.[4] These consist of parallelograms dissected longitudinally by a line. The top, middle and bottom lines of the tablets are in turn transected by smaller lines. The number of courses run is indicated on the projection of the middle line. Within the parallelogram, depending on their place-ment, the smaller transecting lines indicate attaints to, or lances broken on, the body or the head, or lance-thrusts that knocked off pieces of armour, etc. Fouls are generally indicated on the bottom line. In the case of the Field of Cloth of Gold the most common score consists of clusters of small lines transecting the middle line of the parallelogram, which are believed to indicate the number of lances broken on the opponent's body.[5]

No score cheques of English jousts have survived prior to the sixteenth century, and this unique scoring system never took off in Iberia, where preference was always given to narrative discourse for articulating rules as well as rhetorically reconstructing jousting events. It is at this point that the fourteenth-century *Libro de la Orden de la Banda* comes to the fore, since this text devotes an entire statute to the rules of the joust. As I stated in the Introduction, it should come as no surprise that this statute is and was not widely known since the book in which it was written was the exclusive prerogative of the knights who were the members of the order and the custodians of its secret statutes. Given its rarity in the context of the history of jousting, the statute is worth quoting in full:

> The way in which the joust should be staged.
>
> Firstly, we declare that the knights who must joust should run four courses, and no more. And if in these four courses one knight should hit the other, splintering his lance, and the knight upon whom that lance splintered did not break his own lance by striking his oppo-nent, he shall be vanquished, for he did not break his lance.
>
> And furthermore, we declare that, if one knight splinters two lances and the other only one, the winner shall be the knight who breaks the two lances. But if the knight who only splintered one lance knocks off his opponent's helm with the same blow, a tie shall be declared between him and the knight who splintered the two lances.
>
> And furthermore, if a knight shatters two lances by striking

[4] On this MS, see *Making History*, p. 77, fig. 4, and Willetts, *Catalogue of the Manuscripts in the Society of Antiquaries of London*, p. 61, no. 136/2.

[5] On the nuances indicated by the transecting lines, see especially Anglo's detailed analysis, 'Archives of the English Tournament: Score Cheques and Lists'.

his opponent, and the knight who has been struck knocks him off his horse, even though he did not splinter his lance, a tie shall be declared between him and the knight who splintered the two lances.

Furthermore, if one knight knocks down both his opponent and his horse, and the other knocks down the knight but not his horse, we declare that the knight whose horse fell with him shall be the winner, because the fault in this case was the horse's and not the rider's. And in the case of the knight who fell but whose horse did not, the fault rests with the knight and not with the horse.

Furthermore, we declare that lance staves shall not be judged properly broken if they are broken crosswise, but only if they break after striking with the point.

Furthermore, we declare that if in these four courses each knight splinters two staves, or one each, or they each strike in the same place, a tie will be declared between the two. And if in these four courses they never manage to hit each other at all, let the judgement be that they jousted poorly.

Furthermore, we declare that if any knight should drop his lance whilst charging, without ever coming to blows, his opponent should raise his lance and not strike him, for it would be unchivalrous to strike an opponent who had no lance.

And in order to judge these affairs, we declare that there should be four judges in place: two assigned to one team, and another two assigned to the other team, so that they can ensure that the knights who have jousted the best are declared the winners.[6]

---

[6] 'La manera que se debe tener en la justa. ⊄ Primeramente, decimos que los caballeros que hubieren a justar que hagan cuatro venidas, y no más. Y si en estas cuatro venidas el un caballero quebrantare un asta en el otro caballero, y el caballero en quien fue quebrada no quebrare alguna en el otro, este tal que sea vencido, pues no la quebró. ⊄ Y otrosí, decimos que, si quebrare el uno dos astas y el otro no más de una, que haya la mejoría el que quebrare las dos astas. Pero si el que quebró la una derribare el yelmo al otro caballero del golpe que le dio, que sea igualado con el que quebró las dos astas. ⊄ Y otrosí, si un caballero quebrare dos astas en el otro caballero, y el otro caballero en quien las quebró derribare a él, aunque no le quiebre el asta, decimos que este tal que sea igualado con el que quebró las astas. ⊄ Otrosí, si un caballero derribare a otro y a su caballo, si este que cayó derribare a otro sin el caballo, decimos que haya mejoría el caballero que cayó el caballo con él, porque parece que fue la culpa del caballo y no del caballero. Y el que cayó sin caer el caballo con él, fue la culpa del caballero y no del caballo. ⊄ Otrosí, decimos que ninguna de las varas quebradas, que no sean juzgadas por quebrantadas, quebrándolas atravesadas, salvo quebrándolas de golpe. ⊄ Otrosí, decimos que, si en estas cuatro venidas quebrantaren dos varas o sendas, o hicieren golpes iguales, que juzguen los caballeros por iguales. Y si en estas cuatro venidas no se pudieren dar, que juzguen que no tuvieron buen acaecimiento. ⊄ Otrosí, decimos que, si cayere la lanza a algún caballero en yendo

After just over a century of constant practice, and not too long after the introduction of lance-rest and tilt, we find another succinct set of rules for the joust embedded in a chronicle written by Pedro Carrillo de Huete, the royal falconer in the court of King John II of Castile. These rules were applied to the jousts of peace at the Valladolid tournament inaugurated on 26 April 1434, as follows:

> Firstly, that any knight who knocks off any piece of another knight's harness may keep it for himself. But if he were besought by the knight to whom it belonged to loan it to him so that he could joust, let this be at the pleasure of the one who knocked it off; but on the condition that when the joust is over it be returned to the one who knocked it off, and that it stand in the dining hall and be sent to any of the ladies who may be dining there.
>
> Item, that any knight who should fall from an encounter not be allowed to win the prize no matter how much he may have done; rather, let him go wherever the one who unhorsed him should command, and let him say whatever he should command him to say; and let him not joust any more that day.
>
> Item, that whoever should strike a horse or saddle likewise not be allowed to win the prize, and let him joust no more that day.
>
> Item, that whoever should be stunned or be relieved of his shield or helm, let him joust no more that day.[7]

Some six decades later these rules would be expanded upon, perfected and iterated anew by Ponç de Menaguerra. The Catalonians always prided themselves on being more civilised than their Castilian neighbours, which perhaps explains why Menaguerra's rules place no emphasis on the kind of public humiliation that underpinned the Valladolid rules. I summa-

---

por la carrera antes de los golpes, que el otro caballero que le alce la lanza y no le dé, ca no sería caballería herir al que no lleva lanza. ❡ Y para juzgar todo esto, decimos que haya allí cuatro fieles: los dos de la una parte, y los otros dos de la otra parte, por que den la mejoría a los caballeros que justaren mejor'. See Cartagena, *Doctrinal de los caballeros*, in *Tratados Militares*, ed. Fallows, p. 322.

[7] 'Primeramente, que qualquier cauallero que a otro lleuare qualquier pieça de su arnés que la tome para sy. Pero sy rrogado fuere del cauallero cuya era, que ge la preste para justar, que ésto en su plazer sea daquell que la lleuare; pero con condiçión que acauada la justa sea tornada a aquell que la lleuó, e esté en la sala, e la envíe a qualquier señora de las que ay cenaren. ❡ Iten, que qualquier cauallero que de enquentro cayere, que no pueda aver presçio por muy mucho que aya fecho, antes vaya a do quiera que el [que] lo derriuó mandare, e diga lo que le mandare dezir; e aquell día no juste más. ❡ Iten, que el que encontrare cauallo o sylla no pueda essomesmo aver presçio, e no juste más esse día. ❡ Iten, que el que fuere atordido o desmarcado de escudo o yelmo, que no juste más esse día' (Carrillo de Huete, *Crónica del halconero de Juan II*, ed. Mata Carriazo, p. 155; see also Barrientos, *Refundición de la crónica del halconero*, ed. Mata Carriazo, p. 151).

rise below the rules of the joust according to Menaguerra. As points of comparison, and in order to elucidate the Principle of Transferability, I also include similar rules that have survived from other European jousting competitions. They are as follows: the *Regolamento delle giostre*, composed in 1465 by the Duke of Milan, Francesco Sforza Visconti; the *Ordinances for Justes of Peace Royal*, composed by John Tiptoft, Earl of Worcester in 1466; and King Henry VIII's *Challenge for the Tournament* of February, 1511. In the summary below I use the following abbreviations: FS = Francesco Sforza; HR = Henry VIII; JT = John Tiptoft.[8]

I. The principal fouls and reasons why jousters may be disqualified from winning the prize.

(1) If the knight is missing any pieces of armour – with the exception of the (left) tasset – when he comes to the lists (ch. 1).

　　Cp. *FS* 56–8: 'Item, the said jousters must put on their helmets or small helmets when requested to do so, and not take them off until they have finished all their matches, and this with the consent of the judges who have been deputised for the said joust.'[9]

(2) If any pieces of armour hang unevenly or are loosely fastened (ch. 2).

(3) Poor positioning of the legs and body in the saddle (ch. 3).

(4) If the horse's rump hits the tilt after entering the lists (ch. 3).

(5) Any type of lance fumble (ch. 4).

(6) Loss of the stirrups, especially when the prize is to be awarded to the most elegant jouster (chs 3 and 4).

---

[8] For Sforza, see Angelucci, *Armilustre e Torneo con Armi da Battaglia tenuti a Venezia addi XXVIII e XXX Maggio MCCCCLVIII*, pp. 32–5 (in Italian), and Rühl, 'Regulations for the Joust in Fifteenth-Century Europe: Francesco Sforza Visconti (1465) and John Tiptoft (1466)', pp. 195–7 (translation into English). For Henry VIII, see Anglo, *The Great Tournament Roll of Westminster*, vol. I, pp. 109–11 (also edited by Clephan, *The Medieval Tournament*, p. 118–19, and Cripps-Day, *The History of the Tournament*, app. VI, pp. xlix–l). For Tiptoft, see Rühl, 'Regulations for the Joust in Fifteenth-Century Europe: Francesco Sforza Visconti (1465) and John Tiptoft (1466)', pp. 200–2 (also edited by Anglo, *The Great Tournament Roll of Westminster*, vol. I, pp. 108–9; Clephan, *The Medieval Tournament*, pp. 46–7; Cripps-Day, *The History of the Tournament*, app. IV, pp. xxvii–xxx; and Nickel, 'The Tournament: An Historical Sketch', pp. 248–9). My thanks to Ms Elena Borgi of the Biblioteca dell'Accademia delle Scienze in Turin for supplying a photocopy of Angelucci's book.

[9] 'Ancora che li dicti giostratori debbano ponersi l'elmo o l'elmetto quando si sara comandato, et non cauarselo fin che non habbia finito de correre tutte le sue botte, et cum licentia deli iudici saranno deputati in dicta giostra' (Angelucci, *Armilustre e Torneo con Armi da Battaglia tenuti a Venezia addi XXVIII e XXX Maggio MCCCCLVIII*, p. 34).

(7) If the knight has been unhorsed, but returns to joust (ch. 26) or if for any other reason he falls from his horse and subsequently returns to joust (ch. 31).

(8) If the knight makes a foul stroke on his opponent's tasset (ch. 30).

(9) If the knight makes a foul stroke on his opponent's saddle-bow (ch. 30).

Cp. *HR* 100; 'Item, who stryketh his ffelowe beneth the waste or in the sadell with full course by wey of foule ronnyng, he shalbe disallowed of ij speres before well broken'; *JT* 42–3: 'First, whoso breaks on the saddle shall be disallowed for a spear breaking.'[10]

(10) If the knight makes a foul stroke on his opponent's bridle hand (ch. 30).

(11) If the knight makes a foul stroke on his opponent's thigh or anywhere below the thigh (ch. 30).

Cp. *HR* 100 (above, no. 9).

(12) If the knight makes a foul stroke on the head or neck of his opponent's horse (ch. 30).

Cp. *HR* 100: 'Item, if it happe any man as god defend to kyll his ffelowes horse by wey of foule ronnyng, he shalbe bounde that soo doth to gyve the hors that he rydeth on to his ffelowe, or the price of the horse soo kylled, at the discretion of the Juges'; *FS* 38–43: 'Item, if a jouster injures a horse, killing it with the head of his lance, or putting out its eye, or maiming it in such a way that it stays maimed, he is obliged to pay for it according to the verdict of the judges delegated to pronounce judgement: and the maimed horse shall stay with him who had maimed it; and if he did not kill or maim it in the way indicated, he is obliged to have it treated all at his own expense, and he may not joust again or obtain the honours';[11] *JT* 22: 'First, who strikes a horse shall have no prize.'[12]

---

[10] Cp. also Quijada de Reayo: 'When you joust, try not to make a foul stroke, which includes striking below the belt of your opponent or hitting the saddle, and striking the tilt is a serious foul, or striking the shaffron of the horse'.

[11] 'Ancora che se alcuno giostratore ferissi cauallo de punta di lanza amazandolo, o cauandoli lo occhio, o guastandolo in modo che rimanessi guasto, sia tenuto pagharlo a lo iudicio delli iudici deputati a buttare la sententia: et lo cauallo guasto resti ad quello che lo hauessi guasto, et non amazandolo, o non guastando como e dicto, sia tenuto a farlo guarire a tutte sue spese, et non possa giostrare piu, ne hauere lo honore' (Angelucci, *Armilustre e Torneo con Armi da Battaglia tenuti a Venezia addi XXVIII e XXX Maggio MCCCCLVIII*, p. 33).

[12] On this rule, see also Anglo, *The Great Tournament Roll of Westminster*, vol. I, p. 44, n. 2.

II. Forgivable mistakes for which jousters are not disqualified from winning the prize.

(1) Missing the pouch when attempting to place the lance in the pouch at the beginning of the course, i.e. before setting out (ch. 4).

(2) Missing the pouch when attempting to place the stub of the lance in the pouch at the end of the course, i.e. after the encounter (ch. 4).

III.A. Sample jousting scenarios mentioned by Menaguerra for determining a win, a loss or a tie.

Each of the scenarios listed below is course-specific, that is to say, the winner or loser in one scenario would not necessarily be the winner and loser in another scenario by performing the same manœuvres.

(1) Knight no. 1 drops his lance on the approach; Knight no. 2 strikes the tilt. Knight no. 2 wins, since he at least hit something (ch. 6).

(2) Knight no. 1 strikes the tilt with the coronel, breaking his lance; Knight no. 2 does not manage to strike at all. Knight no. 2 wins, since he committed no fouls, such as striking the tilt or dropping the lance (ch. 11).

Cp. *HR* 100: 'Item, if any gentilman, chalenger or defender, breke a staffe on the tylt, to be disallowed a staffe'; *JT* 44–6: 'Item, whoso hits the toil [i.e. the tilt] once shall be disallowed for two. Item, whoso hits the toil twice, for the second time shall be abated 3'; *JT* 25–6: 'Item, whoso hits the toil 3 times shall have no prize.'

(3) Knight no. 1 handles his lance poorly, breaking it on the tilt; Knight no. 2 handles his lance well and attaints, but without breaking the lance. Knight no. 2 wins, since he made an attaint (chs. 8 and 29).

(4) Knight no. 1 and Knight no. 2 both shatter their lances upon each other at the same time. The best, most elegant, rider shall be declared the winner (ch. 9).

Cp. *JT* 59–64: 'Item, if there be any man that fortunes in this wise which shall be deemed longest to have bidden in the field helmeted and to have run the fairest course and to have given the greatest strokes and to have helped himself best with his spear, he shall have the prize.'

(5) Knight no. 1 breaks his lance in a full hit; Knight no. 2 attaints without breaking the lance. Knight no. 1 wins (ch. 29).

Cp. *HR* 100: 'Item, who breketh moost speres is worth the pryse'; *JT* 12–13: 'First, whoso breaks most spears as they ought to be broken shall have the prize.'

(6) Knight no. 1 and Knight no. 2 both fall with their horses in the encounter. The quickest to remount wins (ch. 15).

(7) Knight no. 1 handles the lance poorly on the approach, but manages to splinter it in the encounter; Knight no. 2 handles his lance well, but attaints without breaking. Both are tied (ch. 8).

(8) Knight no. 1 strikes the tilt with the coronel and breaks his lance; Knight no. 2 strikes the tilt crosswise, also breaking his lance. Both knights are tied (ch. 11).

(9) Knight no. 1 splinters his lance, but loses a piece of armour or the reins; Knight no. 2 makes an attaint, but without breaking his lance. Both knights are tied (ch. 17).

(10) Knight no. 1, who is wearing a crest, shatters his lance on his opponent; Knight no. 2, who is not wearing a crest, knocks off the crest of Knight no. 1. Both knights are tied (ch. 27). Exception: in limited or team events the full hit that shatters the lance counts more (ch. 27), in which case Knight no. 1 would be declared the winner.

The paradox in this instance is that the crested jouster, in order to appear more elegant, would be offering his non-crested opponent a scoring option that he himself had been denied. According to the Principle of Equality, it would be unfair for the crest hit to tie with the full hit to the body in a team or limited event because the crest-wearer did not have the option of striking at a crest and, in any case, the full hit on the body that shatters the lance is always considered to be the most praiseworthy stroke when jousting (see III. A.5, above). Hitting a crest would not have been easy to do and, as Menaguerra notes, the crest would have to be knocked off in order to count. Though it is

142 Targeting the crest. From Jost Amman's *Kunstbüchlin* (Frankfurt am Main, 1599)

not overtly stated in the text, it must be assumed that the author is
referring to three-dimensional crests in this instance, as opposed
to one-dimensional crests or plumes, which would have been virtually impossible to hit or knock off. Also, the mere act of striking at a
crest without knocking it off would be tantamount to missing one's
opponent.

Early in his jousting career King John II of Castile bedazzled
all who attended the tournament at Valladolid on 24 May 1428 by
knocking off his opponent's crest in a joust. Whether he did so by
design or by accident, this incident is proof enough that it could be
done.[13] Targeting the crest as a means of earning points lasted well into
the sixteenth century, as evinced by Jost Amman's *Kunstbüchlin* (1599),
in which a jouster is shown engaging in this very activity (fig. 142).

III.B. Sample scenarios not mentioned by Menaguerra, but mentioned by
        other authors.

(1) Both Knights strike coronel to coronel.

See *HR* 110: 'Item, who breketh his spere morne to morne to be
allowed iij speres, after the custume of armes'; *JT* 16–17: 'Item, whoso
meets two times coronal to coronal shall have the prize' and *JT* 55–6:
'Item, he that strikes coronal to coronal 2 times shall have the prize
before him that strikes the sight 3 times.'

The problem with the ordinance as stated by Henry VIII is that it
is not clear which of the two knights would receive the three points,
unless they were both supposed to be awarded the same amount of
points. Tiptoft resolves the issue of a tie by requiring that this be done
twice. Menaguerra is more practical than Henry VIII or Tiptoft and
mentions only the most common fouls with the lance. Most jousters
would have known that hitting a target as small as the tip of their
opponent's lance really was only going to happen by accident and not
by design, and this is undoubtedly why Menaguerra does not mention
it. Zapata mentions striking coronel to coronel as a novel curiosity,
akin in rarity to splitting the lance in two lengthwise from tip to grapper.[14] As Buttin has observed, in order to have a chance of making
such a stroke, both jousters would have to lower their lances suddenly

[13] See Carrillo de Huete, *Crónica del halconero de Juan II*, ed. Mata Carriazo, p. 24;
also Barrientos, *Refundición de la crónica del halconero*, ed. Mata Carriazo, p. 62,
where the date is recorded incorrectly as 24 March 1428. The event is given a
fleeting mention, without providing a day or month and without mentioning the
lance-thrust at the crest, by Pérez de Guzmán, *Crónica del serenísimo príncipe Don
Juan, segundo rey deste nombre en Castilla y en León*, ed. Rosell, p. 447ab. On the
political significance of this tournament, see Ruiz, 'Fiestas, Torneos y Símbolos de
realeza en la Castilla del siglo XV. Las fiestas de Valladolid de 1428'.

[14] Zapata, *Miscelánea*, ed. Carrasco González, ch. 250, p. 349.

and simultaneously just before the moment of impact.[15] As we have seen in the previous chapter, the Iberian masters prefer to avoid this manœuvre, recommending instead that the jousters lower the lances little by little as they are riding down the tilt.

A coronel-to-coronel incident described by Gonzalo Fernández de Oviedo calls attention to the problems that could arise from this type of lance-thrust. The incident occurred during a joust royal staged before King Ferdinand V in Valladolid in 1513 between two accomplished champions: Don Pero Vélez de Guevara and Gutierre Quijada. Although official judges had been deputised to preside over the jousts, each champion had brought along his own loyal judges who had been massaged to declare in favour of their champions; their biased opinions, along with the jousters' own egos, complicated the situation even further. According to Fernández de Oviedo:

> Like others I was watching them, and I saw that in one course the tips of the lances locked rochet against rochet, and Don Pero Vélez's lance broke and with that he equalised or had broken as many lances as Gutierre Quixada. But Gutierre Quixada averred that although Don Pero Vélez's lance had broken, Gutierre Quixada rather than Don Pero Vélez broke it, for because his lance was stronger it remained intact and he had broken the other man's lance, and that that lance should not be counted as a lance broken for Don Pero Vélez but as a lost and weak lance, and it should be counted as a lance broken to Gutierre Quixada. The judges of this joust were the Duke of Alba Don Fadrique de Toledo, and Lord Antonio de Fonseca, who were to judge all the jousters including these two knights since they were two of the jousters. But the private and loyal judges working on behalf of Gutierre Quixada and Don Pero Vélez were other men, and they either could not or would not settle the dispute, and they accepted as arbitrator the opinion of the King. And it turned out to be such a subtle point that no resolution could be reached at that time, because the King insisted on giving careful consideration, but there was no lack of opinions about it and there is much to say for and against.[16]

---

[15] Buttin, 'La lance et l'arrêt de cuirasse', p. 137.

[16] 'Yo estaua como otros mirándolos, e vi que en vna carrera las puntas de las lanças se ajustaron el vn rroquete con el otro, e quebró la lança del don Pero Vélez e con aquella enparejaua o tenía tantas lanças quebradas como el Gutierre Quixada. Pero dezía el Gutierre que avnque la lança de don Pero Vélez se avía quebrado, que no la quebró el don Pero Vélez sino el Gutierre Quixada, que por ser más rezia su lança quedó sana e avía rrompido la del otro, e que aquella lança no se le avía de contar al don Pero Vélez por quebrada sino por perdida e flaca, e dársela por quebrada al

In the case cited above, Menaguerra's rule specified in chapter 9 of *Lo Cavaller* (see above, III. A.4) could well have been applied to settle the dispute: in the event of a tie the best, most elegant, rider shall be declared the winner.

(2) The Knight's horse refuses to run.

See *FS* 44–7: 'Item, if any jouster has a horse which refuses to run, so that, in the opinion of the judges deputised to pronounce judgements in the said joust it is manifestly not able to perform, in such a case, too, the said jouster shall be allowed to change horses only once; and this with the leave of the said judges.'[17]

This scenario is only hinted at by Ponç de Menaguerra, when he states in ch. 4 that the blame for losing the lance can on some occasions be imputed to the knight and on others to 'a bad horse or servant'. It was true that even horses ridden by seasoned jousters stalled occasionally. Cp., however, the description of the fourth course in selection 2 of the *Passo Honroso*. In this case Gonzalo de Castañeda does not raise his lance, strikes his opponent and is chastised by the chronicler. He is chastised because his opponent's horse abruptly stopped in the middle of the course, i.e. the horse was to blame and not the rider. The logic in this case brings to mind the rules from the fourteenth-century Order of the Band which differentiate between types of fall that can be blamed on the horse or the rider.

(3) No points are awarded to those who do not run or gallop.

See *FS* 68: 'Item, the hits of anyone who does not run or gallop his horse will not be recorded.'[18]

Gutierre Quixada. Los juezes desta justa eran el Duque de Alua don Fradrique de Toledo e el señor Antonio de Fonseca, para el juyzio de todos los justadores y destos dos caualleros como dos dellos. Pero los juezes secretos e juramentados para entre Gutierre Quixada y don Pero Vélez eran otros, e no supieron o no quisieron determinar la quistión, e tomaron por tercero el parescer del Rrey. E túuose por tan sotil punto que no se supo la determinación por entonces, porquel Rrey quiso mirar muy bien, pero no faltauan muchos paresceres sobre ello e ay bien que dezir a pro e a contra' (Fernández de Oviedo, *Las Memorias de Gonzalo Fernández de Oviedo*, ed. Avalle-Arce, vol. II, p. 610).

[17] 'Ancora che se alcuno giostratore hauessi cauallo, el quale sciuassi lo andare in modo, che manifestamente se iudicassi per li iudici deputati a sentenziare ne la dicta giostra non essere apto ad andarli, anche in questo caso sia licito al dicto giostratore mutare tal cauallo per vna volta sola, et questo cum licentia de li dicti iudici' (Angelucci, *Armilustre e Torneo con Armi da Battaglia tenuti a Venezia addi XXVIII e XXX Maggio MCCCCLVIII*, pp. 33–4).

[18] 'Ancora che non sia scripto la botta ad alcuno se non corre o galoppa il suo cauallo' (Angelucci, *Armilustre e Torneo con Armi da Battaglia tenuti a Venezia addi XXVIII e XXX Maggio MCCCCLVIII*, pp. 34).

As stated below, V.3., and as indicated by the very title of Mena-guerra's treatise, his principal concern is the knight rather than the horse. Also, he is writing for the seasoned jouster as opposed to the absolute beginner, for the valorous knight as opposed to the poltroon, which perhaps explains why he does not mention obvious details such as this scenario and the scenario described above, III. B.2.

(4) Striking one's opponent in the back is a foul.

JT 23–34: 'Item, who strikes a man his back turned shall have no prize.'

In a joust between two contestants, striking a man in the back would require turning around and thrusting at him after the encounter had taken place. Since such a manœuvre would be not so much a foul as a dirty trick, this is probably why Menaguerra does not mention it. The so-called 'thrust in pursuit' was, however, a legitimate stratagem in mêlée tournaments, as mentioned by Wolfram von Eschenbach in *Parzival*,[19] and may explain the evolution of protective rondels at the back of armets. In Tiptoft's case, then, this rule may be a reminder to the combatants that they are involved in a joust as opposed to a mêlée tournament.

IV. Menaguerra's rules for quantification of performance in the joust.

(1) Knight no. 1 drops the lance when picking it up (ch. 5) = the equivalent of 1 lance broken for Knight no. 2.

(2) Knight no. 1 loses one or both stirrups (ch. 5) = the equivalent of 1 lance broken for Knight no. 2.

(3) Knight no. 1 contracts his legs (ch. 5) = the equivalent of 1 lance broken for Knight no. 2.

(4) Knight no. 1 loses the reins (ch. 17) or a piece of armour, e.g. a gauntlet (ch. 18), a vambrace (ch. 19) or a guard of the vambrace (ch. 19) = the equivalent of 1 lance broken for Knight no. 2 (but Knight no. 2 does not get to keep the lost piece or humiliate Knight no. 1 as in the Valladolid rules of 1434).

(5) Knight no. 1 loses a piece of armour, such as a vambrace, that cannot be refitted without the aid of a hammer (ch. 19) = the equivalent of 4 lances broken for Knight no. 2.

(6) Knight no. 1 suffers irreparable damage to, or loss of, his shield (ch. 20) = the equivalent of 4 lances broken for Knight no. 2 (3 for the loss of the shield + 1 for the encounter itself = 4).

Cp. *FS* 61–3: 'Item, if in the said joust any jouster's lance-rest or shield, or any other part of his armament should be smashed, he can

---

[19] See above, chapter 4, n. 1. See also Crouch, *Tournament*, pp. 149–53.

replace it, provided he does not take off his helmet or small helmet, whichever he is wearing.'[20]

(7) Knight no. 1 gets his helm knocked off (ch. 21) = the equivalent of 10 lances broken for Knight no. 2.

Cp. *FS* 83–5: 'Item, if any jouster strikes his opponent on the head, and touches the helmet or small helmet with the point of his lance, and does not break his lance, this shall be scored as a lance very well broken';[21] *FS* 86–7: 'Item, if a jouster strikes his opponent on the head, and breaks his lance, this shall be scored as two best hits';[22] *JT* 14–15: 'Item, he that or whoso hits three times in the sight of the helmet shall have the prize.'

(8) Knight no. 1 sustains a damaging blow to his helm that causes blunt trauma (ch. 21) = the equivalent of 10 lances broken for Knight no. 2.

Again, in the case of this and the two previous rules, Menaguerra's system is much more nuanced than the Valladolid rules of 1434, which call for the immediate disqualification of the victim and thereby render moot the issue of points.

(9) Knight no. 1 gets his helm knocked off and sustains a bloody injury to his nose, mouth or teeth (ch. 21) = the equivalent of 20 lances broken for Knight no. 2.

(10) Knight no. 1 is unseated so that he either hangs from the stirrups or falls out of the saddle (ch. 26) = the equivalent of 20 lances broken for Knight no. 2.

Cp. *FS* 90–2: 'Item, if any jouster strikes his opponent in such a way that he knocks him out of his saddle, and he falls to the ground, or if he knocks both the horse and his opponent to the ground, this shall be scored as four hits';[23] *HR* 100: 'Item, who striketh doun hors and man is better worth the prise'; *HR* 100: 'Item, who striketh his

---

[20] 'Ancora che rompendosi ad alcuno giostratore in la dicta giostra la resta, lo scudo, o altro pezo d'arme se lo possa mutare non cauandosi l'elmo, o l'elmetto che l'abbia' (Angelucci, *Armilustre e Torneo con Armi da Battaglia tenuti a Venezia addi XXVIII e XXX Maggio MCCCCLVIII*, p. 34).

[21] 'Ancora se alcuno giostratore segnara al compagno in la testa, et che'l tocchi con la punta de la lantia nelelmo siue elmetto, et che'l non rompa la lancia sia posto per lancia rotta bonissima' (Angelucci, *Armilustre e Torneo con Armi da Battaglia tenuti a Venezia addi XXVIII e XXX Maggio MCCCCLVIII*, p. 35).

[22] 'Ancora se alcuno giostratore segnara il compagno in la testa, et che'l rompa la lancia sia posto per botte due bonissime' (Angelucci, *Armilustre e Torneo con Armi da Battaglia tenuti a Venezia addi XXVIII e XXX Maggio MCCCCLVIII*, p. 35).

[23] 'Ancora se alcuno giostratore dara al compagno per modo che lo butti di fuori dela sella, et che caschi per terra, vel che'l buttassi il cauallo et lo compagno per terra, sia posto per botte quattro' (Angelucci, *Armilustre e Torneo con Armi da Battaglia tenuti a Venezia addi XXVIII e XXX Maggio MCCCCLVIII*, p. 35).

ffelowe clene oute of the sadell is best worth the pryse'; *JT* 18–19: 'Item, whoso bears a man down with the stroke of spear shall have the prize'; *JT* 50–4: 'First, whoso bears a man down out of the saddle or puts him to the earth, horse and man, shall have the prize before him that strikes coronal to coronal 2 times.'[24]

(11) Knight no. 1 gets his helm knocked off and sustains an injury to his head or forehead with the result that he is incapacitated (ch. 21) = more points for Knight no. 2 than the total amount of lances taken into account for the prize.

Cp. *JT* 57–8: 'Item, he that strikes the sight 3 times shall have the prize before him that breaks most staves or spears.'

(12) Knight no. 1 is incapacitated by a blow so as he cannot joust any more (ch. 13) = more points for Knight no. 2 than the total amount of lances taken into account for the prize.

Cp. *FS* 66–7: 'Let no-one dare to take it upon himself to assist any jouster who has been injured, whether by a collision or by a lance-thrust, on pain of two strokes of the lash (Let them get up, since everyone is allowed to strike as many people as they want and those who fall can help themselves get up)';[25] *FS* 88–9: 'Item, if any jouster wounds his opponent by the thrusts of his lance in such a way that he can no longer continue in the joust, this shall be scored as three hits';[26] *JT* 35–9: 'Item, whoso breaks a spear so as he strikes him down, or puts him out of his saddle, or dismays him in such a wise as he may not run the next course after, or breaks his spear coronal to coronal shall be allowed 3 spears broken.'

V. Further quantification issues according to Menaguerra.

(1) In mock jousts of war any knight who is knocked unconscious or thrown to the ground with his horse, causing loss of blood or damage to a limb, shall be 'counted as dead' (chs. 13, 24 and 25).

---

[24] Cp. the nuance about falling off or with the horse in the jousting rules of the Order of the Band mentioned above.

[25] 'Ancora che niuno ardisca, ne presuma, se alcuno giostratore, per urto o per colpo di lanza fussi piegato, adiutarlo, sotto pena de duy tratti di corda' (Angelucci, *Armilustre e Torneo con Armi da Battaglia tenuti a Venezia addi XXVIII e XXX Maggio MCCCCLVIII*, p. 34). As noted by Angelucci, the wording in parenthesis appears in the original MS as a marginal note, as follows: 'Leuansi, perchè ciascuno può menare quante persone uuole et aiutasi chi cade'. Since this marginal note is not translated by Rühl the translation in this instance is my own.

[26] 'Ancora se alcuno giostratore facesse male al compagno per la botta della sua lancia per modo che non possesse durare piu a la giostra, sia posto per botte tre' (Angelucci, *Armilustre e Torneo con Armi da Battaglia tenuti a Venezia addi XXVIII e XXX Maggio MCCCCLVIII*, p. 35).

(2) In the case of a knight who breaks his opponent's arm, leg, thigh bone or collar bone, 'points shall be awarded accordingly' (ch. 13). See also above, IV.12.

(3) Deliberately not hitting an opponent (e.g. out of courtesy) who drops his lance on the approach is not recommended due to the potential loss of points (ch. 10).

Menaguerra here seems to be picking up where the *Libro de la Orden de la Banda* left off, that is to say that if his opponent drops his lance, the Knight must determine – in what would have to be a split second – if the lance was dropped because of some misfortune beyond his opponent's control, such as a stumbling horse, or if it was dropped through his own negligence, in which case it is, according to Menaguerra, legitimate to strike. That is to say, elegance in style must always be aggressive and never passive. Cp. above, III. B.2., in cases where the horse is to blame. In contradistinction to Menaguerra, cp. also *HR* 100: 'Item, who striketh his ffelowe vncharged and disgarnysshed of his spere shalbe disallowed at the discretion of the Juges.'[27]

The nuances of this particular issue, where the blame for lance fumbles can be imputed variously to horses, servants and riders, implicitly recognises just how difficult it was to explain mishaps and fouls. These ambiguities also explain why the judges often spent a considerable amount of time discussing each course.

(4) When both knights wear crests, the knight who knocks off his opponent's crest shall win (ch. 27).

(5) Lacerating the hand with the grapper or the lance is of no account, since such a wound is not serious enough to prevent the knight from continuing to joust (ch. 18).

(6) An attaint or full hit that merely causes the knight to lean back in the saddle is of no account, since leaning back in the saddle is a natural part of jousting (ch. 29).

(7) An attaint or full hit that knocks the knight off balance, but without knocking him unconscious, shall be taken into account only if both jousters are tied up to this point (ch. 22).

---

[27] The *Libro de la Orden de la Banda* concurs with Henry VIII on this issue, though knights of the Order are also punished for their infractions by being forced into the unenviable position of jousting with no lance against an opponent who does wield a lance. See Cartagena, *Doctrinal de los caballeros*, in *Tratados Militares*, ed. Fallows, statutes 25, translated above (raising the lance out of courtesy), and 18 and 22 (jousting with no lance as punishment), pp. 322, 319 and 320, respectively.

(8) Striking high or low is of no account unless a pact is made before-hand (ch. 28). If a pact is made to give the advantage to the knight who strikes higher, 'high' is defined as striking on or above the flaon bolt and the vamplate; everything else is low (ch. 28).

This is a common rule, though most other ordinances use either the shield itself or the charnel as the point of reference. Ponç de Mena-guerra is unusual in that he uses the flaon as his reference point. The flaon was affixed next to the charnel, so Menaguerra's choice in fact makes good sense because the charnel would not have been as easily visible as the flanged head of the flaon bolt once the shield was secured in place.

Cp. *HR*: 'Item, who breketh his spere aboue the Charnell to be allowed ij speres well broken, after the olde custume of armes'; *FS* 72–4: 'Item, every jouster must have his shield marked and a line drawn across it one third of the way from the bottom, and in this third part of the shield there shall not be recorded a single hit';[28] *FS* 78–80: 'Item, if any jouster strikes his opponent's shield between the line marking the bottom third and the mid-point between that line and the top edge of the shield, and if he breaks his lance, this shall be scored as a lance well broken';[29] *JT* 33–4: 'Item, whoso breaks a spear from the charnel upward shall be allowed for 2.'

(9) The length or amount of lance-shaft broken is of no account, since the way in which the lance breaks depends on the stave as opposed to the jouster's own skill (ch. 23).

Cp. *JT* 47–9: 'Item, whoso breaks a spear within a foot of the coronal shall be judged as no spear broken, but a fair attaint.'

(10) Leaving shards of lance in the helm, the shield or the armour is of no account (ch. 23).

(11) Striking sparks upon dealing a blow is of no account (ch. 23).

(12) When royals joust against royals these jousts shall be judged according to the rules (ch. 14).

(13) When royals joust against non-royals, the rules are irrelevant, for the royals always win (ch. 14).

---

[28] 'Ancora che ciascuno giostratore facci segnare et fare una lista al trauerso del scudo al terzo del scudo de sotto, et dal dicto terzo de scudo in giu non sia scripta botta alcuna' (Angelucci, *Armilustre e Torneo con Armi da Battaglia tenuti a Venezia addi XXVIII e XXX Maggio MCCCCLVIII*, p. 34).

[29] 'Ancora se alcuno giostratore segnassi al compagno di sopra dal segno del scudo insino al mezo tra esso segno, et la cinta de lo scudo, et che'l rompa la lancia, sia posto per lancia rotta bona' (Angelucci, *Armilustre e Torneo con Armi da Battaglia tenuti a Venezia addi XXVIII e XXX Maggio MCCCCLVIII*, p. 35).

VI. Foreign peculiarities as noted by Menaguerra.

(1) In Germany and Hungary: Knight no. 1 falls as a result of the impact from the blow he delivers; Knight no. 2 misses, but remains in the saddle from the blow received. Knight no. 2 wins because he demonstrates that he is able to withstand the force of the blow (ch. 16).

(2) In Lombardy: Falling off the horse for whatever reason = disqualification from winning the jewel (ch. 31).

Cp. *FS* 35–7: 'Item, if one of the jousters falls, he may not joust again, except if he falls through a collision, or if his horse is injured or maimed by an opponent, or if he falls by himself without being struck, in such cases he may continue jousting, and change horses.'[30]

O N E thing that the various rules for quantification of performance have in common is the emphasis they place on the physicality of jousting. Given this physicality, we are left wondering what recourse the wounded jousters had. Suero de Quiñones affords a tantalising glimpse when he grants the following assurance in Article 12 of his passage of arms: 'be certain that to all those who should incur wounds in said passage, I shall give them everything that they shall need, and as plenteously as if it were for my own person, and for as much time as shall be necessary, and for longer if they wish to have more time'. In doing so, he is, he says, taking into account 'the dangers of arms with which we are all familiar'. Leaving aside fatalities caused by freak accidents, with what injuries would jousters have been familiar? References to non-fatal injuries sustained in the jousts of the Middle Ages and the Renaissance as well as to the treatment of those injuries are much rarer than references to the wounds incurred in war.[31] For modern scholars this can be quite frustrating, though the reasons for the paucity of descriptions should not come as a surprise. Readers of

---

[30] 'Ancora che se alcuno de detti giostratori cascasse non possa giostrare piu, excepto se cascasse per urto, o per essere il cauallo ferito o guasto dal compagno, o che'l cascassi da per si stesso sanza essere urtato che in questi casi possino giostrare, et mutare cavallo' (Angelucci, *Armilustre e Torneo con Armi da Battaglia tenuti a Venezia addi XXVIII e XXX Maggio MCCCCLVIII*, p. 33).

[31] Michael Prestwich once observed that 'there is surprisingly little information on the wounds incurred in battle'. See Prestwich, *Armies and Warfare in the Middle Ages: The English Experience*, p. 332. There are now some informative studies on the subject. On the types of wound incurred in battle, see especially Boardman's sensitive discussion of the grave associated with the battle of Towton (29 March 1461) in *The Medieval Soldier in the Wars of the Roses*, pp. 181–94; also Mitchell, *Medicine in the Crusades*, pp. 137–83. On military surgery, see also: Edgington, 'Medical Knowledge in the Crusading Armies: the Evidence of Albert of Aachen and Others'; Fallows, 'Aproximaciones a la medicina militar en la Edad Media'; Paterson, 'Military Surgery: Knights, Sergeants and Raimon of Avignon's Version of the *Chirurgia* of Roger of Salerno (1180–1209)'; and Siraisi, *Medieval and Early Renaissance Medicine: An Introduction to Knowledge and Practice*, pp. 181–6.

medieval chronicles were probably no more interested in such matters than readers of modern newspapers. Like medieval chroniclers, modern sports commentators, for example, are simply not expected to describe in minute detail the techniques of medicine and surgery used by the sports doctors. The best we can do is to read the surgical literature of the day and hope that the practitioners in the field were also following the literature. Since it was a common belief in the Middle Ages that 'a practical physician is better than one crammed with book-learning',[32] that is to say, that medicine was above all experiential, what is perhaps surprising is the lack of descriptions of innovations applied in the heat of the tournament and the relative frequency of descriptions that do in fact follow the procedures outlined in contemporary medical manuals.

Cleaning the wound and extracting foreign objects is the first in a list of recommendations compiled by doctor Guido Lanfranco of Milan in his surgical treatise entitled *Chirurgia Magna*. This treatise, composed in Latin in 1296, was translated into Castilian around 1481 with the title *Compendio de cirugía* (Compendium of Surgery).[33] The first ten chapters are dedicated to the treatment of wounds sustained in battle, some of which would not have been dissimilar to those sustained at tournaments. For bruises and flesh wounds the author recommends poultices consisting of one egg yolk, two parts rosewater and a half measure of vinegar, followed by much rest. Similar advice is repeated in other medical treatises. The influential *Fasciculus Medicinae*, for example, by the Austrian doctor Johann von Kirchheim, also known as Johannes de Ketham, was published in Venice in 1491. A Castilian version entitled *Compendio de la humana salud* (Compendium of Human Health) was published in 1496. Ketham, like Lanfranco, insists that wounds be cleaned with linen cloths soaked in a variety of curative unguents.[34] Such remedies were standard practice at tournaments. At a tournament held in Nancy in 1445, for example, the French knight Philippe de Lenoncourt was struck in the visor during a joust and knocked

[32] 'es más cierto médico el esperimentado que el letrado' (Rojas, *Comedia o Tragicomedia de Calisto y Melibea*, ed. Russell, p. 329). For the translation, see Rojas, *The Celestina*, trans. Simpson, p. 60.

[33] Two Castilian translations of *Chirurgia Magna* have survived, both of which are currently in the Biblioteca Nacional, Madrid: MSS 2147 and 2165. Both codices have been edited. See Ardemagni, ed., *Text and Concordance of Biblioteca Nacional MS 2147: 'Compendio de cirugia' by Guido Lanfranc of Milan*, and Ardemagni and Wasick, eds., *Text and Concordance of Biblioteca Nacional MS 2165: 'Arte complida de cirugia'*. On the career of Lanfranco, see Gordon, *Medieval and Renaissance Medicine*, pp. 350 and 437–51, and Siraisi, *Medieval and Early Renaissance Medicine: An Introduction to Knowledge and Practice*, pp. 166–72. I cite directly from Biblioteca Nacional MS 2147 in this chapter. This MS was copied by Alonso Fernández de Guadalupe in 1481.

[34] Ketham, *Compendio de la humana salud*, ed. Herrera, p. 164.

senseless by his opponent, Gaston de Foix. In one of the most incredible jousting accidents ever recorded, Gaston's lance pierced Philippe's helm, but missed his head. The force of the blow was enough to lift Philippe out of the saddle and leave him dangling over the crupper on the end of his opponent's lance for several minutes until his aiders were able to extricate him from this predicament. Although paralysed by shock, surprisingly, he sustained only minor cuts and bruises in the accident. Guillaume Leseur, one of the chroniclers of this event, remarks that Philippe de Lenoncourt was carried from the field to his pavilion where, after being treated with a mix of vinegar and rosewater, the patient spent the rest of the afternoon in bed.[35] The fact that he was apparently up and around in the early evening would indicate that Philippe had miraculously not suffered a serious stretch to the neck. Similarly, in a tournament at Ávila in 1423, Ruy Díaz de Mendoza dealt his opponent, Fernando de Castro, such a heavy blow to the shield that Fernando was knocked out of the saddle and lay unconscious for almost three hours. Their joust was temporarily postponed while the young knight spent three days in his quarters recovering from his concussion.[36] According to Menaguerra's scoring system Ruy Díaz de Mendoza would have won more points than the total amount of lances taken into account for the prize for knocking his opponent unconscious, plus twenty points for unhorsing him and another 4 for causing irreparable damage to his shield.

In the premodern era it was believed that the complexion played a role in the cure of sicknesses, infections and wounds. This belief can be traced to theories postulated by the Greek doctor Galen (d. c. 210), whose writings were widely diffused in the Middle Ages. The complexion was in turn believed to consist of four humours: fire corresponded to the choleric temperament; water to the phlegmatic temperament; air to the sanguine temperament; and earth to the melancholic temperament. That is to say, the complexion was hot, dry, cold or moist.[37] As can be seen from the accidents described above, surgeons at tournaments stressed the importance of rest and repose in pavilions not only so that they could observe the patient, but also so that they could modify the environment (the temperature, for example) with a view to controlling the humours.

---

[35] See Leseur, *Histoire de Gaston IV, comte de Foix*, ed. Courteault, vol. I, pp. 159–60. This incident is also discussed by Anglo, 'How to Win at Tournaments: The Technique of Chivalric Combat', pp. 260–1.

[36] Pérez de Guzmán, *Crónica del serenísimo príncipe Don Juan, segundo rey deste nombre en Castilla y en León*, ed. Rosell, p. 424a.

[37] For a comprehensive fifteenth-century Castilian discussion of the complexions and humours, see Martínez de Toledo, *Arcipreste de Talavera o Corbacho*, ed. González Muela, pp. 180–279; also available in English: Martínez de Toledo, *Little Sermons on Sin: The Archpriest of Talavera*, trans. Simpson, pp. 167–97.

The chances of recovering from wounds incurred in the lists were higher than the chances of recovery on the battlefield, for the fighting was nowhere near as brutal, muddy and bloody as the fighting in pitched battle, and there was less opportunity for wound contamination. As we have seen, the purpose of the rules that governed sport in the lists was ostensibly to protect the combatants. Also, at a tournament the surgeons themselves would not be under fire, and events such as jousts could be halted temporarily while injured participants were examined, usually *in situ*, then carried from the field pending further examination and professional care in the comfort of their own quarters. This was the case, for example, with Diego de Mansilla, who sustained a horrific injury at the Pass of Honour of Suero de Quiñones in a joust with Lope de Aller. Both are described as wearing white armour, indicating their low level of skill. The accident is so gruesome that the chronicler slips in a rare simile to emphasise the extent of the victim's blood loss:

> In the very first course Lope de Aller struck Diego de Mansilla on the rondel, and glanced off it, and then hit him in the right arm, beneath the vambrace around the biceps, near the armpit, where no armour could be worn, and he pierced through it to the other side, in such a way that he inflicted a gaping wound on him, from which a lot of blood flowed. And he broke his spear upon him in three pieces, from which encounter Diego de Mansilla suffered a very serious reversal of fortune. And he bore a piece of the spear with the spearhead in his arm until he was not quite three paces from the stand where the judges were, at which point he could grasp it no more, and there they removed the spearhead and broken spear from his arm. And upon removing it, a great gush of blood spurted out of his arm, as wine flows from the cask when the spigot is turned, from which the knight Diego de Mansilla fainted. ... Then all the surgeons arrived there, at the command of the captain, to take his blood and cure the knight Diego de Mansilla, whose colour had greatly changed.[38]

Even though the blood-letting administered by the surgeons in this case would have weakened the patient's condition, there can be little doubt that Diego de Mansilla survived, because not just one, but a whole team of surgeon-spectators was paying close attention to the chromatic spectacle, with the result that these surgeons were able to tend to his wounds immediately after the accident. Although the description of Mansilla's injury mentions spurting blood, it is not obvious whether any arteries or critical nerves in the armpit area were severed in this case. What is clear is that, following the recommendations that are proposed in the medical treatises of the epoch, the splinters of lance were extracted from the wound.

---

[38] See below, Part II, *Passo Honroso* Selection 8, course 1.

The subject pronoun 'they' in the sentence 'they removed the spearhead and broken spear from his arm' possibly refers to Mansilla's aiders, who would have arrived at the scene before the surgeons. The spearhead was apparently extracted by the aiders without severing the patient's arteries, thereby staving off infection and avoiding fatal haemorrhage. For this type of injury Lanfranco of Milan would prescribe a restrictive poultice of egg white and powdered lime to staunch the flow of blood. The wound would subsequently be cauterised by applying heat and then stitched. Lanfranco stresses above all that no hair or oil should enter the wound if infection is to be avoided.[39] The fact that teams of surgeons were regularly deployed at tournaments suggests that resorting to a variety of professional opinions on potential cures and remedies mattered as much in the medieval period as it does in the modern era. Medieval medical treatises also often stress the importance of consulting with others and seeking varied opinions when it comes to tending wounds, curing illnesses and building up the diagnostic armoury.

In all cases, no matter what the wound, phlebotomies were administered as a matter of routine.[40] According to Lanfranco of Milan, bloodlettings were to be administered by strong young men with a steady hand and a keen eye that would enable them to distinguish between veins, arteries and nerves. They were administered initially in order to diagnose and determine the patient's complexion. Samples, usually taken from the basilic vein above the elbow, could be taken as the blood flowed, as it was clotting or after it was fully caked. Haematoscopy was then practised with the samples taken. Blood samples could be analysed for three main reasons: 'To study the patient's condition, to preserve a sample of the illness, and to cure the illness once it has been diagnosed.'[41] That is to say, the analysis of blood in the Middle Ages was a clinical analysis based on criteria such as the colour of the blood itself and the volume drawn from the vein. Without the aid of a microscope it was not possible to make any sort of qualitative analysis. And yet, despite the lack of twenty-first-century equipment, the teams of doctors who attended to the broken jousters had a reasonably high success rate. These men were prime examples of scientists who applied their collective intellect to what their eyes would allow them to see and perforce developed what Nobel-

---

[39] Lanfranco of Milan, *Compendio de cirugía*, Madrid, Biblioteca Nacional, MS 2147, fol. 11r.

[40] See Gil-Sotres, 'Derivation and revulsion: the theory and practice of medieval phlebotomy'.

[41] 'Para observar la sanidat, e para preservaçión de enfermedat conseguida, e por quitar la enfermedat ya complida' (Lanfranco of Milan, *Compendio de cirugía*, Madrid, Biblioteca Nacional, MS 2147, fol. 109r).

Prize winning geneticist Barbara McClintock would call 'a feeling for the organism'.[42]

As is abundantly clear from Menaguerra's treatise, striking at the head was a key way of winning large amounts of points at the joust, and it is in this vicinity that fatal wounds sometimes occurred. In the case of injuries to the cranium and the brain, the best advice offered by renowned thirteenth-century surgeon Theodoric of Lucca is that 'our hope must be placed in Him who does not desert those who have hope'.[43] What is even more disconcerting is that as late as 1689 the English surgeon Hugh Ryder would alert his readers to beware of 'some Knavish and Covetous Surgeons, who dishonestly extract from their unwary Patient a quantity of Gold or Silver, pretending therewith to make a Plate to supply the Defect of the Skull in that part'.[44] The honest doctor Lanfranco of Milan prescribes reinvigorating sage-based poultices and potions for serious head trauma, on the understanding that trepanation would invariably prove fatal. Ketham does the same and he cautions that it generally requires a miracle for serious head wounds to heal.[45] I know of only one documented example of a victim who survived a serious wound to the cranium in early modern Europe, thanks to the intervention of a team of expert doctors who were paid to devote their complete and undivided attention to the patient in question. The case is that of Prince Carlos, eldest son of King Philip II of Spain, who in 1562 cracked open his skull after falling down a flight of stairs. To be sure, the prince survived, but he spent the rest of his short life suffering from chronic migraines. He died in 1568 at twenty-two years of age.[46]

Fortunately in jousting, percussion to the head was always tempered by the protective helmet and, unless the victim was unlucky enough to be struck directly through the visor, the types of injury sustained in this area ranged from loosened teeth and bloodied noses to varying degrees of concussion. In the *Passo Honroso* the chronicler records Diego de Bazán's own description of his symptoms in the wake of a powerful blow to the head as follows: 'As he began to ride out, with his spear in the rest, he was already feeling drowsy in the head before they reached the point of the encounters, so much so that he could not see a thing and he felt as

---

[42] See Keller, *A Feeling for the Organism: The Life and Work of Barbara McClintock*, esp. pp. 197–207.

[43] Theodoric of Lucca, *The Surgery of Theodoric ca. A.D. 1267*, trans. Campbell and Colton, vol. I, p. 110.

[44] Ryder, *Practical Chirurgery*, p. 8.

[45] Ketham, *Compendio de la humana salud*, ed. Herrera, p. 176.

[46] This case has been studied by Villalon, 'Putting Don Carlos Together Again: Treatment of a Head Injury in Sixteenth-Century Spain'.

though flames of fire were shooting out of his eyes.'[47] Bazán's description is remarkably consistent with that of Pero Niño when he too was struck on the head during a duel with Gómez Domao in 1397, as follows: 'At length they came to grips one with the other and gave each other such sword blows upon the head, that Pero Niño averred that sparks flew from his eyes.'[48] In these two cases the flames of fire or sparks suggest what in current medical terminology is called visual scotoma. The headache, drowsiness (torpor) and visual scotoma all fit with a closed head injury or concussion, which in a joust of peace would add up to many points for the victim's opponent.

On a slightly more cryptic note, another jouster at the Pass of Honour of Suero de Quiñones is described as follows after having suffered a powerful blow to the head in a previous course: 'And when Pedro de Silva was at the head of the lists, he sent for another horse. And while they went for it, he took his helmet off his head and tended to himself. And when they brought him the horse, he mounted it and put the helmet back on.'[49] It would appear from this description that whatever the precise symptoms, this jouster was still reeling from the blow he had sustained earlier on and was slightly concussed. Sending for another horse would have enabled him to stall for time and have a few moments to gather his bearings, without losing face. When the chronicler states that he 'tended to himself' it is not too difficult to imagine Pedro de Silva splashing some restorative rose-water in his face with his back turned to his opponent so as not to spoil the final anagnorisis.

Johannes de Ketham states that in the case of a patient who has suffered a head wound: 'You must ensure, with extreme care, that he does not drink strong wine, or eat meat that is not well done, or come close to a woman, or if possible even see one; moreover, let him not talk a lot lest he lose his reason.'[50] Mistrust of women is due to the perennial fear of luxury, the perils of lovesickness and the effects of sexual excitation, all of which had long since been associated with the tournament because of the presence of female spectators.[51] On the other hand the question of strong wine is one of the issues addressed by Gutierre Díaz de Games in *El Victorial*, as

---

[47] See below, Part II, *Passo Honroso* Selection 31, course 1.

[48] 'E una vez se juntó tanto con él Pero Niño, e él con él, que se vinieron a dar tan fuertes golpes de las espadas por ençima de las cabeças, a que dixo Pero Niño que de aquel golpe le fizo saltar las çentellas de los ojos'. See Díaz de Games, *El victorial*, ed. Beltrán Llavador, pp. 349–50. For the translation, see *The Unconquered Knight*, trans. Evans, p. 36.

[49] See below, Part II, *Passo Honroso* Selection 30, course 9.

[50] 'Hay que procurar, con extremo cuidado, que no beba vino fuerte, ni coma carne que no esté muy bien cocida, ni se acerque a mujer, e incluso, si fuera posible, ni la vea; además, que no hable mucho porque no aparte de sí la razón' (Ketham, *Compendio de la humana salud*, ed. Herrera, p. 166).

[51] See Barber, *The Knight and Chivalry*, p. 191.

follows: 'Inebriation is the mother of all calumny, it seizes the head, decays the brain, storms the tongue, plagues the body, violates chastity, sullies fame, corrupts the virtues of the soul.'[52] Díaz de Games even attributes the root of all sin not to pride but to intemperance. According to medieval logic, as much the female sex as alcohol could have an adverse affect on the complexions and delay or otherwise have a detrimental impact on the recovery process. On a purely practical note, without thinking of wounds, but given the expense of bespoke armour, it will be recalled from chapter 1 that Luis Zapata avoided wine because it is fattening.[53]

A summary of the wounds sustained during the tournaments at Binche in 1549 is helpfully provided by eyewitness chronicler Juan Cristóbal Calvete de Estrella. With reference to the jousts, no-one was killed and the injuries constitute a typical overview of what could happen at a major international competition:

> Don Juan Manrique de Lara was struck such a blow that his horse subsequently fell down dead, and Jacobo de Herbaix (= Jacques de Marnix) was struck so intensely that his left arm was broken by the blow, and no less happened in another encounter to François de Montmorency, who was wounded through the thigh by a fragment from a lance. Besides them, many sustained injuries to the hands, and no wonder, because the lances were very thick, the square very small and narrow, and there could not have been one more disaster had not the heavens made them scatter with a downpour that happened so suddenly that it was highly amusing to see those who were on the roofs, in the stands and behind the barriers run for shelter.[54]

This account was subsequently plagiarised by a variety of contemporary and successive chroniclers. One such example highlights the difficulties that are often involved in deciphering the chronicles. In this example

---

[52] 'Enbriaguez es madre de toda caloña, travaçión de la cabeça, menguamiento del seso, tenpestad de la lengua, pestilençia del cuerpo, quebrantamiento de la castidad, fealdad de la fama, corronpimiento de las virtudes del alma' (Díaz de Games, *El victorial*, ed. Beltrán Llavador, p. 599).

[53] Zapata, *Miscelánea*, ed. Carrasco González, ch. 47, p. 59.

[54] 'A don Juan Manrique de Lara se dio tal encuentro que el cavallo cayó luego muerto, y Jacobo de Herbaix fue encontrado tan fuertemente que del encuentro le rompieron el braço yzquierdo, y no menos se hizo de otro encuentro a Francisco de Montmoransi que fue herido por un troço de lança por el muslo. Uvo allende d'éstos muchos heridos en las manos, y no era maravilla, porque las lanças eran muy gruessas, la plaça muy pequeña y angosta, y no pudiera dexar de aver algún desastre si el cielo no los despartiera con una agua que hizo tan súbita, que era gran passatiempo ver recogerse los que estavan en los tejados, tablados y tras las ballas' (Calvete de Estrella, *El felicíssimo viaje del muy alto y muy poderoso Príncipe don Phelippe*, ed. Cuenca, pp. 351–2).

virtually everything that happened is distorted. The joust is turned into a tourney; all the details of the injuries sustained by the majority of the jousters are suppressed, whilst those sustained by the minority are sensationalised. One jouster's name, Jacques de Marnix, is further butchered to the extent that it is virtually unrecognisable, and François, Duke of Montmorency (1530–79), is stripped of his identity so that the chronicler can grossly exaggerate his fate:

> Four calamities happened at that tourney: the first was that it rained, which was odd; the second, that Don Juan Manrique de Lara's horse was struck down dead by a blow; the third, that Monsieur de Arbes, a gentleman of His Majesty's royal chamber and Chief Justice of Antwerp, got his arm broken; the fourth, that a Burgundian knight was dealt a blow to the thigh which was pierced by a splinter from the lance, from which he died.[55]

An important surgical issue not readily apparent from the tournaments at Binche, but described in Rodríguez de Lena's detailed account of the jousting at the Pass of Honour of Suero de Quiñones, is that the same blow that caused some sort of head trauma to an opponent would often also cause trauma to the hand of the jouster who delivered the blow. In fact dislocated hands, or lacerated hands as Menaguerra calls them, were without doubt the most common jousting injuries, though they seldom make an appearance in the chronicles due to the fact that hand injuries are nowhere near as sensational or spectacular as the much less common but much more frequently documented lethal blow through the visor. So, for example, in the joust between Diego de Sanromán and Gómez de Villacorta the following accidents occur simultaneously:

> In the ninth course Diego de Sanromán struck Gómez de Villacorta on the bevor, and he dealt him such a mighty blow that he stunned him, and he made him suffer a serious reversal of fortune. And he broke his spear upon him, and the spearhead and a piece of the broken spear flew very high over the lists. And Gómez de Villacorta struck Diego de Sanromán on the reinforcing breastplate, without breaking the spear, and he dislocated his right hand.[56]

---

[55] 'Acontecieron en aqueste torneo cuatro desgracias: la primera fue que llovió, cosa extraña; la segunda, que de un encuentro dieron con el caballo de D. Juan Manrique de Lara en el suelo muerto; la tercera, que a monsieur de Arbes, gentilhombre de la cámara de Su Majestad y Justicia mayor de la villa de Envers, le rompieron un brazo; la cuarta, que a un caballero borgoñón le dieron un encuentro en el muslo que se le metió una astilla de la lanza por él, de que murió' (Santa Cruz, *Crónica del Emperador Carlos V*, ed. Blázquez y Delgado-Aguilera and Beltrán y Rózpide, vol. V, p. 285).

[56] See below, Part II, *Passo Honroso* Selection 29, course 9.

Similarly, when Pedro de los Ríos jousts against Pero Vázquez, a blow to the head results in both a minor concussion as well as a dislocation, as follows:

> In the fourth course Pedro de los Ríos struck Pero Vázquez on the left pauldron, and he dealt such a mighty blow upon it that he hoisted it off him, and he hit him in the teeth with the same blow, and he stunned him, and made him suffer a serious reversal of fortune. And from the point at which he was struck up to the head of the lists he almost fell off his horse. And Pedro de los Ríos broke his spear into pieces upon him. And Pedro de los Ríos, from the stroke that he delivered, dislocated his hand.[57]

From these descriptions, and the fact that both men continued to joust, the dislocations sustained do not seem to have been too serious. On the understanding that without actually examining the patient it is only possible to speculate, these may have been straightforward dislocations of the fingers. Such dislocations are common and consistent with an axial load type of mechanism such as a spear, and would have been easily relocated. Alternatively, Gómez de Villacorta and Pedro de los Ríos could have sustained carpo-metacarpal dislocations, that is, dislocations between the fingers and the metacarpal bones of the wrist, similar in intensity to the fingers but more difficult to reduce.

The most serious dislocation in this passage of arms was sustained by the host, Suero de Quiñones. The extent of the injury and its treatment are described in some detail. Since descriptions such as this are rare, it is worth quoting in full, as follows:

> And the king-of-arms went to the pavilion where Suero de Quiñones was disarming himself and found that they were dressing his hand, and he saw how he was in much distress from the pain it was causing, and likewise he saw how his arm and hand were trembling, for it looked as if it might have been palsy.
>
> And here speaks the author, and he says that, upon hearing that Suero was injured, and so as to find out how, he had to go in person so as to verify further and write the truth of the matter. And he asked Suero, on his knightly oath, if he was injured whilst performing the deeds of arms he had performed with Juan de Merlo, and Suero replied that he had a disjointed hand and two bloody wounds in the biceps of his right arm, but he did not know if they had been sustained from the spikes of his grapper which had broken from the blow he dealt, or if Juan de Merlo had injured him with the spearhead or some splinter of his spear which Juan de Merlo broke

---

[57] See below, Part II, *Passo Honroso* Selection 22, course 4.

upon him, and that he could not think of anything else, nor had the surgeons been able to tell him. And that the greatest damage that he had suffered from those wounds had been that the third night after the wounds were sustained, lying in bed because of them, he was dreaming about writing letters of challenge in order to perform deeds of arms to the death, when blood had spurted out of the wounds and he had lost so much that the surgeons, when they visited him the following day, were fearful that he was in danger because of the large amount of blood lost.[58]

One of the remarkable features of this description is that the reader is allowed to move beyond the public space where the jousts occur and where pain is eschewed, to the inside of Suero's pavilion. Here the chronicler, Pero Rodríguez de Lena, is to Vergil as the reader is to Dante, leading us by the hand until we find ourselves 'nel mezzo', as it were, of Suero's private quarters. Once inside his pavilion we are afforded the rare privilege of hearing Suero's own description of his dream and his agonising pain – intimate details that would otherwise be denied to us. Given the intense force of this encounter – the grapper of one of the thickest, most powerful spears available snapped in Suero's own hand from the recoil – and Suero's symptoms – excruciating pain, compounded by a previous hand injury,[59] and an inability to hold a spear – it is possible that he sustained a serious lunate or peri-lunate dislocation. Dislocations of the lunate bone require a good deal of force, such as that described, and typically cause lots of late problems, such as those described by Suero three days later. It is also possible that he sustained a displaced fracture that is being referred to incorrectly as a dislocation; Zapata, for example, notes that 'hands get broken' when knights joust with 'loads of wood'. What is certain is that there were so many dislocations at this passage of arms that Suero de Quiñones, in accordance with Article 12, sent for a master of algebra, that is, a specialist in bone setting and the treatment of fractures.[60]

Suero being Suero, he openly celebrated the most common injuries of the joust by wearing a chemise embroidered with Catherine Wheels. The Catherine Wheel is often depicted in medieval iconography as an eight-spoked wheel with knives or spiked teeth radiating from the rim and it is, of course, associated with the martyrdom of St Catherine. As macabre as it seems to modern sensibilities, this wheel would have been recognised by all the contestants as the torture device that involved dislocating and breaking

---

[58] See below, Part II, *Passo Honroso* Selection 20, course 3.

[59] This dislocation was suffered on 28 July, but Suero had already dislocated his hand and shoulder in his joust against Pere Daviu on 15 July.

[60] The algebraist arrived on 4 August 1434. See Rodríguez de Lena, *El Passo Honroso de Suero de Quiñones*, ed. Labandeira Fernández, p. 357.

the victim's bones and then braiding the limbs through the spokes of the wheel. Since the most common injuries at jousts were contusions, dislocations and fractures, the Catherine Wheel was a fitting device for evoking the pain that this knight and his comrades in arms had already suffered and were still prepared to endure in the sacred name of their emprise.[61] To the medieval mind the wheel also connoted the Wheel of Fortune, which in the case of jousts between peers underscored the exciting inability to predict the end result of each course. The heralds depicted in the woodcuts of the sixteenth-century *Theuerdank* and *Thournier Kampff unnd Ritterspiel* sport wheels on their tabards, as illustrated in chapter I, figs. 13–14 for example, which suggests that this was a universally recognised symbol in jousting lore.

Of additional interest to the present discussion is the ingenious attempt by Rodríguez de Lena to quantify the physical intensity of the encounters in the jousts that took place at the Pass of Honour of Suero de Quiñones. The passage of arms was informed by seventy-eight jousts in which 747 courses were run by a total of seventy-seven knights: an average of 9.6 courses per joust. As I stated in the Introduction, Rodríguez de Lena's chronicle constitutes a rhetorical equivalent of the slow-motion action replay so that the competitors could relive the experience as they dissected each and every manoeuvre, and he thus goes far beyond the diagrammatic English score cheques. In his descriptions of each encounter the chronicler either uses the term 'reversal of fortune' ('revés') qualified by a variety of descriptors as a means of reflecting varying degrees of physical intensity or he makes the point that despite the intensity of the encounter the contestant(s) did not suffer a reversal of fortune. In other cases, most often when the contestants fail to make an encounter, there is no mention at all of reversals of fortune. Although one man died in one of the jousts at the Pass of Honour of Suero de Quiñones, what has euphemistically been called being 'beyond any need of a physician' is not quantified by Rodríguez de Lena, as this was not supposed to happen.[62]

Statistically, the author's stratagem for gauging the intensity of the jousts can be broken down as follows:

(1) *No reversal of fortune*, i.e. a respectable course was run, an encounter was made but no injuries were sustained: 106 times, or 14% of the jousts.

---

[61] See below, Part II, *Passo Honroso* Selection 20. Suero arrives at the lists on 28 July with this device on his chemise.

[62] The delightful euphemism 'beyond any need of a physician' ('no ouo menester maestro') for describing the dead is peppered throughout *Amadís de Gaula*. See Rodríguez de Montalvo, *Amadís of Gaul*, trans. Place and Behm, vol. I, pp. 182, 264, 356, etc.

(2) *A slight reversal of fortune* ('tomó un poco revés'), i.e. the rider sustained a contusion or was jerked sideways or backwards in the saddle: 1 time, or 0.1% of the jousts.

(3) *A moderate reversal of fortune* ('tomó un comunal revés'), i.e. the rider sustained a dislocation or minor flesh wound of some sort: 27 times, or 4% of the jousts.

(4) *A serious reversal of fortune* ('fízole tomar un gran revés'), i.e. the rider sustained a concussion or was severely winded and had trouble remaining in the saddle: 23 times, or 3% of the jousts.

(5) *A very serious reversal of fortune* ('tomó un muy gran revés'), i.e. the rider sustained a serious injury: 3 times, or 0.4% of the jousts.

(6) Nothing at all recorded: 79% of the jousts.

This simple but ingenious rhetorical formula is one of the first systematic attempts in Western Europe to quantify intensity of performance. Given that the knights of the Pass of Honour of Suero de Quiñones were fighting in jousts of war in field armour, with no shields and with sharp spearheads, the statistics debunk once and for all the myth that jousting was overly dangerous.

If jousting acquired a reputation for danger, the blame must in large part be imputed to the medieval and renaissance chroniclers – the writers of what we now call primary sources – who selectively recorded chivalric deeds for posterity and thereby validated, perpetuated and fossilised their own image and brand of knightly conduct. A case in point is the official chronicle of the reign of King John II of Castile by Fernán Pérez de Guzmán, which reduces the magnificent spectacle that was the Pass of Honour of Suero de Quiñones to a postscript at the end of a chapter. Of this event we are told only that 'a German knight died from a blow through the sight ... and some knights were wounded',[63] and that allegedly Suero de Quiñones, Lope de Stúñiga and Diego de Bazán jousted the best. Here the chronicler obviously confuses the German knight Arnold von Rottenwald with the Catalonian knight Asbert de Claramunt, and he omits the not very sensational fact that hundreds of courses were run with little or no injury. Similarly, his opinion about the men who jousted the best is debatable. In the case of jousting, Pérez de Guzmán is unfortunately typical of the medieval and renaissance chroniclers of the sport. Unlike Rodríguez de Lena, the vast majority of the chroniclers cared not a

---

[63] 'Murió un caballero alemán de un encuentro por la vista ... e fueron en él feridos algunos'. See Pérez de Guzmán, *Crónica del Serenísimo Príncipe Don Juan, segundo rey deste Nombre en Castilla y León*, ed. Rosell, p. 514b. Some six years later, in 1440, the Castilian knight Pedro Puertocarrero was killed in a comparable incident at a passage of arms held in Valladolid. His death was also considered worthy of note by Pérez de Guzmán, p. 567b.

jot about technical virtuosity in the lists and stressed the most horrific or sensational aspects of the joust. Consequently the data provided by them on this particular subject must be approached with a degree of caution. And even in the case of the *Passo Honroso* chronicle, despite the original author's emphasis on technique, the anonymous amanuensis of the most complete copy of this text to have survived, Escorial MS f.II.19, took the liberty of writing the words 'Blood!' ('Sangre') and 'Death!' ('Muerte') in large, bold letters in the margin of the codex whenever blood is shed and when Asbert de Claramunt is killed (figs. 143 and 144). Although there were no exclamation marks in the fifteenth century, the amanuensis' intent here is clearly hyperbolic, perhaps as a means of alerting his patron and any other interested readers to the goriest parts of the narrative.[64]

Between the Pass of Honour of Suero de Quiñones and publication of *Lo Cavaller*, that is, from 1434 to 1493, the alleged dangers of the joust had been diluted even further. By the 1490s Ponç de Menaguerra was writing on the one hand primarily about jousts of peace and on the other hand about mock jousts of war. In Menaguerra's mock jousts of war every effort was made to imitate the type of jousts described in detail by Rodríguez de Lena, but every precaution was also taken to ensure the safety of the jousters. Menaguerra chooses his words carefully, noting that in the mock jousts of war the combatants would at the very worst be knocked unconscious and therefore 'counted as dead', the idea being that fatal injury was a thing of the past. Even in the mock jousts of war it can be inferred from Menaguerra's treatise that the most common injuries were, once again, those to the hands, such as lacerations or dislocations of fingers and wrists; knights were also occasionally winded or concussed and often bruised. The least common injuries were those that proved fatal.

The sundry contusions, concussions and dislocations suffered by the jousters discussed in this book certainly demonstrate that these were the men who put the pain in Spain, but they also underscore that by the second half of the fifteenth century jousting was not nearly as dangerous or simplistic as has been thought. The safety precautions and concomitant scoring systems that began to play such a prominent role in the joust royal evolved out of the great innovations in armour and weaponry in the fifteenth century and beyond. These innovations meant that jousting had finally evolved into the first technically sophisticated contact sport in the Western world, one that was governed and defined by its distinctive high-performance kit and complex rules, and by sound strategy and vigorous athleticism: a precedent that would inform all future contact sports.

---

[64] See below, Part II, *Passo Honroso* Selection 12, course 5; Selection 15, course 3; Selection 16, course 2; Selection 27, course 5; Selection 32, course 9.

;Eansi mesmo yuan con viego de baçam el ya nonbrado don Juan de bena
uente quele seruia, e otros asaz gentiles homes, e tocando tronpetas de
lante del, e ansi honrrasa mente llegaro a sus tiendas

Capitulo que fabla de como ya el nonbrado cauallero diego
Debaçam torno al campo luego a poca de ora con Ro
drigo quexada. antes desto nonbrado. El qual le sirio A la
sazon que estas armas fizieron

luego a poca de ora en este ya nonbrado sabado torno al campo, el ya
dicho honrrado cauallero diego de baçam armado con las mesmas
armas que antes hauia fecho, e a cauallo, e de la otra parte contra el Ro
drigo quexada de la compaña del ya nonbrado gutier quexada e
como fueron en el campo pusiero sus lancas en los Riestres a guisa de
buenos caualleros, como aquellos que bien parecia que tenian en voluntad de
se delibrar ayna el vno al otro en aquel fecho de armas, e mouiero el vno
contra el otro e esta primera carrera non se encontraron .

A las dos carreras encontro Rodrigo quexada a diego de baça
por la vista del el mete cerca del ojo yzquierdo, e rompio su lança
en el, e quedole en la vista vn pedaço della sta con el fierro fasta quatro
dedos, e todos pensaron que era mal ferido de muerte. e tocole con el
fierro por cerca del ojo e fizole sangre, e plugo a dios que non gelo quebro
, e como se sintio ferido diego de baçam echo mano de la sta con el
fierro por la sacar, e non pudo, e dixo non es nada non es nada como
quiera q tomo muy gran rreues, e di. de baçam encontro a Rodrigo qua
da, e diole vn tan gran golpe en el guardabraço yzqierdo q por muy poco ge
lo falsara, e fizole tomar vn gra rreues e Rompio en el su lanca en dos ptes

143, 144 Two folios from Pero Rodríguez de Lena, *El Passo Honroso de*

Sangre,

Muerte:

A las nueue carreras encontro suero fijo de aluar goñez al ya montado
sin ventura esberte de claramonte por la vista del elmete, e dio
le vn tan gran golpe quele lanço todo el fierro dela lança por el ojo y desos
tales sesos, e fizole saltar el ojo fuera del casco, e tronpio su lança enel
con vn palmo della asta e conel fierro el qual leuaua metido por la vista del
elmete conel pedaço della asta e por el ojo segun vos es deuisado, e a
si fue acostado vn poco por la liça fasta que cayo del cauallo muerto
enel suelo, e tan supitamente murio que por muy apriesa quele acorri
eron nunca le oyeron fablar, ni bollir braço, ni pierna, e como le
quitaron el elmete dela cabeça fallaronle el otro ojo derecho tan in
chado, como vn gran puño que queria parezer enla cara que
hauia dos oras que era muerto, e luego aquellos caualleros
catalanes que alli eran Mosen franci, e mosen Rienbau de
corbera antes desto nonbrados, e otros asaz que alli eran natu
rales de su tierra mostraron gran sentimiento por su muer
te ser tan supita, e Rogauan a dios quele huuiesse md al
anima, e en especial se qxaua mucho por su muerte vn gentil ho
me que ala saçon enel fecho de aquellas armas le seruia, el qual
se llamaua por su nonbre Jufre Jardin, el qual antes desto hauia
muy bien fecho sus armas segun eneste libro es escrito, e dezia
a altas bozes o exberte de claramonte que en fuerte ventura, e
punto fueste nacido por morir tan supitaña muerte, e fuera dela tierra donde
eras plega anro señor dios q te aya el anima, e destas cosas dezia muchas
e muy doloriosas mostrando gra pesar por su muerte, e luego traxieron

Suero de Quiñones with the words 'Blood!' And 'Death!' written in the margins

~: 6 :~
War: A Brief Excursus

MODERN scholars have presented arguments for and against the idea that the tournament was intended as training for war. Vale and Cripps-Day before him have argued that from the twelfth through the fifteenth century the tournament was always ostensibly a training-ground for real war. Without presenting as explicit an argument as Vale, Juliet Barker has pointed to the militaristic strategies that informed the early mêlée tournament if not its later incarnations.[1] On the other hand Lucien Clare, Carroll Gillmor and Sydney Anglo have argued cogently that tournaments were a type of physical exercise – equestrian sporting activities that were never meant to train knights for real war – and certainly beyond the thirteenth century they underwent a metamorphosis into what Anglo calls 'a distinct medium of artistic expression'.[2] Within the general context of the tournament, and specifically in the case of the joust, the texts discussed in this volume confirm that this activity was an end unto itself, with the result that jousters trained above all to be good jousters. Since jousts were callisthenic, physical fitness could help a man endure the rigours of combat, though one of the ironies of the sport is that the worst jousters, those who had been smashed repeatedly in the face and body whilst running as many as twenty-seven courses in a single competition, may well have been the least likely to panic or fall apart if this happened in a real battle. Beyond callisthenics, Capwell observes that jousts did provide knights with an opportunity to practise their aim and tourneys provided them with an opportunity to practise fighting in teams.[3] Both activities were ideal for showing off certain skills in a specific, controlled context, and logically some competitors took them more seriously or performed better in them than others. As we saw in chapter 2, however, even if some men believed that by jousting they could inoculate themselves in preparation for the rigours of real combat, Cartagena made the point

---

[1] Barker, *The Tournament in England, 1100–1400*, pp. 17–44; Vale, *War and Chivalry*, pp. 63–99; Cripps-Day, *The History of the Tournament in England and in France*, pp. 3–6.

[2] Anglo, *The Great Tournament Roll of Westminster*, vol. I, p. 26 (also p. 21). See also Clare, 'Fêtes, jeux et divertissements à la cour du Connétable de Castile Miguel Lucas de Iranzo (1460–1470). Les exercises physiques', Gillmor, 'Practical Chivalry: The Training of Horses for Tournaments and Warfare', and Anglo, *The Martial Arts of Renaissance Europe*, pp. 227–52.

[3] Capwell, *The Real Fighting Stuff*, pp. 33 and 36.

that 'on occasion the good tourneyer is a timorous and cowardly warrior'. With this sober comment in mind, the difference between tournaments and formal training for war cannot in my view be emphasised too strongly.

Formal training for warfare was and still often is a distinctly private – even a clandestine – activity, and the central plaza where jousts often took place has been described appropriately by James Casey not as a secretive arena but as 'a theatre of display'.[4] Casey's description echoes that of Chaucer, who would also use the word 'theatre' to refer broadly to the lists in which the jousts in 'The Knight's Tale' take place.[5] Medieval and renaissance tournaments are just that, a theatre of display, and they are not by any stretch of the imagination a verisimilar representation of the role of mounted soldiers on the battlefield.

If, within the context of tournaments, jousting was not training for war, this did not mean that the amateurs of the pen who wrote jousting manuals were not also avid polemologists. Thus in his *Doctrina del arte de la cavallería*, as well as discussing jousting, Juan Quijada de Reayo devotes a chapter to the art of fighting in war. With the exception of Zapata's comment on the ash and beech lances that are used in combat, which he keeps brief since he had never fought in a battle, Quijada de Reayo is the only Iberian jousting master to dwell on real war. This should not come as a surprise, since his book is about the art of chivalry, and in purely practical terms 'chivalry' denoted the art of war as much as it did the art of jousting. I agree with Vale that these were two distinct activities in which knights were expected to participate. Unlike Vale, however, who contends that the one activity constituted formal training for the other, I would argue that in the *Doctrina del arte de la cavallería* there is no implied connection between the joust and war. On the contrary, the fifth chapter of the book describes in detail how the knight should prepare for war because war is not characterised by etiquette and rules, as are jousting competitions. Although medieval and renaissance battles were predicated upon well-calculated, overarching strategies, once the combatants met face to face on the battlefield no score was kept, as the Catalan author Gabriel Turell stresses in his 1471 treatise entitled *Arbre d'Honor* (Tree of Honour), for 'in battle no-one is judged greater nor lesser; every man is equal in his exercise'.[6] Turell's position would subsequently be reiterated at, of all places, a tournament. At the tournament held at Valladolid in July 1527 to celebrate the birth of Charles V's son and heir, Prince Philip, the participants in a tourney

---

[4] Casey, *Early Modern Spain: A Social History*, p. 114.

[5] Chaucer, *The Canterbury Tales*, ed. Robinson *et al.*, p. 50b line 1885 and p. 51a line 1901.

[6] 'en la batalla no és conegut mejor ni menor, tothom és agual en son axersisi' (Turell, *Arbre d'Honor*, ed. Burgaya, p. 140).

were reminded of the difference between this activity and real combat, as follows:

> In none of these deeds of arms shall you squeeze in arm-locks or twist with the hands the neck or any other part, nor shall you deliver estoc-thrusts or wrest swords or pull out the horses' bits or use any other combat techniques for war, that are not considered proper among friends and in matters of pleasure.[7]

Contemporary accounts of warfare underscore the chaos of battle as well as the dangers and the suffering endured by the mounted soldiers. One example just a year before publication of Quijada de Reayo's treatise is the disturbing description of the battlefield after the first engagements at the battle of Wurttemberg (24 April 1547). The author of the testimony is Luis de Ávila y Zúñiga, Knight Commander of the Order of Alcántara, who participated in the carnage:

> There were many men, some who looked more experienced than others, lying dead in the field; others were still alive, groaning and rolling around in their own blood; and there were still others whose fate was being sealed by the victors, who were arbitrarily killing some and taking others prisoner. In some places the dead were piled on top of one another while in others they were scattered about, and this was how they had met their fate, fleeing or standing their ground.[8]

The reality of being in the midst of a battle was not so much that it was imperative to win but rather that it was imperative that the knights kill and disable efficiently lest they themselves be killed or disabled. With surviving and killing firmly in mind, Quijada de Reayo notes that knights

---

[7] 'En ninguna destas armas se abraçarán ni asirán de las manos ni del pescueço ni de otra parte, ni darán estocadas ni tomarán las espadas ni desenfrenarán cavallos ni usarán de otras maneras de conbates de guerra, las quales no se tienen por onestas entre amigos y en cosas de plazer' (Ruiz García and Valverde Ogallar, 'Relación de las fiestas caballerescas de Valladolid de 1527: un documento inédito', p. 182).

[8] 'Había muchos hombres, que parecían ser de más arte que los otros, muertos en el campo, otros que aun no acababan de morir, gimiendo y revolviéndose en su misma sangre; otros se veía que se les ofrecía su fortuna como era la voluntad del vencedor, porque a unos mataban y a otros prendían, sin haber para ello más elección que la voluntad del que los seguía. Estaban los muertos en muchas partes amontonados, y en otras esparcidos, y esto era como les tomaba la muerte, huyendo o resistiendo' (Ávila y Zúñiga, *Comentario de la guerra de Alemania hecha por Carlos V, Máximo Emperador Romano, Rey de España, en el año de 1546 y 1547*, ed. Rosell, p. 443a). Sandoval plagiarises this account in his own description of the battle of Wurttemberg. See Sandoval, *Historia de la vida y hechos del Emperador Carlos V*, ed. Seco Serrano, vol. III, p. 295b.

should be heavily armed and equipped with a variety of accoutrements and weapons with a view to making appropriate use of them all. Firstly, the bit must be held securely in the horse's mouth by use of a head stall, and the reins must be reinforced with chains consisting of the smallest links possible. Not only must the horse's head be protected by a shaffron as in the joust, but also its neck must be protected by a closed crinet. This chapter of *Doctrina del arte de la cavallería* is of interest as much because of what is omitted as because of what is included. Thus for unknown reasons Quijada de Reayo does not mention two other useful pieces of the horse bard: the peytral, which protects the horse's belly; and the crupper, which protects its hind quarters.

In order to contextualise this chapter of Quijada de Reayo's treatise fig. 145 shows a complete war bard made for Johann Ernst (1521–63), Duke of Saxony-Coburg, which bears embossed on the peytral the same date as the year in which the treatise was published: 1548.[9] Similarly, fig. 146 shows a complete war bard with shaffron, closed crinet, peytral and crupper, probably made in Brescia *c.* 1580–90 for Count Antonio IV Collalto (1548–1620). This bard is of particular interest because it includes a set of original rein-chains, exactly as described by Quijada de Reayo (fig. 147).[10] To go back to the 1527 Valladolid tournament rules quoted above, yet another item that Quijada de Reayo does not mention is a special type of curb bit for war, the shanks of which were garnished with sharp prickers to prevent the bit from being yanked out of the horse's mouth. Like the gupfe mentioned in chapter 3, extant examples and images confirm that these bits were not uncommon, even though they are not mentioned in the Iberian treatises. Fig. 148 shows a sixteenth-century pen and wash illustration of such a bit, the caption of which translates as follows: 'In order to lighten the hand and in order to pull quickly and in order to extend the tongue. And a defence in time of war so that the enemy cannot not grab onto it with his hand.'[11] As a complement to this image fig. 149 shows a fine extant example from the sixteenth century, possibly of French origin. It measures 45.1 × 26 cm (1 ft 5¾ in × 10¼ in).[12]

---

[9] See Pyhrr *et al.*, *The Armored Horse in Europe, 1480–1620*, pp. 24–5 and fig. 18.

[10] On this bard, see Pyhrr *et al.*, *The Armored Horse in Europe, 1480–1620*, pp. 27–9 and fig. 25.

[11] 'Per allegerire la mano e per tirare soelto e per portare lingua for a. E guardia per guerra per che dainimigi non possino piglliar con mano'. This is one of a series of unnumbered original pen and wash illustrations of bits with captions in Italian that have been bound between folios 36 and 37 of the copy of *La Mareschalerie de Laurens Ruse translatée de Latin en francoys* (Paris: Chrestien Ussechel, 1533) in the library of the Department of Arms and Armor at the Metropolitan Museum of Art, New York, call number 147.13.R89.

[12] This bit is illustrated in a line drawing in Viollet-le-Duc, *Dictionnaire raisonné du mobilier français de l'époque carlovingienne à la renaissance*, vol. VI, p. 75.

145 Armour for man and horse made for Johann Ernst (1521–63), Duke of Saxony-Coburg,
by Kunz Lochner (*c.* 1510–67) of Nuremberg and dated 1548

146 Horse armour made in Brescia *c.* 1580–90 for Count Antonio IV Collalto (1548–1620). View of left profile

147 Close-up view of a rein-chain

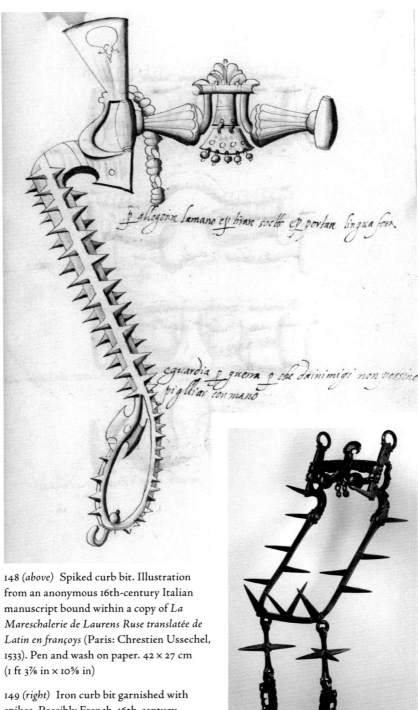

p ahegem lamano eſ hiave soclɔ eⱷ portan lingua fora.

eguardia p guem p che daínimigi non vessine
pigllíav con mano

148 (*above*) Spiked curb bit. Illustration
from an anonymous 16th-century Italian
manuscript bound within a copy of *La
Mareschalerie de Laurens Ruse translatée de
Latin en françoys* (Paris: Chrestien Ussechel,
1533). Pen and wash on paper. 42 × 27 cm
(1 ft 3⅞ in × 10⅝ in)

149 (*right*) Iron curb bit garnished with
spikes. Possibly French, 16th-century.
45.1 × 26 cm (1 ft 5¾ in × 10¼ in)

150   Albrecht Altdorfer, *Battle with the Huns outside Regensburg*, 1518

In the event of a full-blown charge, Quijada de Reayo urges his protégé
to lower his lance until it points directly at the belly of his opponent. A
1518 painting by Albrecht Altdorfer entitled *Battle With the Huns Outside
Regensburg* (fig. 150) shows squadrons of heavily armoured knights in the
foreground in the midst of a charge in formation, their lances couched
in a variety of positions as they approach the enemy, as Quijada de
Reayo recommends. As powerful a weapon as an ash or beech lance was,
however, the infantry tactician Diego Montes, whose literary patron was
also the third Duke of Alburquerque, questions the efficacy of the lance
in mounted combat, observing that it is good for one charge only, after
which it is useless.[13] Quijada de Reayo of course would have known this.
Without actually dialoguing with Montes, whose treatise was published
eleven years earlier, Quijada de Reayo stresses that once the lance is lost

---

[13] 'Las lanças de ristre no se pueden aprouechar dellas más de vn encuentro' ('Lances
couched in rests are of benefit for but one encounter'). Montes, *Instruçión y
regimiento de guerra*, fol. 10v.

the knight should reach for his estoc, strapped onto the left-hand side of the saddlebow. By the 1540s the estoc was a specialised thrusting sword used almost exclusively in cavalry combat.[14] The thrusts, says Quijada de Reayo, should be concentrated on the most vulnerable parts of the enemy's body: face, armpits and groin.

So many estocs were carried by Spaniards during the sixteenth century – in peace as well as war – that legislation was drafted and approved in the various *Cortes* during the reigns of Charles V and Philip II with a view to determining the most appropriate length for blades. Petitions to explore the issue of a standard blade size were approved initially at the *Cortes* held at Valladolid between 25 January and 22 May 1542. Petition number nine argues that the length of blades should be regulated so as to avoid dangerous accidents. Although this petition was approved, a specific length had yet to be determined.[15] Subsequently, in the *Cortes* held at Valladolid between 28 February and 6 May 1544, the petition of 1542 was restated with the supplication that all swords currently on the market be recalled and cut down to a prescribed length. On this occasion the monarch agreed that a committee would be convened whose task it would be to evaluate the feasibility of such a proposal.[16] In the *Cortes* of 4 April to 8 November 1548 the same petition was further developed to include all imported swords, especially estocs. The matter was, once again, referred to the committee that had been established in the previous *Cortes*.[17] The petitions as they are set down in the proceedings of the *Cortes* do not, unfortunately, include the suggested length for sword blades, however, the chronicler Alonso de Santa Cruz in his own transcription of what he perceived as the salient petitions of these *Cortes* states that the length finally decided upon was five palms.[18] Five palms would be at most an approximate equivalent of 106 cm (3½ ft) and less than 121 cm (4 ft).[19] The five-palm limit was reiterated in the first *Cortes* convened during the reign of Philip II. According to Petition 31 of the *Cortes* held at Valladolid between 27 April to 30 September 1558, sword blades of unequal length had in the past been the cause of much injury and death, therefore the laws passed during the reign of Charles V concerning the length of blades should be upheld during the reign of his successor. The king approved the petition.[20] Writing in 1589, infantry tactician Sancho de Londoño recommended a conservative 4½ palms as

---

[14] See Oakeshott, *European Weapons and Armour*, p. 126.

[15] *Cortes de los antiguos reinos de León y de Castilla*, vol. V, p. 175, petition 9.

[16] *Cortes de los antiguos reinos de León y de Castilla*, vol. V, p. 307, petition 6.

[17] *Cortes de los antiguos reinos de León y de Castilla*, vol. V, pp. 435–6, petition 146.

[18] Santa Cruz, *Crónica del Emperador Carlos V*, ed. Blázquez y Delgado-Aguilera and Beltrán y Rózpide, vol. IV, p. 354.

[19] On blade lengths, see also Anglo, *The Martial Arts of Renaissance Europe*, p. 100.

[20] *Cortes de los antiguos reinos de León y de Castilla*, vol. V, p. 750, petition 31.

a suitable length. He incidentally concurred with Quijada de Reayo when he noted that scabbards should be tightly strapped to the leg on the understanding that when marching, trotting or standing still, drawing the sword from a loosely hanging scabbard was an impediment for infantry as well as cavalry.[21]

Although laws were passed, a single fixed length for blades would prove difficult to regulate in practice, not least because the length, weight, and the general dimensions of a sword depended on the height and strength of the individual who carried the weapon as well as his preferred methodology for fighting. It would seem, however, that Spanish lawmakers were generally successful in restricting the length of blades to below the five palm stipulation. For example, six sixteenth-century swords in the Victoria and Albert Museum with Spanish inscriptions on the blades all fall within the limitations imposed by the *Cortes*. The blades of these six swords measure 86.4 cm or 2 ft 10 in (German manufacture, 1550), 91.5 cm or 3 ft (Saxon manufacture, 1550), 96 cm or 3 ft 1⅘ in (French manufacture, 1590, and English manufacture, 1630), 97.3 cm or 3 ft 2¼ in (Saxon manufacture, 1590) and 104.4 cm or 3 ft 5¹⁄₁₀ in (German manufacture, 1600).[22] Figs. 151–3 show three views of an attractive, well-balanced estoc made in Germany about 1525–40, much like the one that Quijada de Reayo would have carried into battle. The blade is of hollow triangular section and measures 100.5 cm (3 ft 3⅜ in) long and 2.6 cm (1 in) wide; the grip measures 19.5 cm (7⅝ in) long; and the estoc weighs 1,495 g (3 lb 5 oz).[23]

When the knight's estoc is lost or broken Quijada de Reayo states that he should have an arming sword strapped onto the left-hand side of his belt. It could be said that this weapon more than any other symbolised the essence of chivalric combat. In the Middle Ages, authorities such as Ramon Llull and Juan Manuel saw in the geometric shape of the arming sword a symbol of the Cross and the knight's spiritual mission as a defender of the faith. In the words of Llull: 'Unto the knight is given a sword, which is made in the shape of a cross to signify that just as our Lord Jesus Christ vanquished on the Cross the death into which we had fallen because of the sin of our father Adam, so the knight must vanquish and destroy the enemies of the Cross with the sword.'[24] Juan Manuel would add that: 'This

---

[21] Londoño, *Discurso sobre la forma de reducir la disciplina militar a mejor y antiguo estado*, p. 32.

[22] North, *An Introduction to European Swords*, pp. 11–13, plates 8, 10, 16, 18, 13 and 9.

[23] Mann, *Wallace Collection Catalogues: European Arms and Armour*, vol. II, pp. 259–60, inv. A505; Norman, *Wallace Collection Catalogues: European Arms and Armour: Supplement*, p. 120, inv. A505.

[24] 'A cavaller és donada espaa, qui és feta en semblança de creu, a significar que enaixí con nostro senyor Jesucrist vencé en la creu la mort en la qual érem caüts per lo

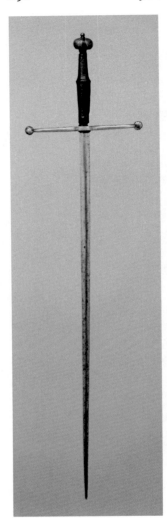

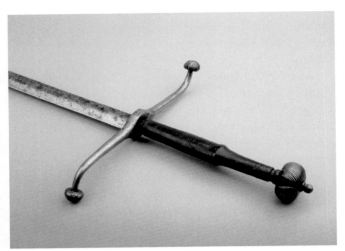

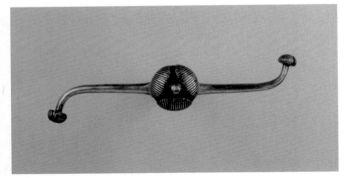

151–3 Study of an estoc. German, *c.* 1525–40.
Total length: 120 cm (3 ft 11 in)

sword signifies three things: firstly, strength, because it is made of iron; secondly, justice, because it is double-edged; thirdly the Cross.'[25] Unlike the estoc, the arming sword would be used for cutting as well as thrusting.[26] Figs. 154–6 are a study of an arming sword with Spanish blade of about

pecat de nòstron pare Adam, enaixí cavaller deu vençre e destruir los enemics de la creu ab l'espaa' (Llull, *Llibre de l'Orde de Cavalleria*, ed. Gustà, p. 69).

[25] 'Esta espada sinifica tres cosas: la primera, fortaleza, porque es de fierro; la segunda, justiçia, porque corta de amas las partes; la terçera, la cruz' (Juan Manuel, *Libro de las armas*, ed. Blecua, p. 124).

[26] See Anglo, *The Martial Arts of Renaissance Europe*, p. 253, and Soler del Campo, *La evolución del armamento medieval en el reino castellano-leonés y al-Andalus (siglos XII–XIV)*, pp. 14 and 177.

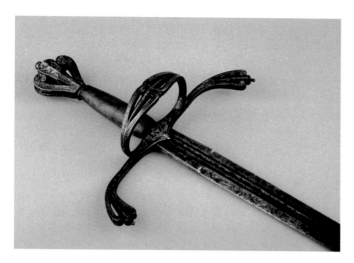

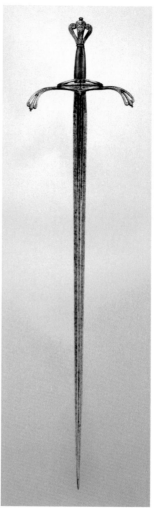

154–6 Study of an arming sword with a Spanish blade, *c.* 1605–15.
Total length: 104.3 cm (3 ft 5⅛ in)

1605–15. This quite beautiful example measures 104.3 cm (3 ft 5⅛ in) long,
3.4 cm (1⅜ in) wide and weighs 1,340 g (2 lb 15 oz).[27]

In addition to the estoc and arming sword, the mounted knight should
have a hammer fastened onto the right-hand side of his belt by a belt-
hook. Although the detail is not stated by Quijada de Reayo, undoubtedly because to him it would have been obvious, the long belt-hook of
the hammer would always be fitted at the top, the reason being that if
the hammer were suspended from the belt by the grip, the head would

---

[27] Mann, *Wallace Collection Catalogues: European Arms and Armour*, vol. II, p. 267,
inv. A517; Norman, *Wallace Collection Catalogues: European Arms and Armour:
Supplement*, p. 123, inv. A517; Norman, *The Rapier and Small-Sword, 1460–1820*,
p. 73.

swing dangerously, banging into the rider's own leg and possibly injuring him. By Quijada de Reayo's time the type of hammer used in cavalry combat would typically consist of an opposing head and a sharp, lethal back spike known as a 'bec-de-corbin' ('crow's beak').[28] The war hammer could thus be used for concussing the enemy or piercing the weak points of his defensive armour. Fig. 157 illustrates the reverse side of a high-quality example showing the belt-hook. Made of steel with a solid silver grip, this hammer was produced in Saxony in the second half of the sixteenth century. It measures 57.2 cm (1 ft 10½ in) long and weighs a pleasing 1,230 g (2 lb 11 oz).[29] Last but by no means least, the knight should also carry a dagger, so that if the estoc, arming sword and hammer are lost, he can grapple and stab his way out of the mêlée. Fig. 158 shows a dagger with sheath which is dated 1595. It measures a compact but lethal 26 cm (10¼ in) long, 2.5 cm (1 in) wide and weighs 333 g (12 oz).[30]

At the end of the fifth chapter of *Doctrina del arte de la cavallería*, Quijada de Reayo reiterates that it is imperative to direct all attacks to the opponent's hands, face and groin in order to secure a swift victory. He adds that some believe that it is a legitimate practice to attack the opponent's horse, and he endorses this strategy in war if it leads to victory. As a general rule, he observes, a knight on horseback has a significant tactical advantage over an adversary on foot. There were, of course, always those who would take such counsel a little too far. In a tourney between thirteen Spanish knights and thirteen French knights that took place on the outskirts of Barlette in 1503, the Spanish knights attacked and slaughtered eleven of the French horses on the grounds that 'once his horse is killed the man-at-arms is lost'. The outraged chronicler of the event, Pierre de Bourdeille, contends that

157 Reverse side of a cavalry war hammer showing the belt-hook. Saxony, 16th century. Length: 57.2 cm (1 ft 10½ in)

---

28 On the *bec-de-corbin*, see Waldman, *Hafted Weapons in Medieval and Renaissance Europe*, pp. 161–3. On cavalry hammers, see also Oakeshott, *European Weapons and Armour*, pp. 69–72. The hammers used in foot combats often also had a top spike and were sometimes two-handed. See Soler del Campo, *La evolución del armamento medieval en el reino castellano-leonés y al-Andalus (siglos XII–XIV)*, p. 57, and Waldman, *Hafted Weapons in Medieval and Renaissance Europe*, pp. 159–63.

29 On this hammer, see Nickel et al., *The Art of Chivalry*, p. 128.

30 Mann, *Wallace Collection Catalogues: European Arms and Armour*, vol. II, p. 386, inv. A757; Norman, *Wallace Collection Catalogues: European Arms and Armour: Supplement*, pp. 170–1, inv. A757; Norman, *The Rapier and Small-Sword, 1460–1820*, p. 252.

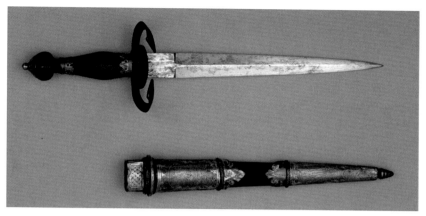

158 Dagger and sheath, 1595. Length: 26 cm (10¼ in)

while such a nefarious ruse might ensure survival on the battlefield, it is inappropriate in organised tourneys.[31]

Other contemporary chronicles confirm not only the frenzy of pitched battle and the type of action that inspired Quijada de Reayo's opinions concerning warfare, but also the vulnerability of armoured knights on horseback. One very human detail mentioned by Juan Manuel, which underscores the physical discomfort of wearing armour for extended periods of time, is that in any long campaign armoured knights were destined to be plagued as much by the fleas within their armour as by the enemy without.[32] That said, in battle even the simplest preventive measures, such as Quijada de Reayo's statement about reinforcing the reins with chains, could mean the difference between life and death. Quijada de Reayo refrains from buttressing his argument by mentioning the disastrous consequences that could befall any knight who failed to heed his advice. The chronicler Fray Prudencio de Sandoval, however, does describe such a case: that of Fernando de Castrionte, Marquis of Civita Sant Angelo, who was fatally wounded in the battle of Pavia in 1525. The marquis failed to reinforce his reins, which were cut during the fray. He lost control of his horse almost immediately and it bolted into a platoon of enemy French troops. Although he fought valiantly, the marquis was ultimately run through with a lance and died instantly.[33] Proof enough that a strong theoretical background was an asset in the kind of battles

[31] 'Muerto el cavallo, perdido el hombre d'armas'. Bourdeille, *Œuvres complètes de Pierre de Bourdeilles, abbé et seigneur de Branthôme*, ed. Mérimée, vol. V, pp. 91–4 and vol. VIII, pp. 91–2.

[32] Juan Manuel, *Livro del cavallero et del escudero*, ed. Blecua, p. 89.

[33] Sandoval, *Historia de la vida y hechos del Emperador Carlos V*, ed. Seco Serrano, vol. II, pp. 79a–83b.

that were being fought throughout Europe in the late Middle Ages and the early Renaissance; and proof enough that a well-placed single thrust with a stout lance could be lethal. As a point of comparison to this incident, Rodríguez de Lena describes an incident at the Pass of Honour of Suero de Quiñones whereby jouster Gómez de Villacorta lost the reins of his horse. The difference is that he managed to survive the accident unscathed because his horse was constrained by the tilt and the enclosure, and retainers were at hand to ensure that the animal did not bolt.[34]

Getting knocked off the horse could have disastrous consequences in the midst of a battle; hence in his description of the garniture Quijada de Reayo avers that in battle knights should wear half-greaves with mail sabatons. By half-greaves he means greaves that cover the front of the legs only, without a hinged rear plate. Full-greaves imposed constrictions that many knights believed were to be avoided at all costs on the battlefield. According to this school of thought the full-greaves were appropriate only for the joust because they limited the flexion of the knee and the rotation of the ankle, thereby enabling (almost forcing) the knight to keep his legs straight. In war, however, knights would be expected to wear their armour for unlimited periods of time and mobility was a key factor for ensuring survival. Mounting and dismounting were easier without the back plates of the greaves as was getting up from the ground if unhorsed or knocked over in combat. Despite the fact that half-greaves made the calves vulnerable, using the front plates only in war was a practical concession made by many knights in the name of comfort and manœuvrability. Fig. 159 shows a page from the Sorg pattern-book which depicts the garniture for the field of the Spanish nobleman Bernardino Manrique de Lara made in 1549, possibly by the German master armourer Matthaus Frauenpreis. Sorg has included key exchange pieces in the margin, arranged clockwise as follows: splinted vambraces for the arms; hinged rear plates of the greaves to be used in this case for jousting but not for war; a front saddle steel; a rear saddle steel; a pauldron with haute-piece for heavy cavalry combat; a right mitten gauntlet; a circular shield; a demi-shaffron for the horse; an articulated reinforcing bevor for the tourney; a burgeonet peak and falling buffe for medium or heavy cavalry combat; and an open-face burgeonet for infantry or light cavalry combat. This drawing is evidence that other prominent noblemen of the period shared the same view as Quijada de Reayo as far as the greaves were concerned.

Peter N. Jones and Alan Williams have shown that in pitched battle there is little doubt that the metal plate of a well-crafted harness did offer adequate protection from piercing blows.[35] But one is still left wondering

---

[34] See below, Part II, *Passo Honroso* Selection 24, course 5.

[35] Jones, 'The Metallography and Relative Effectiveness of Arrowheads and Armor during the Middle Ages'; Williams, *The Knight and the Blast Furnace*, pp. 945–9.

159 Garniture for the field of Bernardino Manrique de Lara, 1549, possibly by
Matthaus Frauenpreiss of Augsburg. From the pattern-book of Jörg Sorg, c. 1548–63

how stable the many straps and fastenings were, given the type of frenetic movements and contortions that characterised close combat with edged weapons. From the vantage point of the twenty-first century, armour looks impressive on static mannequins in museums, but in real battle as well as the jousts of war that attempted to mimic real battle, some pieces evolved because they were a liability – this seems to have been the case in particular in the first half of the fifteenth century when plate armour was still in its early stages of evolution. So, for example, in the San Romano battle panel illustrated in chapter 2, fig. 18, broken and lost arms and armour litter the ground. Likewise Gutierre Díaz de Games notes in his description of an attack launched against the isle of Jersey in 1401, that:

> There many powerful lance thrusts were delivered, as a result of which many were wounded on both sides, and some of them even overthrown. Abandoning the lances, they laid hands on their axes and swords, and a great mêlée ensued. There you could see the visors[36] of some men's bascinets flying off, and vambraces and mail voiders[37] getting ripped off; and others lost their grip on their swords and axes, and grappled with their arms and daggers.[38]

In the context of the joust of war, in Rodríguez de Lena's *El Passo Honroso de Suero de Quiñones* the reader encounters the verb 'desguarnecer', which describes the act of ripping off a piece of armour, on almost every folio. The most vulnerable pieces of armour, that is to say, the pieces most likely to be lost or to fly off in the fray, were those secured in place with leather

---

[36] *the visors*: Cp. medieval Castilian *las corazas*. The word 'coraza' usually means 'cuirass', which would make no sense in this context. In his critical edition of the text, Beltrán Llavador includes the textual variant 'saltar las *caras* de los baçinetes' (Díaz de Games, *El victorial*, ed. Beltrán Llavador, p. 624), which makes it clear that, however unusual the terminology (*corazas*), the author is indeed referring to the visors in this instance.

[37] *mail voiders*: Cp. medieval Castilian *musequines*. Beltrán Llavador defines the word as 'discos o láminas protectores' (Díaz de Games, *El victorial*, ed. Beltrán Llavador, p. 775), that is, 'protective disks or lames'. Corominas and Pascual suggest 'pauldrons' or 'cuisses' (Corominas and Pascual, *Diccionario crítico etimológico castellano e hispánico*, vol. I, p. 624a, s.v. 'borceguí'). Leguina provides concrete evidence that the term refers to the mail voiders. See Leguina, *Glosario de voces de Armería*, pp. 660–1.

[38] 'Allí se dieron muy fuertes golpes de las lanças, de que fueron feridos muchos de amas partes, e aun dellos caýdos. Dexadas las lanças, pusieron manos a las hachas e a las espadas, e bolvióse un torneo muy grande. Allí podría honbre ver a unos saltar las corazas de los baçinetes, e desguarneçer braçales e musequines; e a otros caer las espadas e las hachas de las manos, e venir a los braços, e a las dagas' (Díaz de Games, *El victorial*, ed. Beltrán Llavador, pp. 623–4). The translation in this case is my own. Cp. also (but, unusually, with a few mistakes) Díaz de Gamez, *The Unconquered Knight*, trans. Evans, p. 176.

straps or rivets: the visor, the bevor, upper and lower cannons of the vambrace, pauldrons, rondels, elbow guards or couters, gauntlet reinforces, and tassets.[39] The vulnerability in particular of visor, bevor, vambrace and gauntlets in the early fifteenth century not only explains the subsequent evolution of the exchange pieces for the joust that were secured in place by stout bolts, but also Quijada de Reayo's advice to strike at the hands and face in time of war.

Hernando del Pulgar notes that in the thick of battle it was often impossible even to wield the sword and therefore, without ever losing the sword, it was necessary to stab at the enemy with the dagger. His description of the vicious fighting in the battle of Lobon in 1479 is eerily reminiscent of Díaz de Games' account of the mêlée in Jersey:

> And the knights on both sides, having lost their lances, drew their swords, and they were all tangled with each other, attacking each other so mercilessly that many of them, because they were fighting in such close quarters, were unable to avail themselves of their swords and they fought with their daggers.[40]

Alonso de Maldonado's description of the sack of Alegrete in 1476 is not dissimilar:

> The Grand Master began to strike at them with the tip of his lance. Hernando de Monrroy, lord of Monrroy, who was also carrying a lance, did nothing but shove men over the parapet; and in view of the fact that the lance of the Grand Master, Don Alonso de Monrroy, did not last long due to the fact that he was being pushed on, because in that area many people had charged, he laid hands on his sword and he tossed his adarga shield, which was smashed to pieces, from his arm.[41]

---

[39] On the visor, see Pero Niño, above. On the other pieces, see Rodríguez de Lena, *El Passo Honroso de Suero de Quiñones*, ed. Labandeira Fernández, pp. 226, 280, 305 (bevor), 167, 188, 221, 322 (vambraces), 151, 164, 173, 185, 196, 201, 205, etc. (pauldrons), 205, 207, 211 (rondels), 315, 318, 342 (couters), 201, 300, 376 (gauntlets), 340 (tasset).

[40] 'E los caballeros de la una parte e de la otra, perdidas las lanzas vinieron a las espadas, e andaban mezclados unos con otros, firiéndose tan crudamente, que muchos dellos por estar tan juntos, no se podían aprovechar de las espadas, e peleaban con los puñales' (Pulgar, *Crónica de los señores Reyes Católicos Don Fernando y Doña Isabel de Castilla y de Aragón*, ed. Rosell, p. 343b).

[41] 'El Maestre ... comenzó a darles con el hierro de la lança. Hernando de Monrroy, el señor de Monrroy, que con otra lança estaua, no hazía sino derrocar hombres del adarue abaxo; y como quiera que el maestre Don Alonso de Monrroy le durase poco la lança de la priesa que le dauan, porque por aquella parte auía cargado mucha gente, echó mano a su espada, y la adarga echó del braço hecha pedaços' (Maldonado, *Hechos de Don Alonso de Monrroy, Clavero y Maestre de la Orden de Alcántara*, p. 99).

As postscripts to their descriptions of the battle of Lobon and the sack of Alegrete, both Pulgar and Maldonado observe that few horses on both sides were left standing after the fighting. Their comments expose not only the brutality of fighting in close quarters, but also the fragility of horses – even fully armoured horses – in combat.

So dangerous was the battlefield that the simple act of raising the arm to wield a weapon could in itself prove fatal, for mail voiders were vulnerable to penetration from stray arrows or determined thrusts from weapons such as the estoc. Thus Rodrigo Téllez Girón, Grand Master of the Order of Calatrava was killed by an arrow that hit him directly in the armpit during a skirmish at the siege of Loja in 1482.[42] Like raising the arm, raising the visor could have catastrophic consequences. Don Juan de Cardona, Count of Colosa, Sicily, was killed at the battle of Bicocca on 7 April 1522 by an arrow that struck him in the eye and penetrated his brain when he raised the visor of his helmet the better to see the battlefield.[43] This minor episode of war tucked away in a chronicle reveals an important detail about the dynamics of armour in the context of the lists as well as the battlefield. The count raised his visor because, when he was standing still, the eye-slit allowed for limited vision. When charging, however, the rhythmic movement up and down in the saddle meant that the eyes co-ordinated with the brain to register a field of vision three to four times as deep as the actual width of the eye-slit; hence it was not necessary to raise the visor when charging as it was possible to see much more than at first might seem possible.

Getting killed by an arrow through the head is a sinister leitmotiv in the chronicles and popular ballads of the Middle Ages and the Renaissance and even assumes the form of a heraldic device known as the 'tête affrontée'. Such was the fate of Martín Pérez Puerto Carrero, who was killed instantly when an arrow pierced his eye at the siege of Almazán in 1289. Fifty-four years later, during the siege of Algeciras in 1343, one Per Álvarez met his demise when a stray arrow landed directly on top of his head. The unfortunate victim lingered in agony for three days before succumbing to his injury. In the fifteenth century Juan de Guzmán lost his life at the siege of Utrera in 1477 when a sniper perched atop the walls of the besieged city shot an arrow directly into his face.[44] Finally, in a

---

[42] Pulgar, *Crónica de los señores Reyes Católicos Don Fernando y Doña Isabel de Castilla y de Aragón*, ed. Rosell, p. 372b.

[43] Sandoval, *Historia de la vida y hechos del Emperador Carlos V*, ed. Seco Serrano, vol. I, p. 503b.

[44] *Crónica del Rey Don Sancho el Bravo*, ed. Rosell, p. 81a (Pérez Puerto Carrero); *Crónica del Rey Don Alfonso el Onceno*, ed. Rosell, p. 367b (Álvarez); Bernaldez, *Memorias del reinado de los Reyes Católicos*, ed. Gómez-Moreno and Mata Carriazo, p. 71 (Guzmán).

popular ballad about the siege of Álora (1434), a treacherous Arab cross-bowman shouts in fluent Castilian from the battlements of the besieged city, tricking his victim into raising the visor of his helmet. He then shoots an arrow with deadly accuracy from an acute angle with the result that it enters the victim's forehead and exits through the back of his neck, as follows:

> Between the top turrets
> stands one of the Moors,
> he holds up his crossbow,
> an arrow instals,
> and shouts out aloud
> so they hear as he calls:
> 'Don Diego, a truce!
> The castle is yours!'
> He lifts up his visor
> when he hears what was said,
> and the arrow that strikes him
> goes right through his head.[45]

Ironically, Quijada de Reayo's treatise was published at the dawn of a new era in the military history of Spain, an epoch in which few mounted knights would fight each other in single combat or engage in meticulously planned cavalry charges. The end of the Reconquest in Spain heralded a new era, not only of imperial consolidation, but also of further imperial expansion and conquest. The sworn duty of Spanish military commanders was twofold. They were to strengthen the security of the state and resist potential incursions, either from Calvinists and Lutherans in the north or from Moslems in the south and east. The suppression of the *Comunero* revolt in 1520–1, the defeat of Barbarossa in Tunisia in 1535, the capitulation of the German Princes and the death of King Francis I of France in 1547 meant that most of the serious threats to the political and military stability of the Hapsburg empire had been eliminated, from Europe to the New World. By the second half of the sixteenth century, Charles V's empire was witnessing a period of relative peace, punctuated by very few pitched battles. Between 1522 and 1558 imperial troops fought seven pitched battles during the emperor's campaigns in Europe: Bicocca (1522), Pavia (1525),

---

[45] The Spanish original stresses that the arrow entered through the forehead ('la frente') and exited at the back of the neck ('al colodrillo'): 'Entre almena y almena / quedado se había un morico / con una ballesta armada / y en ella puesto un cuadrillo. / En altas voces decía / que la gente lo había oído: / "¡Treguas, treguas, adelantado, / por tuyo se da el castillo!" / Alza la visera arriba / por ver el que tal le dijo; / asestárale a la frente, / salido le ha al colodrillo' (Smith, ed., *Spanish Ballads*, n° 34 lines 19–30, pp. 63–4). For the English translation, see Wright, ed. and trans., *Spanish Ballads*, n° 63 lines 19–30, pp. 107–8.

Mohacs (1526), Cérisoles (1544), Mühlberg (1547), Saint Quentin (1557) and Gravelines (1558).

As a member of the personal bodyguard of Ferdinand and Isabella it is possible that Quijada de Reayo had seen action in the 1490s in Granada; likewise he may well have been at Beltrán de la Cueva's side in the Navarrese campaigns of the early 1520s and at the battle of Pavia. He thus would have been aware of the power of artillery and firearms and yet he mentions neither in his chapter on war, which is otherwise a pragmatic disquisition on the need for survival at all costs. In the context of the Iberian Peninsula it was in the fifteenth century in Castile that the seeds were sewn for the progress in military technology and organisation that would blossom in the sixteenth century. These innovations have been called the 'military revolution', a term coined by Michael Roberts in a lecture delivered in 1955 and subsequently expanded upon by Geoffrey Parker. Although some historians have argued that the military revolution is in fact a distinctly medieval phenomenon, my own viewpoint is consonant with that of Parker, for the use of gunpowder, new military tactics and organisation would not be truly systematised in Spain until the sixteenth century.[46]

Although systematic use of gunpowder and firearms by no means guaranteed victory in the field, their increased use in the sixteenth century certainly affected the way battles were fought. Peter Krenn has shown that unlike arrows, harquebus and musket balls could penetrate between 2–4 mm of plate armour from as far away as 100 m (108 yd 1 ft).[47] These weapons were not without their faults, however. Alonso Enríquez de Guzmán, for example, describes a frightening encounter with some roisterers armed with harquebuses in the back streets of Cuzco in 1538. The muggers shot twice at his heart at point-blank range with two different harquebuses. On both occasions the harquebuses misfired because they were not properly armed. A relieved Enríquez de Guzmán could only kneel and pray after this unsettling incident.[48] Firearms were often also ineffective in sandy areas as, for example, in Charles V's campaigns in Tunis, where weapons jammed virtually every time sand was blown about by the wind and the harquebusiers found it difficult to take aim.[49] In the European

---

[46] See Parker, *The Military Revolution*, p. 1. For the medieval view, see especially the article by Rogers, 'The Military Revolution of the Hundred Years War', and García Fitz, *Castilla y León frente al Islam: Estrategias de expansión y tácticas militares (siglos XI–XIII)*, esp. p. 75.

[47] Krenn, 'Test-firing Selected 16th–18th Century Weapons'.

[48] Enríquez de Guzmán, *Libro de la vida y costumbres de don Alonso Enríquez de Guzmán*, ed. Keniston, p. 178b.

[49] García Cerezeda, *Tratado de las campañas y otros acontecimientos de los ejércitos del Emperador Carlos V en Italia, Francia, Austria, Berbería y Grecia, desde 1521 hasta 1545*, ed. Cruzada Villaamil, vol. II, p. 38.

arena, however, the harquebusiers of the sixteenth century were often able
to hit their targets with the result that the gunshot wound replaces the
arrow in the head as the fatal leitmotiv of the renaissance military world.
Unlike arrows, the balls fired from harquebuses and wheelock pistols were
small and difficult to extract; they shattered bones and ligaments as well
as penetrating and slicing through them, and most soldiers who suffered
comminuted fractures after being shot invariably died of gangrene and
infection shortly thereafter.[50]

As far as the later Middle Ages are concerned it is only in recent years
that military historians such as Andrew Ayton and Kelly DeVries have
been able to determine that the hegemony and strategic importance of
mounted knights on the battlefield is a fallacy. Likewise the role of infantry
in medieval warfare has often been understated by scholars in large part
because the grandiose appearance of the fully armoured mounted knight
and the excitement of the cavalry charge have always had more appeal
than the often pitiable existence and the equally grim appearance of the
humble infantryman.[51] By the mid-sixteenth century, the decline in the
use of heavy cavalry was commensurate with the rise of the harquebusier
and the musketeer conjoined with the revolutionary phalanx tactics of
the infantry in Spain, in particular the innovation of the Tercios.[52] In 1536,
thirteen years before the publication of Quijada de Reayo's treatise, the
infantry and artillery tactician Captain Diego de Salazar admonishes the
Spanish heavy cavalry for wasting the army's precious resources, for each
knight takes as many as four war horses to the battlefield, but only ever

---

[50] Victims of fatal gunshot wounds litter the pages of the chronicles. To cite but one
chronicle, see García Cerezeda, *Tratado de las campañas y otros acontecimientos de
los ejércitos del Emperador Carlos V en Italia, Francia, Austria, Berbería y Grecia,
desde 1521 hasta 1545*, ed. Cruzada Villaamil, vol. I, pp. 235, 261, 406, and vol. II,
pp. 174, 208, 222, 258, 314.

[51] Ayton notes that: 'At the heart of English tactics from the early 1330s … was a much
diminished role for the warhorse. Its battlefield function was usually confined to
the closing stages of an engagement' (*Knights and Warhorses: Military Service and
the English Aristocracy under Edward III*, p. 21). See also DeVries, *Infantry Warfare
in the Early Fourteenth Century: Discipline, Tactics and Technology*, pp. 191–7.
Compare Webb's assertion, made in 1965, that in Elizabethan England 'a return
to Roman military science was a definite improvement over medieval methods
of warfare, with its emphasis on heavy cavalry and its minimization of infantry'
(*Elizabethan Military Science: The Books and the Practice*, p. 145).

[52] The tactics of the *tercios* are discussed by Oman, *A History of the Art of War in the
Sixteenth Century*, pp. 51–62, and Martínez Laínez and Sánchez de Toca, *Tercios de
España*, pp. 89–96. On the decline of the use of heavy cavalry in battle, see Parker,
The Military Revolution: Military Innovation and the Rise of the West, 1500–1800,
pp. 69ff. On gunpowder and the rise of the harquebusier, see Hale, 'Gunpowder
and the Renaissance: an Essay in the History of Ideas', and Hall, *Weapons and
Warfare in Renaissance Europe*, pp. 105–200.

rides one of them, which often performs poorly in battle. At the same time
he applauds the German knights he has seen in action for they, like the
ancient Romans, allow for just one horse per knight and in the interests of
economy they allocate a single wagon for carrying the equipment of every
twenty knights.[53] Salazar was bold enough to assert that cavalry would be
put to shame by armed and organised infantry any time the two forces
clashed.[54] He was forcing home a point that had been hinted at two centuries earlier: the anonymous chronicler of the reign of King John I of Castile
(1358–90; ruled 1379–90) had once remarked that heavy cavalry was of
little use without support from crossbowmen, 'for without crossbowmen
the heavy cavalry cannot effectively wage war'.[55]

By 1582 yet another infantry and artillery tactician, Diego García de
Palacio, insisted that the army's strength lay 'in the use of gunpowder'.[56]
García de Palacio sees the role of the heavy cavalry as purely defensive.
Withstanding the enemy 'like a fort or bastion', their function is, according
to this theorist, to protect the infantry and, only if absolutely necessary, to
disrupt and break the enemy ranks.[57]

Mounted knights, argues García de Palacio, should practise fighting on
foot for extended periods in full harness, as well as marching and mounting
and dismounting horses without the help of retainers and without the use
of stirrups. In addition to these activities, they should practise carrying
lances. García de Palacio also makes the dangerous recommendation
that mounted knights should practise swimming across rivers whilst clad
in full harness. He does not explain why they should do this, but it can
be assumed that the exercise would build strong muscles, especially the
pectorals and the biceps, which would in turn facilitate combat with the
lance and sword. García de Palacio was certainly familiar with Vegetius
(on swimming, see Vegetius I.10), and perhaps also with *Las Siete Partidas*,
which state that: 'He who falls from a ship, must, necessarily, go to the
bottom of the sea, and the more heavily armed he is, the more rapidly he
descends and is lost',[58] in which case the ability to swim could be a useful
chivalric survival skill. It is worth pointing out, however, that exposure
to fresh or salt water would not be particularly healthy for armour or for

---

[53] Salazar, *Tratado de Re Militari*, ed. Botella Ordinas, p. 162.

[54] Salazar, *Tratado de Re Militari*, ed. Botella Ordinas, pp. 136–7.

[55] 'ca las lanzas sin los ballesteros non pueden facer gran guerra'. See *Crónica del Rey
Don Juan, primero de Castilla e de León*, ed. Rosell, p. 133b.

[56] 'en el uso de la pólvora'. See García de Palacio, *Diálogos militares*, fol. 93r.

[57] García de Palacio, *Diálogos militares*, fol. 56r.

[58] 'El que cae del navío por fuerza ha de ir hasta en fondo de la mar, e cuanto más
armado fuere tanto mas aína desciende e se pierde'. *Las Siete Partidas*, II.xxiv.10, ed.
Sánchez-Arcilla, p. 323b. For the English translation, see *Las Siete Partidas*, trans.
Scott and Burns, vol. II, p. 468.

the leather straps that held the armour in place. On horseback, García de Palacio continues, the heavy cavalry should train with the lance, the sword and a weapon not mentioned by Quijada de Reayo, the mace. Perhaps taking into account the dangers described by Pulgar and Maldonado in their chronicles, García de Palacio argues that they should be skilled in the art of retreating from the enemy as well as charging at and into them.[59] The feigned retreat has been described by one modern historian as 'the single most important tactic in the repertoire of the medieval mounted fighting man'.[60] Although this assertion has been challenged,[61] it is worthy of note that by the Renaissance retreating as a legitimate tactic is mentioned only in passing in García de Palacios' treatise, which is devoted primarily to infantry and artillery strategies. Quijada de Reayo does not mention it at all.

By 1548, the year Quijada de Reayo's treatise was published, instances of single combat or organised cavalry charges on the battlefield were few and far between. In the face of a new tactical situation in the Iberian Peninsula, namely the possibility of incursions by Protestant aggressors from the north or Moslem aggressors from the south and east, there was a need for a new type of mounted warrior, not one who fought frenetically in pitched battles, but one who could engage the enemy in short skirmishes. The heavy cavalry was becoming obsolete because the tactic of charging in formation was cumbersome and inefficient when confronted with any kind of oppositional guerrilla tactics.

In the descriptions of battles and skirmishes in the chronicles produced during or shortly after the reign of Charles V, the reader is struck by the scant number of single combats and the lack of close contact between opposing armies. According to the adventurer-cum-chronicler, Martín García Cerezeda (fl. 1550), the sword and lance, that is, the two preferred weapons of the medieval knight, were losing their prestige in battle in favour of firearms, in particular the harquebus. Whereas in the past mounted knights who fought and vanquished members of the enemy camp in single combat were destined to have their deeds recorded for posterity in contemporary chronicles and memoirs, this particular bellicose ideal of the medieval knight was already an anachronism by the second half of the

---

[59] García de Palacio, *Diálogos militares*, fols. 56rv.

[60] Bachrach, '*Caballus et Caballarius* in Medieval Warfare', p. 188.

[61] Gillmor, for example, observes that there are in fact very few examples of feigned retreats in the battles of the Middle Ages ('Practical Chivalry: The Training of Horses for Tournaments and Warfare', p. 17). Bachrach recently refined his statement, which he limits to the Carolingians, as follows: 'The ability to execute a feigned retreat was well developed and a frequently practiced exercise in the armamentarium of the Carolingians' (*Early Carolingian Warfare: Prelude to Empire*, p. 127).

sixteenth century. If the fifteenth-century chronicler Hernando del Pulgar extols the virtues of the noble mounted knight Rodrigo de Villandrando (d. 1448) for his exploits and victories in single combat on the battlefield, the sixteenth-century chronicler García Cerezeda showers praise upon an infantry officer, Captain Baltasar de Soma, who, at the siege of the town of Coni in 1542, ordered his troops to focus on effecting an expeditious entry into the town by not breaking rank and fighting in single combat with those who challenged them to do so.[62]

Captain Baltasar de Soma doubtless knew that the reality of single combat was that it was not at all glamorous or noble, at least not while the combat was actually taking place. Descriptions through the ages of single combat on the battlefield are as remarkable for their similarity as for their brutality and desperation. The following description by Diego García de Paredes of a single combat in the city of Ravenna in 1533 is but one representative example from the sixteenth century:

> In this battle a French captain turned to face me because I killed two of his brothers on the battlefield, and we fought in the middle of the two camps armed as men-at-arms with some iron maces that I brought out. The Frenchman, seeing the weight of them, threw his to the ground, being unable to wield it well, and seized hold of an estoc and lunged at me, thinking that I would not be able to wield the mace either. He stabbed me through the tasset and wounded me, and I then struck him on the armet with the mace and I sank it into his head, from which he fell down dead.[63]

---

[62] García Cerezeda, *Tratado de las campañas y otros acontecimientos de los ejércitos del Emperador Carlos V en Italia, Francia, Austria, Berbería y Grecia, desde 1521 hasta 1545*, ed. Cruzada Villaamil, vol. III, pp. 66–7. On Rodrigo de Villandrando, see Pulgar, *Claros varones de Castilla*, ed. Tate, p. 34. Pulgar provides a list of other Castilian knights famous for their victories in single combat in *Claros varones de Castilla*, p. 56.

[63] 'Sobre este combate se revolvió un capitán francés conmigo porque le maté dos hermanos suyos en el campo, y combatimos en medio de los dos campos armados de hombres de armas con unas porras de hierro que yo saqué. En viendo el francés la pesadumbre de ellas, hechó la suya en el campo no pudiéndola bien mandar y echó mano a un estoque y vino a mí, pensando que tampoco pudiera mandar la porra. Dióme una estocada por entre la escarcela e hirióme, y yo le di luego con la porra sobre el almete y se le hundí en la cabeza, de que cayó muerto'. See García de Paredes, *Chrónica del Gran Capitán, Gonzalo Hernández de Córdoba y Aguilar*, ed. Rodríguez Villa, p. 257b. This description was plagiarised by López de Gómara, *Annales del Emperador Carlos Quinto*, ed. Merriman, p. 227. Luis Zapata also describes this episode in his epic poem *Carlo Famoso*. See Zapata, *Carlo Famoso*, facsimile, ed. Terrón Albarrán, fol. 150rb; also Sánchez Jiménez, *El Sansón de Extremadura: Diego García de Paredes en la literatura española del siglo XVI*, pp. 128–9.

The violence of such encounters changed little over the centuries as, for example, in the following account of single combat between Sergeant-Major Blackwood of the 71st Highland Light Infantry and a nameless Pathan warrior in the Umbeyla campaign of 1863:

> A Homeric single combat, reminiscent of the days of the Roman circus, took place between Sergeant-Major Blackwood and a huge Pathan who overtopped him by at least a foot. It was one of those strange affairs which happen from time to time in war, even nowadays, when the friends of the combatants feel powerless to intervene, and can only stand and stare. The Sergeant-Major thrust and parried, dodged and ducked, with the sweat pouring down his face and his eyes narrowed to mere slits, while his gigantic opponent bounded about making great sweeps with his tulwar. The end came suddenly. Grinding his teeth, the Pathan toppled over backwards grasping the bayonet, the point of which stuck out of the small of his back. Pulling the Sergeant-Major down on top of him, he wielded his tulwar with a last mighty effort, shearing through his enemy's pouch and mess-tin and cutting his buttocks to the bone. Sergeant-Major Blackwood thus received a wound such as every soldier hopes to avoid, but his Distinguished Conduct Medal was none the less well deserved.[64]

Since the sergeant-major was attacked and did not seek out single combat in this instance, he was awarded one of Britain's highest awards for gallantry in the field for the wound he sustained in this fierce fight.

By the mid-sixteenth century audacious acts of valour invariably had disastrous consequences beyond the relatively controlled environments of the lists, and Quijada de Reayo's advice on war was sound. In particular the tactic of engaging the enemy in close formation had devastating consequences. Luis de Ávila y Zúñiga's eye-witness account of the siege of Ingolstadt in 1546 echoes the theoretical position taken by Captain Diego de Salazar ten years earlier. The chronicler argues that the German heavy cavalry was massacred by the Spanish infantry because 'the siege was unfair, for cavalry was pitted against harquebusiers'.[65] As always, however, a handful of knights in the early Renaissance in Spain were foolhardy and stubborn enough to resist change on the battlefield and they paid dearly for their reckless arrogance.

---

[64] Oatts, *Proud Heritage: The Story of the Highland Light Infantry*, vol. 1: *The 71st Highland Light Infantry, 1777–1881*, p. 230.

[65] 'el sitio era desigual, siendo caballería contra arcabuceros'. See Ávila y Zúñiga, *Comentario de la guerra de Alemania hecha por Carlos V, Máximo Emperador Romano, Rey de España, en el año de 1546 y 1547*, ed. Rosell, p. 419a.

I conclude this chapter with an account of a dramatic but futile chivalric gesture in the face of technology and inexorable change; that of the
Marquis of Saluzzo, who, at the siege of Carmagnola in 1537, against the
advice of his officers and men, cantered on his horse before the walls of
the heavily defended city, lance in rest, openly defying the enemy harquebusiers. In another epoch the marquis might have expected the enemy to
issue a challenge from the battlements to fight in single combat.[66] At the
very least he might have demonstrated his own prowess as he stood firm
in the face of the arrow-volleys shot by enemy troops, relatively safe in the
knowledge that a knight clad in a full harness was impervious to this type
of assault. Times, alas, had changed, and it was no longer wise to tempt
Providence on the battlefield. The marquis was in the way. His officers
and men knew what he either did not know or refused to accept, namely,
that a mounted knight at a protracted siege who deliberately drew enemy
fire to an exposed position was as out of place as a tin-tack in a codpiece.
Instead of being admired for his impetuosity or of being afforded the
dubious privilege of exhibiting a battle scar at some future date, a reminder
to all of his valorous conduct at Carmagnola, the Marquis of Saluzzo was
blasted out of the saddle at close range by a volley of harquebus fire and
was killed instantly. As the chronicler Fray Prudencio de Sandoval laconi-
cally remarked: 'Few lamented his passing.'[67]

---

[66] For examples of such challenges in medieval Europe, see Barber and Barker,
Tournaments, pp. 42–3; Barker, *The Tournament in England, 1100–1400*, pp. 30–3;
and Prestwich, *Armies and Warfare in the Middle Ages*, pp. 232–3.

[67] 'No pesó a muchos su muerte'. Sandoval, *Historia de la vida y hechos del Emperador
Carlos V*, ed. Seco Serrano, vol. III, p. 35a. The incident is also described by
García Cerezeda, *Tratado de las campañas y otros acontecimientos de los ejércitos del
Emperador Carlos V en Italia, Francia, Austria, Berbería y Grecia, desde 1521 hasta
1545*, ed. Cruzada Villaamil, vol. II, p. 246.

~: 7 :~

From Sport to Spectacle:
Jousts, Cane Games and Tauromachy

I F the Iberian Peninsula followed comparable trends to the rest of continental Europe in so far as the evolution of armour was concerned, the
Peninsula was in a unique position in so far as riding techniques were
concerned. By the time Quijada de Reayo was writing, two diametrically
opposed styles of riding competed for dominance: the north-western European bridle style, known in Spanish as 'la brida'; and the autochthonous
jennet style called 'la jineta'.[1]

One of the most marked characteristics of the bridle style was the position of the legs. As we have seen in the previous chapters, whether he was
using a war saddle or a jousting saddle, the medieval knight rode with
long stirrup leathers and straight legs. The earliest documentary evidence
of this style of riding dates from the beginning of the thirteenth century.[2]
In addition to riding in the war saddle, the jousting saddle, and with no
saddle at all, Duarte of Portugal mentions two other methods that Iberian
horsemen must master. One of these – which is exclusive to Duarte's
treatise – involves riding in what he calls the Brabazon saddle ('sella de
Bravante'). From Duarte's description this style is a permutation of the

---

[1] On these two riding styles, see: Clare, 'Les deux façons de monter à cheval en
Espagne et au Portugal pendant le siècle d'or'; Fallows, 'Un debate caballeresco del
Renacimiento español: "caballeros estradiotes" y "caballeros jinetes"'; Mercier, 'Les
Écoles espagnoles dites de la Brida et de la Gineta (ou Jineta)'; Rubin de la Borbolla,
'Origins of Mexican Horsemanship and Saddlery', esp. pp. 26–8; Soler del Campo,
*La evolución del armamento medieval en el reino castellano-leonés y al-Andalus (siglos
XII–XIV)*, pp. 157–72; Sommer D'Andrade, *A Short History of the Spanish Horse
and of the Iberian 'Gineta' Horsemanship for which this Horse is Adapted*; and Soria,
El recado cordobés: Su origen, historia y estado actual, pp. 13–27. On cavalry treatises
in England, France and Spain, respectively, see the following bibliographical
guides: Huth, *Works on Horses and Equitation: A Bibliographical Record of
Hippology*; Menessier de la Lance, *Essai de bibliographie hippique*; and Marqués de la
Torrecilla, *Libros, escritos o tratados de equitación, jineta, brida, albeitería, etc.: Índice
de bibliografía hípica española y portuguesa*. On sixteenth-century Spanish printed
treatises, see Fallows, *Un texto inédito inédito sobre la caballería del Renacimiento
español: 'Doctrina del arte de la cauallería', de Juan Quijada de Reayo*, pp. 91–2. The
renaissance English treatises are discussed by Webb, *Elizabethan Military Science:
The Books and the Practice*, pp. 108–23.

[2] Soler del Campo, *La evolución del armamento medieval en el reino castellano-leonés y
al-Andalus (siglos XII–XIV)*, p. 185.

160 Curb bit with molinets and rings. Europe, 16th century. Length of shanks: 30.5 cm (12 in)

bridle style whereby the legs are pointed slightly forwards instead of straight down. The Brabazon saddle, then, was probably a bastard saddle that combined elements of the war saddle for use on the large Brabant horses in the Portuguese monarch's stable.

Riding in the war saddle, Brabazon saddle or jousting saddle required additional use of another defining accoutrement of the bridle style: the curb bit. The stallions of the Middle Ages and Renaissance could be quite fractious in each other's company with the result that the bits used to control these horses in times of peace were almost as torturous as those used in time of war.[3] Each shank of the curb bit would be connected by the mouthpiece, which consisted of thin, horizontal iron bars attached to a small ring in the middle. Some bars would have an arched protrusion in the middle known as the port. Rollers would be placed on the bars, and keys would often be affixed to the port. Made of metals such as cold-milled steel or sweet iron, which are porous, susceptible to rust and favourable to the taste, these devices were intended to induce sweet mouth, or salivation, and sometimes to occupy the horse and redirect its attention. Salivation was of crucial importance, for once the horse salivated and moved its tongue, the lower jaw relaxed and this in turn allowed the horse to accept the bit and communicate with the rider. For further control a twisted curb would often be attached to the bit as a means of causing severe pressure under the horse's mouth.

The rollers could be smooth and cylindrical in shape, or they could take the form of molinets, scatch-rollers and melon-rollers. The molinets were small, thick, striated wheels placed in clusters in the middle or on either side of the port; they were sometimes also used to link the curb chain. Fig. 160 is an extant example of a sixteenth-century European bit with clusters of molinets on either side of the high, arched port, beneath which are clusters of smooth rings and another three molinets on the curb chain.

3 On the temperament of the medieval stallion, see Davis, *The Medieval Warhorse*, p. 83.

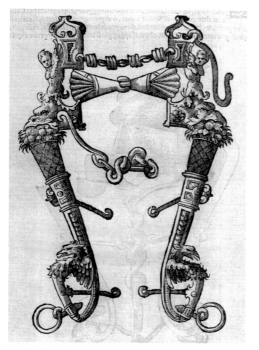 

161 *(left)* Curb bit with ridged scatch-rollers and four clusters of three molinets. Illustration from Pirro Antonio Ferraro, *Cavallo frenato diviso in quattro libri* (Venice: Francesco Prati, 1620; 1st edn 1576), part II, bk I, p. 53

162 *(right)* Curb bit with smooth scatch-rollers. Europe, 16th century. Length of shanks: 33 cm (13 in)

The shanks of this bit are 30.5 cm (12 in) long.[4] Scatch-rollers consisted of two cones set on each bar of the mouthpiece, the points of which would be connected by a small ring. The vertex of each cone was smooth and the frustum could either be smooth or decorated with striated, ridged edging. The finely drafted example of the ridged-edge type on the left in fig. 161 is from the 1620 edition of a book composed originally in 1576 by Pirro Antonio Ferraro, royal equerry of King Philip II of Spain.[5] The example with smooth cones in fig. 162 also dates to the sixteenth century; the shanks of this bit are 33 cm (13 in) long.[6] Melon-rollers, so called because

[4] See ffoulkes, *Inventory and Survey of The Armouries of the Tower of London*, vol. I, p. 215.

[5] The illustration is from Pirro Antonio Ferraro, *Cavallo frenato diviso in quattro libri* (Venice: Francesco Prati, 1620; 1st edn 1576), part II, bk I, p. 53. Ferraro is described as Philip's equerry on the frontispiece. A caption on the page opposite the illustration clarifies that this is a 'Figura di Scaccia' ('Figure of a Scatch-bit').

[6] See ffoulkes, *Inventory and Survey of The Armouries of the Tower of London*, vol. I, p. 215.

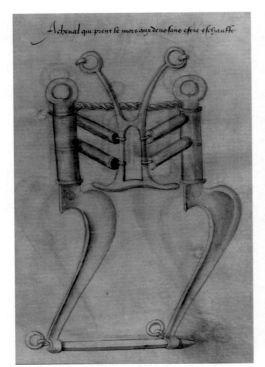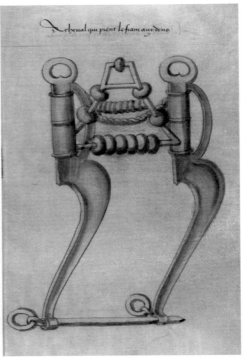

163, 164 Curb bits with high ports shaped like pincers and the arch of a lantern.
Illustrations from *Dessins de Mors* (1547), fols. 18r and 41r.
Vellum and wash. 36.19 × 26.67 cm (14¼ × 10½ in)

of their shape, could be smooth or grooved, depending on the disposition
of the horse.

For horses that clamped their jaws shut, special bits were developed
with very high ports shaped like pincers or the arched cage of a lantern,
which would force the mouth open. Figs. 163 and 164 show examples of
these types of bit from the unique and beautiful *Dessins de Mors* (Drawings of Mouthpieces), a manuscript commissioned in 1547 by Jacques de
Genouillac, Governor of Languedoc during the reign of King Henry II
of France, with the following captions: 'For the horse that clamps the
mouthpiece in its teeth without getting excited'; and 'For the horse that
clamps the bit in its teeth'.[7] Like the high port, a special wide, rounded
port, known as 'espejuelo' in Spanish, was used on horses with thick
tongues so that the animal could dip its tongue comfortably through the

___

[7] See *Dessins de Mors*, fols. 18r and 41r: 'À cheval qui prent le mors aux dens sans
estre eschauffé'; 'À cheval qui prent le frain aux dens'. On this manuscript, see
Catalogue de Livres, dessins et estampes de la Bibliothèque de feu M. J.-B. Huzard,
p. 454, no. 4951.

middle.[8] For horses that rear up, Quijada de Reayo recommends a tie-down in addition to the curb bit. And finally, for horses that refuse to close the mouth he refers to a 'mugerola'. This is an aleatory spelling that reflects Quijada de Reayo's accent, since the accepted modern spelling in Spanish of this technical term is 'muserola'. For training purposes he may be referring here to a drop noseband, which even now is the meaning imputed to the noun 'muserola' in Spanish. Made of soft leather, this accoutrement puts pressure on the horse's air passage and allows for more head control. In the context of sixteenth-century tournaments, however, he may also be refer-

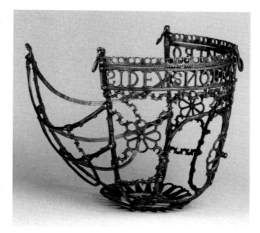

165 Iron horse muzzle. German, 1552

ring to an elaborate muzzle made of chased steel, designed to control the head and to stop particularly restive stallions from biting. In the sixteenth century this type of steel muzzle was also referred to as a 'muserola'. An example is illustrated in fig. 165. Of German manufacture, it dates from 1552. It is inscribed as follows:

S I D E V S N O B I S C V B M C A N T R O.

This cryptic inscription may mean: 'Si[t] Deus Nobiscu[m]. B[eata] M[aria]. Cant[o/a]ro'. That is: 'May God be with us. Blessed Mary. Cantoro (or Cantaro)', the last word being the name of the nobleman who commissioned the locksmith or spurrier to make the muzzle.[9] The surnames Cantoro and Cantaro are quite common in Milan, so perhaps this muzzle was ordered by an Italian jouster from that city. From a practical point of view muzzles of this type would have been incompatible with a shaffron,

---

[8] Several illustrations of this type of port, on jennet snaffle bits, are included in Aguilar, *Tractado de la cavallería de la gineta*, facsimile, fols. 75v–78r. The first edition of this treatise was published in 1572 and a second, expanded edition, was published in 1600. There are two facsimile editions of the 1572 printing, published in 1960 and 2006, respectively. Unless otherwise stated I cite from the 2006 facsimile.

[9] Chodynski, 'Horse Muzzles', p. 6, clarifies that these muzzles were the work of master locksmiths and spurriers. He resolves the inscription on Metropolitan Museum 14.25.1685 (fig. 165) as 'Si Deus Nobiscum Quis Contra Nos' ('If God [is] With Us, Who [could be] Against Us?', p. 19, no. 8), which strikes me as too big of a stretch. Chodynski does not mention in his article that it is not uncommon to find the owner's name worked into the inscription, as is the case, for example, with some comparable muzzles in The Wallace Collection. See Mann, *Wallace Collection Catalogues: European Arms and Armour*, vol. I, pp. 238–9, inv. A450 and A453.

requiring instead a demi-shaffron to protect the upper part of the horse's head.

In addition to the riding styles described above, Duarte recommends that the prospective knight know how to ride in the 'gyneta' saddle. The salient point to be made about this saddle, he says, is that it requires 'keeping the legs always flexed, staying well seated on the saddle and with both feet firm on the stirrups'.[10] The medieval Portuguese noun 'gyneta' and medieval Spanish 'gineta' (cp. modern Spanish 'jineta'; English 'jennet') are derived from the Arabic 'zanâta', a Berber tribe famous as horsemen.[11] This style of riding is first documented in the Iberian Peninsula in the tenth and eleventh centuries, and most likely has an even earlier origin.[12] Unlike the heavily armed knights of north-west Europe, the Arab jennets rode light coursers. They used a snaffle bit and, as stated by Duarte, often rode with short stirrup leathers and bent legs.

What remains unsaid in Duarte's treatise, and what is important to note in Quijada de Reayo's treatise, is the following recommendation that Quijada de Reayo makes in chapter two:

> It is necessary to practise two or three times a week, and in my opinion the man-at-arms should ride somewhat short rather than long, and fitting well in the saddle in the Spanish style, and leaning on the stirrups and pressing in the thighs, the legs taut.

That the prospective jouster should learn how to ride 'in the Spanish style' ('a la española') is suggestive. Soler del Campo cites an almost identical statement made approximately four centuries earlier in the *Historia Silense* (History of Santo Domingo de Silos), whereby King Ferdinand I of Castile and Leon (*c.* 1010–65; ruled 1035–65) recommends that his sons be educated in 'the Spanish way of riding horses'.[13] In an unnumbered chapter appended to the last page of his *Exercitiorum Atque Artis Militaris Collectanea*, Monte also discusses riding 'in the Spanish way', which, he clarifies, means riding 'in the jennet style'.[14] Although Quijada de Reayo's

---

[10] 'trazer as pernas sempre encolhidas, e asseentado na sella, e firmado nos pees' (Duarte I, King of Portugal, *Livro da ensinança de bem cavalgar toda sela que fez El-Rey Dom Eduarte de Portogal e do Algarve e Senhor de Ceuta*, ed. Piel, p. 17). For the translation, see *The Royal Book of Horsemanship, Jousting and Knightly Combat*, trans. Preto and Preto, p. 23.

[11] On the etymology of the words *jineta* and *jinete*, see Maíllo Salgado, 'Jinete, jineta y sus derivados: Contribución al estudio del medievo español y al de su léxico'.

[12] Soler del Campo, *La evolución del armamento medieval en el reino castellano-leonés y al-Andalus (siglos XII–XIV)*, pp. 159–62.

[13] 'more ispanorum equos cursare'. See Soler del Campo, *La evolución del armamento medieval en el reino castellano-leonés y al-Andalus (siglos XII–XIV)*, p. 159.

[14] Monte, *Exercitiorum Atque Artis Militaris Collectanea*: 'in modo hyspano qui ad gianetam vocari solet' ('in the Spanish way, which is wont to be called *in the*

statement is as circumstantial as ever, the other references cited serve to
clarify that although the ultimate goal of masters like Quijada de Reayo
was to teach prospective knights how to ride in the traditional north-west
European bridle style, be it in the war saddle, the Brabazon saddle or the
jousting saddle, the best way to train them was to teach them initially
how to ride in the home-grown jennet style. In other words, according
to one Iberian school of thought, mastery of the various western European riding techniques was predicated upon mastery of the jennet style of
riding.

Since the fourteenth century there had been contingents of jennets in
the Castilian army stationed in the southernmost regions of the Chris-
tian-occupied territories. As noted by Soler del Campo, these were rugged
frontiersmen and not always titled nobility.[15] Their role in combat situations tended to be a secondary one, acting as a vanguard that prepared the
terrain and cleared the way for the advance of the heavy cavalry, or inter-
cepting the enemy in sporadic raids. Their role as vanguard is explained
by the chronicler Álvar García de Santa María in his description of the
preparatory activities for the siege of Ronda in 1408:

> And then he wished to know how many men there were, and he
> discovered that there were a total of sixty-six horsemen, twenty-nine
> heavy cavalry and thirty-seven jennets. And he said: 'My lords, there
> are enough of you to go and raid Ronda, for there are few horsemen
> there'. And they set out from there on Thursday, 15 March, and they
> all arrived at Mercadillo de Ronda. And Fernando Arias stayed
> there with the heavy cavalry and he ordered the jennets to go and
> raid Ronda, and to kill all the Moors they could find in the open
> country. The jennets obeyed the order and, raiding the countryside,
> they came across Moorish foot soldiers, and it is said that they killed
> some thirty Moors, in full view of Fernando Arias.[16]

jennet style'). The neologism 'ad gianetam' (cp. Spanish 'a la jineta') would have
been impenetrable without first knowing the Spanish noun, and lends credence to
Anglo's belief that Monte was in fact a Spaniard.

[15] Soler del Campo, *La evolución del armamento medieval en el reino castellano-leonés y
al-Andalus (siglos XII–XIV)*, p. 167.

[16] 'E entonçes quiso saber qué gente heran, e falló que heran todos sesenta e seis de
cauallo, los veinte e nueve omes de armas e los treinta e siete ginetes. E díxoles:
"Señores, asaz gente sodes quanto para yr a correr a Ronda, que ay está poca gente
de cauallo." E partieron dende jueves quinze días de março, e llegaron todos al
Mercadillo de Ronda. E quedó allí Fernand Arias con gente de armas, e mandó a
los ginetes yr correr a Ronda, e que matasen los moros que fallasen en el campo.
Los ginetes fiziéronlo ansí, e corriendo por el campo fallaron omes de pie moros,
e diz que mataron vnos treinta moros, a vista de Fernand Arias' (García de Santa
María, *Crónica de Juan II de Castilla*, ed. Mata Carriazo, pp. 226–7).

The ruthlessness of the jennets implied in this quotation is made explicit in the fifteenth-century chronicle of the deeds of the Constable of Castile, Don Miguel Lucas de Iranzo (birth date unknown; assassinated in 1473), which juxtaposes to great effect innocuous jennet riding spectacles, referred to as 'honest pleasures' and confined to pretty palace courtyards and town squares, with brutal long- and short-range jennet incursions and raids into Moorish territory. One such raid into the kingdom of Granada in the year 1467 by a squadron of Iranzo's jennets based out of Jaén and captained by knight commander Fernando de Quesada, culminates in the pursuit and slaughter of twelve Moors and concludes with mutilation and robbery, as follows:

> And the said knight commander and the other knights who were with him took three or four heads off the Moors who died there, and five or six horses from said Moors, and the ears of another three or four who died there, and weapons, and all the loot that the Moors left behind.[17]

The enlightened Bishop of Burgos, Alonso de Cartagena, had lauded the contributions of this unique mounted force in his brilliant response to English diplomats in a debate over Castilian versus English military and political superiority at the Council of Basle in 1434. England, he argued, was protected by plenty of heavily armoured knights, but could boast no corps of jennets.[18] Subsequently Cartagena would pin his hopes for a definitive end to the Reconquest of the Nasrid kingdom of Granada on King Henry IV of Castile (1425–74; ruled 1454–74) who early on in his reign was known above all for his abilities in the jennet saddle.

Yet despite Cartagena's isolated defence both of Henry and the jennet riding style, prior to the sixteenth century in the Iberian Christian kingdoms, beyond the covert operations at the frontier this particular style was associated almost exclusively with Moorish culture and for jingoistic reasons it was considered worthy of contempt. The principal reasons for this contempt had to do with riding technique on the one hand, and apparel on the other. As far as technique is concerned, as we see in Quijada de Reayo's treatise, although the jennet style was perfectly acceptable for training purposes, there was an expectation that with experience the rider

---

[17] 'Y el dicho comendador e los otros caualleros que con él yvan tomaron tres o cuatro cabeças de los moros que allí murieron, e çinco o seys cauallos de los dichos moros, e las orejas de otros tres o quatro que murieron allí, e armas, e todo el despojo que los moros dexaron'. For similar raids that end in pursuit, slaughter and mutilation, see *Hechos del Condestable Don Miguel Lucas de Iranzo*, ed. Mata Carriazo, p. 355; also pp. 417–18, 442 and 460. For the term 'honest pleasures' ('placeres honestos'), see p. 98; also pp. 36 and 259. On the location of Jaén, see Map I.

[18] Cartagena, *Discurso sobre la precedencia del Rey Católico sobre el de Inglaterra en el Concilio de Basilea*, ed. Penna, p. 220a.

would eventually graduate to the more serious and prestigious bridle style. And as for cloth apparel, this was of course anathema to those who aspired to be armoured knights. This contempt is evident in a medieval chronicle written by Alonso de Palencia about King Henry IV of Castile. Despite Cartagena's high hopes for King Henry, the young monarch unfortunately failed to consummate his first marriage, acquired as a result the sobriquet 'The Impotent' and was plagued by accusations of homosexuality throughout his tempestuous reign. By association, his riding and dressing habits were routinely condemned as unmanly. So, for example, Palencia, in a characteristically vituperative description of the king, declares that:

> Rather in fact, he rejected the royal system of riding, and he preferred the form of Moorish horsemen – as suitable to robberies, incursions and skirmishes – to our nobler system or that of the Italians which is to be respected in peace and powerful in warlike expeditions and exercises.[19]

Focusing not on riding technique but on arms and armour, Palencia continues his attack in the following vein:

> But with a few horsemen armed with a light shield, he, also armed with a light shield, was roving contrary to ancient teaching which not only forbids light armour to kings and commanders, but also to any and all knights of the Kingdom of Castile, wherever they may be, except those residing in the Baetican Province.[20]

Old traditions really did die hard. And yet, despite the negative opinion about jennets shared by most Castilian equestrian theorists in the Middle Ages, in the sixteenth-century post-Reconquest era a new generation of young Spanish knights would reinvent themselves, appropriating tactics and accoutrements and, in the tradition of the jousting masters, using the printed word to forge new, legitimate identities as distinctly Spanish jennets. And in this chapter, it should be pointed out, I use the verb 'to forge' not only in the sense of giving form to and advancing an agenda, but also in the sense of counterfeiting.

---

[19] 'Quin etiam apparatum regium in equitando respuit, et pretulit Maurorum equitum formam latrociniis incursionibusque et leuibus preliis aptam generosiori nostro uel Italorum apparatui in pace uenerando atque in bellicis expeditionibus exercitationibusque robusto' (Palencia, *Gesta Hispaniensia*, ed. Tate and Lawrance, p. 5).

[20] Palencia's 'Baetican Province' is Andalusia. The Latin reads as follows: 'Sed paucis cum equitibus cetratis ipse quoque uagabatur cetratus, preter disciplinam ueterem quae non tantum regibus ducibusque nostris prohibet armaturam leuem, uerumetiam quibusuis equitibus regni Castellae ubicumque preterquam in prouincia Betica residentibus' (Palencia, *Gesta Hispaniensia*, ed. Tate and Lawrance, p. 111).

The first jennet treatise published in Spain is the *Tractado de la cavallería de la gineta* by Hernán Chacón, written in 1549 and published in Seville in 1551.[21] This book reflects an age of radical changes as much in the chivalric-military arena as in the consequences of those changes in the lives of Renaissance Spanish horsemen. The second half of the sixteenth century was an appropriate moment for publication of Chacón's treatise. In the court of Charles V, ostentation was in vogue. In an effort to promote a degree of austerity at court, as early in his reign as 1537 the emperor had promulgated in the *Cortes* of Valladolid a series of sumptuary laws prohibiting excessive adornment on clothing and equestrian trappings. The intention behind the laws was to impose a code of courtly etiquette, and the promulgation of the sumptuary laws was inspired in large part by the protests of those who 'implored His Majesty to order that all those who did not have a master at court and who attended court be banished, for there were many who went about dressed as knights and their only occupation was to gamble and chase after lovelorn ladies'.[22] Only those who rode in the jennet style were exempt from following the letter of the new law. With regards to equestrian trappings, for example, the emperor issued the following decree: 'The jennet knights may carry packs and silk caparisons embroidered with gold and silver bullion and backstitched with silver and gold, and cords and other trappings of golden silk.'[23] This law echoes a law promulgated much earlier, during the first year of the reign of King John I of Castile, at the 1379 *Cortes* of Burgos, according to which only knights are permitted to wear gilded adornments, with the notable

---

[21] Chacón's book was the only printed jennet treatise in circulation for just over twenty years, and it certainly had an influence on subsequent treatises. Aguilar in his *Tractado de la cavallería de la gineta* plagiarised not only the title of Chacón's treatise, but also an entire chapter (see below for further details). By 1643 Chacón's treatise had disappeared from view. A treatise entitled *Exercicios de la gineta* (Jennet Exercises, 1643), by Gregorio de Tapia y Salzedo, includes an 'Índice de los autores que han escrito de la Gineta' ('Index of authors who have written about the jennet style'), which refers to Aguilar, but not to Chacón. Chacón's treatise was rediscovered in 1950 by professor Eugenio Asensio. There are three modern editions: Chacón, *Tractado de la cavallería de la gineta*, facsimile, ed. Asensio; Chacón, *Tratado de la caballería de la jineta*, ed. Peragón; and Chacón, *Tractado de la cavallería de la gineta*, ed. Fallows.

[22] 'Suplicaron a Su Majestad mandase que todos los que no tuviesen señor en la Corte y anduviesen en ella los desterrasen de ella, porque había muchos que andaban en hábitos de caballeros y no tenían otro oficio sino de jugar y andarse con mujeres enamoradas' (Santa Cruz, *Crónica del Emperador Carlos V*, ed. Blázquez y Delgado-Aguilera and Beltrán y Rózpide, vol. II, p. 390).

[23] 'Los caballeros de la jineta pudiesen traer las mochilas y caparazones de seda con rapacejos de oro y de plata y pespuntada de lo mismo, y las cuerdas y otros aderezos de gusanillo de oro' (Santa Cruz, *Crónica del Emperador Carlos V*, eds Blázquez y Delgado-Aguilera and Beltrán y Rózpide, vol. III, p. 447).

exception of Andalusia, where both jennet knights and squires could orna-
ment clothing and horse trappings with gilt embroidery,[24] further formal
recognition that the jennet horsemen would always be associated primarily
with cloth apparel instead of metal armour. The jennet style allowed for a
certain amount of flexibility and freedom of expression among knights and
squires whilst at the same time it adhered to the sumptuary laws sanctioned and decreed by the *Cortes*.

It is clear from reading the sundry treatises published on jennet riding
techniques and accoutrements in the sixteenth and seventeenth centuries
in Spain that the authors were unsure about the actual practices of their
fifteenth-century Nasrid counterparts. This makes perfect sense, since
by the mid-sixteenth century, when the first printed treatises appear in
print, the frontier that separated and differentiated Christian Spain from
Moslem Spain had long since evanesced. By this time few Spaniards had
actually had the chance to see Moorish (or Turkish) cavalry in action.
Beltrán de la Cueva, the duke who commissioned *Doctrina del arte de
la cavallería*, is a typical example of a Spanish nobleman who had experienced more combat than most, but always on European soil and never
against an Arabic foe. And those old-timers (perhaps like Juan Quijada de
Reayo) who had long ago experienced real combat with a Moorish enemy
were most likely not focusing in the frenzy of battle on the precise ways in
which the enemy rode or wielded weapons, so their own memories would
be nebulous at best.

An example of the renaissance Spanish iteration, or forging, of Moorish
practice is the large bivalve shield called the adarga; 'the light shield', as
Palencia described it in his critique of Henry IV.[25] All the Spanish jennet
treatises, without exception, state that the adarga is to be held on the
arm. Chacón, for example, states that: 'The knight shall clutch the adarga
with his arm', and he 'should clutch his adarga with his arm through both

---

[24] *Ordenamiento de leyes hecho en las Cortes celebradas en Burgos en la era MCCCCXVII
(año 1379)*, statute 1. See *Cortes de los antiguos reinos de León y de Castilla*, vol. II,
pp. 283–6, at p. 284.

[25] An admirer of Cicero, Palencia uses classical Latin 'cetratis … cetratus' ('armed
with a light shield') to describe the adarga. Always game for a catchy neologism,
Pietro Monte invents the term 'darghi' (Monte, *Exercitiorum Atque Artis Militaris
Collectanea*, bk I, ch. I, sig a1v), which once again would have been virtually
impossible to understand without knowledge of Spanish. On the Arabic origin of
the adarga, see especially Buttin, 'Les adargues de Fès', pp. 409–19; also Corominas
and Pascual, *Diccionario crítico etimológico castellano e hispánico*, vol. I, pp. 50b–51a;
and Nicolle, *Arms and Armour of the Crusading Era, 1050–1350*, vol. II, p. 583a. The
ardaga continued to be used by Spanish troops in the American West well into
the eighteenth century. See Faulk, *The Leather Jacket Soldier: Spanish Military
Equipment and Institutions of the late 18th Century*, pp. 59–61.

166 Nasrid adarga, c. 1490

straps up to his elbow'.[26] Chacón's assumption, then, is that the adarga would be held on the arm and he seems to mean that one enarme, or grip, should loop over the left forearm and the other should be gripped in the left hand. Thus in their efforts at equestrian *imitatio* the Spanish jennets of the sixteenth century and beyond seem to have considered the adarga a defensive weapon, the principal purpose of which was to shield and protect. This, however, was a fundamental misunderstanding, since the documentary and pictorial evidence that has survived from Nasrid Granada and other sources indicates that adargas were not held on the arm at all, but that both grips were clutched firmly in the left hand, allowing for greater flexibility in their use as an offensive weapon to parry or deflect.[27] It is interesting to note, given the popularity of chivalric romance in the sixteenth century, that the adarga *is* held correctly by a fictitious character in one of the early texts: on going into battle, the King of Persia in *Las sergas del muy esforzado caballero Esplandián* is described as carrying 'an adarga in his left hand and a dagger in his other hand'.[28] The detail was obviously overlooked by certain readers.

Whereas many sixteenth-century Spanish adargas have survived, only two original fifteenth-century Nasrid examples are known to have survived the vicissitudes of history. These are in the collections of the Real Armería in Madrid and the Kunsthistorisches Museum in Vienna.[29] Fig. 166 illustrates the example in the Real Armería, which dates from the late fifteenth

---

[26] 'El cauallero se embraçará el adáraga'… 'se ha de embraçar su adáraga por ambas manijas hasta el cobdo'. Chacón, *Tractado de la cauallería de la gineta*, ed. Fallows, pp. 29, 37. Identical advice is given by Suárez Peralta, *Tratado de la jineta y brida*, ed. Álvarez del Villar, p. 59 and Tapia y Salzedo, *Exercicios de la gineta*, facsimile, ed., p. 14.

[27] Buttin, 'Les adargues de Fès', pp. 428, 444 and 453.

[28] 'en su mano siniestra una adarga, y en la otra un cuchillo'. See Rodríguez de Montalvo, *Las sergas del muy esforzado caballero Esplandián*, ed. Gayangos, p. 461a. For the translation, see Rodríguez de Montalvo, *The Labors of the Very Brave Knight Esplandián*, trans. Little, p. 229.

[29] Valencia de Don Juan, *Catálogo histórico-descriptivo de la Real Armería de Madrid*, p. 161, inv. D86, Thomas and Gamber, *Kunsthistorisches Museum, Wien: Waffensammlung: Katalog der Leibrüstkammer, I: Der Zeitraum von 500 bis 1530*, pp. 128–9, inv. C195. See also Buttin, 'Les adargues de Fès', pp. 449–50, and Soler

167 Sixteenth-century Spanish adarga bearing the arms of the Fernández de Córdoba family

168 Sixteenth-century Spanish adarga with the impresa 'Slave of María'

century. Made of leather, it is white on the outside and tawny-coloured on the inside. The inner circumference of the shield is decorated with alternating oval and circular medallions. Inside each oval medallion an inscription in Arabic reads: 'And God is but the only victor.' Similarly, an inscription in each of the circular medallions reads: 'Happiness for my master'. Fig. 167 shows an early sixteenth-century Spanish adarga that is a respectable imitation of the Arabic style. It serves as a gentle reminder that even though only two original Nasrid examples have survived to the twenty-first century, many more examples were probably available to inquisitive sixteenth-century Spanish noblemen who were seeking to make authentic reproductions. Made of leather, this shield is also white on the outside and tawny-coloured on the inside, decorated with arabesques along the inner circumference within which are four heraldic shields of arms of the Fernández de Córdoba family embroidered in silk.[30] Fig. 168 is yet another iteration of the Spanish adarga, from the mid-sixteenth century. This is a typical Spanish example of the period, in that it is decorated on the outside. In this case the device consists of a wide diagonal stripe in red flanked on either side by an impresa. A monogramme for the name María

del Campo, *La evolución del armamento medieval en el reino castellano-leonés y al-Andalus (siglos XII–XIV)*, p. 90.

[30] Valencia de Don Juan, *Catálogo histórico-descriptivo de la Real Armería de Madrid*, p. 161, inv. D87.

is painted in red above the stripe. Below the stripe a large letter 'S' is inter-
twined with a nail. Since the noun for nail in Spanish is 'clavo' the impresa
is believed to mean: 'Esclavo de María', or 'Slave of María'.[31]

With the notable exception of the Fernández de Córdoba shield, the
principal difference between the Nasrid adargas and their Spanish counterparts is that the Arabic shields are consistently decorated on the inside,
for the personal enjoyment of the owner, whereas the Spanish shields are
mostly decorated on the outside,[32] following long-established European
heraldic traditions. Iconographic evidence that depicts the inside of shields,
either when carried by Christians or by Moslems, is extremely rare,[33] so the
sixteenth-century jennets had little to go on in the plastic or fine arts as
regards proper usage.

By the mid-sixteenth century the Moorish adarga as conceived and
carried by Spanish noblemen had been conceptually turned around a
full 180 degrees so that the Spanish iteration at once embraced – literally
and therefore inauthentically – and yet rejected the shield upon which it
was modelled. The case of the adarga illustrates that the extent to which
the Spanish jennets were faithful in their appropriation of Moorish techniques and accoutrements is a matter open to debate. In the context of
a Renaissance aristocratic society and culture saturated by the influence
of humanism, this Spanish forging of Moorish practices was a complex
question of *imitatio* versus *exercitatio*, one that paradoxically embraced
and rejected Moorish practice in a quest for national identity that would
capture the imagination of such a broad swath of the populace that it
would ultimately destroy the joust.

As with the shield, the sixteenth-century Spanish iteration of the jennet
saddle was innovative in the sense that it allowed for a variety of possibilities as to the placement of the legs. Such possibilities vastly increased the
comfort level of the mounted knight. I mentioned above that old habits
died hard, however, which is why, in the earliest treatise Hernán Chacón
still argues in favour of long stirrup leathers, which would have required
the legs to be stretched out.[34] As the fashion of riding in the jennet style
swept across Spain, so jennet riders became more familiar with the saddle
and perfected their techniques. Writing in 1572, twenty-one years after the
publication of Chacón's treatise, Pedro de Aguilar, echoing Duarte, states

---

[31] As suggested by Valencia de Don Juan, *Catálogo histórico-descriptivo de la Real
Armería de Madrid*, p. 164, inv. D105.

[32] I say 'mostly' because several examples of European shields are known with small
votive images or phrases painted on the inside. These are the exception rather than
the norm.

[33] For examples of Western European targes, see Blair, *European Armour*, p. 225, and
Hoffmeyer, *Arms and Armour in Spain: A Short Survey*, vol. II, p. 133.

[34] Chacón, *Tractado de la cauallería de la gineta*, ed. Fallows, p. 21.

that it is best to ride in the jennet style with the legs slightly bent at the knee, with short stirrup leathers.[35] Still other theorists declare that it is licit to ride in the jennet style either with the legs stretched out or slightly bent at the knee. This is the opinion of the anonymous author of *Pintura de un potro* (Portrait of a Colt), a treatise composed in the second half of the seventeenth century.[36]

Unlike Juan Quijada de Reayo, Chacón argues that the cantles of the jennet saddle should be of a sufficient height simply to secure the rider so that he cannot fall. The saddle tree of jennet saddles was typically higher at the pommel than the cantle so that the rider could apply the necessary force with his legs in order to control the horse without falling out of the saddle. In his 1590 treatise entitled *Discurso para estar a la Gineta con gracia y hermosura* (Discourse on How to Ride in the Jennet Style with Grace and Splendour), Juan Arias Dávila Puertocarrero recommends that the pommel should measure two fingers above the crotch when the rider is standing in the stirrups. In this way, cautions Puertocarrero, the rider will be certain that when he is sitting in the saddle there will be little chance of flipping forward over the pommel.[37] That the jennet saddle was innovative is confirmed by the anonymous author of *Pintura de un potro*, who cites anecdotal evidence which coincidentally confirms just how skilled and astute a riding master was Quijada de Reayo. According to the anonymous author, while it is easy for a jennet to learn how to ride in the bridle style favoured by the mounted knights of north-west Europe, it is difficult in the extreme for riders accustomed only to the bridle style to learn how to ride in the jennet style, their main fear being that they will flip over the pommel while riding.[38] In a much less serious vein, and poking fun at the theorists in both camps, Cervantes would push this type of argument to its surreal extreme by having Don Quixote ride in both styles at the same time.[39] Examples of jennet saddles are illustrated from different angles below, in figs. 170–5.

Whereas Quijada de Reayo tells his protégé not to insert his feet too much into the stirrups, Chacón recommends that the stirrups for jennet riding be heavy and that they encase the rider's feet. He is referring to the type of stirrups associated with this style of riding, known in Spanish as 'mariño' stirrups, an example of which is illustrated in fig. 169.[40] Further-

---

[35] Aguilar, *Tractado de la cavallería de la gineta*, facsimile, ed., fol. 25v.

[36] Balenchana, ed., *Libros de jineta*, p. 42. The treatise was composed some time after 1665, according to Balenchana in the introduction to his edition of the text (p. viii).

[37] Sanz Egaña, ed., *Tres libros de jineta de los siglos XVI y XVII*, p. 19.

[38] Balenchana, ed., *Libros de jineta*, pp. 31–2.

[39] Cervantes, *El ingenioso hidalgo Don Quijote de la Mancha*, ed. Murillo, vol. I, pp. 83–4.

[40] Valencia de Don Juan, *Catálogo histórico-descriptivo de la Real Armería de Madrid*, pp. 179–80, inv. F104.

169 Jennet 'mariño' stirrup

more, states Chacón, 'the thighs should be very steady and firm against the saddle, and on no account should the thighs become detached or separated from the saddle'.[41] This detail is of fundamental importance because the jennet controls and guides the horse as much with his legs as with the reins. In order to facilitate control of the horse, the bit used by jennet riders had short shanks and a circular mouthpiece known in Spanish as a 'bocado'. The short shanks of the bit, short reins, short stirrup leathers with heavy stirrups, and the saddle would be conducive to agile and quick movement. The steeled front and rear arçons of the bridle-style war saddle which protected the rider's abdomen and cupped his buttocks to keep him in his seat were irrelevant since the jennet riders were never supposed to charge with heavy ash lances or meet the enemy head-on. From a technical standpoint the jennet style was ideal for training purposes, for this style allowed the rider better to understand the ergonomics of his horse. Learning the rudiments of equine ergonomics by riding in the jennet saddle would in turn have been essential in order to be able to ride successfully in the bridle-style military saddle or the high jousting saddle, which alienated the rider from the horse.

In addition to technical justifications for riding in the jennet style, in the fourth chapter of Chacón's *Tractado de la cauallería de la gineta* the jennet style is recommended 'in order to look good'.[42] This observation underscores the courtly theme of this treatise and attests to the enduring attraction of the Principle of Pulchritude. If as a warrior Chacón rejects the bridle style for its obsolescence and lack of comfort on the field of battle, as an aristocrat he rejects it for its lack of aesthetic appeal at court.

For jennet horsemen the practical implementation of chivalry revolves primarily around courtly etiquette. While Quijada de Reayo includes in his own treatise on knighthood detailed descriptions of the different pieces of the knight's armour and the function or purpose of these pieces in the lists and on the battlefield, always with the pragmatic intention of developing preventive measures that will ensure the knight's protection, Chacón picks up where Menaguerra left off, pushing the Principle of Pulchritude to an almost absurd extreme. He devotes six chapters to the topic of the

---

[41] 'los muslos han de estar muy fixos e firmes con la silla, y en ninguna manera los muslos se han de despegar ni apartar de la silla'. Chacón, *Tractado de la cauallería de la gineta*, ed. Fallows, p. 24.

[42] 'para parescer bien'. Chacón, *Tractado de la cauallería de la gineta*, ed. Fallows, p. 18.

etiquette that should be observed in cane games and bull-running,[43] with emphasis on composure, posture and the way the jennet rider carries himself in public; hence:

> My opinion is that running with the lance wearing the cape open should be done like this. The knight should put on his cape, and he shall throw the right flap over his left shoulder, and the left flap over the same shoulder, and he shall take the hem of the cape and tuck it beneath his legs so that when he is running it does not hang over the horse's rump. And likewise he will fasten on his bonnet or his hood very tightly; and let him not wear a cap, for this is not the way of the jennet and it has nothing to do with it. The knight should do all of this nonchalantly and covertly whenever he wishes to go and run the course, because if his hat falls off or the skirt of his cape hangs over the rump of his horse whilst running it is a misfortune and looks bad, and it gives the people who are watching something to laugh at.[44]

In the wake of Chacón's treatise, authors such as Juan Arias Dávila Puertocarrero and Bernardo de Vargas Machuca would manage to describe six subtly different ways of wearing the cloak when riding in the jennet style.[45] It is this type of description that precedes the core of Chacón's treatise and the core of jennet philosophy. Chapters 12 and 13,

---

[43] On the term 'bull-run' (Spanish 'corrida', 'correr toros'), see Kamen, *Philip of Spain*, p. 349, n. 103. The bullfight as it is known today is a later permutation of the bull-run. On bullfighting manuals, see the following bibliographical guides: Carmena y Millán, *Bibliografía de la tauromaquia*; and Díaz Arquer, *Libros y folletos de toros: Bibliografía taurina*. The earliest manuals have been edited by Cossío, ed., *Advertencias y reglas para torear a caballo (siglos XVII y XVIII)*. On cane games, see Clare, 'Un jeu équestre de l'Espagne classique: le jeu des "cannes"'; Fuchs, *Exotic Nation: Maurophilia and the Construction of Early Modern Spain*, pp. 88–102; and Toro Buiza, *Noticias de los juegos de cañas reales tomadas de nuestros Libros de Gineta*, pp. 8–21. On the Arabic origins of the cane game, see especially García-Valdecasas and Beltrán Llavador, 'La maurofilia como ideal caballeresco en la literatura cronística del XIV y XV', pp. 132–4.

[44] 'Corriendo sin lança con capa abierta, me paresce que se ha de hazer desta manera. El cauallero se ha de cubrir su capa, y echará el álaue derecha sobre el hombro yzquierdo, y del yzquierdo echará sobre el mismo yzquierdo, y tomará la halda de la capa y meterla ha debaxo las piernas, porque corriendo no salga sobre las ancas del cauallo. Y assimismo se apretará el bonete o caperuça muy bien; y no sea gorra, porque no es cosa de la gineta ni tiene deudo con ella. Todo esto ha de hazer el cauallero descuydada e dissimuladamente quando quiera yr a correr la carrera, porque cayéndosele el bonete o tendiéndosele las faldas sobre las ancas del cauallo yendo corriendo es azar y paresce mal, y da que reýr a la gente que lo mira'. Chacón, *Tractado de la cauallería de la gineta*, ed. Fallows, p. 25.

[45] Sanz Egaña, ed., *Tres libros de jineta de los siglos XVI y XVII*, pp. 39–43 (Puertocarrero), and pp. 170–3 (Vargas Machuca).

the central chapters of his book, describe the practical implementation of
Chacón's theories of riding in the jennet style as they apply to cane games
and bull-runs.[46]

By the mid-sixteenth century in Spain cane games and bull-runs would
typically take place one immediately after the other in the same arena,
usually a town square – Casey's 'theatre of display'[47] – and they formed
part of the same courtly spectacle.[48] In the cane games, team was pitted
against team in what was little more than a carefully choreographed, innocuous courtly display with no clearly defined scoring system. Quadrilles of
horsemen on each team would ride in synchronisation in a semicircle. As
each one passed the other, the riders would hurl light-weight, short spears
or canes with the intention of striking the opposing team's adargas as
that team retreated, the winning team being the one that beat the hast-
iest and most orderly retreat.[49] Etiquette was of crucial importance. For
example, when the knights file past the spectators it is necessary, declares
Chacón, that they carry their canes in precise formation, otherwise they
will look bad.[50] Likewise each quadrille of riders should be identified by an
appropriate colour in order to avoid confusion between teams during the
game. At a time of aggressive empire-building, the irony of a national spectacle that revolved around retreating has not gone unnoticed by modern
scholars.[51]

In bull-running, which stood at the intersection of hunting and jousting,
man and horse were pitted against raging bull. The bull-runs were somewhat more dangerous than cane games in that the mounted bullfighter
was expected to stand still as he was charged by the bull, and then deliver
the *coup-de-grâce* with his spear (Spanish 'rejón') as the bull delivered its
own attack. This, then, was a new era of pure, unadulterated spectacle.
Indeed, even in the twenty-first century the bullfight is always referred to
in Spanish as a spectacle and never as a sport. Unlike jousting, as the cane

---

[46] These two chapters are edited and translated in Part II, below.

[47] See above, chapter 6, n. 4.

[48] For representative examples, see Mexía, *Historia del Emperador Carlos V*, ed. Mata
Carriazo, p. 426, and Santa Cruz, *Crónica del Emperador Carlos V*, ed. Blázquez y
Delgado-Aguilera and Beltrán y Rózpide, vol. II, p. 92 and vol. III, p. 465.

[49] The spear was known variously in Spanish as the 'azagaya' or 'zagaya' and the cane
was known as the 'caña'. On the Arabic origins of the 'azagaya', see Corominas
and Pascual, *Diccionario crítico etimológico castellano e hispánico*, vol. I, p. 431a,
and Nicolle, *Arms and Armour of the Crusading Era, 1050–1350*, vol. II, p. 627a.
Hoffmeyer, *Arms and Armour in Spain*, vol. II, p. 86, translates 'azagaya' as 'assagay'.
I have opted not to follow this lead as it may cause confusion with the quite different
Zulu weapon of the same name.

[50] Chacón, *Tratado de la caualleria de la gineta*, ed. Fallows, p. 36.

[51] See especially Clare, 'Un jeu équestre de l'Espagne classique: le jeu des "cannes"'.

games and bull-runs evolved, the scoring became obsolete in favour of the choreography.

The choreography that characterised the cane games and bull-runs translated smoothly to the pages of the printed manuals in which these two activities were presented to the reading public. Whereas the jousting treatises of Menaguerra and Quijada de Reayo are both printed in gothic type, the Spanish jennet authors and their printers always marketed their books in variations of elegant roman or antiqua type-founts in their push to move away from the Middle Ages and medieval equestrian mores. Various roman type-founts had been in use in European printing centres since the 1470s. In Spain, these founts were considered to be the most eloquent and desirable way of transmitting knowledge about the jennet style; one more way of forging a particular identity and of widening the gap between jennets and jousters, between new and old.[52] And the greatest innovation of all – Spanish jennet treatises would eventually be illustrated with technical rather than dramatic drawings so that the reader could match pictures to words and gain a better understanding of this equestrian style. Figs. 170–3 are technical illustrations of a cane game in progress, with close-ups of riders carrying their canes, preparing to throw them and beating the retreat in formation. Fig. 174 depicts a massive bull charging a genteel jennet who stands perfectly still on his blindfolded horse, skilfully delivering the *coup-de-grâce* in fig. 175. These sets of illustrations by María Eugenia de Beer (fl. 1640–52) are included in Gregorio de Tapia y Salzedo's magnificent *Exercicios de la gineta* (1643).

It is in the sections of the jennet treatises that deal with chivalric spectacle that the authors push a distinctly nationalistic agenda. Both bull-runs and cane games were peculiarly Spanish spectacles and neither one took off in other European countries. In the debate that took place at the Council of Basle in 1434 Alonso de Cartagena had used the jennets to great effect, though he had emphasised the usefulness of jennets on the battlefield; not in the realm of spectacle. The English delegates at the Council were crushed when the Pope presiding, Pious II, declared Castile the winner of this debate.[53] The English dealt their own crushing blow over a century later when Philip II's Spanish entourage introduced the cane game to London. It was considered a tepid affair at best, though, significantly, the spectators could not deny the beauty of the cloth garments worn by the Spanish jennets. One observer remarked that the game 'left the spectators cold, except for the fine clothes of the players, and the English made fun of it'.[54] Despite this comment it is fair to say that the

---

[52] On the victory of antiqua over gothic type, see Steinberg, *Five Hundred Years of Printing*, pp. 31–40.

[53] On the Council of Basle, see chapter 4, n. 19, above.

[54] Quoted by Anglo, *Spectacle, Pageantry and Early Tudor Policy*, p. 340.

170 View of a cane game. From Gregorio Tapia y Salcedo, *Exercicios de la gineta*
(Madrid: Diego Díaz, 1643). Illustrated by María Eugenia de Beer

171 Carrying the spear in formation. From Gregorio Tapia y Salcedo, *Exercicios de la gineta*
(Madrid: Diego Díaz, 1643). Illustrated by María Eugenia de Beer

172 Preparing to throw the cane in formation. From Gregorio Tapia y Salcedo, *Exercicios de la gineta*
(Madrid: Diego Díaz, 1643). Illustrated by María Eugenia de Beer

173 Beating the retreat in formation. From Gregorio Tapia y Salcedo, *Exercicios de la gineta*
(Madrid: Diego Díaz, 1643). Illustrated by María Eugenia de Beer

174 The bull-run. From Gregorio Tapia y Salcedo, *Exercicios de la gineta* (Madrid: Diego Díaz, 1643). Illustrated by María Eugenia de Beer

175 Delivering the *coup-de-grâce*. From Gregorio Tapia y Salcedo, *Exercicios de la gineta* (Madrid: Diego Díaz, 1643). Illustrated by María Eugenia de Beer

176 Baiting the ostrich. From Gregorio Tapia y Salcedo, *Exercicios de la gineta*
(Madrid: Diego Díaz, 1643). Illustrated by María Eugenia de Beer

campaign launched by sixteenth-century Spanish theorists to promote
cane games and bull-runs as national spectacles was ultimately a success.
The only enclave in Spain that is known to have deliberately resisted cane
games in favour of jousts until well into the seventeenth century is the
great bastion of armour manufacture, Saragossa, thanks to the efforts of
a group of noblemen known as the Brotherhood of St George.[55] And even
though the cane games themselves eventually became extinct, they were
always considered uniquely Spanish. Similarly, the macabre spectacle of
the bullfight survives even today and is synonymous with 'Spain', though
in its modern form the mounted picadors play a subordinate role to the
unmounted matador, whose final struggle with the bull constitutes the
highlight of the spectacle.

By way of a footnote wherein the ludic meets the ludicrous, few Spaniards are aware of the attempts by Tapia y Salzedo in his *Exercicios de la
gineta* to eschew the bull and instead to promote fighting with ostriches
and other exotic animals.[56] Fig. 176 is a depiction of two Spanish jennets
disguised as Moors unmercifully transfixing a terrified ostrich that is also
being attacked by dogs just for good measure. This image shows that not

[55] On this Brotherhood see, especially Marín, 'Fiestas caballerescas aragonesas en la
Edad Moderna'.

[56] Luis Zapata notes that Aranjuez, just outside of Madrid, was a well known ostrich
breeding centre. See Zapata, *Miscelánea*, ed. Carrasco González, ch. 188, p. 263.

unlike the cloth apparel that had usurped the privileged place of armour as
the centre-piece of the knight's panoply, the point of reference of knightly
disguise that played such a prominent role in jousting competitions – the
visor of the armet or close-helmet – was ousted by inexpensive phoney
facial furniture: stick-on beards and moustaches.[57] Unlike their uncommon
handsome counterparts in figs. 169–74, these men wear a look of fiendish
glee as they assail and perforate the wretched ratite. Although the fake
beard has survived as the quintessential male disguise, fortunately for
ostriches everywhere, Tapia y Salzedo's ideas on ostrich-running never
caught on in the Peninsula.

   Some aspects of the joust did make the crossover to cane games. Thus,
as in jousting, it was frowned upon in cane games if accoutrements fell off
while riding. As noted above, Chacón considers that those whose bonnets
fall off are laughable. Suárez Peralta, author of the *Tractado de la cavallería
de la Gineta y Brida* (1580), concurs and expresses his displeasure at those
whose caps, capes, gloves and other falderals come flying off when they are
riding, and we see shades of Menaguerra when he adds that they should
be disqualified from winning the prize.[58] Like jousting, these ceremonial
details would become an integral part of riding in the jennet style, and
both cane games and bull-runs were intended to be more spectacles of
aesthetics than of physical prowess. One other vestige of the joust that
made the transition to the bull-run is that, like jousters, renaissance bullfighters were not expected to fight for money.[59]

   Chacón suggests various preventive measures in order to ensure the
well-being and safety of the contestants in cane games. He recommends,
for example, that all the stones and pebbles be removed from the square
where the cane game is scheduled to take place and that the square be

---

[57] On fake beards (and fake lances), see the following detail from a description of the
   Castilian cane games celebrated in 1464 near the frontier town of Jaén: 'Y luego
   salieron fasta quinientos roçines muy ajaezados e tocados a la morisca, e con barvas
   postizas; los quales trayán vnas cañas muy gruesas e vnos corchos plateados que
   verdaderamente paresçían lanças' ('And then about five-hundred horsemen came
   out wearing Moorish-style trappings and headdresses, and with false beards; who
   were carrying some very thick canes and silvered corks which really looked like
   lances'). See *Hechos del Condestable Don Miguel Lucas de Iranzo*, ed. Mata Carriazo,
   p. 195; also p. 102.

[58] Suárez Peralta, *Tractado de la cavallería de la Gineta y Brida*, fol. 28v; also Suárez
   Peralta, *Tratado de la jineta y de la brida*, ed. Álvarez del Villar, p. 48.

[59] See *Las Siete Partidas*, VII.vi.4: 'E aún decimos que son enfamados los que lidian
   con bestias bravas por dineros que les dan' ('We also decree that those are infamous
   who fight with wild beasts for money which is paid them'). *Las Siete Partidas*, ed.
   Sánchez-Arcilla, p. 903b. For the translation, see *Las Siete Partidas*, trans. Scott
   and Burns, vol. V, p. 1334. This law was reiterated by Diego de Valera in the
   fifteenth century in his *Tratado de las armas*, ed. Penna, p. 128a.

sprinkled with water so that the dust will not rise and impair the riders' vision.[60] This advice is repeated c. 1567 by Pedro Camacho de Morales in his manuscript treatise entitled *Tractado de la gineta*.[61] Over a century earlier, in 1463, the Castilian nobleman Don Miguel Lucas de Iranzo had all the stones cleared as well as the trees uprooted and some contiguous walls demolished in the Plaza de Santa María in Jaén in order to reduce the possibility of accidents at the cane games staged regularly in the square.[62] Remarking upon the untimely deaths of two participants during a cane game, Zapata notes that this rare, fatal accident was caused by dust which obscured the view of two riders, with the result that they suffered a head-on collision.[63] Ever the courtly gentleman, Chacón adds that dust is considered an irritant not only because it gets into the eyes of the riders, but also because it obscures the view of the female spectators who watch the spectacle from their privileged positions in the upper-storey windows and balconies overlooking the square.

Since cane games and bull-runs were far removed from the judicial solemnity of the joust, spectator etiquette was called into question. As in certain contemporary sports, such as snooker, tennis and golf, where cheering and catcalling are permitted at certain completed points in the game, at least one liberal-minded jennet theorist was willing to allow spectators to express their enthusiasm at certain times during the cane game. Pedro de Aguilar states that it is inappropriate to shout or curse during the spectacle, but it is permissible for fans to shout 'Make way, make way!' and 'Clear the way, clear the way!' as the riders enter the square, and to shout 'St James, St James!' and 'Charge, charge!' during the spectacle itself.[64] Others, such as Luis de Bañuelos y de la Cerda, reflect the long tradition in Iberian treatises that spectators should watch cane games with undivided attention and in complete silence.[65] Along similar lines, Bernardo de Vargas Machuca suggests putting cotton balls in the horses' ears during bull-runs so that the horses will not be able to hear the shouts of the bullfighters and the roar of the bulls.[66]

There was little room for shenanigans in a spectacle that revolved around teams of fast-moving riders throwing canes, and the cane games themselves were taken seriously by the players. The chronicler Lorenzo de

[60] Chacón, *Tractado de la cauallería de la gineta*, ed. Fallows, pp. 35–6.

[61] Quoted by Toro Buiza, *Noticias de los juegos de cañas reales tomadas de nuestros Libros de Gineta*, pp. 7–8.

[62] *Hechos del Condestable Don Miguel Lucas de Iranzo*, ed. Mata Carriazo, p. 118.

[63] Zapata, *Miscelánea*, ed. Carrasco González, ch. 141, p. 188.

[64] '¡Aparta, aparta!'; '¡Afuera, afuera!'; '¡Sanctiago, Sanctiago!'; and '¡A ellos, a ellos!' (Aguilar, *Tractado de la cavallería de la gineta*, facsimile, ed., fol. 40r).

[65] Balenchana, ed., *Libros de jineta*, p. 44.

[66] Sanz Egaña, ed., *Tres libros de jineta de los siglos XVI y XVII*, p. 215.

Padilla describes an incident when King Ferdinand of Castile and Aragon lost his patience with a young Portuguese competitor during a cane game that took place in Burgos in 1497. This man, Joan de Castelblanco, stepped forward and threw a cane while the king was in the process of choosing the teams. According to Padilla the king was so incensed at Castelblanco that he chased after him and gave him a sound thrashing with the king's own cane.[67]

As was the case with jousts, cane games and bull-runs could hardly be considered formal training exercises for war. Skirmishes were, in fact, dangerous and highly unpredictable affairs. In the fifteenth century Alonso de Palencia in a rare moment of fear commingled with respect would state that: 'For Moorish armies especially in combats of this type ought to be avoided rather than attacked and it has been established among veterans of our people that they should not voluntarily engage in skirmishes with the Granadans.'[68] A century later the chronicler Fray Prudencio de Sandoval would explain why, cautioning that: 'Because of one skirmish battlefields are wont to turn completely around, and without warning battles are won and lost.'[69] Bull-runs and cane games were events that did enable jennets to show off and hone their riding skills, but, with Sandoval's comment in mind, the relationship between real war and colourful teams of riders hurling canes at each other in precise formation across manicured town squares, or between real war and mounted bullfighters majestically skewering raging bulls, is tangential at best. And yet, having said all of this, one of the principal marketing strategies of the jennet authors was to cast their treatises in terms of the relevance of jennets in war. Thus Chacón rewrites history by claiming that thanks exclusively to the jennets 'the Catholic and fortunate Monarchs of glorious memory, Don Ferdinand and Doña Isabella, conquered and subjugated these kingdoms of Spain', even though the Reconquest of Granada was in fact a meticulously planned artillery campaign.[70] Likewise Aguilar cites the threat of Moorish aggression and

---

[67] Padilla, *Crónica de Felipe I llamado el hermoso*, ed. Sainz de Baranda, p. 45.

[68] 'Nam exerciti apprime Mauri in huiusmodi certaminibus pocius cauendi quam inuadendi sunt, et ueteranis nostrae gentis institutum est ne conserant sponte leuia certamina cum Granatensibus' (Palencia, *Gesta Hispaniensia ex annalibus suorum dierum collecta*, ed. and trans. Tate and Lawrance, p. 109; also p. 131, n. 62 for examples of other Castilian theorists who shared the same view).

[69] 'Suelen por una escaramuza revolverse los campos, y sin querer, darse y perderse las batallas' (Sandoval, *Historia de la vida y hechos del Emperador Carlos V*, ed. Seco Serrano, vol. III, p. 253b).

[70] 'con ella los cathólicos y bienauenturados Reyes de gloriosa memoria, don Fernando y doña Ysabel, ganaron y sojuzgaron estos reynos de España'. Chacón, *Tractado de la cauallería de la gineta*, ed. Fallows, p. 6. Ladero Quesada, *Castilla y la conquista del Reino de Granada*, p. 13, summarises the Reconquest of Granada as 'a war of sieges par excellence'. On the fundamental importance of artillery in this campaign, see

the need for a sound defensive strategy spearheaded by jennets as his reason for writing: 'I was compelled to compose this work', he states in the prologue of his own *Tractado de la cavallería de la gineta*, 'upon considering the close distance, the frontiers and war between the Spanish and the Moors of Africa.'[71] Thus the treatise that promotes the jennet style was apparently written as a reaction against the Moorish jennets. Barbara Fuchs rightly points out that in sixteenth-century Spain Maurophilia always ran parallel to Maurophobia, and this dynamic was not a fad, but a complex endeavour that she summarises as 'an ongoing and conflictive dimension of Spain's national identity'.[72] Aguilar's comment shows that the theory and the practice would mesh in a clever dance negotiated around Moorish custom and culture, at once pulling it in and turning it away as the national identity was forged.

Despite Aguilar's tough talk, what had once been the exclusive domain of rufty-tufty frontiersmen had, by the mid-sixteenth century, been entirely gentrified. By then even the most highly placed aristocrats flirted with the cane games, though not necessarily with the more dangerous bull-runs. The dedicatee of Chacón's text, Juan Vázquez de Molina, Charles V's personal secretary, participated in a cane game in Toledo in the year 1539. His performance is described by Martín de Salinas in an epistle written on 19 February of that year, as follows:

> Either to celebrate the marriage of the Duke of Sesa or to please his father-in-law, which I think is most likely, the Grandees arranged a festival with bull-runs and cane games that was as impressive as the people who were going to participate in that festival. And for this reason they decided that it should take place on the plain because there was not enough space in the plaza due to the large amount of knights, who surpassed 150 in number. And so they ordered that a plaza made of platforms be constructed on the plain, and it would not have been a bad idea to leave it standing permanently as a theatre because it accommodated the court and the city. And their majesties came and the bull-runs and cane games took place and all the Grandees who were there – who just happened to be all the Grandees in the kingdom – participated. Among them was Juan

Ladero Quesada, *Castilla y la conquista del Reino de Granada*, pp. 123–8; Cook, 'The Cannon Conquest of Nasrid Spain and the End of the Reconquista'; and López Martín, 'La evolución de la Artillería en la segunda mitad del siglo XV. El reinado de los Reyes Católicos y el contexto europeo'.

[71] 'Mouióme mucho a tomar este trabajo considerar la vezindad, fronteras y guerra que tenemos los españoles con los moros de África'. Aguilar, *Tractado de la cavallería de la gineta*, facsimile, ed., unnumb. fol.

[72] Fuchs, *Exotic Nation: Maurophilia and the Construction of Early Modern Spain*, p. 114.

Vázquez, his majesty's secretary, who was there for two reasons: firstly because he was a relative of the bride; secondly because he was secretary for war.[73]

I have argued that the authors of the first technical manuals were pioneers and early adapters, so it is only natural that they learned from each other's mistakes and omissions. Menaguerra, for example, barely mentions the horse at all, because he took it for granted that his readers were not absolute beginners. Zapata skirts the issue by making note of the principal coat colours with the qualifier that 'when they are covered in silks and brocades a horse's colour is not revealed'. Quijada de Reayo is writing ostensibly for a little boy, but although his book begins with a chapter on the saddle and ends with a chapter on bits and bridles, he has very little to say about horses *per se*. If these authors do not dwell on coat colour, this was due to the fact that they did not have to: the riding style described by them was already held in high esteem throughout north-west Europe and needed no introduction, publicity or marketing.

Chacón's book is not only the first jennet treatise, but the treatise that set the trend for those that followed in that the nucleus of the text is a description of the two jennet spectacles – cane games and bull-runs – and this nucleus is framed by chapters on horse selection and veterinary medicine. On the enduring influence of the jennet treatises and the success of the authors in marketing this style as the one most suitable for the military arena it is appropriate to quote Charles Gladitz who, in his study of medieval stud management and horse breeding, concludes that 'military requirements played a very important part in the development of certain breeds'.[74] Certainly chapters in vernacular cavalry manuals devoted to the rudiments of veterinary science, as well as entire treatises devoted to the subject, were on the rise in the sixteenth century.[75] The manuals constituted

---

[73] 'Por solemnizar el desposorio del Duque de Sesa o por complacer a su suegro, que creo ser lo más cierto, concertaron los Grandes de hacer una fiesta de toros y cañas muy solemne, como las personas que en ella habían de ser; y a la causa acoradron que fuese en la Vega, porque en la plaza no había lugar por ser grande la cantidad de los caballeros, que pasaron de 150. Y para ello mandaron hacer una plaza de cadahalsos en la dicha Vega, que no fuera mal acertado dexarla perpetua como teatro, porque en ella cupo la Corte y cibdad, a donde vinieron SS. MM. y se corrieron los toros y se jugó el juego de las cañas de todos los Grandes que aquí se hallaron, que fueron los que hay en el reino; y entre ellos Juan Vázquez, secretario de S. M., por dos respectos: el primero, por el deudo que tiene con la dama; y segundo, por ser secretario de la Guerra' (Rodríguez Villa, 'El Emperador Carlos V y su corte (1522–1539). Cartas de D. Martín de Salinas', *Boletín de la Real Academia de la Historia* 46 (1905), p. 182).

[74] Gladitz, *Horse Breeding in the Medieval World*, p. 215.

[75] On Renaissance Spanish veterinary treatises, see especially the bibliographical guide by Palau Claveras, *Bibliografía hispánica de veterinaria y equitación anterior*

the formal written recognition and legitimation of what in north-west Europe was previously considered an unconventional method of riding. In order to combat prejudice, jennet riders needed to seek ways to promote and validate their style. Besides the actual layout of the books in which they presented themselves there were various ways of doing this. Fuchs highlights the least convincing way, a convoluted etymological approach whereby the jennet style – which was clearly of Arabic origin – was alleged to have derived from the riding style of classical Troy and Rome. As Fuchs ably demonstrates, the arguments presented in favour of this theory are so forced as to be painful to read.[76] The much cleverer way was to promote the concrete rather than the abstract, the most obvious concrete element of the jennet preference being horses, in particular those of Andalusian stock. Andalusians had been tried and tested on the amorphous frontier between Christian and Moslem Spain for centuries and had acquired a reputation for excellence throughout Europe.

The author of the first formal treatise on the art of bull-running, Luis de Trexo, declares that: 'When a knight decides to bullfight with the spear, the first thing he must do is know the horses that he will ride.'[77] In so far as horses are concerned, the principal marketing strategy of the Spanish jennet riders, including Chacón, is to promote chestnuts and greys – colours that are unrelated to the actual breed of horse – as the best Spanish horses. Most likely coincidentally, but still worthy of interest is the fact that in the campaigns that had led to the defeat of the Aztecs and the conquest of Mexico (1519–21) the conquistador Hernán Cortés rode two dark chestnuts: one by the name of 'El Arriero' (The Muleteer); the other called 'El Romo' (Pudgy).[78] On the tenuous success of the campaigns Cortés himself wrote with these two animals in mind that 'after God, our only security was the horses'.[79]

a 1901, as well as the overview by Sanz Egaña, *Historia de la veterinaria española: albeitería, mariscalería, veterinaria*, pp. 97–128. On medieval and renaissance hippic science in general, see especially Davis, *The Medieval Warhorse*, pp. 100–7; Prévot, 'Le Cheval malade: l'hippiatrie au XIIIème siècle'; and Prévot and Ribémont, *Le Cheval en France au Moyen Âge: Sa place dans le monde médiéval; sa médecine: l'exemple d'un traité vétérinaire du XIVème siècle, la 'Cirurgie des chevaux'*, pp. 321–48.

[76] Fuchs, *Exotic Nation: Maurophilia and the Construction of Early Modern Spain*, pp. 99–102.

[77] 'Quando un cauallero determinare torear con el rejón, lo primero ha de reconocer los cauallos de que se ha de seruir' (Trexo, *Advertencias y obligaciones para torear con el rejón*, ed. Butler, p. 1). A facsimile edition of the first ed. of Trexo's manual has been published by Librerías París-Valencia.

[78] Díaz, *The Conquest of New Spain*, trans. Cohen, pp. 116 and 342.

[79] 'no teníamos después de Dios otra seguridad sino la de los caballos'. See Cortés, *Cartas y Documentos*, ed. Hernández Sánchez-Barba, p. 100. For the translation, see Cortes, *Letters of Cortes*, trans. MacNutt, vol. I, p. 301.

In the twenty-first century almost all Andalusians (that is, the breed) are chestnut, bay or grey, so it is feasible that Andalusians of Spanish origin, originally derived from horses the Moors brought to Spain in the eighth century and established as an official breed in 1579,[80] were the breed preferred by jennets. It is probable that the variety of colours was limited in the thoroughbred horses that were being bred at the time, and that the 'lesser' colours – such as white, morel and sorrel – mentioned by authors such as Chacón were a sign of crossbreeding or undesirable blood.[81] Whites allegedly had weak mouths and hooves, morels were short-sighted and often in rut, while sorrels were fundamentally flawed because of their 'burning mouths',[82] which probably refers to inflammation of the gum tissue on the bar space caused by pressure from the bit. The bar space or inter-dental space is the area of bone on the inside of the horse's mouth between the incisor and the molar, about 7 cm (2¾ in) long, which is a particularly sensitive pressure point. Since the bar cushions the pressure when the rider pulls on the bit, problems in this area could impede a jennet's ability to control his mount.

When describing the horse, Chacón gives consideration first to points of beauty, then to points of conformation. It is at this point, as with the adarga, that we note another mistake that betrays once again the dilettantism of these technical pioneers. As far as beauty is concerned, according to Chacón the ideal chestnut has black shanks, a broad tail, a full mane and a blaze or star on the forehead, with no white spots on the points. The mistake he makes here is that, at least by modern-day stand-ards, a brown horse with black legs or a black mane or a black tail would be described as bay, for a true chestnut would have brown legs, a brown mane and a brown tail. Chacón is correct by modern standards when he states that the ideal grey should be dappled, with a broad tail and a full mane.[83] Chestnuts and greys are preferred for two particular points of conforma-tion: they have a well-proportioned mouth, ideally suited for the seating of the snaffle bit; and they have strong hooves. They also reputedly run faster than horses of other colours. The hooves are an important consid-eration, for as well as colour, renaissance veterinary science dwelt primarily on hoof quality. When purchasing a horse, prospective buyers are advised to check the hooves and to steer clear of horses with hooves like those

---

[80] Jiménez Benítez, *El caballo en Andalucía*, p. 216.

[81] Different populations in East and West Europe preferred horses of different colours. English breeders, for example, preferred black (morel) and bay coloured horses. See Gladitz, *Horse Breeding in the Medieval World*, p. 203.

[82] Chacón, *Tractado de la cauallería de la gineta*, ed. Fallows, pp. 10–11. Zapata also notes that sorrels 'often have bad mouths and in many courses they overheat and will not stop'.

[83] Chacón, *Tractado de la cauallería de la gineta*, ed. Fallows, pp. 11–12.

of a mule.[84] This descriptor refers to the fact that mules often have small, upright, steep-angled hooves. This was and is not desirable because the combination of steep angle and small hoof would increase the strain on tendons in the leg and lead to lameness problems. In general, riders would look for hooves with a large diameter that could spread the horse's weight over a larger surface area. As well as the width of the hoof, riders would look for a strong hoof wall that would not chip or crack easily. The angle of the hoof wall varies according to breed, but the ideal dorsal hoof wall angle would be between 53 and 56 degrees. This would allow the horse to move without placing excessive strain on tendons and ligaments. Horses are fragile animals and any condition that puts excessive force or wear on the foot, such as bruising on too much weight from a hard object, or cracks or splits in the wall that make the soft tissue of the foot painful, can lead to lameness. In fact, the fragility and expense of horses coupled with the rugged Iberian terrain led the Spanish nobility to prefer mules to horses for general transportation needs.[85]

Chapter 2 of Chacón's treatise dwells upon the proportion of the horse. The best greys and chestnuts, argues Chacón, have small heads and strong lungs that enable them to endure the rigours of combat. In a similar vein, besides the description of the horse from a veterinary point of view, in the same chapter Chacón follows the lead of the jousters and highlights the Principle of Pulchritude, indicating that the animal should have 'good grace and elegance in its step and gait'.[86] These details underscore the trend in appropriation that characterises sixteenth-century Spanish jennet culture – the same emphasis on decorum as in tournaments, but a cunning marketing strategy which stresses that the horses and the courtly and chivalric etiquette associated with them are new and unique to the jennet way of doing things.

It is no coincidence that while Juan Quijada de Reayo's treatise on jousting was printed in the northern town of Medina del Campo, all the early jennet treatises were printed in southern cities, such as Seville and Málaga, that is, the areas where skirmishes with a mounted Moorish foe had occurred in the past and where the seeds could most readily be sewn for a gentrified jennet revival. By 1590, as the jennet riding style gained

[84] The Spanish adjective which describes this condition is 'patimuleno', sometimes spelt as 'patimuleño'. See Chacón, *Tractado de la cauallería de la gineta*, ed. Fallows, p. 13.

[85] On the expenses of travel by mule, as well as approximate distances covered in various case studies, see Ringrose, *Transportation and Economic Stagnation in Spain, 1750–1850*, pp. 43–8, and Ruiz, *Crisis and Continuity: Land and Town in Late Medieval Castile*, pp. 224–5.

[86] 'buena gracia y donayre en el passo y andamio'. Chacón, *Tractado de la cauallería de la gineta*, ed. Fallows, p. 14.

acceptance, jennet treatises were being printed in the north as well as the south. The first jennet treatise published in a northern city is Juan Arias Dávila Puertocarrero's *Discurso para estar a la Gineta con gracia y hermosura* (Madrid: Pedro Madrigal, 1590). In the year 1599, Pedro Fernández de Andrada would make clear the jennet nationalistic agenda by adding a conspicuous qualifier to the title of his own jennet treatise, the *Libro de la gineta de España* (Book of the Jennet Style of Spain), published in Seville by Alonso de la Barrera. It could be said that the jennet style received the national stamp of approval and recognition in 1600, when two jennet treatises were published in northern and southern cities that same year: the second edition of Pedro de Aguilar's *Tratado de la cavallería de la gineta* (Málaga: Juan René, 1600); and Bernardo de Vargas Machuca's *Libro de Exercicios de la Gineta* (Madrid: Pedro Madrigal, 1600). The enormous success of the books and the fashion statements they promoted would lead the protagonist of Cervantes' masterpiece to lament in chapter 1 of part II (published in 1615) that: 'Most of our knights nowadays prefer to rustle in damasks, brocades, and other rich clothes that they wear, than in armoured coats of mail. There are no knights now to sleep in the open, exposed to the rigour of the skies, in full armour from head to foot.'[87]

There was some disagreement between riding masters as to the most appropriate way for the novice to learn how to ride. Picking up where Quijada de Reayo leaves off, Chacón recommends a gradual approach, stating that at two-and-a-half years old colts should be bitted and trained to trot, amble and gallop for a few hours per day in a variety of different terrains.[88] Horses should be taught to proceed 'slowly, and not in haste',[89] that is, the horses should be trained to walk, speeding up for the trot only for skirmishes proper. Just over half a century later Luis de Bañuelos y de la Cerda advocates for a more direct approach. He declares more than once that the best way to learn how to ride in the jennet style is to choose a horse that runs with determination at a quick pace.[90] Both Simón de Villalobos, author of a treatise entitled *Modo de pelear a la gineta* (Method of Fighting in the Jennet Style, 1605), and the anonymous author of *Pintura de un potro* contribute the sound piece of practical advice that in wartime

---

[87] 'Los más de los caballeros que agora se usan, antes les crujen los damascos, los brocados y otras ricas telas de que se visten, que la malla con que se arman; ya no hay caballero que duerma en los campos, sujeto al rigor del cielo, armado de todas armas desde los pies a la cabeza' (Cervantes, *El ingenioso hidalgo Don Quijote de la Mancha*, ed. Murillo, vol. II, p. 48). For the translation, see Cervantes, *Don Quixote*, trans. Cohen, p. 477.

[88] Chacón, *Tractado de la cauallería de la gineta*, ed. Fallows, p. 15.

[89] 'passo a passo, y no de priessa'. Chacón, *Tractado de la cauallería de la gineta*, ed. Fallows, p. 49.

[90] Balenchana, ed., *Libros de jineta*, pp. 29 and 73.

skirmishes horses should always trot and never gallop, as it is essential that they not run out of breath on the battlefield.[91] Another danger of galloping at full speed on the battlefield is that horses cannot all gallop at the same maximum speed at the same time, which would in turn make for a disorganised, uneven and ineffective line of attack. The detail is suppressed by jennet theorists because their role on the battlefield was always to harass the enemy in small cohesive units and never to charge en masse. On the other hand, the detail is not suppressed by the infantry strategist Bernardino de Mendoza, who states that: 'The infanterie … indeed is the verie strength of the fielde, in respect that the force standeth more vnited in the footmen then in the horse, because that they moue by reason, and horses by the spurrs, and helde backe by the bridle, and both the one and the other cannot bee alike in all, as in men which haue discretion.'[92]

At the end of his treatise Chacón revisits the lameness issue. Chapter 14 includes a basic list, with no further explanation, of the most common types of hippic ailments, which he divides into two broad categories: lesions and lameness problems.[93] This chapter is little more than a checklist for prospective buyers and riders. The conspicuous absence of definitions indicates that the serious jennet was expected to be conversant with the rudiments of equine physiology. And however basic, Chacón's list was certainly impressive enough for Pedro de Aguilar to plagiarise it in Aguilar's own *Tractado de la cavallería de la gineta*.[94]

Most of the lameness problems refer to hoof and hock abnormalities. The lesions mentioned in the list are scabies, lice, mange and 'pox' ('alvarazes'),[95] which could refer simply to cold sores or to the more serious equine herpes virus III. Chacón also refers to a condition known as strangles ('lamparones'), which is an inflammation of the lymph nodes at the junction of the jaw and neck. Herpes and strangles are the only contagious diseases mentioned in Chacón's treatise. The problems listed underscore once again the fragility of horses, especially in so far as the hoof and hock are concerned. Unlike town squares, battlefields were never manicured before engagements with the enemy; thus by implication the medical

---

[91] Sanz Egaña, ed., *Tres libros de jineta de los siglos XVI y XVII*, p. 85 (Villalobos), and Balenchana, ed., *Libros de jineta*, p. 61 (*Pintura de un potro*).

[92] 'La infantería … realmente es la firmeza de los campos, por respecto del poder estar en los infantes más unida la fuerza que en la caballería a causa que ellos se mueven por la razón y los caballos por las espuelas, reteniéndolos el freno, y lo uno y lo otro no puede ser en todos con igualdad, como en los hombres por la consideración' (Mendoza, *Teórica y práctica de guerra*, ed. Saavedra Zapater and Sánchez Belén, pp. 76–7. For the translation, see Mendoza, *Theorique and Practise of Warre*, trans. Hoby, p. 54).

[93] Chacón, *Tractado de la caualleria de la gineta*, ed. Fallows, pp. 42–6.

[94] Aguilar, *Tractado de la cavallería de la gineta*, facsimile, ed., fols. 59v–60r.

[95] Chacón, *Tractado de la caualleria de la gineta*, ed. Fallows, p. 46.

conditions specified by Chacón also highlight the acute risks involved in real combat on horseback.

In the fifteenth century Diego de Valera described the horse as a naturally proud animal that could only be controlled with bridle and whip.[96] In order to train horses for skirmishing manoeuvres the sixteenth-century theorists in both camps concur that it is necessary to get the animal used to the bit in addition to riding it daily in different terrains. The jennet also had to get the horse accustomed to the pull on the reins and sudden changes of direction. The importance of the horse's mouth and the bit is stressed in chapter six of Chacón's treatise in which the author describes the most common defects in horses' mouths. Like Quijada de Reayo, Chacón recommends a curb bit for horses that suffer from parrot mouth, a condition where the top incisors overshoot the bottom incisors. Otherwise he focuses on horses with 'burning mouths' or 'sensitive mouths'. This is where he differs from Quijada de Reayo, for in these cases Chacón is alluding to conditions that would have a detrimental impact on snaffle bits, which had short shanks or no shanks at all, with the reins attached directly to the mouthpiece. Recognising that the snaffle bit communicates directly with the horse's mouth, but that all horses are different, he adds that the rein should be held in the left hand 'and fitted in whichever way best suits the horse's mouth, for on some occasions it will be necessary to place it low and on others high, on some occasions loose, on others tight'.[97] Fig. 177 shows an example of a snaffle bit from this period with the circular mouthpiece associated with the quintessentially Spanish jennet method of riding. The caption reads: 'Spain. For the horse that has a very big and only slightly slit mouth.'[98]

In addition to the saddle and stirrup leathers, the bit became the most important element of all the trappings of the jennet rider, as it was with the

---

[96] Valera, *Tratado en defenssa de virtuossas mugeres*, ed. Penna, p. 65a: 'El cavallo … naturalmente es sobervio. Onde por el cavallo el Salmista quiso entender aquí la no domada sobervia de los gentiles … pues los que tales opiniones tienen deben ser enfrenados como bestias e castigados con açote' ('The horse … is naturally proud. Whence by the horse the Psalmist meant here the unbridled pride of the gentiles … for those who have such opinions must be bitted like beasts and punished with the whip'). Valera's comment is reminiscent of and possibly influenced by Quintus Curtius Rufus' *Historiae Alexandri Magni*, which was widely circulated in the fifteenth century. See *Historiae Alexandri Magni*, ed. and trans. Rolfe, VII.iv.18 (vol. II, pp. 154–7): 'Nobilis equus umbra quoque virgae regitur, ignavus ne calcari quidem concitari potest' ('A noble horse is guided by the mere shadow of the whip, a worthless one cannot be aroused even by the spur').

[97] 'puesta en aquel lugar que a la boca del cauallo conuiene, que a las vezes será menester baxa y a las vezes alta, otras vezes blanda y otras vezes rezia'. Chacón, *Tractado de la cauallería de la gineta*, ed. Fallows, p. 24.

[98] *Dessins de Mors*, fol. 110r: 'Pour cheval qui a la bouche bien large et peu fendue'.

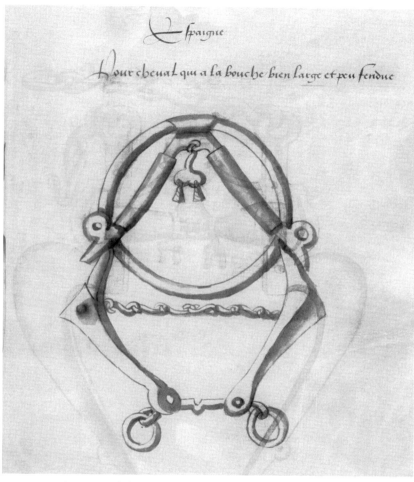

177 Jennet snaffle bit. Illustration from *Dessins de Mors* (1547), fol. 110r.
Vellum and wash. 36.19 × 26.67 cm (14¼ × 10½ in)

bit and the short reins that the jennet would learn to have greater control
over the horse. So important did the bit become that it was the object of a
separate genre of specialised studies. The most comprehensive sixteenth-
century Spanish work on the subject of bits is Eugenio Mançanas' *Libro
de enfrenamientos de la gineta* (Book of Jennet Bits), the first edition of
which was published in Toledo by Francisco de Guzmán in the year 1570.[99]

99 The title of Mançanas' treatise is somewhat misleading, for the author also
   provides a systematic and well-informed analysis of horses' hooves and the art
   of shoeing. See Mançanas, *Libro de enfrenamientos de la gineta*, fols. 6r–23v and
   32v–42v (on the bit), and fols. 24r–32r (on the hoof). See also, Sanz Egaña, 'El libro
   de enfrenamientos de Eugenio Manzanas'.

His treatise was followed by Pedro Fernández de Andrada's *De la natu-*
raleza del cavallo (On the Nature of the Horse, Seville: Fernando Díaz,
1580), which was in turn followed by a second edition of Mançanas' treatise, published in Toledo by Juan Rodríguez in 1583. All these treatises are
heavily illustrated.

As far as bitting is concerned, the illustrations in treatises such as those
by Mançanas and Aguilar reveal that jennet snaffle bits relied on iron
frothers and rollers for exerting pressure and enhancing salivation and in
this sense were as overly complicated as the bridle-style curb bits.[100] It would
not be until the 1660s that the anonymous author of *Pintura de un potro*
would question the use of complex keys and rollers, but without offering
an alternative.[101] This author was a voice in the wilderness, and the type of
snaffle bit used by renaissance Spanish jennet riders would undergo no
serious changes until the publication in 1855 of Juan Segundo's treatise on
the revolutionary 'new method' of bitting, that is, with the simple snaffle
or shank bits that are still used to this day.[102]

Losing control of a horse due to bit problems during a skirmish could
have catastrophic consequences that could be avoided only by the most
skilled riders. The chronicler García Cerezeda describes one such rider,
Don Sancho de Leyva, during the siege of Marseille in 1536. Don Sancho
spurred on his horse in a charge against the enemy, at which point a piece
of his horse's head stall snapped off. A seasoned rider, he had the presence
of mind to lean forward and seize hold of the bit just as it was coming
loose from the horse's mouth. So that Don Sancho's horse would not bolt
out of control into the enemy horde, he leaned over the pommel, flung his
arms around the neck of his horse, grabbed its chin and distracted the
animal until other riders could come to his assistance and help him replace
the bit in the horse's mouth.[103] This ruse, which Zapata refers to with wry
understatement as 'a useful skill',[104] worked, and Don Sancho survived this
skirmish relatively unscathed.

Despite the dangers mounted soldiers faced when confronted with
platoons of harquebusiers, the sixteenth-century jennet authors, like

---

[100] For the illustrations, see Mançanas, *Libro de enfrenamientos de la gineta*, fols. 34r–42v,
    and Aguilar, *Tractado de la cavallería de la gineta*, facsimile, ed., fols. 66v–84r. See
    also Chacón, *Tractado de la cauallería de la gineta*, ed. Fallows, p. xl.

[101] Balenchana, ed., *Libros de jineta*, p. 21.

[102] See Segundo, *Nuevo método para embocar bien todos los caballos y tratado sucinto de
    equitación*. The book was reprinted in 1857 and 1858.

[103] García Cerezeda, *Tratado de las campañas y otros acontecimientos de los ejércitos del
    Emperador Carlos V en Italia, Francia, Austria, Berbería y Grecia, desde 1521 hasta
    1545*, ed. Cruzada Villaamil, vol. II, p. 176.

[104] 'Una útil habilidad'. Zapata, *Miscelánea*, ed. Carrasco González, ch. 30, p. 42. He
    describes a similar incident with a broken bridle in ch. 250, p. 350.

Quijada de Reayo before them, do not mention firearms. One can only assume that it was a matter of personal prejudice that prevented them from commenting on the existence of firearms, let alone the devastation caused by these weapons, in which case the writers of jennet treatises were suffering from a condition that is now popularly known as being 'in denial'. Or could it be that the sixteenth-century authors knew that they would seldom if ever actually be expected to engage in front-line combat? As I mentioned above, they came to terms with the fact that the cavalry in the military arena had long since diminished in strategic importance firstly by rewriting their history on the battlefield and secondly by redirecting attention to the importance of national spectacle.

It would be up to writers such as Diego García de Palacio in his treatise on infantry and artillery tactics to give some idea of the complexities involved in skirmishing on horseback with firearms, noting that in wartime the mounted harquebusiers are to be deployed for the not very glamorous task of spying on the enemy and acting as scouts who discover the enemy's position. According to García de Palacio they should also be responsible for the mundane chores of bringing up supplies and guarding thoroughfares and passes. The light cavalry, he adds, are used principally for escort duties and to provide back-up support in skirmishes.[105] The infantry tactician goes on to say that the jennets should be skilled at skirmishing, wielding the spear in either hand, riding and controlling their horses. In addition to being able to fight with the sword and other weapons they must be able to ride with speed up and down hills and in rugged mountainous terrain. Mounted harquebusiers should differ from those on foot only to the extent that mounted harquebusiers must be able to ride up and down sierras and mountains at high speeds and in formation. As well as being skilled swordsmen, harquebusiers on foot and on horseback should be ambidextrous so that they can fire the harquebus with either hand.[106]

In *The Arte of Warre*, published in 1591, the English theorist William Garrard – who had served in the Spanish army for fourteen years – concurs with García de Palacio on the role of the cavalry, and he adds a shrewd note to the effect that in the case of mounted ambuscades, where a stealthy approach is essential, geldings are preferable to 'stoned', or uncastrated horses, as geldings tend not to neigh as much as their stoned counterparts.[107] Garrard, having noted that at best the cavalry constitutes 'a great commoditie and reputation to a Prince, and sharpe spurs to a well ordered armie',[108] reaches the following general conclusion about the role

[105] García de Palacio, *Diálogos militares*, fol. 56r.
[106] García de Palacio, *Diálogos militares*, fol. 56v.
[107] Garrard, *The Arte of Warre*, p. 231; also p. 5 for his service in Spain.
[108] Garrard, *The Arte of Warre*, p. 231.

of cavalry in sixteenth-century warfare, and the undeniable power of pike and musket:

> Their seruice is commonly espying aduantage, to breake vpon the squadrons of pikes, to encounter the enemies horse, and to relieue their owne light horse if by hap they bee put to a retrait. But a good squadron of pikes, of resolute men, well empaled and girdled with musket, doth greatly discredit their auncient reputation now in these our dayes.[109]

The jennets, in forging their new identity, had come to play a central rather than a peripheral role in courtly, peacetime equestrian activities. Yet despite the wealth of information supplied by the authors of the vernacular manuals on equestrian technique, by the sixteenth century the chivalric ideal of the mounted knight was, on the European battlefield, obsolete. It would be up to the infantry tacticians such as García de Palacio and Garrard to point out the urbane truth, however, which was that the cavalry were expected to bring up supplies for the infantry, guard passes and spy on the enemy, with the result that in battle their role was quite literally relegated to that of the spectator.

---

[109] Garrard, *The Arte of Warre*, p. 142.

Conclusion

THE treatises commissioned or composed by royalty that contain sections on jousting, such as Alfonso XI's *Libro de la Orden de la Banda* and Duarte's *Livro da ensinança de bem cavalgar toda sella* are generically allied to the treatises of Menaguerra, Quijada de Reayo and Zapata in terms of content. What distinguishes the three texts under discussion in this book from the royal books is the question of form. Ponç de Menaguerra, Juan Quijada de Reayo and Luis Zapata were not kings aided by notaries, but three practising jousters who took up the pen and wrote as they spoke, even, in the case of Menaguerra, despite official attempts at regularisation and censure. Their elliptic style and quirky phraseology is forgivable given that they were linguistic and technical pioneers. It was as though the isolated old hermit who was a pivotal motif of chivalric literature had emerged from the forest, but an important transformation had taken place. Iberian chivalric theory was saturated with Aristotelianism with the result that Menaguerra, Quijada de Reayo and Zapata, whether consciously or not, present themselves as wise, experienced, virtuous counsellors in whom other men have placed their trust in the quest for the Truth about jousting. The confluence of physical and consultative practice in this quest was born of the felicitous alliance between the joust, the new technology of the printing press and Aristotelian philosophy. Thus in these three authors the reclusive hermit was transformed into a born-again prophet seeking salvation for the joust in the vernacular and through the medium of print. On the one hand, the conversational style of *Lo Cavaller*, *Doctrina del arte de la cavallería* and 'Del Justador' can sometimes make for difficult reading. On the other hand, when Richard Kaeuper laments the fact that 'we have no oral history of chivalry',[1] these texts come remarkably and tantalisingly close.

In the sporting arena, as Alan Young has argued, the demise of the tournament in renaissance England can be attributed to the increasingly high expenditure involved in staging such lavish events and the economic burden placed upon individual participants.[2] This is a sound theory that can be applied equally well to the demise of tournaments in other countries, including Spain. Even leaving aside the costs of staging these sumptuous events, the armour required for jousting in particular had always

---

[1] Kaeuper, *Chivalry and Violence in Medieval Europe*, p. 34.

[2] Young, *Tudor and Jacobean Tournaments*, pp. 43–73.

been an extremely expensive commodity that only the very wealthy could hope to afford.[3]

As we have seen in chapter 5, jousts of peace were characterised by a complex scoring system. However, most of the chronicles that describe jousting tend not to emphasise the score as much as they exploit the tabloid aspects of the sport. Typically the chronicles focus either on the pageantry, the luxurious, refulgent attire of the contestants or any juicy disasters that befell them in the lists. Similarly, the miniatures in illuminated manuscripts and the woodcuts in early printed books that depict jousts almost always highlight the most dramatic moment of the encounter: the impact. Indeed, one sure-fire way of achieving immortality in the pages of a chronicle was to get killed jousting. Thus, as well as the economic burden, it is very probable that another reason jousting fell out of favour was that due to bad public relations via the chronicles it was ultimately considered altogether too dangerous for the practitioners and its supposed irrelevance became too obvious to ignore.

Unlike other nations, however, sixteenth-century Spain presented a unique set of circumstances whereby innocuous and vastly entertaining alternatives were possible; in the case of the cane game, an alternative that could be cleverly justified, exploited and legitimated for its connection, tangential though it in fact was, with real war. These were spectacles that followed no complex rules to speak of, certainly none that needed to be embarrassingly suspended for the benefit of royal participants. Kings and their sons could join in with impunity and without fear of being abruptly killed, protecting both honour and primogeniture. Ironically, it is this very situation that helps explain the sudden appearance of printed jousting treatises. The idea of disseminating and sharing knowledge that had been a secret closely guarded by an élite group of custodians for several centuries validated the issue at hand: jousting. The need to go public was especially urgent at a time when other spectacles competed for dominance. This is one reason why the authors of the jousting manuals opted for the medium of print. The fact that Menaguerra's *Lo Cavaller* went through a second edition in 1532 suggests that in addition to validating the sport the intention was to sell jousting to as large an audience as possible at the time.

Although bull-runs and cane games had existed for centuries in the Iberian Peninsula, as far as courtly happenings and displays were concerned they had always played a subordinate role to the more élite joust. With the notable exception of Saragossa, the fate of Western Europe's most élite sport was gradually sealed throughout the Peninsula when, spearheaded by authors such as Chacón and Aguilar in the 1550s and 1570s via the medium of the printing press, jennet aficionados successfully marketed a

---

[3] On the costs of jousting armour in comparison to field armour, see Williams, *The Knight and the Blast Furnace*, pp. 904–10.

kind of 'democratised' chivalry, as Cátedra would put it;[4] one that had been validated by the *Cortes* and had historically been accessible to a wide spectrum of social classes, including frontiersmen and squires as well as knights. Their treatises promoted cane games and bull-runs, aureate yet eminently affordable spectacles in which choreography and unabashed display took precedence over physical strength, technical virtuosity and nuanced scoring systems. A watered down version of the Principle of Pulchritude that had characterised combat in the lists would survive and triumph once more in the public plazas and the bullrings, much to the chagrin of men such as Luis Zapata, for whom the joust would always be the superior – the royal – activity. Conversely, the Principle of Equality would become a thing of the past the moment the jennets started baiting bulls. The end result of this spectacle was not in the least bit stochastic, for the bull always died.

By the late sixteenth century, the reality of Spanish imperial expansion in the form of invasion and conquest was now a topic of heated discussion and debate beyond the country's own borders, especially in England. Ten years after the disastrous Armada attack of 1588, in Robert Barret's *The Theorike and Practike of Moderne Warres*, a dialogue between a naïve civilian gentleman and an astute military captain best captures the fears of many Europeans at that time. The dialogue reads as follows:

> CAPTAIN: And first, concerning mine opinion touching the ambitious and proud minded Spaniard, I say; that besides her Maiestie and her honourable Counsell, it is not vnknowne vnto a number of honest gentlemen and souldiers of our nation, that the Spaniard hath aboue these thirtie years, as well as by his owne naturall imperious inclination, as by the Satanicall suggestion of the Romain Pope and Clergie, and continuall instigation of our English and Irish Papists, both desired, pretended and practised the vtter ruine, subuersion and conquest of our religion, state, and realme: the experiment whereof in Anno 1588 last, with his Inuincible Nauie, so by him termed, attempting our seas and coasts, we haue yet fresh in memorie: whereof wee may well say: *Deus pro nobis pugnabat.*
>
> GENTLEMAN: But do you thinke that he will yet attempt the like, considering his soyles, and losses then receiued?
>
> CAPTAIN: Why sir, doe you thinke that so mightie a Prince, so proud and ambitious a Nation, possessing so many mightie Kingdomes, such inestimable Indies, such plentie of wealth, such readie subiects, such skilfull warriors, such braue conductors, such store

---

[4] Cátedra, *El sueño caballeresco*, pp. 93, 103 and 125; Cátedra, 'Fiesta caballeresca: ideología y literatura en tiempos de Carlos V'. p. 83; Cátedra, 'Fiestas caballerescas en tiempos de Carlos V', pp. 99–100.

of shipping, and hauing such an egger on as is the pestiferous Pope, will not yet attempt what he can, were it but to recouer his honour and reputation lost in the last action?[5]

Such sentiments were echoed by military and political theorists until well into the seventeenth century. In addition to – or perhaps because of – the debates that played themselves out in treatises on warfare, translations of original Spanish manuals became increasingly popular reading matter. A fact often ignored by modern scholars is that the works of Spanish military tacticians such as Bernardino de Mendoza, Francisco de Valdés, Luis Gutiérrez de la Vega and others, while hardly known today, were among the first European best-sellers and as well as going through several editions in Spain the books written by these authors were translated into English, French and Italian.[6] John Thorius, the English translator of Valdés' *Dialogo militar … en el qual se trata del oficio del Sargento mayor*, implicitly recognises the value of this treatise by the very fact that he deemed it worthy of translation.[7] The importance of the treatise on the Sergeant Major is made explicit in the following statement in Thorius' own prologue:

> And forasmuch as thys booke was written to instruct those that are professed enemyes to our estate, I thoght that we might reap some profite by them, if this theyr Sergeant Maior were as well knowen vnto our men as vnto themselues. I haue therefore bestowed some pains in vnarming this Spanysh Sergeant and doffing his Castilian and hostile armour, and haue clothed him in English apparel, to the end that our men may vse him to theyr pleasure, and he finding himself metamorphosed, learne how to serve Englishmen.[8]

The translations underscore the fact that in the area of military theory as well as that of armour the sixteenth century was a time of cultural exchange. And yet, unlike the infantry treatises, not a single Spanish cavalry treatise was ever translated into another language. There are two paradoxical reasons for this. Firstly, there was no interest outside of Spain in the jennet riding style because of its nationalistic affiliations; it

[5] Barret, *The Theorike and Practike of Moderne Warres, Discoursed in Dialogue Wise*, pp. 1–2.

[6] The English translations of Mendoza, Valdés and Gutiérrez de la Vega are discussed by Webb, *Elizabethan Military Science: The Books and the Practice*, pp. 228, 232, and 227, respectively.

[7] Thorius had an intellectual affinity with Iberia, for he had been a pupil of the Spanish monk Antonio del Corro, who lectured at Oxford, 1578–86. Both Corro and Thorius were the authors of some of the first Spanish grammar books printed in England. See Blaylock, 'The Study of Spanish in Tudor and Stuart England', esp. p. 65.

[8] Thorius, *A Dialogue of the Office of a Sergeant Maior*, fol. A2.

was retailed as a Spanish style that did not translate physically or liter-
arily to other nations and cultures. The Principle of Transferability that
had characterised the international tournament circuit would be doomed
the moment the bull-runs and cane games were consciously promoted as
national spectacles in the pages of the printed manuals. The adarga shield,
the light-weight cane carried by jennets and the bullfighting spear gradually replaced the accoutrements that had characterised the jouster: the
bouched shield (latterly the grandguard and targetta) and the lance. As
early as 1528 the nationalistic ethos that underpinned the cane games and
bull-runs was anticipated in the pages of the first edition of Castiglione's
Book of the Courtier. The ideal courtier, we are informed, should be able
to joust like an Italian, tourney like a Frenchman and excel at cane games
and bull-runs like a Spaniard.[9] In this sense, the strategy of marketing
national styles and spectacles succeeded. Secondly, however, there was
quite probably no interest in these treatises outside of Spain because for
all the militaristic bombast the treatises were perceived for what they were:
equestrian manuals that posed no serious threat at all. In this sense the
strategy of rewriting history by overstating the importance of the jennets
on the battlefield – a strategy that was undermined by the contemporary
infantry treatises written by Spaniards that were translated into other
languages – failed.

King Henry IV of Castile's affinity for the jennet style was considered in
a negative light by the upper echelons of court society because this style had
always required a minimal amount of armour, even when Castilian jennets
had engaged real enemies during the Reconquest on the amorphous Chris-
tian-Moslem frontier. The equestrian activities of the sixteenth-century
distant cousins of the fifteenth-century jennets consisted of participation
in delightful cane games and bull-runs, with emphasis on apparel made of
cotton, velvet, satin, wool, leather and brocades. This was a style that was
affordable not only to the aristocrats but also to the swelling ranks of the
bourgeoisie who strove to imitate and emulate their socio-political supe-
riors. Rips and tears could be stitched and cloth apparel could – horror of
horrors – be altered, borrowed or purchased second-hand with the expectation of a reasonable fit. The garments and accoutrements that characterised the jennet style had also received official sanction in the sumptuary
laws of the *Cortes*. They thus constituted both a formal and a final rejection of expensive, sculpted plate armour and, by extension, of the élite
sport that for hundreds of years had been indissolubly linked to it: the
joust.

---

[9] Castiglione, *The Book of the Courtier*, trans. Opdycke, p. 26.

~: PART II :~

Texts, Translations and Glossaries

Introduction to the Texts

The Editions

Lo Cavaller

My edition of *Lo Cavaller* is based on the only known copy of 1493 printing, currently in The Hispanic Society of America in New York. This is the first time that the 1493 edition has been made available in a modern edition. Textual variants from the 1532 edition are provided in footnotes.

Doctrina del arte de la cavallería

My edition of *Doctrina del arte de la cavallería* follows the text of the only surviving original copy in the Biblioteca de Palacio.

'Del Justador'

In the case of 'Del Justador' my edition is based on the original manuscript in the Biblioteca Nacional.

Passo Honroso – Selections

Although a modern edition of the *Passo Honroso* is currently available, based on Biblioteca del Monasterio de San Lorenzo de El Escorial MS f.II.19, it contains many mis-transcriptions and errors of interpretation.[1] The chapters edited below are based on my own transcription of Escorial MS f.II.19. Written in Castilian in two different hands, this manuscript was copied between 1516 and 1576 and contains the most complete text of the *Passo Honroso*.[2] Two later copies, both of which have some lacunae, have been taken into account in the collation: Madrid, Real Academia de la Historia, MS 9–2-4/213;[3] and Santander, Biblioteca Menéndez y Pelayo, MS m-104.[4] Textual variants are included in the notes to the Spanish edition.

---

[1] Rodríguez de Lena, *El Passo Honroso de Suero de Quiñones*, ed. Labandeira Fernández. In the not too distant future Dr Tobias Capwell and I plan on preparing a new critical edition in Spanish and an English translation of the *Passo Honroso*.

[2] For a description of the MS see *BETA*, Manid 3057, and Zarco Cuevas, *Catálogo de los manuscritos castellanos de la Real Biblioteca de El Escorial*, vol. I, pp. 139–41. On the dates see Mulertt, 'La fecha del manuscrito Escurialense del *Paso Honroso*'.

[3] *BETA*, Manid 2117, and *Índice de la colección de Don Luis de Salazar y Castro*, vol. XI, p. 80.

[4] *BETA*, Manid 3058.

In the notes I abbreviate the manuscripts as follows:

ESC – Escorial, Biblioteca del Monasterio de San Lorenzo de El Escorial, MS f.II.19.

RAH – Madrid, Real Academia de la Historia, MS 9-2-4/213.

BMP – Santander, Biblioteca Menéndez y Pelayo, MS m-104.

A much-abbreviated printed edition of the *Passo Honroso* was published by Fray Juan de Pineda in 1588. This text has been edited by Martín de Riquer.[5] I have taken Pineda's abbreviated chronicle into account in the case of the occasional *lectio difficilior* in the Escorial MS or note of interest in the English translation. Other manuscripts are listed in the *Bibliografía Española de Textos Antiguos (BETA)* online database. These are so fragmentary that I have discounted them from the collation. The MSS are as follows: Madrid, Biblioteca Nacional, MS 7012 is a late sixteenth-century copy of Pineda's abbreviated chronicle; Madrid, Biblioteca Nacional, MS 746, fols. 222v–224v contains a list of the participants in the passage of arms, a summary of how the judges were elected and a summary of the challenge issued by the Fabras brothers to Suero de Quiñones requesting that they alone be allowed to fight the defenders; Madrid, Biblioteca Nacional, MS 7809, fols. 148v–151r and 151v–165r, contains a translation of the twenty-two Articles into Catalan followed by the Fabras' brothers challenge and Suero's response, in Catalan and Castilian respectively; Madrid, Biblioteca Nacional, MS 7811, fols. ccxvi^v–ccxxxv^v, from which MS 7809 is copied, contains the same text; and Madrid, Biblioteca Nacional, MS Res. 27, fols. 63vb–67vb and 94rb–95rb contains Suero's explanation to King John II of Castile of his emprise on 1 January 1434, the twenty-two Articles, and two responses from Don Juan de Benavente to the Fabras brothers.[6]

For each test case scenario edited I refer in the Castilian version to the folio numbers of Escorial MS f.II.19, and in the English translation I include the date of the joust and the relevant passage in Menaguerra's text in which the rules are explained.

Tractado de la cavallería de la gineta – Selections

Written by Hernán Chacón in 1546 and published in 1551 this is the first of many treatises which describes the art of riding in the jennet style and the spectacles associated with this style. I have edited and translated two chapters devoted to cane games and bull-runs, respectively. As with the *Passo Honroso* selections my aim in this case is once again to complement

[5] Pineda, *Libro del Passo Honroso*, ed. Riquer.

[6] For detailed descriptions of these MSS, see *BETA*, Manid 3070 (MS 7012), Manid 4297 (MS 746), Manid 2173 (MS 7809), Manid 1565 (MS 7811), Manid 2736 (MS Res. 27).

the theoretical manuals on jousting. The chapters edited are from the first and only edition of the text, of which one copy survives in Salamanca, Biblioteca Universitaria, 49.391.[7]

Editorial Criteria

The texts edited below are characterised by a high incidence of aleatory spellings, haplography and elision, as well as by an almost total lack of punctuation. On the understanding that the placement of a single comma can radically alter the meaning of a sentence, it is my hope that the texts as I have edited them make logical sense. In making sense of the texts, and in order to facilitate comprehension, I have adhered to the following editorial criteria:

(1) I have resolved all abbreviations used in the original texts without further indication, e.g. the abbreviation 'q̃' is transcribed as 'que' as opposed to '*que*'.

(2) I change -u- to -v- when used as a consonant, and -v- to -u- when used as a vowel; hence 'cavallero' instead of 'cauallero', 'usança' instead of 'vsança', etc.

(3) I have modernised accents and punctuation, which are erratic or non-existent in the originals. Similarly, I have joined or separated, according to modern usage, words that are separated or joined in the original texts.

(4) In the case of *Lo Cavaller*, following the long established editorial practices of the series 'Els Nostres Clàssics', I use the 'punt volat' to indicate elision ('bé·m', 'si·l', 'perquè·l', etc.). While I may be accused of overkill, I also provide the extended wording in a footnote, always with a view to facilitating comprehension.

Translations

All the translations are my own. They constitute another first, since none of the texts edited in this book has previously been translated into English.

Every effort has been made to translate the original texts as accurately and as literally as possible. Indeed, the reader should know that faced with such a difficult undertaking I did make a private chivalric vow to complete them or die trying. Each text poses its own unique problems of interpretation. Firstly, certain technical terms, such as Catalan *encontre* and Spanish *encuentro*, have several different meanings which I have endeavoured to

---

[7] For the complete text in Spanish see Chacón, *Tractado de la cauallería de la gineta*, ed. Fallows.

translate correctly based on context. Other technical terms are mind-bogglingly obscure and have required many years of research in order to decipher. Last but by no means least, still other technical terms can only be inferred by studying the context, discussing with colleagues, and then making what I hope are logical deductions. Many of my interpretations are discussed in Part I; others are explained in the notes to the translations.

Bibliographic Notes

Ponç de Menaguerra • *Lo Cavaller*

(1) Ponç de Menaguerra, [*Lo Cavaller*] (Valencia: n.p., 16 September 1493).

LOCATION: New York, Hispanic Society of America, Reserve Incunabula (no call number); previous call number hc397 no. 805.

BIBLIOGRAPHIC REFERENCES: *Bibliografia de Textos Catalans Antics (BITECA)*, Manid. 1759; Fustér, *Biblioteca Valenciana*, vol. I, pp. 37b–38a; Goff, *Incunabula in American Libraries: A Third Census of Fifteenth-Century Books Recorded in North American Collections*, p. 415b, Item M-487; Haebler, *Bibliografía ibérica del siglo XV*, vol. I, p. 199, no. 419; Palau y Dulcet, *Manual del librero hispano-americano*, vol. IX, p. 6a; Penney, *List of Books Printed Before 1601 in the Library of The Hispanic Society of America*, p. 166; Penney, *Printed Books, 1468–1700, in The Hispanic Society of America*, p. 362; Ribelles Comín, *Bibliografía de la lengua valenciana*, vol. I, p. 436a.

NOTES: 8 blank + 8 + 8 blank folios. The frontispiece of this copy is missing. On the first extant page (fol. a ij r) a modified title is written in Spanish by a contemporary hand:

Libro:– de –: Justas:~
(Book of Jousts).

The same hand has written other marginalia throughout the text. The author of this marginalia also accidentally spilled some of his ink, which has stained the bottom right-hand corner of every folio. The pages measure 140 × 206 mm (5½ × 8 in). The book is printed in a fifteenth-century Gothic font, the exhortative sentence at the top of the first page in red, the rest of the text in black. Small woodcut initials are added at the beginning of some chapters, but not others. Woodcut initials are missing from chapters 2, 4, 8, 10, 13, 18, 23, 25, 28, 29 and the first paragraph of the section entitled 'Scola del junyidor'.

The book was rebound in the nineteenth century in green morocco leather embossed in gold leaf along the inner edges. The spine is embossed in gold leaf as follows: 'MENAGUERRA LO CAVALLER 1493'. Eight extra end pages were added to the original text when it was re-bound. Glued to the verso side of the first added page is the French sales catalogue description of the book.

Writing between 1903 and 1917, Haebler notes that there are some doubts as to whether this edition actually exists, but none the less suggests that Nicolás Spindeler is the printer.[8]

(2) Ponç de Menaguerra, *Lo Cavaller* (Valencia: n.p., 13 July 1532).

LOCATION: Madrid, Biblioteca de Palacio, 1/c/199.

BIBLIOGRAPHIC REFERENCES: *BITECA*, Manid. 2093; Gallardo y Blanco, *Ensayo de una biblioteca española de libros raros y curiosos*, vol. III, p. 736b, no. 3016; Marqués de la Torrecilla, *Libros, escritos o tratados de equitación, jineta, brida, albeitería, etc.*, p. 234, no. 365; Palau y Dulcet, *Manual del librero hispano-americano*, vol. IX, p. 6a; Ribelles Comín, *Bibliografía de la lengua valenciana*, vol. I, p. 435ab.

NOTES: 2 blank + 9 + 2 blank folios. The pages measure 125 × 183 mm (4⅞ × 7¼ in). All the folios of this edition have at one time been guillotined and strengthened along the inner edge. On the frontispiece of this copy a previous owner, the bibliophile and grammarian Benito Martínez Gayoso (*c.* 1710–87), has signed his last name in ink with a flourish below. The frontispiece includes the title at the top, below which are two woodcuts. The first woodcut, set directly below the title, depicts two knights jousting. Behind the two jousters is a tilt decorated in a lozenge pattern. For added perspective there are some mountains in the background. The second woodcut, at the bottom of the page, consists of a generic vase flanked on either side by sumptuous foliate designs.

Like the 1493 edition, this book is printed in a fifteenth-century Gothic font, the exhortative sentence at the top of the first page in red, the rest of the text in black. Small woodcut initials are added at the beginning of every chapter. The book is bound in brown leather with a red leather spine embossed in gilt as follows: 'PORI [*sic*] LO CAUALLER'. This binding was added in the late eighteenth century, most likely by Gayoso.

Ribelles Comín suggests that the printer of this edition is either Nicolás Spindeler or Miguel Albert.[9]

---

[8] Haebler, *Bibliografía ibérica del siglo XV*, vol. I, p. 199.

[9] Ribelles Comín, *Bibliografía de la lengua valenciana*, vol. I, p. 435b.

(3) Ponç de Menaguerra, *Lo Cavaller*, facsimile, ed. José León Sancho Rayón (Madrid: J. Sancho Rayón, 1874).

> LOCATION: London, British Library, 899.f.16 (bound in 1923, this volume contains fifteen of the Rayón facsimiles; the facsimile edition of *Lo Cavaller* is the thirteenth text in the volume); New York, Hispanic Society of America, no call number (the verso side of the frontispiece states that this is the twenty-first copy in the run of forty-six copies); Princeton, Firestone Library, 3166.269 (four volumes of the Rayón facsimiles bound *c.* 1915; the facsimile edition of *Lo Cavaller* is the fourth text in vol. I).

> BIBLIOGRAPHIC REFERENCES: Infantes, *Una colección de burlas bibliográficas*, pp. 51–2, no. XXII; Ribelles Comín, *Bibliografía de la lengua valenciana*, vol. I, p. 436a.

> NOTES: This is a facsimile of the 1532 edition. As noted by Infantes, forty-six copies of this edition were printed in 1874.[10] Publication was announced in the *Revista de Archivos, Bibliotecas y Museos* 4 (1874), p. 207.

(4) Ponç de Menaguerra, *Lo Cavaller*, ed. Ignacio Janer, Ernesto Moliné y Brases, Luis Faraudo, Recull de textes Catalans antichs, vol. III (Barcelona: La Academica, de Serra germans y Russell, 1906).

> LOCATION: Chicago, University of Chicago Library, PC3937. M5C4. 1906; Madrid, Biblioteca Nacional, R/100136.

> NOTES: Although it is handsomely printed in a fifteenth-century-style gothic font, this book should not be mistaken for a facsimile edition. In fact it is a transcription based on the 1532 printing. The edition itself is preceded by a brief introduction written collaboratively by the editors. This edition is quite rare in that it was limited to 200 copies.

(5) Ponç de Menaguerra, *Lo Cavaller*, ed. Pere Bohigas, in *Tractats de cavalleria* (Barcelona: Barcino, 1947), pp. 177–95. Reprinted without changes in 1982.

> NOTES: Bohigas states in his introduction that his edition follows the 1906 edition prepared by Janer *et al.*[11] Consequently Bohigas reproduces many of the same mistakes made by the previous editors. The editors of the modern editions were aware of the existence of the 1493 incunable, though in fairness to them it would not have been at all easy in the years 1906 and 1947 to have travelled to New York to study this text in person, or even to have ordered copies.

---

[10] Infantes, *Una colección de burlas bibliográficas*, p. 52.

[11] Menaguerra, *Lo Cavaller*, ed. Bohigas, p. 42.

(6) Ponç de Menaguerra, *Lo Cavaller*, trans. Constantí Llombart (Valencia, 1870).

> BIBLIOGRAPHIC REFERENCES: Giner, *Constantí Llombart i el seu tempo*, p. 38; Infantes, *Una colección de burlas bibliográficas*, p. 51; Ribelles Comín, *Bibliografía de la lengua valenciana*, vol. I, p. 436a.

> NOTE: Despite these references, I have yet to locate a copy of this translation into Spanish. It is possible that it was a privately printed keepsake with a very limited print run.

Juan Quijada de Reayo • *Doctrina del Arte de la Cavallería*

(1) Juan Quijada de Reayo, *Doctrina del arte de la cauallería* (Medina del Campo: Pedro de Castro, 1548).

> LOCATION: Madrid, Biblioteca de Palacio, I/c/198.

> BIBLIOGRAPHIC REFERENCES: Marqués de la Torrecilla, *Libros, escritos o tratados de equitación, jineta, brida, albeitería, etc.*, pp. 251–2, no. 428; Palau y Dulcet, *Manual del librero hispano-americano*, vol. XIV, p. 450b; Pérez Pastor, *La imprenta en Medina del Campo*, pp. 52b–53a; Vindel, *Manual gráfico-descriptivo del bibliófilo hispano-americano*, vol. VII, p. 331.

> NOTES: 2 blank + 7 + 2 blank folios. The pages measure 130 × 180 mm (5⅛ × 7¹/₁₆ in). All the folios of this edition have at one time been guillotined. As with the 1532 edition of *Lo Cavaller* (Palacio Real, I/c/199), on the frontispiece of this copy the bibliophile Benito Martínez Gayoso has signed his last name in ink with a flourish below. The binding is also similar to I/c/199, embossed in gilt on the spine as follows: 'QUIXADA ARTE DE CAVALLERIA'. This is the only original copy of Quijada de Reayo's text that is known to have survived and is not to be confused with the facsimiles mentioned below.

(2) Juan Quijada de Reayo, *Doctrina del arte de la cauallería*, facsimile, ed. José León Sancho Rayón (Madrid: J. Sancho Rayón, 1874).

> LOCATION: Ann Arbor, University of Michigan Special Collections Library, PQ6425. Q7. 1548a; London, British Library, 899.f.16 (the facsimile edition of *Doctrina del arte de la cauallería* is the fourteenth text in the volume); Madrid, Biblioteca de Palacio, 1/B/247; Madrid, Biblioteca Nacional, R/3634; New York, Hispanic Society of America, no call number; Princeton, Firestone Library, 3166.269 (the facsimile edition of *Doctrina del arte de la cauallería* is the third text in vol. I).

> BIBLIOGRAPHIC REFERENCES: Infantes, *Una colección de burlas bibliográficas*, pp. 59–60, no. XXVIII; Palau y Dulcet, *Manual del librero hispano-americano*, vol. XIV, p. 450b.

> NOTES: This edition is almost as rare as the one known original. A mere forty-four copies were printed, some of them on sixteenth-century paper, making them quite difficult to distinguish from the original. According to Infantes, Sancho Rayón added the crest of the printer, Pedro de Castro, on the recto side of the last folio of the facsimiles, and this is how they can be distinguished from the original, which does not include this crest. This is the case, for example, with Biblioteca Nacional R/3634, British Library 899.f.16, and the Hispanic Society copy, which include the crest. There is another twist to these facsimiles, however, in that Sancho Rayón also created minor variations within each print run (different types of paper, addition of printers' crests in some copies but not others, etc.). Palau y Dulcet confirms that the first twenty of the forty-four facsimiles were printed on genuine sixteenth-century paper; hence I would qualify Infantes' statement by adding that only the copies printed on this type of paper include the printer's crest. Thus Biblioteca de Palacio 1/B/247 and University of Michigan Special Collections Library PQ6425. Q7. 1548a do not include the tell-tale crest, but they are known to be facsimiles because they are printed on paper from later epochs.

(3) Noel Fallows, *Un texto inédito sobre la caballería del Renacimiento español: 'Doctrina del arte de la cauallería', de Juan Quijada de Reayo*, Hispanic Studies TRAC (Textual Research and Criticism) 14 (Liverpool: Liverpool University Press, 1996).

Luis Zapata de Chaves ◆ 'Del Justador' (*Miscelánea*, ch. 125)[12]

(1) Luis Zapata, 'Del Justador', in *Miscellánea de Zapata*.

LOCATION: Madrid, Biblioteca Nacional, MS 2790, fols. 182r–188v.

BIBLIOGRAPHIC REFERENCE: *Inventario general de manuscritos de la Biblioteca Nacional de Madrid*, vol. VIII, p. 355.

NOTES: The pages measure 210 × 310 mm (8¼ × 12³/₁₆ in). The MS is bound in red Morocco leather, embossed in gilt on the spine: 'MISCELLANEA [*sic*] DE ZAPATA'. The MS was most likely dictated by Zapata to approximately six different amanuenses. Zapata himself also intervenes in the text, making comments and accretions, mostly of a personal nature. In addition to the text, there are numerous ink drawings, or doodles, throughout the MS. According to fols. IIIr and 1r, this MS belonged to Don Bernabé de Gaynza and Doña Ana de Arcas y Mendoza.

Martín de Riquer has stressed the point that it was the task of the medieval and renaissance amanuensis not merely to copy, but also to correct and even to improve his text.[13] Never was this assertion truer than in the case of MS 2790, which is full of corrections, alternate readings and some very cryptic abbreviations.

All the modern editors have followed Gayangos' 1859 edition of the text, thereby perpetuating the (unfortunately, and unusually, for Gayangos) many mistakes made in that edition. The moral is that it is imperative to check original sources, which is precisely what I have done for the new edition included below.

---

[12] I only include in this list the complete editions of *Miscelánea* which include the chapter entitled 'Del Justador'. There are numerous partial editions, none of which includes this chapter, as follows: (1) 'Extremeñerías (De la *Miscelánea de Zapata)*', *Revista de Extremadura* 12 (1910), pp. 63–92; (2) Luis Zapata, *Miscelánea (selección)*, Letras Españolas 11 (Madrid: Bruno del Amo, 1926); (3) Luis Zapata, *Miscelánea: silva de casos curiosos*, Las cien mejores obras de la literatura española 94, ed. Antonio R. Rodríguez-Moñino (Madrid: Compañía Ibero-Americana de Publicaciones, n.d.; reprinted by Artes Gráficas, n.d); (4) Luis Zapata, *Varia historia (Miscelánea)*, vol. 1, ed. Geertruida Christine Horsman (Amsterdam: H. J. W. Becht, 1935). This is an excellent critical edition, but only one volume was published, which ends at chapter 118. Since 'Del Justador' is chapter 125, it is not included in the volume. The second volume was never published.

[13] This task of the amanuensis is underscored by Riquer, 'La fecha del Ronsasvals y del Rollan a Saragossa según el armamento', p. 195, n. 90.

(2) Luis Zapata, 'Del Justador', in *Miscelánea*, ed. P. de G. [= Pascual de Gayangos], Memorial Histórico Español: Colección de Documentos, Opúsculos y Antigüedades 11 (Madrid: Real Academia Española, 1859), pp. 212–18.

(3) Luis Zapata, 'Del Justador', in *Varia historia (Miscelánea)*, 2 vols., ed. Isidoro Montiel (Madrid: Ediciones Castilla, 1949), vol. II, pp. 64–72.

NOTE: Although Montiel states that his edition is based on the original MS, he in fact tends to follow the Gayangos edition of 1859.

(4) Luis Zapata, 'Del Justador', in *Miscelánea*, facsimile, ed. Manuel Terrón Albarrán (Badajoz: Institución Pedro de Valencia, CSIC, 1983), fols. 182r–188v.

(5) Luis Zapata, 'Del Justador', in Fallows, *Un texto inédito sobre la caballería del Renacimiento español: 'Doctrina del arte de la cauallería', de Juan Quijada de Reayo*, pp. 77–83.

NOTE: This edition follows the Gayangos edition of 1859, to which are added explanatory notes about the text.

(6) Luis Zapata, 'Del Justador', in *Miscelánea o Varia Historia*, ed. Antonio Carrasco González (Llerena: Editores Extremeños, 1999), pp. 162–7.

NOTE: This edition also follows the Gayangos edition of 1859.

Ponç de Menaguerra
Lo Cavaller
(1493)

[Lo Cavaller]*

Los del estament militar en la noble ciutat de València preguen a mossèn Ponç de Menaguerra ab estil de semblants paraules:

Manifesta speriència nos ha clarament mostrat la veritat que de vós, Cavaller Strenu, ab alta veu de gloriosa Fama, les nostres no envejoses orelles hoyt havien. Car sóu una encesa falla, a la claredat de qui les leges ombres y defalts de les armes, en nosaltres, mirant-se, prenen esmena. E sóu la luminosa entorcha que acompanya, guia y descobre la honorosa senda per hon al terme de tota perfectió, ab gest, passos y continença de singular triunfo, los justadors cavallers, exercitant-se en l'orde y actes de milícia, ab facilitat y breu promptitud atènyer esperen. Sóu, encara, la scola, doctrina y excel·lent magisteri que a nosaltres, deixebles nodrits en los daurats breços de vostre gentil saber y entendre, per obres pràtiques y exemples governar acostumen.

A vós, donchs, Magnànim Cavaller, nostre dir se presenta, pregant-vos per gentilea nostres prechs accepteu, y la ploma,† per a pintar del armat cavaller la pintada bellea y concertada pintura, per a linear, encara, y allimitar del plantat rench e intangible com se deu collir lo fruyt de maravellosa‡ destrea. Y perquè lo nombre dels dubtes y disputes per a egualar la desegualtat, avantatges y milloria dels qui justen, és tan gran com la diversitat de les carreres, encontres, vicis, desastres y ventures, affectadament demanam que capituleu les estimacions y valor del que junyint, per destrea o per colpa, per sort o per desventura del cavaller, és possible se segueixca.

The Knight

The members of the military estate in the noble city of Valencia beseech Lord Ponç de Menaguerra with words of the following tenor:[1]

Manifest experience has clearly revealed to us the truth which, Enterprising Knight, thanks to the loud voice of glorious Fame, our not invidious ears had heard about you.[2] For you are a burning fire, in whose light the loathsome shadows[3] and martial blunders, exposing themselves, are ours to correct.[4] And you are the shining torch that accompanies, guides and reveals the honourable pathway that leads to total perfection which, with a singularly triumphant demeanour, gait, and mien, chivalrous jousters, practising the order and deeds of chivalry, strive to attain as easily and quickly as possible.[5] In you, furthermore, is the school, the doctrine and the distinguished teaching, through whose expert deeds and examples we, disciples nurtured in the gilded cradles of your exquisite knowledge and understanding, are accustomed to being guided.

To you, then, Magnanimous Knight, is our address presented, beseeching you gracefully[6] to accept our requests and the pen in order to depict the vivid beauty and a harmonious portrait of the armoured knight; in order, moreover, to describe and delineate how the fruit should be plucked with awesome skill from the steadfast and intangible lists. And because the number of doubts and disputes about equalling out inequality,[7] advantages and ranking[8] amongst those who joust is as great as the diversity of courses, encounters, vices, disasters and chance occurrences, we affectionately petition you to document in chapters the esteemed qualities and value of the jouster which may ensue in consequence of the knight's skill or negligence, of his luck or misfortune.[9]

---

* The frontispiece of Ed. 1493 is missing. The title is taken from the frontispiece of Ed. 1532.
† *ploma: pluma* – Ed. 1532.
‡ *maravellosa: maravillosa* – Ed. 1532.

Prometent per vostre treball restar-vos en obligació infinida, y que·ns* tenrem per contents de vostres decretades leys, regint-nos per aquelles; puix† lo que teniu vist, lest, hoyt y praticat ab la disposició de vostre gran esperit y clara vista, nos asegura que de just juhí y dreta sentència lo vostre armat y fort braç no pot torçre‡ la ralla.

Respòn mossèn Menaguerra:

Si força de ignorància no m'enpachava, desig de servir-vos, bé·m§ consent que·l¶ treball no refusse, perquè scrivint satisfés al que la mercè de vosaltres graciosament me demana. Cavallers virtuosos, inclinats per natura al que vostres engendradors** de excel·lent manera entenent-ho practicaven: ¿Qui pot creure vos fallgua†† lo que naturalea no us denega, ne qui, affigint en la mar una gota d'aygua, presumeix augmentar aquella? Baix és lo meu dir per atènyer la altitud del vostre elevat entendre, ni la mia poca e antiga tapesceria‡‡ bastaria jamés, fornint, empaliar les noves sales de vostra estimada modernitat e sciència. Mas puix, manant-me, voleu que desplegue les bales de la mia grossa roba en mans de vostra prima intel·ligència, obeynt-vos com a senyors

We swear that we shall be forever in your debt for writing this work, and that we shall be contented with the laws decreed by you, by which we shall govern ourselves; for what you have seen, read, heard and practised with the disposition of your great mind and your clear vision assures us that with fair judgement and an honest sentence, your sword-wielding and strong arm[10] is incapable of twisting the line.[11]

Lord Menaguerra Responds

If the power of ignorance were not preventing me from doing so, the desire to serve you well compels me not to refuse this task, for in writing I shall satisfy the elegant request that it is your pleasure to make. Virtuous Knights, naturally inclined to the very practices that your forefathers understood so well: Who can believe that you lack what nature does not deny you, and who, by spilling a drop of water into the ocean, can presume to increase its volume? My diction is too poor to reach the heights of your exalted knowledge, nor would my humble and antiquated tapestry ever be sufficient, once having supplied you with it, to palliate the new rooms of your esteemed modernity and science. Since you wish, however, ordering me to do so, that I unfurl the bales of my inferior cloth into the hands of your superior intelligence,[12] obeying you as lords and

* *que·ns*: que ens.
† *puix*: *puixs* – Ed. 1532.
‡ *torçre*: *tòrcer* – Ed. 1532.
§ *bé·m*: bé em.
¶ *que·l*: que el.
** *engendradors*: *engendradores* – Ed. 1532.
†† *fallgua*: *fallgau* – Ed. 1532. The verb form *fallgua* is an antiquated present subjunctive form of the verb *fallir* (cp. modern Catalan *falleixi*). Janer *et al.* emend to the third-person plural *fallgan* (fol. Vr), which is incorrect; Bohigas emends to *fallga* (p. 179). The -*u*- in the verb ending is strictly orthographical and has no phonetic value. The addition of this -*u*- is quite frequent in medieval Navarrese and Aragonese texts (see also the variant form *jutjuar*, below, ch. 19).
‡‡ *tapesceria*: *tapisceria* – Ed. 1532.

y mestres,* sotsmet a la correctió vostra, que esmene,† la sentència y mal estil dels capítols que recite, ab protest que de presumtuós lo sobrenom no matenga;‡ car bé conech pertànyer a mi lo demanar y apendre, puix lo determenar a vosaltres és propri offici.

masters, I submit to your corrections, so that you can emend the grammar and poor style of the chapters that I narrate, protesting so that I not be called presumptuous; for I know well that beseeching and learning pertain to me, whilst correcting is your own craft.

Capítol primer

Lo cavaller, venint al rench armat de totes aquelles defensives armes que al junyidor són acostumades, al cap del rench pot pendre la scarcella. E si alguna altra peça li fallia, ordena la ley que emperadors, reys e prínceps manat han se observe, tal cavaller lo pris guanyar no puixa; y la rahó, que no consent en res que defalt sia, vol que semblant libertat no·s§ done al qui dóna occasió scandalosa en lo plaer de tant pomposa festa.

Chapter One

The knight, coming to the lists[13] clad in all of the defensive armour that befits the jouster, can pick up his tasset at the head of the lists.[14] And if he is missing any other piece of armour, the law states that emperors, kings and princes have ordered that the rule be observed that this knight cannot win the prize;[15] and reason, which tolerates nothing that may be in error, dictates that such licence not be given to one who would occasion such scandal in the enjoyment of so magnificent a festival.[16]

Capítol segon

Quant pris se dóna al més gentil, mire atentament lo jutge – puix lo millor ataviat, més rich, pompós, guanyar deu y s'espera – si los paraments decanten o pengen més a una part que a altra, e la cimera si va dreta y ben posada, puix tals mancaments, notats, a perdre lo pris ajuden.

Chapter Two

Whenever the prize is to be awarded to the most elegant knight, let the judge watch attentively – since the knight who wears the best, most expensive, magnificent armour should be expected to win –[17] if the trappings lean or hang more unevenly on one side than the other, and if the crest is straight and fastened firmly,[18] for such mistakes, once noticed, can lead to the loss of the prize.[19]

---

* *mestres: maestres* – Ed. 1532.
† *esmene: esmena* – Ed. 1532.
‡ *matenga: mantenga* – Ed. 1532.
§ *no·s: no es.*

Capítol terç

No menys se deu mirar l'orde y mesura del cavaller entrant en la plaça, per ésser vist y loat de singular destrea; com arremet, com dóna los sperons, com porta les cames y com lo cors sobre la sella, ne ab quin temps voltarà, perquè·l* rench no·s† deu tocar ab lo cavall de anques, al girar, ni en qualsevol altra manera.

Chapter Three

No less attention should be paid to the knight's orderliness and restraint when he makes his entrance in the lists,[20] in order that he be seen and praised for his outstanding skill; how he sallies forth, how he puts spurs to his horse, how he holds his legs and his body in the saddle, and the way in which he turns, because the horse's rump should not touch the tilt[21] on turning around nor in any other way.

Capítol quart

Sia vist al cap del rench lo cavaller com pren la lança, com parteix en la sella, com van les cames, si pert estreps.

Si pert la lança, passats tres ponts, exínt-li‡ de la bossa, com ans de tres ponts, no·s§ puga jutjar perduda, a nostra usança. Car és presumidor del mal cavall o del qui serveix, deu ser la colpa. Lança perduda a colpa¶ del cavaller, se eguala, se cobra y compensa per altra lança rompuda.

Chapter Four

Let it be seen at the head of the lists how the knight grasps the lance, how he sits in the saddle, how he holds his legs, if he loses the stirrups.

If he loses the lance, the three stages having been passed,[22] because it slips out of the pouch, or likewise before the three stages, the lance cannot be judged lost, according to our rules. Since this is a sign either of a bad horse or servant, the blame should be imputed accordingly. If it is the knight's fault for losing the lance, he can equalise, recover and compensate by breaking another lance.[23]

Capítol cinquè

Per sostenir la polícia e noble exercici del júnyer,** y per millor estimar del bon junyidor la destrea, segons tenor de molts capítols fermats en passos de córrer puntes, sien condempnats†† los vicis de perdre lança al pendre, o perdre strep o streps, e cames arronçades, a arbitre del jutge; perquè tals‡‡ legees, no esmenades, valen a la part altra per una lança rompuda.

Chapter Five

In order to maintain decorum and the noble exercise of jousting, and in order best to judge the good jouster's skill, following the tenor of many chapters devoted to running with sharp lances,[24] let the vices of dropping the lance when picking it up, or losing one or both stirrups, and contracted legs be censured at the judge's discretion; because these fouls, if they are not redressed, are worth a lance broken to the opposing jouster.

* *perquè·l*: perquè el.
† *no·s*: no es.
‡ *exínt-li*: exín-li – Ed. 1532.
§ *no·s*: no es.
¶ *colpa*: culpa – Ed. 1532.
** *júnyer*: júnyr – Ed. 1532.
†† *condempnats*: condemnats – Ed. 1532.
‡‡ *tals*: tales – Ed. 1532.

Capítol sisè

De dos cavallers, la hu perdent la lança, l'altre qui encontrant al rench fa bona carrera, guanya lo qui encontra, perquè exercint fa més e millors actes necessaris per al júnyer; car los Arbres o Capítols qui tracten de les valors y drets de les armes així ho volen: que nengun acte sia pres per no fet; ans sia remunerat lo digne de premi, e punit lo mereixedor* de pena.

Chapter Six

In a joust between two knights where one loses his lance and the other strikes the tilt but runs a good course, the one who strikes shall be the winner, for by making an effort he is doing more and performing better manœuvres that are necessary in jousting; for the Trees[25] or Chapters that deal with the rules and laws of arms wish it to be so: let no action be treated as if it had not been done; rather let what is worthy of a prize be rewarded, and what is deserving of a penalty be penalised.

Capítol setè

Com en les armes lo dan s'esguarde al qui toca, és determenat que si lo cavaller, partint ab la lança en la bossa, passats los tres ponts, li's rompia en la mà damunt o davall la roda, o metent-la o portant-la en lo rest, tal carrera no·s† deu dir vana, tornant per aquella a fer-ne altra; mas deu anar per carrera correguda.

Chapter Seven

Since in passages of arms the knight who is struck is the one who risks injury, it is determined that if the knight, setting out with the lance in the pouch, the three stages having been passed, got his lance broken in his hand above or below the vamplate, either when placing it or carrying it in the rest, such a course should not be discounted, so that he gets to run another because of what happened in that one; rather, it should count as one course run.[26]

Capítol huytè

Si al cavaller, partint, li surtrà la lança de la bossa, y, fent legees en la carrera la met en lo rest, y, fent calades que toquen al rench ve a rompre la lança d'encontre, e l'altre, fent bona carrera, encontrarà e no romprà, tals‡ encontres són eguals.§ Mas si la hu, donant de pla o de punta en lo rench, romprà, guanya l'altre qui encontra fent bona carrera, encara que no rompa.

Chapter Eight

If, on setting off, one knight's lance should slip out of the pouch and, committing fouls during the course, he places it in the rest and, swooping[27] the lance so that it touches the tilt, he manages to splinter the lance in the encounter, and the other knight, running a good course, attaints[28] and does not break, these encounters are tied. But if the first knight, striking the tilt crosswise or with the point, breaks the lance, the other knight who attaints while running a good course shall win, even though he does not break the lance.

---

* *mereixedor: merexedor* – Ed. 1532.
† *no·s:* no es.
‡ *tals: tales* – Ed. 1532.
§ *eguals: eguales* – Ed. 1532.

Capítol novè

Dels cavallers qui ensemps s'encontraran y rompran les lances, deu guanyar lo qui millor és anat, y pert l'altre qui en la carrera haurà fet una o moltes legees.

Chapter Nine

Of the knights who strike each other at the same time and break the lances, the one who has charged the best must win, and the one who has committed one or more fouls in the course shall lose.

Capítol deè

E per maior declaració dels sobredits capítols, per quant en la determinació de les gentiles e legees en les festes de júnyer són vàries opinions de cavallers seguint l'orde e stil de les armes, si·l* cavaller passant carrera† la lança alçarà per no encontrar al altre venint desbaratat o ab lança perduda, tal alçar de lança no és de alguna estima, car seria prejuhí de un altre, qui haurà encontrat o romput lança. E, per semblant, lo cavaller qui haurà encontrat o romput lança fent calades e legees, donant de la lança davall lo rest, per tals legees no pert encontre ni lança rompuda, car en armes retretes alguna gentilea no augmenta lo nombre dels colps, ni alguna legea‡ en l'orde de ferir sobre les armes diminueix lo nombre de aquells, exceptat quant los cavallers seran eguals de encontres o lances rompudes, que en tal cars lo pris deu ésser partit en parts, donant milloria al qui haurà fet la gentilea, e la menor part al qui haurà fet la legea, remetent la tal partició a arbitre del jutge.

Chapter Ten

And by way of further explanation of the aforementioned chapters, inasmuch as the knights who are familiar with different strokes and styles of weapon have various opinions about determining what constitutes elegance and fouls in jousting festivals, if the knight should raise his lance when charging so as not to strike his opponent who is riding shoddily or who has lost his lance, raising the lance in this way has no value, for it would mean losing points to another knight who did make the attaint or shattered his lance.[29] And, likewise, the knight who has made the attaint or splintered his lance by swooping and committing fouls, having placed it poorly in the rest, despite these fouls, loses no points for the attaint or for the splintered lance; for in combats with rebated arms[30] elegance in style does not increase the number of blows, nor do clumsy methods of striking armour diminish the number of blows, except when knights are tied for the number of attaints or lances broken, for in such a case the prize should be partly shared, giving the advantage to the one who has jousted most elegantly, and the lesser share to the one who has committed the foul, remitting this division to the discretion of the judge.

---

* *si·l*: si el.

† *carrera: carreres* – Ed. 1532.

‡ *legea: legeea* – Ed. 1532.

Capítol onzè

Quant lo cavaller romprà de punta de billeta en lo rench, encara que vinga de bona carrera, guanya l'altre sens encontre, ab tot que haja fet legees e calades donant al rench de pla. E si donant de pla al rench, romprà la lança, és egual ab lo qui encontra en lo rench de punta de billeta.

Chapter Eleven

When the knight strikes the tilt with the coronel,[31] breaking the lance, even though he is charging well up to this point, his opponent shall win without encountering, even if he has committed fouls, swooping and striking the tilt crosswise. And if his opponent should break his own lance by striking the tilt crosswise, he is tied with the knight who strikes the tilt with the coronel.

Capítol dotzè

Fent bona carrera lo cavaller, si per desastre encontrarà en lo rench o perdrà lança, pot-se acabalar avançant un encontre, rompent lança o fehent perdre peça o la regna a l'altre – deixant-ho a arbitre del jutge –, levant-li aquell avantage que haurà guanyat o la carrera que haurà encontrat, axí que una bona carrera vaja per la mala.

Chapter Twelve

Whilst riding a good course, if through some disaster the knight should hit the tilt or lose his lance, it can be equalled out[32] by forging ahead with another encounter,[33] breaking the lance or making the opponent lose a piece of armour or let go of the reins – leaving this to the judge's discretion –, thereby taking away from him that advantage that he will have gained or the successful course that he will have run, so that a good course may replace the bad one.

Capítol tretzè

És dit fora de rench lo cavaller naffrat qui no pot tornar a júnyer. E per aquella sanch, lo qui encontrat haurà, guanya més de aquelles lances que són en lo pris, exceptant-ne cavaller qui ab sanch o sens sanch serà tret de tot recort no podent tornar a les armes, y exceptant-ne cavaller qui ab lo cavall serà caygut en terra, perduda sanch o desbaratat de algun membre, car són estimats com morts. E si al cavaller per encontre li serà trencat lo braç, la cama, la cuixa o l'ansa del coll, val segons és jutgat,[*] puix aquell encontre deu ésser de maior valor que fa més acostar lo cavaller a morir.

Chapter Thirteen

Any injured knight who cannot joust anymore is declared out of the lists. And on account of the blood shed, the knight who had struck him wins more points than the total amount of lances that are taken into account for the prize, except for the knight who, with or without losing blood, is knocked completely unconscious so that he cannot return to joust, and except for the knight who has fallen to the ground with his horse, suffering loss of blood or damage to a limb, for they are counted as dead. And if any knight sustains a broken arm, leg, thigh or collar bone in an encounter, points shall be awarded accordingly,[34] for that stroke should be of greater value which brings the knight closer to death.[35]

---

[*] *jutgat: jutjat* – Ed. 1532.

Capítol quatorzè

Reys o fills de reys, si uns contra de altres junyiran, sien jutjats per les leys que·ls* altres cavallers se jutgen, perquè exercint tals actes militars no són més que cavallers.

E si algun rey o fill de rey, carrera corrent ab lança, passarà, encara que no encontre ni sia altra cosa que lança correguda, val més que tots los encontres, actes, cassos ni lances que·ls† altres cavallers de qualsevol títol baix de rey hajen fet, e açò havent respecte a la altitud de real dignitat.

Chapter Fourteen

If kings or the sons of kings should joust against each other, let them be judged according to the same rules by which other knights are judged, for when they are performing such feats of arms they are nothing more than knights.

And if a king or one of his sons should run the length of the course[36] without scoring, even though he does not make the encounter, nor is there anything other than a course run with the lance, it is worth more points than all of the encounters, manœuvres, actions and lance strokes that the other knights of any other rank beneath the king may have made, and thus shall they have respect for the pre-eminence of his royal office.

Capítol quinzè

Cahent per encontre dos cavallers en terra ab los cavalls, lo qui menys mal se fa y pus prest torna a cavalcar‡ per a júnyer, guanya, segons costum de ungres e alamanys e seguint los estils de les armes d'ultrança, que donen milloria al combatent restant de tal encontre més dispost per a batallar.

Chapter Fifteen

When both knights and their horses fall to the ground in an encounter, the one who is hurt the least and who is the quickest to re-mount and return to joust wins, according to the custom of the Hungarians and the Germans and in accordance with the rules for jousts of war,[37] which give the advantage to the combatant who emerges from such an encounter the most prepared for battle.

Capítol setzè

En Alamanya y Ungria no estimen sinó aquell encontre del qual los cavallers cahen en terra. E axí, si fent bones carreres dos cavallers, la hu de aquells, del seu encontre, caurà de la sella en terra o caurà ab lo cavall, guanya lo qui no encontra, puix tal encontre no té valor per a qui·l§ fa, mas per al cavaller qui ab tanta virtut lo mostra sostenir y reebre.¶

Chapter Sixteen

In Germany and Hungary they only count that encounter which makes the knights fall to the ground. And thus, if two knights are running good courses and one of them, as a result of the stroke he delivers, falls from his saddle to the ground or falls with the horse, the one who does not strike wins, since such a stroke is of value not to the one who delivers it, but to the knight who shows that he has enough power to withstand and receive it.

---

* que·ls: que els.
† que·ls: que els.
‡ cavalcar: cavalgar – Ed. 1532.
§ qui·l: qui el.
¶ reebre: rebre – Ed. 1532.

Capítol desetè

Com perdre peça o regna sia gran defalt al cavaller, si, per encontre rebut o embarrerada, se pert la regna y no·s* cobra fins lo cavall és reposat al cap de la carrera, tal encontre val com lança rompuda. E si lo qui romprà perdrà peça o regna, e l'altre, no rompent, encontrarà, tals encontres són eguals.

Chapter Seventeen

Since losing a piece of armour or the reins is a serious mistake for the knight, if, because of a recoil from an attaint or a full hit,[38] the rein is lost and not recovered until the horse has stopped at the end of the course, such a stroke counts as one lance broken. And if the knight who splinters his lance loses a piece of armour or the reins, and his opponent makes an attaint, but without breaking, these strokes are tied.

Capítol dehuytè[†]

És peça perduda, y val com lança rompuda, si·l[‡] cavaller pert lo guant dret per encontre de billeta; e si en lo guant no s'i mostrarà encontre, val per peça perduda encara que·s[§] perda per un reverssar o per fort encontre del cavaller mateix. Mas si lo gocet o la lança, remordent la mà del cavaller, li feya naffra, tal sanch no és de alguna stima, puix per aquella no·s[¶] deixe de júnyer.

Chapter Eighteen

If the knight loses the right gauntlet from a strike by his opponent's coronel,[39] this piece is counted as lost, and it is worth the same as one lance broken; and if there is no evidence on the gauntlet that it was struck,[40] it still counts as a piece lost even though it is lost through being bent backwards or through the force of the knight's own encounter. But if the grapper or the lance,[41] lacerating the knight's hand, injured him, the blood shed is of no account, since despite that injury he should not stop jousting.

Capítol denovè[**]

Val una lança rompuda al cavaller quand l'altre, per encontre o per embarrerada, perdrà lo braçalet[††] o la guarda, e aximateix s'estima peça perduda. E si serà encontrat en lo braçal dret o esquerre tant desmarchat que sens martell tornar a armar no·s[‡‡] puga, és fora de rench tal cavaller, e val quatre lances rompudes. Mas

Chapter Nineteen

It is worth a lance broken to the knight when his opponent, because of an attaint or a full hit, loses the vambrace or the guard,[42] and likewise both pieces are counted as lost. And if he were struck such a damaging blow on the right or left vambrace that the armour cannot be re-fitted without a hammer, this knight is out of the lists and the blow is worth four lances broken. But if the vambrace loses the guard

---

* *no·s*: no es.
† *dehuytè*: dehuit – Ed. 1532.
‡ *si·l*: si el.
§ *que·s*: que es.
¶ *no·s*: no es.
** *denovè*: denou – Ed. 1532.
†† *braçalet*: bracelet – Ed. 1532.
‡‡ *no·s*: no es.

si·l* braçal pert la guarda (o rompent les altres peces) – sens traure'l del† braç ab tiretes se adoba, no és en alguna estima.

E axí se deu jutjar‡ de totes les peces, puix no·s§ parteixca lo cavaller del cap del rench per adobar aquelles.

(or breaking the other pieces) – without flying off the arm it is fixed with leather straps, this is of no account.

And all the pieces should be judged in this way, as long as the knight does not leave the head of the lists to mend them.

Capítol vintè

Perdre lo scut⁋ per encontre o embarrerada val tres lances al qui encontra, e una del encontre són quatre, y és fora de rench lo cavaller, segons és determenat** per nostre senyor lo Rey don Ferrando,†† huy pròsper regnant. E aximateix val, segons és dit, si per qualsevol cars lo scut era esclafat, partit o trocejat, axí que per tal desmarchament no pogués tornar a júnyer, remetent açó a arbitre del jutge.

Chapter Twenty

Losing the shield because of an attaint or a full hit is worth three lances to the knight who delivers the stroke, plus one for the encounter itself makes four, and the knight is out of the lists,[43] as is determined by our lord King Ferdinand, whose prosperous reign continues to this day.[44] And it is worth the same, as is stated, if for any reason the shield was crushed, split, or smashed to pieces, with the result that it is so damaged that the knight cannot return to joust, remitting such determination to the judge's discretion.

Capítol vint-e-hu

Lo elm levat del cap val deu lances al cavaller que·l‡‡ leva. E si li fa perdre sanch del nas o de la boca, perdent alguna dent, val vint lances. E si haurà sanch en lo cap o en lo front, per la qual naffra no puixa tornar a júnyer, val segons és dit en lo capítol [XIII].§§ E si serà lo elm desmarchat, axí que no·s⁋⁋ puga ni dega ab aquell tornar a júnyer, val com si fos levat del cap.

Chapter Twenty-One

If the helm is knocked off the head it is worth ten lances to the knight who knocks it off. And if this causes him to bleed from the nose or the mouth, losing any teeth, it is worth twenty lances. And if it causes bleeding from the head or the forehead, because of which injury he cannot return to joust, it is worth the same as the situation described in Chapter Thirteen. And if the helm were damaged with the result that the wearer could not or should not return to joust, it counts as though it had been removed from his head. And since in jousts much heed is paid to equality, if a set number of

---

* *si·l:* si el.

† *del:* omit – Ed. 1532.

‡ *jutjar: jutjuar* – Ed. 1532.

§ *no·s:* no es.

⁋ *scut: escut* – Ed. 1532.

** *determenat: determinat* – Ed. 1532.

†† *Ferrando: Ferrnando* – Ed. 1532.

‡‡ *que·l:* que el.

§§ Ed. 1493 and Ed. 1532 both refer incorrectly to *capítol XII* instead of *capítol XIII*. Neither Janer *et al.* (fol. IXv) nor Bohigas (p. 189) correct the mistake.

⁋⁋ *no·s:* no es.

Y com en les armes se mire molt la egualtat, si·l* rench serà cridat a carreres comptades, lo cars seguit en la derrera† val com si fos seguit en la primera carrera o qualsevol de les altres.

courses were proclaimed for this tilt,[45] if this[46] happens in the last course it is worth the same as if it happened in the first course or any of the others.

Capítol vint-e-dos

Tot encontre o embarrerada que faça anar lo cavaller torbat, puix no ixca de recort y puga tornar sens molt espay a júnyer, sia remès a arbitre del jutge, perquè finit lo rench, si tals cavallers de lances o encontres seran eguals, tal cars deu ser posat en compte.

Chapter Twenty-Two

Let any attaint or full hit that knocks the knight off his balance, without knocking him unconscious so that he can return in a short while to joust, be referred to the judge's discretion, so that once the tilt is over, if both knights tie in lances broken or attaints, this situation can be taken into account.

Capítol vint-y-tres‡

Deixar troç de lança en lo elm, en lo scut o en qualsevol altra part, no és d'alguna estima, ni menys traure foch per encontre, perquè, encontrant e rompent, los tals desastres no donen més valor que lança rompuda, y són eguals ab altre qui romp, encara que semblant cars no li sdevinga.§ Aximateix, trencar les lances per encontre, la hu fins a la roda, l'altre a un palm de la billeta, no és més ni menys, com se prenga en lo fust la tal manera⁋ de rompre.

Chapter Twenty-Three

Leaving a shard of the lance in the helm, in the shield or in any other part of the armour, is not worth any points, neither is making fire fly in an encounter,[47] since, upon encountering and shattering, these disasters add no further value to a broken lance, and they are tied with any other knight who breaks his lance, even though a similar circumstance does not happen to him. Likewise, breaking the lances in an encounter, one down to the vamplate, the other a palm's length below the coronel,[48] counts neither more nor less, since the way in which they are broken depends on the stave.

Capítol vint-e-quatre

Si lo cavaller serà encontrat en qualsevol loch que no sia prohibit encontrar e exirà de tot recort, no podent tornar a júnyer, val més que tots los altres** casos que poden guanyar lo pris, e més que totes les lances; e val més que açò si per tal encontre perdia sanch, com ja és dit en lo capítol XIII.

Chapter Twenty-Four

If the knight were struck in any place where it is not prohibited to strike[49] and he were knocked unconscious so that he was unable to return to joust, this counts more than all the other instances that can win the prize, and more than all the lances; and it counts even more than this if blood is shed in the encounter, as is already stated in Chapter Thirteen.

* *si·l*: si el.
† *derrera: darrera* – Ed. 1532.
‡ *vint-y-tres: vient-y-tres* – Ed. 1532.
§ *sdevinga: esdevenga.* – Ed. 1532.
⁋ *manera: manere* – Ed. 1532.
** *los altres: lo altres* – Ed. 1532.

Capítol vint-y-cinch

Lo qui derroca cavaller ab lo cavall per terra per encontre o embarrerada, guanya més de aquelles lances que seran en lo pris, exceptant los encontres del capítol XXIIII. Perquè lo encontre trahent sanch, o seguint per aquell algun dan en la persona e membres* del cavaller, és en† lo nombre dels encontres intitulat segon, car en armes d'ultrança qui cau ab lo cavall és reputat com a mort.

Chapter Twenty-Five

Whomsoever knocks a knight and his horse to the ground because of an attaint or a full hit, wins more points than the total amount of lances that are taken into account for the prize, with the exception of the encounters described in Chapter Twenty-Four.[50] Whenever blood is drawn in this encounter, or if an injury of some kind is inflicted upon the knight's body or limbs, this falls into what is called the second class of encounters,[51] for in jousts of war he who falls with his horse is counted as dead.[52]

Capítol vint-e-sis

Quand lo cavaller per encontre o per embarrerada serà tret de la sella, penjant en los arçons o estreps, o del tot posat en terra, és dit fora de rench, e lo qui encontra guanya vint lances. E si lo caygut volia tornar a júnyer, no pot guanyar pris per la vergonya de ser exit de sella closa, segons lo stil en passos de córrer puntes.

Chapter Twenty-Six

Whenever the knight is unseated because of an attaint or a full hit so that he hangs from the arçons or stirrups, or is knocked completely to the ground, he is declared out of the lists, and the knight who unhorses him scores twenty lances. And if the unhorsed knight wishes to return to joust, he cannot win the prize because of the disgrace of being knocked out of the close saddle,[53] following the style for jousts with sharp lances.

Capítol vint-y-set

Iunyint dos cavallers ab les cimeres, qui pert la cimera per encontre o embarrerada pert la carrera.

E si, anant-hi mesions, la hu, per parer més galant,‡ passarà ab cimera e l'altre no, si·l§ portant cimera, fent bona carrera, romprà, e l'altre, fent no menys¶ bona carrera de punta de billeta, la cimera li levarà, són eguals, exceptat quant junyiran a carreres comptades o partida,

Chapter Twenty-Seven

When two knights joust, both of whom are wearing crests, the one who loses his crest because of an attaint or full hit loses the course.

And if, having the wherewithal,[54] one of them, so as to appear more elegant, jousts with a crest and the other does not, if the one who is wearing a crest splinters his lance upon running a good course and the other, upon running no less of a good course, knocks off his opponent's crest with the coronel,[55] they are tied, except when they should be jousting for a set number of courses or in teams, in which case the splintered lance counts more,

---

* membres: menbres – Ed. 1532.

† en: eu – Ed. 1532.

‡ galant: galan – Ed. 1532.

§ si·l: si el.

¶ menys: meyēs – Ed. 1532. Janer et al. (fol. Xv) transcribe as meyēs, which makes no sense; Bohigas (p. 191) emends correctly to menys.

hon val més la lança rompuda,* perquè en les armes retretes los colps† o encontres donats ans del finit nombre són de estimar.

for in combats with rebated arms the blows or strokes made towards the fixed number that has been set for the joust are what count.

Capítol vint-e-huyt

Si per les encontres‡ no·s§ segueix altre que rompre les lances en les carreres ben fetes, rompudes les lances, los dos cavallers són eguals, encara que la un cavaller haja encontrat pus alt que l'altre; car rompre en lo elm o en lo scut – o damunt lo caragol o davall – no és més ni menys, si ja entre·ls⁋ cavallers no s'era fet pacte donant milloria al qui pus alt encontra. Axí, per ben jutjar los encontres, del caragol en amunt són dits alts, y los d'entorn de tota la roda aximateix; tots los altres són baixos. Açò per esquivar contrast.

Chapter Twenty-Eight

If in the encounters nothing else happens other than breaking the lances in well-run courses, having broken the lances, the two knights are tied, even if the one knight has struck higher than the other; for splintering the lance on the helm or on the shield – either above or below the flaon bolt – counts neither more nor less, unless a pact had been made between the knights beforehand giving the advantage to the one who strikes higher. Thus, in order to judge the encounters fairly, strokes on or above the flaon bolt are declared high, as are those that strike anywhere around the vamplate; all the rest are low. In this way disputes shall be avoided.

Capítol vint-e-nou

Passant bones carreres, si dels dos cavallers la hu romprà lança d'embarrerada, e l'altre, encontrant, no romp, guanya lo que romput haurà, exceptat que no haja fet calades e legees tocant al rench, qu·en** tal manera guanya lo qui encontra e no romp. E si per encontre o embarrerada la hu reversava més que l'altre, tornant en la sella sens altre cars, no és de fer-ne stima. Seguint-se altre, sia jutjat segons és dit en los damunt dits capítols.

Chapter Twenty-Nine

Upon running good courses, if one of the two knights breaks his lance in a full hit, and the other one attaints without breaking, the one who broke wins, unless he swooped it or committed other fouls such as touching the tilt, in which case the one who attaints without breaking is the winner. And if because of an attaint or a full hit one knight leaned back more than the other, returning to the saddle without further consequences, this counts for nothing.[56] Should anything else occur,[57] let it be judged as is stated in the chapters above.

---

* *rompuda: ronpuda* – Ed. 1532.
† *colps: cops* – Ed. 1532.
‡ *les encontres: los encontres* – Ed. 1532.
§ *no·s*: no es.
⁋ *entre·ls*: entre els.
** *qu·en*: que en.

Capítol XXX

Són encontres* prohibits en les festes de júnyer encontrar en la scarcella, en l'arçó de la sella, en la mà de la regna, en lo cap o en lo coll del cavall, en la cuixa del cavaller o d'aquí† avall; en axí que per tal encontre, lo que encontra no deu ni pot guanyar pris algú aquell dia, encara que sia exit al rench lo pus rich pompós ataviat; e açò per esquivar escàndels, com per tals encontres se sien seguides morts de junyidors e grans dans, destorbant de les ju[s]tes‡ la alegr[e]§ festa.

Chapter Thirty

Prohibited strokes in jousting festivals include striking the tasset, the arçon of the saddle, the bridle hand, the head or the neck of the horse, the thigh of the rider or from here on down;[58] so that for any such encounter, the one who makes the stroke must not and cannot win any prizes that day, even if he were the richest and most splendidly dressed knight who went out to the lists; and in this way scandals can be avoided, since because of strokes like this jousters have died or sustained serious injuries, spoiling the merriment of the jousts.

Capítol XXXI

E perquè en les festes són de mal comport los escàndels, si lo cavaller caurà en terra, ab lo cavall o sens lo cavall, per desastre o per defalt o en qualsevol altra manera, no pot gaunyar¶ pris, encara que puga tornar a júnyer. Axí, fon declarat en Lombardia que si·l** cavaller, entrant en la plaça per tornejar, cahia en terra arremetent lo cavall,†† ab colpa o sens colpa,‡‡ no devia guanyar joya aquell dia, perquè seguint-li tal desastre guastava la festa.

Chapter Thirty-One

And because scandals at festivals shall not be tolerated, if the knight falls to the ground, with or without the horse, because of some disaster or mistake or for any other reason whatsoever, he cannot win the prize, even though he may be able to return to joust. Thus it was declared in Lombardy that if the knight, entering the lists to tourney, fell to the ground whilst spurring on his horse, whether it was his fault or not, he would be disqualified from winning the jewel that day, because by meeting with such a disaster he spoiled the festival.

* encontres: encontrats – Ed. 1532.
† d'aquí: d'aquel – Ed. 1532. Janer et al. (fol. XIv) and Bohigas (p. 192) did not emend, but the masculine demonstrative pronoun does not make sense, given that the point of reference is a feminine noun (la cuixa). Ed. 1493 reads correctly daq̃, which is a common abbreviation for d'aquí.
‡ justes: juntes – Ed. 1493; jũtes (a standard abbreviation for juntes) – Ed. 1532. Clearly a mistake for justes, as also noted by Janer et al. (fol. XIv) and Bohigas (p. 193).
§ alegre: alegra – Ed. 1493; alegre – Ed. 1532.
¶ gaunyar: guanyar – Ed. 1532.
** si·l: si el.
†† cavall: cabal – Ed. 1532. The error was transmitted to Janer et al. (fol. XIv) and thence to Bohigas (p. 193).
‡‡ ab colpa o sens colpa: ab culpa o sens culpa – Ed. 1532.

Scola del junyidor

En la scola del junyidor que es pratica, Art és lo mestre. Enteniment, Disposició e Natural Inclinació són los dexebles, perquè sens companyia de aquests és impossible al cavaller exir destre famós de tal estudi. Venint, donchs, lo cavaller per dar lició als miradors, volent mostrar lo que natura y fortuna li mostren, deu exir al rench de aquesta manera:

Preceheixquen trompetes, atavals, tamborins e ministrés; segueixquen ben ataviades persones de honor, servidors o patges que porten les lances; aprés, ben acompanyat de cavall y de peu, arremeta lo cavaller junyidor* per alguna part, que, prompte apareixent† de les gents a la vista, done delit e admiració la gentilesa‡ e disposició de la sua pomposa bellea. Volte ab temps y mesura, guardant-se de tocar al rench del cap del cavall, de anques ni en altra manera. No s'oblide portar guarnició ben concertada,§ o paraments chapats, brocats o de seda, lo més rich y pompós que li sia possible, les armes netes, febrides, ben guarnides d'or y de seda. Lo scut,¶ brodat** o pintat de alta y galant†† invenció, vaja cenyt per lo mig a la usança. Y sobre tot, bella cimera, la letra de la qual, si serà ben acertada, en moltes parts escrita la done, en lo primer arremetre, a les gents que saber la declaració de les invencions naturalment desigen.

School of Jousting[59]

In the school of jousting practice, Skill is the master. Intellect, Aptitude and Natural Inclination are the disciples, for without these companions it is impossible for the knight to graduate as a renowned expert. The knight, then, coming to give a lesson to the spectators, wishing to demonstrate what nature and fortune demonstrate to him, should enter the lists in the following manner:

Let the trumpeters, kettledrummers, tabor players and minstrels lead the way; let well-dressed persons of honour, the servants or the pages who carry the lances follow; then, well accompanied on horseback and on foot, let the noble jouster spur his horse forward from some place so that, as he suddenly comes into view before the spectators, the elegance[60] and disposition of his majestic beauty inspires joy and admiration. Let him turn in good time and with restraint, being careful that his horse does not touch the lists with its head, its rump, or in any other way.[61] Let him not forget to wear a well-fitted garniture, or horse trappings covered with the richest and most splendid brocades or silks possible, his armour clean, polished, nicely decorated with gold and silk. Let his shield, emblazoned or decorated with a sublime and elegant device, be girt in the centre as is customary. And above all, let him not forget to wear[62] a beautiful crest, the motto for which, if it should be well conceived, shall be widely distributed in writing, at the first charge, to those who naturally wish to know the explanation of inventions.[63]

---

* *junyidor: junydor* – Ed. 1532.
† *apareixent: aparexient* – Ed. 1532.
‡ *gentilesa: gentileza* – Ed. 1532.
§ *concertada: consertada* – Ed. 1532.
¶ *scut: escut* – Ed. 1532.
** *brodat: brodad* – Ed. 1532.
†† *galant: galan* – Ed. 1532.

E axí, batent la guarda per son orde, faça per lo rench la acostumada volta. E perquè·s[*] conega ser gran cavaller de la sella de la guisa, porte lo cors ert e algun poch pandó; lo braç dret no deixe anar penjant, mas[†] porte la mà posada del escut sobre la mossa (e, alguna vegada, sobre lo fals de la correja); les cames dretes, exint del cors per son endret, no lançant-les per avant ni corves per atràs, mas ertes y molt acostades al ventre del cavall; los peus seguits, punta e taló per un egual; los esperons mirant a hon se deu batre.

Al cap del rench no estiga fluix, abandonat, ne li cayga la lança de la mà; dreta la porte en la bossa, acostada envés lo elm. La mà, alta prop la roda; lo colze, ubert; e al traure la lança de la bossa, cale la mà prop los gocets. Sia lo metre alt e sens galtada, no donant davall lo rest. Parteixca ab tento, no arrebatat, car dels esperons lo cavall no·s[‡] deu molt batre. Corrent ab lança en rest, cale poch a poch, perquè no faça calades ni toque de pla en lo rench, ni de punta de billeta hi encontre. Portant la lança en lo rest, no vaja uberta, mas sobre lo rench, mirant al muscle dret del altre, girant-se algun poch al encontre; no ature lo cavall ans del encontre ni cride davall lo elm. Mas, aprés de haver encontrat, alce la lança y escórrega la mà fins a la roda, deixant[§] per espatles aquella, sobre lo rench, als servidors de peu, que la prenguen. E aprés, passejant reposadament, al cap del rench se ature.

And thus, taking care over his proper deportment, let him ride the customary lap around the lists.[64] And so that he may be recognised as a great knight of the jousting saddle, let him hold his body straight and slightly rigid; let him not hang his right arm down, but rather hold his hand in place on the bouche of the shield (and, at one time, on the buckle of the guige); his legs straight, hanging directly in line with his torso, neither pushing them forward nor bending them backwards, but rigid and very close to the horse's belly; his feet well placed, the toes level with the heels; watching where to prick with the spurs.

At the head of the tilt he should be neither slack nor slovenly, nor should the lance fall out of his hand; he should hold it vertical in its pouch, with the stave standing close to his helm. His hand high, close to the vamplate; his elbow opened;[65] and upon taking the lance out of the pouch let him slide his hand close to the grappers. Let him lift the lance high without clumsily hitting the lance-rest or dropping below it. Let him set off carefully, not hastily, because the horse should not be pricked a lot with the spurs.[66] Riding with the lance in the lance-rest, let him lower it little by little, so that he does not swoop or touch the tilt crosswise or hit it with the coronel.[67] Holding the lance in the lance-rest, let him not ride wide open, but along the tilt, watching his opponent's right shoulder, turning slightly at the encounter;[68] let him not bring his horse to a halt before the encounter or shout inside of his helm. But rather, after having encountered, let him raise his lance and slide his hand toward the vamplate, passing what is left of the lance back over the tilt to his footmen so that they can take it.[69] And then, riding at a gentle pace, let him come to a halt at the end of the lists.[70]

---

[*] *perquè·s: perquè es.*

[†] *mas: més* – Ed. 1532.

[‡] *no·s: no es.*

[§] *deixant: dexant* – Ed. 1532.

Les altres subtilitats, deixant* a vostres senyories, seran com a diamants que faran rica la brodadura de aquesta mal guarnida roba.

The remaining subtleties, left up to your lordships, shall be like diamonds that will enrich the embroidery of this poorly trimmed cloth.[71]

Deo gracias.[†]

Thanks be to God.

Fon acabat de empremptar[‡] e effigiar lo present tractat en la nobilissima ciutat de València, a xvj de setembre,[§] any de la salutífera nativitat de Nostre Senyor Déu Jesuchrist. Mil.cccc.lxxxxiij.[¶]

Printing and duplicating of the present treatise was completed in the most noble city of Valencia, on 16 September, in the year of the salutiferous birth of Our Lord God Jesus Christ, 1493.

---

* *deixant: dexant* – Ed. 1532.
† Janer *et al.* end their edition at this point. Consequently, the colophon is not included either in their edition or in that of Bohigas.
‡ *empremptar: empremtar* – Ed. 1532.
§ *a xvj de setembre: a xiij de Juliol* – Ed. 1532.
¶ *Mil.cccc.lxxxxiij: M.D.xxxij* – Ed. 1532.

NOTES TO THE TRANSLATION

1 In the 1493 incunable owned by The Hispanic Society of America, this sentence is preceded by a modified title, written in Spanish in a contemporary hand, as follows: 'Libro:– de –: justas:~' ('Book of Jousts').

2 The wording of the exordium is equally as stylised in Catalan.

3 *the loathsome shadows*: Cp. medieval Catalan *les leges ombres*. Coromines, *Diccionari etimologic i complementari de la llengua catalana*, vol. V, p. 140a, notes that Old Catalan *leges* (cp. modern Catalan *lleig/lletja*) is derived from the same etymological root as English 'loath'; hence my choice of adjective in this case.

4 The sentence plays on the idea of Menaguerra imparting wisdom to his disciples. Cp. the words of Christ: 'For there is nothing hid, except to be made manifest; nor is anything secret, except to come to light' (Mark 4:22; also Matthew 10:26 and Luke 12:2).

5 The rhetoric of these two sentences is reminiscent of *Tirant lo Blanc*. Tirant, the personification of the chivalric ideal, is described in the Epistle Dedicatory in terms of brilliance, light and magnanimity: 'aquell tan famós cavaller, que, com lo sol resplandeix entre los altres planets, així resplandeix aquest en singularitat de cavalleria entre·ls altres cavallers del món, apellat Tirant lo Blanch, qui per sa virtut conquistà molts regnes e províncies donant-los a altres cavallers.' ('That famous knight Tirant lo Blanc, whose brilliance among knights was like the sun's among planets, and who, conquering by his powers many kingdoms and provinces, gave them all to other knights.') See Martorell, *Tirant lo Blanch*, ed. Hauf, [Dedicatòria], p. 61. For the translation, see *Tirant lo Blanc*, trans. LaFontaine, p. 37.

6 *gracefully*: Cp. medieval Catalan *per gentilea*. Forms such as *gentilea*, *bellea* ('beauty'), *destrea* ('skill') and *naturalea* ('nature'), as opposed to *gentilesa*, *bellesa*, *destresa* and *naturalesa*, are an accurate reflection of actual pronunciation, underscoring the Valencian heritage of Ponç de Menaguerra and his patrons.

7 The Principle of Equality applies to scoring opportunities (see chapters 21 and 27, below), rank

(see ch. 14, below) and weaponry, which Ponç de Menaguerra does not address in this book. On the Principle of Equality as it applies to weapons, see Quijada de Reayo, ch. 4: 'It behoves the judges to assure that the lance-maker provide lances of equal length so that one is not longer than another, for if one is one digit longer than another, the one that strikes first will splinter, and the other may or may not break at all.'

8 As is clear from this and other jousting treatises, the issue of ranking or determining who jousted best was often not an easy task.

9 *in consequence of the knight's skill or negligence, of his luck or misfortune*: In the quest for 'the truth' (*la veritat*) mentioned in the first sentence of the exordium, the application of dialectic to jousting, in the form of these simple *Sic et Non* ('Aye and Nay') formulae, is rhetorically appropriate.

10 *your sword-wielding and strong arm*: The terminology in this instance refers literally to Menaguerra's physical prowess and metaphorically to his noble lineage. Since in medieval Catalan *mena* means 'battlement' and *guerra* means 'war', the Menaguerra family arms are appropriately bellicose, as follows: a field *gules*, a cubit dexter arm in armour proper *argent*, issuing from the sinister and grasping a sword of arms *argent*, the pommel *or*. The blazon is reproduced in *Lo Cavaller*, ed. Janer *et al.*, fol. IIIv. See also Riquer, *Heràldica catalana des l'any 1150 al 1550*, vol. I, p. 284.

11 *is incapable of twisting the line*: Cp. medieval Catalan *no pot torçre la ralla*. That is, he delivers firm, straight cuts. In modern-day parlance Menaguerra would be considered a 'straight shooter'. The language is reminiscent of that used by Ramon Llull, who states that of all the knight's weapons it is the lance that symbolises the truth, 'car veritat és cosa dreta e no es torç' ('for truth is a straight thing and it is not twisted'). See Llull, *Llibre de l'Orde de Cavalleria*, ed. Gustà, part V, p. 69.

12 *that I unfurl the bales of my inferior cloth into the hands of your superior intelligence*: This is a modesty topos typical of the exordium. The elliptic metaphor should be understood in the context of Catalonia's long-standing reputation as a centre for the textile industry (chiefly the export of wool cloth and

the import of cotton, linen and luxury cloths), the meaning being that Ponç de Menaguerra's written expression is akin to course cloth, and this will be immediately obvious to his patrons, for their keen intelligence allows them to discern coarse from fine material. Rhetorically, Menaguerra's use of the adjectives *grossa* ('inferior') and *prima* ('superior') forms a neat antithesis. As noted in the *Rhetorica Ad Herennium*: 'Hoc genere si distinguemus orationem, et graves et ornati poterimus esse' ('Embellishing our style by means of this figure we shall be able to give it impressiveness and distinction'). See *Rhetorica Ad Herennium*, ed. Caplan, pp. 282–3

13 *lists*: Cp. medieval Catalan *rench*. For Menaguerra the word *rench* has different meanings in different contexts. On the one hand *rench* is used to refer to the lists within which the jousts actually take place (see also below, n. 64). In this sense the word has the same meaning as Old French *renc*, which referred to a jousting course scattered with sand (see Crouch, *Tournament*, pp. 84–5). On the other hand, it can denote the wooden tilt that separates the competitors (see below, n. 20). In this sense it has the same meaning as medieval Castilian *renque*. See, for example, Rodríguez de Lena, *El Passo Honroso de Suero de Quiñones*, ed. Labandeira Fernández, p. 100: 'por medio de la liça estava fecho un renque de maderos' ('in the middle of the lists a tilt was constructed out of wooden planks'). One further meaning of *rench* in Menaguerra's text is 'tilting competition' (below, n. 45).

14 The tasset in question is the left tasset.

15 The same hand that penned the modified title to the 1493 ed. has bracketed this sentence and added the following marginal note in Spanish: 'cómo se pierde el precio o la joia' ('how the prize or jewel is lost').

16 *to one who would occasion such scandal in the enjoyment of so magnificent a festival*: Cp. medieval Catalan *al qui dóna occasió scandalosa en lo plaer de tant pomposa festa*. The anonymous writer of marginalia in ed. 1493 has underlined this clause.

17 Another marginal note in Spanish by the same hand is included in the 1493 ed. at this point. It has been cut off where the page was at one time guillotined: 'cómo se da el precio [al] más jentil que se [ha

de] mirar' ('how the prize is awarded to the one who looks the most elegant').

18 Menaguerra returns to the issue of crests below, ch. 27.

19 Ed. 1493 has another marginal note in Spanish by the same hand: 'perder del precio' ('loss of the prize').

20 *lists*: Cp. medieval Catalan *plaça*. The lists, or jousting enclosure, would often be erected temporarily in the main public plaza of a city or town, or in the courtyard of a palace or castle. Permanent tiltyards were also usually located adjacent to a castle or in or close to a major city, the tiltyard at Smithfield near London being one example.

21 *tilt*: Cp. medieval Catalan *rench*. In this instance *rench* clearly denotes the tilt that separates the competitors (cp. notes 13, 45 and 64).

22 *the three stages having been passed*: Cp. medieval Catalan *passats tres ponts*. In ch. 2 of his treatise Quijada de Reayo refers to these three stages as *tres partes* ('three parts'). See also below, ch. 7.

23 On compensating for mistakes, see also below, ch. 12.

24 *running with sharp lances*: Cp. medieval Catalan *passos de córrer puntes*. The equivalent expression existed in medieval Castilian ('correr puntas') and Portuguese ('correr pomtas'). In the *Cancionero de Baena* (c. 1430), for example, we are told that kings, princes and grandees enjoy watching and engaging in the following activities: 'justar e tornear e correr puntas' ('jousting and tourneying and running with sharp lances'). See *Cancionero de Juan Alfonso de Baena*, eds Dutton and González Cuenca, p. 6. Portuguese jousts of this type are described in Fernão Lopes' *Crónica de D. João I*, ed. Sérgio, vol. II, chs CI and CXI, pp. 232–3 and 250–1.

25 *Trees*: Menaguerra is referring to a rule of judicial combat, as discussed in several medieval 'trees', or books of laws. See, for example, Honoré Bouvet (also known as Bonet), *L'Arbre des Batailles* (1387), ed. Nys, p. 231: 'En ceste bataille les armeures sont en figure de tesmoings par lesquelles chascun d'eulx entend de prouver son entente.' ('In this kind of battle arms stand for the witnesses by which each man means to prove his case.') For the translation, see *The Tree of Battles of Honoré Bonet*, trans. Coopland, p. 200. *L'Arbre des Batailles* was translated into

Catalan and Castilian in the early fifteenth century so Menaguerra would have had access either to a version in French or to a translation. Bouvet's point is reiterated and expanded upon by the Catalan author Gabriel Turell in his own *Arbre d'Honor* (1471). See Turell, *Arbre d'Honor*, ed. Burgaya, pp. 133–42.

26 The meaning of this chapter is that if the knight runs a course and accidentally breaks his lance without actually striking his opponent, this course must still count as one course run. This type of illegal break might be caused by a jouster barricading his lance in an encounter. However, since a similar break could also be caused by a very powerful direct blow, Menaguerra is here stressing the importance of determining the exact cause – legal or illegal – of a break. Ch. 8 provides further clarification on how the lance might accidentally get broken whilst running the course.

27 *swooping*: Cp. medieval Catalan *fent calades*. The equivalent Spanish expression *hazer calada* is used by Quijada de Reayo in chapters 2 and 4 of his treatise.

28 *the other knight … attaints*: Cp. medieval Catalan *l'altre … encontrarà*. In Catalan and Spanish jousting treatises the verb *encontrar* can mean 'to encounter', 'to collide', 'to strike' or, as in this case, 'to attaint'. The verb 'to attaint' is an equivalent technical term defined as follows: 'To touch, get at with a blow, to hit in tilting' (*OED*). An attaint is a stroke with the lance which does not make it shatter. The text repeatedly makes distinctions between these attaints versus hits which do actually break the lance (see chapters 10, 22, 25, 26, 27 and 29, for example). Of interest here is the advice contained in ch. 4 of Quijada de Reayo's treatise: 'It behoves the judges sitting on the bench to require that one of them have some red ochre and that he smear this on the single-pointed heads or the mournes so that a mark will be left wherever they attaint or strike.'

29 Note that a distinction is being made between attainting, on the one hand, *or*, shattering the lance, on the other hand.

30 Cp. medieval Catalan *armes retretes*, literally 'withdrawn arms', that is to say, lances for the joust of peace, in which the safety of the participants was paramount.

31 *with the coronel*: Cp. medieval Catalan *de punta de billeta*. This is, specifically, a four-prong coronel used in jousts of peace. See also below, chapters 18, 23 and 27.

32 *it can be equalled out*: Cp. medieval Catalan *pot-se acabalar*. The verb *acabalar* in this instance is used as a synonym of *igualar* ('to equalise'), with the specific nuance of scoring the exact amount of winning points required to cancel out the losses incurred.

33 *another encounter*: The Catalan text reads as follows: *un encontre*. This literally means 'an encounter', which I have taken the liberty of clarifying, since the author is referring to the fact that the knight can compensate for making a foul in one course by running another, more successful course. See also chapters 6, 7 and 11.

34 This is an example of Menaguerra's elliptic style. The points are awarded to the knight who inflicts the disabling wounds rather than to the knight who sustains them, for the knight who sustains serious injury is either declared 'out of the lists' or he is 'counted as dead'. On being counted as dead, see also ch. 25, below.

35 This chapter gives a good impression of some of the dangers that were still present even in the jousts of peace as practised at the end of the fifteenth century, even though efforts to increase levels of safety had been ongoing for well over a hundred years.

36 *should run the length of the course*: That is to say, against a non-royal.

37 Cp. medieval Catalan *armes d'ultrança*, literally 'arms of the extreme', in other words, jousts of war. As is clear from ch. 25, below, the jousts of war mentioned by Menaguerra were in fact a kind of mock joust *à outrance* and not at all the true (and much more dangerous) version that had been practised up until around 1450.

38 *full hit*: Cp. medieval Catalan *embarrerada*. The meaning of this word can only be inferred, since Ponç de Menaguerra is the only author who has ever used it in the context of jousting and, frustratingly, he does not provide a definition. In his edition Bohigas (p. 208) conjectures that *embarrerada* means that the knight is pushed into the tilt so that he cannot move, but this would constitute a foul as

opposed to a praiseworthy hit. Menaguerra always uses the word *embarrerada* in conjunction with, and as a direct alternative to, the word *encontre* ('attaint'). Alcover, *Diccionari català-valencià-balear*, vol. IV, p. 714b, defines the Old Catalan verb *embarrerar* as follows: 'circuir l'enemic impedint-li la fuita o retirada' ('to surround the enemy preventing his escape or retreat'). In the context of jousting it seems logical that the type of blow from which there is no escape would be an unavoidable full hit. One further inference to be made from the text is that this type of full hit causes the lance to shatter. The author, then, is once again distinguishing between an attaint – a light or average hit which is perfectly respectable but which does not break the lance – and a full hit – an especially powerful blow of the sort all jousters aspire to, which shatters the lance and perhaps also crushes the opponent's armour or draws blood.

39 *coronel*: Cp. medieval Catalan *billeta*, as mentioned in ch. 11, above.

40 Cp. Quijada de Reayo's advice quoted above, n. 28, on smearing the lance-head with red ochre in order to provide evidence of a palpable hit.

41 *the grapper or the lance*: Cp. medieval Catalan *lo gocet o la lança*. Bohigas, in the notes to his ed., confuses 'lo gocet' ('the grapper') with the gusset, the mail that protected the armpit. Riquer, *L'Arnès del cavaller*, p. 169, n. 48, suggests emending to 'lo gocet [de] la lança' ('the grapper *of* the lance'), but the injuries sustained at the Pass of Honour of Suero de Quiñones confirm that the hand could be injured either by the grapper or by the lance stave itself. The Pass of Honour of Suero de Quiñones also makes it clear that the most common grapper injuries were in fact dislocations rather than lacerations.

42 *guard*: Cp. medieval Catalan *guarda*. In medieval Catalan and medieval Castilian, 'la guarda' can refer to the gardbrace or the guard of the vambrace. In the context of this chapter Menaguerra is referring ostensibly to the guard of the vambrace. The guard of the vambrace, or couter reinforcing plate, is a separate reinforce or double plate rather than the integral couter wing itself. He may, however, also be inferring the gardbrace in his effort to quantify performance whilst taking into account the evolution of jousting armour and the reality that no two kits were ever exactly alike.

43 That is to say, the knight upon whom the attaint or direct hit is dealt and who loses his shield as a result is declared out of the lists.

44 Ferdinand V of Aragon (1452–1516; King of Aragon-Catalonia, 1478–1516).

45 *tilt*: Cp. medieval Catalan *rench*, which is now used to refer to a tilting competition. See also notes 13, 20 and 64.

46 *this*: That is, a damaged or dislodged helm.

47 *making fire fly*: Cp. medieval Catalan *traure foch*. This is Menaguerra's way of describing the striking of sparks.

48 *coronel*: Cp. medieval Catalan *billeta*, as mentioned in chapters 11 and 18, above.

49 On the prohibitions see below, ch. 30.

50 Cp. also ch. 13.

51 *the second class of encounters*: The first class, or category, of encounters are the jousts of peace and the second class, as is clarified in the next clause of the sentence, are the jousts of war.

52 *is counted as dead*: Cp. also ch. 13, above. The wording here indicates that these were not real jousts *à outrance*, that is, judicial combats fought to the death. Rather, the jousters were mimicking this type of joust, and even though they were following the rules for judicial combat, the various measures taken to guarantee safety would – hopefully! – prevent them from getting killed. The mock joust *à outrance* would often take place in the open field, without the aid of a tilt, with single-pointed (but not necessarily sharp) lances and with armour that was designed to be reminiscent of the field armour worn in previous centuries. This chapter underscores above all the ludic nature of jousting.

53 *close saddle*: Cp. medieval Catalan *sella closa*. Cp. *The School of Jousting*, where Menaguerra refers to the *sella de la guisa*, which I translate as 'jousting saddle'.

54 *having the wherewithal*: Cp. medieval Catalan *anant-hi mesions*. This expression is quite vexing. According to Alcover, *Diccionari català-valencià-balear*, vol. VII, p. 387ab, the meaning of *messió* in modern Catalan is 'bet' or 'wager', but it is doubtful that the expression concerns betting, since chivalric treatises routinely condemn all games of chance. See, for example, the *Libro de la Orden de la Banda*,

statute 5 (Cartagena, *Doctrinal de los caballeros*, in *Tratados Militares*, ed. Fallows, p. 313): 'Mucho es de extrañar que ningún caballero de la Banda no juegue los dados en cuanto anduviere en guerra y en menester. Y por ende, decimos que cualquier que los jugare, si fuere sabido en verdad, que le den por pena que le quiten el sueldo de un mes y que no beba vino en tres días. Y, señaladamente, si fuere sabido que jugare armas o caballo, que le tiren el sueldo por dos meses y que no traiga banda por cuatro meses.' ('It is expressly forbidden for any knight of the Band to play dice when he is on campaign or on official duty. And therefore, we declare that any knight who plays dice, if it were proven beyond a doubt, shall be punished by having his salary docked for one month and he shall not be allowed to drink wine for three days. And, in particular, if it were proven that he was betting his arms or his horse, his salary shall be docked for two months and he shall not be allowed to wear the band for four months.') Alcover also notes that in medieval Catalan the word often meant 'costs' or 'expenses' (cp. medieval Castilian *misión*). Similarly, Coromines, *Diccionari etimologic i complementari de la llengua catalana*, vol. V, p. 655a, states that Old Aragonese *messió* can refer to a person with extravagant tastes or spending habits; hence my interpretation, which is that the author is referring to knights who have the financial means to ride in full-dress regalia, complete with elaborate crest on helm. There was certainly an incentive to spend as much money as possible on one's harness and other accoutrements, given the statement in ch. 2, for example: 'Whenever the prize is to be awarded to the most elegant knight … the knight who wears the best, most expensive, magnificent armour should be expected to win.'

55 *coronel*: Cp. medieval Catalan *punta de billeta*, as mentioned in chapters 11, 18 and 23, above.

56 *this counts for nothing*: The immutable laws of physics dictate that the knight upon whom the blow is dealt will lean or be pushed back in the saddle due to the force of the impact. Conversely, the knight who deals the blow might lean sideways out of the saddle and into the tilt in order to adjust his angle of attack. Since leaning in the saddle is an integral part of jousting technique, Menaguerra's opinion is that it should not warrant any special consideration or extra points.

57 *Should anything else occur*: Such as being unseated, losing the lance or a piece of armour, etc.

58 Cp. Quijada de Reayo, ch. 4: 'When you joust, try not to make a foul stroke, which includes striking below the belt of your opponent or hitting the saddle, and striking the tilt is a serious foul, or striking the shaffron of the horse.'

59 In ed. 1493 two hand-drawn hands point from the left margin to the first two paragraphs of this section, underscoring their importance. It was common in the fifteenth century to refer to jousts as 'Schools of Prowess'. See Anglo, *The Great Tournament Roll of Westminster*, vol. I, p. 19, n. 2, and Barker, *The Tournament in England, 1100–1400*, p. 24.

60 *elegance*: Cp. medieval Catalan *gentilesa*. This is the only occasion in the text that the author uses the grammatically correct form *gentilesa* instead of *gentilea* (see above, n. 6).

61 See also above, ch. 3.

62 *let him not forget to wear*: This phrase is only implied in the original. It is a necessary addition to the translation, which otherwise would make little sense.

63 Cp. Castiglione, *Il Libro del Cortegiano*, ed. Maier, pp. 205–6: 'E se poi se ritroverà armeggiare nei spettaculi publici, giostrando, torneando, o giocando a canne, o facendo qualsivoglia altro esercizio della persona, ricordandosi il loco ove si trova ed in presenzia di cui, procurerà esser nell'arme non meno attillato e leggiadro che sicuro, e pascer gli occhi dei spettatori di tutte le cose che gli parrà che possano aggiungergli grazia; e porrà cura d'aver cavallo con vaghi guarnimenti, abiti ben intesi, motti appropriati, invenzioni ingeniose, che a sé tirino gli occhi de' circonstanti, come calamita il ferro.' ('If he happens to be playing at arms in public shows – such as jousts, tourneys, cane games, or any other bodily exercise–, mindful of the place and presence in which he is, he will contrive to be not less elegant and graceful than unerring with his weapons, and to feast the spectators' eyes with all those things which he thinks may give him an added grace. He will take care that his horse is bravely caparisoned, that his attire becomes him, that his mottoes are appropriate and his devices clever, so that they may attract the eyes of the bystanders as the loadstone attracts iron.') For the translation see Castiglione,

The Book of the Courtier, trans. Opdycke, pp. 80–1. Note that Opdycke translates 'giocando a canne' as 'stick-throwing', which is not quite right. I have taken the liberty of emending to 'cane games', which more accurately reflects the original Italian.

64 Here the meaning of the word *rench* (see also above, n. 13) is the lists that would often be erected in the middle of the courtyard or the public plaza.

65 As pointed out by Riquer, *L'Arnès del cavaller*, p. 170, the elbow needs to be open in order to hold the lance vertically at this point.

66 Cp. Zapata, whose words echo Menaguerra's three stages of the course: 'On setting out, spurs should be put to it one time, and once again in the middle of the course, as if to remind it to run, and once again on stopping, if one wants it to stop in double-quick time.' Duarte of Portugal is just as specific: 'E algūs em justando continu(av)am sempre dar com as sporas ao cavallo, abalando as pernas atee os encontros. E aquesto he feo e faz mais fraco o justador; por que em este tempo dévesse de dar com as sporas poucas vezes, e ryjo ou passo, segundo a besta for. E os tempos em que lhe devem de dar, som estes: hū ao aballar, pera o fazer entrar naquele galope ou correr como lhe mais praz que leve; e outra vez tanto que assessegar a vara de soo-braço.' ('Some riders are using the spurs continu-ously – from the starting of the final run until the moment of collision. This is not only ugly but it also makes the rider weaker; actually, in these situations we should use the spurs as few times as possible, strongly or lightly, in accordance with the beast's temper. And the appropriate moments to use the spurs are only two: to start the final run (to get from the beast the proper galloping pace); and just a moment before the collision (when we have the spear already aiming at the other jouster).') See Duarte I, King of Portugal, *Livro da ensinança de bem cavalgar toda sela que fez El-Rey Dom Eduarte de Portogal e do Algarve e Senhor de Ceuta*, ed. Piel, pp. 79–80. For the translation, see *The Royal Book of Horsemanship, Jousting and Knightly Combat*, trans Preto and Preto, p. 79. The need to spur the horse in particular at the moment of impact is sound advice, as this is the crucial moment when it needs the most encouragement.

67 *coronel*: Cp. medieval Catalan *punta de billeta*, as mentioned in chapters 11, 18, 23 and 27.

68 At this point some jousters might also lean sideways out of the saddle and into the tilt in order to press home their attack. See above, ch. 29. Cp. also Zapata: 'What looks really good is to turn the body slightly at the moment of impact, for better strokes are made this way and it looks graceful, for anything that stirs movement in an armoured man looks good, since it makes that fantastic figure seem like he is alive and not just a piece of iron.'

69 The blame may be imputed to clumsy footmen if the lance is dropped at this point. See above, ch. 4.

70 This paragraph constitutes an excellent descrip-tion of the three stages of the course mentioned in chapters 4 and 7, above.

71 Thus Ponç de Menaguerra neatly concludes his treatise by returning to the textile metaphor of the exordium.

There follows on pp. 347–62 an actual-size facsimile of the 1st edition of Ponç de Menaguerra, *Lo Cavaller*, (Valencia, 1493).

Libro :- de -: juſtas :-

Los del eſtament militar en la noble ciutat de valencia pre guen a moſſen Ponc de mena guerra ab eſtil de ſemblants paraules.

Aniſeſta ſperiencia nos ha cla= ramēt moſtrat la veritat que de vos Caualler ſtrenu ab alta veu de glorioſa fama les noſtres no enuejoſes orelles hoyr hauien . Car ſou vna enceſa falla a la claredat de qui. les leges ombres y defalts deles armes en noſaltres mirant ſe prenen eſmena . E ſou la luminoſa ētorcha q̃ acompanya guia y deſco bre la honoroſa ſenda p̃ hon al terme de to= ta perfectio ab geſt/paſſos y cōtinença de ſin gular triunfo los juſtadors cauallers exerci= tant ſe en lorde y actes de milicia ab facilitat y breu promptitud atenyer eſperen Sou enca ra la ſcola doctrina y excellent magiſteri que a noſaltres deixebles nodrits en los daurats breços d̃ voſtre gentil ſaber y entēdre p̃ obres pratiques y exemples gouernar acoſtumen. A vos dōchs magnanim caualler: noſtre dir ſe preſenta : pregant vos per gentilea noſtres prechs accepteu y la ploma pera pintar d̃l ar mat caualler la pintada bellea y concertada pintura/pera linear encara y allimitar d̃l plā

a ij

tat rench e intãgible com se deu collir lo fru꞊
pt de marauellosa destrea.Y per que lo nom
bre dls dubtes y disputes pera egualar la des
egualtat auantatges y millozia dels qui justẽ
es tan gran com la diuersitat deles carreres/
encõtres/vicis desastres y ventures. Affecta
dament demanam que capituleu les estimaci
ons y valoz del que junyint per destrea o per
colpa/per sozt/o per desuentura del caualler
es possible se segueixca Promerẽt y vostre tre
ball restar vos en obligacio ĩfinida.y quens
tenrem y cõtents de vostres decretades leys:
regint nos y aquelles : puix lo que teniu vist/
lest/hoyt y praticat ab la disposicio de vostre
gran esperit y clara vista nos asegura:que de
just jubi yozeta sentẽcia lo vostre armat y fozt
braç no pot tozpre la ralla.

¶ Respon mossen Menaguerra.

Si força de ignozãcia no menpacha
ua : desig de seruir vos beni consent
quel treball no refusse : per que scri꞊
uint satisfes al que la merce de vosal
tres graciosamẽt me demana .Cauallers vir
tuosos inclinats per natura al que vostres en
gendzadozs d excellent manera entenent bo
praticauen : qui pot creure vos fallgua lo q̃
naturalea nous denega : ne qui affigint en
lamar vna gota daygua psumeix augmẽtar
aquella : baix es lo meu dir y atenyer la alti꞊
tud del vostre eleuat entendze ni la mia poca

e antiga tapeſceria baſtaria jantes foꝛnint
empaliar les noues ſales de voſtra eſtimada
modernitat e ſciencia. Mas puix manant me
voleu que deſplegue les bales dela mia groſ=
ſa roba en mans de voſtra pꝛima intelligen=
cia: obeynt vos com a ſenyoꝛs y meſtres ſots
met ala coꝛrectio voſtra que eſmene la ſenten
cia y mal eſtil dels capitols que recite/ab pꝛo
teſt que de pꝛeſumtuos lo ſobꝛe nom no mate̅
ga: car be conech ptanyer a mi lo demanar
y apendꝛe puix lo determenar a voſaltres es
pꝛopꝛi offici.

⁋ Capitol pꝛimer.

O caualler venint al re̅ch armat de
totes aquelles defe̅ſiues armes que
al junyidoꝛ ſo̅ acoſtumades: al cap
del rench pot pe̅dꝛe la ſcarcella. E ſi alguna al
tra peça li fallia/oꝛdena la ley q̅ emperadoꝛs
reys/e pꝛinceps/manat han ſe obſerue tal ca
ualler lo pꝛis guanyar no puixa. Y la raho q̅
no co̅ſent en res q̅ defalt ſia/vol que ſembla̅t
libertat nos done/al qui dona occaſio ſca̅da
loſa en lo plaer de tant pompoſa feſta.

⁋ Capitol ſegon.

Tant pꝛis ſe dona al mes ge̅til/mi
re atentame̅t lo jutge/puix lo mi=
lloꝛ atauiat/mes rich pompos gua
nyar deu y ſeſpera. Si los parame̅ts decan=
ten o pengen/mes a vna part que a altra/e
la cimera ſi va dꝛeta y ben poſada/puix tals

q

a iij

mancaments notats/a perdre lo pris ajuden.

¶ Capitol terç.

Omēys se deu mirar lorde y mesura del caualler entrāt en la plaça p es=ser vist y loat o singular ostrea : com arremet/com dona los sperons com porta les cames/y com lo cors sobre la sella/ne ab quin temps voltara per quel rench nos deu tocar ab lo cauall de anques al girar / ni en qualsevol altra manera.

¶ Capitol quart.

Ja vist al cap ol rech lo cauall'r com prē la lança/com parteix en la sella=com vā les cames/si pert estreps /si pert la lança passats tres ponts exint li dela bossa : com ans de tres ponts nos puga jut jar pouda a nostra vsança : Car es presumi=dor del mal cauall o del qui serueix deu ser la colpa . Lança pouda a colpa del caualler/se eguala se cobra y cōpēsa p altra lāça rōpuda.

¶ Capitol cinque .

Er sostenir la policia e noble exerci = ci del junyer y p millor estimar ol bō junyidor la destrea:segons tenor de molts capitols fermats en passos de correr puntes sien condempnats los vicis de per=dre lança al pendre/o perdre strep/o streps/e cames arronçades/ a arbitre del jutge : per que tals legees no esmenades valen ala part altra per vna lança rompuda.

¶ Capitol sise.

E dos cauallers la hu perdēt la lã
ça, laltre qui encontrant al rēch fa
bona carrera : guanya lo qui encō=
tra/per que exercint fa mes e millors actes
necessaris per al junyer : car los arbres o ca
pitols qui tracten deles valors y drets deles
armes ati ho volen que nengū acte sia pres p
no fet : ans sia remunerat lo digne de premi
e punit lo mereiredor de pena.

¶ Capitol sete.

Om en les armes lo dan sesguarde
al qui toca. Es determenat que si lo
caualler partint ab la lãça en la bos=
sa passats los tres ponts lis rompia en la ma
damunt o dauall la roda o metent la o por=
tant la en lo rest/tal carrera nos deu dir va=
na/tornant per aquella a fer ne altra : mas
deu anar per carrera correguda.

¶ Capitol huyte.

J al caualler partint li surtra la lãça
dela bossa y fēt legees en la carrera
la met en lo rest y fēt calades que to
quen al rench ve aromprela lança dencontre
E laltre fent bona carrera encontrara e no
rompra/tals encōtres son eguals. Mas si la
hu donant d pla o de punta en lo rench rom
pra guanya laltre qui encontra fent bona car
rera encara que no rompa.

¶ Capitol noue.

a   iiij

Els cauallers qui enfemps fencõtra
ran y rompzan les lançes. Deu gua
nyar lo q̃ millo: es anat y pert laltre
q̃ en la carrera haura fet vna o moltes legees
℟ Capitol dee.

Per maio: declaracio d̃ls fobze dits
e   capitols : per quant en la d̃termina=
cio d̃les gentilees e legees en les fe=
ftes de junyer fon varies opiniõs d̃ cauallers
Seguint lo:de e ftil d̃les armes. Sil caualler
paffant carrera la lança alçara per no encon
trar al altre venint defbaratat o ab lança per
duda tal alçar de lança no es de alguna efti=
ma. Car feria pzejubi d̃ vn altre qui haura en
contrat o romput lança. E per femblãt lo ca=
ualler qui haura encontrat o romput lança
fent calades e legees donant dela lança da
uall lo reft, per tals legees no pert encon=
tre ni lança rõpuda Car en armes retretes al
gũa gẽtilea no augmẽta lo nõbze dels colps
ni algũa legea ẽ lo:de d̃ ferir fobze les armes
diminueix lo nõbze de aq̃lls. Exceptat quant
los cauallers ferã eguals de encõtres o lãces
rõpudes : q̃ en tal cars lo pris deu effer par=
tit ẽ parts donãt millo ria al qui haura fet la
gẽtilea e la meno: part al qui haura fet la le=
gea remetẽt la tal particio a arbitre d̃l jutge.
℟ Capitol onze.
Uant lo caualler rompza d̃ pũta de
bületa en lo rẽch encara que vinga

de bona carrera/guanya laltre sens encon̄
tre/ab tot que baja fet legees e calades do̅
nant al rench de pla. E si donant de pla al
rench rompra la lança es egual ab lo qui en̄
contra en lo rench de punta de billeta.

¶Capitol dotze.

Ent bona carrera lo caualler si per
desastre enco̅trara en lo rench o po̅ra
lança: pot se acabalar aua̅çant vn en
contre rompent lança o fehent perdre peça o
la regna a laltre/deixant ho a arbitre del jut
ge: leuant li aquell auantage que haura gua
nyat o la carrera que haura enco̅trat/axi que
vna bona carrera vaja per la mala.

¶Capitol tretze.

S dit fora de rench/lo caualler naf
frat qui no pot tornar a junyer/e per
aquella sanch lo qui encontrat haura
guanya mes de aquelles lances que son en lo
pris.Exceptāt ne caualler qui ab sanch o se̅s
sanch sera tret o̅ tot recort no podent tornar
ales armes.Y exceptant ne caualler qui ab lo
cauall sera caygut en terra/perduda sanch o
desbaratat de algū niembre/car son estimats
com morts.E si al caualler per encontre li se
ra trencat lo braç/la cama/la cuixa/o lansa o̅l
coll val segons es jutgat/puix aquell encon
tre deu esser de maior valor que fa mes aco̅
star lo caualler a morir.

¶Capitol quatorze.

a   v

Eys o fills de reys si vns cõtrã de al tres junyirã/sien jutjats per les leys quels altres cauallers se jutgen/per que exercint tals actes militars no son mes q̃ cauallers. E si algũ rey o fill õ rey carrera cor rent ab lança passara encara que no encõtre ni sia altra cosa que lãça corregruda val mes que tots los encontres/actes/cassos/ni lan= ces quels altres cauallers de qualseuol titol baix õ rey hajen fet/e aço bauent respecte a la altitud de real dignitat.

Capitol quinze.

Abent per encõtre dos cauallers en terra ab los caualls/lo qui mẽys mal se fa y pus prest torna a caualcar per a junyer guanya/segons costum de vngres e alamanys. E seguint los estils deles armes dultrança que donẽ milloria al combatent re stãt de tal encõtre mes dispost pera batallar.

Capitol setze.

N alamanya y vngria no estimẽ sino aq̃ll encontre del qual los cauallers cahen en terra. E axi si fent bones car reres dos cauallers la bu õ aquells õl seu en contre caura dela sella en terra o caura ab lo cauall: guanya lo qui no encõtra puix tal en cõtre no te valor pa quil fa mas y al cãualler qui ab tãta virtut lo mostra sostenir y reebre.

Capitol desete.

Om perdre peça o regna sia gran de=
falt al caualler Si per encontre rebut
o embarrerada se pert la r̄gua / y nos
cobra fins lo cauall es reposat al cap d̄la car
rera / tal encontre val com lança rompuda.
E si lo qui rompra pdra peça o regna e laltre
no r̄opent encōtrara / tals encōtres sō eguals
℣ Capitol debuyte.

S peça pōuda y val com lança rom=
puda sil caualler pert lo guant dret p
encōtre de billeta / e si en lo guant no
si mostrara encontre / val per peça pōuda en=
cara ques perda p vn reuerssar o per fort en=
contre del caualler mateix . Mas si lo gocet
o la lança remordent la ma del caualler li fe=
ya naffra / tal sanch no es de algūa stima puix
per aquella nos deixe de junyer.
℣ Capitol denoue.

Al vna lança rompuda al caualler /
quand laltre per encontre o p embar
rerada perdra lo braçalet o la guar =
da / e axi mateix sestima peça perduda E si se=
ra encontrat en lo braçal dret o esquerre tant
desmarchat que sens martell tornar a armar
nos puga / es fora de rench tal caualler e val
quatre lances rōpudes. Mas sil braçal pert la
guarda o rompēt les altres peces sens trau=
rel del braç ab tiretes se adoba no es en algu
na estima. E axi se deu jutjar de totes les pe=
ces puix nos parteixca lo caualler del cap del

a   vj

rench per adobar aquelles.

¶ Capitol vinte.

Erdre lo scut per encontre o embarre rada val tres lances al qui encontra e vna del encontre son quatre y es fora de rench lo caualler: segons es determe⁓ nat per nostre senyor lo Rey don Ferrando huy prosper regnant. E aximateix val segons es dit si per qualseuol cars lo scut era esclafat partit o trocejat axi que p tal desmarchamēt no pogues tornar a junyer remetent aço a ar bitre del jutge.

¶ Capitol vint e hu.

O elm leuat del cap val deu lances al caualler quel leua. E si li fa perdre sanch del nas o dela boca perdent al guna dent val vint lances. E si haura sanch en lo cap o en lo front per la qual naffra no puixa tornar a junyer val segons es dit en lo capitol. xij. E si sera lo elm desmarchat axi q̃ nos puga ni dega ab aq̃ll tornar a junyer⁄ val com si fos leuat del cap. Y com en les ar mes se mire molt la egualtat⁄ sil rêch sera cri dat a carreres cōptades⁄ lo cars seguit en la derrera val com si fos seguit en la p̃mera car rera o qualseuol deles altres.

¶ Capitol vint e dos.

Ot encontre o embarrerada que faça anar lo caualler torbat puix no ixca d̃ recort y puga tornar sens molt espay

a junyer⸝ sia remes a arbitre del jutge p̄ que
finit lo rench⸝si tals cauallers:de lances o en
contres seran eguals⸝tal cars deu ser posat
en compte.

℀Capitol vint y tres.

Eixar troç d̄ lāça en lo elm en lo scut
o en q̄lseuol altra part no es dalgu⸝
na estima ni mēys traure foch p en⸝
contre: p̄ que encontrant e rompēt los tals
desastres no donē mes valor que lança rom⸝
puda y son eguals ab altre qui romp encara
q̄ semblāt cars no li sdeuinga Axi mateix trē
car les lāces p encōtre la bu fins ala roda lal
tre a vn palm dela billeta no es mes ni mēys
℀om se prēga ē lo fust la tal manera d̄ rōpre.

℀Capitol vint e quatre.

Si lo caualler sera encōtrat en qual⸝
seuolloch q̄ no sia prohibit encōtrar
e exira d̄ tot recort no podēt tornar
a junyer val mes que tots los altres casos q̄
poden guanyar lo pris⸝e mes que totes les
lances.E val mes que aço si per tal encōtre
perdia sanch⸝ com ja es dit en lo capitol.xiij.

℀Capitol vint y cinch.

O qui derroca caualler ab lo cauall
p terra p encōtre o embarrerada⸝gu
nya mes de aquelles lāces que serā
en lo pris Exceptāt los encontres del capitol
xxiiij.p̄ que lo encōtre trahent sanch o seguint
p aq̄ll algun dan en la psona e mēbres del ca

ualler ⁄ es en lo nombre dels encōtres intitu⁄
lat segon. Car en armes dultrāça ⁄ qui cau ab
lo cauall es reputat com amort.

¶ Capitol vint e sis.

Uād lo caualler p encōtre o per em
barrerada sera tret dela sella penjāt
en los arçōs o estreps o dl tot posat
en terra ⁄ es dit fora de rench. E lo qui encon
tra guanya vint lances. E si lo caygut volia
tornar a junyer no pot guanyar pris ⁄ per la
vergonya deser exit de sella closa ⁄ segōs lo stil
en passōs de correr puntes.

¶ Capitol vint y set.

Unyit dos cauallers ab les cimeres
qui pert la cimera p ēcōtre o embar⁄
rerada pt la carrera. e si anāt hi me⁄
sions la hu per parer mes galant passara ab
cimera e laltre no ⁄ sil portāt cimera fent bo⁄
na carrera rōpra e laltre fent no mēys bona
carrera d pūta d billeta la cimera li leuara sō
eguals Exceptat quāt junyirā a carreres cōp
tades o partida hon val mes la lāça rōpuda ⁄
p q̄ en les armes retretes los colps o encōtres
donats ans del finit nombre son de estimar.

¶ Capitol vint e huyt.

I per los encōtres nos segueix altre
q̄ rōpre les lances en les carreres ben
fetes rompudes les lāces los dos ca
uallers sō eguals : encara que la vn caualler
haja encōtrat pus alt quel altre ⁄ car rōpre en

lo elm o en lo scut/o damūt lo caragol/o da
uall no es mes ni menys.Si ja entrels caua
llers no sera fet pacte donant milloria al qui
pus alt encōtra.Axi p ben jutjar/los encon ⸗
tres del caragol en amunt son dits alts p los
dentorn de tota la roda/axi mateix tots los
altres son baixos/aço p esquiuar cōtrast.

¶ Capitol vint e nou.

Assant bones carreres si ōls dos ca
p   uallers la hu rōpra lāça dembarrera
da e laltre encōtrāt no romp/guāpa
lo q̃ rōput haura/exceptat q̃ no haja fet cala⸗
des e legees tocant al rēch/quen tāl manera
guanpa lo qui encōtra e no romp.E si per en
contre o embarrerada la hu reuersaua mes
quel altre tornant en la sella sens altre cars:
no es de fer ne stima.Seguint se altre sia jut
jat segōs es dit en los damūt dits capitols.

¶ Capitol.xxx.

On encontres prhibits en les festes
de junper/encōtrar en lascarcella/en
larço ōla sella/en la ma ōla regua en
lo cap o en lo coll del cauall/en la cuira del ca
ualler o daq̃ auall.En axi q̃ p tal encōtre lo q̃
encōtra no deu ni pot guāpar pris algu aq̃ll
dia: ēcara q̃ sia exit al rēch lo pus rich pōpos
atauiat.e aço p esq̃uar escādels com p tals en
ōtres se siē seguides morts ō jūpidors e grās
dans.destorbant deles juntes la alegra festa.

¶ Capitol.xxxj.

Per que en les festes ſõ de mal com
port los eſcãdels Si lo caualler cau
ra en terꝛa ab lo cauall o ſens lo ca⸗
uall/ꝑ deſaſtre o ꝑ defalt o en qualſeuol al⸗
tra manera no pot gaunyar pꝛis : encara que
puga toꝛnar a junper Açi fõ declarat en lom
bardia que ſil caualler entrãt en la plaça ꝑ toꝛ
nejar cabia en terꝛa arꝛemetët lo cauall ab col
pa o ſens colpa : no deuia guanyar joya aꝗ̃l
dia Perque ſeguint li tal deſaſtre guaſtaua la
feſta.

¶ Scola del junyidoꝛ.

A la ſcola del junyidoꝛ que es pꝛati
ca. Art es lo meſtre. Entenümët. Di⸗
ſpoſicio E natural ínclinacio ſõ los
deꝝebles/ꝑ que ſens compãyia de aqueſts es
ímpoſſible al caualler eꝝir deſtre/famos⸗ de
tal eſtudi. Venínt donchs lo caualler ꝑ dar li
ço als miradoꝛs/volent moſtrar lo que natu
ra ꝑ foꝛtuna li moſtren/deu eꝝir al rench de a
queſta manera.

Recebeiꝝquẽ trompetes atauals tã
boꝛíns e miniſtres. Segueiꝝquen bẽ
atauiades perſones de honoꝛ ſerui⸗
doꝛs o patges ꝗ poꝛtẽ les lãces. A⸗
pꝛes ben acõpanyat ð cauall ꝑ ð peu/arreme
ta lo caualler junyidoꝛ ꝑ alguna part ꝗ pꝛom
pte apareiꝝent de les gents a la viſta done de
lit e admiracio la gentileſa e diſpoſicio dela
ſua pompoſa bellea. Volte ab temps ꝑ meſu⸗

rá guardāt se de tocar al rench del cap del cā
uall de anques ni en altra manera. Nos obli
de portar guarnicio ben concertada o para=
mēts chapats brocats o de seda/lo mes rich
p pompos que li sia possible. Les armes ne=
tes febrides ben guarnides dor p de seda. Lo
scut brodat/o pintat de alta p galant inuen=
cio. Uaja cenyt per lo mig ala vsança : p sobre
tot bella cimera/la letra dela qual si sera ben
acertada/en moltes parts escrita la done ē lo
primer arremetre/ales gents que saber la de=
claracio deles inuenciōs naturalment desigē
E axi batent la guarda p son orde faça per lo
rench la acostumada volta. E p ques conega
ser gran caualler dela sella dela guisa / porte
lo cors ert e algun poch pādo lo braç dret no
deixe anar penjāt mas porte la ma posada/ōl
escut sobre la mossa e alguna vegada sobre lo
fals dela correja. Les cames dretes exint del
cors p son endret no lançant les p auāt ni cor
ues p atras mas ertes p molt acostades al vē
tre del cauall. Los peus seguits/punta e ta=
lo p vn egual. Los esperons mirant a hon se
deu batre. Al cap ōl rench no estiga fluix abā
donat. Ne li caygala lança de la ma/dreta la
porte en la bossa acostada en ves lo elm . La
ma alta prop la roda . Lo colze vbert / e al=
traure la lança dela bossa cale la ma prop los
gocets/sia lo metre alt e sens galtada/no do
nant dauall lo rest. Partexca ab tento/no ar

rebatàt/càr dels esperons lo cauall nos deu
molt batre. Corrent ab làça en rest cale poch
a poch p que no faça calades/ni toque ò pla
en lo rench ni de punta de billeta hi encontre.
Portant la lança en lo rest no vaja vberta
mas sobre lo rench mirant al nuscle dret del
altre girant se algun poch al encôtre/no atu
re lo cauall ans del encontre/ni cride dauall
lo elm. mas apres de hauer encôtrat alce la
lança y escorrega la ma fins ala roda/deitàt
per espatles aquella sobre lo rench als serui
dors de peu que la prenguen. E apres passe
jant reposadament al cap del rench se ature.
Les altres subtilitats deitàt a vostres senyo
ries/seran com adiamàts q faran rica la bro
dadura de aqsta mal guarnida roba.

Deo gracias.

℣ Fon àcàbat de empremptar e effigiar lo p
sent tractat En la nobilissima ciutat de Valê
cia.a.xvj.de setembre Any dela salutifera na
tiuitat de nostre senyor deu Jesu christ. Mil.
cccc.lxxxiiij.

Juan Quijada de Reayo
Doctrina del arte de la cavallería
(1548)

Doctrina del arte de la cavallería

Doctrina del arte de la cavallería, ordenado por Juan Quixada de Reayo, vezino de la villa de Olmedo, hombre de armas de la capitanía del muy illustríssimo señor el Duque de Alburquerque, a fin de dar consejo a un hijo suyo, como más viejo en las guardas de los reyes passados, de gloriosa memoria. So correctión de otros cavalleros que lo saben mejor hazer y dezir.

Comiença la obra:

Capítulo primero

En el nombre de Dios y de la sacratíssima Virgen María, sin el ayuda de los quales no puede cosa alguna aver próspero fin.

Hijo, primeramente conviene que si has de usar el ábito militar de la cavallería, tener buen caballo que corra claro.

Y que la silla sea de barras y contrabarras por que vaya más fuerte, una madera sobre otra. Y que la evilla do se ponen las aciones esté en el medio de la barra, y dos dedos más adelante que atrás, y midiéndolo con una cuerda desde una madera a otra y desde las barras abaxo sobre muy poca lana, quando más dos dedos.

Y has de mirar que si el cavallo fuere alto de aguja o baxo, que puesta la silla encima del cavallo esté del assiento de la cavallería un poco más abivada de detrás que no de delante, porque en aquellas cinchuelas sobre que van assentado yendo cavalgando, se pueden clavar más altas de un cabo que de otro para ygualar la cavallería por que cayga bien en la silla, porque si van clavadas muy altas de detrás mucho más que de delante, haze hechar el cuerpo adelante y las piernas atrás y, si va muy abivada de delante haze caer el cuerpo atrás y las piernas. Conviene que sea[n]* casi ygual

* The original text reads: *sea.*

Doctrine of the Art of Chivalry

Doctrine of the Art of Chivalry, composed by Juan Quijada de Reayo, resident of the town of Olmedo, man-at-arms under the command of the most illustrious lord Duke of Alburquerque,[1] in order to give advice to one of his sons, being the oldest in the bodyguard of the former monarchs, of glorious memory.[2] Under the correction of other knights who know better than I what to do and say.

Here begins the work:

Chapter One
[On the Saddle][3]

In[4] the name of God and the holiest Virgin Mary, without whose succour nothing can reach a successful conclusion.

My son, it behoves you[5] firstly, if you wish to join the order of chivalry and be a knight, to have a good horse that can run freely.

And the saddle should be made of bars and crossbars so that it is as strong as can be, with one board on top of the other.[6] And the buckle that holds the stirrup leathers in place should be at the middle of the bar, and two digits in front rather than behind, and measuring the distance with a string from one end of the board to the other and below the bars to just a little above the woollen lining pad, two digits maximum.

And you should check that whether the horse has high or low hindquarters, when the saddle is placed upon the horse, it is set slightly more elevated upon the frame[7] at the back than at the front, because on those tabs[8] upon which they rest when you are riding, they can be set higher at one end than the other in order to level out the frame so that it accommodates the saddle well, for if the tabs are set very high at the back much more so than at the front, it will make the body be thrown forward and the legs backward, and if the frame is set too high at the front it makes the body and the legs lean back. It behoves those tabs to be set almost level so that if possible there is no gap in the

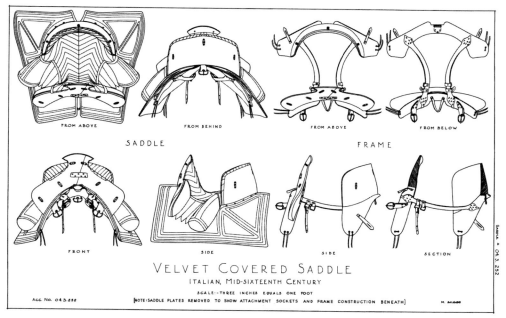

Fig. 178 Construction drawing of saddle shown in fig. 70. Drawn by M. Salgado for the Metropolitan Museum of Art, Arms and Armor Department, *c.* 1940. Ink on paper. 73.66 × 48.26 cm (29 × 19 in)

clavadas aquellas cinchuelas que si ser pudiere no haga oyo en medio, aunque esté cinchado el cavallo, y poco más abivada de detrás que no de delante.

Y conviene que el arzón delantero sea ancho y cruzado, por que vaya más fuerte, una madera sobre otra, que siendo ancho es más provechoso para buen encuentro y guarda más la barriga. Y el arzón trasero, si fuere de conteras, sean algo baxas azia baxo, y cortas – por manera que estorban mucho siendo altas y largas – por que vengan en ygual. Y redondo el torno del fuste de detrás, y algo más baxas las conteras que lo d'en medio, y caýdo un poco hazia dentro antes que atrás. La borrena de delante conviene que esté vazía en el medio de la señal de la silla do se pone la contera de la lança porque [es]* su lugar.

middle, even though the horse may be girthed, and slightly more elevated at the back than at the front.

And it behoves the front arçon to be wide and broad across, so that it is stronger, with one board over another, for being wide it is more beneficial for a good encounter and it protects the belly more. And the rear arçon, if it should be fitted with saddle steels,[9] let them be lower at this end, and narrow – for they are a hindrance if they are high and wide – so that they are level. And the edge of the bow rounded, and the saddle steels somewhat lower than the centre and canted slightly inward rather than outward. It behoves the front bolster[10] to be recessed at the middle of the outer edge of the saddle[11] where the butt[12] of the lance is positioned because it is its place.

* *es*: Omitted in the original text.

Conviene que siempre que cavalgares lleves dos cinchas, y la cincha orcada no ha de tener [...]* porque hazen estorvo al cavalgar y al apear; antes ha de aver en la tajuela de la silla, por debaxo, una ebilla clavada con su correón todo lo más alto que ser pudiere, para que vayan bien cubiertas con la ropa de la silla. Y apretando la cincha orcada lo que fuere menester.

Y la cincha grande por la parte derecha ha de ser hendida, y guarnecida la hendidura con un poco de cuero, y sacar por allí el estribo porque, como arriba he dicho, que ha de yr la ebilla† de las barras de los estribos casi en el medio. Conviene abrir la cincha para que cayga el estribo derechamente. Por la otra parte yzquierda ha de yr el estribo detrás del látigo, y no ha de baxar el hierro de la cincha abaxo. De la ebilla de las barras do se ponen los aciones, suba el otro hierro de la cincha de abaxo para arriba, apretando lo que fuere menester.

Y cavalgando, has de caer tan derechamente en la silla como si estuviesses delante del rey en pie, y con esto ha de ser corta de tajuelas y corta de ropa porque haze más largo de piernas al hombre de armas.

Las sillas mantuanas son mejores y más descansadas para cavalgar y apear.

It behoves you whenever you ride to have two cinches, and the crupper[13] should have no [slack][14] because it is a hindrance when riding and dismounting; instead there should be on the saddletree, underneath, a buckle riveted with its leather strap as high as can be, so that they are well covered by the saddle cloth. And tighten the crupper as should be necessary.

And the breast strap should be slit on the right-hand side, and the slit trimmed with a piece of leather, and pass the stirrup through it for, as I have stated above, the buckle on the bars for the stirrups should be almost in the middle. It behoves you to make the slit in the breast strap wide enough for the stirrup to hang straight down. On the left-hand side the stirrup should hang behind the latigo,[15] and the stirrup iron should not hang any lower than the breast strap. Through the buckle on the bars that fastens the stirrup leathers, thread the other metal-tipped tongue of the breast strap from the bottom to the top, tightening as should be necessary.

And when riding, you should stand as straight in the saddle as if you were standing at attention before the king,[16] and for this reason it should have short saddletrees and a short saddle cloth because it makes the man-at-arms' legs look longer.

Mantuan saddles are better and more comfortable for riding and dismounting.

---

* The plural direct object of the verb *tener* has been inadvertently omitted by the printer.
† *ebilla* is accidentally repeated in the original.

Capítulo segundo
De cómo se h[a]* de enseñar el hombre de armas

Combiene que deprendas las cosas del principio, como el niño que deprende a leer por el A.B.C. Y assí ha de hazer el tal cavallero para que deprenda y salga buen maestro, que si quisiere ser maestro primero que discípulo nunca será buen cavallero del hábito militar de la cavallería. Usándolo y porfiándolo se alcançan las cosas – como dizen: 'Uso haze maestro' – y tomando buen padrino que lo sepa hazer y amostrar.

Es menester ensayarse cada semana dos o tres vezes, y paréceme que el tal hombre de armas cavalgue algo corto que no largo, y cayendo bien en la silla, a la española, y cargando sobre los estribos y apretando los muslos, las piernas tiestas. Y no meneallas, y no meter mucho los estribos, aunque algunos engargantan mucho: cada uno haga como mejor le pareciere. Y si fuere menester herir el cavallo conviene que hieras con ambas piernas ygualmente, de la rodilla abaxo, luego tornar a endereçar las piernas en su ser. Ay cavallos que con hazer un acometimiento se abivan y no han menester herillos para esso. Es el buen conoscimiento del cavallero conoscer lo que ha menester su cavallo.

Conviene que el tal hombre de armas sea primero cavallero de la silla y sepa bien menear un cavallo, correlle y paralle primero que tome la lança en la mano, armado o desarmado. Y luego, desque esto sepas hazer, armado con todas armas, tu vista calada, tome la lança en la mano y póngala en su lugar, y póngase al cabo de la carrera, y segura tu cavallo, y cargando sobre antes un poco baxa que alta y queriendo partir, apercibe tu cavallo y la persona, y levantándote sobre los estribos. Y harás tres partes la carrera. Y saliendo con galope no has de hechar tu lança abaxo ni enrristralla

Chapter Two
On How the Man-at-Arms Should Be Taught

It behoves you to learn things from scratch, like the child who learns how to read by the ABC's.[17] And this is what the knight should do so that he may learn and become a good expert, for if he should wish to be a master before being a pupil he will never be a good knight of the order of chivalry. New things are mastered through practice and perseverance – as they say: 'Practice makes perfect' – and under the tutelage of a good aider[18] who knows what to do and how to explain it.

It is necessary to practise two or three times a week, and in my opinion the man-at-arms should ride somewhat short rather than long, and fitting well in the saddle in the Spanish style, and leaning on the stirrups and pressing in the thighs, the legs taut. And do not swing them, and do not insert the feet too much into the stirrups, even though some do insert their feet as far as the instep: let each rider decide what works best for him. And should it be necessary to goad the horse it behoves you to strike it with both legs at the same time, from the knee down, then straighten out your legs again. Some horses get excited when making an attack and it is not necessary to goad them for this. The knowledgeable knight understands his horse's needs.

It behoves the man-at-arms firstly to be a horseman and to know how to ride a horse well, to race it and bring it to a halt before he ever takes the lance in his hand, either armed or unarmed. And then, after you know how to do this, armed with all your weapons, your visor lowered, take the lance in your hand and put it in its place, and stand at the head of the lists, and hold your horse steady, and preferably leaning the lance a little lower than higher[19] as you are getting ready to set off, prepare your horse and yourself, and stand on the stirrups. And you shall run the course in three parts.[20] And when you are charging at a gallop you should not point the lance downwards or hold

---

* The original text reads: *he*.

de sobaco, y levantando la lança hazia arriba y hechándola en el ristre, requerilla, y baxalla poco a poco, como pesa de relox, y baxándola y emendando el abiesso, no hazer calada ni santiguada. Y atrabessándola, que cayga sobre la oreja izquierda del c[a]vallo.* Passado el encuentro y llegando a la tercia parte de la carrera, sacar la lança del ristre y tornalla a la cuxa.

Y conviene que deprendas de un muy buen hombre de armas y no de muchos, porque como somos de muchas opiniones, cada uno te lo dirá de su manera y podría ser no tomar nada de nenguno. Por esso es mejor tomar lición de un buen hombre de armas y no de muchos.

Y al correr de las lanças has de bolver sobre la mano hizquierda, y a los golpes de espada, sobre la mano derecha.

Capítulo tercero
De cómo se ha de hazer un arnés

La pasta que ha de llevar para que sea perfecto: dos partes de hierro y una de azreo.

Las grevas han de ser largas de abaxo porque parece mejor, y de arriba como conviene, y gruessas, porque como andan más cerca del lodo y del suelo siempre ay más que limpiar. Y no han de ser abiertas por abaxo; antes ha de aver una ventanica por do salga el rodete del espuela (para en la guerra usan medias grebas), con escarpe de malla, y quixote y medio quixote.

Las platas han de ser de pieças y justas a tu persona y ligeras. El faldaje venga justo y no venga arregaçado, y escarcelas de tres o quatro pieças porque son más sueltas, y aforradas en paño. El ristre ha de ser rezio, y haga conoscimiento en torno hazia arriba y antes

it in rest underarm,[21] and raising the lance upwards and placing it in the lance-rest, couch it, and lower it little by little, like the weight of a clock, and as you are lowering it and correcting any mistakes, do not swoop or make the sign of the Cross.[22] And when pointing it diagonally, let it fall over the left ear of the horse. After the encounter and as you reach the third part of the course, remove the lance from the lance-rest and return it to the pouch.

And it behoves you to learn from one very good man-at-arms as opposed to many, for since we have different opinions, each will explain in his own way and you could end up learning nothing from anyone. Therefore it is better to receive instruction from one good man-at-arms instead of many different ones.

And when running with lances you should aim to the left, and when fighting with swords, aim to the right.

Chapter Three
On How a Harness Should Be Made

The compound that must be made in order for it to be perfect: two parts iron and one part steel.[23]

The lower plate of the greaves should be long because this looks better, and the top plate as befits the wearer, and sturdy, for since they are nearer to the mud and the ground there is always more to clean. And they should not be open at the bottom; instead there should be a vertical slit[24] through which the rowel arm of the spur shall project (in battle half-greaves are used), with mail sabatons, and cuisse and demi-cuisse.

The cuirass should consist of separate pieces[25] and be close-fitting and light-weight. Let the fauld fit closely and let it not be too high, and tassets of three or four pieces because they are more loose-fitting, and lined with cloth.[26] The lance-rest should be strong, and make sure that it is bolted on pointing upwards and its arm[27] short rather than long.

---

* The original reads: *cruallo.*

corto que no largo con su coz. Los braçales han de ser de torno y la guarda ha de ser que cubra bien el braço con su juego de pieças. Los guardabraços de buena manera: el derecho con sus barras; y el yzquierdo algo más gruesso.

El almete ha de venir justo a la cabeça y quepa harta estofa, con su* barascudo detrás. Y armado, puedas comer y bever con él. Y en las quixeras en ygual de las orejas, cinco agujericos en cruz, y la estofa por la parte de dentro, en ygual de los cinco agujeros, sacado un bocado tan redondo como la oreja por que puedas bien entender lo que te dixeren. Y la vista sea ancha acá baxo que cubra bien las quixeras del almete, y medio barbote con su alpartaz de malla.

Las manoplas un poco anchas y a tu medida y aforradas por la parte de dentro con un poco de cuero. Las platas con su alpartaz de malla (y en la guerra conviene lleves gocetes de malla porque son provechosos); y testera.

Las pieças dobles de justa son ocho. Han de ser gruessas, las quales son: bolante y escarcelón y guardabar[r]iga;† y la gran pieça; que tenga poco encuentro el baverón; y la vista, que tenga poco encuentro en la calva; la sobreguarda sea grande que cubra bien el braço; y la sobremanopla.

Y abiendo de justar ha de ser clavada la gran pieça con un clavo de cabeça redonda que tiene por debaxo del guardabraço y por çima muy rebatido el clavo por que lança ninguna no pueda cevar en él. Y ha de llevar dos correones, y el uno con una evilla, clavados; y la gran pieça se ha de apretar por las espaldas bien por que del encuentro no te dé bofetón. La sobreguarda ha de yr clavada con un clavo de cabeça redonda, y ha de yr metido por un agujero que ha de aver en la guarda del braçal yzquierdo, y se ha de clavar la sobreguarda encima de la

The vambraces must have threaded holes[28] and the couter should have its pieces arranged in such a way that it protects the arm well. The pauldrons well made: the right one with its bars; and the left one somewhat thicker.

The armet should fit tightly on the head and it should have enough room to be fitted with a full lining, with its rondel at the back. And when you are armed you should be able to eat and drink with the armet on. And on the cheek pieces aligned over the ears, five small holes in the shape of a cross, and the lining on the inside, aligned over the five holes, should have a piece cut out in the shape of the ear so that you can hear clearly what is said to you. And the visor should be wide below so that it fully covers the cheek pieces of the armet, and a half-wrapper with its mail aventail.

The gauntlets somewhat wide and in your correct size and lined on the inside with some leather. The breastplate and backplate with their mail skirt (and in battle it behoves you to wear mail voiders because they are useful); and a shaffron.

There are eight double-pieces for the joust. They should be thick, as follows: plackart and over-tasset and waist lame; and the grand-guard; may the reinforcing bevor seldom be struck; and the visor, may it seldom be struck on the brow; let the pasguard be big so that it protects the arm fully; and the manifer.

And when you joust the grandguard should be bolted in place with a round-headed bolt[29] pushed up from beneath the pauldron and with a very rebated head so that no lance may gain a purchase on it.[30] And it should have two straps, and one with a buckle, riveted in place; and the grandguard should fit tightly around the shoulders so that it does not buffet into you from the encounter.[31] The pasguard should be bolted in place with a round-headed bolt, and it should be pushed through a hole that should be in the couter of the left vambrace, and the pasguard should be bolted over the couter, and

---

* Text: *sus*.
† The text reads as follows: *guardabariga*.

guarda, y bien rebatido el clavo que la lança no pueda cevar en él.

Estos arneses encampronados son muy galanes, mas nengún bien he visto quien ha justado con ellos, porque en mi tiempo he visto muchos muertos por la vista de rencuentro. El primero, el hijo del Conde de Oñate, en la casa de la reyna; Don Luys Osorio, en Tafalla de Navarra; y en Çaragoça, Don Gaspar, hijo del Conde de Sástago; y Gerónimo Dansa. Todos estos e visto morir de rencuentro, y más que no escrivo.

Yo nunca justé encampronado porque siempre me hallé bien con lo castellano. Cada uno puede justar como mejor le parescerá.

Capítulo quarto
Que trata de la justa

Si ovieres de justar, conviene que tengas cavallo que corra claro y salga con galope. Y hazle estar junto al cabo de la tela, y antes que tengas la lança en la mano ha de mirar tu padrino que vaya tiesto el borne o evilla. Conviene que si fuere evilla, que al guarnecer, el hastero le haga assiento en la madera tiesta que encaxe muy justa y que no passe de la meytad y poco más de la evilla. Por que encontrando sea tiesta la evilla, tocará a la madera y no cevará: por tanto, se entiende que de yr guarnecida la evilla o borne muy justo y atestado con un maço que entre por debaxo muy justa, porque si encuentra y cabecea tantico a un cabo o a otro, no romperá.

Conviene que los juezes tengan tal aviso que el hastero las dé por medida que no sea más una que otra, porque si una es un dedo más larga que otra, la que llegare primero romperá,

the bolt very rebated so that the lance cannot gain a purchase on it.

These reinforced[32] harnesses are very gamely, but I have seen nothing good come to those who have jousted in them, for in my time I have seen many men killed by blows through the visor. First, the son of the Count of Oñate, at the Queen's palace; Don Luis Osorio, at Tafalla in Navarre; and in Saragossa, Don Gaspar, son of the Count of Sástago; and Hieronymus Dansa. I have seen all of these men die after being hit, as well as others whose names I shall not mention.

I never jousted with a reinforced harness because I was always comfortable with the Castilian style. Each one should joust in the way that best suits him.

Chapter Four
Which Concerns the Joust

If you should have occasion to joust, it behoves you to have a horse that can run freely and that will gallop. And have it stand next to the end of the tilt, and before you take hold of the lance your aider should check that the mourne or single-pointed head is fitted tightly. In the case of the single-pointed head, it behoves the lance-maker, on accoutring the lance, to place it tightly onto the seat of the stave so that it fits very snugly in place and so that the shaft of the lance-head is no more than half the length of the tip of the lance stave. This way, in the case of an encounter the single-pointed head will remain tightly in place, pressure will be exerted on the stave, and it will not penetrate:[33] thus, it is understood that the single-pointed head or the mourne should be driven tightly and firmly in place with a mallet, for if it strikes and wobbles even slightly from one side to the other, it will not break.

It behoves the judges to assure that the lance-maker provide lances of equal length so that one is not longer than another, for if one is one digit longer than another, the one

y la otra estará en duda. Conviene que los juezes manden a una persona en su assiento que[*] tenga almagre y toque las evillas o bornes por que dondequiera que tocare o encontrare quedará señalado.

Conviene que esté al cabo de la tela con su lança en la mano y su vista calada, y llamando la trompeta, respondiendo, partir con galope, y si vees que tu contrario no sale, buélvete al cabo de la tela, que si partes de tropel, quando no te cates eres al cabo de la tela y haste de tornar de donde partieres. Y si vieres que tu contrario sale, echa tu lança en el ristre, requiriéndola y atravessándola, y hazle el encuentro a la cabeça o a la gran pieça y al arandela, por no herralle.

No has de cerrar los ojos porque si los cierras no encontrarás ni verás por dónde va tu lança; ni tampoco has de mirar la lança de tu contrario, porque si la miras, parecerte ha que te la quiere meter por los ojos. Y has de mirar a tu borne o evilla, y pon[er]la[†] en medio de donde le quisieres encontrar, sea a la cabeça o al arandela, que puedas dezir a tu padrino: '¡Anda! ¡Mira el almagre, que en tal parte le encontré!'

Conviene que el tal justador ha de engocetar la lança, porque si encuentra y no va engocetada, torna atrás hasta engocetar y no ceva el borne ni evilla y pierde el encuentro de no romper.

that strikes first will splinter, and the other may or may not break at all.[34] It behoves the judges sitting on the bench to require that one of them have some red ochre and that he smear this on the single-pointed heads or the mournes so that a mark will be left wherever they attaint or strike.

It behoves the knight to stand at the end of the tilt with his lance in hand and his visor lowered, and at the sound of the trumpet he should respond by galloping forth, and if you see that your opponent does not set off, turn back to the end of the tilt, for if you gallop forth in haste, before you know it you are at the other end of the tilt and you must go back to your own end. And if you see that your opponent is setting off, place your lance in the lance-rest, couching it and pointing it crosswise, and make the encounter to the head or the grand-guard and the vamplate, so as not to miss him.

You should not close your eyes for if you do close them you will neither encounter nor will you see where your lance is going; nor should you focus on your opponent's lance, for if you do, it will look as though he is aiming right for your eyes. And you should focus on your mourne or single-pointed lance-head, and aim for the centre of the point you wish to hit, be it the head or the vamplate, so that you may say to your aider: 'Look there! Look at the red ochre, I struck him in such-and-such a place!'

It behoves the jouster to affix a grapper on the lance[35] because if he encounters and it has no grapper, it will recoil backwards to the point where the grapper is affixed[36] and neither the mourne nor the single-pointed lance-head will gain a purchase and he will lose the encounter for not breaking the lance.

---

* *que* is accidentally repeated in the original.

† The typeface makes it difficult to distinguish between *pónsela* or *ponrela*. Since this paragraph is predicated upon the construction *has de* + *infinitive*, I believe that the text reads *ponrela*, which is a typographical error for *ponerla*; hence I have changed the text accordingly.

Y si rompieres, no sueltes el troço de la mano hasta que te lo tomen.

Por tres cosas no rompen los que justan: la primera, por cerrar los ojos y mirar la lança del contrario; y también por no engocetar que encuentra y torna atrás la lança hasta engocetar y si no ceva el borne ni evilla; la tercera es por no yr bien justo y guarnecido en la madera el borne, y si afloxó en encontrando, cabecea a un cabo o a otro y desbara y no ceva. Por esso, deven de mirar los padrinos que el tal justador que la lança vaya bien guarnecida y el borne tiesto y engocetada y requerida la lança y no cerrar los ojos al tiempo del encuentro y parecerse ha con yr almagrado el borne y el tal justador tenga conoscimiento dónde le encuentra y diga dónde le encuentra.

Maravíllanse mucho algunos cavalleros porque un buen hombre de armas da buen encuentro. También le puede dar como otro que no sea buen hombre de armas, porque no es en mano del buen hombre de armas dexar de dar encuentro feo, que la culpa del encuentro feo tiénela el cavallo o la carrera. Porque corriendo el cavallo tantico que entropieça, haze sentimiento al cavallero, y assí la lança mimbra azia baxo, y lo que es al ristre un dedo es al borne dos palmos. Y assimesmo, corriendo el cavallo, levantando las dos manos pone la una más baxa que la otra, y házele hazer señal a la mano que pone más baxa, y si acierta al tiempo del encuentro, puede dar encuentro feo, porque la mesma señal que el cavallo haze esso haze el cavallero. Si la carrera fuesse tan llana y tan tiesta que no tropeçando el cavallo, el buen hombre de armas no daría encuentro feo.

And if you should break the lance, do not let go of the fragment left in your hand until it is taken from you.

Jousters fail to break their lances for three reasons: the first, because they close their eyes and focus on the opponent's lance; and next because they do not affix a grapper so that it strikes and recoils backwards to the point where the grapper is affixed and neither the mourne nor the single-pointed lance-head gains a purchase; the third is because the lance-head is not tightly mounted and affixed to the stave, and if it came loose upon encountering, it will wobble from side to side and it will slip and will not bite. Therefore, aiders should make sure that the jouster's lance is well fitted and the lance-head taut and the grapper affixed and the lance couched and the eyes not closed at the moment of impact and that he comes to joust with the lance-head smeared with red ochre and that the jouster be cognisant of where he is striking his opponent and that he be able to say where he is striking.

Some knights are truly amazed whenever a good man-at-arms makes a good encounter. It is also possible for such a man to fare as badly as those who are not good men-at-arms, because making a foul encounter is out of the hands of the good man-at-arms, for the blame for the foul encounter rests upon the horse or the lists. For if the horse stumbles slightly while running, the rider feels this, with the result that the lance droops downward, and a movement of one digit at the lance-rest equates to two palms at the lance-head. And likewise, when the horse is running, should it place one front hoof lower than the other, this is transferred to the lance hand so that it is placed lower, and if this happens at the moment of the encounter, it can lead to a foul encounter, for the same movement that the horse makes the rider makes as well.[37] If the lists were so smooth and so firm that the horse never stumbled, the good man-at-arms would not make a foul encounter.

Algunos justadores llevan la lança alta hasta el tiempo del encuentro y báxanla de un golpe y puede blandear hazia baxo y dar encuentro feo. Por esso es mejor, so emienda de otros pareceres, enrristralla presto e requerilla y baxalla poco a poco, como pesa de relox, que baxar y encontrar sea todo a un tiempo. A mí me paresce que es mejor enrristrar temprano porque [si]* acontesce en la carrera un revés con la lança, como perdella [u]† otra cosa, tenéys lugar de remedialla y podréys hazer encuentro, y si enrristráys tarde, no tenéys lugar de remedialla, y si la perdéys porque viene el contrario tan de presto, que no da lugar que la cobréys. Si al hombre de armas acontesce perder la lança y, por ser buen hombre de armas, la cobra y haze encuentro a su contrario, no la daré por perdida aquella tal lança, porque por ser buen hombre de armas la cobró e hyzo encuentro a su contrario.

[Si]‡ acontesce, al parar el cavallo, salirse la lança de la cuxa por descuydo o al enrristrar aver algún revés, no es de maravillar, porque a muchos buenos hombres de armas acontesce. Juzgan los juezes, que no pueden dexar de juzgar sino conforme a las condiciones del cartel. Y mucho aprovecha llevar buenos padrinos el tal justador para dezir a su ahijado lo que le[s]§ paresce y demandar a los juezes el derecho de su ahijado. Y acontesce los padrinos tomar la demanda por los ahijados, por esso conviene que en justa o torneo lleves padrinos que lo sepan hazer y dezir.

Some jousters hold the lance upright until the moment of the encounter and they lower it in one sudden motion[38] and it can drop low and lead to a foul stroke. Thus it is better, in accordance with others who are of the same opinion, to place the lance in the lance-rest right from the start and couch it and lower it little by little, like the weight of a clock, so that you are lowering and striking at the same time. In my opinion it is better to place the lance in the lance-rest sooner because if a setback with the lance occurs during the course, such as losing your grip on it or something else, you will have time to compensate for it and you will be able to make the encounter, and if you place the lance in the lance-rest later, you will not have time to compensate for it, and if you lose your grip on it because the opponent reaches you too quickly, there will be no time for you to recover it. Should the man-at-arms lose his grip on the lance and, by virtue of being a good man-at-arms, he recovers it and strikes his opponent, I shall not consider that a lost lance, because by virtue of being a good man-at-arms he recovered it and struck his opponent.

If, when your horse comes to a halt, the lance should fall out of the pouch by accident, or should there be some mishap when placing the lance in the lance-rest, it is nothing to worry about, for this happens to many a good man-at-arms. The judges are the ones who judge, and they must do so strictly according to the conditions of the cartel.[39] And it benefits the jouster a great deal to take good aiders who can tell their apprentice[40] what they think and who can petition the judges on behalf of their apprentice's rights. And aiders should always argue in favour of their apprentice, thus it behoves you to take aiders to a joust or tourney who know what to do and say.

---

* *si*: Omitted in the original text.
† *u*: Omitted in the original text.
‡ *Si*: Also omitted in the original text.
§ Text: *le*.

Y para que no te haga mal ni estorbo justando en tela o en contratela, tengas [que]* poner en los estrivos unas barras, de manera de puente, clavadas en cada estrivo por la parte de dentro y por manera que puedas bien meter el estrivo con el escarpe, y estas barras que se puedan quitar y poner con sus clavos.

Justando, trabaja de no dar encuentro feo, que es el encuentro encontrar de la cinta abaxo a tu contrario o encontrar en la silla, y encontrar en la tela es mucha fealdad, o encontrar en la testera del cavallo. Ay cavallos que quando corren llevan la cabeça alta hasta el tiempo del encuentro y dan ocasión que los encuentren en la testera, y tocar con la lança en ella ni barrear lança no es bueno porque acontesce romper lanças atravessadas y son mal rompidas porque los juezes las juzgan por malas. Entiéndese lança barreada atravessalla mucho por la otra parte que no encuentra y rómpese mal rompida. Calada es menear la lança de arriba para baxo y de abaxo para arriba en la carrera. Santiguada es menear la lança a man derecha y a man hizquierda. Todo esto es malo y feo. El que pudiere justar sin hazer nenguna fealdad destas será buen cavallero del hábito militar.

And so that no injury or hindrance may befall you on the tilt or counter-tilt during the joust you must place some bars on the stirrups, like a bridge, affixed to the inside of each stirrup and in such a way that you can fit the stirrup easily over the sabaton, and these bars should be fitted so that they can be put on or taken back off with their rivets.

When you joust, try not to make a foul stroke, which includes striking below the belt of your opponent or hitting the saddle, and striking the tilt is a serious foul, or striking the shaffron of the horse.[41] When they run, some horses hold the head high until the moment of the encounter and this causes them to be struck on the shaffron, and attainting it with the lance or barricading the lance is not good because it makes lances split crosswise and they are poorly broken because the judges judge them to be so.[42] Barricading the lance means crossing it too far sideways so that it does not strike and breaks poorly.[43] Swooping means that the lance does nothing but waver up and down when you are charging. Making the sign of the Cross means that the lance wavers from side to side, from right to left. These are all bad fouls. The man who can joust without committing any fouls like these will be a good knight of the order of chivalry.

Capítulo quinto
Que trata de la guerra

Chapter Five
Which Concerns War

Si te hallares en guerra, conviene que lleves unas cabeçadas de visagras bien labradas a la medida del cavallo y asidas en el freno y puestas con unas cintas por debaxo de las cabeçadas, y de cuero, y las riendas de cadena y bien labradas y cortos los eslavones. Y unos estribos, que salga vuestro anillo por donde se metan los aciones, o una media visagra que salga del estribo para que se hagan unos aciones de† visagras bien l[a]

If you find yourself at war, it behoves you to use well-made, hinged head stalls tailored to fit the horse and attached firmly to the bridle and held in place by some leather straps beneath the head stalls, and the reins with chains and well made and with small links. And some stirrups, made so that your ring comes out, through which the stirrup leathers thread, or a small hinge which comes out of the stirrup so that some leathers can be made with well-made and tinned[44] hinges, and they can interlock with that small hinge, and they should

---

* *que*: Omitted in the original.
† *de* is repeated in the original text.

brados* y estañados de paella, y se enclaven en aquella media visagra, y de largor que lleguen encima de la mitad de la ropa de la silla. Y la postrera visagra ha de ser el cabo della de manera de evilla, do se pueda poner un pedaço de ación con su evilla por que se puedan acortar y alargar los estribos. Y llevarás la silla armada, y encubertado tu cavallo con cuello y testera.

Y has de llevar tu lança en la mano y puesta en la cuxa. Y partiendo con galope, heechando tu lança en el ristre, hazle el encuentro a la barriga, y rompida la lança, hecharás mano al estoque, que ha de estar colgado en el arzón delantero a la mano hizquierda, puesto de manera que aunque heches mano no se te salga la vayna tras él. Y peleando con ellos, [los]† golpes a la vista y a las escotaduras, que es la barriga y los sobacos. Deque le ayas perdido o quebrado, echarás mano al espada de armas, la cual llevarás ceñida al lado yzquierdo, y peleando desque la ayas perdido o quebrado, hecharás mano al martillo, que ha de yr asido de la cinta con su presa al lado derecho. Hechando el braço hazia baxo, toparás con él, y alçando para arriba, soltará la presa, y allándote con él en la mano, harás lo que podrás hasta que le pierdas. Y después de perdido, bolverás la mano atrás y tomarás la daga de las espaldas.

Y aferrarás con tu enemigo con todas estas armas que has de pelear, los golpes y el encuentro a las escotaduras, que es la barriga y los sobacos, y a la vista, con el estoque o espada y con el martillo a las manos, porque atormentando la cabeça y las manos luego te será rendido.

hang just over halfway down the length of the saddle cloth. And the other hinge should be at the top of the saddle cloth like a buckle, where you can attach a piece of the stirrup leather with its buckle so that the stirrups can be shortened and lengthened. And you shall use the armoured saddle, and your horse barded with a closed crinet[45] and shaffron.

And you must hold your lance in your hand and placed in the pouch. And setting off at the gallop, placing your lance in the lance-rest, aim for the enemy's belly, and once the lance is broken, you shall take hold of the estoc, which should be strapped onto the left-hand side of the front arçon, secured in place in such a way that when you draw it the scabbard does not come with it. And when fighting with these weapons, strike at the visor and the voids, that is, the belly and the armpits. After you have lost or broken the estoc, you shall take hold of the arming sword, which shall be girded on your left-hand side, and fighting until you have lost or broken it, you shall take hold of the hammer, which shall be attached to the right-hand side of the belt with its hook. Reaching down, you shall find it, and pulling upwards, the hook will release and, with hammer in hand, you shall do what you can with it until you lose it.[46] And after it is lost, you shall reach behind you and draw the dagger from behind your back.

And you shall grapple with your enemy with all these weapons that you have at your disposal, striking and aiming at the voids, that is, the belly and the armpits, and at the visor, with the estoc or sword and with the hammer in hand, for by wounding the head and the hands he will inevitably surrender.[47]

---

* The text reads as follows: *lsbrados*.
† *los*: Omitted in the original text. I emend based on the similar wording in the following paragraph.

Algunos tienen por opinión que es bien matar el cavallo a su contrario. Todo me parece bien en disfavor de tu contrario. Si en tal te vieres, harás como mejor te paresçerá, porque el contrario a pie y tú a cavallo, en gran señorío le tienes.

Some are of the opinion that it is licit to kill your enemy's horse.[48] In my view anything that puts your enemy at a disadvantage is acceptable. If you should ever find yourself in this type of situation, you will do whatever seems best to you, for if the enemy is on foot and you are on horseback, you will be master over him.[49]

Capítulo sexto
Para enfrenar cavallos desbocados

Para un cavallo que tuviere la quixada gruessa y junta una con otra de lo alto, que le hagan un freno a tenazas con dos barvadas, y si por que él no se quisiere regir, que le hagan un freno con dos lanternas, los pilaretes torcidos, y una pieça en el medio con tres molinetes arriba y las camas algo larguillas.

[Para]* un cavallo boquiconejuno, que le hagan un freno de scacha delgada, y si por aquel no se quisiere regir, que le hagan un freno de melones rajados, y los tiros de buena manera.

Para un cavallo que es blando de boca y se va, que le hagan un freno de melones lisos, las camas un poco larguillas, con dos barvadas, y sea corto de anillos.

Para un cavallo que abaxa la cabeça, que le hagan un bocado trabado de coscojos, con sus saliberas para que sabore[e],† y los tiros cortos y derechos que sean metidos adelante.

Para un cavallo que tiene la lengua gruessa, que le hagan un freno de espejuelo para que meta su lengua y para que la bañe, y unos melones lisos, los tiros un poco larguillos, y el bocado no sea ancho.

Para un cavallo que beve el freno, que le hagan los tiros de la parte de arriba del juego algo largo, con una barreta al trabés y llena de coscojos rajados y junto a los anillos de

Chapter Six
How to Bridle Spirited Horses

For a horse that has strong jawbones and that clamps them shut from the top, let them make[50] a pincer-bit with two curb chains, and if it should refuse to be controlled with it, let them make a bit with two lanterns,[51] the pillars twisted in a spiral and a piece in the middle with three molinets overhead and the shanks somewhat long.

For a horse with parrot mouth, let them make a bit with thin scatch-rollers,[52] and if it should refuse to be controlled by that, let them make a bit with grooved melon-rollers, and the pulls[53] of an appropriate disposition.

For a horse that has a sensitive mouth and bolts, let them make a bit with smooth melon-rollers, the shanks somewhat long, with two curb chains, and let it have small rings.

For a horse that lowers its head, let them make a bit with rollers on either side, with its frothers so that it may salivate, and short and straight pulls which should be set forward.

For a horse that has a thick tongue, let them make a bit with a rounded port[54] into which it can insert and dip its tongue, and smooth melon-rollers, the pulls somewhat long, and let the mouthpiece not be wide.

For a horse that swallows the bit, let them make the pulls of the upper part of the rig somewhat long, with a bar in between and outfitted with grooved rollers and set next to

---

* *Para*: Omitted in the original.
† The text reads as follows: *sabore*.

a[r]riba,* y si por dicha quisiere tomar la cama con el beso, que le pongan una cadenica y d'en medio de aquella que salga otra que asga en la barbada.

Para un cavallo que sea natural de boca y se fuere, que le hagan un freno de escachuela delgada y una barbada torcida, y si no quisiere bolver, tanto a una mano como a otra, que le pongan la barbada al revés, con dos molinetes rajados.

Para un cavallo que se empina, que le echen una gamarra.

Para un cavallo que abre la boca, que le echen una mugerola.

Para un cavallo que junta la barba con el pecho y se va, que le hagan una bola algo gruesa y se la pongan junto a la gola. Y ha de tener un agujero algo grande por do se meta un cordón con que se ate arriba a la cabeçada junto al cocote para que cayga bien debaxo de la gula. Y puesta, no le dará lugar que junte la barba con el pecho y podrá ser que no se vaya a otros cavallos. Lo he provado, y les ha aprovechado y no [...]† yrse. Esta bola se puede aforrar en terciopelo y atado arriba el cordón que no se vaya al pescueço, y ha de ser de seda y gruesso.

Y parésceme que es bien tener los cavallos o quartagos con suelta rata porque están más quedos y engordan más estando assí, y un cavallo estando con sueltas en el campo, si se suelta, luego le pueden tomar, porque he visto en mi tiempo, estando en campo, soltarse un cavallo sin sueltas y hazer soltar a otros veynte. Por esso es bien tener en el campo o en la villa con sueltas los cavallos, y adondequiera que estén, porque abren los braços y levantan más estando acostumbrados a tener suelta rata.

the posterior rings, and if it should try to suck on the shank, let them put on a small chain with enough room in the middle of that for another chain to clasp onto the curb chain.

For a horse with a normal mouth and that bolts, let them make a bit with thin scatch-rollers and a twisted curb chain, and if it should refuse to turn, as much to one side as to another, let them place the curb chain on upside down, with two striated molinets.

For a horse that rears up, let them put a tie-down on it.

For a horse that opens its mouth, let them put a muzzle on it.

For a horse that rubs its chin on its chest and that bolts, let them make a fairly thick ball and place it next to the horse's throat. And the ball should have a fairly large hole in it through which a cord can be threaded with which it is tied to the top of the head stall at the nape of the neck so that the ball hangs straight below the throat. And once it is in place, the horse will not be able to rub its chin on its chest and hopefully it will not bolt after other horses. I have tried it and it was good for them and they did not [try to][55] bolt. This ball can be wrapped in velvet and the cord tied on top so that it does not hang down to the neck, and the cord should be made of silk and be thick.[56]

And in my opinion it is a good idea to secure horses or ponies with a firm tether because they stand more still and they fatten better standing like this, and a horse standing in the pasture on tethers, if it breaks loose, can then be caught, for I have seen in my time, out in the pasture, a single untethered horse break loose and cause another twenty to break loose. For this reason it is a good idea to tether horses in the country or in the city, and wherever they may be, because they stretch their legs and they stand taller once they are used to being secured with a firm tether.[57]

---

* The text reads as follows: *ariba.*

† A conjugated auxiliary verb has been inadvertently omitted from this sentence by the printer.

Esto es lo que me ha parescido que se requiere para que el hábito militar de la cavallería se acierte a exercitar. Si yo en ello no he tenido aquel juyzio que en tal obra se requería, suplico a los que este libro vieren que le den perfectión y a ti enseñen, para que por medio de todo esto yo cobre fama y tú ganes honrra, que es lo que un bueno para esta vida ha de procurar.

Fue impressa la presente obra, llamada Doctrina del arte de la cavallería, en la noble villa de Medina del Campo, por Pedro de Castro, impressor de libros, en la calle de Salinas. Acabóse a veynte y dos días del mes de octubre, de este presente año de mil e quinientos y quarenta y ocho años.

This is what I think is required in order to be able to master the profession of knighthood. If I have not demonstrated the kind of intelligence required for a task such as this, I implore those who read this book to improve upon it and to teach you, so that by dint of all this I might acquire fame and you might gain honour, which is what any good knight should strive for in this life.[58]

The present work, entitled *Doctrine of the Art of Chivalry*, was printed in the noble city of Medina del Campo, by Pedro de Castro, master printer, in Salinas Street. It was finished on the twenty-second day of the month of October, in the present year of 1548.

NOTES TO THE TRANSLATION

1 Don Beltrán de la Cueva, Third Duke of Alburquerque (1478?–1559). The Duke had two daughters – Doña Francisca and Doña Leonor – and three sons – Don Gabriel, Don Juan and Don Francisco. This book is most likely dedicated to Don Gabriel.

2 The reference is to Ferdinand V of Aragon (1452–1516) and Isabella of Castile (1451–1504). Known as The Catholic Monarchs, they ruled as King and Queen of Aragon-Castile, 1474–1516 and 1474–1504, respectively.

3 There is no chapter heading in the original, which I believe is a printer's error.

4 *In*: Cp. Spanish *En*, the letter *E* of which contains a small woodcut of two knights sitting together reading a book. This woodcut constitutes a subtle pictorial link, perceived by the printer Pedro de Castro, between Quijada de Reayo's treatise and Ramon Llull's treatise on knighthood, wherein the prospective knight is given a little book to read by an older, experienced knight (in Llull's case a hermit who was once a knight).

5 In the Spanish text Quijada de Reayo repeatedly uses the impersonal expression 'conviene que' as a signature rhetorical strategy. In the English version I translate this expression as 'it behoves you to'.

6 The terminology 'bars and crossbars' (Spanish 'barras y contrabarras') refers to the basic structure of the saddletree, which consists of four wooden parts: two arched bridges (Quijada de Reayo's crossbars) at the pommel and cantle, joined by pegs and glue to two lateral supports known as sideboards (the bars).

7 *the frame*: Cp. Spanish *la caballería*. On this term see Leguina, *Glosario de voces de Armería*, p. 182. The nomenclature refers specifically to iron struts that would strengthen the saddle tree. Extant saddles of the period often show two struts running parallel from the front to the rear arçon, supporting the seat of the saddle. They constitute a type of frame that holds the tree together; hence my translation. See also the construction drawing below.

8 *tabs*: Cp. Spanish *cinchuelas*. Saddles of the period are often equipped on the underside at one or both ends with little leather tabs with button

slits that would not have been strong enough for a cinch or the crupper; rather, they would have helped secure a pad or light-weight attachment for adjusting the height of the saddle. It is apparent from the context that in this paragraph Quijada de Reayo is using the word 'cinchuela' to describe the tabs for securing a wedge-shaped specialty pad used for adjustment of the saddle. The pads are known in modern English as riser pads. The tabs to which Quijada de Reayo is referring are clearly visible at the underside of the rear arçon in the construction drawing below. This saddle is illustrated in Part I, chapter 3, fig. 70.

9 *saddle steels*: Cp. Spanish *conteras*. The noun 'contera' typically refers to the metal chape at the tip of a scabbard or a cane. See Leguina, *Glosario de voces de Armería*, p. 253. I infer from the context that Quijada de Reayo is using this term to describe the saddle steels.

10 The padded bolster at the saddlebow was also sometimes known in sixteenth-century English as the burr, not unlike Spanish 'borrena'.

11 *at the middle of the outer edge of the saddle*: Cp. Spanish *en el medio de la señal de la silla*. Quijada de Reayo is describing the lance cut-out in the right side of the front saddle steel, used to brace the lance when the butt rests in the saddle recess near the underside of the right thigh. The word 'señal' in medieval Spanish was occasionally used to refer to the extremity or outer edge (usually of a territory, but used here with reference to the front saddle steels and the padding at the bow). See Kasten and Nitti, *Diccionario de la prosa castellana del Rey Alfonso X*, vol. III, p. 1642a.

12 *butt*: Cp. Spanish *contera*, used here to refer to the butt of the lance.

13 *the crupper*: Cp. Spanish *la cincha orcada* (modern Spanish *ahorcada*). Literally, 'the noosed cinch'.

14 A plural direct object is missing from this clause in the Spanish original. The most straightforward possibility, given especially what follows, is that a plural noun was being used to indicate that the crupper should have no slack, which would certainly be a hindrance and would require

tightening. Other possibilities: the crupper should have no breeching or narrow radiating straps as are often found on cruppers of the period (though this possibility conflicts with the woodcut on the title page); or – as the author implies by omission in ch. 5 – the leather crupper should not be complemented by an armoured crupper and tail-guard.

15 The latigo is a leather strap to which the front cinch is secured.

16 In order for the rider to be able to stretch out his legs Quijada de Reayo has already recommended in the third paragraph of this chapter that the stirrup leathers be fastened near the bow, two digits in front of the middle of the sidebar of the saddletree.

17 by the ABC's: Cp. Spanish por el A.B.C. The expression could also be an allusion to learning from an abecedario, or primer.

18 aider: Cp. Spanish padrino. The noun 'padrino' in modern Spanish means 'godfather'. English 'aider' is the comparable technical term used in roughly contemporary English accounts of jousts. See, for example, Anglo, The Great Tournament Roll of Westminster, vol. I, p. 50, n. 4, and Clephan, The Medieval Tournament, pp. 114–15. These were experienced knights who served as personal tutors, assistants, advisors and advocates to the aspiring jouster.

19 and preferably holding the lance a little lower than higher: Cp. Spanish y cargando sobre antes un poco baxa que alta. Since the feminine adjectives 'baxa' and 'alta' are used in this clause I infer that the author is talking about holding the lance, which is a feminine noun ('la lanza').

20 you shall run the course in three parts: Cp. Spanish harás tres partes la carrera. On the three parts, or stages, of the course, cp. Menaguerra, chapters 4 and 7.

21 or hold it in rest underarm: Cp. Spanish ni enrristralla de sobaco. The author means that the jouster should always engage the lance in the lance-rest and he should never attempt to use his own arm in lieu of the rest.

22 The meaning of these terms is explained in ch. 4 of the treatise.

23 Anglo, The Martial Arts of Renaissance Europe, p. 216, suggests that this cryptic statement refers to the mixing of the billet prior to forging the sheet of metal from which the armour is made. It is also possible that Quijada de Reayo is referring to a lamination technique for hardening the metal, whereby steel was forge-welded onto iron between two iron laminas. On this technique, see Karlsson, 'Iron and Steel Technology in Hispano-Arabic and Early Castilian Written Sources', p. 242. The complexities of the manufacturing process are described by Pfaffenbichler, Medieval Craftsmen: Armourers, pp. 62–6, and Williams, The Knight and the Blast Furnace, pp. 877–910.

24 vertical slit: Cp. Spanish ventanica. Whereas Quijada de Reayo refers to the slit literally as a 'little window', his contemporary Gonzalo Fernández de Oviedo uses the terms 'slot' ('muesca') and 'aperture' ('abertura'). See Fernández de Oviedo, Las Memorias de Gonzalo Fernández de Oviedo, ed. Avalle-Arce, vol. I, p. 215.

25 That is to say, a breastplate and backplate.

26 The linings prevent chafing and, as Zapata makes clear, they prevent the armour from clanking.

27 arm: Cp. Spanish coz. This is an extremely rare meaning of the noun 'coz' and is not registered in standard dictionaries.

28 The vambraces must have threaded holes: Cp. Spanish Los braçales han de ser de torno. Anglo, The Martial Arts of Renaissance Europe, p. 216, suggests: 'The rerebraces have to be made with turning joints'. However, 1548 was a little too early for turning joints, which in any case were often purposefully omitted from jousting armour since the arm would be immobilised if the turning joint was bent or twisted out of shape by a lance-thrust. It makes more sense to me that Quijada de Reayo is here describing the threaded holes into which the bolts of the exchange pieces would screw. He goes on to describe the exchange pieces and the bolts below.

29 bolt: Cp. Spanish clavo. The word means 'nail' in modern Spanish, but is used variously by Quijada de Reayo to mean 'rivet' or 'bolt', depending on context. As noted by ffoulkes, The Armourer and his Craft, p. 52: 'Up to the sixteenth century the rivet as we know it today is always called an "arming-nail", and it is only in the middle of the sixteenth century that we find the word rivet used as part of the armourer's stock-in-trade'. Quijada de Reayo's terminology is thus appropriate for the time period.

30 Almost identical language is used in the 1446 French *Traité du costume militaire* when describing the rivets on the jousting helm: 'la teste du clou limée affin que le rochet ny prengne' ('the head of the rivet filed flat so that the coronel will not bite on it'. See Reverseau, 'L'Habit de guerre des français en 1446. Le manuscrit anonyme fr. 1997 de la Bibliothèque Nationale', p. 191.

31 The recoil from a particularly powerful blow could cause blunt trauma much more serious than a bruise, such as fractured or sprained bones, and haemorrhages.

32 *reinforced*: Cp. Spanish *encampronado*. This is an aleatory spelling of *encambronado*, which literally means 'reinforced with iron'.

33 That is to say, the lance stave will break because of the pressure exerted on it.

34 On the fundamental Principle of Equality, see Menaguerra, chapters 14, 21 and 27.

35 *to affix a grapper on the lance*: Cp. Spanish *engocetar la lança*. The verb refers to the action of affixing the grapper (Spanish 'gocete') onto the lance so that it will engage with the lance-rest.

36 That is to say, the lance will recoil dangerously into the lance-rest.

37 The jousters of Quijada de Reayo's day would have charged at a canter at around 16–27 km/h (10–17 mph). In this sentence the author is touching upon the horse's ability to canter on the correct lead and the rider's understanding of the complex sequence of the movement of the horse's feet during the canter. Cantering gaits were not understood entirely until it was possible to film horses in motion, so Quijada de Reayo is attempting to explain as best he can what feels right to him, based on years of experience.

38 Cp. Zapata: 'There are those who lower the lance in one sudden motion, which is called fishing; I do not approve of this, because the encounter goes awry a thousand times over and the opponent and the tilt get struck with lance staves, and the tilt and the horse get hit, and other foul and very unfortunate strokes are made'.

39 Menaguerra, ch. 4, is equally forgiving.

40 *apprentice*: Cp. Spanish *ahijado*. Literally, 'godson'. The relationship between aider(s) and apprentice was obviously a close one, given the terminology.

41 Cp. Menaguerra, ch. 30: 'Prohibited strokes in jousting festivals include striking the tasset, the arçon of the saddle, the bridle hand, the head or the neck of the horse, the thigh of the rider or from here on down'.

42 An example of a horse raising its head can be seen *Passo Honroso* Selection 33, Course 3.

43 The barricaded lance 'breaks poorly' because it does not strike with the point.

44 *tinned*: Cp. Spanish *estañados de paella*. The meaning of *paella* is unclear. The word is often used to describe the special tin-plated pan in which paella is made, so it is possible that the author is using it here as a synecdoche to describe the process of plating anything with tin. Tinning of horse tack was certainly quite common at this time. The procedure was of much benefit on blood-spattered, muddy battlefields, since the tin helped prevent oxidisation. Stirrups were also susceptible to oxidisation from horse sweat. Another remote possibility is that Quijada de Reayo is referring to hinges with some sort of patina (the word 'patina' is a derivative of Latin *patella*), though I err more towards the synecdoche in this case.

45 *closed crinet*: Cp. Spanish *cuello*. Literally, 'neck'. The nomenclature suggests a crinet that covers all of the horse's neck and not just the top, which certainly makes sense in battle.

46 Martial arts expert Pietro Monte recommends carrying two hammers in battle. See Monte, *Exercitiorum Atque Artis Militaris Collectanea*, bk II, ch. 72, sig. e1r.

47 On the loss of weapons and horses in battle, see *Las Siete Partidas*, II.xxvii.5: 'Pérdidas hacen los hombres en guerras porque merecen haber galardón con lo que cobran; e como quiera que esto sea como en manera de galardón por pérdida, todavía entiéndese que debe ser mejor que lo que perdió porque la pérdida fue en guerra, pues de otra guisa no sería galardonado. E esto aviene cuando a alguno muere el caballo, o otra bestia, andando en guerra en servicio de su señor, no muriendo ni se lo matando en hecho de armas mas por enfermedad o por otra ocasión que aviniese; pues tal como éste, según fuero antiguo de España, débenselo pechar

tan bueno o mejor. Mas si se lo matasen en hecho de armas, ayudando a honrar su señor o vencer a sus enemigos, débele pechar, aquél cuyo vasallo fuere, otro que valga tanto e medio, o haber para comprarlo. E si lo perdiese amparando a su señor débele dar otro por él que valga dos tanto. E eso mismo sería de las armas de su cuerpo que en tales hechos como estos perdiese.' ('Men suffer losses in war on account of which they deserve to be rewarded, in addition to the booty which they secure. Although this may resemble a recompense for loss sustained, yet it is understood that it should be greater than what was lost because it was sustained in war; for if made in any other way, he would not be entitled to compensation; and this happens when anyone's horse or other animal dies while he is engaged in the military service of his lord, where it is not killed in battle, but perishes through sickness, or through some other accident; for, in a case of this kind, according to the ancient fueros of Spain, the owner should be provided with as good a one, or a better. But where the animal is killed in action, while the owner is fighting for the honor of his lord, he should provide his vassal with one which is worth one and a half times as much, or give him the money with which to purchase it. If he loses his horse while defending his lord, the latter should give him another in place of it, which is worth twice as much. This same rule applies to arms lost under similar circumstances.') *Las Siete Partidas*, ed. Sánchez-Arcilla, pp. 346–7. For the translation, see *Las Siete Partidas*, trans Scott and Burns, vol. II, p. 501.

48 Monte concurs with this opinion. See Monte, *Exercitiorum Atque Artis Militaris Collectanea*, bk II, ch. 74, sig. e1rv.

49 For a notable exception to this general rule, see the following account by the English footsoldier Richard Pyke, who was ambushed and charged by 'a Spanish Horseman' during an expedition to Cádiz in the early 1600s: 'As therefore his horse was violently breaking in upon me, I struck him into the eyes with the flap of my cloak, upon which, turning sideward, I took my advantage, and as readily as I could, stepping in, it pleased God that I should pluck my enemy down, and have him at my mercy for life, which notwithstanding I gave him'. See Pyke, *Three to One*, sig. B4r.

50 The author in this chapter repeatedly uses the expressions 'que le hagan' and 'que le echen', quirky turns of phrase that mark him as an aristocratic amateur of the pen. I translate as 'let them make' and 'let them put on', respectively. The idea is that Quijada de Reayo is advising his pupil to order the saddlers or harness-makers to forge or put on the items in question.

51 *two lanterns*: Cp. Spanish *dos lanternas* (modern Spanish *linternas*). I have not been able to locate any other contemporary references to this term and can therefore only speculate as to the meaning. In the case of this bit, the two curb chains would put pressure on the flesh under the horse's mouth and – if one imagines the construction of a sixteenth-century lantern – elongated, arched mouthpieces would put pressure on the tongue.

52 Horses with parrot mouth have thin or low palates in which case the conical scatch-rollers would be appropriate, for they would exert pressure on the corners of the mouth.

53 *the pulls*: Cp. Spanish *los tiros*. The curb bits of the time would have two sets of reins attached to the posterior and anterior terminals of the shanks, known respectively as the rein and the curb rein. Occasionally the anterior terminal would consist of pendants to which the curb rein would attach. Quijada de Reayo is referring to these important parts of the curb bit by their function in relation to the reins.

54 *rounded port*: Cp. Spanish *espejuelo*. This is a type of wide, circular port designed to accommodate horses with particularly thick tongues.

55 A conjugated verb is missing from this clause. From the context it seems clear that the author is saying that the horses did not try or wish to bolt.

56 Quijada de Reayo is describing a practice associated with the jennet style, or what he calls 'the Spanish style' (above, ch. 2), deemed by him to be the most appropriate for training purposes. Stylised versions of this type of ball hanging from the neck can be seen on the horses illustrated in Part I, chapter 7, figs. 169–73. The ball was known as the Turkish beard ('barba turca'). See Soler del Campo, 'Arreos y jaeces para caballería en al-Andalus', pp. 94–5.

57 Although it is true, as Quijada de Reayo ascertains, that a tether or tie-down can be used to teach a horse to stand, a certain degree of expertise is required since improper tethering can be harmful to the animal.

58 The desire for fame and honour in word (written or spoken) and deed was an integral part of the chivalric ethos. To cite but one eloquent example, cp. Martorell, *Tirant lo Blanch*, ch. 318, p. 1154: '¿E qui és aquell miserable cavaller qui per dubte de mort se dexa de fer lo que la humana natura ha ordenat, morint virtuosament, car és reviure per aquest miserable de món en fama gloriosa?' ('What miserable knight, out of fear of death, would keep from doing that which human nature has ordained – dying bravely – by which means he can obtain the eternal life of glorious fame?') For the translation, see *Tirant lo Blanc*, trans. La Fontaine, p. 611.

Luis Zapata de Chaves

Del Justador

(1589–93)

Del Justador

De las fiestas hordinarias que se hazen la justa
es la más galana y más hermosa y más vizarra,
y con razón, pues la más hermosa cosa del
mundo dijo El Oráculo que era un cavallero
a cavallo armado. Por lo que Curctio se echó
en aquel boquerón que en Roma se avía avierto
en la Plaza por donde toda se yba asolando; y
con aquel tapador se tapó al abertura grande la
voca y se le abrió perpetuamente a la fama. Y
aun por el desseo della su misma madre le tapó
con su manto los ojos al cavallo, que rrehusava,
harto más rracional en ello que no entrambos.

Pues si uno parece así, ¿quánto mejor
parecerán a una tela muchos cavalleros armados,
las armas luzientes y doradas, los paramentos
enbutidos y rrecamados, la variedad de las
colores, penachos y plumas altas, y borlas de
varias colores colgadas, las divisas diversas, las
trompetas, menistriles y atabales, los padrinos,
los lacayos llenos de colores, con sus bastones
pintados en las manos, los paxes con sus libreas
y caballos encubertados? Vien la llaman real,
porque es fiesta de reyes, y si no es en las cortes
y por señores y cavalleros que todo lo tienen,
y hallan guisado es gran cansera esta en una
ciudad, que de otros se traen los cavallos, de
otros las armas, a uno le prestan la silla, a otros
los aderezos, y si a cada uno le quitassen los
empréstidos quedarían sin plumas, como el
páxaro falsario que hurtava las plumas a las
aves, y desque cayeron en la qüenta, quedó de
todos pelado. Como tanvién estos que se meten
en exercicio ageno son pelados, aunq'esto
en los presidios y en las guarniciones donde
ay gente de armas vien se haze, aunque se
comvienen mal las armas con las calzas de
paño y con los mozos de los que van a justar
rotos y desharrapados. En fin, ella es fiesta
real, como es tan yllustre y claro el exercicio de
las armas. Porque los toros y juegos de cañas,
aunque son de mucho contento y rregocijo,

On the Jouster[1]

Of the currently popular festivals that people
organise the joust is the most elegant and
most impressive and most splendid,[2] and
with reason, for the Oracle said that the
most impressive thing in the world was an
armoured knight on horseback.[3] Which is why
Curtius threw himself into that chasm which
had opened in the Forum in Rome causing
the whole place to fall apart; and with that
blockage the mouth of the great abyss was
blocked and he was opened up to everlasting
fame. And still out of the desire for fame his
own mother blocked the eyes of the horse with
her cloak, for it was refusing,[4] so much[5] more
rational was it about the situation than either
of them.[6]

Thus if one knight looks like this, how much
better must many armoured knights look at a
tilt,[7] the armour shining and gilded, the trappings inlayed and embroidered, the variety of
colours, panaches and tall plumes,[8] and orles
hung with varied colours,[9] the sundry devices,
the trumpeters, minstrels and kettledrummers, the aiders, the footmen awash with
colours, holding their painted staffs in their
hands, the pages in their livery and caparisoned
horses? They call it royal for good reason, for it
is a festival of kings, and unless it takes place at
court and for the benefit of lords and knights
who own all their own things, they do find[10]
that staging this in a city is a lot of bother, for
the horses are obtained from other people, the
armour from others, one man is loaned the
saddle, others the equipment, and if the items
on loan were taken away from each of them
they would be stripped of their plumage, like
the counterfeit bird that pilfered the feathers
from the birds, and when they found out, it was
stripped bare by all of them.[11] Likewise those
who get involved in other people's business are
stripped bare, if indeed this actually happens
in the fortresses and garrisons where there are
men-at-arms, for armour badly befits cloth
breeches and the type of lads who go to joust
ragged and tatty.[12] In short, it is a royal festival,

al fin, ver toros por esos campos es cosa muy común a todos, y tanvién ber xinetes correr la carrera y escaramuçar. Aunque son bonísima fiesta los regozijos, que no se les quita su valor porque aya otra cosa más, y sean las justas y fiestas más raras y reales.

El justador a de tener lo primero buen cavallo, aunque parezca esto al juego de los muchachos; y el cavallo a de ser grande, ancho y fuerte, espesso, que por muchos enqüentros no se resavian ni cansan. De la color no me enpacho, porque cubiertos de sedas e de brocados no se echa de ver la color de un cavallo como paseando. Mas aunque sea para ruar, la color es lo menos que hace al caso, aunque dicen que en un año se parecen el cavallo y su amo, y por eso sería vien y por el contento que fuese de buena color el cavallo, más que para justar. En el pisar muy sobervio y muy gallardo, que a la entrada parezca que no cave en toda la plaza. Que entre como señor del campo, aviertas las narizes y bufando. Que después se arrime muy vien a la tela, y qu'esté a ella muy quieto y muy sosegado. Que parta muy seguro y no de tranco, y que corra con gran furia y muy menudo sobre los pies, y tan llano que se pudiese llevar, a manera de dezir, una taza llena de agua en la mano. Que pare vien y no sobre los brazos.

Son muy fuertes y muy hermosos rruzios rodados y tordillos, castaños escuros, vayos y alazanos tostados, aunq'estos suelen ser de malas bocas y a muchas carreras se les calientan y no paran. El caballo no a de pensar parar ni a de ser menester que le vayan perneando, qu'es gran fealdad ir haldeando en un hombre de armas como milano a la dormida, como yr coleando el cavallo, sino que, al partir, le toquen una vez las espuelas, y otra en medio de

since the exercise of arms is so illustrious and noble. For bull-runs and cane games, whilst they are very pleasing and merry, in the end, seeing bulls in fields is a very common thing for everyone, as is seeing[13] jennets run the course and skirmish. Whilst these festivities are wonderful entertainment, it should not detract from their value that there be something even better, and that jousts and festivals be rarer and more royal.

The first thing a jouster needs is a good horse, even though this may seem like child's play; and the horse must be big, broad and strong, steadfast, so that after many encounters they get neither intemperate nor worn out. I shall not dwell on colour, for when they are covered in silks and brocades a horse's colour is not revealed as much as when it is out walking.[14] But even when parading on city streets,[15] the colour is of the least importance, although they say that within a year the horse and its master look alike, and so it would be beneficial and felicitous for the horse to be of a good colour, beyond the case of jousts. It should tread very proudly and very gracefully, so that when it makes its entrance it seems as though the whole enclosure will not be big enough to hold it. It should enter as if it were master of the field, the nostrils flared and snorting. It should then stand very close to the tilt, and let it stand there very still and very steady. It should set off very confidently yet smoothly, and it should run at full speed and very nimbly on its feet,[16] and so steady that you could hold, in a manner of speaking, a level cup of water in your hand. It should stop well and not on the forelegs.

Silver greys and dappled greys, dark chestnuts, bays and dark brown sorrels are very strong and very handsome, although the latter often have bad mouths and in many courses they overheat and will not stop. The horse should not be the one who thinks of stopping nor should it be necessary for it to be prodded on, for it is ugly in the extreme for a man-at-arms to look like he is flying by in a skirt[17] like a dozy kite,[18] or for his horse to be stumbling,

la carrera, como quien le acuerda el correr, y al parar otra, si quieren que pare rredoblando.

Los pies a de llevar el cavallero yguales, como cuando un hombre anda, y un poco las puntas afuera, porque si las llevase, como dezían los del tiempo viejo, las puntas adentro, mal se podría picar y dar de las espuelas al cavallo.

Las armas an de ser nuevas, porque tanvién como todas las cossas se embexecen, como una capa y un sayo. Las armas doradas y justas a la persona, y ellas entre sí que unas y otras ajusten, y donde una con otra junta, por que no suenen ni chapeen, con cuero delgado del enbés estofadas. Porque es gran deslustre a un justador yrle las armas como calderas sonando, o como un armado de monumento.

La celada no muy picuda, que parece gallo, y ni muy fea, ni muy roma, que paresce mochuelo, sino de hermosa proporción y talle, estofada por de dentro por que no suenen los enqüentros, y bridada la cabeza, qu'es con un doblez de la misma estofa de tafetán u de rasso, que tome un poco de la frente, con dos cintas, apretada la caveza hacia el colodrillo de la celada por que con el baivén del enqüentro no llegue a la celada la cara. La vista segura y pequeña y pegada a los ojos por que juntos a ella se vea todo quanto ay. Y para el peligro guárdeos Dios que no entre raxa, que si entra, no haze al caso para matar que entre un dedo menos u más.

El peto un poco salido afuera en justa proporción para que pueda el justador alentar. La targeta pequeña y de buen talle, que hace a los hombres galanes. Los braçales no anchos. La coraza y el talle más alto que los huesos de los quadriles, y que no le toquen las armas, que matarían en los lados. De brazales y grevas,

but rather, on setting out, spurs should be put to it one time, and once again in the middle of the course, as if to remind it to run, and once again on stopping, if one wants it to stop in double-quick time.

The knight should hang his feet evenly, as when a man walks, and the tips pointed slightly outwards, because if he were to point them inwards, as those in olden days used to recommend, he would scarcely be able to prick and put spurs to the horse.

Armour should be new, because it gets old just like everything else, such as a cape and a tunic. The armour gilded and tight fitting, and arranged in such a way that one piece fits with the next, and at the point where one joins with another, so that they do not clatter or catch on each other, padded on the reverse side with thin pieces of leather.[19] For it tarnishes a jouster's image if his armour clangs like kettles each time he moves, or if it makes him stand as stiff as a statue.

The close-helmet not too pointed, for this looks like a rooster, nor too unsightly, nor too blunt, for this looks like an owl, but handsomely proportioned and sized, padded on the inside so that the blows do not resound, and the head bridled, which is by means of a fold of the same taffeta or silk padding, so that it secures part of the brow, with two strips, the head tightened towards the back of the helmet so that in the erratic movements of the encounter the face does not strike the helmet. The visor secure and small and fitted close to the eyes so that everything there is can be seen when looking through it. And may God protect you from the danger of a splinter entering, for if it does, it goes without saying that in order to be fatal it only needs to enter one digit less or one more.

The breastplate protruding out slightly just the right amount so that the jouster can breathe. The targetta[20] small and well shaped, which makes men look elegant. The vambraces not wide.[21] The cuirass and the waist-line resting on the pelvic bones, and may it never be struck by weapons, for blows to the sides would

chicas las rodajas. Los escarpes no puntiagudos ni anchos como zapatos de alemanes, sino romos como una bota. Y nadie juste sin arnés de piernas, porque pareze caçador y no justador el caballero que no va todo armado, y es bueno y conviniente para no topar con los pies en la tela y contratela y quebrárselos y para entrar seguro entre las coces de otros cavallos. En la pierna derecha no quixote entero, sino medio, para asentar bien la lança. La arandela no muy cub[a],* ni muy plana, ni muy chica, sino en medio, donde la virtud está.

El ristre, en que consiste la mayor parte de el vien justar: si muy baxo hácense mill calados con la lanza, dánse mill enqüentros feos; si muy alto no se puede enrristrar vien ni, para encontrar, vaxar bien la lanza; sino el medio antes dicho, y antes un poco alto el rristre que vaxo, y no muy adelante en el peto ni muy atrás.

Los vestidos y paramentos galanes, rricos y vizarros. Las divisas hermossas, discretas, nuevas, y a las personas y casos acomodadas. Los sayetes, si largo el cavallero, largos, si pequeño, cortos, si mediano, en proporción razonable.

La silla, si es largo de piernas el cavallero, larga de ropa por que no parezca çanquibano; si es corto, corta de rropa por que el cavallero parezca más grande en ygual proporción, y al justo de la corva, remediando la falta. Como dicen: 'Que donde falta natura obre pintura', como quando un navío se acuesta a un lado es el seso acostarse los nabegantes a la parte contraria, y por eso es buen carguío el de los cavallos, porque es esto lo que hacen de buen asiento. La silla no ancha, porque yría el cavallero espernancado; no echada detrás, porque yrá echado atrás – muy feo y mal puesto y aparejado, para derrivarle –, sino que cayga en ella el hombre derecho, como en sus

prove fatal. On vambraces and greaves, small wings.[22] The sabatons neither sharp-pointed nor wide like German shoes, but rounded like a boot. And let no-one joust without legharness, for the knight who is not fully armoured looks like a hunter rather than a jouster, and legharness is fitting and proper so as not to hit the tilt or counter-tilt with your feet and break them and so as to enter safely amidst the kicks of other horses.[23] On your right leg not an entire cuisse, but a demi-cuisse, in order to brace the lance well. The vamplate not too capacious, nor too flat, nor too small, but in moderation, where virtue is.

The lance-rest, which is the key to jousting well: if too low, a thousand flourishes with the lance will be made, a thousand foul strokes will be dealt; if too high[24] it will be impossible to couch the lance properly or, in order to encounter, to lower the lance properly; but in moderation as stated above, and the lance-rest preferably slightly higher than lower, and neither too far towards the front of the breast-plate nor too far towards the back.

Clothes and horse trappings elegant, fine-quality and splendid. Heraldic devices impressive, tasteful, original, and well suited to people and occasions. Surcoats, if the knight is big, long, if he is small, short, if of medium height, of an appropriate length.

The saddle, if the knight has long legs, on a long saddle cloth so that he does not look lanky; if he is short, on a short saddle cloth so that the knight looks bigger in even proportion, and aligned parallel to the back of each knee,[25] making up for the shortcoming. As they say: 'Where Nature should fail, let Art prevail', as when a ship lists to one side reason dictates that the sailors station themselves on the opposite side, and that is why horses make good cargo, since this is what they do willingly.[26] The saddle not wide, because the knight would ride doing the splits; not placed too far back, for he will be slung backwards – very ugly and badly positioned and harnessed, with the result that he will be thrown –, but

* MS: *cubo.*

propios pies. Anda con un poco de asiento para el descanso, y no tan sobre el arçón delantero, qu'el hombre como maleta se vaya adelante. En fin, la postura del cavallero consiste en la silla; en mala silla no puede yr vien puesto por ningún caso.

Las lanzas an de ser cortas, gruesas, tiestas y livianas, que ser muy rezias y fuertes no sirven de nada – deslómanse los cavallos, desconciértanse los cavalleros y quiébranse las manos. Y tener mucha madera es (como aquellos bestiales yndios de Arauco) más que de cavalleros y reyes, de ganapanes, que diferente es el entendimiento y virtud para gobernar que de ser uno para príncipe, que como azémila bueno de carga, diciéndose el peso que un rrey tiene a cuestas por metáphora. La lança de pino, porque de fresno u de haya para justar (que al fin es burla) entre amigos sería la burla muy pesada; y para enemigos desotras.

La tela a de ser de ciento y cincuenta pasos, vien larga, que el buen hombre de armas hará mill lindezas con la lanza y el malo mill fealdades.

Agora el cómo se a de justar, dígalo quien lo save. Citara yo aquí a grandes maestros deste arte, mas mi *Carlo Famoso* los dice vien a la larga. Mas sólo diré lo que e oýdo y visto a grandes cavalleros en esto muy áviles, como el moço del çurujano que cura a falta de quien lo haga, aunque yo en esto (quiérolo dezir) he sido de los más exercitados y venturosos de España.

El justador a d'estar y pasear por la tela puesto sobre los estribos y no sentado en la silla ni encoxidas las piernas como gallina asada, sino derecho y estacado, y la medida de los estrivos

rather, the rider should sit straight in the saddle, as if he were standing on his feet. He shall walk with some room in the seat to rest, and without leaning on the front arçon, otherwise the rider will proceed looking like a travelling bag. In sum, the posture of the knight depends on the saddle; in a poorly fitted saddle there is no way that he will ever sit well.

Lances should be short, sturdy, rigid, and light, as there is no point in their being thick and weighty – horses get exhausted, riders get flustered, and hands get broken. And carrying loads of wood (like those bestial Araucanian Indians)[27] is more the stuff of odd-job men[28] than of knights and kings,[29] for a different kind of intellect and virtue is required to govern than that which is required to be a prince, or than that required to be a good pack mule, the latter being a metaphor for the load that a king must bear. The lance made of pine, because using lances made of ash or beech for jousting (which when all is said and done is a game) among friends would be a cruel game indeed; and lances made of those woods are for enemies.[30]

The tilt should be 150 paces,[31] quite long, where the good man-at-arms will make a thousand elegant strokes with the lance and the bad one a thousand foul strokes.

Now as for how to joust, allow one who knows to explain how. At this point I could have cited great masters of this art, but my *Carlo Famoso* mentions them at great length.[32] But I shall only say what I have heard and seen of great knights who are very skilled jousters, like the surgeon's apprentice who performs the operation only because the doctor himself is absent,[33] although I myself (I do feel compelled to point out) have been one of the most consummate and successful jousters in Spain.[34]

The jouster should stand and walk towards the tilt standing on the stirrups and not sitting on the saddle or contracting his legs like a roasted chicken,[35] but upright and erect, and the length of the stirrups should be such that

a de ser que quepa entre el asiento del cavallero y la silla una mano, porque si va larga va feo y floxo y desgraciado. Pues, partiendo sobre los estrivos, después que be qu'el contrario se anda para partir, meneando de* las espuelas a su cavallo, y salga muy ynhiesto, la lanza en cuja, cargado el cuerpo un poco sobre la lanza – y con mucha disimulación –, con tanta fuerça sobre ella que como yo del mucho uso tenía en el muslo saltada la sangre del cuento de la lanza. Y llevando la lanza un poco en cuxa, en asentando el curso el cavallo, sáquela, retorciéndola alta, y póngala, con un repulgo y más arriba torciendo la mano con buen ayre, en el ristre, y con otro la rrequiera, y poco a poco sesga la vara, vaxando sin calada. Y para no hacer caladas, aprovecha, como e dicho, el ristre un poco alto, que no se abraza el brazo con la lanza. Y aprovecha tanvién para que con facilidad, sin hacer desdén, barreando, le salga la lanza de la mano, aunque el barrear se deve de escussar, porqu'es de las cosas feas que en el caso pasan. Pues, baxando poco a poco, a de acavar de baxar al punto que llega al enqüentro al contrario.

Otros hay que baxan de golpe, que llaman pescar; esto no lo apruevo, porque mill vezes se hierra el enqüentro y se da en el contrario y en la tela palos, y se enqüentra la tela y el cavallo, y se hazen otros enqüentros feos muy desgraciados. Lo que parece muy vien es bolverse un poco el cuerpo al encuentro, que se dan mayores enqüentros y da buena gracia, que cualquiera cossa que menee un hombre armado parece vien, que parece que está vibo aquel cuerpo fantástigo y que no es todo hierro. Esto hazía galanamente el señalado cavallero Don Diego de Córdova, que se sacudía muy graciosamente con las armas, con la loçanía

* MS: de de.

there is a palm's breadth[36] between the knight's seat and the saddle, for if the stirrups are too long he will look ugly and weak and graceless. So, setting out on the stirrups, after seeing that the opponent is preparing to set off, putting spurs to his horse, let him sally forth standing perfectly straight, the lance in the pouch, leaning the body slightly over the lance – and without revealing any emotion –, with as much force as possible on it that, like I used to have through long experience, the butt makes a permanent bruise on the thigh. And carrying the lance for a while in the pouch, as the horse gets ready to run the course, lift it out, raising it high with a twist of the hand, and place it, with a lunge[37] and twisting your hand higher with proper gracefulness,[38] into the lance-rest, and with another lunge couch it, and little by little the lance will incline,[39] lowering without swooping.[40] And in order to avoid swooping, it is worthwhile, as I have stated, to set the lance-rest slightly high, for your arm should not be clutching the lance. And this is also worthwhile so that you can let go of the lance with ease, without hesitating,[41] if you barricade it,[42] although barricading must be excused, for it is the kind of foul stroke that happens when jousting. So then, lowering little by little, it should be fully lowered the moment you make the encounter with the opponent.

There are those who lower the lance in one sudden motion, which is called fishing; I do not approve of this, because the encounter goes awry a thousand times over and the opponent and the tilt get struck with lance staves, and the tilt and the horse get hit, and other foul and very unfortunate strokes are made.[43] What looks really good is to turn the body slightly at the moment of impact, for better strokes are made this way and it looks graceful, for anything that stirs movement[44] in an armoured man looks good, since it makes that fantastic[45] figure seem like he is alive and not just a piece of iron.[46] The distinguished knight[47] Don Diego de Córdoba[48] used to do this elegantly, for he used to acquit himself very gracefully with weapons, with

que se sacude un halcón en el ayre. Mas de postura en la silla ninguno de los hombres a el Rey Don Phelipe, mi amo, hiço ventaja. No quebrava muchas lanzas, porqu'esto es más que zerteza, caso.

Pasado el enqüentro a de tornar a la cuxa el cavo de lanza, y luego echarle y sin daño de los circunstantes. Luego correr otra y otra sin parar, de manera que tan presto corra como buelva, mas esto a de ser quebrando la lança, porque si fuese una y otra sin quebrarla, antes sería cosa de* rissa y embaraçar la tela sin hacer nada, y le podrían desçir: 'Justar mal y porfiar'.

Si se desalentare el justador por correr muchas carreras con el savor de justar, ase de apartar a una parte con hachaque de que le alargue u acorte el estrivo un lacayo u que el padrino u el armero le apriete la llave, como que lleva desguarnecido algo, como hacen los músicos que, quando están cansados u no se les acuerda qué dezir, encomienzan a templar. Lo que no hize yo en una justa partida, una bez, en la folla del Parque de Bruselas en Flandes, que me aparté a una parte de aver corrido muchas carreras, tan desalentado qu'estando echado sobre el arzón de mi cavallo me llegó Don Francisco de Mendoza, hijo del marqués de Mondéxar, con mandado del Emperador nuestro señor que justase, que se perdía mi parte, que yva de ganancia; lo que yo no pude obedezer en gran rato. Como dicen que no le obedezió una vez un cavallero justando, que pensando que lo hacía de cortés el no encontrar a su Magestad, le envió muy de beras a mandar que le encontrase, y el cavallero le rrespondió que ni savía ni podía encontrarle y que jurava a Dios que no deseava por entonces otra cossa más.

* MS: *de de.*

the self-assurance with which a falcon acquits itself in the sky.[49] But where posture in the saddle is concerned no man ever outclassed my master,[50] King Philip. He never used to break many lances, for this is not just the truth, it is a known fact.[51]

After the encounter he should return the lance stub to the pouch, and subsequently discard it and without injuring any spectators. He should then run one course after another without stopping, so that he sets off on a new course as soon as he returns from another, but this should only be after breaking the lance,[52] because if he were to run one course after another without breaking it,[53] this would on the contrary be the stuff[54] of laughter and clogging up the lists without doing anything, and they could say of him: 'A jouster wrapped up in himself makes a very small parcel'.[55]

If the jouster should get out of breath because of running many courses whilst savouring in the joust, he should stand to one side under the pretext that a footman must lengthen or shorten the stirrup or that the aider or the armourer must tighten a joint, as if something has come undone, like musicians who, when they are tired or cannot remember the tune, pretend to tune up. Which is what I did not do once on a jousting team in the mêlée at The Brussels Park in Flanders, for I moved to one side after having run many courses, so out of breath that as I was leaning over the arçon on my horse Don Francisco de Mendoza, son of the Marquis of Mondéjar,[56] came over with an order from our lord the Emperor[57] that I joust, for my side, which had been winning, was beginning to lose; and I was physically unable to obey for some time. Similarly they say that there was once a knight who refused to obey the king during a joust, and thinking that he was refusing to joust against His Majesty[58] out of courtesy, he sent an order to him that he truly wished to fight, and the knight replied that he was neither mentally nor physically able to fight him and that he swore to God that he wished for nothing more at that time.

Las follas son muy agradables, que se ben quebrar muchas lanzas, y el que la corriere a de encontrar a uno y a otro hasta que no le quede sino la enpuñadura y el cavo de la lanza. Y hasta* el húltimo fin de la carrera no a de sacar del ristre el cabo, porque por allí no le entre ningún enqüentro, hallando sin arandela desarmada aquella parte.

Y si perdiere la lanza por barrear y por aberla en la folla acabado, buelva atrás el brazo y pase así la carrera por que no se lo quiebren y hagan pedazos. Por eso las justas partidas son más agradables, porque lo que la gente ama es ber quebrar a priesa muchas lanzas, y en la mantenida no se puede esto hacer porque a cada carrera es menester esperar cómo se an de oýr a justicia las partes.

Así qu'el justar vien consiste, si es un hombre de buen entendimiento y no maníaco, en buen cavallo y buenas armas, y las armas en tres cosas: vien concertadas; bien puesto el rristre que cumple para el encontrar y llebar buenas lanzas; bien hecha la silla para la postura del cuerpo y la vista de las armas vien conzertada para ber lo que se haze.

Ay justa de guerra, y de targeta y de Roe, que todo entra devaxo de unos mismos casos. Mas justo es con la justa acavar ya, y que yo me salga de la tela, y que pues de barios hilos es la tela de mi ystoria, sea ya de otra hurdiembre la trama.

Mêlées are very enjoyable, for you get to see many lances shatter, and anyone who participates in them will encounter one knight after another until all he has left is the grip and the stub of the lance. And he must not remove the stub from the lance-rest until the very end of the course has been reached, lest he be injured by some blow, that area having been left exposed by disarming the vamplate.

And if you should lose the lance because you barricaded it and destroyed it in the mêlée, put your arm behind your back and ride the rest of the course in this position so as it does not get hit and broken. This is why jousting in teams is more enjoyable, because what people love is to see many lances being splintered in rapid succession, and in one-on-one jousts it is impossible to do this because after each course it is necessary to wait until the judges have evaluated each jouster's performance.

Thus jousting well, assuming the man is of good judgement as opposed to a maniac, consists of a good horse and good armour, and the armour consists of three things: a good fit; the lance-rest well sited so that it serves its purpose for encountering and supporting strong lances; the saddle well suited[59] to the body's posture and the visor on the armour well fitted so that you can see what is going on.

There are jousts of war, and with the targetta and of peace,[60] which all fall under the same rudiments. But it is fitting to conclude with jousting at this point, and that I take my leave of the cloth-covered tilt, and since the fabric of my history is made of sundry threads, let the weft of its plot now weave in a different direction.[61]

* *hasta*: The MS reads incorrectly *hasta qu'el*, with *qu* struck through to correct the grammar.

NOTES TO THE TRANSLATION

1 This chapter of the MS is written in four different hands, one of which is Zapata's. I clarify the different scribal interventions as follows: Amanuensis 1; Amanuensis 2; Amanuensis 3 (Zapata); and Amanuensis 4. Amanuensis 1 is responsible for the bulk of the text. Amanuensis 2 has reviewed the work of Amanuensis 1, making corrections, additions, deletions and stylistic changes to the text. Amanuensis 3 (Zapata) makes some personal accretions. Amanuensis 4, obviously a later hand, makes one annotation regarding authorship.

2 *most splendid*: Cp. Spanish *más vizarra*. The MS originally read *más vizarra de cuantas ay* ('the most splendid of them all'), but *de cuantas ay* ('of them all') has been struck through, it is not clear by which amanuensis.

3 *an armoured knight on horseback*: Cp. Spanish *un cavallero a cavallo armado*. The syntax, which is more flexible in Spanish than in English, originally read *un cavallero armado a cavallo*, which was changed by Amanuensis 1.

4 *was refusing*: Cp. Spanish *rrehusava*. This word is difficult to decipher in the MS. In his edition Gayangos (p. 211) mistranscribes as 'retoçaba' ('was frolicking'). Montiel (vol. II, p. 64) and Carrasco González (p. 162) do the same, following Gayangos. In fact Zapata is saying that the horse was refusing to jump into the chasm since it was not blinded by passion like Curtius and his mother.

5 *so much*: Cp. Spanish *harto*. Amanuensis 1 had written *arto*, which he then crossed out and spelled correctly as *harto*.

6 In order to save his country and in obedience to an oracle from the gods, Marcus Curtius leapt fully armed and on horseback into a chasm that opened up in the midst of the Roman Forum for him, an event that took place in 362 BCE. This topographical legend is mentioned by a variety of authorities whose works would have been accessible to Zapata, such as Livy, Valerius Maximus and St Augustine. See Poucet, *Recherches sur la légende sabine des origines de Rome*, pp. 241–63. The Bellini sketch illustrated in Part I, chapter 2, fig. 28 has been associated with this myth. See Eisler, *The Genius of Jacopo Bellini*, p. 219.

7 Zapata is using the word 'tilt' ('tela') to refer metaphorically to the tilting competition or the joust itself. Menaguerra uses the Catalan term 'rench' in the same way in ch. 21 of his treatise.

8 The panache is a cluster of plumes on the helmet.

9 The orle (Spanish 'borla') was a chaplet or wreath around the helmet, bearing the crest. It might be hung with colourful pennants called lambrequins. Note that in Zapata's day the noun 'colour' could be feminine ('la color'); in modern Spanish it is always masculine ('el color'). On the orle see also ffoulkes, *Armour & Weapons*, p. 45: 'The orle was made by wrapping the lambrequin or mantling – which hung from the back of the helmet and which is still used in heraldic drawings – much in the same manner as the modern puggaree is worn in India'.

10 *they do find*: Cp. Spanish *y hallan guisado*. The conjunction *y* is here being used at the beginning of a clause for the purposes of emphasising the verb.

11 This is a pertinent allusion to one of Aesop's fables about a jackdaw (Zapata's 'counterfeit bird'). The fable is worth quoting in full, as follows: 'Intending to set up a king over the birds, Zeus appointed a day for them all to appear before him, when he would choose the most handsome to reign over them. They all went to a river bank and proceeded to do their toilet. A jackdaw, realising how plain he was, went about collecting the feathers which the others moulted, and fastened them all over his body so that he was the gayest of them all. On the appointed day they all paraded in front of Zeus, including the daw in his motley plumage. Zeus was just going to award the throne to him because of his striking appearance, when the others indignantly plucked off his finery, each one taking the feathers that belonged to it. So he was stripped bare and changed back into a jackdaw. Men in debt are like this bird. They cut a dash on other people's money. Make them pay up, and you can recognize them for the nobodies they always were.' See *Fables of Aesop*, nuo. 72, p. 76.

12 By referring to ragged and tatty lads in breeches Zapata is cocking a very deliberate snook at the radical changes that had taken place in the military

arena by the late 1580s. These lads were humble infantrymen for whom jousting was a mere lark. The same year Zapata started writing the *Miscelánea*, the infantry tactician Sancho de Londoño published the first edition of his influential *Discurso sobre la forma de reduzir la disciplina militar a mejor y antiguo estado* (Brussels, 1589). Londoño makes the point that armour had been reduced to seven essential pieces, known collectively as corselets: the breastplate, pauldrons, tassets, upper and lower cannons of the vambrace, gauntlets and helmet. This light armour protected the head, torso, shoulders and arms; the legharness had been replaced by voluminous cloth breeches known as *gregüescos*. Similarly the helmets with plumes and large, ornate crests that were so admired by Zapata and other noble jousters were condemned by Londoño for practical reasons, for they now made ideal targets for harquebusiers. See Londoño, *Discurso sobre la forma de reduzir la disciplina militar a mejor y antiguo estado*, pp. 29–30.

13 *seeing*: Cp. Spanish *ber*. Amanuensis 1 had written *aber* ('having'), and then crossed out the initial *a-* in order to correct to *ber*.

14 Zapata is referring to the fact that horses were often covered by caparisons during the joust. The caparison often only left the eyes, ears, nose and lower legs exposed.

15 *But even when parading on city streets*: Cp. Spanish *Mas aunque sea para ruar*. On the 'silla de rúa' see Part I, chapter 3, fig. 127.

16 *on its feet*: Cp. Spanish *sobre los pies*, added by Amanuensis 2.

17 *flying by in a skirt*: Cp. Spanish *ir haldeando*, added by Amanuensis 2.

18 *like a dozy kite*: Cp. Spanish *como milano a la dormida*, added by Amanuensis 2. The author is referring here to the bird of prey. Zapata was an avid hunter and had written a falconry treatise entitled *Libro de cetrería* (1583). For his discussion of the kite, see Zapata, *Libro de cetrería*, facsimile ed. Terrón Albarrán, vol. I, pp. 138–44.

19 A perfect fit was essential since the proverbial chink in the armour would be a liability to the wearer. One of the most poignant moments in the *Miscelánea* is the chapter in which Zapata describes how his father, Francisco Zapata de Chaves, was

drenched with boiling oil which seeped through the gaps in his armour at the siege of Fuenterrabía in 1522. The author alleges that he has a birth-mark on his neck in the exact same spot where his father was scalded. See Zapata, *Miscelánea*, ed. Carrasco González, ch. 58, p. 77.

20 Whereas Quijada de Reayo refers in 1548 to the grandguard ('la gran pieça'), Zapata is here using the latest terminology to refer to the shield used in the jousts of his day.

21 That is to say, they should fit snugly to the contour of the wearer's arm.

22 *wings*: Cp. Spanish *rodajas*. This word is registered by Leguina, *Glosario de voces de Armería*, p. 758, as a part of the spur, which is clearly not the meaning here. At the time Zapata was writing the arms (vambraces) almost always had shaped tendon-guards at the elbow, which might appear circular when viewed from the side, and the poleyns at the knee usually had basic circular wings.

23 As Zapata has already stated: 'The knight should hang his feet evenly, as when a man walks, and the tips pointed slightly outwards.' With the tips of the feet pointing outwards, and therefore more prone to slamming into the tilt and counter-tilt than if they were pointing inwards, there would indeed be a need to protect them with armour.

24 *high*: Cp. Spanish *alto*. Amanuensis 1 had written *baxo* ('low'), which he then crossed out and corrected to *alto*.

25 *the back of each knee*: Cp. Spanish *de la corva*, added by Amanuensis 2.

26 Coincidentally, Duarte of Portugal also uses the listing ship analogy in his own discussion of saddles. See Duarte I, King of Portugal, *The Royal Book of Horsemanship, Jousting and Knightly Combat*, trans Preto and Preto, p. 34.

27 Zapata had never seen any action in battle. He had certainly not fought in any of the campaigns of the Arauco War, the first of which took place in the 1530s. In keeping with Zapata's interest in epic poetry, his immediate source for this remark is *La Araucana*, the epic poem published in three installments (1569, 1578 and 1589) by Alonso de Ercilla y Zúñiga, a soldier who had participated in the war. One of the most memorable moments in the work is the scene in which Caupolicán becomes

chief of the Araucanian Indians by winning a test of strength and endurance which involves lifting a massive cedar log and holding it up for as long as possible. See Ercilla, *La Araucana*, eds Morínigo and Lerner, Canto 2, vol. I, pp. 158–64. In English, *The Araucaniad*, trans. Lancaster and Manchester, pp. 45–7. See also Zapata, *Miscelánea*, ed. Carrasco González, ch. 46, p. 58, for another reference to this same scene. Clearly it had made an impression.

28 *odd-job men*: Cp. Spanish *ganapanes*. In Zapata's time *ganapanes* were odd-job men or hired hands who ran errands or made deliveries with a mule.

29 A notable exception is the astonishing feat by the English knight Nicholas Carew at a tournament staged by King Henry VIII on 7 July 1517. One account states that immediately after the jousting, three retainers hoisted a huge tree into Carew's lance-rest at which point he set off down the lists, impressing all who were present with his great strength. Another account avers that he ran the course with the tree balanced on his head. See Anglo, *The Great Tournament Roll of Westminster*, vol. I, p. 65, n. 3.

30 *and lances made of those woods are for enemies*. Cp. Spanish *y para enemigos desotras*, added by Amanuensis 2. Zapata is describing one of the fundamental differences between jousting in the lists for pleasure and fighting in war with the intention of killing the enemy.

31 150 paces = approx. 226.5 m (245 yd 1ft 1½in).

32 The following marginal note is written by Amanuensis 4: 'mi Carlo Famoso'. Esta es obra de D. Luis Zapata, por consiguiente este es el autor de esta Miscelánea ('"my *Carlo Famoso*". This is a work by Don Luis Zapata, therefore he is the author of this Miscellany'). For the catalogue of champion jousters see Zapata, *Carlo Famoso*, facsimile ed. Terrón Albarrán, Canto 33, fols. 180rb–180va.

33 A similar metaphor, borrowed from the writings of Saint Jerome, is used by Alonso de Cartagena in his *Doctrinal de los caballeros* (c. 1444): 'así como a los médicos pertenece saber las cosas de la medicina, y a los herreros tratar las de la herrería, así a los caballeros las reglas de lo militar' ('just as it is the doctors' job to know all about medicine and it is the blacksmiths' job to know about the craft of the smith, so it is the knights' job to know the rules

of war'). See Cartagena, *Doctrinal de los caballeros*, in *Tratados militares*, ed. Fallows, p. 63.

34 *although I myself (I do feel compelled to point out) have been one of the most consummate and successful jousters in Spain*: Cp. Spanish *aunque yo en esto (quiérolo decir) he sido de los más exercitados y venturosos de España*, added somewhat immodestly by Amanuensis 3 (Zapata).

35 Cp. Menaguerra, ch. 5: 'Let the vices of dropping the lance when picking it up, or losing one or both stirrups, and contracted legs be censured at the judge's discretion; because these fouls, if they are not redressed, are worth a lance broken to the opposing jouster'.

36 Approximately 10.16 cm (4 in).

37 *a lunge*: Cp. Spanish *un repulgo*. This is an aleatory spelling of *un repullo*.

38 *and twisting your hand higher with proper gracefulness*: Cp. Spanish *y más arriba torciendo la mano con buen aire*, added in the margin by Amanuensis 2.

39 *little by little the lance will incline*: Cp. Spanish *poco a poco sesga la vara*. In his edition, Gayangos (p. 216) has 'poco a poco siga la raya' ('little by little let him follow the line'). Montiel (vol. II, p. 69) and Carrasco González (p. 165) follow Gayangos. The original MS reads *sesga la vara*, the point being that if the jouster follows all of the instructions mandated by Zapata in this sentence he will be able to lower the lance without making the common mistake of dropping the lance-head too low. This point is reiterated in the last sentence of the paragraph. As noted by Riquer, 'Las armas en el *Victorial*', p. 249, the term 'la vara' refers specifically to the jousting lance as opposed to the war lance.

40 Cp. Quijada de Reayo, ch. 4: 'Swooping means that the lance does nothing but waver up and down when you are charging.' Cp. also Menaguerra, ch. 8.

41 *without hesitating*: Cp. Spanish *sin hacer desdén*. Corominas and Pascual, *Diccionario crítico etimológico castellano e hispánico*, vol. II, p. 495a (s.v. 'digno'), register the expression as it is used in this context.

42 Cp. Quijada de Reayo, ch. 4: 'Barricading the lance means crossing it too far sideways so that it does not strike and breaks poorly'.

43 Cp. Quijada de Reayo, ch. 4: 'Some jousters hold the lance upright until the moment of the

encounter and they lower it in one sudden motion and it can drop low and lead to a foul stroke'.

44 *stirs movement*: Cp. Spanish *menee*. Amanuensis 1 had written *se bulla*, which Amanuensis 2 strikes and substitutes with *menee*. The verbs *menear* and *bullirse* are synonyms.

45 *fantastic*: Cp. Spanish *fantástigo*, added in the margin by Amanuensis 2.

46 *and not just a piece of iron*: Cp. Spanish *que no es todo hierro*. Amanuensis 1 had written *que no es todo un pedazo de armas* ('and not just pieces of armour'). Amanuensis 2 strikes *un pedazo de armas* and substitutes *hierro*.

47 *The distinguished knight*: Cp. Spanish *El señalado cavallero*, added in the margin by Amanuensis 3 (Zapata).

48 Don Diego de Córdoba is included in the catalogue of jousting champions mentioned above, n. 32. See Zapata, *Carlo Famoso*, facsimile ed. Terrón Albarrán, Canto 33, fol. 180va. He participated in many of the same tournaments as Zapata during the royal tour of Italy, Germany and the Low Countries in 1549–51. Elsewhere Zapata states that this knight was a protégé of 'The Academy of The Great Captain', Gonzalo Fernández de Córdoba (1453–1515). See Zapata, *Miscelánea*, ed. Carrasco González, ch. 112, p. 149. On the so-called Academy of The Great Captain see also Ruiz-Domènec, *El Gran Capitán: Retrato de una época*, pp. 654–7. By 1570 Don Diego de Córdoba was serving as Equerry to King Philip II, a testimony to his riding skills. In November of that year he gave his seal of approval for the subsequent publication (in 1572) of Pedro de Aguilar's *Tractado de la cavallería de la gineta*. See Aguilar, *Tractado de la cavallería de la gineta*, facsimile, fol. *2v.

49 This is an appropriate simile, as Zapata had dedicated his falconry treatise, *Libro de cetrería*, to Don Diego. In the preface he addresses Don Diego as 'rraro y cierto justador' ('rare and sure jouster'). See Zapata, *Libro de cetrería*, facsimile ed. Terrón Albarrán, vol. I, p. 21.

50 *my master*: Cp. Spanish *mi amo*, added in the margin by Amanuensis 3 (Zapata).

51 King Philip II of Spain (1527–98; ruled 1556–98). Zapata is repeating an opinion he had expressed in his poem *Carlo Famoso*. In the catalogue of

champion jousters (see above, n. 32) he says of King Philip that: 'ninguno en gracia ni en postura / le fue ygual, ni jamás fue así en la silla' ('no-one in grace or in posture was equal to him, never moreso than in the saddle'). See Zapata, *Carlo Famoso*, facsimile ed. Terrón Albarrán, Canto 33, fol. 180va.

52 *the lance*: Cp. Spanish *la lança*, added by Amanuensis 2.

53 *breaking it*: Cp. Spanish *quebrarla*. The pronoun *la* is added by Amanuensis 2.

54 *the stuff*: Cp. Spanish *cosa*. Amanuensis 1 had written *materia*. Purely for stylistic reasons (the meaning does not change), Amanuensis 2 strikes the word *materia* and substitutes *cosa de* (thereby accidentally repeating the preposition *de*).

55 *and they could say of him: 'a jouster wrapped up in himself makes a very small parcel'*. Cp. Spanish: *y le podrían desçir: 'justar mal y porfiar'*. Gayangos emends the grammar of this sentence and radically alters it as follows: 'y le podrían decir que es justar mal y porfiar' (p. 217). Montiel (vol. II, p. 71) and Carrasco González (p. 166) do the same. In doing so these editors miss the point. In the Baroque, paremiological literature was in vogue. Zapata is playing with the maxim 'cantar mal y porfiar', wittily substituting the verb 'justar' for 'cantar'. Literally the maxim means 'to sing [joust] badly and persist'. Figuratively it describes those who presume to be experts when in fact they are pedants and poseurs. I have endeavoured to capture the spirit and intent behind the Spanish maxim by playing with a similar one in English, coined originally by John Ruskin (1819–1900). The Spanish maxim is well documented. See O'Kane, *Refranes y frases proverbiales españolas de la Edad Media*, p. 73b. Another aspect of this pun is that the verb 'porfiar' ('to persist') in the maxim, and its antonym 'desviar' ('to flinch'), are standard jousting terms. Cp. the crest of the Valencian jouster Francí de Castellví (d. 1506): A tilt with the motto 'Razón es que desvía, / Voluntad la que porfía' ('Reason flinches, / Will does not'). See Macpherson, *The 'Invenciones y Letras' of the 'Cancionero general'*, no. 62, p. 77.

56 In his edition Montiel, vol. II, p. 384, identifies Don Francisco de Mendoza as the fourth son of the third Marquis of Mondéjar, who accompanied Philip II to Flanders in 1595, but this date is far too late for the event described here, which

took place in 1549 during the reign of Charles V. The Francisco de Mendoza in question is in fact Don Francisco Hurtado de Mendoza, the second son of Don Luis Hurtado de Mendoza, the second Marquis of Mondéjar. A fellow Knight of the Order of St James, Don Francisco was known as 'El Moro' ('The Moor'). He perished tragically on 19 October 1562 aboard one of the twenty-five Spanish galleys that sank in Herradura Bay, Spain, during a violent storm. See López de Haro, *Nobiliario Genealógico de los Reyes y Títulos de España*, vol. I, p. 370b.

57 A reference to Charles V (1500–58), King of Spain, 1516–56, crowned Holy Roman Emperor at Aachen in 1520.

58 On the protocol for mixed jousts bewteen royals and non-royals, see Menaguerra, ch. 14.

59 *well suited*: Cp. Spanish *bien hecha*, added by Amanuensis 3 (Zapata).

60 *with the targetta and of peace*: Cp. Spanish *de targeta y de Roe*. In his edition Gayangos (p. 218) substitutes the noun *Roe* with *regocijos* ('festivities'). Montiel (vol. II, p. 72) and Carrasco González (p. 167) do the same, obviously following Gayangos. This solution is incorrect for three reasons: (1) If *Roe* really were an abbreviation of *regocijos* it would make more sense for the vowels to be arranged differently: *-eo* as opposed to *-oe*; (2) The singular and plural forms *regocijo/regozijos* appear twice in the second paragraph of this chapter, and in both instances in the original MS an abbreviation

is not used; rather, the word is spelled out; and (3) Gayangos' interpretation implies that Zapata is distinguishing between three types of joust (jousts of war, jousts with targettas and jousts that form part of festivities), when in fact there were but two main types of joust: the jousts of war; and the jousts of peace characterised in Zapata's day by the distinctive targetta. On the term 'justa de roel' used to describe the jousts of peace see Cátedra, *El sueño caballeresco*, p. 73. Also of interest is Leguina, *Glosario de voces de Armería*, p. 761, who registers the noun *roela*, along with a definition from a mid-nineteenth-century source followed by a question mark, which means that he does not understand it. The definition reads as follows: 'Guarnición de metal que se ponía alrededor del pavés para sujetar la tablazón y resistir los golpes de las armas blancas' ('Metal edging that was put about the pavise in order to strengthen the base and withstand the blows of edged weapons'). As poor as this definition is, it seems to be an attempt to describe the trellis-work on the targetta. If *Roe* is an abbreviation of *roela*, the meaning could be: 'There are jousts of war, and with the targetta and with trellis-work.'

61 The last sentence is a witty pun. In Spanish, *tela* refers both to cloth in general and to the tilt barrier in particular, which was usually draped in cloth. Similarly, the word *trama* refers both to the weft of the cloth as well as the plot or trajectory of a story or history.

Pero Rodríguez de Lena
El Passo Honroso de Suero de Quiñones
(1434)
SELECTED PASSAGES

El Passo Honroso
de Suero de Quiñones

The Pass of Honour
of Suero de Quiñones

1.

Escorial MS f.II.19, fols. 16r–18v

1.

[Rules of the Passage of Arms]

En el nombre de Dios e de la bienaventurada
Virgen Nuestra Señora
e del Apóstol Señor Sanctiago.

In the name of God and of the blessed Virgin
Our Lady and of Saint James the Apostle.[1]

Yo, Suero de Quiñones, cavallero, natural
vasallo del muy alto e muy poderoso rey
de Castilla, Señor nuestro, e de la casa del
magnífico señor Condestable suyo, notifico
e fago [saber]* las condiciones de una mi
empresa, la qual yo notifiqué día primero del
año presente, ante el muy poderoso rey y señor
mío ya nombrado, [las]† quales parecen por
orden en los [capítulos]‡ deyuso scritos, de los
quales el primero es el que se sigue.

I, Suero de Quiñones,[2] knight, natural vassal
of the most high and most mighty king of
Castile, our lord, and of the household of his
magnificent lord Constable,[3] do declare and
make known the conditions of this my emprise,
which I declared the first day of the present
year,[4] before my aforenamed most powerful
king and lord, which conditions are arranged
in order in the Articles written below, the first
of which is as follows:

[§1.] [Que]§ todos los cavalleros o
gentileshombres a cuya noticia verná el
presente fecho, será manifiesto que yo seré con
nueve cavalleros gentileshombres que conmigo
serán en la deliberación de la dicha mi prisión
y empresa, en el paso cerca de la puente de
Órbigo, arredrado del camino quantía de cinco
passos, poco más o menos, quince días antes
del Apóstol bienaventurado ya dicho, en el que
yo estaré fasta quinze días después de la fiesta
suya si antes en el dicho plazo mi rescate no
fuere cumplido. El qual es trezientas lanças
rompidas por el hasta, con fierros fuertes, en
arneses de guerra, sin scudo ni targa, nin más
de una dobladura sobre cada pieza.

[§1.] That to all of the knights or gentlemen
to whose attention the current deed of arms
is brought, it shall be made clear that I shall
be accompanied by nine gentlemen knights
who shall be with me in the deliverance from
my said prison and emprise,[5] at the passage
near the Orbigo bridge, a distance of five
paces from the road, more or less, two weeks
before the aforenamed blessed Apostle's day,[6]
where I shall remain up to two weeks after
his festival if before that time my release
should not be attained. Which release shall
be attained by breaking at the shaft three-
hundred[7] spears with strong spearheads, in
war harnesses, without shields or targes, nor
any more than one reinforcing piece[8] over
each piece of armour.

---

* *saber: sobre – ESC.*

† *las: los – ESC.*

‡ *capítulos: apítulos – ESC.*

§ *Que*: omit – ESC; emended following Pineda
(ed. Riquer, p. 33).

[§2.] [El]* segundo capítulo es que allí fallarán todos [los]† gentileshomes e cavalleros estrangeros arneses e cavallos e lanças, sin ninguna ventaja ni mejoría de mí nin de los cavalleros que allí conmigo serán. E si algún cavallero e gentilhome pluguiere de traer su arnés, podrá fazer con él.‡

[§3.] El tercero capítulo es que correrán con cada uno de los cavalleros o gentileshomes que allí vernán tres lanças rompidas por el hasta, contando la que derribare el cavallero por rompida, y la que fiziere sangre.

[§4.] El quarto capítulo es que qualquier señora de honor que passare por aquel lugar donde yo estaré, e los cavalleros e gentileshomes ya nombrados, o a media legua dende, que si non lleva cavallero o gentilhome que faga las armas ya divisadas por ella, que pierda el guante de la mano derecha.

[§5.] El quinto capítulo es que si dos cavalleros o más, por salvar el guante de una señora, vinieren a fazer armas las susodichas, que será recibido el primero.

[§6.] El sexto capítulo es que, porque ay algunos que no aman verdaderamente, e querrían salvar el guante de más de una señora, que non lo pueda[n]§ fazer, e que después que oviere[n]§ rompido las tres lanças de su parte del que con él fiziere, que non seamos tenudos, yo ni los que conmigo allí estuvieren, a fazer las armas con el tal cavallero o gentilhome.

[§2.] The second article is that all foreign gentlemen and knights will find harnesses and horses and spears there, without any advantage or melioration over me or the knights who shall be there with me. And if it should please any knight and gentleman to bring his own harness, he may perform deeds of arms in it.[9]

[§3.] The third article is that they shall run courses against each knight or gentleman who should come there until three spears are broken at the shaft, counting the spear that knocks down a knight and the spear that draws blood as broken.

[§4.] The fourth article is that any lady of honour who should pass by that place where I and the aforenamed knights and gentlemen shall be, or within half a league thereof, if she is not accompanied by a knight or gentleman who shall be performing pre-arranged deeds of arms for her, let her forfeit the glove of her right hand.[10]

[§5.] The fifth article is that if two knights or more, to save the glove of a lady, should come to perform the above-mentioned deeds of arms, the first of them shall be received.

[§6.] The sixth article is that because there are some men who are not truly in love, and they would wish to save the glove of more than one lady, let them not be allowed to do so, and after they have broken the three spears on their part against the man who performs deeds of arms with them, let us not, neither I nor those who should be there with me, have to perform deeds of arms with this knight or gentleman.

---

* El: En el – ESC.
† los: omit – ESC.
‡ con él: con él. El tercero, with El tercero struck through – ESC.
§ puedan … ovieren: pueda … oviere – ESC.

[§7.] El seteno capítulo es que por mí serán nombradas tres señoras deste reino a los farautes que allí conmigo serán para dar verdadera fee de lo que pasare, entre las quales aseguro que no será nombrada la señora cuyo yo [so],* salvo por sus grandes virtudes. El primero cavallero o gentilhome que viniere a salvar el guante de qualquier dellas, que fará las armas susodichas conmigo, e le daré un diamante.

[§8.] El octavo capítulo es – porque tantos podrán requerir a un solo cavallero de los que allí estuviésemos, o dos, que sus personas no lo vastarían, o si lo vastasen podría[n]† romper tantas lanças de las por mí limitadas que los otros quedasen sin fazer armas –, sepan todos los cavalleros e gentileshomes que allí por fazer las armas vernán que non podrían requerir a ninguno de los cavalleros que en la guarda del paso serán señalados, nin sabrán con quién fazen fasta las armas cumplidas, salvo tanto que sean ciertos que farán con cavallero o gentilhome de cota de armas sin reproche.

[§9.] El nono capítulo es que, non obstante esto, si algún cavallero o gentilhome que después de las tres lanças rompidas quisiere requerir a alguno de los del paso señaladamente, embíemelo dezir, e si el tiempo lo adebdare, romperá con él otra lança.

[§10.] El dézimo capítulo es [que],‡ si qualquier cavallero o gentilhome de los que allí vernán a fazer armas quisieren quitar qual pieza de arnés de las que por mí son nombradas para correr las dichas lanças, o alguna dellas, embíemelo a dezir, que él será respondido a su grado si la razón [e]§ el tiempo lo adeudare.

[§7.] The seventh article is that three ladies of this realm shall be nominated by me to the heralds who shall be there with me to bear true witness to what shall happen, amongst whom I swear that the lady to whom I belong shall not be nominated, her great virtues notwithstanding.[11] The first knight or gentleman who comes to save the glove of any of them, he shall perform the above-named deeds of arms with me, and I shall give him a diamond.

[§8.] The eighth article is – because so many shall be able to challenge a single knight among those of us who are there, or two, that their body could not take it, or if they could take it they could break as many spears as those set by me that the others would never get to perform any deeds of arms –, let all of the knights and gentlemen who shall come there to perform deeds of arms know that they could not challenge any of the knights who shall be chosen to guard the passage, nor shall they know with whom they are performing the deeds of arms until they are completed, on the understanding that they may be certain that they shall perform deeds of arms with a knight or gentleman with a coat of arms beyond reproach.[12]

[§9.] The ninth article is that, despite this, if some knight or gentleman who, after having broken the three spears, should wish to issue a special challenge to one of the Defenders of the passage, let him send word of it to me, and if time permits, he shall break another spear with him.[13]

[§10.] The tenth article is that, if any knight or gentleman amongst those who come there to perform deeds of arms should wish to remove any of those pieces of the harness designated by me for running with said spears, or just one of them, let him send word of it to me, for he shall be answered to his liking if reason and time should permit.

---

* *cuyo yo so: cuyo yo seré – ESC.*

† *podrían: podría – ESC.*

‡ *que: omit – ESC.*

§ *e: omit – ESC.*

[§11.] El onzeno capítulo es que con ningún cavallero [o]* gentilhome de los que allí vernán, non serán fechas armas si antes no dize quién es e dónde.

[§12.] El dozeno capítulo es que, por [que]† algún cavallero o gentilhome movido con buen desseo, cayendo en los peligros de las armas que son a todos comunes, yendo al dicho paso, no duden su salud, sean ciertos que todos los que en el dicho paso fueren feridos, que yo les daré todas las cosas que les serán menester, e assí e tan cumplidamente como para mi persona mesma, e todo aquel tiempo que menester les será, e más si recibirlo querrán.

[§13.] El trezeno capítulo es que asseguro, a fee de cavallero, que si acaesciere, assí de los cavalleros como de los gentileshomes, [en]‡ las armas que fizieren, llevar ventaja o ferir a mí o a alguno de los cavalleros que conmigo serán, que nunca les será demandado por nosotros, ni parientes ni amigos nuestros.

[§14.] El catorceno capítulo es que qualquier cavallero o gentilhome que fuere camino derecho de la sancta romería, non acostándose al dicho lugar del paso do yo e los dichos cavalleros que conmigo serán, estaremos, podrá ir, sin contraste de mí e de los cavalleros ya dichos, a cumplir su romería.

[§15.] El quinceno capítulo es que qualquier cavallero o gentilhome que, desviando el derecho [camino],§ se llegare al lugar del paso que yo y los míos guardáremos, no podrá partir del dicho paso sin primero fazer las armas ya devisadas, o dexar una arma de las que llevare, o la spuela derecha, so fee de jamás traer aquella arma o spuela hasta que se vea en fecho de armas tan peligroso o más que aquél do la dexara.

[§11.] The eleventh article is that deeds of arms shall not be performed with any of those knights or gentlemen who come there if he does not state beforehand who he is and where he is from.

[§12.] The twelfth article is that, so that no knight or gentleman motivated by good intentions, falling into the dangers of arms with which we are all familiar, by going to the said passage, be concerned about his health, be certain that to all those who should incur wounds in said passage, I shall give them everything that they shall need, and as plenteously as if it were for my own person, and for as much time as shall be necessary, and for longer if they wish to have more time.

[§13.] The thirteenth article is that I swear, on my knightly oath, that if it should come to pass, either to the knights or the gentlemen, in the deeds of arms that they shall perform, that they take the advantage or wound me or any of the knights who shall be with me, they shall never be sued by us, nor by relatives or friends of ours.

[§14.] The fourteenth article is that any knight or gentleman who were travelling the holy pilgrims' route,[14] who does not come to the said place where I and the said knights who shall accompany me will be, shall be allowed to go, without a challenge from me or the aforenamed knights, to complete his pilgrimage.

[§15.] The fifteenth article is that any knight or gentleman who, leaving the pilgrims' route, should arrive at the place of the passage that my men and I are guarding, shall not be allowed to depart from said passage without first performing pre-arranged deeds of arms, or leaving behind one of the arms that he is carrying, or the right spur, on his oath that he will never bear that arm or don the spur until he participates in a deed of arms as dangerous as, or more dangerous than, that at which he left it.[15]

---

* *o*: omit – *ESC.*
† *que*: omit – *ESC.*
‡ *en*: *e* – *ESC.*
§ *camino*: omit – *ESC.*

[§16.] El deziséis capítulo es que [si yo o]* qualquier cavallero o gentilhome de los que conmigo serán matáremos cavallo de los que allí vinieren o de qualquier dellos a fazer armas, que yo se lo pagaré, e si ellos mataren cavallo a qualquiera de nós, vástele la fealdad del† encuentro por paga.

[§17.] El dezisiete capítulo es que qualquier cavallero o gentilhome de los que armas fizieren que encontrare [cavallo],‡ si el que corriere con él encontrare poco o mucho en el arnés, que se qüente la lança por rompida por la fealdad del encuentro.

[§18.] El deziocho capítulo es que si algún cavallero o gentilhome de los que allí fazen armas vernán, después de la una lança o de las dos rompidas, por voluntad non quisiere fazer más armas, que pierda la arma o la spuela ansí como si non fiziese ningunas.

[§19.] El dezimonono capítulo es que allí darán lanças e fierros sin ventaja a todos los del reyno que llevaren armas e cavallos para fazer las dichas armas. Non podrán fazer con las suyas, en caso que las lieven, por quitar la ventaja.

[§20.] El veynte capítulo es que si algún cavallero o gentilhome de los que allí serán por fazer las armas ya dichas, oviere ferida de la primera lança o segunda, tal que aquel día no pueda más armas fazer, que después non seamos tenudos a fazer más armas con él, aunque las demande, e las armas sean acavadas.

[§16.] The sixteenth article is that if I or any knight or gentleman of those who shall accompany me should kill the horse of anyone at all of those who come to perform deeds of arms, I shall pay him for it, and if they should kill any of our horses, let the ugliness of the encounter be payment enough.

[§17.] The seventeenth article is that any knight or gentleman of those who perform deeds of arms should strike a horse, if the man who is running against him should deal a light or heavy blow on his harness, let the spear be counted as broken because of the ugliness of the encounter.

[§18.] The eighteenth article is that, if any knight or gentleman of those who shall come there to perform deeds of arms, after the first or second spears have been broken, should willingly refuse to perform more deeds of arms, let him lose the arm or the spur as if he had not performed any deeds of arms.

[§19.] The nineteenth article is that spears and spearheads shall be given out without advantage to all men of the realm who should bring arms and horses to perform the said deeds of arms. They shall not be allowed to use their own, in the event that they bring them, in order to remove the advantage.

[§20.] The twentieth article is that if any knight or gentleman of those who shall be there to perform the aforesaid deeds of arms should sustain a wound from the first or second spear, such that he can perform no more deeds of arms that day, let us not have to perform more deeds of arms with him afterwards, even if he demands them, and let the deeds of arms be declared over.

---

* *si yo o*: omit – *ESC*. Labandeira Fernández, p. 93 emends to *si*. I emend to *si yo o*, based on the first person singular verb, *matáremos*.
† *fealdad del*: *fealdad que del*, with *que* struck through – *ESC*.
‡ *cavallo*: *cavallero* – *ESC*. This mistake was not caught by Labandeira Fernández.

[§21.] El veynte y un capítulo es que – por que los cavalleros e gentileshomes, por sospecha de recebir engaño, non [dexen]* de venir† al dicho passo –, [a]‡ todos sea manifiesto que allí estarán presentes dos cavalleros antiguos, provados en armas e dignos de fee, e dos farautes, a los quales, cavalleros e gentileshomes que allí a fazer armas vernán, farán juramento apostólico e omenaje d'estar a todo lo quellos mandasen cerca de las dichas armas, a los quales [los]§ dichos cavalleros [e]¶ farautes ygual juramento farán de los guardar de engaño, [e]** que juzgarán verdad, según razón [e]†† derecho de armas. Que si alguna dubda de nuevo, allende de aquello que yo en mis capítulos aquí screví, acaeciere, quede a discreción de aquellos juzgar sobre ello. Por que a ninguno non sea escondido el bien o ventaja que en las dichas armas fará, los farautes que allí estarán darán signado, a qualquier que lo demandare, lo que con verdad cerca [de lo]‡‡ que fizo demandar querrá.

[§22.] El capítulo postrimero de mi deliberación es que sea notorio a todas las señoras del mundo, e assí a los cavalleros e gentileshomes que los capítulos susodichos oyrán, que si la señora cuyo soy passare por aquel lugar por mí ya nombrado ado yo seré, que podrá yr segura su mano derecha de perder el guante, que no fará armas nengún cavallero nin gentilhome por ella sino yo, pues que en el mundo no ay quién tan verdaderamente las pueda fazer como yo.

[§21.] The twenty-first article is that – so that knights and gentlemen, for fear of being tricked, not be dissuaded from coming to the said passage –, let it be clear to all that there shall be present two old knights, proven in arms and worthy of trust, and two heralds, to whom the knights and gentlemen who shall come there to perform deeds of arms shall swear an apostolic oath and homage to submit to everything that they may order about said deeds of arms, to whom the said knights and heralds shall swear a similar oath to protect them from trickery, and that they will judge the truth, in accordance with reason and the law of arms.[16] For if some new doubt, beyond that which I have written here in my articles, should arise, let it be left to the discretion of those men to pass judgement about it. So that the benefit and advantage which shall be gained in the said deeds of arms may not be concealed from anyone, the heralds who shall be there shall provide a signed statement, to anyone who should request it, concerning the truth that he shall wish to request about what he did.

[§22.] The last article of my deliberation is that it be publicly known to all the ladies in the world, and likewise to the knights and gentlemen who shall hear the aforesaid articles, that if the lady to whom I belong should pass through that aforenamed place where I shall be, her right hand can be sure of losing its glove, for no knight or gentleman shall perform deeds of arms for her except me, since there is no-one in the world who can perform them as faithfully as I.[17]

---

* dexen: dexe – ESC.
† venir: convenir, with con struck through – ESC.
‡ a: e a – ESC.
§ los: omit – ESC.
¶ e: omit – ESC.
** e: omit – ESC.
†† e: de – ESC.
‡‡ de lo: dello – ESC.

2.

Escorial MS f.II.19, fol. 67v

Capítulo que fabla de las armas que fizo Pedro de los Ríos, uno de los defensores del paso ya nonbrado, en este ya nonbrado martes en la tarde,* con Antón de Funes, aragonés.

Luego este dicho día† martes,‡ treze días del dicho mes de julio, en la tarde, entró en el campo e liça Pedro de los Ríos, uno de los defensores del paso, e de la otra parte contra él, Antón de Funes, aragonés.

E anduvieron [seis]§ carreras e⁋ non se encontraron.

A las** siete carreras que anduvieron, tocó Antón de Funes a Pedro de los Ríos en la calva del almete, e non prendió nin rompió lança.

E a las ocho carreras encontró por esta misma vía.

E anduvieron otra carrera que no se encontraron.

A las†† diez carreras encontró Antón de Funes a Pedro de los Ríos en la guarda de la manopla yzquierda, e falsó la guarda e la manopla e el piastrón e el peto, e quebró su lança fasta tres palmos del fierro.

2.

Tuesday, 13 July 1434
Pedro de los Ríos vs. Antón de Funes
[*Use of a reinforcing piece: above, Article 1*]

Chapter which speaks about the deeds of arms which Pedro de los Ríos, one of the Defenders of the aforenamed passage of arms, performed with Antón de Funes, from Aragon, in the afternoon of this aforenamed Tuesday.

Later this said Tuesday, the thirteenth day of the said month of July, in the afternoon, Pedro de los Ríos, one of the Defenders of the passage of arms, entered the field and lists, and on the other side opposite him, Antón de Funes, from Aragon.

And they rode six courses and they did not encounter.

In the seventh course which they rode, Antón de Funes attainted Pedro de los Ríos on the brow reinforce of the helmet, and the spear neither gained a purchase nor broke.

And in the eighth course Antón de Funes encountered in this same way.

And they rode another course in which they did not encounter.

In the tenth course Antón de Funes struck Pedro de los Ríos on the reinforce of the left gauntlet,[18] and he pierced the reinforce and the gauntlet and the plackart and the breastplate, and he broke his spear three palms below the spearhead.[19]

---

*   *en este ya nonbrado martes en la tarde: antes en la tarde – RAH.*
†   *día: omit – BMP.*
‡   *martes: martes ya nombrado,* with *ya nombrado* struck through *– RAH.*
§   *seis: sus – ESC, RAH; seis – BMP.*
⁋   *e: que – BMP, RAH.*
** *A las: E a las – BMP.*
†† *A las: E a las – BMP, RAH.*

A las[*] once carreras encontró Pedro de los Ríos al catalán en el peto del piastrón, e pasólo, e entró en el otro peto de las platas, e despuntó el fierro de la lança. E rompió su lança en él por medio en pieças.

E luego los juezes, deque vieron los arneses assí falsados, guardando los capítulos ya nombrados antes desto, mandaron[†] que saliesen de la liça e que[‡] non fiziesen más armas hasta que tomasen otros arneses o adereçasen aquéllos. E luego salieron de la liça e desarmáronse e fizieron adereçar los mesmos arneses con que primero fazían. E adovados, tornáronse a armar[§] e bolvieron al campo a cumplir sus armas.

E anduvieron tres carreras que no se encontraron.

A las[¶] quinze[**] carreras que anduvieron, encontró Antón de Funes a Pedro de los Ríos en el borde del guardabraço yzquierdo, e quebró su lança. E Pedro de los Ríos encontró a Antón de Funes en meitad del guardabraço ezquierdo, e desguarneciógelo, e non rompió lança.

E aquí[††] acabaron de cumplir sus armas. E luego los juezes les mandaron que saliesen de la liça e se fuesen[‡‡] a sus tiendas. E luego Pedro de los Ríos combidó a cenar[§§] a[¶¶] Antón de Funes, según[***] costumbre de los cavalleros e gentilhomes del passo.

De[†††] lo que dixo el auctor destas armas:

In the eleventh course Pedro de los Ríos struck the Catalonian on the reinforcing breastplate,[20] and punctured it, and went into the other breastplate, and the spearhead blunted. And he broke his spear in half upon him.[21]

And then the judges, when they saw the harnesses pierced in this way, following the aforenamed Articles above, ordered them to leave the lists and not to perform any more deeds of arms until they donned other harnesses or mended those ones. And then they left the lists and disarmed themselves and they had the same harnesses that they were initially using mended. And once they were ready, they rearmed themselves and returned to the field to complete their deeds of arms.

And they rode three courses in which they did not encounter.

In the fifteenth course which they rode, Antón de Funes struck Pedro de los Ríos on the stop-rib of the left pauldron, and he broke his spear. And Pedro de los Ríos struck Antón de Funes in the middle of the left pauldron, and he ripped it off him, and he did not break the spear.

And at this point they finished completing their deeds of arms. And then the judges ordered them to leave the lists and go to their pavilions. And then Pedro de los Ríos invited Antón de Funes to dinner, according to the custom of the knights and gentlemen at the passage of arms.[22]

What the author said about these deeds of arms:[23]

[*] *A las: E a las – BMP, RAH.*

[†] *mandaron: después mandaron – BMP.*

[‡] *e que: o que – BMP.*

[§] *tornáronse a armar: tornáronse armar – BMP.*

[¶] *A las: E a las – BMP.*

[**] *quinze: doze – RAH.*

[††] *aquí: omit – BMP.*

[‡‡] *e se fuesen: e que se fuessen – BMP, RAH.*

[§§] *cenar: comer – BMP.*

[¶¶] *a: omit – BMP.*

[***] *según: según de – BMP.*

[†††] *De: E de – BMP.*

Aquí[*] dize el autor que, comoquiera quel nonbrado Pedro de los Ríos andava maravilloso cavallero e traía muy buena lança, que Antón de Funes llevó lo mejor por rronper dos lanças en Pedro de los Ríos, e esto pone a la ventura serle contraria.

Here the author says that, even though the aforenamed Pedro de los Ríos rode like a marvellous knight and wielded the spear well, Antón de Funes carried the advantage by breaking two spears on Pedro de los Ríos, and he attributes this to the fact that good fortune was against Pedro de los Ríos.[24]

3.
Escorial MS f.II.19, fols. 72rv

3.
Wednesday, 14 July 1434
Sancho de Rabanal vs. Jofre Jardí
[On the fragility of the 'arrêt à vervelles']

Capítulo que fabla [de][†] cómo este ya nonbrado Sancho de Ravanal, uno de los defensores de aquel paso,[‡] tornó en este día otra vez a fazer armas con Jufre Jardí, ya dicho.

Chapter which speaks about how this aforenamed Sancho de Rabanal, one of the Defenders of that passage of arms, returned once again on this day[25] to perform deeds of arms with said Jofre Jardí.

Después[§] desto, a poca de ora, entró en el campo e liça el ya nombrado antes desto Sancho de Ravanal, defensor, el qual havía fecho las armas con el ya dicho Juan de Estamarín. E venía armado con las mismas [armas][¶] que havía fecho e en el cavallo [en][**] que havía andado. E de la otra parte vino armado[††] contra él a cavallo[‡‡] Jufrei Jardín. E dentro en el campo, amos a dos movieron el uno contra el otro, sus lanças enrristradas, muy rreyciamente.

A short while after this, the aforenamed Defender, Sancho de Rabanal, who had performed deeds of arms with the aforesaid Juan de Estamarín, entered the field and lists. And he came armed with the same arms that he had used and on the same horse he had ridden. And on the other side Jofre Jardí came armed on horseback opposite him. And inside the field, they both charged against each other very vigorously, their spears in the rests.

---

  * *Aquí: E aquí – BMP.*
  † *fabla de: fabla – ESC; fabla de – BMP, RAH.*
  ‡ *de aquel paso: del paso – RAH.*
  § *Después: E después – BMP.*
  ¶ *armas: omit – ESC; armas – BMP, RAH.*
  ** *en: omit – ESC; en – BMP, RAH.*
  †† *RAH adds the following, which is struck through: contra él el ya nombrado Jufre Jardín que el día antes con él avía enpeçado a fazer sus armas armado en blanco e a cavallo. E como amos a dos fueron dentro en el campo fuesse el uno contra el otro, sus lanças enristradas, con muy buenas continencias de cavallería. E a esta primera carrera encontró Jufre Jardín a Sancho de Ravanal en la guarda del braçal ezquierdo e fa…*
  ‡‡ *contra él a cavallo: a cavallo contra él – BMP, RAH.*

E a esta primera carrera encontró Sancho a Jufrei Jardín en el peto de las platas, e fízole una buena señal, e rrompió su lança en él en pedaços, e non hovo revés ninguno. E de su mesmo encuentro quebráronse* las pontecillas de su rriestre e desguarneciósele una lama del guardabraço.†

E por quanto era ya noche e non havía tiempo para aderéçar las piezas assí desconcertadas, nin se podían ya examinar los encuentros, mandaron los juezes e rei de armas e faraute que se fuesen a sus tiendas, e otro día, en amaneciendo, quando oyesen tocar las trompetas, fuesen luego armados e puestos en el campo e liça para conplir sus armas. E ellos les rrespondieron que pues havían prometido de estar a su mandamiento en el fecho de las armas, que les plazía de lo facer, comoquiera que amos a dos‡ dixieron que si a los juezes pluguiese, que ellos esperarían a que se aderéçasen las piezas de arneses que estavan desconcertadas e que allí cumplirían sus armas antes que del campo saliesen. E los juezes dixieron lo que primero havían dicho, e deque esto vieron que más a la sazón non podían fazer, fuéronse cada uno dellos a su tienda.

E antes que se fuesen, combidó Sancho de Rabanal a cenar§ a Jufrey Jardín, según¶ la costumbre del paso, e él dixo que le plazía. E assí salieron, el uno por la una puerta de la liça e el otro por la otra.

E esta noche non se fizieron más armas.

And in this first course Sancho de Rabanal struck Jofre Jardí on the breastplate, and he made a good mark on him, and he broke his spear into pieces upon him, and neither one suffered a reversal of fortune. And from his own encounter the vervelles[26] of his rest broke off and a lame of his pauldron[27] was ripped off.

And since night had already fallen and there was no time to repair the damaged pieces, nor by this time could the encounters be examined, the judges and king-of-arms and herald ordered them to go to their pavilions, and the next day, at dawn, when they heard the sound of the trumpets,[28] they should at that time go armed and ready to the field and lists in order to complete their arms.[29] And they replied that since they had promised to be at their command in the deed of arms, that they would be pleased to do so, even though they both said that if it pleased the judges, they would wait until the pieces of the harnesses that were damaged were repaired and that they would complete their arms right there before they left the field. And the judges said what they had said in the first place, and when they realised that at that time they could do no more, each one went to his pavilion.

And before they went, Sancho de Rabanal invited Jofre Jardí to dinner, according to the custom of the passage of arms, and he said that he would be pleased to accept. And thus they left, one through one gate of the lists and the other through the other.[30]

And no more deeds of arms were performed on this night.

---

* *quebráronse: quebráronsele – BMP.*
† *guardabraço: guardabraço derecho – BMP, RAH.*
‡ *a dos: omit – BMP.*
§ *a cenar: a cena – RAH.*
¶ *según: según de – BMP.*

4.
Escorial MS f.II.19, fols. 72v–73r

Jueves, a quinze días del ya nonbrado jullio. Capítulo de las armas[*] que el ya nonbrado Sancho de Ravanal otra vez fizo con[†] el ya nonbrado Jufrei Jardín, por quanto el miércoles de antes no las havían acabado.

El dicho jueves siguiente, quinze días del ya nonbrado mes de jullio, luego de mañana, como fueron tocadas las trompetas, entró en el canpo e liça el ya nonbrado Sancho de Ravanal, defensor del paso, armado en blanco e a cavallo, el qual havía compeçado a fazer las armas el día de antes con el ya dicho Jufrei Jardín, según[‡] vós es devisado. E de la otra parte contra él, [el][§] ya nombrado Jufrey Jardín, que el día de antes con él avía empeçado a fazer sus armas, armado en blanco e a cavallo. E como amos a dos fueron dentro en el campo,[¶] fuése el uno contra el otro, sus lanças enristradas, con muy buenas continencias de cavallería.

E a esta primera carrera encontró Jufrei Jardín a Sancho de Ravanal en la guarda del braçal yzquierdo, e falsóla, e salió de allí e tocó en el piastrón, e falsólo. E rrompió su lança en él por dos partes. E fue forçado que se desarmase el dicho Sancho. E quedó la punta del fierro en el peto de las platas. E adovadas las dichas armas, armóse Sancho luego.

4.
Thursday, 15 July 1434
Sancho de Rabanal vs. Jofre Jardí
[Conclusion of the joust:
see Selection 3, above]

Thursday, the fifteenth day of the aforesaid July. Chapter about the deeds of arms which the aforenamed Sancho de Rabanal performed once again with the aforenamed Jofre Jardí, since they had not finished them on the previous Wednesday.

That following Thursday, the fifteenth day of the aforenamed month of July, later in the morning, when the trumpets were sounded, the aforenamed Sancho de Rabanal, Defender of the passage of arms, entered the field and lists in white armour and on horseback, who had begun to perform the deeds of arms the day before with the aforesaid Jofre Jardí, as is described to you. And on the other side opposite him, the aforenamed Jofre Jardí, who had begun to perform his deeds of arms with him the day before, in white armour and on horseback. And now that they were both in the field, they ran at each other, their spears in the rests, with great chivalric composure.

And in this first course Jofre Jardí struck Sancho de Rabanal on the left couter wing, and pierced it, and glanced off there and hit the plackart, and pierced it. And he broke his spear in two upon him. And said Sancho was forced to disarm himself. And the tip of the spearhead was stuck in the breastplate. And once the said armour was mended, Sancho then armed himself.

---

[*] *de las armas*: omit – BMP.
[†] *fizo con*: fizo de las armas con – BMP.
[‡] *según*: según de – BMP.
[§] *el*: omit – ESC; el – BMP, RAH.
[¶] *en el campo*: del campo – BMP.

A las* dos carreras encontró Jufrey Jardín a Sancho de Ravanal en la falda del guardabraço, e de allí salió e fue rrayando el fierro por encima del piastrón hasta que llegó adonde primeramente lo havía falsado. E si non estuviera adobado, pudiera por allí ser mal ferido. E allí despuntó el fierro e rrompió su lança.

E luego los juezes dixieron que havían complido sus armas, pues aquel día havían rronpido† dos lanças, e el día de antes la una, por ende, que les mandavan que saliesen del campo e se fuesen a sus tiendas. E‡ ellos assí lo fizieron, e fue conbidado a cenar Jufrei Jardín, según la costumbre del passo.

E en estas armas fabla el auctor, que dize que según él vio, que ellos amos a dos andavan muy buenos cavalleros e con ardideza de cavallería. Comoquiera que da lo mejor destas armas que amos fizieron al ya nonbrado Jufrei Jardín, por quanto él rompió las dos lanças en Sancho de Ravanal. E bien parece que en este fecho de armas que amos fizieron que tovo un poco contraria la ventura Sancho de Ravanal, e non puede saber más deste fecho porque los secretos de Dios son muy encubiertos a todas personas.

In the second course Jofre Jardí struck Sancho de Rabanal on the edge of the pauldron, and glanced off there, and the spearhead scraped right across the plackart until it landed at the spot where he had initially pierced it.[31] And if it had not been mended, he could have been badly injured in that spot. And at that point the spearhead blunted and he broke his spear.

And then the judges said that they had completed their deeds of arms, for that day they had broken two spears, plus the one the day before, therefore, they ordered them to leave the field and go to their pavilions. And that is what they did, and Jofre Jardí was invited to dinner, according to the custom of the passage of arms.

And the author speaks of these deeds of arms, and says that from what he saw, they were both riding like very good knights and with chivalric verve. However, he gives the advantage in these deeds of arms which they both performed to the aforenamed Jofre Jardí, since he broke the two spears on Sancho de Rabanal. And it truly seems that in this deed of arms which they both performed good fortune was slightly against Sancho de Rabanal, and the author can have no further knowledge of this fact because God's secrets are closely guarded from all people.

---

* A las: E a las – BMP.
† rronpido: complido – BMP.
‡ E: omit – BMP.

5.
Escorial MS f.II.19, fols. 73r–74r

Pedro de Nava.
Capítulo de las armas que hizo el ya nonbrado
Pedro de Nava, uno de los defensores de aquel
passo, en este ya nonbrado jueves, con el ya
antes desto nonbrado Francisco de Fazes.

Después* desto, este día jueves nonbrado,
entró en el campo e liça Pedro de Nava, uno
de los defensores del paso, armado en blanco e
a cavallo, e de la otra parte, contra él, Francisco
de Faces, hermano de Mossén Luis de Faces,
assimesmo armado en blanco e a cavallo. E
amos a dos dentro en el campo, movieron muy
reciamente el uno contra el otro, sus lanças
enristradas.

E a esta primera carrera† encontró Pedro de
Nava a Francisco de Faces en el guardabraço
yzquierdo, e non prendió nin rompió lança.
Comoquiera que ambos a dos pasaron esta
carrera con muy buenas continencias e
ardideza de cavallería.

E anduvieron otras quatro carreras que non
se encontraron, salvo en‡ la una dellas que
barrearon las lanças.§

A las¶ seis carreras encontró Pedro de
Nava a Francisco de Faces en el guardabraço
ezquierdo, e rompió su lança en él por cerca del
fierro. E Francisco de Faces encontró a Pedro
de Nava en la calva del almete, e non prendió
nin ronpió lança.

E anduvieron otras tres carreras que non se
encontraron.

5.
Thursday, 15 July 1434
Pedro de Nava vs. Francisco de Faces
*[The longest joust of the passage of arms:
27 courses]*

Pedro de Nava.
Chapter about the deeds of arms which
the aforenamed Pedro de Nava, one of the
Defenders of that passage of arms, on this
aforementioned Thursday, performed with
the aforenamed Francisco de Faces.

After this, on this aforenamed Thursday,
Pedro de Nava, one of the Defenders of the
passage of arms, entered the field and lists, in
white armour and on horseback, and on the
other side, opposite him, Francisco de Faces,
brother of Lord Luis de Faces, likewise in
white armour and on horseback. And now
that they were both in the field, they charged
against each other very vigorously, their spears
in the rests.

And in this first course Pedro de Nava
struck Francisco de Faces on the left pauldron,
and the spear neither gained a purchase nor
broke. Even so, they both ran this course with
great composure and chivalric verve.

And they rode another four courses in
which they did not encounter, except that in
one of them they barricaded the spears.[32]

In the sixth course Pedro de Nava struck
Francisco de Faces on the left pauldron, and
he broke his spear upon it near the spearhead.
And Francisco de Faces struck Pedro de Nava
on the brow reinforce of the helmet and the
spear neither gained a purchase nor broke.

And they rode another three courses in
which they did not encounter.

* *Después: E después – BMP.*
† *a esta primera carrera: a estos primeros encuentros – BMP.*
‡ *en: omit – BMP.*
§ *las lanças: sus lanças – RAH.*
¶ *A las: E a las – BMP.*

A las* diez carreras encontró Francisco de Faces a Pedro de Nava en el arandela, e rompió su lança en él† por dos partes. E Pedro de Nava barreó su lança.

E anduvieron otras cinco carreras que‡ non se encontraron, salvo en las dos dellas que barrearon sus lanças.

A las§ diez y seis carreras encontró Pedro de Nava a Francisco de Faces en el guardabraço yzquierdo, e despuntó el fierro en él,¶ e non ronpió ninguno dellos lança.

E passaron otra carrera que non se encontraron.

A las** diez y ocho carreras encontró Pedro de Nava a Francisco de Faces en la bavera, e non prendió nin rrompió lança.

E passaron otras dos carreras que non se encontraron, salvo en la†† una dellas que barreó su lança Pedro de Nava por debaxo de la bavera.

A las‡‡ veinte e una carreras encontráronse amos a dos en las arandelas, e barrearon las lanças sin ronper ninguna dellas§§ ni tomar revés.

E anduvieron otras quatro carreras que non se encontraron, salvo en las dos dellas que barrearon las lanças.

A las¶¶ veinte e seis carreras encontró Pedro de Nava a Francisco de Faces encima de la vista del almete, e non prendió nin ronpió lança.

A las*** veinte y siete carreras encontró Francisco de Faces a Pedro de Nava en la

In the tenth course Francisco de Faces struck Pedro de Nava on the rondel, and he broke his spear in half on it. And Pedro de Nava barricaded his spear.

And they rode another five courses in which they did not encounter, except that in two of them they barricaded their spears.

In the sixteenth course Pedro de Nava struck Francisco de Faces on the left pauldron, and the spearhead blunted on it, and neither one of them broke a spear.

And they ran another course in which they did not encounter.

In the eighteenth course Pedro de Nava struck Francisco de Faces on the bevor, and the spear neither gained a purchase nor broke.

And they ran another two courses in which they did not encounter, except that in one of them Pedro de Nava barricaded his spear beneath Francisco de Faces' bevor.

In the twenty-first course they both struck each other on the rondels, and they barricaded the spears without breaking either one of them[33] or suffering a reversal of fortune.

And they rode another four courses in which they did not encounter, except that in two of them they barricaded the spears.

In the twenty-sixth course Pedro de Nava struck Francisco de Faces above the eye-slit of the helmet, and the spear neither gained a purchase nor broke.

In the twenty-seventh course Francisco de Faces struck Pedro de Nava on the couter

---

* *A las: E a las – BMP.*
† *en él: omit – BMP.*
‡ *que: e – BMP.*
§ *A las: E a las – BMP.*
¶ *en él: omit – BMP.*
** *A las: E a las – BMP.*
†† *salvo en la: salvo la – BMP.*
‡‡ *A las: E a las – BMP.*
§§ *ninguna dellas: ninguno dellos – BMP.*
¶¶ *A las: E a las – BMP.*
*** *A las: E a las – BMP.*

guarda del braçal, e salió della e tocó en el peto e rrompió en él su lança por cerca del fierro.

E mandaron los juezes que pues havían cunplido sus armas, que saliesen del campo e se fuesen a sus tiendas. E ellos dixeron que les plazía, pues [en]* esto [estavan]† a su mandamiento.‡

E aquí dize el auctor, por quanto era presente al fazer de las armas, que bio que andavan muy buenos cavalleros amos a dos, con ardideça de coraçones. Comoquiera que da lo mejor a Francisco de Faces, por quanto rompió las dos lanças en Pedro de Nava, e Pedro de Nava la una en él. E esto piensa que fue la ventura non querer ser al presente en fabor de Pedro de Nava.

wing, and glanced off it and hit the breast-plate, and he broke his spear upon it near the spearhead.

And the judges ordered that since they had completed their deeds of arms they should leave the field and go to their pavilions. And they said that they would be pleased to do so, since on this matter they were at their command.[34]

And here says the author, since he was present when the deeds of arms were being performed, that he saw that both knights were riding very well, with passionate hearts.[35] However, he gives the advantage to Francisco de Faces, since he broke the two spears upon Pedro de Nava, and Pedro de Nava the one upon him. And he believes that this was because good fortune did not at the time wish to favour Pedro de Nava.

6.
Escorial MS f.II.19, fols. 75v–76v

Lope de Stúñiga.
Viernes, diez y seis días del ya nonbrado jullio.§ Capítulo de las armas que el honrrado cavallero Lope de Stúñiga, ya nonbrado, fizo con el honrrado cavallero Mossén Francés Daviu, catalán, antes desto nonbrado.

El dicho viernes diez y seis de jullio, entró en el campo el ya nonbrado cavallero Lope de Stúñiga, uno de los defensores del passo, armado e a cavallo, e encima de sus armas media uça¶ de aceitoní brocado, vellud vellutado, azul la meitad, e la otra meitad de damasco verde e blanco. E de la otra parte, contra él, Mossén

6.
Friday, 16 July 1434
Lope de Stúñiga vs. Francés Daviu
[On the fragility of the 'arrêt à vervelles']

Lope de Stúñiga.[36]
Friday, the sixteenth day of the aforesaid July. Chapter about the deeds of arms which the aforenamed honourable knight Lope de Stúñiga performed with the above named honourable Catalonian knight Lord Francés Daviu.

On the aforesaid Friday, 16 July, the aforenamed knight Lope de Stúñiga, one of the Defenders of the passage of arms, entered the field, armed and on horseback, and wearing over his armour a tabard of satin brocade and épinglé velvet, one side blue, and the other green and white damask. And on the other side, opposite him, Lord Francés Daviu,

---

* en: omit – ESC; a – RAH.
† estavan: estava – ESC; estavan – BMP, RAH.
‡ E se fuessen a sus tiendas e ellos dixeron que les plazía: added and struck through – RAH.
§ jullio: sábado – BMP.
¶ uça: omit – BMP.

Francés Daviu, hermano del ya nonbrado Mosén Pere Daviu. E ambos a dos dentro en el campo,[*] pusieron sus lanças [en los riestres],[†] e movieron muy rreciamente el uno contra el otro, a guisa de muy buenos cavalleros.

E a esta primera carrera encontró Mosén Francés de Aviu a Lope de Astúñiga en el guarda del braçal izquierdo, e despuntó el fierro e quedó la punta del fierro[‡] en ella. E Lope de Stúñiga [encontró][§] a Mosén Francés en el asta de la lança, cerca del fierro, e levóle una racha della, e fue por ella e tocóle[¶] en el arandela, e fizo una señal en ella. E de su[**] encuentro se desguarneció todo el riestre e quebráronse las pontecillas dél,[††] e desguarneciósele el gocete e la manopla, por tal manera que se hovo a desarmar. E non rompió ninguno dellos lança.[‡‡]

E, acabadas de guarnecer las armas[§§] de Lope,[¶¶] anduvieron otras tres carreras que non se encontraron.

A las[***] cinco carreras que passaron encontró Mossén Francés a Lope de Stúñiga en el arandela, e salió della e tocó en el guardabraço derecho e desguarneciógelo. E rompió su lança en él en dos pedaços, e del encuentro abrió el fierro por el ojo.

brother of the aforenamed Lord Pere Daviu. And now that they were both inside the field, they placed their spears in the rests, and they charged against each other very vigorously, like very good knights.

And in this first course Lord Francés Daviu struck Lope de Stúñiga on the left couter wing, and the spearhead blunted, and the point bit[37] on it. And Lope de Stúñiga struck Lord Francés on the shaft of the spear, near the spearhead, and took a slice out of it, and slid down the spear and attainted the vamplate,[38] and made a mark on it. And from the blow he delivered the entire rest was ripped off and its vervelles broke, and his grapper[39] and gauntlet were ripped off him, in such a way that he had to disarm himself. And neither one of them broke a spear.

And, after having finished mending Lope's armour, they rode another three courses in which they did not encounter.

In the fifth course which they ran, Lord Francés struck Lope de Stúñiga on the rondel,[40] and glanced off it and hit the right pauldron and ripped it off. And he broke his spear in two upon him, and from the encounter the spearhead snapped off at the eye.[41]

---

  [*] *en el campo: del campo* – BMP.
  [†] *en los riestres:* omit – ESC; *en los riestres* – BMP, RAH.
  [‡] *e quedó la punta del fierro:* added in margin – RAH.
  [§] *encontró:* omit – ESC; *encontró* – BMP, RAH.
  [¶] *tocóle: tocó* – BMP; *tocóle,* with *le* struck through – RAH.
  [**] *de su: deste* – BMP.
  [††] *dél: della* – RAH.
  [‡‡] *lança: la lança,* with *la* struck through – RAH.
  [§§] *guarnecer las armas: guarnecer e las armas* – ESC, RAH.
  [¶¶] *de Lope: a Lope* – BMP.
  [***] *A las: E a las* – BMP, RAH.

E passaron otras siete carreras que non se encontraron, salvo la una dellas que cruzaron.*

A las treze carreras encontró Lope de Stúñiga a Mosén Francés en la guarda del braçal yzquierdo. E non ronpió lança ninguno dellos.

E passaron otras tres carreras que non se encontraron.

A las† diez y siete carreras que passaron, encontró Lope de Stúñiga a Mossén Francés en el guardabraço yzquierdo, e non lo falsó, e rompió su lança en él en dos pedaços.

E passaron otras cinco carreras que non se encontraron, salvo en la una dellas que barreó su lança Lope de Stúñiga.

A las‡ veinte e tres carreras que passaron, encontró Lope de Stúñiga a Mossén Francés en la guarda del braçal yzquierdo, e fízole una buena señal, e non la falsó, e quebró el perno della e echógela§ en el suelo, e rrompió¶ su lança en él en pieças, e salió el fierro muy alto, con un pedaço de la asta, por encima del cadafalso de los juezes, e fue a caer fuera de la liça, más de seis passos della.

E assí cumplieron sus armas, e los juezes mandaron que se fuesen a sus tiendas. E estando Mossén Francés al cabo de la liça para se yr, dixo estas palabras que se siguen, delante de los cavalleros e gentilesomes que allí eran. Que fazía voto a Dios de jamás en su vida nunca dormir con monja, ni la amar, porque él fasta allí havía amado una, por amor de la qual él era allí venido** a fazer aquellas armas. E que qualquiera que ge lo supiese que él amava

And they ran another seven courses in which they did not encounter, except that in one of them they crossed.[42]

In the thirteenth course Lope de Stúñiga struck Lord Francés on the left couter wing. And neither one of them broke a spear.

And they ran another three courses in which they did not encounter.

In the seventeenth course which they ran, Lope de Stúñiga struck Lord Francés on the left pauldron, and he did not pierce it, and he broke his spear in two on it.

And they ran another five courses in which they did not encounter, except that in one of them Lope de Stúñiga barricaded his spear.

In the twenty-third course which they ran, Lope de Stúñiga struck Lord Francés on the left couter wing, and he made a good mark on it, and he did not pierce it, and he broke its retaining bolt[43] and cast it to the ground, and he broke his spear into pieces on it, and the spearhead flew very high, with a piece of the shaft, over the judges' stand, and it came to rest outside of the lists, over six paces away.

And thus did they complete their deeds of arms, and the judges ordered them to go to their pavilions. And standing at the head of the lists as he was about to go, Lord Francés said the following words, in front of the knights and gentlemen who were there. That he made a vow to God never again in his life to sleep with a nun, nor to love one, because up until now he had loved one, for whose love he had come to perform those deeds of arms. And that anyone who should find out that he loved that or any

---

*   * cruzaron: trasaron, struck through and emended to crusaron – RAH.
*   † A las: E a las – BMP.
*   ‡ A las: E a las – BMP.
*   § echógela: se echógela – BMP.
*   ¶ rrompió: quebró – BMP.
*   ** él era allí venido: él avía venido allí – RAH.

aquella monja o a otra, que lo pudiesse reuctar*
por malo – pues él por tal vía las armas havía
fecho; por su amor –, e que a la tal persona que
le requestase quél non le pudiese responder en
ningún lugar e fuese acusado por malo.

E luego amos a dos vinieron ante los juezes e
alçaron las caras de los almetes e conociéronse
el uno al otro. E Mossén Francés gradeció
mucho a Lope de Stúñiga porque tan noble
cavallero quiso fazer con él las armas,† e
diole muchas gracias por ello. E Lope le
respondió que assimesmo hazía a él.‡ E aquí
se offrecieron§ sus offrecimientos el uno al
otro. E luego Lope de Stúñiga combidóle⁋ a
cenar, según la costunbre del passo. E Mossén
Francés salió luego del campo, e con él yvan
asaz trompetas e gente a pie e a cavallo. E assí
fue, armado e a cavallo, fasta el lugar de la
puente donde posava,** e esta honrra le dieron
porque era estrangero (e non havía llevado lo
mejor). E asimesmo salió Lope de Stúñiga del
campo, e†† tocando trompetas delante dél, e assí
muy honrrosamente llegó a su tienda.

E aquí dize el auctor e fabla en este fecho
destas armas, e da‡‡ lo mejor a Lope de Stúñiga
por tres razones: la primera, porque rompió dos
lanças en Mossén Francés, e Mosén Francés
en Lope non más de una; e la segunda razón
es por quanto Lope de Stúñiga encontró más
carreras; e la tercera, porque fue causa de quitar
de peccado a dos almas, la del§§ Mossén Francés

other nun could challenge him as a sinner – for
he had in this way performed deeds of arms;
for the sake of their love –, and that no matter
where he were accused as a sinner, he would
not be able to respond to the man who challenged him.[44]

And then they both came before the judges
and they raised the visors of the helmets and
they recognised each other. And Lord Francés
was very beholden to Lope de Stúñiga because
such a noble knight wished to perform deeds of
arms with him, and he thanked him profusely
for this. And Lope answered him that likewise he thanked him. And at this point each
one offered boons to the other. And then Lope
de Stúñiga invited him to dinner, according
to the custom of the passage of arms.[45] And
then Lord Francés left the field, and with him
went many trumpeters and people on foot
and on horseback. And thus did he go, armed
and on horseback, to the place where he was
lodging at the bridge,[46] and they gave him this
honour because he was a foreigner (and he had
not carried the advantage).[47] And likewise
Lope de Stúñiga left the field, and trumpeters
played before him, and thus did he arrive very
honourably at his pavilion.

And here the author tells and speaks about
these deeds of arms, and he gives the advantage to Lope de Stúñiga for three reasons:
firstly, because he broke two spears on Lord
Francés, and Lord Francés no more than one
on Lope; and the second reason is because
Lope de Stúñiga made the encounter in
more courses; and thirdly, because he was
the cause of two souls being absolved of sin,
that of Lord Francés and that of the nun, his

---

   * *reuctar: reputar – BMP; reutar – RAH.* The
    verb in this instance is an aleatory spelling of
    retar, as clarified in Pineda (ed. Riquer, p. 81).

  † *las armas: armas – RAH.*

  ‡ *hazía a él: fagan a él – BMP.*

  § *offrecieron: fizieron – BMP, RAH.*

  ⁋ *combidóle: combidólo – RAH.*

 ** *donde posava: omit – BMP.*

 †† *e: omit – RAH.*

‡‡ *e da: que da – RAH.*

§§ *la del: la de – RAH.*

e a la de la monja, su amiga ya nonbrada, de lo qual cree seguirse gran servicio a Dios. E dize que estos dos cavalleros anduvieron sus carreras muy bien, e con ardideça de cavallería.

aforementioned lover, for which he believes a great service to God shall follow. And he says that these two knights rode their courses very well, and with chivalric verve.

7.
Friday, 16 July 1434
Sancho de Rabanal vs. Juan de Soto
[The Principle of Pulchritude; shouting
inside one's helmet: cp. Menaguerra, ch. 10
and the School of Jousting]

7.
Escorial MS f.II.19, fols. 84r–85r*

Luego a poca hora en este día viernes que desuso vos es dicho, entró en el campo e liça por deffensor el honrrado gentilhome Sancho de Ravanal, bien armado e cavalgando encima de su cavallo. Contra él, de la otra parte, por conquistador, Juan de Soto, de la casa del honorable Ruy Díaz de Mendoza, ansimesmo bien armado. E amos en el campo entrados, e sus lanças enristradas, con buenas continencias reciamente bolvieron el uno contra el otro.

A la primera carrera encontró Sancho de Ravanal a Juan de Soto en el barascuro. E Juan de Soto encontró a Sancho encima del guardabraço yzquierdo, cerca de la buelta. E non rompió ninguno dellos lança ni tomaron rebés.

E passaron otra carrera que no se encontraron.

A las tres carreras encontró Sancho de Ravanal a Juan de Soto por cima de la cara del almete, e llegando al encuentro dixo alto: '¡Agora le daré!' E non prendió ni rompió lança.

E pasaron otra carrera que no se encontraron, maguer la† passaron con buenas continencias.

A las cinco carreras que andubieron, quando venían al cercano lugar de los encuentros, volbióse el cavallo a Juan de Soto, que adelante yr non quiso. E alçó luego Sancho su lança

A short while later on this Friday as stated to you above, the honourable gentleman Sancho de Rabanal entered the field and lists as Defender, well armed and riding his horse. Against him, on the other side, as Contender, Juan de Soto, of the household of the honourable Ruy Díaz de Mendoza,[48] likewise well armed. And having both entered the field, and their lances in the rests, with great composure they vigorously turned towards each other.

In the first course Sancho de Rabanal struck Juan de Soto on the besagew.[49] And Juan de Soto struck Sancho de Rabanal on the left pauldron, near the haute-piece. And neither one of them broke a spear or suffered a reversal of fortune.

And they ran another course in which they did not encounter.

In the third course Sancho de Rabanal struck Juan de Soto on the visor of the helmet, and upon approaching the encounter he shouted: 'Now I've got him!' And the spear neither gained a purchase nor broke.

And they ran another course in which they did not encounter, although they did run it with great composure.

In the fifth course which they rode, as they were getting close to the point of the encounters, Juan de Soto's horse turned, for it refused to go forward. And then Sancho raised his

---

* This entire chapter is omitted in *BMP*.
† *la: las* – *ESC*.

que le non quiso encontrar, lo qual todos lo tuvieron por gran gentileza.

A las seis carreras tocó Sancho a Juan de Soto cerca de la vista del almete sin prender ni romper lança.

A las siete carreras encontró Juan de Soto a Sancho de Ravanal en la falda del guardabraço yzquierdo, e rompió su lança en él en pedazos, sin ninguno dellos tomar rebés.

E anduvieron otras dos carreras que no se encontraron, salvo la una que varreó su lança Sancho.

A las treze carreras embió Juan de Soto pedir por merced a los juezes que le diesen licencia para que tomase otro cavallo por quanto el que tráya non andava a su voluntad. E los juezes diéronle luego licencia y embió luego por otro cavallo allende la puente donde possavan. En tanto que se lo truxeron e adereçaron y ensillaron, estuvo Sancho a cavallo en el campo, e con su almete e armado, que quitar no lo quiso, esperando que veniese recaudo al honrrado Juan de Soto. E venido su cavallo que quería cavalgar, alçó un poco la cara del almete para ver cómo cavalgava, e desque cavalgado, movieron el uno contra el otro, sus lanças enristradas.

Y anduvieron tres carreras que no se encontraron.

A las dezisiete carreras encontró Sancho a Juan de Soto, barreando su lança, e saltó el fierro della sin la romper.

A las deziocho carreras encontráronse amos a dos en los guardabraços yzquierdos, sin romper ninguno dellos lança.

A las dezinueve carreras encontró Sancho a Juan de Soto en el barrascuro del guardabraço, e desguarnecióselo, e rompió su lança en él en dos pedazos, e arrojó el fierro de la lança.

E passaron otra carrera que no se encontraron.

spear for he did not wish to strike him, which everyone considered a great courtesy.[50]

In the sixth course Sancho attainted Juan de Soto near the eye-slit of the helmet without the spear either gaining a purchase or breaking.

In the seventh course Juan de Soto struck Sancho de Rabanal on the edge of the left pauldron, and he broke his spear into pieces on him, without either one of them suffering a reversal of fortune.

And they rode another two courses in which they did not encounter, except that in one Sancho barricaded his spear.

In the thirteenth course[51] Juan de Soto sent to beseech the judges that they allow him to take another horse since the one he had was not doing his bidding. And the judges then granted him permission and he then sent for another horse across the bridge where they were stabled. While they brought it to him and got it ready and put the saddle on, Sancho was on his horse in the field, and wearing his helmet and armour, for he refused to take it off, waiting for the honourable Juan de Soto to receive what he had requested. And when the horse that he wished to ride arrived, he raised his visor a little so as he could see to mount, and when he had mounted, they charged against each other, their spears in the rests.

And they rode three courses in which they did not encounter.

In the seventeenth course Sancho struck Juan de Soto, barricading his spear, and the spearhead flew off without breaking it.

In the eighteenth course they both struck each other on the left pauldrons, without either one of them breaking a spear.

In the nineteenth course Sancho struck Juan de Soto on the besagew of the spaulder, and he ripped it off him, and he broke his spear upon him in two pieces, and sent the spearhead flying.

And they ran another course in which they did not encounter.

A las veynte y una carreras encontró Sancho a Juan de Soto en el barrascuro de la manopla, sin romper lança.

Y a las veynte y dos carreras encontró Juan de Soto a Sancho en el guardabraço yzquierdo, e no rompió lança.

E passaron otra carrera que no se encontraron.

A las veynte y quatro carreras encontró Juan de Soto a Sancho en el arçón delantero* de la silla, e rompió su lança.

E aquí acabaron de fazer sus armas. E luego los juezes los fizieron traer ante sí al rey de armas e faraute. E deque traýdos, dieron sus armas por cumplidas e les mandaron salir del campo e yrse a sus tiendas. E ante que saliesen, offreciéronse el uno al otro, e combidó Sancho de Ravanal a Juan de Soto para cenar. E assí salieron del campo honradamente, cada uno por su puerta. E se fueron a sus tiendas, e con cada uno los trompetas, según que era costumbre.

In the twenty-first course Sancho struck Juan de Soto on the rondel of the gauntlet,[52] without breaking the spear.

And in the twenty-second course Juan de Soto struck Sancho on the left pauldron, and he did not break the spear.

And they ran another course in which they did not encounter.

In the twenty-fourth course Juan de Soto struck Sancho on the front arçón of the saddle, and he broke his spear.[53]

And at this point they finished performing their deeds of arms. And then the judges had the king-of-arms and the herald bring them before them. And when they had been brought, they declared their deeds of arms completed and they ordered them to leave the field and go to their pavilions. And before they left, each one offered boons to the other, and Sancho de Rabanal invited Juan de Soto to dinner. And thus they left the field honourably, each one through his gate. And they went to their pavilions, each accompanied by trumpeters, as was the custom.

8.
Escorial MS f.II.19, fols. 85r–86r†

Sábbado siguiente, [diecisiete]‡ días contados del susodicho mes de julio del año de treynta y quatro, después del alvorada por los trompetas tocada, e otrosí acabada la primera missa del día en la tienda acostumbrada que desuso avedes oýdo, entró en el campo e liça por defensor, el honrrado gentilhome Lope de Aller, bien armado en blanco encima de un buen cavallo. E de la otra parte entró por conquistador,

8.
Saturday, 17 July 1434
Lope de Aller vs. Diego de Mansilla
[On wounding one's opponent: cp. Menaguerra, ch. 13; above, Article 3]

That Saturday, the seventeenth day of the aforesaid month of July in the year 1434, after the trumpeters announced the break of day, and furthermore when the first mass of the day in the usual pavilion that you have heard of above had ended, the honourable gentleman Lope de Aller entered the field and lists as Defender, well armed in white armour on a good horse. And on the other side Diego de Mansilla, knight of the household of the

---

* *arçón delantero: guardabrazo ezquierdo*, struck through and emended to *arçón delantero* – ESC.

† This entire chapter is omitted in *BMP*.

‡ *diecisiete: deziséis* – ESC.

dentro en el campo e liça, el cavallero Diego de Mansilla, de la casa del famoso Ruy Díaz de Mendoza, e assimesmo bien armado, a punto, encima de un buen cavallo, todo paramentado de unos paramentos de buen paño figurados todos de fuegos. E deque dentro en el campo, sus lanças enristradas, con buenas continencias movieron el uno contra el otro bien de rrezio en sus cavallos como esforçados cavalleros.

Luego la primera carrera, encontró Lope de Aller a Diego de Mansilla en el arandela, e surtió della, e fuele a dar en el braço derecho, deyuso el brazal de los morcillos, cerca del sobaco, donde armadura poner non se podía, e falsóselo de la otra parte, por tal vía que le dio una gran ferida, de que mucha sangre le salió. E rompió su lança en él en tres pedazos, del qual encuentro tomó muy gran rebés Diego de Mansilla. E llevó un pedazo de la lança con el fierro en su brazo hasta tres passadas no complidas allende del cadahalso do los juezes estavan, que adelante más asir non pudo, e allí le sacaron el fierro e troço del braço. Y en sacándoselo, corrióle su brazo un gran chorro de sangre, a manera como sale vino de cuva en poniéndole la canilla, de lo qual tomó gran desmayo el cavallero Diego de Mansilla. E non lo ayades por maravilla que un home que lo vio, el qual, cavalgando encima de una aca fuera de la liça junto con el cadafalso de los juezes, cayó luego en el suelo amortezido, y estuvo cerca de media hora que retornar non podía, aunque le travavan de las narizes, cuydando que alguna mala cosa le avía* tomado.

Luego allí fueron llegados todos los cirujanos, por mandado del capitán, a tomar la sangre e a curar del cavallero Diego de Mansilla, que fue mucho de su color mudado. E todos cuydaron que a vida no escaparía.

E luego los juezes dieron sus armas por cumplidas e le mandaron yrse a su tienda, y assimismo el defensor, los quales cada uno por su puerta del campo e liça salió. E aquí no

famous Ruy Díaz de Mendoza, entered the field and lists as Contender, and likewise well armed, ready, on a good horse, completely caparisoned with fabric trappings of good cloth all emblazoned with flames of fire.[54] And when they were inside the field, their spears in the rests, with good composure they charged against each other on their horses with much vigour like strenuous knights.

In the very first course Lope de Aller struck Diego de Mansilla on the rondel, and glanced off it, and then hit him in the right arm, beneath the vambrace around the biceps, near the armpit, where no armour could be worn, and he pierced through it to the other side, in such a way that he inflicted a gaping wound on him, from which a lot of blood flowed.[55] And he broke his spear upon him in three pieces, from which encounter Diego de Mansilla suffered a very serious reversal of fortune. And he bore a piece of the spear with the spearhead in his arm until he was not quite three paces from the stand where the judges were, at which point he could grasp it no more, and there they removed the spearhead and broken spear from his arm. And upon removing it, a great gush of blood spurted out of his arm, as wine flows from the cask when the spigot is turned, from which the knight Diego de Mansilla fainted. And do not be amazed that a man who saw this, riding a mare outside the lists next to the judges' stand, fell to the ground unconscious, and it took about half an hour for him to regain consciousness, even though they blocked his nostrils, thinking that something bad had happened to him.[56]

Then all the surgeons arrived there, at the command of the captain, to take his blood and cure the knight Diego de Mansilla, whose colour had greatly changed. And everyone thought that he would not escape alive.

And then the judges declared their deeds of arms completed and they ordered Diego de Mansilla to his pavilion, and likewise the Defender, each of whom left the field and lists through his respective gate. And no trumpets

* avía: avían – ESC.

tocaron ningunas trompetas; antes el capitán por su persona fue luego a la tienda donde Diego de Mansilla se desarmó, e fízolo curar con buena diligencia.

played here; rather the captain then went in person to the pavilion where *Diego de Mansilla* disarmed himself, and he very diligently had him cured.

9.
Monday, 19 July 1434
Pedro de Nava vs. Joan de Camós
[Use of a helm instead of the usual sallet or armet, and a reinforcing piece: Article 1]

9.
Escorial MS f.II.19, fols. 90rv

Lunes siguiente, diez y nueve de jullio.
Pedro de Nava.
Capítulo que fabla de las armas que el ya nonbrado Pedro de Nava
en este día fizo con Johan de Camós, aragonés, antes desto nonbrado.

The following Monday, 19 July.
Pedro de Nava.
Chapter which speaks about the deeds of arms which the aforenamed Pedro de Nava performed on this day with the above named Joan de Camós, from Aragon.

En* el ya nonbrado lunes siguiente, diez y nueve días de jullio, de mañana,† entró en el campo e liça el ya antes desto nonbrado Pedro de Nava, uno de los diez defensores del passo, armado e a cavallo. E de la‡ otra parte contra él, Juan de Camós, ya antes desto dicho, vezino de Barcelona, assimesmo armado e a§ cavallo. E como fueron dentro en el campo e liça, pusieron sus lanças en los riestres, e movieron el uno contra el otro con ardideza de cavallería.

On the aforesaid following Monday, 19 July, in the morning, the aforenamed Pedro de Nava, one of the ten Defenders of the passage of arms, entered the field and lists, armed and on horseback. And on the other side opposite him, the aforenamed Joan de Camós, a resident of Barcelona, likewise armed and on horseback. And now that they were inside the field and lists, they placed their spears in the rests, and they charged against each other with chivalric verve.

E a esta primera carrera encontró Pedro de Nava a Juan de Camós en el guardabraço yzquierdo, e verdugó la lança. E non rompió nin tomó ninguno dellos revés.

And in this first course Pedro de Nava struck Joan de Camós on the left pauldron, and the spear bowed.[57] And it did not break, nor did either one of them suffer a reversal of fortune.

E passaron otras dos carreras que non se encontraron, salvo en la una dellas que barrearon las lanças.

And they ran another two courses in which they did not encounter, except that in one of them they barricaded the spears.

A las quatro carreras encontró Pedro de Nava a Juan de Camós en cabo del guardabraço yzquierdo,¶ e de allí sortió e diole en la bavera,

In the fourth course Pedro de Nava struck Joan de Camós on the top of the left pauldron, and from there it glanced off and hit him in the bevor, and the spearhead blunted and he broke

---

* *En*: omit – *BMP.*
† *de mañana*: luego de mañana – *BMP, RAH.*
‡ *E de la*: E a la – *BMP.*
§ *a*: omit – *RAH.*
¶ *yzquierdo*: omit – *BMP.*

e despuntó el fierro e rompió su lança por[*] dos partes. E tomó Juan de Camós un buen revés.

A las[†] cinco carreras encontró Pedro de Nava a Juan de Camós[‡] en la charnela[§] del almete, de guisa que le fizo tomar un gran revés, de que fue atordido un rato[¶] por la liça, sin romper lança.

A las seis carreras encontró Pedro de Nava a Juan de Camós en el guardabraço yzquierdo un poco, sin romper lança.

A las siete carreras que passaron, encontró Pedro de Nava a Juan de Camós en el guardabraço yzquierdo, e desortió[**] de allí e diole en la bavera, e fízole tomar un gran revés, e desguarnecióle el guardabraço, sin rromper lança.

A las ocho carreras encontró Pedro de Nava a Juan de Camós en el peto del piastrón, que por muy poco le[††] passara, e rrompió su lança en él en dos pedaços. E fue forçado de desarmar[‡‡] Juan de Camós para adereçar el piastrón, e como fue adereçado, tornóse armar.

A las nueve carreras que pasaron, encontró Pedro de Nava a Juan de Camós en el piastrón, e falleció muy poco que non lo[§§] falsó por derecho del coraçón, e rompió su lança en él por tres partes, e fízole tomar un gran[¶¶] revés.

E aquí[***] fueron cumplidas sus armas. E los juezes diéronlas por complidas, e mandáronles que se fuesen a sus tiendas. E luego Pedro de

his spear in two. And Joan de Camós suffered quite a reversal of fortune.

In the fifth course Pedro de Nava struck Joan de Camós on the charnel of the helm,[58] in such a way that he made him suffer a serious reversal of fortune, from which he was dazed for a while in the lists, without breaking the spear.

In the sixth course Pedro de Nava struck Joan de Camós lightly on the left pauldron, without breaking the spear.

In the seventh course which they ran, Pedro de Nava struck Joan de Camós on the left pauldron, and glanced off there and hit him in the bevor, and he made him suffer a serious reversal of fortune, and he ripped off his pauldron, without breaking the spear.

In the eighth course Pedro de Nava struck Joan de Camós on the reinforcing breastplate,[59] which he almost would have pierced, and he broke his spear in two upon him. And Joan de Camós was forced to disarm in order to mend the reinforcing breastplate, and when it was mended, he rearmed.

In the ninth course which they ran Pedro de Nava struck Joan de Camós on the reinforcing breastplate, and only just missed piercing it directly over the heart, and he broke his spear upon him in three pieces, and he made him suffer a serious reversal of fortune.

And at this point their deeds of arms were completed. And the judges declared them completed, and they ordered them to go to their pavilions. And then Pedro de Nava

---

[*] *por: en – RAH.*

[†] *A las: E a las – RAH.*

[‡] *a Juan de Camós: omit – BMP.*

[§] *charnela: caravela, struck through and emended to charnela – RAH.*

[¶] *un rato: omit – BMP.*

[**] *desortió: sortió – BMP, RAH.*

[††] *le: lo – BMP, RAH.*

[‡‡] *de desarmar: de se desarmar – BMP, RAH.*

[§§] *lo: le – BMP.*

[¶¶] *gran: grande – RAH.*

[***] *E aquí: En que – BMP.*

Nava combidó a cenar a Juan de Camós, e salieron del campo e fuéronse a sus tiendas.

E aquí no cumple que mucho fable el autor, que todos los que estas armas leyeren, que amos a dos fizieron, darán la ventaja a Pedro de Nava, pues cada carrera encontró, e todas tres lanças rompió en Juan de Camós. E bien parece que [a]* Juan de Camós non le quiso al presente ayudar la ventura, comoquiera que passava sus carreras con buena voluntad.

invited Joan de Camós to dinner, and they left the field and went to their pavilions.

And it does not behove the author to talk much here, for everyone who may read these deeds of arms which they both performed will give the advantage to Pedro de Nava, for he made the encounter in each course, and broke all three spears on Joan de Camós. And it truly seems that at present good fortune refused to help Joan de Camós, though he did run his courses most willingly.

10.
Escorial MS f.II.19, fols. 96v–97r

Lope de Stúñiga.
Capítulo que fabla de las armas que el ya nonbrado honrrado cavallero Lope de Stúñiga fizo en este nonbrado viernes, de mañana, con Juan de Villalobos, de la conpañía de Gutier Quixada antes desto nonbrado.

10.
Friday, 23 July 1434
Lope de Stúñiga vs. Juan de Villalobos
[Jousting saddles versus war saddles; the Principle of Equality]

Lope de Stúñiga.
Chapter which speaks about the deeds of arms which the aforenamed honourable knight Lope de Stúñiga performed this said Friday, in the morning, with Juan de Villalobos, on the aforementioned Gutierre Quijada's team.

En el ya nonbrado viernes a veinte e tres de jullio, luego† de mañana, entró en el campo e liça el ya nonbrado noble cavallero Lope de Stúñiga, uno de los diez defensores de aquel passo,‡ armado e a cavallo. E estovo esperando un gran rrato a que viniese cavallero que fiziesse con él. E assí, estando esperando, llegó de la otra parte contra él, a cavallo e armado, Juan de Villalobos, ya antes desto dicho, de la compañía de Gutier Quixada. E como fueron dentro en el campo, pusieron sus lanças [en los ristres],§ e movió¶ muy reciamente el uno contra el otro, como cavalleros que bien parecían de ardides coraçones.

On the aforesaid Friday, 23 July, later that morning, the aforenamed noble knight Lope de Stúñiga, one of the ten Defenders of that passage of arms, entered the field and lists, armed and on horseback. And he stood waiting a good while for a knight to come and perform deeds of arms with him.[60] And thus, standing there waiting, the aforesaid Juan de Villalobos, on Gutierre Quijada's team, came to the other side opposite him. And now that they were inside the field, they placed their spears in the rests, and they charged against each other very vigorously like knights who truly seemed to be of passionate hearts.

---

* *a*: omitted in the MSS.
† *luego*: omit – *BMP*.
‡ *de aquel passo*: del passo – *BMP, RAH*.
§ *en los riestres*: omit – *ESC*; en los ristres – *BMP, RAH*.
¶ *movió*: movieron – *BMP, RAH*.

E a esta primera carrera encontró Lope de Stúñiga en el pescuezo del cavallo de* Juan de Villalobos, cerca de las crines, e fízole una comunal ferida, e rrompió su lança en él. E Juan de Villalobos encontró por cerca del pescueço del cavallo, e rrasgólle los paramentos, e de allí topó† en la chapa della, la de la silla, e de allí sortió al basto en medio de la silla, a lo hueco que está encima de la cruz del cavallo. E allí rrompió su lança, e quedó el fierro con un poco del hasta en la silla, que por muy poquito‡ falleció que non ferió§ tan bien el cavallo del otro tan bien como el suyo. E como fue ferido su cavallo, non quiso más fazer en él, e demandó licencia a los juezes para que le pudiesen traer otro cavallo. E los juezes mandáronlo assí. E¶ en tanto que ge lo truxeron, estuvo esperando Lope de Stúñiga en el campo, armado.

E como fue traído el cavallo, passaron otra carrera que non se encontraron.

E los juezes vieron que era ya** ora de comer e que havía entrellos debate sobre una silla de justa muy alta e fuerte, e muy boltados†† los arçones traseros, qu'el dicho Juan de Villalobos traýa. Mandáronles que saliesen del campo e se fuesen a comer, e que después tornarían a cumplir sus armas. E ellos assí lo fizieron.

And in this first course Lope de Stúñiga struck Juan de Villalobos' horse in the neck, near the mane, and he inflicted a fair-sized wound, and he broke his spear on it. And Juan de Villalobos struck near the neck of Lope de Stúñiga's horse, and he tore its caparison, and from there he attainted on the steel, the saddle steel, and from there skated down to the saddle pad in the middle of the saddle, in the space over the horse's withers. And he broke his spear there, and the spearhead with a piece of the shaft bit on the saddle, so that it barely missed injuring his opponent's horse as much as his own had been injured. And since Juan de Villalobos' horse was injured, he did not wish to perform more deeds of arms on it, and he requested permission from the judges that they allow him to be brought another horse. And the judges ordered it so. And while it was brought to him, Lope de Stúñiga stood waiting in the field, armed.

And when the horse was brought, they ran another course in which they did not encounter.

And the judges saw that it was now time to eat lunch and that there was a debate going on between them about a very high and sturdy jousting saddle, and with amply vaulted rear arçons, which said Juan de Villalobos was using. They ordered them to leave the field and go and eat, and that they could return to complete their deeds of arms afterwards. And this is what they did.[61]

---

* *de: a – RAH.*

† *topó: tocó – BMP, RAH.*

‡ *poquito: poco – BMP; poco*, struck through and emended to *poquito – RAH.*

§ *ferió: rompió*, struck through and emended to *ferió – RAH.*

¶ *E:* omit *– BMP.*

** *era ya: ya era – BMP.*

†† *e fuerte, e muy boltados: e fueron muy boltados – BMP.*

E dixieron los juezes que ellos le* dezían e mandavan a Juan de Villalobos que non truxese† más aquella silla, que non era de guerra, e en‡ los capítulos de§ Suero se contenía que las armas se fiziessen en arnés¶ de guerra, e sin vantaja ninguna. E que pues havía vantaja en la silla quél trabýa, que [si diessen]** lugar a quél fiziesse armas en ella, que por ellos non sería guardada la ygualdad que prometido tenían. E que por ende, queriéndoles guardar ygualdad, que non davan nin darían lugar a que más fiziessen él ni otro en aquella silla. E si las armas quería†† acabar, que echase en su cavallo otra silla que fuese de guerra; si no, que no le darían lugar a las acabar.

E por Lope de Stúñiga les fue respondido que conociese la avantaja que trabýa en la silla, e que [a él]‡‡ plazía de fazer con él. E el dicho Juan de Villalobos dixo que la non conocería, nin faría sino con aquella silla con que havía començado. E a esto respondió Lope de Stúñiga, e dixo que pedía de merced a los juezes que le dexasen complir sus armas en aquella silla, e que non dezía en aquella, mas aún si ciento pudiesse poner encima de su cavallo que fuesen más fuertes que aquélla, que las pusiese, que él faría las armas con él, e aún con otro si viniese.

E los juezes, deque vieron la voluntad de§§ Lope, dieron lugar a que fiziesse con él en aquella silla, e con condición que otro ninguno non fiziese más armas en ella en aquel passo,¶¶ que lo non consentirían.

E luego todos fueron a comer.

And the judges said that they declared and ordered that Juan de Villalobos not use that saddle any more, for it was not a war saddle, and in Suero's Articles it was stated that the deeds of arms be performed in war harness, and without any advantage. And that since there was an advantage in the saddle he was using, if they allowed him to perform deeds of arms in it, they would not be ensuring the equality that they had promised to maintain. And that therefore, in the interests of ensuring equality, they did not, nor ever would, allow him – or anyone else – to perform more deeds of arms in that saddle. And if he wished to finish the deeds of arms, he should put another saddle on his horse that was a war saddle; otherwise, they would not allow him to finish them.

And the reply Lope de Stúñiga gave them was that he recognised the advantage Juan de Villalobos had by using the saddle, and that it pleased him to perform deeds of arms with him. And said Juan de Villalobos said that he would not recognise it, nor would he perform deeds of arms in any other saddle but that one in which he had started. And Lope de Stúñiga responded to this, and he said that he besought the judges to allow Juan de Villalobos to complete his deeds of arms in that saddle; and not only that, but even if he were allowed to put a hundred saddles on his horse which were sturdier than that one, let him put them on, for he would perform deeds of arms with him, and also with anyone else if they stepped forward.

And the judges, when they saw Lope's pertinacity, allowed Juan de Villalobos to perform deeds of arms with Lope de Stúñiga in that saddle, and on condition that no-one else perform further deeds of arms in it in that passage of arms, for they would not permit it.

And then they all went to lunch.

---

* *le: les – BMP.*

† *truxese: trajesen – BMP.*

‡ *en: omit – BMP.*

§ *de: del – BMP.*

¶ *en arnés: en armas – BMP; con armas*, struck through and emended to *en arnés – RAH.*

** *si diessen: se diesse – BMP, ESC; si diessen – RAH.*

†† *quería: querían – RAH.*

‡‡ *a él: al – BMP, ESC; a él – RAH.*

§§ *de: del – BMP.*

¶¶ *passo: campo – BMP, RAH.*

11.

Escorial MS f.II.19, fols. 97rv

Capítulo que fabla [de]* cómo los suso
nonbrados Lope de Stúñiga e Juan de
Villalobos entraron otra vez en el campo en†
este día, en la tarde, a cumplir sus armas que
de antes havían començado.

Después desto, en este ya nonbrado viernes,
después de comer, en la tarde, e después que los
debates de la silla fueron fenecidos, tornaron al
campo e liça los ya nonbrados Lope de Stúñiga,
defensor, e de la otra parte por aventurero,
Juan de Villalobos.

En esta‡ primera carrera que pasaron,
puestas sus lanças en los rriestres – que son
aquí ya tres carreras con las dos que antes de
comer havían andado – encontró Juan de
Villalobos a Lope de Stúñiga en la guarda del
guardabraço ezquierdo, e falsógela y echógela§
en el suelo, sin romper lança ni tomar ninguno
dellos rreveses.¶

E passaron otras tres carreras que non se
encontraron.

A las siete carreras encontró Lope de
Stúñiga a Juan de Villalobos en la falda del
guardabraço izquierdo, e diole un tan gran
golpe que por muy poco lo falsara, e despuntó el
fierro en él, e quedó la punta en el guardabraço,
e rompió su lança por cabe el fierro.

A las** ocho carreras encontró Juan de
Villalobos en la oreja del cavallo de†† Lope
de Stúñiga, e fízole sangre, e de allí salió e

11.

Friday, 23 July 1434
Lope de Stúñiga vs. Juan de Villalobos
[Jousting saddles versus war saddles;
the Principles of Equality and Pulchritude]

Chapter which speaks about how the above-
mentioned Lope de Stúñiga and Juan de
Villalobos once again entered the field on this
day, in the afternoon, to complete their deeds
of arms which they had begun earlier.

After this, on this aforesaid Friday, after lunch,
in the afternoon, and after the debates about
the saddle had come to an end, the aforenamed
Lope de Stúñiga, Defender, and on the other
side as Answerer, Juan de Villalobos, returned
to the field and lists.

In this first course which they ran, their
spears placed in the rests – which with the
two courses they had ridden before lunch
now makes three – Juan de Villalobos struck
Lope de Stúñiga on the left gardbrace, and he
pierced it and cast it to the ground, without
breaking the spear or either one of them
suffering reversals of fortune.

And they ran another three courses in which
they did not encounter.

In the seventh course Lope de Stúñiga
struck Juan de Villalobos on the edge of the
left pauldron, and he dealt him such a mighty
blow[62] that he almost would have pierced it,
and the spearhead blunted on it, and the point
gained a purchase on the pauldron, and he
broke his spear near the spearhead.

In the eighth course Juan de Villalobos
struck Lope de Stúñiga's horse on the ear,
and he made it bleed, and continued from
there and went on to strike Lope de Stúñiga

---

* fabla de: fabla – BMP, ESC; fabla de – RAH.
† en: omit – BMP.
‡ En esta: A esta – BMP; E desta – RAH.
§ echógela: hechóla – BMP.
¶ rreveses: revés – BMP, RAH.
** A las: E a las – BMP, RAH.
†† de: a – BMP.

fuele encontrar* en el arandela, e non rompió lança. E Lope de Stúñiga encontró a Juan de Villalobos en la guarda de la manopla izquierda, e derribógela sin romper lança. E por quanto Juan de Villalobos havía fecho sangre en el cavallo de Lope, e Lope havía encontrado a él en pieça de arnés, contáronla a Lope por rompida aquella lança.

E assí fueron acabadas de romper todas tres lanças, e fueron cumplidas sus armas. E luego los juezes les mandaron que se fuesen a sus tiendas. E antes que saliesen del campo, Lope de Stúñiga combidó a cenar a Juan de Villalobos, según la costunbre del paso, e fuéronse a sus tiendas.

E el auctor non cura de fablar mucho en este fecho de estas armas que estos dos cavalleros fizieron este día, por quanto él era presente a las ver fazer, e vio que los encuentros que fizieron el uno al otro que non eran muy fermosos en quanto† regla de cavallería. E esto piensa: que fueron menguando sus esfuerços, salvo que la ventura‡ en este caso non los quiso ayudar.

on the rondel, and he did not break the spear. And Lope de Stúñiga struck Juan de Villalobos on the reinforce of the left gauntlet, and he knocked it off without breaking the spear, And since Juan de Villalobos had made Lope's horse bleed, and Lope had struck him on a piece of the harness, they counted that as a spear broken for Lope.[63]

And thus they were finished breaking all three spears, and their deeds of arms were completed. And then the judges ordered them to go to their pavilions. And before they left the field, Lope de Stúñiga invited Juan de Villalobos to dinner, according to the custom of the passage of arms, and they went to their pavilions.

The author does not think of speaking much about this deed of arms which these two knights performed this day, since he was present to see them being performed, and he saw that the encounters they each made were not very becoming in so far as the law of chivalry is concerned. And this is what he thinks: that they were not performing to their abilities, notwithstanding the fact that good fortune in this case refused to help them.

---

* *fuele encontrar: fuele a encontrar* – BMP.
† *en quanto: en quanto a* – BMP.
‡ *ventura: ventaja*, struck through and emended to *ventura* – RAH.

12.

Friday, 23 July 1434
Suero de Quiñones vs.
Gonzalo de Castañeda
[The Principle of Pulchritude;
on wounding one's opponent:
cp. Menaguerra, ch. 13; above, Article 3]

12.

Escorial MS f.II.19, fols. 98rv

Capitán mayor.
Capítulo que fabla de las armas que el
honrrado cavallero Suero de Quiñones,
capitán mayor de aquel paso, fizo la terçera
vez, con Gonzalo de Castañeda.

The Senior Captain.
Chapter which speaks about the deeds of
arms which the honourable knight Suero
de Quiñones, senior captain of that passage
of arms, performed for the third time, with
Gonzalo de Castañeda.[64]

Después[*] desto, en este ya nonbrado viernes,
veinte e tres de jullio, en la tarde, por quanto
el muy honrrado cavallero Suero de Quiñones,
defensor e capitán mayor del passo, haviendo
oýdo dezir la buena fama de cavallería en
que se havía visto el ya antes desto nonbrado
Gonçalo de Castañeda, e como era recio
home de armas, e todas las más vezes que
armas havía fecho havía levado lo mejor, quiso
fazer aquel día armas con él. E vino al campo
armado e a cavallo, e assimesmo vino luego
el dicho Gonçalo de Castañeda armado e a
cavallo.[†] E como fueron amos a dos[‡] dentro en
el campo, pusieron sus lanças en los rriestres, e
movieron amos e dos el uno contra el otro muy
reciamente, como cavalleros que bien parecía
que non era aquella la primera vez que en armas
se havían visto, e assimesmo como aquellos que
gran voluntad mostravan de se delibrar el uno
al otro.

After this, on this aforementioned Friday, 23
July, in the afternoon, the very honourable
knight Suero de Quiñones, Defender and
senior captain of the passage of arms, having
heard tell of the great fame of the chivalric
deeds[65] in which the aforenamed Gonzalo
de Castañeda had been involved, and how he
was a robust man-at-arms, and all the other
times that he had performed deeds of arms
he had carried the advantage, he insisted on
performing deeds of arms with him that day.
And he came to the field armed and on horseback, and likewise then the said Gonzalo de
Castañeda came armed and on horseback. And
now that they were both inside the field, they
placed their spears in the rests, and they both
charged against each other very vigorously, like
knights for whom it truly seemed that that was
not the first time that they had been involved
in deeds of arms, and likewise like those who
showed a great desire to match strength with
each other.

E a esta primera carrera dio un tan gran
encuentro el honrrado cavallero Suero de
Quiñones a Gonçalo de Castañeda en el
guardabraço yzquierdo, en la falda dél, en
derecho del coraçón, que por muy poco lo
falsara, e despuntó el fierro, e quedó la punta

And in this first course the honourable
knight Suero de Quiñones dealt such a mighty
blow upon Gonzalo de Castañeda on the left
pauldron, on the inner edge of it, directly over
his heart, that it almost would have pierced it,
and the spearhead blunted, and the point bit

---

[*] *Después: E después – BMP.*

[†] *e assimesmo vino luego el dicho Gonçalo de*
    Castañeda armado e a cavallo: omit – RAH.

[‡] *amos a dos: amos e dos – RAH.*

en él, e rompió su lança fasta tres palmos cerca del fierro.[*]

E passaron otras dos carreras que non se encontraron, salvo en una[†] dellas que barrearon las lanças.

A las quatro carreras que movían el uno contra el otro, e yendo por la liça adelante volvióse el cavallo de Suero de Quiñones e paróse en meitad de la carrera, e Gonzalo de Castañeda, non qurando[‡] de cortesía que deviera guardar, e alçar la lança, no la alçó. E púsogela por entre el volante de las platas y el arçón delantero de la silla, e a la buelta que dio su cavallo rrompió la lança de Gonzalo por medio, sin tocar con el fierro en pieza de arnés ningun[a].[§]

A las çinco carreras encontró el honrrado cavallero Suero de Quiñones a Gonçalo de Castañeda en el cañón del braçal derecho, e sortió dél por debaxo de la guarda, e pasóle el fierro por meitad de los morcillos del braço e falsógelo, e ansimesmo falsó el braçal, e passóle el fierro quanto un palmo con el asta de la otra parte, e fízole una grande ferida. E rrompió su lança en él, e lebó el troçón de la lança con el fierro fasta que fue descavalgar a su tienda.

E como los juezes vieron esta ferida tan peligrosa, dieron las armas por cumplidas, e antes que de la liça e campo saliesen,[¶] Gonçalo de Castañeda estando ya ferido dixo a altas vozes que él se havía visto en muchos lugares tan peligrosos, e más que aquél, fiziendo armas, e nunca cavallero ni gentilhome que

on it, and he broke his spear three palms below the spearhead.

And they ran another two courses in which they did not encounter, except that in one of them they barricaded the spears.

In the fourth course they were charging against each other, and as he was going forward down the lists, Suero de Quiñones' horse turned and stopped in the middle of the course, and Gonzalo de Castañeda, not thinking of the courtesy which he should observe and raise the spear, did not raise it. And he thrust it in between the reinforcing piece[66] and the front arçon of the saddle, and when his horse rode past, Gonzalo's spear broke in half, without the spearhead touching a single piece of Suero's harness.

In the fifth course the honourable knight Suero de Quiñones struck Gonzalo de Castañeda on the upper cannon of the right vambrace, and it glanced off it beneath the couter wing, and the spearhead passed through the middle of the biceps of his arm and pierced it, and likewise it pierced the vambrace, and the spearhead with a palm's length of the broken spear pierced through to the other side and inflicted a gaping wound. And Suero de Quiñones broke his spear upon Gonzalo de Castañeda, and Gonzalo de Castañeda bore the piece of spear with the spearhead in his arm until he went to dismount at his pavilion.[67]

And when the judges saw a wound as dangerous as this they declared the deeds of arms complete, and before they could leave the lists and the field, Gonzalo de Castañeda being already wounded, said out loud that he had been involved in many such dangerous situations, and more dangerous than that one, performing deeds of arms, and no knight or gentleman who had performed deeds of arms with him had ever carried the advantage from him, with the exception now of Suero de

---

[*] *del fierro: del fierro, e quedó la punta en él*, with *e quedó la punta en él* struck through – *RAH*.

[†] *en una: en la una* – *RAH*.

[‡] *qurando: acatando* – *BMP*.

[§] *ninguna: ninguno* – *ESC, RAH; ninguna* – *BMP*.

[¶] *saliesen: saliese* – *BMP; saliesen*, with the *-n* struck through – *RAH*.

con él hiziesse havía lebado lo mejor dél, sino entonce Suero de Quiñones, capitán e defensor mayor de aquel paso, [pero]* que pues assí era, e a Dios plazía que por tal vía fuese ferido, que le plazía que era ferido de mano de tan noble cavallero como él era.

E entonce dixo el honrrado cavallero† Suero de Quiñones que dava muchas gracias a Dios por ello, e mandó luego a los çurujanos que fuesen a curar dél, según‡ lo tenía§ por costumbre con todos los otros cavalleros e gentileshomes que en¶ aquel campo e liça havían sido o fuesen feridos.

E luego los juezes les mandaron que se fuessen a sus tiendas.

E en estas armas que estos cavalleros** fizieron este día, non cumple que el auctor mucho hable, que bien parece a todos los que lo vieron, e assimesmo los que lo leyeren, quel honrrado cavallero Suero de Quiñones lebó lo mejor. E parece que la ventura que Gonçalo de Castañeda solía tener†† consigo que le fue contraria este día.

Quiñones, captain and principal Defender of that passage of arms, but that since it was thus, and it pleased God that he was wounded in this way, he was pleased that he was wounded by the hand of such a noble knight as Suero was.

And then the honourable knight Suero de Quiñones said that he gave much thanks to God for this, and then he ordered the surgeons to go and attend to Gonzalo de Castañeda, as was their custom with all the other knights and gentlemen who had been or would be wounded in that field and those lists.

And then the judges ordered them to go to their pavilions.

And it does not behove the author to talk much about these deeds of arms which these knights performed this day, for it seems obvious to all those who saw it, and likewise to those who may read it, that the honourable knight Suero de Quiñones carried the advantage. And it seems that the good fortune that Gonzalo de Castañeda used to have on his side was against him on this day.

---

* *pero: para – ESC; pero – BMP, RAH.*
† *cavallero: omit – BMP, RAH.*
‡ *según: e según – BMP.*
§ *tenía: tenían – BMP.*
¶ *en: dentro en – BMP.*
** *estos cavalleros: estos dos cavalleros – BMP, RAH.*
†† *tener: tener, struck through and emended to traer – RAH.*

13.
Escorial MS f.II.19, fols. 105rv

Pedro de los Ríos.
Capítulo de las armas que el ya nonbrado
Pedro de los Ríos, en este nonbrado* viernes,
fizo con Alfonso Quixada, de la compañía de
Gutier Quixada antes desto nonbrado.

Después† desto, este dicho viernes, entró en el
campo e liça Pedro de los Ríos, uno de los diez
defensores de aquel paso, armado e a cavallo. E
de la otra parte contra él, Alfonso Quixada, de
la compañía del ya nonbrado Gutier Quixada,
ansimesmo armado e a cavallo. E como fueron
dentro en el campo, pusieron sus lanças en los
riestres, e movieron el uno contra el otro de
muy buenas continencias.

E a esta primera carrera encontró Pedro de
los Ríos a Alfonso Quixada en el arandela, e
falsóla por tal manera que le rrasgó un poco‡
del jubón cerca del sobaco, e non hizo sangre, e
rrompió su lança en él en dos partes.

E luego como esta carrera passaron,
tomaron otras lanças más gruesas, e passaron
otra carrera con ellas que non se encontraron.

A las tres carreras encontró Pedro de los
Ríos a Alfonso Quixada en la guarda del
guardabraço yzquierdo, e despuntó el fierro, e
qued[ó]§ la punta en él. E rompió su lança en
pieças, sin tomar ninguno rrevés.

E passaron otra carrera que non se
encontraron.

13.
Friday, 23 July 1434
Pedro de los Ríos vs. Alfonso Quijada
[On reaffixing armour:
cp. Menaguerra, ch. 19]

Pedro de los Ríos.
Chapter about the deeds of arms which the
aforenamed Pedro de los Ríos, on this said
Friday, performed with Alfonso Quijada, on
the aforenamed Gutierre Quijada's team.

After this, on this said Friday, Pedro de los
Ríos, one of the ten Defenders of that passage
of arms, entered the field and lists, armed and
on horseback. And on the other side, opposite him, Alfonso Quijada, on the aforenamed
Gutierre Quijada's team, likewise armed and
on horseback. And now that they were inside
the field, they placed their spears in the rests,
and they charged against each other with great
composure.

And in this first course Pedro de los Ríos
struck Alfonso Quijada on the rondel, and he
pierced it in such a way that he tore his jupon
slightly near the armpit, and he did not draw
blood, and he broke his spear upon him in two
pieces.

And after they ran this course, they took
other, thicker spears, and they ran another
course with them in which they did not
encounter.

In the third course Pedro de los Ríos struck
Alfonso Quijada on the left gardbrace, and
blunted the spearhead, and the point bit on
it. And he broke his spear into pieces, without
either one suffering a reversal of fortune.

And they ran another course in which they
did not encounter.

---

* *este nonbrado: este ya nombrado – RAH.*
† *Después: E después – BMP.*
‡ *un poco: un pedaço – RAH.*
§ *quedó: queda – ESC; quedó – BMP, RAH.*

A las* cinco carreras encontró Pedro de los Ríos a Alfonso Quixada en la bavera, e non rompió lança, comoquier que tomó un poco revés Alfonso Quixada.

E passaron otra carrera que non se encontraron.

A las siete carreras encontró Pedro de los Ríos a Alfonso Quixada en la guarda† del guardabraço yzquierdo, e non rrompió lança.

E passaron otras tres carreras que non se encontraron.

A las onze carreras encontró Pedro de los Ríos a Alfonso Quixada en el guardabraço yzquierdo, e desguarneciógelo, e de allí sortió e tocóle un poco en la bavera, por tal manera que se hovo de adreçar el guardabraço. E non rronpió lança ninguno dellos.

Como‡ fue§ armado, a las doze carreras encontró Pedro de los Ríos a Alfonso Quixada, e diole un tan gran golpe en el guardabraço yzquierdo, e¶ por muy poco lo falsara, e rrompió su lança en él por tres partes.

E aquí fueron cumplidas sus armas, e los juezes mandáronles que se fuesen a sus tiendas. E Pedro de los Ríos conbidó luego a cenar a Alfonso Quixada, según la costunbre del paso, como huvieron alçadas las caras de los almetes e se conocieron.

El auctor dize aquí, por quanto era presente al fazer destas armas, que da lo mejor a Pedro de los Ríos, por quanto rrompió todas las tres lanças en el otro. E Alfonso Quixada que le pareció que la ventura que lo tenía olvidado en aquella ora, según por la [esperiencia]** de sus armas parece.

In the fifth course Pedro de los Ríos struck Alfonso Quijada on the bevor, and he did not break the spear, although Alfonso Quijada did suffer a slight reversal of fortune.

And they ran another course in which they did not encounter.

In the seventh course Pedro de los Ríos struck Alfonso Quijada on the left gardbrace, and he did not break the spear.

And they ran another three courses in which they did not encounter.

In the eleventh course Pedro de los Ríos struck Alfonso Quijada on the left pauldron, and he ripped it off him, and the spear glanced off from there and attainted Alfonso Quijada lightly on the bevor, in such a way that he had to repair the pauldron. And neither one of them broke a spear.

When Alfonso Quijada was armed, in the twelfth course Pedro de los Ríos struck him, and he dealt such a mighty blow upon the left pauldron, and almost would have pierced it, and he broke his spear upon it in three pieces.

And at this point their deeds of arms were completed, and the judges ordered them to go to their pavilions. And Pedro de los Ríos then invited Alfonso Quijada to dinner, according to the custom of the passage of arms, when they had raised the visors of the helmets and they recognised each other.

The author says here, since he was present when these deeds of arms were being performed, that he gives the advantage to Pedro de los Ríos, since he broke all three spears upon the other man. And it seemed like good fortune had forgotten Alfonso Quijada at that time, as it would appear from the exercise of his arms.

---

* *A las*: *E a las* – *BMP*.

† *guarda*: *bavera*, struck through and followed by *guarda* – *BMP*.

‡ *Como*: *E como* – *BMP*.

§ *fue*: *fuesse* – *RAH*.

¶ *e*: *que* – *BMP*.

** *esperiencia*: *escriptura* – *ESC, RAH*; *esperiencia* – *BMP*.

14.
Escorial MS f.II.19, fols. 105v–106v

Sábado siguiente, veinte e quatro de jullio.
Gómez de Villacorta.
Capítulo que fabla de las armas que el ya
nonbrado Gómez de Villacorta hizo en este
nonbrado sábado de mañana con Bueso de
Solís, de la compañía de Gutier Quixada
antes desto nonbrado.

En el ya nonbrado sábado siguiente, veinte e
quatro días del ya* dicho jullio, en la mañana,
entró en el campo e liça Gómez de Villacorta,
uno de los diez defensores nonbrados del paso,
armado e a cavallo. E de la† otra parte contra
él, Bueso de Solís, de la conpañía de Gutier
Quixada, asimesmo armado e a cavallo. E
dentro en el canpo, pusieron sus lanças en los
riestres a guisa de buenos‡ cavalleros.

E [passaron]§ cinco carreras que non se
encontraron.

E después desto, luego, estando dentro en el
campo el dicho Bueso, sin rrequerir antes que
en el campo entrase, haviendo pasado ya las
cinco carreras, quitó el guardabraço derecho,
diziendo que havía de fazer sin él con Gómez
de Villacorta. E como el dicho Gómez supo
que havía quitado el guardabraço, luego quitó
el semejante guardabraço suyo. E como los
juezes vieron que havían quitado¶ aquellas
pieças, tomaron gran saña de amos a dos, en
especial de Bueso, que lo havía empeçado,
por quanto no tenía la hordenança de los
capítulos del ya nonbrado Suero, e assimesmo,

14.
Saturday, 24 July 1434
Gómez de Villacorta vs. Bueso de Solís
*[On defying the rules and
amending the Articles]*

The following Saturday, 24 July.
Gómez de Villacorta.
Chapter which speaks about the deeds of
arms which the aforenamed Gómez de
Villacorta performed this said Saturday
morning with Bueso de Solís, on the
aforenamed Gutierre Quijada's team.

On this aforesaid following Saturday, the
twenty-fourth day of the aforesaid July, in the
morning, Gómez de Villacorta, one of the ten
aforenamed Defenders of the passage of arms,
entered the field and lists, armed and on horseback. And on the other side, opposite him,
Bueso de Solís, on Gutierre Quijada's team,
likewise armed and on horseback. And inside
the field, they placed their spears in the rests
like good knights.

And they ran five courses in which they did
not encounter.

And then, after this, when said Bueso was
already inside the field, without petitioning
before he entered the field, having already run
the five courses, he removed the right pauldron, saying that he had to perform deeds of
arms without it with Gómez de Villacorta.
And when said Gómez realised that Bueso
de Solís had removed the pauldron, he then
removed his own corresponding pauldron.
And when the judges saw that they had
removed those pieces, they took great umbrage
at both of them, especially at Bueso, who had
started it, since he was not following the decree
in the Articles by the aforenamed Suero,[68]
and likewise, because they were not keeping

---

* *ya*: omit – BMP.
† *E de la: E a la* – BMP.
‡ *buenos: muy buenos* – BMP.
§ *passaron: pusieron* – ESC; *passaron* – BMP,
RAH.
¶ *quitado: quitando* – BMP.

porque* no tenía[n]† la fe que les havían dado. E luego mandaron al rrei de armas e faraute que presentes eran, que fuesen por ellos e los traxiessen allí, delante del‡ cadafalso donde ellos estavan. E luego los traxieron allí, e como allí fueron, los juezes les mandaron que luego tornasen a poner sus guardabraços; si non, que si los non§ pusiesen, que los mandarían echar del campo luego. E que quando qualquier pieça de arnés quisiesse cada uno dellos quitar, que la pudían¶ quitar antes que en** el campo e liça entrasen.

E cada uno dellos compeçaron a porfiar por fazer sin las piezas. E aún fizieran†† en jubones, según las voluntades mostravan, si los dexaran, pero todavía se huvieron de tornar armar,‡‡ según los juezes les mandaron. E salvándose el dicho Bueso, que si la condición de los capítulos supiera, que quitara aquella pieza antes§§ que en el campo entrara.

E como fueron armados, passaron otras tres carreras que¶¶ non se encontraron.

A las nueve carerras encontró Gómez de Villacorta a Bueso de Solís en el guardabraço yzquierdo, e diole un tan gran golpe en él que por muy poco lo falsara, e despuntó el fierro de la lança, e quedó en él la punta, e rrompió su lança por dos partes.

E passaron otra carrera que non se encontraron.

the oath which they had given to them. And then they ordered the king-of-arms and herald who were present to go and get them and bring them there, before the stand where they were. And then they brought them there, and when they were there, the judges ordered them to put their pauldrons back on; otherwise, if they did not put them on, they would immediately order them to be sent off the field. And whenever either one of them wished to remove a piece of the harness, they could only do so before they entered the field and lists.

And each one of them began to argue so as to perform deeds of arms without the pieces. And they would even have performed them in their jupons, as their intentions showed, if they would have let them, but they still had to put their armour back on, as the judges ordered them. And said Bueso saved face by saying that had he known about the condition of the Articles, he would have removed that piece before he had entered the field.

And now that they were armed, they ran another three courses in which they did not encounter.

In the ninth course Gómez de Villacorta struck Bueso de Solís on the left pauldron, and he dealt him such a mighty blow that he almost would have pierced it, and the spearhead blunted, and the point bit on it, and he broke his spear in two pieces.

And they ran another course in which they did not encounter.

---

* porque: por quanto, struck through and emended to porque – RAH.

† tenía[n]: tenían – BMP, RAH; tenía – ESC.

‡ del: al – BMP.

§ si los non: si non los – BMP.

¶ pudían: podrían – RAH.

** que en: que dentro en – RAH.

†† fizieran: fazerían – BMP.

‡‡ tornar armar: tornar a armar – BMP.

§§ antes: antes antes – ESC.

¶¶ que: e – BMP.

A las once carreras encontró Gómez de Villacorta a Bueso de Solís en el arandela, e falsógela, e así con el arandela como del encuentro de la lança, tocó en el guardabraço derecho, e desguarneciógelo, e rrompió su lança. E Bueso encontró a Gómez de Villacorta en el guardabraço derecho, e desguarneciógelo, e rompió su lança en dos pedaços, sin tomar ninguno dellos rrevés.

E aquí fueron complidas sus armas, e los juezes mandaron[*] que se fuesen a sus tiendas, e luego alçaron las caras de los almetes, e conocidos el uno al otro, Gómez de Villacorta conbidó a cenar a Bueso de Solís, según la constunbre del passo.

E aquí dize el auctor, por quanto era presente, que vio que andavan de muy buenas continencias e con esforçados coraçones, según pareció,[†] pero que da avantaja[‡] a Gómez de Villacorta, por quanto rrompió dos lanças en Bueso de Solís, e Bueso en él non más de una.

E fuéronse a sus tiendas.

Grida.

Luego[§] en aquella mesma ora, en saliendo del campo aquellos dos cavalleros, mandaron los juezes al rei de armas e faraute que presentes eran, que fiziesen esta Grida[¶] que se sigue, e dixeron assí, a altas vozes:

'Que ningún cavallero ni gentilhome non fuese osado de embiar a los juezes embaxada ninguna, salvo si fuese por los ya nonbrados rrei de armas e faraute e[**] persavante alguno; si no, que supiesen que non les sería recebida en ninguna manera, por las faltas que dello havían nacido o podían nacer.'

In the eleventh course Gómez de Villacorta struck Bueso de Solís on the rondel, and he pierced it, and as with the rondel, and because of the stroke with the spear, he hit the right pauldron, and ripped it off him, and broke his spear. And Bueso struck Gómez de Villacorta on the right pauldron, and he ripped it off him, and broke his spear in two, without either one of them suffering a reversal of fortune.[69]

And at this point their deeds of arms were completed, and the judges ordered them to go to their pavilions, and then they raised the visors of the helmets, and each one having recognised the other, Gómez de Villacorta invited Bueso de Solís to dinner, according to the custom of the passage of arms.

And here says the author, since he was present, that he saw that they were riding with great composure and with strenuous hearts, so it seemed, but he gives the advantage to Gómez de Villacorta, since he broke two spears upon Bueso de Solís, and Bueso no more than one upon him.

And they went to their pavilions.

Criee.[70]

At that very moment, as those two knights were leaving the field, the judges ordered the king-of-arms and the herald who were present to make the following Criee, and they said the following out loud:

'That no knight or gentleman should dare to send any messages to the judges, except through the aforenamed king-of-arms and herald and any of the pursuivants;[71] otherwise, they should know that the message would in no way be acknowledged, because of the misunderstandings that had arisen or that could arise because of this.'

---

[*] *mandaron: mandáronles – BMP, RAH.*
[†] *pareció: parecerían – BMP.*
[‡] *avantaja: la ventaja – BMP.*
[§] *Luego: E luego – BMP, RAH.*
[¶] *Grida: Guarda – BMP.*
[**] *e: o – BMP.*

15.
Escorial MS f.II.19, fols. 107v–108v

Diego de Baçám.
Capítulo que fabla de las armas que el
ya nonbrado Diego de Baçám fizo con el
honrrado cavallero Gutier Quixada ya antes
desto nonbrado.

Luego* en este ya nonbrado sábado, veinte y
quatro de jullio, dos oras poco más o menos
antes de sol puesto, entró en el campo e
liça el honrrado cavallero Diego de Baçán,
ya nombrado antes desto, uno de los diez
defensores de aquel paso, el qual entró armado e
a cavallo. E de la otra parte contra él, asimesmo,
el honrrado cavallero Gutier Quixada, el qual
trayá en pos de sí su estandarte verde con
escaques blancos e azules que eran sus armas,
e su tronpeta tocando delante. E trayá una
espada desnuda en la mano, e venían† con él
Juan de Merlo cavalgando, e otros asaz‡ de
su compañía con él, a pie, en derredor de su
cavallo.

E assí muy honrrosamente entró en el campo
e liça, estándole ya esperando el ya nonbrado
Diego de Baçán en el dicho campo. E como allí
dentro fueron, amos a dos§ pusieron sus lanças
en los rriestres, las quales lanças eran de las
medianas, e movieron el uno contra el otro a
guisa de muy buenos cavalleros, como aquellos
que bien parecía¶ querer mostrar e fazer obra
de cavallería, según el linage donde** venían.
E andava Juan de Merlo sirviendo a Gutier
Quixada a cavallo, e otros dos escuderos a pie.

15.
Saturday, 24 July 1434
Diego de Bazán vs. Gutierre Quijada
[On wounding one's opponent: cp.
Menaguerra, ch. 13; above, Article 3.
On making a dramatic entrance: cp.
Menaguerra, the School of Jousting]

Diego de Bazán.
Chapter which speaks about the deeds
of arms which the aforenamed Diego de
Bazán performed with the aforementioned
honourable knight Gutierre Quijada.[72]

Later on this aforementioned Saturday, 24
July, more or less two hours before sundown,
the aforementioned honourable knight Diego
de Bazán, one of the ten Defenders of that
passage of arms, entered the field and lists
armed and on horseback. And likewise on
the other side opposite him, the honourable
knight Gutierre Quijada, who carried behind
him his standard *vert* with lozenges *argent* and
azure which were his arms, and his trumpeter
marching ahead, sounding his instrument.
And he carried an unsheathed sword in his
hand, and Juan de Merlo was accompanying
him on horseback, and many others from his
team, on foot, surrounding his horse.

And thus very honourably he entered the
field and lists, in which field the aforenamed
Diego de Bazán was already awaiting him.
And now that they were inside, they both
placed their spears in the rests, which spears
were of medium size, and they charged against
each other like very good knights, like those
who truly looked like they wished to exhibit
and perform deeds of chivalry, as befitting
their lineage. And Juan de Merlo was riding
as the servant of Gutierre Quijada, along with

---

* *Luego: E luego – BMP.*
† *venían: venía – BMP, RAH.*
‡ *asaz: más – BMP.*
§ *amos a dos: amos et dos – BMP, RAH.*
¶ *parecía: parecían, emended to parecía – RAH.*
** *donde: de donde – BMP.*

E assimesmo andava* con Diego de Baçán don Juan de Benavente, e otros dos gentileshomes a pie.†

E a esta primera carrera, e a la segunda, non se encontraron.

A las tres carreras encontró Diego de Baçám a Gutier Quixada por debaxo del guardabraço derecho, e rresgóle el falso peto por encima del honbro, e la camisa, e un poco de la carne, por tal vía que le fizo‡ sangre, e desguarnecióle el [guarda]braço§ e rrompió su lança por cerca de un palmo del asta con el fierro, e lebó el troçón de la lança puesto por encima del honbro hasta en cabo de la liça. E todos pensaron que yva más ferido de lo que fue. E Gutier Quexada encontró a Diego de Baçám en el guardabraço yzquierdo, e diole un tan gran golpe que por muy poco ge lo falsara, e rompió su lança en él en dos pedaços. E assí de su encuentro, como del que le dio Diego de Baçám, tomó Gutier Quixada un comunal revés.

A las¶ quatro carreras encontró Gutier Quixada a Diego de Baçám en el guardabraço yzquierdo, e rompió su lança en él en pieças. E Diego de Baçám encontró a Gutier Quexada en el guardabraço yzquierdo, e non rompió lança, ni tomó ninguno dellos revés. E aquí cumplieron sus armas.

E luego los juezes les mandaron que se fuesen a sus tiendas. E alçaron las caras de los almetes, e como se conocieron combidó Diego de Baçám** a Gutier Quixada a cenar, según la costumbre del paso. E luego se fueron a sus tiendas.

two other squires on foot. And likewise Juan de Benavente was riding with Diego de Bazán, along with two other gentlemen on foot.

And in this first course, and the second, they did not encounter.[73]

In the third course Diego de Bazán struck Gutierre Quijada beneath the right pauldron,[74] and slashed the arming-doublet over the shoulder, and the shirt,[75] and a bit of the flesh, in such a way that he made him bleed, and he ripped his pauldron off and broke his spear almost a palm's length of the shaft from the spearhead, and Gutierre Quijada bore the piece of the spear over his shoulder up to the head of the lists. And everyone thought that he was more injured than he actually was. And Gutierre Quijada struck Diego de Bazán on the left pauldron, and he dealt him such a mighty blow that he almost would have pierced it, and he broke his spear upon it in two pieces. And thus from the blow he struck, as well as the one that Diego de Bazán dealt upon him, Gutierre Quijada suffered a moderate reversal of fortune.

In the fourth course Gutierre Quijada struck Diego de Bazán on the left pauldron, and he broke his spear into pieces on it. And Diego de Bazán struck Gutierre Quijada on the left pauldron, and he did not break the spear, nor did either of them suffer a reversal of fortune. And at this point they completed their deeds of arms.

And then the judges ordered them to go to their pavilions. And they raised the visors of the helmets, and when they recognised each other Diego de Bazán invited Gutierre Quijada to dinner, according to the custom of the passage of arms. And then they went to their pavilions.

---

  * *andava: andavan – BMP.*
  † *a pie: de a pie – RAH.*
  ‡ *que le fizo: que fizo – RAH.*
  § *guardabraço: braço – ESC; guardabraço –*
    BMP, RAH.
  ¶ *A las: E a las – BMP, RAH.*
  ** *combidó Diego de Baçám: Diego de Baçán*
    combidó – BMP.

E aquí fabla el auctor, e dize que non da la mejoría a uno más que a otro, por quanto vio, estando presente, que amos a dos cavalleros lo fizieron tan bien que non se podiera* mejorar. E si por ventura alguno† de los que leyeren quisiere‡ dar la mejoría a Gutier Quixada por romper dos lanças en Diego de Baçán, deve de parar mientes a§ la una lança que rompió Diego de Baçán en Gutier Quixada, como de aquel encuentro fizo sangre. E aquí cesarán algún tanto los dezidores.

E quando Gutier Quexada se fue para su tienda lebava su espada desnuda en la mano, e acompañado de Juan de Merlo e de otros asaz cavalleros e gentileshomes, e tocando su trompeta delante. E ansí muy honrrosamente llegaron a su tienda. E luego fueron los juezes a catarlo e fallaron que la ferida era pequeña.

E ansimesmo yvan con Diego de Baçám el ya nonbrado Don Juan de Benavente que le servía, e otros asaz gentileshomes, e tocando trompetas delante dél, e ansí honrrosamente¶ llegaron a sus tiendas.**

And here speaks the author, and he says that he gives the advantage neither to one nor to the other, since he saw, being present, that both knights performed so well that there was no room for improvement. And if peradventure someone who may be reading this should wish to give the advantage to Gutierre Quijada for breaking two spears on Diego de Bazán, he should reflect upon the single spear which Diego de Bazán broke on Gutierre Quijada, since in that encounter he drew blood. And the judges shall tarry here for a good while.[76]

And when Gutierre Quijada headed for his pavilion he was carrying his unsheathed sword in his hand, and accompanied by Juan de Merlo and many other knights and gentlemen, and his trumpeter was marching ahead, sounding his instrument. And thus did they arrive very honourably at his pavilion. And then the judges went to examine him and they found that the wound was slight.

And likewise the aforenamed Don Juan de Benavente, who was serving him, and many other gentlemen, went with Diego de Bazán, and the trumpeters marching ahead, sounding their instruments, and thus did they arrive at their pavilions honourably.

---

* *podiera: podía – BMP, RAH.*
† *alguno: algunos – RAH.*
‡ *quisiere: quisieren – BMP, ESC.*
§ *a: omit – RAH.*
¶ *honrrosamente: muy honrrosamente – BMP.*
** *sus tiendas: su tienda – BMP.*

16.
Escorial MS f.II.19, fols. 108v–109r

Capítulo que fabla de cómo [el ya]* nonbrado
cavallero Diego de Baçám tornó al campo,
luego a poca de ora, con Rodrigo Quexada,
antes desto nonbrado, el qual le firió a la sazón
que estas armas fizieron.

Luego a poca de ora, en este ya nonbrado
sábado, tornó al campo el ya dicho honrrado
cavallero Diego de Baçám, armado con las
mesmas armas que antes havía fecho, e a
cavallo. E de la otra parte contra él, Rodrigo
Quexada, de la compañía del ya nonbrado
Gutier Quexada. E como fueron en el campo,
pusieron sus lanças en los riestres a guisa de
buenos† cavalleros, como aquellos que bien
parecía‡ que tenían en voluntad de se delibrar
aýna el uno al otro en aquel fecho de armas.
E movieron el uno contra el otro.

E a [e]sta§ primera carrera non se
encontraron.

A las dos carreras encontró Rodrigo
Quexada a Diego de Baçán por la vista del
elmete, cerca del ojo yzquierdo, e rrompió su
lança en él, e quedóle en la vista un pedaço del
asta con el fierro fasta quatro dedos. E¶ todos
pensaron que era mal ferido de muerte, e tocóle
con el fierro por cerca del ojo e fízole sangre, e
plugo a Dios que non ge lo quebró. E como se
sintió ferido Diego de Baçám, echó mano del
asta con el fierro por la sacar, e non pudo, e
dixo: 'Non es nada. Non es nada.' Comoquiera
que tomó muy** gran rrevés. E Diego de Baçám
encontró a Rodrigo Quixada e diole un tan

* el ya: ya el – ESC; el ya – BMP, RAH.
† buenos: muy buenos – BMP.
‡ parecía: parecían, struck through and
    emended to parecía – RAH.
§ E a esta: E asta – ESC; E a esta – BMP, RAH.
¶ E: Que – RAH.
** muy: un – RAH.

16.
Saturday, 24 July 1434
Diego de Bazán vs. Rodrigo Quijada
[On wounding one's opponent: cp.
Menaguerra, ch. 13; above, Article 3]

Chapter which speaks about how the
aforenamed knight Diego de Bazán returned
to the field, a short while later, with the
aforenamed Rodrigo Quijada, who wounded
Diego de Bazán at the time they performed
these deeds of arms.

A short while thereafter, on this aforementioned Saturday, the aforesaid honourable
knight Diego de Bazán returned to the field,
armed with the same arms that he had used
before, and on horseback. And on the other
side opposite him, Rodrigo Quijada, on the
aforenamed Gutierre Quijada's team. And
now that they were in the field, they placed
their spears in the rests like good knights, like
those who it seemed truly had a desire to match
strength against each other soon in that deed
of arms. And they charged against each other.

And in this first course they did not
encounter.

In the second course Rodrigo Quijada
struck Diego de Bazán through the eye-slit of
the helmet,[77] near his left eye, and he broke
his spear upon him, and four-fingers' length
of the broken spear with the spearhead stuck
in the eye-slit.[78] And everyone thought that
he was fatally injured, and he hit him with the
spearhead near the eye and made him bleed,
and it pleased God that it did not puncture
it. And as soon as Diego de Bazán realised he
was wounded, he grabbed hold of the broken
spear by the spearhead so as to pull it out, and
he could not, and he said: ''Tis nothing. 'Tis
nothing.' He did, however, suffer a very serious
reversal of fortune. And Diego de Bazán struck
Rodrigo Quijada and dealt him such a mighty

gran golpe en el guardabraço yzquierdo que por muy poco ge lo falsara, e fízole tomar un gran revés, e rompió en él su lança en dos partes.

E aquí acabaron de cumplir sus armas, por quanto hovo sangre, e los juezes las dieron por cumplidas, comoquiera que no havían rrompido* más de dos lanças. E mandáronlos yr a sus tiendas, e luego se fue cada uno a su tienda.†

E aquí dize el auctor que da lo mejor deste fecho de armas a Rodrigo Quixada por la sangre que fizo e la lança que rompió tan bien como el otro. E dize que si Diego de Baçám non encontrara a Rodrigo Quexada, [que Rodrigo Quijada]‡ le lançara la lança por el ojo fasta el colodrillo por manera que lo matara.

E§ este día non fizieron más armas por quanto era ya muy noche.

blow upon the left pauldron that he almost would have pierced it, and he made him suffer a serious reversal of fortune, and he broke his spear upon him in two pieces.

And at this point they finished completing their deeds of arms, since blood had been shed, and the judges declared them completed, even though they had broken no more than two spears. And they ordered them to go to their pavilions, and then each one went to his pavilion.

And here the author says that he gives the advantage in this deed of arms to Rodrigo Quijada for the blood that he drew and the spear that he broke as well as the other man. And the author says that, if Diego de Bazán had not struck Rodrigo Quijada, Rodrigo Quijada would have poked the spear through his eye to the back of his neck in such a way that he would have killed him.

And on this day they performed no more deeds of arms since night had long since fallen.

---

* havían rrompido: avían cumplido, struck through and emended to avían rompido – RAH.

† e luego se fue cada uno a su tienda: omit – RAH.

‡ que Rodrigo Quijada: omit – ESC; que Rodrigo Quijada – BMP, RAH.

§ E: omit – BMP.

17.
Escorial MS f.II.19, fols. 109r–110v

Día del bienaventurado apóstol señor
Sanctiago, fue domingo, a veinte e cinco
días del ya nonbrado jullio.
De cómo entró en el campo el capitán este día
sin tres pieças, e de cómo fue detenido.

En el ya nonbrado domingo, a veinte e
cinco días del mes ya dicho de jullio, día del
bienaventurado apóstol* señor Sanctiago –
cuya perdonança e jubileo este año fue, según
que† antes desto la escritura deste libro vos ha
devisado–, en el principio dél, este día, [de]
mañana,‡ llegó al campo e liça donde las armas
se fazían el muy honrrado e famoso cavallero
Suero de Quiñones, defensor e capitán mayor
de aquel paso, según antes desto es declarado.
E la manera como yva armado era ésta: quitada
la cara del elmete, el§ guardabraço yzquierdo
e el piastrón de las platas. E llegó al cadafalso
donde¶ los juezes estavan, e rrei de armas e
faraute. E dixo:

'Señores cavalleros e juezes deste campo:
Plégavos saber que yo mandé a Monrreal,
faraute del rrei nuestro señor, que
presente está, que publicase en la corte
de su muy alta e rreal señoría, a todos los
cavalleros e gentileshomes que allí fuesen,
e a los estrangeros todos que lo quisiesen
saber, que este día presente del ya dicho
bienaventurado   apóstol   Sanctiago,
estaría[n]** en este campo e liça donde las

---

* apóstol: omit – BMP.
† que: omit – BMP, RAH.
‡ día, de mañana: día, mañana – ESC; día, de
   mañana – BMP, RAH.
§ el: et el – BMP, RAH.
¶ donde: en donde – BMP.
** estarían: estaría – BMP, ESC; estarían
   – RAH.

17.
Sunday, 25 July 1434
Suero de Quiñones vs. The Judges
[On removing pieces of armour: cp.
Menaguerra, ch. 1; above, Article 10]

It was the day of the blessed Apostle Saint
James, Sunday, the twenty-fifth day of the
aforenamed month of July.
On how the captain entered the field on this
day missing three pieces of armour, and on
how he was detained.

On the aforementioned Sunday, the twenty-
fifth day of the aforesaid month of July, the day
of the blessed Apostle Saint James – whose
Day of Pardon and Jubilee Year this was,[79] as
the words at the beginning of this book have
informed you –, that morning at daybreak, the
most honourable and famous knight Suero de
Quiñones, Defender and senior captain of that
passage of arms, as is declared above, arrived at
the field and lists where the deeds of arms were
being performed. And the way in which he
was armed was as follows: he had removed the
visor of the helmet, the left pauldron and the
plackart. And he approached the stand where
the judges and the king-of-arms and the herald
were. And he said:

'My lord knights and judges of this field:
May it please you to know that I ordered
Monreal, herald of the king our lord, who
is present, to publish at the court of his
most royal highness, to all the knights
and gentlemen who were there, and to
all of the foreigners who might wish
to know, that on this day of the aforenamed blessed Apostle Saint James, in
this field and these lists where deeds of
arms are being performed, there would
be three knights, each one with a piece
of the harness removed, to wit: one with

armas se fazían, tres cavalleros, cada uno quitada una pieça de arnés,* conbiene a saber: el uno quitada la cara del elmete, e el otro quitado el guardabraço yzquierdo, e el otro quitado el piastrón de las platas, para cada uno dellos correr dos carreras con cada cavallero o gentilhome que allí aquel día viniesse a fazer armas. E yo vos notifico que yo,† Suero de Quiñones, capitán del passo, soi solo estos tres cavalleros'.

E por que lo más conociessen, fízose quitar la bavera, e vieron que era él mesmo. E dixo que él estava presto para cumplir aquello, que por‡ él había sido publicado por el dicho Monrreal, faraute, según antes desto es declarado.

E los juezes rrespondieron que ellos havían bien oýdo lo que él dezía, e assimismo visto en qué manera venía, e que estuviesse quedo, e que haverían su consejo con el rei de armas e faraute que presentes eran, e§ le darían su respuesta. E luego se apartaron los juezes e rey de armas e faraute, e¶ el auctor e escrivano con ellos que presentes eran. E havido su consejo e deliberación sobrello, dixeron a Suero de Quiñones los ya nonbrados juezes:

'Bien sabedes que vós havedes jurado e prometido a fee de cavallero de estar a nuestro mandamiento e hordenança en el fecho de estas vuestras armas contenidas en vuestros capítulos, e más ni menos no queremos que en ellas se faga, porque nos toca a nuestras honrras e peligro de nuestras cabeças. E por quanto en vuestros capítulos non se contiene ni se entiende la semejante cosa que vós queredes fazer, ni a nosotros es dado

the visor of the helmet removed, and the other with the left pauldron removed, and the other with the plackart removed, each one of whom would run two courses against each knight or gentleman who should come here on that day to perform deeds of arms. And I hereby inform you that I alone, Suero de Quiñones, captain of the passage of arms, am these three knights'.

And so that they would recognise him better, he had his bevor removed, and they saw that it was none other than Suero. And he said that he was ready to complete that task, which had been published on his behalf by said Monreal the herald, as is declared above.

And the judges replied that they had certainly heard what he was saying, and likewise they had seen how he was armed, and that he should stay where he was, and that they would take their counsel with the king-of-arms and the herald who were present, and they would give him their reply. And then the judges and king-of-arms and herald, and the author and scribe who were present with them, stepped aside.[80] And having taken their counsel and deliberated over this, the aforementioned judges said to Suero de Quiñones:

'You know very well that you have sworn and promised on your knightly oath to be subject to our command and decree in the matter of these your deeds of arms contained in your Articles, and we wish that neither more nor less be done in these deeds of arms than that which is stated, at the risk of losing our honour and our heads. And in your Articles there is no reference to, nor room for interpretation for such a thing as you wish to do, nor are we invested with such power by

---

* *arnés: armas* – RAH.
† *yo: soy* – BMP.
‡ *por: para* – BMP.
§ *e: que*, struck through and emended to *e* – RAH.
¶ *e:* omit – BMP.

tal poderío por el dicho señor rei para consentir lo que vós queredes fazer, e salides de la hordenança por vós jurada e prometida e por vós al presente tentada a rromper'.

E los juezes, acabando de le dezir esto, decendieron del cadafalso donde estavan, e llegaron a do estava Suero de Quiñones, e otros cavalleros e gentileshomes que con él a pie havían venido, de los quales algunos dellos le tenían el cavallo por las riendas, e dixiéronles que lo dexasen, e dexándolo, los juezes echaron mano de[*] las rriendas del cavallo e dixieron: 'Suero de Quiñones, vós seredes preso'. E mandaron al rei de armas e faraute que le tomasen por las riendas del cavallo e lo levasen preso a su tienda, la qual los juezes le davan por cárcel por todo aquel día, que non saliesse della sin mandamiento dellos. E Suero de Quiñones les respondió[†] que le fazían gran sinrazón e agravio, que pues él lo havía prometido, según havía dicho, que le dexassen cumplir su boto e promesa. E los juezes mandaron todavía al rei de armas e faraute[‡] que lo llevasen preso, según ge lo avía[n][§] mandado, e que non curase[¶] de más razones.

E Suero de Quiñones, deque esto vio que non le consentían fazer lo que quería,[**] empeçóse mucho a[††] agraviar, e dixo al rrei de armas e faraute e escrivanos que presentes eran que ge lo diessen assí por testimonio en la manera e forma que él[‡‡] allí había llegado para cumplir lo que prometido havía, e cómo los juezes non ge lo consintían, ni consintieron, e cómo lo mandavan e mandaron prender sobrello.

the said king our lord to consent to what you wish to do, and you are defying the decree sworn and promised by you and which is being attempted to be broken by you at this time'.

And the judges, as they finished saying this, descended the stand where they were and approached the spot where Suero de Quiñones and other knights and gentlemen who had come with him on foot were standing, some of whom were holding the horse by the reins, and they told them to let it go, and when they let it go, the judges grabbed hold of the horse's reins and said: 'Suero de Quiñones, you shall be taken prisoner'. And they ordered the king-of-arms and the herald to take him by the horse's reins, and to take him prisoner to his pavilion, which the judges made his prison for that entire day, so that he could not leave it without their permission. And Suero de Quiñones answered them that they were doing him a great injustice and injury, for since he had made a promise, as he had said, they should allow him to fulfil his vow and promise. And the judges still ordered that the king-of-arms and herald take him prisoner, as they had ordered them, and that he not think of arguing any more.

And Suero de Quiñones, when he realised that they would not allow him to do what he wished, began to appeal a great deal, and he said to the king-of-arms and the herald and the scribes who were present that they thus serve as his witnesses as to the means and way in which he had come there to fulfil what he had promised, and how the judges considered not allowing him to do it, nor did they allow it, and how they considered ordering, and did order, his arrest because of it. And then, before

---

* *de: a – RAH.*
† *respondió: respondieron, struck through and emended to respondió – RAH.*
‡ *e faraute: omit – BMP.*
§ *avían: avía – ESC; avían – BMP, RAH.*
¶ *curase: curassen – BMP, RAH.*
** *quería: querían, struck through and emended to quería – RAH.*
†† *a: omit – RAH.*
‡‡ *él: omit – BMP, RAH.*

E entonces, antes que del campo lo sacasen, dixo a los juezes que obedecía su mandamiento, pues* ge lo havía† prometido.

E luego lo llevaron preso a su tienda, e començaron a tocar las trompetas e menestriles delante dél. E los juezes mandaron que non tañiesen, si no, que los mandarían tanbién prender a ellos. E como lo llebaron a su tienda, descavalgó de su cavallo, [e]‡ el rrei de armas e faraute diérongela por cárcel, e assimesmo otra tienda donde§ oýa missa, e la sala donde comían, según los juezes lo havían mandado.

E luego Suero de Quiñones dixo al rei de armas e faraute que llegassen¶ a los juezes de su parte, e les dixiessen** quél havría su consejo con cavalleros e gentileshomes que en esto entendían,†† e si‡‡ fallasen que contra su onor era, que él tornaría a fazer las armas que por él eran declaradas, que§§ él sabía bien que allí era venido un cavallero [a] aquel paso non a otra cosa sino a fazer aquellas armas devisadas con él. Por ende, que les pedía por merced que le dexasen correr¶¶ las dos lanças ya devisadas, por que su honor e promessa fuese guardado.

they escorted him out of the field, he told the judges that he would obey their order, since he had promised to do so.

And then they took him prisoner to his pavilion and the trumpeters and minstrels began to march ahead, sounding their instruments. And the judges ordered them to stop playing, otherwise they would order them to be arrested as well. And when they took him to his pavilion, he dismounted his horse, and the king-of-arms and herald delivered him to the pavilion that would be his prison, and likewise another pavilion where he would hear mass, and the dining room, as the judges had ordered.

And then Suero de Quiñones told the king-of-arms and the herald to approach the judges on his behalf, and tell them that he would take his counsel with knights and gentlemen who understood such matters, and if they found that this was an affront to his honour, he would return to perform the deeds of arms that were arranged for him, for he knew very well that one knight had come to that passage of arms for no other reason than to perform those pre-arranged deeds of arms with Suero de Quiñones. Therefore, he besought them to let him run the two courses that were already pre-arranged, so that his honour and his promise would be upheld.

---

* pues: pues que – BMP.
† havía: avían, struck through and emended to avía – RAH.
‡ e: omit – ESC, RAH; e – BMP.
§ donde: que, struck through and emended to donde – RAH.
¶ llegassen: llegasse – RAH.
** dixiessen: dixesse – RAH.
†† que en esto entendían: omit – BMP; que en esto entendiessen – RAH.
‡‡ si: assí, struck through and emended to si – RAH.
§§ que: et que – RAH.
¶¶ correr: correr con él – BMP, RAH.

E el rei de armas e faraute fueron luego con esta embaxada a los juezes,[*] según Suero ge lo havía dicho, e dixiérongelo como él lo[†] havía mandado. E los juezes brevemente le respondieron que tal licencia non la darían, e que por demás le era porfiar más en esta razón, e donde otros cavalleros e gentileshomes estavan armados para fazer las armas que ante eran acostumbradas a fazer. Los dichos juezes, con gran saña que tenían de aquel fecho que Suero de Quiñones quería fazer tan peligroso, en todo aquel día non consintieron que ninguno fiziesse armas, e fuéronse a sus tiendas, e mandaron al rei de armas e faraute que fuessen luego a Juan de Merlo e Gutier Quexada e les dixiessen de su parte que si estavan armados algunos[‡] de su compañía, que se desarmasen, e que huviessen buena paciencia, porque aquel día que estavan enojados, por tal manera que non podían bien ver el fazer de las armas aquel día, ni darían lugar a ello. E que les rogavan que parasen mientes que era domingo, e más día del apóstol Santiago.

E Juan de Merlo e Gutier Quixada les respondieron que, pues ellos havían prometido de estar a hordenança e mandamiento dellos, así como juezes que eran de aquel campo, que les plazía de buena voluntad de los complazer e estar a su mandamiento en esto.

And the king-of-arms and herald then went to the judges with this message,[81] just as Suero had told it to them, and they told it to them as he had ordered. And the judges briefly responded that they would not grant him such licence, and that it was in vain for him to persist further in this argument, and at a time when other knights and gentlemen were armed, waiting to perform the deeds of arms that they were accustomed to doing before this. The said judges took such great umbrage about that deed of arms which Suero de Quiñones wished to make so dangerous, that for the rest of that day they did not allow anyone to perform deeds of arms, and they went to their pavilions, and they ordered that the king-of-arms and the herald go forthwith to Juan de Merlo and Gutierre Quijada and tell them on their behalf that if any of their team-members were armed they should disarm themselves, and that they should have great patience, because that day they were vexed, to such an extent that they could not properly watch deeds of arms that day, nor would they allow it. And they entreated them to reflect upon the fact that it was Sunday, and moreover Saint James the Apostle's day.

And Juan de Merlo and Gutierre Quijada answered them that, since they had promised to be subject to their decree and command, as the judges that they were of that field, it pleased them willingly to oblige them and be at their command in this matter.

---

[*] *con esta embaxada a los juezes: a los juezes con esta embaxada – BMP.*

[†] *lo: omit – BMP.*

[‡] *algunos: o algunos – BMP.*

18.

Escorial MS f.II.19, fols. 113r–114r

Capítulo que fabla [de]* cómo luego a poco
de ora bolvió al campo e liça el ya nonbrado
Pedro de Nava a fazer armas con Diego
Çapata, de la compañía del honrrado cavallero
Gutier Quixada ya nonbrado.

Luego este dicho día, a poca† de ora, tornó
al campo e liça el honrrado Pedro de Nava,
assí armado e a cavallo como havía salido del
campo. E de la otra parte contra él, Diego
Çapata, de la compañía de Gutier Quixada,
assimismo armado e a cavallo. E amos a dos
dentro en el campo e liça donde las armas se
fazían, pusieron‡ sus lanças en los riestres,
e movieron amos a dos§ el uno contra el otro
muy reciamente.

E a esta primera carrera¶ encontró Pedro
de Nava a Diego Çapata en la guarda de la
manopla esquierda e abollógel[a]** un poco, e
rompió su lança en él por dos partes. E Diego
Çapata non lo encontró a él.

E passaron otras quatro carreras que non
se encontraron, salvo en la una dellas que
barrearon las lanças.

A las seis carreras encontró Pedro de Nava
a Diego Çapata un poco en el guardabraço
yzquierdo, e non rompió lança.

18.

Monday, 26 July 1434
Pedro de Nava vs. Diego Zapata
[War saddles versus jousting saddles;
the Principle of Equality]

Chapter which speaks about how a short
while later the aforenamed Pedro de Nava
returned to the field and lists to perform
deeds of arms with Diego Zapata, on the
aforenamed honourable knight Gutierre
Quijada's team.[82]

A short while later on this day the honourable Pedro de Nava returned to the field and
lists, armed and on horseback in the same
way as he had left the field. And on the other
side opposite him, Diego Zapata, on Gutierre
Quijada's team, likewise armed and on horseback. And now that they were both in the field
and lists where the deeds of arms were being
performed, they placed their spears in the
rests, and they both charged against each other
very vigorously.

And in this first course Pedro de Nava
struck Diego Zapata on the reinforce of the
left gauntlet and dented it slightly, and he
broke his spear upon him in two pieces. And
Diego Zapata did not make the encounter
with him.

And they ran another four courses in which
they did not encounter, except that in one of
them they barricaded the spears.

In the sixth course Pedro de Nava struck
Diego Zapata a little on the left pauldron, and
he did not break the spear.

---

* *fabla de: fabla – ESC; fabla de – BMP, RAH.*

† *poca: poco – RAH.*

‡ *pusieron: omit – BMP; e pusieron – ESC,*
  RAH.

§ *amos a dos: amos et dos – BMP, RAH.*

¶ *E a esta primera carrera: E en estas primeras*
  carreras – BMP.

** *abollógela: abollógelo – ESC; abollógela –*
  BMP; doblógela – RAH.

E passaron otra carrera que non se encontraron.

A las* ocho carreras encontró Pedro de Nava a Diego Çapata en el arandela, e non rompió lança.

E assimesmo, a las nueve carreras, encontró Pedro de Nava otra vez en el arandela a Diego Çapata,† e non rompió lanza.

A las diez carreras fizo dos caladas Diego Zapata, e non se encontraron.

E a las onze carreras non se encontraron, pero que‡ barrearon las lanças.

E passaron otra carrera que non se encontraron.

A las§ treçe carreras encontró Pedro de Nava a Diego Çapata en la manopla yzquierda, de partes de dentro, e fízole un poco de sangre, e encobrióla fasta❡ después que ge la vieron. Comoquiera que fue poca cosa.

E passaron otra carrera que** non se encontraron.

E luego traxieron otro cavallo a Diego Çapata, por quanto el cavallo en que fazía non andava a su voluntad.

A las quince carreras encontró Pedro de Nava a Diego Çapata en el guardabraço derecho, e despuntó el fierro, e quedó un poco de la punta en él, e rompió su lança en tres†† partes.

E pasaron otras tres carreras que non se encontraron.

And they ran another course in which they did not encounter.

In the eighth course Pedro de Nava struck Diego Zapata on the rondel, and he did not break the spear.

And similarly, in the ninth course, Pedro de Nava struck Diego Zapata once again on the rondel, and he did not break the spear.

In the tenth course Diego Zapata swooped the spear twice, and they did not encounter.

In the eleventh course they did not encounter, but they did barricade the spears.

And they ran another course in which they did not encounter.

In the thirteenth course Pedro de Nava struck Diego Zapata on the left gauntlet, on the inner parts,[83] and he made him bleed a little, and Diego Zapata concealed it until it was seen afterwards. Even so, it was a minor thing.

And they ran another course in which they did not encounter.

And then they brought another horse to Diego Zapata, since the horse he was riding was not doing his bidding.[84]

In the fifteenth course Pedro de Nava struck Diego Zapata on the right pauldron, and the spearhead blunted, and the point bit on it slightly, and he broke his spear into three pieces.

And they ran another three courses in which they did not encounter.

---

* *A las: E a las – BMP.*
† *Pedro de Nava otra vez en el arandela a Diego Çapata: Pedro de Nava a Diego Çapata otra vez en el arandela – BMP.*
‡ *que: porque – BMP; omit – RAH.*
§ *A las: E a las – BMP, RAH.*
❡ *fasta: fasta que, emended to fasta – RAH.*
** *que: y – BMP.*
†† *tres: quatro – RAH.*

A las[*] diez e nueve carreras encontró Pedro de Nava a Diego Çapata en el arandela e doblógela toda sin ronper lança.

A las veinte carreras encontró Pedro de Nava a Diego Çapata en la calva del elmete, e fízole tomar un comunal rrevés, e non rompió lança, pero despuntó el fierro. E Diego Çapata encontró a Pedro de Nava en el guardabraço yzquierdo, e diole un tan gran golpe que por poco ge lo falsara, e rompió su lança en él por[†] dos partes, e fízole tomar un comunal revés.

E aquí fueron cumplidas sus armas. E luego los juezes e rei de armas decendieron del cadafalso, e como decendieron fueron requeridos por parte de Pedro de Nava que catasen[‡] a Diego Çapata si venía ligado. E[§] ellos luego lo fueron a[¶] catar, e fallaron que traýa metidos los estrivos con las aciones por la cincha[**] a manera de ligadura, e assimesmo traýa borrenas en los arçones çagueros de la silla, de lo qual non traýa cosa alguna Pedro de Nava. E los juezes dixieron luego a Gutier Quixada, por quanto Diego Çapata era de su compañía, que non havía fecho bien en le consentir de traer aquello allí, pues sabía que ninguno de los defensores non[††] traýa ninguna[‡‡] ligadura. E que le mandavan al dicho Gutier Quixada que non consintiese a ninguno de su compañía que traxiesse ligadura ninguna, sino que supiese que en meitad del campo le farían descabalgar al que lo tal traxiesse e[§§] lo echarían dél,[¶¶] mal pareciendo.

In the nineteenth course Pedro de Nava struck Diego Zapata on the rondel and bent the whole thing in half without breaking the spear.

In the twentieth course Pedro de Nava struck Diego Zapata on the brow reinforce of the helmet, and he made him suffer a moderate reversal of fortune, and he did not break the spear, but the spearhead blunted. And Diego Zapata struck Pedro de Nava on the left pauldron, and he dealt him such a mighty blow that he almost would have pierced it, and he broke his spear in two upon him, and he made him suffer a moderate reversal of fortune.

And at this point their deeds of arms were completed. And then the judges and king-of-arms descended the stand, and as they descended they were petitioned at the behest of Pedro de Nava to check if Diego Zapata was riding tied. And they then went to check this, and they found that he had inserted his stirrups and stirrup leathers through the cinch as a means of tying them, and likewise he had bolsters on the rear arçons of the saddle, none of which did Pedro de Nava have. And the judges then said to Gutierre Quijada, since Diego Zapata was on his team, that he had not acted well by allowing him to do that there, since he knew that none of the Defenders was riding with any ties. And they ordered said Gutierre Quijada not to allow any members of his team to use any ties, but that he should know that they would make anyone who used such things dismount in the middle of the field and they would send him off, for being out of order.

---

 [*] *A las: E a las* – *BMP, RAH.*

 [†] *en él por: en* – *BMP.*

 [‡] *catasen: curassen,* struck through and emended to *catasen* – *RAH.*

 [§] *E:* omit – *BMP.*

 [¶] *a:* omit – *BMP, RAH.*

[**] *cincha: cincha forarda* – *BMP; cinta foradada,* struck through and emended to *cincha foranda* – *RAH.*

[††] *non:* omit – *BMP.*

[‡‡] *ninguna:* omit – *BMP.*

[§§] *e: que* – *BMP.*

[¶¶] *dél: del campo,* with *campo* struck through – *BMP.*

E Gutier Quixada dixo que le plazía de estar a su mandamiento dellos en esto.

E luego alçaron las caras de los elmetes Pedro de Nava e Diego Çapata, e allí se conocieron. E luego Pedro de Nava conbidó a cenar a Diego Çapata, según la costunbre del paso. E luego los juezes mandáronlos yr a sus tiendas.

E aquí non cumple que mucho fable el auctor, que bien parece a todos los que leyeren e* oyeron† el fazer destas armas, que Pedro de Nava levó lo mejor dellas.

And Gutierre Quijada said that he would be pleased to be at their command on this issue.

And then Pedro de Nava and Diego Zapata raised the visors of the helmets, and at that time they recognised each other. And then Pedro de Nava invited Diego Zapata to dinner, according to the custom of the passage of arms. And then the judges ordered them to go to their pavilions.

And here it does not behove the author to say much, for it seems right to all those who may read and who heard about the performance of these deeds of arms, that Pedro de Nava took the advantage in them.

19.
Escorial MS f.II.19, fols. 114v–115r

Sancho de Ravanal.
Capítulo que fabla de las armas que el ya nonbrado Sancho de Ravanal, en este lunes en la tarde, fizo con Alfonso de Cabedo, de la compañía de Gutier Quixada.

Después‡ desto, en este ya nonbrado lunes, a veinte e seis de jullio, a la ora de las víspras, entró en el canpo e liça a fazer armas Sancho de Ravanal, uno de los diez defensores de aquel§ passo ya nonbrado, armado e a cavallo. E de la otra parte contra él, Alfonso Quevedo,¶ de la compañía de Gutier Quixada, asimismo armado e a cavallo. E como fueron dentro en el campo donde las armas se acostunbravan fazer, pusieron sus lanças en los rriestres a guisa de gentileshomes, e movieron amos a dos rreciamente el uno contra el otro.

19.
Monday, 26 July 1434
Sancho de Rabanal vs. Alfonso de Cabedo
[On striking the horse: cp. Menaguerra, ch. 30; above, Articles 16–17]

Sancho de Rabanal.
Chapter which speaks about the deeds of arms which the aforenamed Sancho de Rabanal, this Monday afternoon, performed with Alfonso de Cabedo, on Gutierre Quijada's team.

After this, on this aforesaid Monday, 26 July, at the hour of vespers,[85] Sancho de Rabanal, one of the ten Defenders of that aforenamed passage of arms, entered the field and lists to perform deeds of arms, armed and on horseback. And on the other side opposite him, Alfonso Cabedo, on Gutierre Quijada's team, likewise armed and on horseback. And now that they were inside the field where the deeds of arms were customarily performed, they placed their spears in the rests like gentlemen, and they both charged vigorously against each other.

---

* *e: e, struck through and emended to o – RAH.*
† *oyeron: oyeren – BMP.*
‡ *Después: E después – BMP.*
§ *de aquel: del – BMP.*
¶ *Alfonso Quevedo: Alfonso de Cabedo – BMP, RAH.*

E passaron dos carreras que non se encontraron.

A las tres[*] carreras encontró Alfonso de Cabedo en el pezcueço del cavallo de Sancho de Ravanal, e atrabesógelo de parte a parte, e salió mucha sangre dél, e rompió su lança. E Sancho de Ravanal encontró [a][†] Alfonso de Cabedo en la bavera, e fízole tomar un comunal revés, e non rrompió lança, pero por dar[‡] el encuentro feo que Alfonso dio en el cavallo, contaron a Sancho la lança por ronpida, según la condición de los capítulos que sobre esta empresa se fizieron. E truxieron otro cavallo a Sancho.

A las quatro carreras encontró Alfonso de Cabedo a Sancho de Ravanal en el guardabraço yzquierdo, e despuntó el fierro en él sin rromper lança nin tomar ninguno dellos revés. E Sancho non encontró deste camino.

A las cinco carreras encontró Sancho de Ravanal en las ancas del cavallo de Alfonso de Cabedo, e rrompióle los paramentos, e fizo sangre un poco en el cavallo. E Alfonso de Cabedo encontró a Sancho un poco encima del guardabraço ezquierdo, e non rrompió lança, e por quanto Sancho havía fecho sangre en su cavallo, contaron a Alfonso de Cabedo la lança por rrompida.

E passaron otras cinco carreras que non se encontraron.

A las doze carreras encontró Alfonso de Cabedo a Sancho de Ravanal en el guardabraço yzquierdo, e desguarneciógelo sin romper lança ni tomar ninguno dellos revés.

E passaron otra carrera que non se encontraron.

A las catorze carreras encontró Sancho de Ravanal a Alfonso de Cabedo en la bavera, e derribógela en el suelo sin romper lança, e

And they ran two courses in which they did not encounter.

In the third course Alfonso de Cabedo struck Sancho de Rabanal's horse in the neck, and he pierced it from one side to the other, and a lot of blood flowed out of it, and he broke his spear.[86] And Sancho de Rabanal struck Alfonso de Cabedo on the bevor, and he made him suffer a moderate reversal of fortune, and he did not break the spear, but for dealing the foul stroke which Alfonso dealt upon the horse,[87] they counted Sancho's spear as broken, according to the condition of the Articles that were drawn up for this emprise. And another horse was brought to Sancho.

In the fourth course Alfonso de Cabedo struck Sancho de Rabanal on the left pauldron, and the spearhead blunted on it without breaking the spear or either one of them suffering a reversal of fortune. And Sancho did not make an encounter in this course.

In the fifth course Sancho de Rabanal struck Alfonso de Cabedo's horse on the rump, and tore its caparison, and made the horse bleed a little. And Alfonso de Cabedo struck a little high on the left pauldron, and he did not break the spear, and since Sancho had made Alfonso's horse bleed, they counted Alfonso de Cabedo's spear as broken.

And they ran another five courses in which they did not encounter.

In the twelfth course Alfonso de Cabedo struck Sancho de Rabanal on the left pauldron, and he ripped it off him without breaking the spear or either one of them suffering a reversal of fortune.

And they ran another course in which they did not encounter.

In the fourteenth course Sancho de Rabanal struck Alfonso de Cabedo on the bevor and he knocked it to the ground without breaking the spear, and Alfonso de Cabedo suffered a moderate reversal of fortune. And the judges

* tres: quatro – BMP.
† a: omit – ESC; a – BMP, RAH.
‡ dar: omit – BMP.

tomó Alfonso de Cabedo un comunal revés.
E mandaron los juezes, por quanto era ya muy
noche e non se vían los encuentros, que saliesen
del campo e se fuesen a sus tiendas, e que otro
día martes de mañana que tornasen al campo a
cumplir sus armas.

E luego alçaron las caras de los elmetes e
conociéronse, e conbidó Sancho de Ravanal a
Alfonso de Cabedo a cenar, según la costunbre
del paso. E luego se fueron a sus tiendas.

E aquí el auctor non cura de fablar mucho
en estas armas que estos dos gentileshomes
fizieron este* día, por quanto vio, siendo él
presente a ellas, que las non fizieron tan bien
como primeramente lo mostravan, según los
encuentros antes desto devisados.

ordered, since night had long since already
fallen and the encounters could not be seen,
that they leave the field and go to their pavilions, and that they should return to the field
on Tuesday morning to complete their deeds
of arms.

And then they raised the visors of the
helmets and they recognised each other, and
Sancho de Rabanal invited Alfonso de Cabedo
to dinner, according to the custom of the
passage of arms. And then they went to their
pavilions.

And here the author does not think of
speaking much about these deeds of arms
which these two gentlemen performed this day,
since he saw, being present at them, that they
did not perform them as well as they demonstrated earlier, in the encounters described
previously.

20.
Wednesday, 28 July 1434
Suero de Quiñones vs. Juan de Merlo
*[A difficult judgement. On lacerations caused
by the lance: cp. Menaguerra, ch. 18.
On wounding one's opponent:
cp. Menaguerra, ch. 13; above, Article 3]*

20.
Escorial MS f.II.19, fols. 120v–122v

Capitán mayor.
Capítulo que fabla† de las armas que el
ya nonbrado Suero de Quiñones, capitán
mayor del‡ paso, la quarta§ vez hizo con el ya
nonbrado honrrado cavallero Juan de Merlo.

Luego en este ya nonbrado día miércoles,
veinte y ocho de jullio, acabados estos debates
e embaxadas, llegó al campo e liça donde
las armas se hazían el honrrado e famoso

The Senior Captain.
Chapter which speaks about the deeds
of arms which the aforenamed Suero de
Quiñones, Senior Captain of the passage
of arms, performed for the fourth time,
with the aforenamed honourable knight
Juan de Merlo.[88]

Later on this aforementioned Wednesday, 28
July, at the conclusion of these discussions and
embassies, the honourable and famous knight
Suero de Quiñones, Defender and senior
captain of that passage of arms, arrived at the

---

* *este: en este – RAH.*
† *que fabla: omit – BMP.*
‡ *del: de aquel – BMP.*
§ *quarta: tercera, struck through and emended
   to quarta – RAH.*

cavallero* Suero de Quiñones, defensor e capitán mayor de aquel paso, armado e a cavallo, el qual llevava sobre las armas una camisa blanca con unas ruedas de sancta Catalina brosladas en ella. E de la otra parte contra él, el famoso e esforçado cavallero Juan de Merlo antes desto en este libro ya nonbrado. E muy honrrosamante amos a dos† llegaron al campo, con trompetas e menestriles, como cavalleros que eran merecedores de aquello e de mucho más. E como fueron dentro en el campo, amos e dos pusieron sus lanças en los rriestres, las quales eran de las más gruesas que allí havían,‡ como a guisa de cavalleros que bien parecía que eran diestros en armas, e amos a dos§ movieron muy reciamente el uno contra el otro, como aquellos que bien parecía⁋ que querían aína delibrar aquellas armas.

E a esta primera carrera barrearon las lanças.

A las dos carreras encontró el honrrado cavallero Suero de Quiñones al honrrado e famoso cavallero Juan de Merlo en el guardabraço yzquierdo, e non ronpió lança.

A las** tres carreras encontró Suero de Quiñones a Juan de Merlo en la guarda del braçal yzquierdo, e diole un tan gran golpe que ge lo†† falsó, e rronpió su lança en él por la meitad. [E Juan de Merlo encontró a Suero de Quiñones en la mitad]‡‡ del piastrón, e de allí sortió e fue ferido en los morcillos del braço derecho, e hovo dos llagas, e non se supo si fue ferido de los clavos del gocete de su lança que él

field and lists where the deeds of arms were being performed, armed and on horseback, wearing over his armour a white chemise[89] with Catherine Wheels embroidered on it. And on the other side opposite him, the famous and strenuous knight Juan de Merlo, who has been mentioned before in this book. And both of them arrived very honourably at the field, with trumpeters and minstrels, like knights who were worthy of all that and of much more. And now that they were inside the field, they both placed their spears in the rests, which were of the thickest kind that there were,[90] like knights who truly looked like they were skilled in arms, and they both charged very vigorously against each other, like men who truly looked like they wished to match strength soon in those deeds of arms.

And in this first course they barricaded the lances.

In the second course the honourable knight Suero de Quiñones struck the honourable and famous knight Juan de Merlo on the left pauldron, and he did not break the spear.

In the third course Suero de Quiñones struck Juan de Merlo on the left couter wing, and he dealt him such a mighty blow that he pierced it, and broke his spear in half on him. And Juan de Merlo struck Suero in the middle of the plackart, and it skated off there and he was wounded in the biceps of the right arm, and he had two wounds, and it was not known if he was wounded by the spikes[91] of the grapper of his spear which he had broken

---

* el honrrado e famoso cavallero: omit – BMP.

† amos a dos: amos et dos – BMP, RAH.

‡ havían: avía – BMP; avían, struck through and emended to avía – RAH.

§ amos a dos: amos et dos – BMP, RAH.

⁋ parecía: parecían – RAH.

** A las: E a las – BMP, RAH.

†† ge lo: ge la – BMP, RAH.

‡‡ E Juan de Merlo encontró a Suero de Quiñones en la mitad: omit – ESC; E Juan de Merlo encontró a Suero de Quiñones en la mitad – BMP, RAH; E Merlo encontró a él en medio – Pineda (ed. Riquer, p. 127).

havía ronpido en Juan de Merlo – por quanto quebró su gocete–* o si fue del fierro de la lança de Juan de Merlo, o de la racha de la lança que Juan de Merlo en él rompió.

E assí fue rompida la lança de Juan de Merlo en rachas, comoquiera que entonces non se supo como Suero era ferido, que lo encubrió, por† tal manera que non se pudo saber dende a ciertos días. E luego Suero de Quiñones, como estos encuentros fueron passados, enbió dezir a‡ Don Pedro de Acuña, que allí con él andava sirviéndole, que dixiesse a Juan de Merlo que supiesse que él havía entrado en el campo con él§ al fazer¶ de** las armas con la mano derecha desencasada, e que esto fiziera por fazer armas con tan buen cavallero e diestro en armas como él era. E que agora, de los encuentros que él havía fecho, que se le havía otra vez desencasada†† la mano, por tal vía que en ninguna manera la lança non podía tener con ella. Por ende, que le rogava que, pues bien havía[n]‡‡ fecho sus armas, aunque una lança quedava por rromper, que amos a dos juntamente demandasen licencia a los juezes para que fuesen a sus tiendas e diesen sus armas por cumplidas, pues él al presente non las podía fazer, pero que si todavía quisiese porfiar, que él faría con él sin lança, que en ninguna manera non tenía mano para la traer.

E el dicho Juan de Merlo, como oyó las palabras que le dixo Don Pedro de partes§§ de Suero de Quiñones, dixo que le plazía, pero que le rogava de partes de su dama que mandase

on Juan de Merlo – since he broke his grapper –, or if it was from the spearhead of Juan de Merlo's spear, or from the splinter of the spear which Juan de Merlo broke on him.

And thus Juan de Merlo's spear was shattered into splinters; however, at that time it was not known that Suero was wounded, for he concealed it, in such a way that it was not revealed until some days later.[92] And then Suero de Quiñones, when these encounters were over, sent word to Don Pedro de Acuña, who at that time was his servant, that he tell Juan de Merlo that he should know that Suero had entered the field to perform deeds of arms with him with his right hand dislocated, and that he had done this so as to perform deeds of arms with such a good knight and one as skilled in arms as he was. And that now, from the encounters that Suero had made, his hand was dislocated a second time, in such a way that there was no way he could hold the spear with it. Therefore, he entreated him that, since they had performed their deeds of arms well, even though there was still one spear to be broken, the two of them together seek permission from the judges to go to their pavilions and declare their deeds of arms completed, for he was at present unable to perform them, but if he should wish to persist, Suero would fight with him without a spear, for there was no way he could carry one in his hand.

And said Juan de Merlo, when he heard the words which Don Pedro de Acuña told him on behalf of Suero de Quiñones, said that it pleased him, but that he entreated him on behalf of his lady that he order another knight to arm, with whom he could break the other spear, since Suero was unable. And Suero de

* de su lança que él havía ronpido en Juan de Merlo – por quanto quebró su gocete –: omit – BMP.
† por: de – BMP.
‡ a: con – RAH.
§ con él: omit – BMP.
¶ al fazer: a fazer – BMP.
** de: omit – BMP.
†† desencasada: desencasado – BMP.
‡‡ havían: havía – ESC; avían – BMP, RAH.
§§ partes: parte – BMP.

armar otro cavallero con quien rompiesse la otra lança, pues él non podía. E Suero de Quiñones respondió que en ninguna manera con otro cavallero non havía de fazer, sinon con él. E ansí, juntamente, amos e dos demandaron licencia a los juezes. E luego ge la otorgaron, e dieron sus armas por cunplidas, e mandaron que se fuesen a sus tiendas. E luego el honrrado cavallero Suero de Quiñones combidó a cenar a Juan de Merlo, según la costunbre del paso.

E el[*] rrei de armas fuese a la tienda adonde Suero de Quiñones se desarmava e falló que le estavan adereçando la mano, e vio cómo mostrava del dolor della gran sentimiento, e assimesmo vio cómo le tenblava el braço con la mano, que parecía[†] como si fuera perlesía.

E aquí fabla el auctor, e dize que, oyendo que[‡] Suero era ferido, e por saber en qué manera, hovo de llegar a él mismo por se más certificar e escrevir el fecho de la verdad. E le preguntó, a fee de cavallero, si era ferido en el fazer de las armas que[§] con Juan de Merlo havía fecho, e[¶] Suero le respondió que él tenía la mano sacada e en los morcillos [del][**] braço derecho dos llagas a[††] sangre, pero que non sabía si havían sido fechas[‡‡] de los clavos de su gocete que[§§] a la sazón de su encuentro se quebrara, o si Juan de Merlo lo feriera[¶¶] con el fierro o alguna racha de su lança que Juan de Merlo en él rompió, e que non podía haver conocimiento de otra cosa, ni los çurujanos se lo havían sabido dezir. E que el mayor daño que él havía havido de aquellas llagas havía sido que dende a tercera noche que las llagas se fizieron, estando en la cama por

Quiñones replied that there was no way that Juan de Merlo could perform deeds of arms with any other knight except him. And thus, together, they both sought permission from the judges. And they then granted it, and they declared their deeds of arms completed, and they ordered them to go to their pavilions. And then the honourable knight Suero de Quiñones invited Juan de Merlo to dinner, according to the custom of the passage of arms.

And the king-of-arms went to the pavilion where Suero de Quiñones was disarming himself and found that they were dressing his hand, and he saw how he was in much distress from the pain it was causing, and likewise he saw how his arm and hand were trembling, for it looked as if it might have been palsy.

And here speaks the author, and he says that, upon hearing that Suero was injured, and so as to find out how, he had to go in person so as to verify further and write the truth of the matter. And he asked Suero, on his knightly oath, if he was injured whilst performing the deeds of arms he had performed with Juan de Merlo, and Suero replied that he had a disjointed hand and two bloody wounds in the biceps of his right arm, but he did not know if they had been sustained from the spikes of his grapper which had broken from the blow he dealt, or if Juan de Merlo had injured him with the spearhead or some splinter of his spear which Juan de Merlo broke upon him, and that he could not think of anything else, nor had the surgeons been able to tell him. And that the greatest damage that he had suffered from those wounds had been that the third night after the wounds were sustained, lying in bed because of them, he was dreaming about writing letters of challenge in order to perform

---

* *E el: E del – RAH.*

† *que parecía: omit – BMP.*

‡ *oyendo que: oyendo dezir que – BMP, RAH.*

§ *que: omit – RAH.*

¶ *e: que él e, with que él struck through – BMP.*

** *del: de – ESC; del – BMP, RAH.*

†† *a: con – BMP.*

‡‡ *fechas: omit – BMP.*

§§ *que: et que, emended to que – RAH.*

¶¶ *feriera: fiziera, struck through and emended to feriera – RAH.*

causa* dellas, que soñava que [escrivía]† cartas de requesta para fazer armas a todo trance, que se le soltara la sangre de las llagas e se le‡ saliera tanta que los çurujanos, otro día que a él vinieron, huvieron pavor que se viera§ en peligro por causa de la mucha sangre dél salida.

E asimesmo dize el auctor que vio quando a Juan de Merlo dixieron cómo Suero tenía la mano sacada, e si más armas con él havía de fazer al presente que andaría sin lança porque non tenía [mano]¶ para la llebar.** E que estas palabras, oýdas por Juan de Merlo, que mostrara en sí gran sentimiento, diziendo que le pesava mucho de su enojo, e que Dios non quisiese que él tornase a fazer armas con él al presente, pues que así era, que en su fee†† non sabía dezir de haver él mismo recebido aquel enojo a lo haver recebido Suero de Quiñones – de quál fuera más pesante. Comoquier que él quisiera mucho su salud por dar fin a las armas que con él tenía començadas, pero‡‡ que le havría en mucho grado que le diese otro cavallero para las allí acabar.

E Suero le respondió que él creýa que pesava de su enojo e§§ que non havía dello dubda, mas que non le podía dar otro cavallero, según le havía respondido antes desto.¶¶

deeds of arms to the death,[93] when blood had spurted out of the wounds and he had lost so much that the surgeons, when they visited him the following day, were fearful that he was in danger because of the large amount of blood lost.[94]

And likewise the author says that he saw it when they explained to Juan de Merlo how Suero had a disjointed hand, and if Suero had to perform more deeds of arms with him at present that he would ride without the spear because his hand was in no condition to carry it. And that when Juan de Merlo heard these words, he was in much distress himself, saying that Suero's anguish aggrieved him greatly, and since God should not wish Suero to return to perform deeds of arms with him at present, such being the case, that on his oath he could not tell if he himself had suffered that anguish when Suero de Quiñones had suffered it – which was the worst. Even though he truly wished for his recovery so as to conclude the deeds of arms that he had begun with him, he none the less would be extremely grateful to Suero if he would provide him with another knight to finish them right then.

And Suero replied that he believed that Juan de Merlo was aggrieved by his anguish and that he had no doubt of it, but that he could not provide him with another knight, as he had responded previously.

---

* *causa: curarse*, struck through and emended to *causa* – RAH.

† *escrivía: escreví* – ESC; *escrivía* – RAH.

‡ *e se le: e le* – BMP; *e que le* – RAH.

§ *viera: vería* – BMP.

¶ *mano: lança* – ESC; *mano* – BMP, RAH.

** *la llebar: llevarla* – RAH.

†† *fee: fee dezía*, with *dezía* struck through – BMP.

‡‡ *pero: e* – BMP; *et*, struck through and emended to *pero* – RAH.

§§ *e*: omit – BMP.

¶¶ *según le havía respondido antes desto*: omit – BMP.

E de las armas destos dos cavalleros que en este día se fizieron, el ya nonbrado auctor dize que, por non ser bien* certificado si Juan de Merlo fizo aquellas llagas a Suero de Quiñones, según antes desto havéis oýdo, que rremite el juizio dellas a los que lo leyeren e oyeren e más† de fecho de armas entendieren.

E como Juan de Merlo fue en su tienda, antes que acabasen de adereçar la mano a Suero de Quiñones, embióle un guardabraço yzquierdo muy fermoso, e alto de la buelta, e fuerte, que los que le bieron dezían que era el mejor que nunca havían visto. E embióle dezir que le pedía por merced que recibiesse dél aquella pieza de arnés que le embiava con buen amorío, e le‡ perdonase por ser tan poca cosa, pero que se la embiava a condición que él, ni alguno de su conpañía, no fiziessen armas con él allí, [o]§ con¶ ninguno que en su compañía viniesse. E Suero de Quiñones respondió** que él ge lo tenía en mucho grado, e ge lo prometía ansí.

E luego embió Suero de Quiñones a Juan de Merlo una gentil mula, la qual le embió pedir de merced e gracia que la quisiese recebir dél e le†† quisiesse perdonar por ser tan poca cosa, pero que parase mientes a la buena voluntad, e‡‡ porque él sabía como le estava aparejado largo camino para yr fazer sus armas fuera del rreino, e la mula andava muy llano e bien, que para descanso de su trabajo no pudiera al presente pensarle§§ mejor remedio, e que a Dios

And of the deeds of arms that these two knights performed on this day, the aforenamed author says that, since it could not be verified if Juan de Merlo inflicted those wounds on Suero de Quiñones, as you have heard above, he remits the judgement of them to those who shall read and hear it and who better understand deeds of arms.

And when Juan de Merlo was in his pavilion, before they finished dressing Suero's hand, he sent him a very beautiful left pauldron,[95] with a high and stout haute-piece, and those who saw it said that it was the best they had ever seen. And he sent him word that he besought Suero to receive from him that piece of harness which he was sending to him with great affection, and that he forgive him for its being such a trifling thing, but that he was sending it to him on condition that neither he, nor anyone else on his team, would perform deeds of arms with Suero at this time, or with anyone else who should be on Suero's team. And Suero de Quiñones replied that he thanked him profusely for this, and he made the promise to him accordingly.

And then Suero de Quiñones sent Juan de Merlo a charming mule, which he sent to beseech Juan de Merlo that he should receive it from him with thanks and that he should forgive him for its being such a trifling thing, but that he think about the good will, and because Suero knew that he was preparing for a long journey to go and perform his deeds of arms abroad, and the mule rode very smoothly and well, that he could not think at present of a better way to make his trip restful, and that it should please God that he always be happy and healthy and delighted to complete deeds

* *bien*: omit – BMP.
† *más*: *demás* – BMP.
‡ *e le*: *e que le*, with *que* struck through and emended to *e le* – RAH.
§ *o*: Omitted in the MSS.
¶ *con*: *que*, struck through and emended to *con* – RAH.
** *respondió*: *le rrespondió* – BMP.
†† *e le*: *e que le* – RAH.
‡‡ *e*: *e que* – BMP.
§§ *pensarle*: omit – BMP.

pluguiesse que él fuese siempre alegre e sano e gozoso a las cumplir adonde puesto tenía, e le tornase con victoria e onor, como él desseava.

E ansí quedaron estos dos cavalleros muy offrescidos el uno al otro, según ya es devisado.

of arms wherever he had a contest, and that he return victoriously and honourably, as Suero wished.[96]

And thus were these two knights very beholden to each other, as is described above.

21.
Escorial MS f.II.19, fols. 124r–125r

Pedro de los Ríos.
Capítulo que fabla de las armas que en este miércoles* en la tarde fizo el ya nonbrado Pedro de los Ríos con Galaor Mosquera antes desto nonbrado, de la compañía de Juan de Merlo.

Luego† en este ya nonbrado miércoles, veinte e ocho de jullio, en la tarde, después de las armas fechas de los honrrados cavalleros Lope de Stúñiga e Alfonso de Deza, entró en el campo e liça Pedro de los Ríos, uno de los diez defensores de aquel passo, armado e a cavallo. E de la otra parte contra él, Galaor Mosquera, de la compañía de Juan de Merlo, asimesmo armado e a cavallo. E como fueron dentro en el campo, pusieron sus lanças en los riestres, e amos a dos‡ movieron el uno contra el otro, como gentileshomes que bien parecía que tenían en voluntad de ser en breve delibrados.

E a esta primera carrera encontró Galaor Mosquera a Pedro de los Ríos en el guardabraço ezquierdo, e despuntó el fierro de su lança, e quedó la punta en el guardabraço. E Pedro de los Ríos encontró a Galaor encima de la calva del elmete. E non rompió ninguno dellos lança e§ ni tomaron revés.

21.
Wednesday, 28 July 1434
Pedro de los Ríos vs. Galaor Mosquera
[On losing the right gauntlet: cp. Menaguerra, ch. 18]

Pedro de los Ríos.
Chapter which speaks about the deeds of arms which on this Wednesday afternoon the aforenamed Pedro de los Ríos performed with the aforesaid Galaor Mosquera,[97] on Juan de Merlo's team.

Later on this aforesaid Wednesday, 28 July, in the afternoon, after the deeds of arms performed by the honourable knights Lope de Stúñiga and Alfonso Deza, Pedro de los Ríos, one of the ten Defenders of that passage of arms, entered the field and lists, armed and on horseback. And on the other side opposite him, Galaor Mosquera, on Juan de Merlo's team, likewise armed and on horseback. And now that they were inside the field, they placed their spears in the rests, and they both charged against each other, like gentlemen who truly looked like they had a will to match strength as soon as possible.

And in this first course Galaor Mosquera struck Pedro de los Ríos on the left pauldron, and his spearhead blunted, and the point bit on the pauldron. And Pedro de los Ríos struck Galaor on the brow reinforce of the helmet. And neither one of them broke a spear, nor did they suffer a reversal of fortune.

---

* este miércoles: este ya nombrado miércoles
 – BMP.
† Luego: E luego – BMP.
‡ amos a dos: amos e dos – BMP, RAH.
§ e: omit – BMP.

A las dos carreras encontró Galaor Mosquera a Pedro de los Ríos en la guarda del guardabraço yzquierdo, e diole un tan gran golpe que por poco ge la falsara, e rompió su lança en él quanto tres palmos del asta cerca del fierro.

A las tres carreras encontró Pedro de los Ríos a Galaor en la bavera del elmete, e fízole tomar un comunal revés. E Galaor encontró a Pedro de los Ríos en la buelta del guardabraço yzquierdo. E non ronpió lança ninguno dellos.

A las quatro carreras encontró Pedro de los Ríos a Galaor Mosquera en la manopla [derecha],* e echógela en el suelo sin fazer sangre, e rompió su lança en él en dos partes. E Galaor encontró a Pedro de los Ríos en el guardabraço yzquierdo, e diole un tan gran golpe que ge lo echó en el suelo, e rompió su lança en él por tres partes.

E aquí acabaron de cumplir sus armas. E los juezes mandáronles que se fuesen a sus tiendas, pues las havían cumplido. E luego alçaron las caras de los elmetes e conociéronse el uno al otro, e luego conbidó Pedro de los Ríos a cenar a Galaor Mosquera, según la costumbre del passo. E luego se fueron a sus tiendas.

E aquí dize el auctor, comoquiera que vio, siendo presente, que estos dos anduvieron a guisa de buenos cavalleros e diestros,† que todas las más carreras que passaron se encontraron‡ el uno al otro. Comoquiera que levó lo mejor deste fecho de armas Galaor Mosquera, por quanto rrompió dos lanças en Pedro de los Ríos, e Pedro una en él, non más.

In the second course Galaor Mosquera struck Pedro de los Ríos on the left gardbrace, and he dealt him such a mighty blow that he almost would have pierced it, and he broke his spear upon him a length of three palms below the spearhead.

In the third course Pedro de los Ríos struck Galaor on the wrapper of the armet,[98] and he made him suffer a moderate reversal of fortune. And Galaor struck Pedro de los Ríos on the haute-piece of the left pauldron. And neither one of them broke a spear.

In the fourth course Pedro de los Ríos struck Galaor Mosquera on the right gauntlet, and cast it to the ground without drawing blood, and he broke his spear in two upon him. And Galaor struck Pedro de los Ríos on the left pauldron, and he dealt him such a mighty blow that he cast it to the ground, and he broke his spear upon him in three pieces.

And at this point they finished completing their deeds of arms. And the judges ordered them to go to their pavilions, for they had completed them. And then they raised the visors of the helmets and they recognised each other, and then Pedro de los Ríos invited Galaor Mosquera to dinner, according to the custom of the passage of arms. And then they went to their pavilions.

And here the author says, since he saw, being present, that these two men rode like good and skilled knights, for in each and every course which they ran they made the encounter. However, Galaor Mosquera carried the advantage in this deed of arms, since he broke two spears upon Pedro de los Ríos, and Pedro no more than one upon him.

* derecha: izquierda – ESC; derecha – BMP, RAH. Pineda also has derecha (ed. Riquer, p. 131).
† diestros: dispuestos – BMP.
‡ encontraron: encontró – RAH.

22.

Wednesday, 28 July 1434
Pedro de los Ríos vs. Pero Vázquez de
Castilbranco
[*On losing teeth: cp. Menaguerra,*
chs. 13 and 21; above, Article 3]

22.

Escorial MS f.II.19, fols. 125v–126r

Capítulo que fabla de cómo el ya nonbrado
Pedro de los Ríos tornó en este día en la tarde
otra vez al campo a fazer armas con Pero
Bázquez de Castilblanco.

Luego en este miércoles, en la tarde, tornó al
campo e liça el ya antes desto nonbrado Pedro
de los Ríos, uno de los diez defensores de aquel
passo, el qual havía ese día fecho armas antes
de comer con Galaor Mosquera, según ya vos
es* devisado, el qual vino armado e a cavallo.
E de la otra parte contra él, Pero Bázquez de
Castilblanco, de la conpañía del antes desto
nonbrado honrrado cavallero Juan de Merlo,
assimesmo armado e a cavallo.

E como fueron dentro en el campo, pusieron
sus lanças en los riestres a guisa de cavalleros, e
movieron amos a dos† el uno contra el otro.

E a esta primera carrera encontró Pedro de
los Ríos a Pero Bázquez en la cinta del galaro,‡
e non rrompió lança, comoquiera que resgó un
poco del galaro.

E passaron otras dos carreras que non se
encontraron.

A las quatro carreras encontró Pedro de
los Ríos a Pero Bázquez en el guardabraço
yzquierdo, e diole un tan gran golpe que ge
lo alçó, e diole con el mesmo en los dientes, e
atordeciólo, e hízole tomar un gran revés. E
desde el lugar donde fue encontrado hasta en
cabo de la liça fue por caer del cavallo. E rompió

Chapter which speaks about how the
aforenamed Pedro de los Ríos returned once
more to the field this day in the afternoon
to perform deeds of arms with
Pero Vázquez de Castilbranco.[99]

Later this Wednesday afternoon the aforementioned Pedro de los Ríos, one of the ten
Defenders of that passage of arms, who had on
that day performed deeds of arms with Galaor
Mosquera before lunch, as is stated to you,
returned to the field and lists, coming armed
and on horseback. And on the other side opposite him, Pero Vázquez de Castilbranco, on the
aforenamed honourable knight Juan de Merlo's
team, likewise armed and on horseback.

And now that they were inside the field, they
placed their spears in the rests like knights,
and they both charged against each other.

And in this first course Pedro de los Ríos
struck Pero Vázquez in the waist of the
surcoat, and he did not break the spear, though
he did rip the surcoat slightly.

And they ran another two courses in which
they did not encounter.

In the fourth course Pedro de los Ríos
struck Pero Vázquez on the left pauldron, and
he dealt such a mighty blow upon it that he
hoisted it off him, and he hit him in the teeth
with the same blow, and he stunned him, and
made him suffer a serious reversal of fortune.
And from the point at which he was struck up
to the head of the lists he almost fell off his
horse. And Pedro de los Ríos broke his spear

---

* *ya vos es: vos es ya – BMP.*
† *amos a dos: amos et dos – BMP, RAH.*
‡ *cinta del galaro: cara del guardabraço,* struck
   through and emended to *cinta del galaro*
   – RAH.

su lança en él [en pieças].* E Pedro de los Ríos, del encuentro que le dio, desencasósele la mano.

E como los juezes vieron que estava tan mal adereçado Pero Bázquez, e asimesmo Pedro de los Ríos mal de la mano, mandáronles que se fuesen a sus tiendas, e que quando fuesen libres e adereçados que tornarían otro día a cumplir sus armas. Comoquiera que Pedro de los Ríos quisiera, tal qual estava, cumplir sus armas, e los juezes mandáronles todavía que se fuesen. E assí salieron luego del campo e fue conbidado [a cenar Pero Vázquez],† según la costunbre del paso.

E aquí non cumple que mucho fable el auctor, que bien parece a todos que Pedro de los Ríos levó lo mejor en estas pocas carreras que passaron.

into pieces upon him. And Pedro de los Ríos, from the stroke that he delivered, dislocated his hand.

And when the judges saw that Pero Vázquez was in such bad shape, and likewise Pedro de los Ríos had hurt his hand, they ordered them to go to their pavilions, and when they were fit and hardy they could return another day to complete their deeds of arms. Pedro de los Ríos, however, wished, in his present state, to complete his deeds of arms, and the judges still ordered them to go. And thus they then left the field and Pero Vázquez was invited to dinner, according to the custom of the passage of arms.

And here it does not behove the author to say much, for it seems obvious to everyone that Pedro de los Ríos took the advantage in these few courses which they ran.

23.
Escorial MS f.II.19, fols. 126r–127r

Pedro de Nava.
Capítulo que fabla de las armas que el ya nonbrado Pedro de Nava fizo, en este miércoles en la tarde, con Lope de la Torre, escudero de Pedro de Acuña.

E luego en este ya nonbrado miércoles, a poca‡ de ora, entró en el campo e liça a fazer armas Pedro de Nava, uno de los diez defensores de aquel§ passo ya nonbrado, armado e a cavallo. E de la otra parte contra él, Lope de la Torre, escudero de Pedro de Acuña, el qual havía venido en la compañía de Juan de Merlo, assimismo armado e a cavallo.

23.
Wednesday, 28 July 1434
Pedro de Nava vs. Lope de la Torre
[On unhorsing one's opponent: cp. Menaguerra, ch. 25; above, Article 3]

Pedro de Nava.
Chapter which speaks about the deeds of arms which the aforenamed Pedro de Nava performed, this Wednesday afternoon, with Lope de la Torre, Pedro de Acuña's squire.

And a short while later on this aforementioned Wednesday, Pedro de Nava, one of the ten Defenders of that aforementioned passage of arms, entered the field and lists to perform deeds of arms, armed and on horseback. And on the other side opposite him, Lope de la Torre, Pedro de Acuña's squire, who had come on Juan de Merlo's team, likewise armed and on horseback.

---

* *en piezas: empiezas – ESC; en pieças – BMP, RAH.*
† *a cenar Pero Vázquez: omit – BMP, ESC, RAH.*
‡ *poca: poco – RAH.*
§ *de aquel: del – BMP.*

E como fueron dentro en el campo, pusieron sus lanças en los riestres, e amos a dos* movieron el uno contra el otro, a guisa de cavalleros que bien parecía† que tenían [en]‡ voluntad de se delibrar muy en breve el uno al otro en aquel fecho de armas.

E a esta primera carrera tocóle Pedro de Nava a Lope de la Torre un poco en el guardabraço yzquierdo, sin romper lança ni tomar ninguno dellos revés.

A las dos carreras encontró Pedro de Nava a Lope de la Torre en el piastrón, en derecho del coraçón, e diole un tan grand golpe que cayó el cavallo e el cavallero en el suelo, e non rompió lança, comoquiera que ge la contaron por rompida a Pedro de Nava, por quanto havía caído el cavallo de Lope e él en el suelo, porque en los capítulos antes desto dichos se contiene que qualquiera que derribare cavallero, aunque no ronpa su lança, que le sea contada por rompida.

E como fue en el suelo el cavallo, luego Lope de la Torre se levantó muy reciamente sin le ayudar ninguno a levantar. E muy rrecio tornó luego a cavalgar, aunque cavalgó a ezquierdas por más ligereza, e luego a cavallo pasó en cabo de la liça.

E muy reciamente pasaron otras dos carreras que non se encontraron, salvo en la una dellas que barrearon las lanças.

A las cinco carreras encontró Pedro de Nava a Lope de la Torre en el guardabraço yzquierdo, e rompió su lança en él con dos palmos del asta con el fierro, sin tomar ninguno dellos rrevés.

A las siete carreras encontró Pedro de Nava a Lope de la Torre en la bavera e echógela en el suelo, e alçóle un poco la cara del elmete, e

And now that they were inside the field, they placed their spears in the rests and they both charged against each other, like knights who truly looked like they had a will to match strength with each other as soon as possible in that deed of arms.

And in this first course Pedro de Nava attainted Lope de la Torre lightly on the left pauldron, without breaking the spear or either one of them suffering a reversal of fortune.

In the second course Pedro de Nava struck Lope de la Torre on the plackart, right over his heart,[100] and he dealt such a mighty blow upon him that horse and rider fell to the ground,[101] and he did not break the spear, though they did count it as a broken spear for Pedro de Nava, since Lope's horse had fallen to the ground along with Lope, because in the Articles mentioned above it is stated that anyone who should knock down a knight, even though he does not break his spear, it will be counted as broken.

And since the horse was on the ground, Lope de la Torre then got up very vigorously without anyone helping him to get up.[102] And he then returned to ride with much vigour, although in an effort to be swifter he rode crookedly, and having remounted he rode to the head of the lists.

And they ran another two courses very vigorously in which they did not encounter, except that in one of them they barricaded the spears.

In the fifth course Pedro de Nava struck Lope de la Torre on the left pauldron, and he broke his spear upon him a length of two palms of the shaft from the spearhead, without either one suffering a reversal of fortune.

In the seventh course Pedro de Nava struck Lope de la Torre on the bevor and cast it to the ground, and he raised the visor of Lope's helmet slightly, and he broke his spear upon him in two pieces, and he made him suffer a

---

* amos a dos: amos e dos – BMP.
† parecía: parecían, emended to parecía – RAH.
‡ en: e – ESC; en – BMP, RAH.

rompió su lança en él* por dos partes, e fízole tomar un gran revés. E Lope de la Torre encontró a Pedro de Nava en el guardabraço yzquierdo, e diole un tan gran golpe que por muy poco ge lo falsara, e rompió en él su lança en tres partes, e ansí cumplieron sus armas muy bien, por quanto rompieron una lança de más, según las condiciones de los capítulos.

E luego los juezes mandáronles† que se fuesen a sus tiendas, e alçaron las caras de los elmetes, e conociéronse el uno al otro, e Pedro de Nava combidó a Lope de la Torre a cenar, según la costunbre del passo.

E aquí fabla el autor, e dize, según lo que vio, siendo presente al fazer destas armas, que levó lo mejor deste fecho Pedro de Nava, por el romper de las tres lanças que ronpió, e assimesmo por la caída que el cavallo e Lope de la Torre cayeron. E aquí non es maravilla que muchos rrezios cavalleros caen algunas vezes, según se falla por las corónicas de los fechos de armas que en otros tiempos se fizieron, porque las venturas en tales fechos son [verdaderas]‡ a las vezes.

serious reversal of fortune. And Lope de la Torre struck Pedro de Nava on the left pauldron, and he dealt such a mighty blow upon him that he almost would have pierced it, and he broke his spear upon him in three pieces, and thus they completed their deeds of arms very well, since they broke one spear more than is specified in the conditions of the Articles.[103]

And then the judges ordered them to go to their pavilions, and they raised the visors of the helmets, and they recognised each other, and Pedro de Nava invited Lope de la Torre to dinner, according to the custom of the passage of arms.

And here speaks the author, and he says, according to what he saw, being present as these deeds of arms were being performed, that in this deed Pedro de Nava carried the advantage, by breaking the three spears that he broke, and likewise for the fall which the horse and Lope de la Torre suffered. And here it is no surprise that many robust knights occasionally fall, as can be found in the chronicles of deeds of arms that were performed in past times, because chance occurrences in such deeds of arms are, on occasion, a reality.

* *en él*: omit – *RAH.*
† *mandáronles*: *mandaron* – *RAH.*
‡ *verdaderas*: *vanderas* – *ESC, BMP*; *verdaderas*, struck through and emended to *vanderas* – *RAH.* Since *vanderas* makes no sense I have opted to restore *verdaderas*.

24.
Escorial MS f.II.19, fols. 127v–128v

Gómez de Villacorta.
Capítulo que fabla de las armas que el ya
nonbrado Gómez de Villacorta, este jueves de
mañana, fizo con Martín de Almeida.

Luego,* después desto, a poca de ora, en este ya
nonbrado jueves de mañana, entró en el campo
e liça donde las armas se fazían Gómez de
Villacorta, uno de los diez defensores de aquel
paso,† armado e a cavallo. E de la otra parte
contra él, Martín de Almeyda, de la compañía
de Juan de Merlo ya nonbrado, assimesmo‡
armado e a cavallo. E como fueron dentro en
el campo, pusieron sus lanças en los riestres, e
movieron amos e dos el uno contra el otro, con
muy buenas continencias de cavallería.

E a esta primera carrera encontró Gómez de
Villacorta a Martín de Almeida en la guarda
del guardabraço yzquierdo, e diole un tan gran
golpe que por muy poco ge lo falsara. E rompió
su lança en él en dos partes, e saltó el troçón de
la lança con el fierro por cima de un cadafalso
fuera de la liça. E tomó un comunal revés. E de
su encuentro se le desencasó la mano.

E passaron otra carrera que non se
encontraron.

A las tres§ carreras encontró Gómez
de Villacorta a Martín de Almeyda en el
guardabraço yzquierdo. E rompió su lança
en él en dos pedaços. E Martín encontró a
Gómez⁋ un poco en el guardabraço yzquierdo,

24.
Thursday, 29 July 1434
Gómez de Villacorta vs. Martín de Almeida
[*On losing the reins: cp. Menaguerra, ch. 17*]

Gómez de Villacorta.
Chapter which speaks about the deeds of
arms which the aforenamed Gómez de
Villacorta performed this Thursday morning
with Martín de Almeida.

A short while after this, on this aforesaid
Thursday morning, Gómez de Villacorta, one
of the ten Defenders of that passage of arms,
entered the field and lists where the deeds of
arms were being performed, armed and on
horseback. And on the other side opposite
him, Martín de Almeida, on the aforenamed
Juan de Merlo's team, likewise armed and on
horseback. And now that they were inside the
field, they placed their spears in the rests, and
they both charged against each other with
great chivalric composure.

And in this first course Gómez de Villacorta struck Martín de Almeida on the left
gardbrace, and he dealt him such a mighty
blow that he almost would have pierced it.
And he broke his spear in two upon him, and
the big piece of the spear with the spearhead
flew over a stand outside the lists. And Martín
de Almeida suffered a moderate reversal of
fortune. And from the stroke he delivered
Gómez de Villacorta dislocated his hand.

And they ran another course in which they
did not encounter.

In the third course Gómez de Villacorta
struck Martín de Almeida on the left pauldron. And he broke his spear upon him in two
pieces. And Martín struck Gómez lightly on
the left pauldron, without breaking a spear

---

* *Luego: E luego – BMP.*
† *aquel paso: aquel passo ya nombrado – BMP,*
   RAH.
‡ *assimesmo: e assimesmo – BMP.*
§ *tres: quatro – BMP.*
⁋ *Gómez: Gómez de Villacorta – BMP.*

sin romper lança nin tomar ninguno dellos revés.

E passaron otra carrera que non se encontraron.

A las* cinco carreras encontró Martín de Almeida a Gómez de Villacorta en la guarda de la manopla yzquierda, e diole un tan gran golpe que le fizo quebrar las rriendas de su cavallo. E salió el fierro de la lança sin la romper. E tomó Gómez un comunal revés.

E passaron otras tres† carreras que non se encontraron.

A las nueve carreras encontró Martín de Almeida a Gómez en el guardabraço yzquierdo, sin romper lança.

E pasaron otras tres carreras que non se encontraron, salvo en la una dellas que barrearon las lanças.

A las treze carreras encontró Martín de Almeida a Gómez de Villacorta en el arandela, e non rompió su‡ lança nin tomó ninguno dellos revés.

A las catorce carreras encontró Gómez de Villacorta a Martín de Almeyda en el guardabraço ezquierdo, e desguarneciógelo. E rompió su lança en él en dos partes. E Gómez tomó de su encuentro un comunal revés. E Martín de Almeida encontró a Gómez en el guardabraço derecho, e desguarneciógelo.

E así fueron cumplidas sus armas, e alçaron las caras de los elmetes e conociéronse, e combidó Gómez de Villacorta a cenar a Martín de Almeida, según la costunbre del passo. E los juezes mandáronles que se fuesen a sus tiendas, e luego se fueron.

E aquí non es necessario que mucho fable el auctor en este fecho de armas que ambos fizieron, ca claro parece que levó lo mejor Gómez de Villacorta.

or either one of them suffering a reversal of fortune.

And they ran another course in which they did not encounter.

In the fifth course Martín de Almeida struck Gómez de Villacorta on the reinforce of the left gauntlet, and he dealt him such a mighty blow that he made the reins of his horse break apart. And the spearhead fell off the spear without the spear breaking. And Gómez suffered a moderate reversal of fortune.

And they ran another three courses in which they did not encounter.

In the ninth course Martín de Almeida struck Gómez on the left pauldron, without breaking the spear.

And they ran another three courses in which they did not encounter, except that in one of them they barricaded the spears.

In the thirteenth course Martín de Almeida struck Gómez de Villacorta on the rondel, and he did not break his spear nor did either one of them suffer a reversal of fortune.

In the fourteenth course Gómez de Villacorta struck Martín de Almeida on the left pauldron, and he ripped it off him. And he broke his spear upon him in two pieces. And Gómez suffered a moderate reversal of fortune from the blow he delivered. And Martín de Almeida struck Gómez on the right pauldron, and ripped it off him.

And thus their deeds of arms were completed, and they raised the visors of the helmets and they recognised each other, and Gómez de Villacorta invited Martín de Almeida to dinner, according to the custom of the passage of arms. And the judges ordered them to go to their pavilions, and then they went.

And here it is not necessary for the author to speak much about this deed of arms which they both performed, for it seems clear that Gómez de Villacorta carried the advantage.

---

* *A las: E a las – BMP.*

† *tres: dos – RAH.*

‡ *su: omit – BMP, RAH.*

25.
Escorial MS f.II.19, fols. 128v–130r

Sancho de Ravanal.
Capítulo que fabla de las armas que
el ya nonbrado Sancho de Ravanal, en este
jueves, hizo con Gonçalo de León,
escudero de Juan de Merlo.

Luego[*] en este ya nonbrado jueves, a poca[†] de ora, después de cumplidas estas armas, entró en el campo e liça Sancho de Ravanal, uno de los diez defensores de aquel passo, ya nonbrado, armado e a cavallo. E de la otra parte contra él, Gonçalo de León, escudero de Juan de Merlo. E como fueron dentro en el campo, pusieron sus lanças en los riestres, e movieron muy reciamente amos e dos, el uno contra el otro, con muy buenas voluntades.

E a esta primera carrera non se encontraron.

A las dos carreras tocó Sancho de Ravanal un poco a Gonzalo de León en la guarda del guardabraço derecho, e non rompió lança.

E passaron otras tres carreras que non se encontraron.

A las seis[‡] carreras barrearon las lanças, e como echó Sancho su lança en el suelo, tocó con el fierro en una parte de la liça, e metióse[§] el cuento della entre el arçón delantero de la silla y el faldaje de las platas en derecho del bientre, e fízole tomar a él e al cavallo un gran rrevés, que si no topara en la liça, por muy poco cayieran el cavallo e él.

25.
Thursday, 29 July 1434
Sancho de Rabanal vs. Gonzalo de León
[On striking the tilt: cp. Menaguerra, ch. 8]

Sancho de Rabanal.
Chapter which speaks about the deeds of arms which the aforenamed Sancho de Rabanal performed this Thursday with Gonzalo de León, Juan de Merlo's squire.

A short while later on this aforementioned Thursday, after these deeds of arms were completed, the aforenamed Sancho de Rabanal, one of the ten Defenders of that passage of arms, entered the field and lists, armed and on horseback. And on the other side opposite him, Gonzalo de León, Juan de Merlo's squire. And now that they were inside the field, they placed their spears in the rests, and they both charged against each other very vigorously, most willingly.

And in this first course they did not encounter.

In the second course Sancho de Rabanal attainted lightly upon Gonzalo de León on the right gardbrace, and he did not break the spear.

And they ran another three courses in which they did not encounter.

In the sixth course they barricaded the spears, and as Sancho dropped his spear to the ground, he hit a part of the tilt with the spearhead, and the butt of the spear got lodged between the front arçon of the saddle and the skirt of the cuirass over his belly, and it made him and the horse suffer a serious reversal of fortune, so that if he had not collided with the tilt, both horse and rider would almost certainly have fallen.

---

[*] *Luego: E luego – BMP.*
[†] *poca: poco – RAH.*
[‡] *seis: dos,* struck through and emended to *seys – RAH.*
[§] *metióse: metiesse – RAH.*

A las siete carreras encontró Gonçalo de León a Sancho de Ravanal en la buelta del guardabraço yzquierdo, sin ronper lança ni tomar ninguno dellos rrevés.

A las* ocho carreras encontró Gonçalo de León a Sancho de Ravanal en el guardabraço yzquierdo, e diole un tan gran golpe que por poco ge lo [falsara],† e rompió su lança en él en dos partes. E Sancho de Ravanal encontró a Gonçalo de León en la guarda del guardabraço derecho, e lançógela en el suelo sin ge la falsar nin romper lança.

E pasaron otra carrera que non se encontraron.

A las‡ diez§ carreras tocó Gonçalo un poco a Sancho de Ravanal en el guardabraço yzquierdo, sin romper lança ni tomar revés ninguno dellos.

E pasaron otra carrera que non se encontraron.

A las doze carreras encontró Gonçalo de León a Sancho de Ravanal en el guardabraço yzquierdo, acerca de la buelta, e diole un tan gran golpe que rompió su lança por un palmo cerca del fierro, sin tomar ninguno dellos revés.

E passaron otras dos carreras que non se encontraron, salvo en la una dellas que barrearon las lanças.

A las quinze carreras encontró Gonçalo a Sancho un poco en el guardabraço yzquierdo, sin romper lança.

E passaron otras dos carreras que non se encontraron.

A las¶ diez y ocho carerras barreó la lança Sancho de Ravanal. E Gonçalo de León encontró a Sancho en el arandela, sin romper lança ni tomar ninguno dellos revés.

In the seventh course Gonzalo de León struck Sancho de Rabanal on the haute-piece of the left pauldron, without breaking the spear or either one of them suffering a reversal of fortune.

In the eighth course Gonzalo de León struck Sancho de Rabanal on the left pauldron, and he dealt such a mighty blow upon him that he would almost have pierced it, and he broke his spear upon him in two pieces. And Sancho de Rabanal struck Gonzalo de León on the right gardbrace, and he struck it to the ground without piercing it or breaking the spear.

And they ran another course in which they did not encounter.

In the tenth course Gonzalo de León attainted Sancho de Rabanal lightly on the left pauldron, without breaking the spear or either one of them suffering a reversal of fortune.

And they ran another course in which they did not encounter.

In the twelfth course Gonzalo de León struck Sancho de Rabanal on the left pauldron, near the haute-piece, and he dealt him such a mighty blow that he broke his spear a palm's length below the spearhead, without either one of them suffering a reversal of fortune.

And they ran another two courses in which they did not encounter, except that in one of them they barricaded the spears.

In the fifteenth course Gonzalo struck Sancho lightly on the left pauldron, without breaking the spear.[104]

And they ran another two courses in which they did not encounter.

In the eighteenth course Sancho de Rabanal barricaded the spear. And Gonzalo de León struck Sancho on the rondel, without breaking the spear or either one of them suffering a reversal of fortune.

---

* *A las: E a las* – BMP, RAH.
† *falsara*: omit – ESC; *falsara* – BMP, RAH.
‡ *A las: E a las* – RAH.
§ *diez*: *dos* – RAH.
¶ *A las: E a las* – BMP.

E luego el honrrado cavallero Juan de Merlo llegó a los juezes, e les dixo cómo[*] el ya nonbrado Gonçalo estava muy mal de agua que havía bevido, e[†] que al presente que le parecía que non estava para fazer armas, e que viesen en ello qué mandavan fazer. E los juezes e rei de armas[‡] apartáronse[§] luego [a] haver su consejo sobrello, e luego respondieron que, pues Gonçalo non estava al presente para fazer, que se fuesen del campo, e que después de comer, quanto fuese delibre[¶] de aquella ocupación, que[**] tornaría[††] a cumplir sus armas, o[‡‡] otro día de mañana.

E como Sancho de Ravanal sopo esto, fue a los juezes a rrequerirles que non diesen la tal licencia a Gonçalo de León, quél non saldría del campo fasta que sus armas fuesen cumplidas. E los juezes dixieron e mandaron todavía que se fuesen del campo, e después[§§] que el otro bien[¶¶] estuviesse, tornarían a cumplir sus armas. E luego alçaron las caras de los elmetes e conociéronse el uno al otro, e fue conbidado a cenar[***] Gonzalo, según la costunbre del passo.

E aquí non cura mucho el auctor de fablar fasta el tiempo que cumplieren sus armas, que lo mejor destas claro se parece quien lo lieva, que es Gonçalo de León, por quanto rrompió dos lanças.

And then the honourable knight Juan de Merlo approached the judges, and he told them that the aforenamed Gonzalo was very ill from water that he had drunk, and that at present it seemed to him that he was not up to performing deeds of arms, and that they consider what they were going to order to be done about this. And the judges and the king-of-arms then stepped aside to take their counsel about this, and then they responded that, since Gonzalo was at present in no condition to perform, that they leave the field, and that after lunch, or some other day, when he was cured of what ailed him, he could return to complete his deeds of arms.[105]

And when Sancho de Rabanal heard about this, he went to the judges to petition them not to give such licence to Gonzalo de León, for he would not leave the field until their deeds of arms were completed.[106] And the judges still told and ordered them to leave the field, and after the other man was better, they could return to complete their deeds of arms. And then they raised the visors of the helmets and each one recognised the other, and Gonzalo was invited to dinner, according to the custom of the passage of arms.[107]

And here the author does not think of speaking until such time that they complete their deeds of arms, for it seems obvious that the one who carries the advantage thus far is Gonzalo de León, since he broke two spears.

---

[*] *cómo: en cómo – BMP.*

[†] *e:* omit *– RAH.*

[‡] *e rei de armas:* omit *– BMP.*

[§] *apartáronse: apeáronse – RAH.*

[¶] *delibre: libre – RAH.*

[**] *que:* omit *– BMP.*

[††] *tornaría: tornarían – RAH.*

[‡‡] *o: e – BMP; et,* struck through and emended to *o – RAH.*

[§§] *e después: e que después – BMP.*

[¶¶] *bien:* omit *– BMP.*

[***] *cenar: cena – RAH.*

26.
Escorial MS f.II.19, fols. 132rv

Sancho de Ravanal.
Capítulo que fabla de las armas que en este
día viernes el ya nonbrado Sancho de Ravanal
fizo con Pedro de Linares.

Despúes* desto, en este ya nonbrado viernes,[†]
a poca[‡] de ora, entró en el campo e liça a fazer
armas Sancho de Ravanal, uno de los diez
defensores de aquel passo, armado e a cavallo.
E de la otra parte contra él, Pedro de Linares,
de la compañía de Juan de Merlo, assimesmo
armado e a cavallo. E como fueron dentro en
el campo, pusieron sus lanças en los riestres,
e movieron muy reciamente el uno contra el
otro, de[§] muy buenas continencias e ardideça
de cavallería.

E pasaron dos carreras que non se
encontraron.

A las tres carreras encontró Sancho de
Ravanal a Pedro de Linares en el arandela, sin
romper lança.

E passaron otras cinco carreras que non se
encontraron.

A las nueve carreras encontró Sancho de
Ravanal [a Pedro de Linares][ſ] en la guarda
del braçal yzquierdo, e despuntó el fierro de la
lança en él, e rompióla en él** en dos partes, e
derribó la guarda en el suelo.

E passaron otras seis carreras que non
se encontraron, salvo en la una dellas que
barrearon las lanças.

26.
Friday, 30 July 1434
Sancho de Rabanal vs. Pedro de Linares
[On losing the right gauntlet: cp.
Menaguerra, ch. 18]

Sancho de Rabanal.
Chapter which speaks about the deeds of
arms which on this Friday the aforenamed
Sancho de Rabanal performed with
Pedro de Linares.

A short while after this, on this aforesaid
Friday, Sancho de Rabanal, one of the ten
Defenders of that passage of arms, entered the
field and lists to perform deeds of arms, armed
and on horseback. And on the other side opposite him, Pedro de Linares, on Juan de Merlo's
team, likewise armed and on horseback. And
now that they were inside the field, they placed
their spears in the rests, and they charged
against each other very vigorously, with great
composure and chivalric verve.

And they ran two courses in which they did
not encounter.

In the third course Sancho de Rabanal
struck Pedro de Linares on the rondel, without
breaking the spear.

And they ran another five courses in which
they did not encounter.

In the ninth course Sancho de Rabanal
struck Pedro de Linares on the left couter
wing, and the spearhead blunted on it, and he
broke it in two upon him, and he knocked the
couter wing to the ground.

And they ran another six courses in which
they did not encounter, except that in one of
them they barricaded the spears.

---

* *Después: E después – BMP.*
† *desto, en este ya nonbrado viernes: omit*
   – BMP.
‡ *poca: poco – RAH.*
§ *de: con – BMP.*
ſ *a Pedro de Linares: omit – BMP, ESC, RAH.*
** *en él: omit – BMP.*

A las diez y seis carreras encontró Sancho de Rabanal a Pedro de Linares en el braçal derecho, acerca de[*] la sangradera, e falsóle la guarda dél, e del encuentro sacudió tanto el braço que le saltó la manopla de la mano derecha fuera de la liça fasta siete o ocho pasos, sin romper lança ni tomar ninguno dellos revés.

E como era ya ora de comer, los juezes mandáronles que saliesen del campo e se fuesen a comer, e que tornarían después, otro día, a cumplir sus armas. Comoquiera que amos e dos[†] porfiaron que non saldrían del canpo hasta que acabasen de cumplir sus armas, e todavía[‡] los juezes mandaron que se fuesen a comer, pues que mandado lo havían. E desque esto vieron que non podían más fazer, salieron del campo e fuéronse a sus tiendas.

In the sixteenth course Sancho de Rabanal struck Pedro de Linares on the right vambrace, near the mail voider,[108] and pierced his couter wing, and from the encounter he jolted his arm so much that the gauntlet flew off his right hand about seven or eight paces away from the lists, without breaking the spear or either one of them suffering a reversal of fortune.

And since it was now lunch time, the judges ordered them to leave the field and to go and eat, and they could come back later, the following day, to complete their deeds of arms.[109] However, they both insisted that they would not leave the field until they had finished completing their deeds of arms, and the judges still ordered them to go and eat, for ordered it they had. And when they realised that there was nothing else they could do, they left the field and went to their pavilions.

27.
Escorial MS f.II.19, fols. 133rv

Pedro de Nava.
Capítulo que fabla de las armas que, en este día viernes en la tarde, el ya nonbrado Pedro de Nava fizo con Antón de Deça, de la compañía del honrrado cavallero Juan de Merlo ya nombrado.

Después[§] desto, en este ya nonbrado viernes, treinta días de jullio, en la tarde, entró en el campo e liça a fazer las armas devisadas Pedro de Nava, uno de los diez defensores de aquel passo ya nonbrado, armado e a cavallo. E de la otra parte contra él, Antón de Deça, de la compañía de Juan de Merlo, asimesmo armado

27.
Friday, 30 July 1434
Pedro de Nava vs. Antón de Deza
[On wounding one's opponent: cp. Menaguerra, ch. 13; above, Article 3]

Pedro de Nava.
Chapter which speaks about the deeds of arms which, this Friday afternoon, the aforenamed Pedro de Nava performed with Antón de Deza, on the aforenamed honourable knight Juan de Merlo's team.

After this, on this aforementioned Friday, 30 July, in the afternoon, the aforenamed Pedro de Nava, one of the ten Defenders of that passage of arms, entered the field and lists to perform pre-arranged deeds of arms, armed and on horseback. And on the other side opposite him, Antón de Deza, on Juan de Merlo's team, likewise armed and on horseback.

---

[*] *de: omit – BMP, RAH.*
[†] *amos e dos: ambos a dos – BMP.*
[‡] *armas, e todavía: armas, comoquiera que amos et dos, et todavía,* with *comoquiera que amos et dos* struck through – *RAH.*
[§] *Después: E después – BMP.*

e a cavallo. E como fueron dentro en el campo, pusieron sus lanças en los riestres, e movieron con buenas voluntades* el uno contra el otro.

E a esta primera carrera encontró Antón de Deça a Pedro de Nava en el guardabraço ezquierdo, e diole un tan gran golpe que por poco ge lo falsara, e ronpió su lança en él por cabe el fierro.

A las dos carreras encontró Pedro de Nava a Antón de Deça en el guardabraço yzquierdo, e diole un tan gran golpe que rompió su lança en él por dos partes, sin tomar ninguno [dellos]† revés.

E pasaron otra carrera que non se encontraron.

A las quatro carreras encontró Antón de Deça a Pedro de Nava en el guardabraço yzquierdo, e desguarneciógelo sin romper lança. E Pedro de Nava encontró a Antón de Deça un poco en la bavera, e non rompió lança nin tomó ninguno dellos rrevés.

A las cinco carreras encontró Antón de Deça a Pedro de Nava en la meitad del piastrón, e sortió de allí e salió al borde de las platas, e desguarneciógelo, e metióle el fierro [por el braço]‡ derecho, cerca§ de la cojuntura del honbro cabe el sobaco, por tal manera que le apuntó el fierro por¶ la otra parte, de lo qual le fizo una buena herida, e salió dél mucha sangre, de la qual ferida dezían los çurujanos que al presente estava en peligro, comoquiera que después sanó dello.

E los juezes mandaron luego que se fuesen a sus tiendas. E quando Antón de Deça dio esta ferida e encuentro a Pedro de Nava, rompió su

And now that they were inside the field, they placed their spears in the rests, and they charged against each other most willingly.

And in this first course Antón de Deza struck Pedro de Nava on the left pauldron, and he dealt him such a mighty blow that he almost would have pierced it, and he broke his spear upon him near the spearhead.

In the second course Pedro de Nava struck Antón de Deza on the left pauldron, and he dealt such a mighty blow upon him that he broke his spear upon him in two pieces, without either one of them suffering a reversal of fortune.

And they ran another course in which they did not encounter.

In the fourth course Antón de Deza struck Pedro de Nava on the left pauldron, and he ripped it off him without breaking the spear. And Pedro de Nava struck Antón de Deza lightly on the bevor, and he did not break the spear nor did either of them suffer a reversal of fortune.

In the fifth course Antón de Deza struck Pedro de Nava in the middle of the plackart, and glanced off there and went up into the stop-rib of the breastplate,[110] and ripped it off him, and the spearhead stuck through his right arm, near the shoulder joint next to the armpit, in such a way that the spearhead poked through to the other side, which caused a gaping wound, and a lot of blood flowed out of it,[111] from which wound the surgeons said that he was at present in danger, though he did subsequently recover from it.

And the judges then ordered them to go to their pavilions. And when Antón de Deza dealt this wound and blow to Pedro de Nava, he broke his spear upon him a length of two palms below the spearhead, and Pedro de

---

* *con buenas voluntades*: omit – *BMP*.

† *dellos*: de los – *ESC*; dellos – *BMP, RAH*.

‡ *por el braço*: omit – *ESC*; por el braço – *BMP, RAH*; so el braço – *Pineda* (ed. Riquer, p. 143).

§ *cerca*: omit – *RAH*.

¶ *por*: de – *BMP*.

lança en él por dos palmos cerca del fierro, e levó el troço* de la lança metido por el braço fasta en cabo de la liça. E fuéronse a sus tiendas.

E aquí dize el auctor, comoquiera que vio, siendo presente al fazer destas armas, que andavan muy diestros cavalleros amos a dos† e con buenas voluntades, que da lo mejor a Antón de Deça en este fecho de armas.

Nava bore the piece of the spear stuck through his arm until he reached the head of the lists. And they went to their pavilions.

And here says the author, since he saw, being present as these arms were being performed, that both knights were riding very skilfully and most willingly, that he gives the advantage to Antón de Deza in this deed of arms.

28.
Escorial MS f.II.19, fols. 134v–135r

Sábado siguiente, treinta e uno de jullio.
Dama.
Capítulo que fabla de‡ cómo le§ tomaron el guante a esta dama e de cómo lo tomó Pero Carnero, ya nonbrado, para lo delibrar.

Otro día de mañana, sábado, a treinta e un días del mes ya nonbrado jullio, tomó el rei de armas un guante a una dueña que se llamava Ynés Álvarez de Viedma, muger que dixo que era de Pero García del Castillo, vecino de Palencia, el qual venía con ella. E el rrei de armas le dixo que aquel guante le�⁋ tomava por quanto era costunbre de aquel paso que qualquier dueña e doncella de onor e** linaje que por allí pasase, dexase el guante de la mano derecha, [o]†† diese ome de linaje e cota de armas que salvase el guante faziendo armas con un cavallero de los diez defensores de aquel paso fasta rromper tres lanzas por el asta, según se contenía en los capítulos del honrrado cavallero Suero de Quiñones, capitán mayor de aquel paso. E que‡‡ si ella traýa consigo persona tal, que fuese para delibrar su guante, que lo dixiesse luego.

28.
Saturday, 31 July 1434
[Formal arrival of a Lady]

The following Saturday, 31 July.
A Lady.
Chapter which speaks about how they took the glove from this lady and about how the aforenamed Pero Carnero took it, in order to deliver it.

The following Saturday morning, on the thirty-first day of the aforesaid month of July, the king-of-arms took a glove from a lady whose name was Inés Álvarez de Biedma, who stated that she was the wife of Pero García del Castillo, a resident of Palencia, who was accompanying her. And the king-of-arms told her that he was taking that glove from her because it was the custom at that passage of arms that any lady or maiden of honour and nobility who passed that way should relinquish the glove of her right hand, or she should entrust a nobleman with a coat of arms to save the glove by performing deeds of arms with a knight from among the ten Defenders of that passage of arms until three spears were broken at the shaft, as stated in the Articles by the honourable knight Suero de Quiñones, senior captain of that passage of arms. And that if she had such a person with her who would be the one who would deliver her glove, she should say so now.

---

   * *troço: trozón* – BMP.
   † *amos a dos: amos et dos* – BMP, RAH.
   ‡ *de:* omit – BMP.
   § *le:* omit – BMP.
   ⁋ *le: lo* – BMP.
   ** *e: o* – BMP.
   †† *o: e* – ESC; *o* – BMP, RAH.
   ‡‡ *que:* omit – BMP.

E antes que la dueña ya nonbrada respondiesse, llegó luego Pero Carnero, escudero de Pedro de Acuña, e respondió por ella, e dixo al rei de armas e faraute que él quería delibrar el guante de aquella dueña. E ellos le respondieron que lo farían saber a Suero de Quiñones, capitán del paso, e a los juezes dél, e que trabajarían quanto pudiesen por que le fuese otorgado.

E como el rei de armas e faraute fueron al campo e liça donde Suero de Quiñones e los juezes ya nonbrados estavan, dixiéronles cómo havían tomado aquel guante a la dueña desuso nonbrada, e que Pero Carnero, respondiendo[*] por ella, que lo quería delibrar, e que les embiava pedir por merced que se lo quisiesen otorgar.

E Suero e los juezes respondieron[†] que les plazía que lo delibrase mucho en ora buena.

And before the aforenamed lady could reply, Pero Carnero, the squire of Pedro de Acuña, immediately approached, and he replied on her behalf, and he told the king-of-arms and the herald that he wished to deliver that lady's glove. And they replied that they would make it known to Suero de Quiñones, captain of the passage of arms, as well as to the judges, and that they would do everything in their power to see that his request were granted.

And when the king-of-arms and the herald went to the field and lists where Suero de Quiñones and the aforenamed judges were, they explained to them how they had taken that glove from the lady mentioned above, and that Pero Carnero, replying on her behalf, wished to deliver it, and he was sending them to beseech that they grant his request.

And Suero and the judges replied that they were pleasantly pleased that he should deliver it.

29.
Escorial MS f.II.19, fols. 144v–145r

Gómez de Villacorta.
Capítulo de las armas que el ya nonbrado Gómez de Villacorta en este [día][‡] fizo con Diego de Sanromán, de la compañía de Alfonso de Deça.

Luego en este ya nonbrado lunes, como fueron acabadas las armas de los honrrados cavalleros Lope de Stúñiga e Alfonso de Deça ya nonbrados, a poca[§] de ora entró en el campo e liça a fazer armas, armado e a cavallo, Gómez de Villacorta, uno de los diez defensores de aquel paso ya nonbrado.[¶] E de la otra parte

29.
Monday, 2 August 1434
Gómez de Villacorta vs. Diego de Sanromán
[Striking the tasset: cp. Menaguerra, ch. 30]

Gómez de Villacorta.
Chapter about the deeds of arms which the aforenamed Gómez de Villacorta performed on this day with Diego de Sanromán, on Alfonso de Deza's team.

Later on this aforenamed Monday, when the deeds of arms of the honourable aforenamed knights Lope de Stúñiga and Alfonso de Deza were finished, a short while later Gómez de Villacorta, one of the ten aforenamed Defenders of that passage of arms, entered the field and lists to perform deeds of arms, armed and on horseback. And on the other side opposite

---

[*] respondiendo: respondió – RAH.
[†] respondieron: le respondieron – BMP, RAH.
[‡] día: omit – ESC; día – BMP, RAH.
[§] poca: poco – RAH.
[¶] aquel paso ya nonbrado: aquel passo armado et a cavallo – RAH.

contra él, Diego de Sanrromán, escudero del ya nonbrado Alfonso de Deça. E como fueron dentro en el campo e liça, pusieron sus lanças en los riestres, e amos e dos movieron muy reciamente el uno contra el otro.

E a esta primera carrera ni a la segunda non se encontraron.

A las tres carreras encontró Gómez de Villacorta a Diego de Sanrromán un poco en el guardabraço yzquierdo, e non rompió lança nin tomó ninguno dellos revés.

A las* quatro carreras encontró Gómez de Villacorta a Diego de Sanrromán en la escarcela, e desguarneciógela, e rompió su lança en él en piezas.

E pasaron otras quatro carreras que non se encontraron, salvo en las dos dellas que barrearon.

A las† nueve carreras encontró Diego de Sanrromán a Gómez de Villacorta en la bavera, e diole un tan gran golpe que lo aturdió,‡ e fízole tomar un gran revés. E rompió su lança en él, e saltó el fierro con un pedaço del asta muy alto§ por encima de [la] liça.¶ E Gómez de Villacorta encontró a Diego de Sanrromán en el peto del piastrón, sin romper lança, e desencasósele** la mano derecha.

E por quanto amos a dos havían rompido sendas lanças e era ya mediodía e ora de comer, dieron los juezes sus armas por cunplidas, e mandáronles que se fuesen a sus tiendas. Comoquiera quellos porfiaron que non saldrían del campo fasta que sus armas cumpliesen. E los juezes todavía les mandaron que se fuesen, pues davan por cumplidas sus armas. E ellos, deque vieron que más non podían fazer, alçaron

him, Diego de Sanromán, squire of the aforenamed Alfonso de Deza. And now that they were inside the field and lists, they placed their spears in the rests, and they both charged against each other very vigorously.

And neither in this first course nor in the second did they encounter.

In the third course Gómez de Villacorta struck Diego de Sanromán lightly on the left pauldron, and he did not break the spear nor did either one of them suffer a reversal of fortune.

In the fourth course Gómez de Villacorta struck Diego de Sanromán on the tasset, and he ripped it off him, and he broke his spear into pieces on him.

And they ran another four courses in which they did not encounter, except that in two of them they barricaded.

In the ninth course Diego de Sanromán struck Gómez de Villacorta on the bevor, and he dealt him such a mighty blow that he stunned him, and he made him suffer a serious reversal of fortune. And he broke his spear upon him, and the spearhead and a piece of the broken spear flew very high over the lists. And Gómez de Villacorta struck Diego de Sanromán on the reinforcing breastplate, without breaking the spear, and he dislocated his right hand.[112]

And since they had both broken the two spears and it was by now midday and time for lunch, the judges declared their deeds of arms completed, and they ordered them to go to their pavilions. They insisted, however, that they would not leave the field until they completed their deeds of arms.[113] And the judges still ordered them to go, since they were declaring their deeds of arms completed. And, when they realised that they could do no more, they raised the visors of the helmets and

---

* A las: E a las – RAH.
† A las: E a las – BMP.
‡ aturdió: atordeció – BMP, RAH.
§ muy alto: omit – BMP.
¶ de liça: de la liça – BMP, RAH.
** desencasósele: desencasóse – BMP.

las caras de los elmetes e conociéronse el uno al otro. E Gómez de Villacorta conbidó a cenar a Diego de Sanromán, según la costunbre del passo. E assí saliéronse* luego, e fuéronse a sus tiendas.

E aquí non tiene mucho que fablar el auctor en este fecho de armas que estos amos e dos fizieron, por quanto le pareció que muy poca ventaja llevó el uno al otro.†

recognised each other. And Gómez de Villacorta invited Diego de Sanromán to dinner, according to the custom of the passage of arms. And thus they then left, and they went to their pavilions.

And here the author does not have much to speak about in this deed of arms which these two performed, since it seemed to him that the one carried very little advantage over the other.

30.
Escorial MS f.II.19, fols. 147r–148v

Martes, tres días del mes de agosto.
Pedro de los Ríos.
Capítulo que fabla de las armas que en este día martes el ya nonbrado Pedro de los Ríos, de mañana, fizo con el honrrado cavallero Pedro de Silva.

En este ya nonbrado martes, tres días del ya dicho‡ mes de agosto, luego de mañana, entró en el campo e liça a fazer armas, armado e a cavallo, Pedro de los Ríos, uno de los diez defensores de aquel paso ya nonbrado. E de la otra parte contra él, Pedro de Silva, fijo de Arias Gómez de Silva, asimesmo armado e a cavallo. E como fueron dentro en el campo, pusieron sus lanças en los riestres, e amos e dos movieron el uno contra el otro muy fuertemente, con voluntades prestas, a guisa de cavalleros.

E passaron [esta]§ carrera que non se encontraron.

A las dos carreras encontró Pedro de los Ríos a Pedro de Silva en el arandela, e rronpió su lança en él por cerca del fierro.¶ E Pedro de Silva encontró a Pedro de los Ríos un poco en

30.
Tuesday, 3 August 1434
Pedro de los Ríos vs. Pedro de Silva
[A difficult judgement]

Tuesday, 3 August.
Pedro de los Ríos.
Chapter which speaks about the deeds of arms which, this Tuesday morning, the aforenamed Pedro de los Ríos performed with the honourable knight Pedro de Silva.

On this aforenamed Tuesday, on the third day of the aforesaid month of August, later that morning, Pedro de los Ríos, one of the aforenamed ten Defenders of that passage of arms, entered the field and lists to perform deeds of arms, armed and on horseback. And on the other side opposite him, Pedro de Silva, Arias Gómez de Silva's son, likewise armed and on horseback. And now that they were inside the field, they placed their spears in the rests, and they both charged against each other very fiercely, with eager wills, like knights.

And they ran this course without encountering.

In the second course Pedro de los Ríos struck Pedro de Silva on the rondel, and he broke his spear upon him near the spearhead. And Pedro de Silva struck Pedro de los Ríos lightly on the brow reinforce of the helmet,

---

* *saliéronse: salieron – RAH.*
† *al otro: del otro – RAH.*
‡ *ya dicho: ya nombrado – RAH.*
§ *esta: otra – ESC; esta – BMP, RAH.*
¶ *por cerca del fierro. E: omit – BMP.*

la calva del elmete, e non rompió lança, ni tomó ninguno [dellos]* revés.

A las tres carreras tocó un poco Pedro de los Ríos a Pedro de Silva por encima de la vista del elmete, sin rronper lança.

A las† quatro carreras tocó Pedro de Silva un poco a Pedro de los Ríos por encima de la calva del elmete. E Pedro de los Ríos barreó su lança. E ninguno dellos non la rompió nin tomó revés.

E passaron otra carrera que non se encontraron.

E a las seis carreras barreó su lança Pedro de los [Ríos].‡

A las siete carreras encontró Pedro de los Ríos a Pedro de Silva en la guarda del guardabraço yzquierdo, e diole un tan fuerte golpe que ge la falsó e desguarneció, e tocóle un poco en la bavera, e derrivólle una pieça en el suelo, e fízole tomar un gran revés, por tal manera que salió de la silla un poco, e huviera de caer. E ronpió su lança en él en pieças.

A las ocho carreras encontró Pedro de los Ríos a Pedro de Silva en el guardabraço yzquierdo, e non rronpió lança, nin tomó ninguno dellos rrevés.

A las nueve carreras barrearon las lanças, sin rronper ninguna.§ E como fue Pedro de Silva en cabo de la liça, enbió por otro cavallo. E en tanto que por él fueron, quitóse el elmete de la cabeça e adereçóse. E como le traxieron el cavallo, cavalgó en él e tornóse [a] armar¶ del elmete.

E luego pasaron otra carrera que non se encontraron.

and he did not break the spear, nor did either one of them suffer a reversal of fortune.

In the third course Pedro de los Ríos attainted Pedro de Silva lightly upon the eyeslit of the helmet, without breaking the spear.

In the fourth course Pedro de Silva attainted Pedro de los Ríos lightly upon the brow reinforce of the helmet. And Pedro de los Ríos barricaded his spear. And neither one of them broke a spear or suffered a reversal of fortune.

And they ran another course in which they did not encounter.

And in the sixth course Pedro de los Ríos barricaded his spear.

In the seventh course Pedro de los Ríos struck Pedro de Silva on the left gardbrace, and he dealt such a mighty blow upon it that he pierced it and ripped it off, and he attainted him lightly on the bevor, and knocked a piece to the ground, and made him suffer a serious reversal of fortune, in such a way that he came out of the saddle slightly, and almost fell. And Pedro de los Ríos broke his spear into pieces on him.

In the eighth course Pedro de los Ríos struck Pedro de Silva on the left pauldron, and he did not break the spear, nor did either one of them suffer a reversal of fortune.

In the ninth course they barricaded the spears, without either one breaking. And when Pedro de Silva was at the head of the lists, he sent for another horse. And while they went for it, he took his helmet off his head and tended to himself. And when they brought him the horse, he mounted it and put the helmet back on.

And then they ran another course in which they did not encounter.

---

* dellos: dello – ESC; dellos – BMP, RAH.
† A las: E a las – RAH.
‡ Ríos: omit – ESC; Ríos – BMP, RAH.
§ ninguna: ninguno – RAH.
¶ tornóse armar: tornóse a armar – BMP, RAH.

A las* onze carreras barrearon las lanças, e del barrear desguarnecióse a Pedro de los Ríos una pieça del guardabraço derecho e echógela en el suelo, sin ronper lança nin tomar revés ninguno dellos.

A las doze carreras encontró Pedro de Silva a Pedro de los Ríos en el guardabraço yzquierdo, e diole un tan gran golpe que dio con él e con el cavallo† en el suelo. E antes que cayiese Pedro de los Ríos, encontró a Pedro de Silva en el guardabraço izquierdo, cerca de la buelta, e falsóle una pieça dél. E el dicho Pedro de Silva tomó muy gran rrevés. E su cavallo e él fueron arredrados de la liça fasta acerca del palenque, que podía haver tres passos del lugar donde fue encontrado, e por muy poco cayiera el cavallo e él. E‡ comoquiera que Pedro de Silva rronpió su lança en Pedro de los Ríos quanto§ cayó el cavallo e él.

E aquí fueron conplidas sus armas, e los juezes mandáronlos venir ante sí, como¶ luego hovo cavalgado Pedro de los Ríos. E allí alçaron las caras de los elmetes e fueron conocidos. E luego Pedro de los Ríos conbidó a cenar a Pedro de Silva, según la costunbre del passo. E luego los juezes les** mandaron que se fuesen a sus tiendas. E ellos, por obedecer su mandamiento, luego se fueron.

In the eleventh course they barricaded the lances, and from the barricading a piece of Pedro de los Ríos' right pauldron was ripped off and cast to the ground, without either one of them breaking a spear or suffering a reversal of fortune.

In the twelfth course Pedro de Silva struck Pedro de los Ríos on the left pauldron, and he dealt him such a mighty blow that he knocked him and the horse to the ground. And before Pedro de los Ríos fell, he struck Pedro de Silva on the left pauldron, near the haute-piece, and he pierced a piece of it. And said Pedro de Silva suffered a very serious reversal of fortune. And he and his horse were driven back from the tilt almost as far as the palisade, which must have been three paces away from the point where he was struck, and he and the horse almost fell. And even so, Pedro de Silva broke his spear on Pedro de los Ríos when Pedro de los Ríos and the horse fell.

And at this point their arms were completed, and the judges ordered them to come before them, after Pedro de los Ríos had re-mounted. And there they raised the visors of the helmets and they were recognised. And then Pedro de los Ríos invited Pedro de Silva to dinner, according to the custom of the passage of arms. And then the judges ordered them to go to their pavilions. And then they went, in compliance with their order.

---

  * *A las*: *E a las* – *RAH*.
  † *cavallo*: *cavallero*, struck through and
   emended to *cavallo* – *RAH*.
  ‡ *E*: omit – *RAH*.
  § *quanto*: *quando* – *BMP, RAH*.
  ¶ *como*: *e como* – *BMP*.
  ** *les*: omit – *BMP*.

E aquí fabla el auctor, e dize, comoquiera[*] que estos dos[†] anduvieron muy buenos cavalleros, según él vio, que era presente, que si non acaeciera el desastre a Pedro de los Ríos de la caída que cayó su cavallo e él por causa del encuentro que le dio Pedro de Silva, que él diera lo mejor a Pedro de los Ríos, por quanto havía andado bien diestro e havía ronpido dos lanças en Pedro de Silva, e Pedro de Silva non más de una en él. Pero que remite este juicio a los que este fecho de sus[‡] armas leyeren e oyeren e más en fecho[§] de armas supieren.

And here speaks the author, and he says, even though these two rode like very good knights, according to what he saw, for he was present, that if the disaster of the fall that Pedro de los Ríos and his horse suffered because of the blow that Pedro de Silva dealt him had not happened, he would have given the advantage to Pedro de los Ríos, since he had ridden quite skilfully and he had broken two spears on Pedro de Silva, and Pedro de Silva no more than one on him. But he remits this judgement to those who shall read and hear about this deed of arms and who know more about deeds of arms.

31.
Escorial MS f.II.19, fols. 154r–155r

Jueves siguiente, cinco días de agosto.
Diego de Baçám.
Capítulo que fabla de las armas que en este día el honrrado cavallero Diego de Baçám, ya nonbrado, fizo con el honrrado cavallero Mossén Rienbau de Corvera.

31.
Tuesday, 3 August 1434
Diego de Bazán vs.
Lord Riambau de Corbera
[On concussion: cp. Menaguerra, ch. 13]

The following Thursday, 5 August.
Diego de Bazán.
Chapter which speaks about the deeds of arms which on this day the aforenamed honourable knight Diego de Bazán performed with the honourable knight Lord Riambau de Corbera.[114]

En este ya nonbrado jueves, cinco días del dicho mes de agosto, luego de mañana, entró en el campo e liça el antes desto nonbrado honrrado cavallero Diego de Baçám, armado e a cavallo, comoquiera que no estava bien libre aún[¶] de la ferida[**] que avía havido, el qual ya havedes oýdo,[††] que era uno de los diez defensores de aquel paso. E de la otra parte contra él, el ya nonbrado cavallero antes desto, Mossén Rienbau de Corvera, uno de los dos cavalleros catalanes antes desto nonbrados,

On this aforementioned Thursday, the fifth day of the said month of August, later that morning, the above mentioned honourable knight Diego de Bazán, who was one of the ten Defenders of that passage of arms, entered the field and lists, armed and on horseback, even though he was still not fully recovered from the injury which he had sustained, about which you have already heard.[115] And on the other side opposite him, the aforenamed knight Lord Riambau de Corbera, one of the two Catalonian knights mentioned above,[116] likewise armed and on horseback (said Lord

---

* *comoquiera: que comoquiera – RAH.*
† *dos: omit – BMP.*
‡ *sus: omit – BMP.*
§ *en fecho: de fechos – BMP.*
¶ *aún: omit – BMP.*
** *la ferida: una ferida – BMP.*
†† *oýdo: oýdo dezir – BMP, RAH.*

asimesmo armado e a cavallo (el qual Mosén Rienbau traýa un fuerte* cavallo que él e su conpañero havían traído de Aragón, e era muy diestro e seguro, e su color dél era ruzio pedrés, e muy hermoso). E como fueron dentro en el canpo, tomó Mosén Rienbau de las lanças más fuertes e gruesas que allí havía, e asimesmo tomó Diego de Baçán de aquellas mesmas. E pusiéronlas en sus riestres, e movieron de muy buenas continencias el uno contra el otro, a guisa de muy buenos cavalleros.†

E a esta primera carrera encontró Mossén Rienbau de Corvera a Diego de Baçám en la bavera del elmete, e diole un tan gran golpe que rrompió su lança en él en pieças, e quedó la punta del fierro de su lança‡ en la bavera. E fue atordecido Diego de Baçán un rrato por la liça, que pensaron que cayera del cavallo. E§ este atordecimiento dizen, que allende del encuentro quél rrecebió, que fuera del atronamiento que tenía en la cabeça del encuentro de que, antes que estas armas fiziese, fuera ferido, según antes desto havedes ya¶ oýdo.

E luego el rei de armas e faraute decendieron del cadafalso donde estavan e fueron a catar al ya nonbrado Diego de Bazán, pensando que era ferido, e fallaron que non. E como vinieron, dixeron a los juezes de aquel campo que Diego de Baçám les havía jurado, a fee de cavallero, que en** enpeçando a salir, con su lança enrristrada, que ya yva atordecido de la cabeça antes que llegasen al lugar de los encuentros, por tal manera que non vía†† nada de los ojos e que le parecía‡‡ que le salían llamas de fuego por ellos, e que este día muriese él muerte de

Riambau had a strong horse which he and his companion had brought from Aragon, and it was very agile and sure and very handsome, and its colour was silver grey). And now that they were inside the field, Lord Riambau took one of the strongest and thickest spears that were there, and likewise Diego de Bazán took one of those same ones. And they placed them in their rests, and they charged with great composure against each other, like very good knights.

And in this first course Lord Riambau de Corbera struck Diego de Bazán on the wrapper of the armet, and he dealt him such a mighty blow that he broke his spear into pieces on him, and the point of the spearhead of his spear stuck in the wrapper. And Diego de Bazán was stunned for a moment in the lists, and they thought he would fall from the horse. And they say that this torpor, beyond the blow he received, was because of the throbbing that he had in his head from the encounter in which he was injured prior to performing these deeds of arms, as you have already heard previously.

And then the king-of-arms and the herald descended the stand where they were and they went to examine the aforenamed Diego de Bazán, thinking that he was injured, and they found that he was not. And when they arrived, they told the judges of that field that Diego de Bazán had sworn to them, on his knightly oath, that as he began to ride out, with his spear in the rest, he was already feeling drowsy in the head before they reached the point of the encounters, so much so that he could not see a thing and he felt as though flames of fire were shooting out of his eyes, and may he die like a

---

* *un fuerte*: un muy fuerte – BMP.

† *a guisa de muy buenos cavalleros*: omit – RAH.

‡ *en él en pieças, e quedó la punta del fierro de su lança*: omit – RAH.

§ *E*: E a – BMP.

¶ *ya*: omit – RAH.

** *en*: omit – BMP, RAH.

†† *vía*: vio – RAH.

‡‡ *parecía*: parecían – RAH.

villano si non dezía verdad en esto que les havía dicho.

E luego el rei de armas e faraute, como esto huvieron dicho a los juezes, siendo presentes los escrivanos e auctor* que allí eran,† publicaron luego estas palabras a altas vozes a todos los cavalleros e gentileshomes que presentes eran. E luego los juezes mandaron llamar delante de sí el‡ ya nonbrado cavallero Mosén Rienbau,§ e él venido allí, dixiéronle que, por quanto veýan que Diego de Baçám al presente non podía fazer más armas por razón del atordecimiento ya dicho, e ansimesmo por quanto en los capítulos que Suero de Quiñones havía fecho sobre esta enpresa se contenía que quando las semejantes cosas acaeciesen, que fuessen las armas cumplidas, por ende, quellos así las davan por cumplidas, e que les davan licencia que⁋ se fuesen enorabuena a sus tiendas.

E Mossén Rienbau dixo que él estava presto para cumplir sus armas con aquel cavallero que las havía començado a fazer. E los juezes dixieron que bien veýa** que el cavallero non estava para fazer con él al presente, pero que le darían otro cavallero que acabase de fazer las armas con él. E Mossén Rienbau dixo que en ninguna manera con otro cavallero non faría armas, sinon con aquel cavallero que las havía començado a fazer. E como los juezes esto oyeron,†† dieron las armas por cumplidas, e mandáronles que se fuesen a sus tiendas. E ansí salieron luego del campo por su mandamiento.

peasant this day if he were not telling the truth about what he had told them.

And then the king-of-arms and the herald, when they had stated this to the judges, in the presence of the scribes and the author,[117] who were there, these words were proclaimed out loud to all the knights and gentlemen who were present. And then the judges ordered the aforenamed knight Lord Riambau to be called before them, and after he had come, they told him that, since they could tell that Diego de Bazán could not at present perform more deeds of arms because of the aforesaid torpor, and likewise because it was stated in the Articles which Suero de Quiñones had drawn up for this emprise that when anything like this should happen the deeds of arms were completed, therefore, they were thus declaring them completed, and they were granting them permission to go quickly to their pavilions.

And Lord Riambau said that he was ready to complete his deeds of arms with that knight who had begun to perform them. And the judges said that he could see very well that the knight was in no condition to perform deeds of arms with him at present, but that they would authorise another knight to finish performing them with him. And Lord Riambau said that there was no way he would perform deeds of arms with any other knight except that knight with whom he had begun to perform them. And when the judges heard this, they declared the deeds of arms completed, and they ordered them to go to their pavilions. And thus did they then leave the field at their order.[118]

* *e auctor: e el autor,* emended to *e autor* – *RAH.*
† *eran: era* – *RAH.*
‡ *el: al* – *BMP.*
§ *Mosén Rienbau: Mosén Riembau de Corvera* – *RAH.*
⁋ *que: a que,* emended to *que* – *RAH.*
** *veýa: veýan* – *BMP.*
†† *oyeron: vieron* – *BMP, RAH.*

E aquí fabla el auctor, e dize que, según lo que antes desto vio en las armas que Diego de Baçán havía fecho en aquel campo e liça, e asimesmo la fortaleza e valentía dél, que si él non estuviera ocupado de la ferida ya nonbrada que antes desto havía havido, que bien creýa que el cavallero catalán que este día estas armas con él havía fecho, que non saliera tan libre* del campo Mosén Rienbau† como salió. E remite el juizio desta mejoría a los que estas armas leyeren e oyeren e más en el fecho dellas‡ entendieren.§

And here speaks the author, and he says that, according to what he saw before this of the deeds of arms which Diego de Bazán had performed in that field and lists, and likewise of his fortitude and valour, that if he were not encumbered by the aforementioned injury which he had sustained prior to this, he believed that the Catalonian knight Lord Riambau, who had performed these deeds of arms with him on this day, would not have left the field as freely as he did. And he remits the judgement of the advantage in this case to those who shall read and hear about these deeds of arms and who know more about how they are performed.

32.
Escorial MS f.II.19, fols. 156v–159r

Suero, fijo de Álvar Gómez.
Capítulo de las armas que el ya nonbrado Suero fizo¶ con el sinventura Esverte de Claramonte, el qual en aquella sazón allí murió.

Luego en este ya nonbrado viernes, después que la espuela fue tomada a este cavallero de suso escripto, luego de mañana entró en el campo e liça a fazer armas, armado e a cavallo, el antes desto nonbrado Suero, fijo de Álvar Gómez, uno de los diez defensores de aquel paso ya nonbrado. E de la otra parte contra él, el sinventura Exberte de Claramonte, natural del reino de Aragón, según antes desto es escrito, assimesmo armado e a cavallo. E como fueron dentro en el campo, pusieron sus lanças en los rriestres, e amos a dos** movieron el uno contra

32.
Friday, 6 August 1434
Suero Gómez vs. Asbert de Claramunt
[On foul strokes and death:
cp. Menaguerra, ch. 30]

Suero, son of Álvar Gómez.[119]
Chapter about the deeds of arms which the aforenamed Suero performed with the unfortunate Asbert de Claramunt, who died there at that time.[120]

Later in the morning on this aforementioned Friday, after the spur was taken from this knight mentioned above,[121] Suero, son of Álvar Gómez, one of the aforementioned ten Defenders of that passage of arms, entered the field and lists to perform deeds of arms, armed and on horseback. And on the other side opposite him, the unfortunate Asbert de Claramunt, citizen of the kingdom of Aragon, as is written above, likewise armed and on horseback. And now that they were inside the field, they placed their spears in the rests, and they

* tan libre: también – BMP.
† Mosén Rienbau: omit – BMP, RAH.
‡ dellas: de armas – BMP.
§ entendieren: entendiere – RAH.
¶ Suero fizo: Suero, fizo de Álvar Gómez, fizo – BMP.
** amos a dos: amos et dos – BMP, RAH.

el otro muy reziamente a guisa de buenos cavalleros, comoquiera que el ya nonbrado Suero, fijo de Álvar Gómez, aún non era sano de la ferida que en el braço derecho tenía que le havían dado antes desto, según antes desto en este libro vos es devisado.

E desta* primera carrera non se encontraron.

A las dos carreras encontró Exberte de Claramonte a Suero, fijo de Álvar Gómez, en el arandela, e de allí sortió, e diole en el guardabraço derecho, e desguarneciógelo, sin rronper lança nin tomar ninguno dellos rrevés.

E passaron otras quatro carreras que non se encontraron. E porque el cavallo en que Exberte andava se deviaba, diole este nonbrado Suero el cavallo en que andava, e él† tomó otro.

A las siete carreras encontró Suero a Exberte de Claramonte en el elmete encima de la vista, e doblósele la lança, e non la rrompió, nin tomó rrevés ninguno dellos.

A las ocho carreras encontró Suero, fijo de Álvar Gómez, al ya nonbrado sinventura Esberte de Claramonte en el guardabraço yzquierdo, e desguarneciógelo, e quedó la punta del fierro en él, e abrió, del encuentro que le dio, e rrompió su lanza en él en piezas, comoquiera que non tomó ninguno dellos revés.

A las nueve carreras encontró Suero, fijo de Álvar Gómez, al ya nonbrado sinventura Esberte de Claramonte por la vista del elmete, e diole un tan gran golpe que le lançó todo el fierro de la lança por el ojo yzquierdo fasta los sesos, e fízole saltar el ojo fuera del casco, e rronpió su lança en él con un palmo del asta, e con el fierro, el qual levava metido por la vista del elmete con el pedazo del asta, e por el ojo, según vos es devisado, e así fue acostado un poco por la liça fasta que cayó del cavallo

* desta: a esta – BMP, RAH.
† e él: e Suero – BMP, RAH.

both charged against each other very vigorously like good knights, even though the aforenamed Suero, son of Álvar Gómez, was not yet cured of the wound in his right arm which had been inflicted upon him beforehand, as is described to you above in this book.

And in this first course they did not encounter.

In the second course Asbert de Claramunt struck Suero, son of Álvar Gómez, on the rondel, and glanced off there and hit him in the right pauldron, and he ripped it off him without breaking the spear or either one of them suffering a reversal of fortune.

And they ran another four courses in which they did not encounter. And because the horse that Asbert was riding was swerving, this said Suero gave him the horse which he was riding, and he took another.

In the seventh course Suero struck Asbert de Claramunt on the helmet, on the eye-slit, and his spear bent, and he did not break it, nor did either one of them suffer a reversal of fortune.

In the eighth course Suero, son of Álvar Gómez, struck the aforenamed unfortunate Asbert de Claramunt on the left pauldron, and he ripped it off him, and the point of the spearhead bit on it, and it snapped off, from the blow he dealt upon him, and he broke his spear into pieces upon him; however, neither one of them suffered a reversal of fortune.

In the ninth course Suero, son of Álvar Gómez, struck the aforenamed unfortunate Asbert de Claramunt through the eye-slit of the helmet, and he dealt him such a mighty blow that he pushed the entire head of the spear through his left eye into his brains, and he made his eye pop out of the socket, and he broke his spear in it with a palm's length of the shaft,[122] and with the spearhead, which Asbert de Claramunt bore stuck through the eye-slit of the helmet with the piece of the broken spear, and through his eye, as is described to you, and thus he leant a little over the tilt until he fell dead from his horse to the ground.[123]

muerto en el suelo. E* tan súpitamente murió que, por muy aprisa que le acorrieron, nunca le oyeron fablar, ni bollir braço ni pierna. E como le quitaron el elmete de la cabeça falláronle el otro ojo derecho tan inchado como un gran puño, que quería parezer en la cara que havía dos oras que era muerto.

E luego aquellos cavalleros catalanes que allí eran – Mosén Francí e Mosén Rienbau de Corvera antes desto nonbrados, e otros asaz que allí eran naturales de su tierra – mostraron gran sentimiento por su muerte ser tan súpita, e rogavan a Dios que le huviesse merced al ánima.† E en especial se quexava mucho por su muerte un gentilhome que a la sazón en el‡ fecho de aquellas armas le servía, el qual se llamava por su nonbre Jufre Jardín, el qual antes desto havía muy bien fecho§ sus armas, según en este libro es escrito. E dezía a altas bozes: ¡O Exberte de Claramonte! Que en fuerte ventura e punto fueste nacido por morir tan supitaña muerte, e fuera de la tierra donde eras, plega a Nuestro Señor Dios que te aya el ánima'. E destas cosas dezía muchas e muy dolorosas, mostrando gran pesar por su muerte

E luego traxieron una tabla larga, e pusiéronlo⁋ así armado encima della, e tomáronlo aquellos cavalleros e gentileshonbres que allí eran presentes, e llebáronlo a una tienda, e allí le sacaron** el fierro con el asta de los sesos. E tenía el ojo sacado del casco, colgando fasta la barva, e como le sacaron el fierro, començó a salir mucha sangre que de antes non le havía salido ninguna, comoquiera que havía rato que era muerto.

And he died so suddenly that as quickly as they managed to go to his aid, they never heard him utter a word, nor move an arm or leg. And when they removed the helmet from his head they discovered that his right eye was as swollen as a giant fist, so that it looked from his face as though he had been dead for two hours.[124]

And then those Catalonian knights who were there – the aforementioned Lord Francí Desvalls and Lord Riambau de Corbera, and many other citizens of his land who were there – showed great sorrow at his death being so sudden,[125] and they prayed to God that He have mercy on his soul. And in particular a gentleman by the name of Jofre Jardí, who before this had performed his deeds of arms very well, as is written in this book, who at the time of those deeds of arms was his servant, greatly bemoaned his death. And he said out loud: 'O Asbert de Claramunt! Who was born in great fortune and at a special moment, only to die such a sudden death, and outside of the country where you were from, may it please Our Lord God to receive your soul'. And he said many very painful things such as this, showing great sorrow for his death.

And then they brought a long board, and they put him thus armed on top of it, and those knights and gentlemen who were present picked it up, and they carried him to a pavilion, and there they took the spearhead with the broken spear out of his brains. And his eye was hanging out of the socket down to his beard, and as they took the spearhead out, a lot of blood began to flow out, when before there had not been a drop, even though it had been a while since he died.

---

* E: omit – BMP.
† al ánima: del ánima – RAH.
‡ el: aquel – BMP.
§ muy bien fecho: fecho muy bien – BMP.
⁋ pusiéronlo: pusiéronle – BMP.
** le sacaron: lo sacaron – BMP.

E entonze el honrrado cavallero Suero de Quiñones, capitán mayor del passo[*] ya nonbrado, mostró muy gran sentimiento, e todos los otros cavalleros e gentileshomes que allí con él estavan, diziendo que non quisiera que muriera aquel cavallero por quanto en el mundo podía haver, e que le pesava tanto de su muerte que dezir non lo podía. E assimesmo como el ya nonbrado Suero, fijo de Álvar Gómez, fue desarmado, començó a llorar tan fuertemente como sy su padre delante tuviera muerto, diziendo que non quisiera ser nacido para allí ser venido por le haver acaecido aquella desdicha que acaecido le havía.

E en esto el ya nonbrado capitán enbió por ciertos freiles que allí en el passo estavan e[†] dezían las oras cada día, para lo levar a enterrar a la yglesia. E luego como fueron venidos, les dixo que le cantasen sus rresponsos que acostunbravan cantar a los muertos. E[‡] ellos le dixieron que [a] aquel home non le podían fazer aucto ninguno que fiel cristiano devía haver, por ser muerto en el hávito que moriera. E Suero les rogó e pedió quanto pudo de gracia, con muy[§] gran affición, que así lo quisiese[n][¶] honrrar, e[**] non quisiese[n][††] poner escusa más que si a él mismo aquella muerte acaeciera. E los freiles le respondieron que fuese cierto que non fizieran más a él si le aquello[‡‡] acaeciera, e como esto oyó Suero, rogó a un doctor freile que ende estava que luego fuese al Obispo de Astorga, por quanto la puente era de su diócesis e obispado, e le demandase licencia para lo

And then the honourable knight Suero de Quiñones, senior captain of the aforenamed passage of arms, showed very great sorrow along with all of the other knights and gentlemen who were there with him, saying that he did not wish that knight to die for all the world, and that words could not express how much sorrow his death caused him. And likewise when the aforenamed Suero, son of Álvar Gómez, was disarmed, he began to weep so intensely as if his own father were lying dead before him, saying that he wished he had not been born rather than to have reached this point at which that misfortune which had happened, had happened to him.[126]

And at this moment the aforenamed captain sent for certain friars who were there at the passage of arms and who led prayers every day, in order to take him to be buried at the church. And after they had come, he told them to sing the prayers that were traditionally sung for the dead. And they said that they could not perform any service for that man that should be performed for a faithful Christian, due to his getting killed in the manner in which he had died. And Suero de Quiñones begged and besought them as much as he could, most earnestly, that this was how they should strive to honour him, and that they should refrain from giving excuses, any more than if that death had happened to him. And the friars replied that they certainly would have done no more for him if that had happened to him, and when Suero heard this he begged a judicial vicar who was there to go then to the Bishop of Astorga, since the bridge was in his diocese and bishopric, and that he seek his permission to bury him in hallowed ground, for he would

---

[*] *del passo: de aquel passo – RAH.*

[†] *e: que – RAH.*

[‡] *E: omit – BMP.*

[§] *muy: omit – BMP.*

[¶] *quisiese[n]: quisiesen – BMP; quisiese – ESC, RAH.*

[**] *e: que – RAH.*

[††] *quisiese[n]: quisiesen – BMP; quisiese – ESC, RAH.*

[‡‡] *le aquello: aquello le – BMP, RAH.*

enterrar en sagrado, [que él]* le prometía, si la†
traýa, de lo enbiar a León al dicho Esberte para
lo fazer enterrar e sepultar en la capilla e lugar
donde el enterramiento de su linaje estava, tan
honrradamente [quanto]‡ más§ él pudiesse, así
como si fuese un pariente su bien propinco.
E el freile le prometió de luego partir e fazer
en ello quanto pudiese porque su voluntad se
cumpliese. E luego partió para Astorga, que
era a tres leguas de aquel passo.

E él partido, Suero de Quiñones, con todos
los cavalleros e gentileshomes que allí estavan,
llebaron muy honrradamente al ya nonbrado
Esberte de Claramonte, defunto ya nonbrado,
e pusiéronlo en una ermita que está en el cabo
de la puente de Órvigo, acerca del lugar ya
escripto, que non era consagrada, e allí estovo
fasta la noche esperando la licencia si se podría⁋
haver. E desque vino el doctor que por ella era
ydo, e dixo como la non** quería dar, fizieron
una fuesa en el cabo†† de la puente enfrente
de la dicha hermita, e ardiendo muchas
antorchas, siendo presentes a lo enterrar por
le honrrar el ya nonbrado Suero e todos los
más de los cavalleros e gentileshomes que en
el paso eran defensores dél, e otros asaz que
allí eran venidos así a fazer armas como a las
ver fazer. E así lo enterraron en la manera que
oýdo havedes, e en aquel lugar que devisado vos
es, perdónele‡‡ Dios. Por que§§ Dios perdone a
todos aquellos que esta hystoria leyeren, el
auctor les encomienda que digan por su ánima
– por que Dios aya piedad della – sendos
Paternostres e sendas Avemarías, que Dios

promise, if permission were granted, to send
said Asbert to León to have him buried and
entombed in the chapel and place of burial that
was reserved for Suero's family, as honourably
as he were able, as if he were one of his closest
relatives. And then the vicar promised to set
out and do what he could about this so that
his will were done. And then he set out for
Astorga, which was three leagues away from
that passage of arms.

And after he had left, Suero de Quiñones,
with all of the knights and gentlemen who
were there, carried the aforenamed deceased
Asbert de Claramunt very honourably, and
they put him in a hermitage which is at the end
of the Orbigo bridge, near the place already
mentioned, which was not consecrated, and
there he remained until nightfall waiting to
see if permission would be granted.[127] And
when the judicial vicar who had left for this
reason returned, and said that the Bishop did
not wish to grant it, they dug a ditch at the end
of the bridge facing the said hermitage, and
burning many torches, the aforenamed Suero,
and all the rest of the knights and gentlemen
who were Defenders of the passage, and many
others who had come as much to perform deeds
of arms as to watch them being performed,
being present to bury him and honour him.
And thus they buried him in the way you have
heard, and in that place that is described to
you, may God forgive him. So that God may
forgive all those who should read this history,
the author entreats them that they say for his
soul – so that God may have mercy on it – two
Our Fathers and two Ave Marias, so that God

---

* que él: el qual – ESC; que él – BMP; et que
  – RAH.
† la: lo – RAH.
‡ quanto: quanta – ESC; quanto – BMP, RAH.
§ más: omit – RAH.
⁋ podría: podía – BMP.
** la non: non la – BMP.
†† en el cabo: en cabo – RAH.
‡‡ perdónele: perdónelo – BMP; et perdónele
  – RAH.
§§ Por que: Et por que – BMP, RAH.

depare quien las diga por ellos al tiempo de su fin e muerte.*

E el ya nonbrado auctor destas armas dize que non conbiene más fablar de lo que por ellas parece, salvo que los secretos de Dios son muy ascondidos, e la muerte non puede ser recebida sinon en el lugar que por Él está hordenada.†

E lo porque el auctor nonbró en el primero capítulo destas armas que estos dos cavalleros fizieron, a este Esberte de Claramonte 'sinventura', es por quanto quatro días antes desto‡ que estas armas fiziesse, le§ levaron para se armar todas las armas que el ya nonbrado capitán e los de su capitanía¶ en aquel passo tenían para la defensión dél. E según la grande** e altura de su persona nunca le fizieron armas ningunas, en†† especial arnés de piernas e braçales. Ca‡‡ este Esberte era un home tan alto que era marabilla, e tan seguido que cosa en sí non parecía mal puesta, e muy ancho d'espaldas, e de muy fuertes mienbros, ca dubda sería si en mill homes escogidos se pudiera fallar cuerpo de home tan fuerte ni tan aventajado. E era home muy fermoso, e a la sazón que este día se començó armar§§ se armó del arnés del ya nonbrado antes desto Diego de Baçám, uno de los defensores de aquel passo, el qual arnés era el primero que se había ensayado, e aquel día que dél se armó¶¶ para venir a la liça e campo para fazer las armas, dixo que non havía fallado arnés en su vida que le ansí viniesse, ni elmete de que mejor se armase. E por tanto le

may provide for those who say them at the time of their demise and death.

And the aforenamed author of these deeds of arms says that it does not behove him to speak further of what he thinks about them, except that God's secrets are closely guarded, and death cannot be received except in the place which is ordained by Him.

And the reason why the author described this Asbert de Claramunt as 'unfortunate' in the first paragraph of these deeds of arms that these two knights performed, is because four days before he performed these deeds of arms, they took him to put on all of the armour which the aforenamed captain and those on his team at that passage of arms had for his defence.[128] And because of the size and height of his person no armour ever fit him, especially the legharness and vambraces. For this Asbert was such a tall man that it was amazing, and so straight that nothing in and of itself looked bad on him, and very broad in the shoulders, and he had very strong limbs, for it would be doubtful that out of a thousand men you could find such a strong or such a tall man. And he was a very handsome man, and at the time on this day that he began to arm himself, he put on the harness of the aforenamed Diego de Bazán, one of the Defenders of that passage of arms, which harness was the first one he had tried on, and that day when he put it on to come to the lists and the field to perform deeds of arms, he said that he had never in his life found a harness that suited him so well, nor a helmet that fit better.[129] And therefore the author says that he is unfortunate because

* *e muerte*: omit – BMP, RAH.
† *hordenada*: *ordenada*, emended to *ordenado* – RAH.
‡ *desto*: *deste* – BMP.
§ *le*: *lo* – BMP.
¶ *capitanía*: *compañía* – BMP.
** *la grande*: *las grandes* – BMP; *grandes* – RAH.
†† *en*: *et en* – RAH.
‡‡ *Ca*: *E* – BMP.
§§ *començó armar*: *començó a armar* – BMP, RAH.
¶¶ *que dél se armó*: omit – BMP.

dize el auctor ser sinventura por la muerte que vio que aquel día hovo. E que según su juizio le llamó la Fortuna a lo* traer allí, porque la ventura lo tenía juzgado.

of the death that he saw him suffer that day. And in his opinion Fortune called upon him to bring him there, because fate had him judged.[130]

33.
Escorial MS f.II.19, fols. 161r–162r

Lope de Stúñiga.
Capítulo que fabla de las armas que en este día el honrrado cavallero ya nonbrado Lope de Stúñiga† fizo con el honrrado cavallero Miçer Arnao, bretón, según deyuso vos será devisado.

33.
Saturday, 7 August 1434
Lope de Stúñiga vs. Monsieur Arnaut Bojue
[*On striking the horse: cp. Menaguerra, ch. 30; above, Articles 16–17.*
On losing the reins:
cp. Menaguerra, chs. 12 and 17]

Lope de Stúñiga.
Chapter which speaks about the deeds of arms which on this day the aforenamed honourable knight Lope de Stúñiga performed with the honourable knight Monsieur Arnaut the Breton, as will be described to you below.

Luego como esta Grida fue dada, entró en el campo e liça a fazer armas el honrrado cavallero antes desto nonbrado Lope de Stúñiga, uno de los diez defensores de aquel passo, armado e a cavallo. E de la otra parte contra él, Arnao, bretón, de la casa del Duque de Bretaña, asimesmo armado e a cavallo. Siendo presente el muy famoso e generoso cavallero Don Pedro de Velasco, Conde de Faro, el qual ese día allí havía llegado, e otros asaz cavalleros e gentileshomes de su casa que con él allí havían venido, los quales venían de romería de la casa del ya nonbrado bienaventurado apóstol Sanctiago, e asimesmo todos los otros cavalleros e gentileshomes que antes desto ya nonbrados son, que allí en el passo solían estar.

E como fueron dentro en el campo a fazer las armas, pusieron sus lanças en los riestres a guisa de buenos cavalleros que bien parecía‡

After this Criee was given, the aforenamed honourable knight Lope de Stúñiga, one of the ten Defenders of that passage of arms, entered the field and lists to perform deeds of arms, armed and on horseback. And on the other side opposite him, Arnaut the Breton, from the household of the Duke of Brittany,[131] likewise armed and on horseback. Being present the most famous and generous knight Don Pedro de Velasco, Count of Haro,[132] who had arrived there that day, and sundry other knights and gentlemen of his household who had come with him, all of whom were coming from a pilgrimage from the house of the aforenamed blessed Apostle Santiago,[133] and likewise all of the other aforementioned knights and gentlemen, who were always there at the passage of arms.

And now that they were inside the field to perform deeds of arms, they placed their spears in the rests like good knights who truly looked like they had a will to match strength as

---

* *lo: le – BMP.*

† *ya nonbrado Lope de Stúñiga: Lope de Stúñiga ya nonbrado – BMP, RAH.*

‡ *parecía: parecían – RAH.*

que tenían en voluntad de ser en breve delibres[*] en aquel fecho de armas que començavan.

E a esta primera carrera encontró el honrrado cavallero[†] Lope de Stúñiga al ya nonbrado Mosén Arnao, bretón, en el borde de las platas, e rompió su lança en él en rachas, e fízole tomar un gran revés,[‡] e levava el ya nonbrado Mosén Arnao una racha con el fierro de la lança por so el sobaco derecho, e otra racha metida por debaxo de la bavera. E todos pensaron que yva ferido, e deque lo cataron el rrey de armas e faraute, fallaron que non fuera[§] ferido nin havía sangre.

A las dos carerras barrearon las lanças, comoquiera que perdió las rriendas[¶] el bretón.

A las tres carreras encontró Mosén Arnao, bretón, a Lope de Stúñiga en el guardabraço yzquierdo, e diole un tan gran golpe que rompió su lança en él en pieças, e fízole tomar un gran revés.^{**} E Lope de Stúñiga encontró en el pezcueço del cavallo del bretón por cerca de las crines, e passóle el fierro de la otra parte, e rrompió su lança en él e salió mucha sangre de la ferida. E este encuentro dizían que fue^{††} por quanto dio el bretón una sofrenada al cavallo, de la qual alzó la cabeça, e que por eso fuera^{‡‡} ansí encontrado, comoquiera que non morió el cavallo de [aquella]^{§§} ferida ni dexó el cavallero de yr^{¶¶} en él a su tienda.

soon as possible in that deed of arms that they were commencing.

And in this first course the honourable knight Lope de Stúñiga struck the aforenamed Monsieur Arnaut the Breton on the stop-rib of the breastplate, and he shattered his spear into pieces on him, and he made him suffer a serious reversal of fortune, and the aforenamed Monsieur Arnaut was carrying a splinter with the spearhead of the spear under his right armpit, and another splinter stuck beneath the bevor. And everyone thought he was wounded, and when the king-of-arms and the herald examined him they discovered that he had not been wounded nor was there any blood.

In the second course they barricaded the spears; however, the Breton lost the reins.

In the third course Monsieur Arnaut the Breton struck Lope de Stúñiga on the left pauldron, and he dealt him such a mighty blow that he broke his spear into pieces upon him, and he made him suffer a serious reversal of fortune. And Lope de Stúñiga struck the Breton's horse in the neck, near the mane, and the spearhead pierced through to the other side, and he broke his spear in it and a lot of blood flowed from the wound. And they said that this encounter happened because the Breton gave a sudden jerk on the reins of his horse, causing it to raise its head, and for this reason it was struck thus, even though the horse did not die from that wound nor did it prevent the knight from riding it to his pavilion.

---

[*] *delibres: delibrantes – RAH.*
[†] *cavallero: omit – RAH.*
[‡] *e fízole tomar un gran revés: omit – BMP.*
[§] *fuera: era – BMP, RAH.*
[¶] *las rriendas: las rriendas del cavallo – BMP.*
^{**} *un gran revés: un buen revés – BMP, RAH.*
^{††} *que fue: omit – BMP.*
^{‡‡} *fuera: fue – BMP, RAH.*
^{§§} *aquella: aquela – ESC; aquella – BMP, RAH.*
^{¶¶} *de yr: omit – BMP.*

E luego los juezes dieron sus armas por cumplidas, e mandáronlos que saliesen* del campo e se fuesen a sus tiendas. E luego allí, antes que saliesen del campo, vinieron delante los juezes, e alçaron las caras de los almetes e conociéronse el uno al otro. E allí le dixo Mosén Arnao Dojue a Lope de Stúñiga que dava muchas gracias a Dios e a él, porque tan noble† cavallero como él era le havía delibrado de aquellas armas. E Lope de Stúñiga le rrespondió que él era mereciente dello, e de mucho más, e digno de [mucho]‡ onor, e que así fazía él que era muy ledo e alegre por haver fecho las armas con él. E luego lo conbidó a cenar, según la costunbre del passo,§ e ansí se partieron del campo.

E aquí fabla el auctor e dize, según lo que vio, siendo presente, que andavan amos a dos¶ muy diestros en aquellas armas. Comoquiera qu'el honrrado cavallero Lope de Stúñiga parecía andar más fuerte cavallero e havía llebado lo mejor del bretón, salvo porque encontró** el cavallo, como ya es devisado, e por ser el encuentro así fecho, es rregla†† de cavallería de dar lo mejor quando las tales cosas acaecen, al que el tal encuentro recibe como este [cavallero]‡‡ recebió, e§§ por ende le da lo mejor.

And then the judges declared their arms completed, and they ordered them to leave the field and go to their pavilions. And then while still there, before leaving the field, they came before the judges and raised the visors of the helmets and recognised each other. And there Monsieur Arnaut Bojue told Lope de Stúñiga that he gave many thanks to God and to him, because such a noble knight as he had matched strength with him in those deeds of arms. And Lope de Stúñiga replied that he was deserving of this, and of much more, and worthy of much honour, and Lope de Stúñiga did the same, for he was most content and happy for having performed deeds of arms with Arnaut Bojue. And then he invited Arnaut Bojue to dinner, according to the custom of the passage of arms, and this is how they left the field.

And here speaks the author and he says, according to what he saw, being present, that they were both riding very skilfully in those deeds of arms. However, the honourable knight Lope de Stúñiga seemed to be a stronger knight and he had been carrying the advantage over the Breton, but for the fact that he struck the horse, as is described above, and because the encounter was made in this way, it is the law of chivalry to give the advantage when such things happen to the one who receives a blow such as the one this knight received, and thus he gives the Breton the advantage.

---

* *saliesen: se saliesen – BMP.*
† *noble: notable – RAH.*
‡ *mucho: mucha – ESC; mucho – BMP, RAH.*
§ *E luego lo conbidó a cenar, según la costunbre del passo: omit – BMP.*
¶ *amos a dos: amos et dos – BMP, RAH.*
** *encontró: entonce – BMP.*
†† *es rregla: es en regla – BMP, RAH.*
‡‡ *cavallero: cavallo – ESC; cavallero – BMP, RAH.*
§§ *e: omit – BMP.*

34.
Escorial MS f.II.19, fols. 164r–165r

Domingo siguiente, ocho días de agosto.
Capítulo que fabla de cómo en este domingo,
en la tarde, entró en el campo e liça a fazer
armas* el ya nonbrado Gómez de Villacorta
con Lope de Ferrera antes desto nonbrado.

En este ya nonbrado domingo siguiente, ocho
días del ya dicho mes de agosto, de mañana
non se fizieron ningunas armas.† E en la tarde
entró en el campo e liça otra vez el ya antes
desto‡ nombrado Gómez de Villacorta, que el
día de§ antes las armas havía fecho con Alfonso
Fraijoo, uno de los defensores del passo, armado
e a cavallo. E de la otra parte contra él, Lope
de Ferrera, hermano de Sancho de Ferrera, ya
antes desto nonbrado, de la conpañía de Don
Juan de Portugal, asimismo armado e a cavallo.
E como fueron dentro en el campo, pusieron
sus lanças en los riestres de muy buenas
continencias e ardideça de cavallería, e amos a
dos¶ movieron muy reziamente el uno contra
el otro.**

Comoquiera que passaron quatro carreras
que non se encontraron.

A las cinco carreras encontró Gómez de
Villacorta a Lope de Ferrera en la buelta del
guardabraço yzquierdo, e desgranó el fierro de
su lança sin la romper ni tomar ninguno dellos
revés.

34.
Sunday, 8 August 1434
Gómez de Villacorta vs. Lope de Ferrera
[*On striking the horse: cp. Menaguerra, ch. 30; above, Articles 16–17*]

The following Sunday, 8 August.
Chapter which speaks about how on this
Sunday afternoon, the aforenamed Gómez
de Villacorta entered the field and lists to
perform deeds of arms with the aforenamed
Lope de Ferrera.

On this aforesaid following Sunday, the eighth
day of the aforesaid month of August, no deeds
of arms were performed in the morning. And
in the afternoon the aforenamed Gómez de
Villacorta, one of the Defenders of the passage
of arms, who the day before had performed
deeds of arms with Alfonso Freijos, entered
the field and lists once again,[134] armed and
on horseback. And on the other side opposite
him, Lope de Ferrera, the brother of the aforenamed Sancho de Ferrera, on Don Juan of
Portugal's team, likewise armed and on horseback. And now that they were inside the field,
they placed their spears in the rests with great
composure and chivalric verve, and they both
charged against each other very vigorously.

However, they ran four courses in which
they did not encounter.

In the fifth course Gómez de Villacorta
struck Lope de Ferrera on the haute-piece of
the left pauldron, and the head of his spear tore
off[135] without breaking it or either one of them
suffering a reversal of fortune.

---

* *fazer armas: fazer las armas – BMP.*
† *ningunas armas: más armas – RAH.*
‡ *antes desto: omit – BMP.*
§ *de: omit – BMP.*
¶ *amos a dos: amos et dos – BMP, RAH.*
** *movieron muy reziamente el uno contra el otro:*
    movieron el uno contra el otro muy rreciamente
    – BMP.

A las seis carreras encontró Lope de Ferrera en la cara del cavallo de Gómez de Villacorta con su lança, debaxo del ojo yzquierdo quanto tres dedos, e passóle el fierro con un pedaço del asta de la otra parte quanto un palmo. E como le dio el encuentro, dio un relincho el cavallo, e asimesmo relinchó otra vez quando le sacaron el asta con el fierro de la cara. E rompió su lança en él. E este encuentro dizen que non encontrara Lope en el cavallo salvo porque, en* empeçando a salir de la liça, tocó el cavallo con las camas del freno en un palo de la liça e alçó la cabeça. E dizen que por aquella causa le encontró en la cara, según juraron ciertos escuderos que allí eran presentes a la sazón. E por quanto Gómez de Villacorta encontró un poco en esta carrera† a Lope de Ferrera en el guardabraço yzquierdo, contaron a Gómez la lança que firió el‡ cavallo por rrompida.

E luego los juezes dieron sus armas por cumplidas, e mandáronles que se fuesen a sus tiendas. Comoquiera que porfiaron amos a dos§ que non saldrían del campo fasta que sus armas fuesen cumplidas. E los juezes todavía les mandaron que saliesen del campo e se fuesen a sus tiendas.¶ Comoquiera que si tiempo huviesse adelante, antes que el plazo** se cumpliesse, que les darían lugar a que las cumpliesen. E ellos, por cumplir su mandamiento,†† huviéronlo de fazer.

In the sixth course Lope de Ferrera struck Gómez de Villacorta's horse in the face with his spear, as much as three digits below the left eye, and the spearhead and a piece of the shaft pierced as much as a palm's length through the other side. And when he delivered the blow, the horse gave a whinny, and likewise it whinnied once more when the shaft and spearhead were removed from its face. And Lope de Ferrera broke his spear on it. And they say that Lope would not have delivered this stroke upon the horse but for the fact that, as Gómez de Villacorta was starting to ride down the lists, the horse clipped a post of the lists with the shanks of the bit and raised its head. And they say that for that reason he struck it in the face, according to the testimony of certain squires who were present in that place at that moment. And since Gómez de Villacorta struck Lope de Ferrera lightly on the left pauldron in this course, they counted the spear that injured the horse as one spear broken for Gómez.

And then the judges declared their deeds of arms completed, and they ordered them to go to their pavilions. However, they both insisted that they would not leave the field until their deeds of arms were completed. And the judges still ordered them to leave the field and go to their pavilions, on the understanding that if there were still time before the deadline arrived,[136] they would allow them to complete them. And so as to comply with their order, they had to do the judges' bidding.

---

* *en*: omit – *BMP, RAH.*
† *en esta carrera*: omit – *BMP.*
‡ *el*: omit – *BMP.*
§ *amos a dos*: amos e dos – *BMP.*
¶ *comoquiera que porfiaron amos a dos que non saldrían del campo fasta que sus armas fuesen cumplidas. E los juezes todavía les mandaron que saliesen del campo e se fuesen a sus tiendas*: omit – *RAH.*
** *plazo*: paso, emended to *plazo* – *ESC.*
†† *mandamiento*: mandado – *RAH.*

E alçaron las caras de los elmetes, e conociéronse el uno al otro. E luego Gómez de Villacorta conbidó a cenar a Lope de Ferrera, según la costunbre del passo, e fuéronse a sus tiendas.

E el autor non cumple que mucho aquí* fable en estas armas que estos dos cavalleros ficieron, por quanto por ellas parece que lieva lo mejor el ya nonbrado Gómez de Villacorta.

And they raised the visors of the helmets, and each one recognised the other. And then Gómez de Villacorta invited Lope de Ferrera to dinner, according to the custom of the passage of arms, and they went to their pavilions.

And it does not behove the author to speak much here about these deeds of arms which these two knights performed, since it seems that the aforenamed Gómez de Villacorta is carrying the advantage in them.

* *aquí*: omit – BMP.

NOTES TO THE TRANSLATION

1 St James was at the core of the Pass of Honour of Suero de Quiñones. Firstly, the passage of arms was staged close to the pilgrim route to the Cathedral of Santiago de Compostela, the saint's alleged burial site. Secondly, the timeline, as indicated below, hinged on St James' Day. Thirdly, St James had long since been associated with martial activity in Castile, having reputedly appeared before Christian knights and urged them on to victory at the battle of Calahorra in 844, so he was an appropriate patron for these jousts of war. St James' miraculous appearance at the battle of Calahorra and subsequent battles of the Reconquest is discussed by Fallows, *The Chivalric Vision of Alfonso de Cartagena*, p. 178, n. 5, and Martínez Ruiz, 'Notas sobre las supersticiones de los caballeros castellanos medievales'.

2 Suero de Quiñones (1409–58). Biographical sketches are provided by Evans, 'A Spanish Knight in Flesh and Blood: A Study of the Chivalric Spirit of Suero de Quiñones'; Mingote Tarazona, *Varones ilustres de la Provincia de León*, pp. 69–89; and Rodríguez de Lena, *El Passo Honroso de Suero de Quiñones*, ed. Labandeira Fernández, pp. 46–51. Álvarez Álvarez, *El condado de Luna en la Baja Edad Media*, offers a well-documented study of the political and economic fortunes of the Quiñones family in the fifteenth century and beyond (on Suero see pp. 85–97). The longer biographical works vary in

quality. For example, without providing a shred of documentary evidence, the thrust of Camín's book *Don Suero de Quiñones* is that Suero was a madman who was Cervantes' model for Don Quixote. The chapters meander from one disconnected topic to another, from local geography and personalities of the fifteenth century to the author's own supposedly stellar reputation as a poet – a most irritating read that must be treated with a great deal of caution. Alonso Luengo, *Don Suero de Quiñones, el del Passo Honroso*, is written in a novelistic style buttressed by solid documentation; Marqués de Alcedo y de San Carlos, *Un olvidado pleito del siglo XV: La herencia de Suero de Quiñones*, provides transcriptions and facsimiles of documents pertaining to the family lineage, without dwelling on Suero's biography. This book includes a facsimile of Suero's signature, between pp. 122–3.

3 Suero is addressing King John II of Castile (ruled 1406–54) and the royal favourite, Álvaro de Luna (c. 1390–1453), who held the title Constable of Castile.

4 That is, on 1 January 1434.

5 The ten Defenders of this passage of arms were: Suero de Quiñones (Senior Captain), Lope de Aller, Diego de Bazán, Diego de Benavides, Lope de Stúñiga, Suero, son of Álvar Gómez, Pedro de

Nava, Sancho de Rabanal, Pedro de los Ríos and Gómez de Villacorta.

6 Saint James' Day falls on 25 July. The first jousts took place on 10 July 1434 and the last jousts on 9 August.

7 In fact, a total of 180 spears were broken or counted as broken in this passage of arms (on spears being counted as broken, see below, Article 17).

8 *reinforcing piece*: Cp. medieval Castilian *dobla-dura*. In 1434 these reinforcing pieces would have been fairly rudimentary and nowhere near as complex as the exchange pieces used in the jousts of the sixteenth century.

9 Instances are known of foreign contestants being prohibited from participating in hastiludes because, for example, of the potential political and legal ramifications of accidental death. See Barber and Barker, *Tournaments*, p. 25, and Barker, *The Tournament in England, 1100–1400*, pp. 54–5. On the myriad problems generated by accidental death, see below, Selection 32.

10 For an example of the formal arrival of a lady, see below, Selection 28. The glove is associated with the literary conceit of the love token. The earliest examples of such tokens in courtly literature can be found in Marie de France's twelfth-century lais *Chaitivel* and *Eliduc*, where the French term used is 'druërie'. See Marie de France, *Chaitivel* and *Eliduc*, in *Les Lais de Marie de France*, ed. Rychner, p. 145 line 57 and p. 168 line 431, respectively. In the early thirteenth-century Castilian lyric poem *Razón de Amor* one of the love tokens exchanged is, specifically, a lady's glove. See *Razón de Amor*, in Michalski, *La 'Razón' de Lupus de Moros: Un poema hermético*, pp. 165–78, at p. 168 line 37a.

11 Suero's love was Doña Leonor de Tovar, whom he married in 1435. Legend has it that he requested that Doña Leonor relinquish her glove as a token at a passage of arms in Madrid in 1433 and she had refused him the honour. See Camín, *Don Suero de Quiñones*, p. 167; also Alonso Luengo, *Don Suero de Quiñones, el del Passo Honroso*, pp. 225–34.

12 *with a coat of arms beyond reproach*: That is to say, with a member of the titled nobility whose family arms are depicted on a 'coat of arms', or heraldic crest. The coat of arms was always associated with war and was therefore appropriate for

this passage of arms. See Barker, *The Tournament in England, 1100–1400*, pp. 183–6, and Vale, *War and Chivalry*, pp. 96–8. In the context of the fifteenth-century Christian kingdoms in Iberia, the term 'beyond reproach', as well as signifying martial reputation, may be interpreted to mean that these knights are 'true' Christians with no Jewish or *converso* ancestry.

13 The judges attempted to veto this Article on the grounds that too many knights would issue special challenges. Suero de Quiñones ultimately won the debate for its inclusion on the grounds that these articles had already been widely publicised and distributed and were therefore binding. For the debate, see Rodríguez de Lena, *El Passo Honroso de Suero de Quiñones*, ed. Labandeira Fernández, pp. 121–2.

14 The reference is to the pilgrimage route to the Cathedral of Santiago de Compostela.

15 Cp. the following Article of the Passage of Arms of Charlemagne's Tree held near Dijon in 1443: 'Item, no prince, baron, knight or esquire, shall pass within a quarter of a league of the spot assigned for these combats without entering the lists and taking part, or otherwise leaving as pledges his sword or spurs, according to his pleasure'. Quoted by Clephan, *The Medieval Tournament*, p. 60.

16 The judges were Pero Barba and Gómez Arias de Quiñones.

17 Note that the Articles begin and end with an empirical 'I' (Spanish 'yo'), underscoring Suero's omnipresence at and personal investment in this passage of arms. Although it is not known if the original Articles for this passage of arms were signed by the ten Defenders or not, the practice of adding signatures to the end of the Articles which regulated passages of arms was certainly not uncommon. See Anglo, *The Great Tournament Roll of Westminster*, vol. I, p. 52.

18 Cp. Menaguerra, ch. 30, where striking the bridle hand (i.e. the left hand) is considered a 'prohibited stroke'. Despite Menaguerra's viewpoint, however, see also the comment made by Sir John Paston in a letter he sent to his brother in March, 1467: 'My hand was hurt at the tourney at Eltham upon Wednesday last, I would that you had been there and seen it, for it was the goodliest sight that was seen in England this forty years of so few

men.' See Davis, ed. *Paston Letters and Papers of the Fifteenth Century: Part I*, p. 396, no. 236.

19 Miraculously, despite having his armour pierced in four different places, Pedro de los Ríos is not recorded as sustaining a single injury in this course. It can be inferred that Funes' spear pierced the reinforce of the gauntlet, then the gauntlet itself, whence it skated over to the plackart, piercing it at an oblique angle in such a way that it then pushed its way back out from beneath the breastplate, piercing it from the inside out and snapping in the process.

20 *the reinforcing breastplate*: Cp. medieval Castilian *el peto del piastrón*. Leguina omits this term in his *Glosario de voces de Armería*. Blair notes that in jousts of war: 'As far as can be judged from the scanty information available at present the ordinary field armour ... probably with the addition of certain reinforcing-pieces, seems to have been used until *c.* 1440' (*European Armour*, p. 159). From the context, the terminology in this instance is referring to a second breastplate worn over the regular breastplate. Cp. below, Selection 29, Course 9.

21 In this and the previous course, the fact that their harnesses were so easily skewered calls into question the defensive properties and, by extension, the quality of the armour they are both wearing.

22 An invitation to dinner was often the culmination of the jousting ritual, the idea being that the combatants would now socialise in a peaceable manner whilst sharing food. See Contreras Martín, 'Comida y cortesía: los rituales alimenticios en la sociedad caballeresca de los siglos XIV y XV'.

23 Note that the chronicler records the judges' decision in the previous paragraph, in his official capacity, to which he now appends his own opinion.

24 Pero Rodríguez de Lena's running commentary at the end of each series of jousts brings to mind the following comment made by Oren Falk about judicial combat: 'Bystanders, in a very real sense, come first; only when this pivotral role has been manned can other, secondary participants in the violence – viz. the combatants themselves – assume their positions. We ought to be thinking not of witnesses to a fight, then, but of fighters to a witness.' See Falk, 'Bystanders and Hearsayers First: Reassessing the Role of the Audience in Duelling', p. 99.

25 This was Sancho de Rabanal's first joust against Jofre Jardí, but his second joust of the day, having just run eight courses against Juan de Estamarín.

26 *vervelles*: Cp. medieval Castilian *pontecillas*. Literally, 'little bridges'. The vervelles, or staples, were arranged vertically on the right-hand side of the breastplate. The bracket of the lance-rest was then secured to the vervelles with a retaining pin.

27 That is, a lame of the right pauldron.

28 On the importance of music as part of the established ceremonial in fifteenth-century tournaments and passages of arms, see Anglo, *The Great Tournament Roll of Westminster*, vol. I, p. 29, n. 2.

29 Here we have an unusual confluence of nature, the courtly ethos and rhetoric. In so far as literary works are concerned, the notion that 'we must stop because night is coming on' is a rhetorical topos of the conclusion. See Curtius, *European Literature and the Latin Middle Ages*, pp. 90–1. In courtly culture night was traditionally associated, as at this passage of arms, with the banquet, repose and sleep (sometimes also love-making). Torch-lit jousting festivals which defied rhetorical convention, and nature itself, were rare, but not without precedent. See Barber and Barker, *Tournaments*, pp. 35, 58, 98–9 and 102.

30 On the two entrances to the lists, see Anglo, *The Great Tournament Roll of Westminster*, vol. I, p. 29, and Barber and Barker, *Tournaments*, p. 51.

31 Instances of striking twice in the same spot were rare and therefore noteworthy. Cp. Zapata, *Miscelánea*, ed. Carrasco González, ch. 250, p. 349: 'Otra vez vimos un mal justador dar encuentro feo en la tela, y hacer en ella agujero, y volver luego y meter otra carrera por el mismo agujero la lanza.' ('Another time we saw a bad jouster deal a foul stroke on the tilt cloth, and rip a hole in it, and ride another course later on in which he stuck the lance through the same hole.')

32 *they barricaded the spears*: Cp. Quijada de Reayo, ch. 4: 'When they run, some horses hold the head high until the moment of the encounter and this causes them to be struck on the shaffron, and attainting it with the lance or barricading the lance is not good because it makes lances split crosswise and they are poorly broken because the judges judge them to be so. Barricading the lance means crossing

it too far sideways so that it does not strike and breaks poorly.'

33 This is a pertinent aside, since a barricaded spear typically would snap the moment the opposing jouster charged into and through it.

34 Assuming that the weather in medieval Spain was the same as it is today, running twenty-seven courses on a hot July afternoon must have required tremendous fortitude and endurance, a testimony to the fact that these men, and their horses, were at the peak of physical fitness.

35 As noted by Kaeuper, *Chivalry and Violence in Medieval Europe*: 'The heart was the seat of prowess, the point of origin for the arteries which in Galenic theory carried the animal vitality of the body' (p. 247).

36 Lope Ortíz de Stúñiga (c. 1410–c. 1477) was an accomplished *cancionero* poet as well as a jouster. On his life and poetry see Benito Ruano, 'Lope de Stúñiga: Vida y cancionero'.

37 In the original Castilian the chronicler alternates between 'prendió' and 'quedó', which I translate as 'gained a purchase' and 'bit', respectively.

38 *vamplate*: Cp. medieval Castilian *arandela*, which can refer either to a defensive 'rondel' worn on the armour or to the protective 'vamplate' of the lance. Here it refers to the vamplate, into which Lope de Stúñiga's spear would have slammed after it continued its trajectory down the shaft of his opponent's spear. Although the vamplate is also known in English as the rondelle, I avoid this term in order to prevent confusion with rondel. On the terminology see Hoffmeyer, *Arms and Armour in Spain*, vol. II, pp. 207–8.

39 On the grapper, see Menaguerra, ch. 18.

40 *rondel*: Cp. medieval Castilian *arandela*. In this case the chronicler is clearly talking about the rondel, as opposed to the vamplate.

41 This happens only once in this entire chronicle, from which it can be inferred that it was highly unusual for the spear to snap at the eye.

42 *they crossed*: Cp. medieval Castilian *cruzaron*. Since the chronicler does not say that the spears barricaded, it can be inferred that they knocked against each other crosswise as they were being lowered, but without breaking.

43 *retaining bolt*: Cp. medieval Castilian *perno*. The couter wing, or guard of the vambrace, was in this case attached by a staple and retaining bolt. See Blair, *European Armour*, p. 83. The retaining bolts are visible on the Avant armour in Part I, chapter 2, fig. 17.

44 This episode requires some explanation. Firstly, in 1434 political relations between the king of Castile's powerful royal favourite Álvaro de Luna and the King of Aragon, Alfonso V the Magnanimous (ruled 1416–58), were rather strained. Suero de Quiñones was at this time an ardent supporter of Álvaro de Luna. As Riquer notes, many of the Catalonian knights were prompted by the political situation to travel to this passage of arms with the intention of doing everything in their power to spoil the festivities (Riquer, *Caballeros andantes españoles*, pp. 98–9). In this instance the Catalonian knight Francés Daviu is alluding to a 'wayward nun', a stock figure in medieval comic tales, the two most famous of whom were Doña Garoza and Madame Eglentyne, both created in the fourteenth century by Juan Ruiz and Geoffrey Chaucer, respectively. Bawdy tales of wayward nuns (and other stock figures, such as gluttonous friars, shrewish wives, henpecked husbands, etc.) were often told or sung by minstrels and troubadours for the entertainment of those who travelled the pilgrim routes of Europe (see Daichman, *Wayward Nuns in Medieval Literature*, pp. 115–60). Since the Pass of Honour of Suero de Quiñones took place near the pilgrim route to Santiago de Compostela it is not too fanciful to suggest that Daviu and his colleagues had heard such a tale en route. Daviu, then, is making a mockery of the very premise of this passage of arms, since he is not jousting for love of a chaste lady, as stated in the Articles, but for love of a lascivious nun. In shattering the illusion he conforms to Huizinga's description of the spoilsport (see Part I, Introduction). It is significant that his comment goes largely ignored by the Castilians.

45 The notion of jousting incognito or in disguise, followed by an anagnorisis when each contestant recognises his opponent, and the notion of delaying the invitation to dinner until some adventure has taken place or been described, are both leitmotivs borrowed directly from medieval chivalric romance. For sundry examples, see Anglo, *The Great Tournament Roll of Westminster*, vol. I, pp. 23–32; Barker,

The Tournament in England, 1100–1400, pp. 86–7; and Kaeuper, *Chivalry and Violence in Medieval Europe,* pp. 49, 113, 148 and 191.

46 *to the place where he was lodging at the bridge*: Cp. medieval Castilian *fasta el lugar de la puente donde posava.* The verb *posar* suggests lodging at an inn (Spanish *posada*). It was quite common for visiting jousters to be hosted at local inns. See Anglo, *The Great Tournament Roll of Westminster,* p. 98, n. 1, and Muhlberger, *Jousts and Tournaments,* p. 22.

47 In this instance the chronicler cocks his own parenthetical snook at Francés Daviu, i.e. the man who publicly admitted to having fun with a nun *and* who lost the joust still got to enjoy the luxury of staying at an inn. All of this jocularity was lost on the author of the abbreviated chronicle, the ecclesiastic Fray Juan de Pineda, who makes the following comment: 'Al igual digo yo que si él tuviera alguna nobleza de Christiano, o siquiera la vergüença natural con que todos procuran encubrir sus faltas, no pregonara un sacrilegio tan escandaloso y tan en deshonra del estado monachal y tan injurioso para Iesu Christo.' ('Whereas I say that if he had any Christian nobility, or even the natural shame with which everyone strives to conceal their shortcomings, he would not have proclaimed such a scandalous sacrilege and such a dishonour to the monastic estate and such an affront to Jesus Christ.') See Pineda, *Libro del Passo honroso,* ed. Riquer, p. 81.

48 Ruy Díaz de Mendoza (d. 1479), First Count of Castrojeriz. From 1432–3 he had held the prestigious position of royal standard bearer to King John II of Castile. See also below, Selection 8.

49 *on the besagew*: Cp. medieval Castilian *en el barascuro,* referring to Juan de Soto's 'ursus'-type spaulders with integral besagews made in one piece with the pauldron. The same term (with the variant spelling *barrascuro*) is used in course 21 of this joust to refer to the rondel on the gauntlet. Over a hundred years later in 1548, Quijada de Reayo (ch. 3) would use the term (with the variant spelling *barascudo*) to refer to the rondel at the back of the armet.

50 For the exact opposite scenario, see Selection 12, course 4

51 The author inadvertently omitted to describe courses 10–12. The same omission occurs in the abbreviated chronicle. See Pineda, *Libro del Passo honroso,* ed. Riquer, p. 83.

52 *the rondel of the gauntlet*: Cp. medieval Spanish *el barrascuro de la manopla.* Typically the chronicler refers to the 'guarda de la manopla'. The nuance refers to the fact that Juan de Soto is wearing a mitten gauntlet on his left hand, to which is attached a protective rondel on a short stem.

53 Cp. Menaguerra, ch. 30, where striking the front arçon, or saddle-bow, is a 'prohibited stroke'.

54 As we have seen in the Introduction to Part I, Pero Rodríguez de Lena was a master of hypotyposis, dissecting and interpreting each and every joust with great precision. He shows much less enthusiasm for what might be called the semiotics of jousting and most often – as in this case – simply describes what the contestants or their horses were wearing but without explaining the meaning. The colours of the caparison of Diego de Mansilla's horse were most likely *gules* and *or*. From a heraldic point of view, both Honoré Bouvet and Christine de Pizan note that flames of fire denote loftiness and nobility. See Bouvet, *The Tree of Battles,* trans. Coopland, IV.cxxix, p. 206a, and Pizan, *The Book of Deeds of Arms and of Chivalry,* trans Willard and Willard, p. 219. The actual design on the caparison might have been reminiscent of the flamboyant tracing which characterised the stained glass windows of the great Gothic cathedrals of the time. The flames of fire could also signify that Diego de Mansilla is riding on a veritable hell of passion – perhaps a common thread joining this to the Marqués de Santillana's *Infierno de los enamorados* (The Lovers' Inferno), an allegorical poem composed *c.* 1437, some three years after this passage of arms. The flames on the caparison, when considered alongside the armour worn by the knight, may also symbolise accident and injury, reminiscent of the Castilian knight Don Miguel Lucas de Iranzo, who is described at a siege as 'tomando por estremo remedio el fuego y el fierro, como facen los çirujanos e físicos, que curan las llagas quando por melecinas blandas sanar no las pueden' ('taking as an extreme remedy fire and iron, as surgeons and physicians do, who treat wounds with them when they cannot heal them with mild medicines'). See *Hechos del Condestable Don Miguel Lucas de Iranzo,* ed. Mata Carriazo, p. 268–9 (for the year

1465). What can be stated with certainty is that as Diego de Mansilla's horse gathered speed and the caparison flowed, the overall effect must have been truly spectacular. The motif seems to have been popular: not unlike Diego de Mansilla, the future King Henry IV of Castile and his team of twelve knights all wore matching red surcoats embroidered with gold bullion flames of fire at the jousts staged in Valladolid on 24 May 1428. See Carrillo de Huete, *Crónica del halconero de Juan II*, ed. Mata Carriazo, p. 24; also Barrientos, *Refundición de la crónica del halconero*, ed. Mata Carriazo, p. 64.

55 *from which a lot of blood flowed*: Cp. medieval Castilian *de que mucha sangre le salió*. Such stock phraseology to describe the pouring forth (Latin 'effusio') of blood was used throughout medieval Europe to denote 'immoderate interpersonal violence'. See Meyerson, Thiery and Falk, 'Introduction', p. 3.

56 Most likely the unconscious passer-by in this case had his mouth closed, in which case it would have been difficult to tell if he was breathing. Pinching the nostrils would have been a simple yet effective way of forcing him to open his mouth to breathe.

57 *bowed*: Cp. medieval Castilian *verdugó*. Leguina, *Glosario de voces de Armería*, p. 858, merely cites this passage (from the Pineda edition of the *Passo Honroso*) and shies away from a definition of the verb *verdugar*. Corominas and Pascual, *Diccionario crítico etimológico castellano e hispánico*, vol. V, pp. 783a–785a, do not register the verb *verdugar* in their extensive treatment of the noun *verdugo*. Since *verdugo* refers to a branch stripped of its leaves, I interpret the meaning of the verb to be that these two knights were jousting with the thin spears. The shafts would have been cut by hand and, with so many spears required for this passage of arms, it makes sense that one or two of them were defective in some way. Given the meaning of the noun *verdugo*, this spear may well have been cut from a tree that was too young, or it may have been cut too thin, or it had not been properly dried out, with the result that it bowed or flexed on impact instead of breaking.

58 *the charnel of the helm*: Most of the knights at this passage of arms were wearing sallets with bevors or armets with wrappers. Here we have a rare exception, since reference to the charnel indicates that Joan de Camós is wearing a helm. Given the effect of this particular spear stroke, it can be inferred that he was struck high on the charnel, near the neck, which would have made him choke or gag.

59 Since Joan de Camós is wearing a helm, it makes sense that he is also wearing a reinforcing breastplate over his main breastplate, which would have been equipped with a vertical alignment of pegs to which the charnel of his helm would have attached.

60 At first glance it seems that Lope de Stúñiga is such a strenuous, resolute knight that the Contenders are afraid to fight him. However, as is demonstrated below and in Selection 33, Course 3, a pattern emerges which reveals that Stúñiga had a nasty habit of hitting horses. This is perhaps the real reason why no-one wishes to joust with him.

61 At this passage of arms lunch was apparently not as exotic as dinner, and was never preceded by a formal invitation. Typically it is the judges who simply order a break for lunch.

62 It is often (though by no means always) the Defenders of the passage of arms who are recorded as delivering these 'mighty blows'. To cite Kaeuper once more: 'Chivalry is repeatedly equated with deeds done with weapons, with feats of arms (*chevaleries*); prowess is equated with nobility, great blows being noted specifically as proof of nobility' (*Chivalry and Violence in Medieval Europe*, p. 265).

63 See above, Article 17.

64 This is Suero's first joust against Gonzalo de Castañeda, but it is the third time he has jousted at the passage of arms. His two previous jousts were fought against the German knight Arnold von Rottenwald (Monday, 12 July 1434) and the Catalonian knight Pere Daviu (Thursday, 15 July 1434).

65 *chivalric deeds*: Cp. medieval Castilian *caballería*. As shown by Kaeuper (with reference to the equivalent French term *chevalerie*), this term often refers specifically to deeds of prowess. See Kaeuper, *Chivalry and Violence in Medieval Europe*, pp. 135–49.

66 *reinforcing piece*: Cp. medieval Castilian *el volante de las platas*. The term *el volante* has traditionally been defined as the reinforcing breastplate. See, for example, Leguina, *Glosario de voces de Armería*, p. 865, and Valencia de Don Juan, *Catálogo*

histórico-descriptivo de la Real Armería de Madrid, p. 166. It is clear from the text, however, that the term for the reinforcing breastplate is in fact *el peto del piastrón* (see above, n. 20) and that what is being described here is a reinforce for the lower part of the breastplate or perhaps for the plackart. Riquer, *L'Arnès del cavaller*, pp. 114–15, suggests that *el peto del piastrón* and *el volante de las platas* are synonyms. What can be stated with certainty is that Gonzalo de Castañeda's lance got lodged in between the front arçon of Suero de Quiñones' saddle and the reinforcing piece of the lower breastplate.

67 The word 'Sangre' ('Blood!') is written in large, bold letters in the left margin of *BMP*, fol. 43v and *ESC*, fol. 98v.

68 See above, Article 10.

69 This encounter would have been catastrophic for both parties had not the judges insisted that they reaffix their right pauldrons.

70 The Criee was a formal announcement. In this case it is a clarification on the part of the judges with reference to Article 10, which states that those who wish to remove pieces of armour should 'send word of it' to Suero, without specifying that word needs to be sent to the judges via the king-of-arms, the herald or the pursuivants. On the Criee, see Muhlberger, *Jousts and Tournaments*, pp. 22–7.

71 One of the principal duties of the pursuivants was to record and keep track of the score. See Clephan, *The Medieval Tournament*, p. 129, n. 1.

72 The fictitious knight Don Quixote claimed to be a direct descendent of Gutierre Quijada, such was his renown. Quijada's chivalric career is discussed in detail by Riquer, *Caballeros andantes españoles*, pp. 117–23, and Riquer, *Cavalleria fra Realtà e Letteratura nel Quattrocento*, pp. 170–9. Gutierre Quijada would ultimately be responsible for Suero de Quiñones' death when he struck Suero through the visor during a joust of war in 1458. See Alonso Luengo, *Don Suero de Quiñones, el del Passo Honroso*, pp. 265–70.

73 Two misses in a row must have been most anticlimactic after the pomp and ceremony of the entrance.

74 The word 'Sangre' ('Blood!') is written in large, bold letters in the left margin of *ESC*, fol. 107v.

75 *shirt*: Cp. medieval Castilian *camisa*. From the context, the shirt in this instance is a soft linen under-garment.

76 As Rodríguez de Lena makes clear, it was ultimately the task of the judges ('los dezidores'; cp. French 'les diseurs') to sort out these knotty scoring issues.

77 The fact that the jousters were occasionally struck right through the eye-slit clarifies that they were jousting with single-pointed spearheads as opposed to coronels which terminated in tines.

78 The word 'Sangre' ('Blood!') is written in large, bold letters in the left margin of *ESC*, fol. 108v.

79 The Cathedral of Santiago de Compostela declares a Holy or Jubilee Year whenever St James' Day falls on a Sunday, as it did in 1434.

80 A marginal note in *RAH*, fol. 96r reads as follows: 'Juezes, Rey de armas, Faraute, Auctor' ('Judges, King-of-Arms, Herald, Author').

81 Procedurally this is correct. See the Criee in Selection 14, above.

82 This was Pedro de Nava's first (and only) joust with Diego Zapata, but it was the fifth time he had jousted in the passage of arms.

83 I translate the Castilian *de partes de dentro* literally. It is the author's way of referring both to the under side and the lining-glove of the gauntlet.

84 Clearly Diego Zapata has been jousting poorly up to this point. On the pretext of an obedience problem he exchanges horses (cp. Selection 7, Course 13). In fact he must have known that the new horse was kitted out with a jousting saddle instead of the war saddle that all contestants were supposed to use (see Article 1, above). This in turn would have given him an advantage over Pedro de Nava, who himself was not the best of jousters. The irony is that even though Diego Zapata is cheating, he is still a rotten jouster and does not manage to perform remotely well until the twentieth course.

85 This would have been in the early evening, around 6:00 p.m.

86 As stated above in Article 2, all foreign visitors would be loaned a horse if necessary. Since Sancho de Rabanal was one of the ten Defenders and hosts of this passage of arms, the horse in this case was probably his own steed. That said, he remains

remarkably calm in the wake of this disaster. Such phlegmatic reserve is a fine example of what Menaguerra (ch. 3) calls *mesura*.

87 A marginal note in *RAH*, fol. 102v reads as follows: 'Enqüentro feo' ('Foul stroke').

88 That is to say, it is Suero's fourth joust at the passage of arms. This was his one and only joust against the Portuguese knight Juan de Merlo. Juan de Merlo was quite famous in his own lifetime, and was ultimately killed in action during a skirmish at Arjona in 1443. On his chivalric career, see Riquer, *Caballeros andantes españoles*, pp. 110–17.

89 *chemise*: Cp. medieval Castilian *camisa*. The garment in this case could well be a 'chemise de Chartres', a quilted fabric defence worn over the armour. See Barker, *The Tournament in England, 1100–1400*, p. 167. Wearing chemises and jupons decorated with symbolic embroidery over the armour is yet another motif of chivalric fiction. See, for example, Martorell, *Tirant lo Blanc*, trans. LaFontaine, ch. 132, p. 276.

90 A marginal note in *RAH*, fol. 110r reads as follows: 'Lanças de las más gruessas' ('Lances of the thickest kind').

91 *spikes*: Cp. medieval Castilian *clavos*. This is the chronicler's way of referring to the cog-like teeth that assisted the fixed interaction of the grapper with the rest. See Menaguerra, ch. 18.

92 A marginal note in *RAH*, fol. 110r reads as follows: 'Encubrió Suero su herida.' (Suero concealed his wound.')

93 Public duels in Castile and Catalonia were always preceded by a formal epistolary duel in which the combatants would exchange letters of challenge, or cartels of defiance. In these letters they explained their motives, insulted each other and decided upon the weaponry for the duel, amongst other things. The last public duel in Spain was fought between Hieronymus Dansa (mentioned by Quijada de Reayo, ch. 3) and Pedro Torrellas in Valladolid, on 29 December 1522.

94 The syntax is somewhat abstruse. Suero was dreaming about writing letters of challenge, only to be rudely awoken by the blood spurting out of his wounds.

95 A marginal note in *RAH*, fol. 111v reads as follows: 'Guardabraço' ('Pauldron').

96 The abbreviated chronicle specifies that Juan de Merlo was preparing for a trip to France and Burgundy, where he is known to have acquitted himself well in numerous jousts. See Pineda, *Libro del Passo honroso*, ed. Riquer, p. 128. It was common for Castilian noblemen to travel by mule, so Suero's gift is entirely appropriate. See the following observation by a fifteenth-century observer: 'In Spain when a landed gentleman rides abroad, he rides on a mule while all his servants, often thirty or forty, have to run on foot as long as their master rides, at times twelve or fourteen miles a day.' See *The Travels of Leo of Rozmital through Germany, Flanders, England, France, Spain, Portugal, and Italy, 1465–1467*, p. 90. See also Part I, ch. 7, n. 85.

97 Galaor Mosquera was another knight of the Portuguese contingent.

98 The chronicler most often refers to 'the bevor' ('la bavera'). The fact that sometimes bevors get knocked off or are displaced (see below, Selection 23, Course 7, for example) suggests that the combatants in these cases are wearing a separate bevor and sallet combination. In this joust, however, the chronicler refers to 'la bavera del elmete' (literally, 'the bevor of the helmet'), a nuance which suggests that the bevor is considered more of an integral component of the helmet; hence it can be inferred that Galaor Mosquera (and because of the Principle of Equality, probably Pedro de los Ríos as well) is wearing an armet with wrapper.

99 Pero Vázquez de Castilbranco was yet another Portuguese knight who attended this passage of arms.

100 The terminology here is problematic. High plackarts with stepped or cusped borders are a unique feature of Spanish armour in the 1470s (see Mann, 'Notes on the Armour worn in Spain from the tenth to the fifteenth century', pp. 298–9). In the 1430s, however, the plackart would have been set too low for it to have covered the heart. Furthermore, a blow to the heart may have been sufficient to unhorse the rider, but probably not to knock down the horse as well (cp. the description of the first course run by Suero de Quiñones and Gonzalo de Castañeda in Selection 12, above, where neither rider nor horse falls). A strong blow to the plackart on the other hand, would have been close enough to the rider's centre of gravity to knock both horse

and rider to the ground. The technical mistake in this instance may be a scribal error that Rodríguez de Lena did not catch as he collated notes. On the scribes see below, Selection 31.

101 A marginal note in *RAH*, fol. 116v reads as follows: 'Gran enqüentro' ('Great encounter').

102 Cp. the Sforza ordinance quoted in Part I, ch. 5: 'Let no-one dare to take it upon himself to assist any jouster who has been injured, whether by a collision or by a lance-thrust, on pain of two strokes of the lash (Let them get up, since everyone is allowed to strike as many people as they want and those who fall can help themselves get up)'.

103 As stated above in Article 3, the idea was to break three spears total in each joust (i.e. not three spears per jouster), or to call off the joust when it was too dark to see or when someone was seriously injured. Pedro de Nava broke two spears and was allowed one more for knocking down Lope de la Torre and his horse = three total. Lope de la Torre also broke one spear, making a grand total of four spears broken in this particular contest, that is, one more than the amount specified in Article 3.

104 Given Rodríguez de Lena's close involvement with everyone and everything at this passage of arms, it is only natural that he became friendly with some of the jousters, which explains the occasional use of first names only, as in his description of this course.

105 Although leaving the field at this point was clearly a disappointment for Sancho de Rabanal, after running eighteen courses with a stomach virus on a hot July afternoon it was most likely a relief for Gonzalo de León who, significantly, is not recorded as making any effort to challenge the judges' decision.

106 Sancho's reaction is predictable since he is currently losing.

107 In this instance the rhetoric rings rather hollow, since it is unlikely that Gonzalo de León would have felt like eating dinner.

108 *the mail voider*: Cp. medieval Castilian *la sangradera*. On the Spanish term see Leguina, *Glosario de voces de Armería*, p. 661, s.v. *musequíes*.

109 As stated above, it is the judges who call for lunch breaks, often when both parties are jousting atrociously. As the judges must have known,

Sancho de Rabanal was simply not one of the best jousters, having in this case made the encounter in a mere three of sixteen courses, in which he broke just one spear. Despite repeated poor performances, however, Sancho de Rabanal participated in the greatest number of jousts at this passage of arms: sixteen total. He never did return to finish this joust with Pedro de Linares. This episode brings to mind Zapata's comment: 'He should then run one course after another without stopping, so that he sets off on a new course as soon as he returns from another, but this should only be after breaking the lance, because if he were to run one course after another without breaking it, this would on the contrary be the stuff of laughter and clogging up the lists without doing anything, and they could say of him: "A jouster wrapped up in himself makes a very small parcel"'.

110 *the stop-rib of the breastplate*: Cp. medieval Castilian *el borde de las platas*. Leguina, *Glosario de voces de Armería*, p. 154, registers the term 'el borde', but without providing a definition. From the context it is clear that the chronicler is referring to the 'lisière d'arrêt', or stop-rib. See also below, Selection 33, Course 1.

111 The word 'Sangre' ('Blood!') is written in large, bold letters in the left margin of *ESC*, fol. 133v.

112 See above, Selection 22, Course 4, for a similar dislocation. Also, in this case Diego de Sanromán's reinforcing breastplate does its job, unlike the one worn by Antón de Funes in Selection 2, above.

113 It is difficult not to agree with the jousters in this instance, since just one more course may have yielded the third broken spear which would have broken the tie.

114 Riambau de Corbera (d. 1442) was well known for his contumacy and intemperance. Out of sheer malice he and his companion Francí Desvalls had actually written to Suero de Quiñones requesting that they alone be allowed to break all the spears with the ten Defenders of the Pass of Honour, at the exclusion of every other Challenger. See Riquer, *Caballeros andantes españoles*, pp. 75–89; Riquer, *Cavalleria fra Realtà e Letteratura nel Quattrocento*, pp. 113–31; and Riquer, *Caballeros catalanes y valencianos en el Passo Honroso*, pp. 34–47. Their request was denied.

115 See above, Selection 16.

116 Riambau de Corbera had travelled to the passage of arms with his colleague Francí Desvalls.

117 The scribes were taking notes throughout the Pass of Honour of Suero de Quiñones, as was Pero Rodríguez de Lena. He subsequently collated all of the notes as he wrote this official chronicle.

118 Here we witness a deliberate snub of a knight who hails from Aragon-Catalonia. Diego de Bazán does not issue the customary invitation to dinner to his obtuse opponent.

119 Suero, the son of Álvar Gómez de Quiñones, was Suero de Quiñones' nephew.

120 A marginal note in *RAH*, fol. 150r reads as follows: 'El sinventura Asbert de Claramonte' ('The unfortunate Asbert de Claramunt').

121 The reference is to the formal arrival of the Aragonese knight Lord Francés Pero Bast. As stated in Article 15, above, all contestants had to relinquish their right spur to the judges in order to be allowed to compete in the passage of arms. The spur was returned to contestants only when it was their turn to fight in the lists.

122 The word 'Sangre' ('Blood!') is written in large, bold letters in the left margin of *ESC*, fol. 157v.

123 The word 'Muerte' ('Death!') is written in large, bold letters in the left margin of *ESC*, fol. 157v.

124 Suero's lance would have penetrated Asbert's left eye at an oblique angle, thereby causing severe trauma behind the right eye, which would account for the swelling.

125 Their sorrow was due at least in part to the fact that those who suffered sudden, violent deaths in the Middle Ages were often accused of having lived a life of iniquity. See Fernández Gallardo, *Alonso de Cartagena: Una biografía política en la Castilla del siglo XV*, p. 318, n. 157.

126 Suero here shows a lack of restraint, though in all fairness he had just killed a man.

127 A marginal note in *RAH*, fol. 152r reads as follows: 'No le dieron sepultura en sagrado' ('They did not give him a consecrated burial').

128 Asbert de Claramunt has also been called, appropriately, 'the martyr of chivalry' ('el mártir de la caballería'). See Riquer, *Tirant lo Blanch, novela de historia y de ficción*, pp. 13–14 and *Caballeros andantes españoles*, p. 98.

129 From this statement it can be deduced that Diego de Bazán was himself a tall man.

130 Zapata makes the pertinent point that armour should always be bespoke so that the pieces fit perfectly. Elsewhere in the *Miscelánea* he adds that: 'Después de armado queda como una ciudad cercada de fuerte muro, y aun es su muro de acero.' ('After he is armed he is like a city surrounded by a strong wall, and yet his wall is made of steel.') See Zapata, *Miscelánea*, ed. Carrasco González, p. 259. His words echo those of Ramon Llull, who used the same analogy to describe a well fitted mail hauberk. See Llull, *Llibre de l'Orde de Cavalleria*, ed. Gustà, part V, p. 70. This would be especially important in the case of an unusually large man who could not always expect to borrow a well-fitted harness. Given, however, that Article 2 concerns loaning equipment, horses and weapons, it can be inferred that knights must often have travelled to hastiludes on the understanding that armour and weapons would be provided by the hosts or sponsors. On bespoke armour, see also Anglo, *The Martial Arts of Renaissance Europe*, p. 217.

131 Depending on how they interpret the mind-bogglingly complex events of the Breton War of Succession, modern scholars refer to the Duke of Brittany at this time either as Jean V or Jean VI (1389–1442).

132 Don Pedro Fernández de Velasco (1399–1470), First Count of Haro.

133 These men were returning from their pilgrimage to the tomb of St James at the Cathedral of Santiago de Compostela.

134 Gómez de Villacorta fought in a total of twelve jousts at this passage of arms.

135 *tore off*: Cp. medieval Castilian *desgranó*. According to Covarrubias, *Tesoro de la lengua castellana o española*, p. 415a, *desgranar* is a variant spelling of the verb *desgreñar*, which in turn is a synonym of *desguarnecer*, 'to rip off'. I translate as 'tore off' in order to capture the slight nuance.

136 On the timeline, see Article 1, above. The last jousts of the Pass of Honour of Suero de Quiñones took place on 9 August 1434. Gómez de Villacorta and Lope de Ferrera did not have the chance to complete their deed of arms.

Hernán Chacón
Tractado de la cavallería de la gineta
(1551)
SELECTED PASSAGES

Tractado de la cavallería de la gineta　　　*Treatise on Jennet Cavalry*

Capítulo XII
De cómo se ha de jugar a las cañas

Ya que avemos dicho de las cavallerías, diremos aquí cómo se ha de jugar a las cañas, según lo que yo he visto. Y me he hallado en muchos juegos de cañas, en ordenarlos, assí por mandado de Su Magestad como por ruego de algunos cavalleros y señores que en la corte avían por bien que yo les dixesse cómo lo avían de hazer. Y lo que yo aprendí siendo mancebo en la ciudad de Úbeda, donde yo nascí y se precian desta cavallería de la gineta, diré aquí lo más breve que pueda.

Cuando los cavalleros quisieren jugar cañas se deven juntar y ordenar sus quadrillas de cinco en cinco, o más o menos, según uviere cavalleros, y vestirse cada quadrilla de su color. Y el día de la fiesta, juntarse han todos en una plaça antes que vayan donde han de jugar. Y dende allí se ygualarán cada quadrilla de su color, y assí yrán de dos en dos hasta llegar a la boca de la plaça donde han de jugar.

La plaça ha de estar limpia de piedras y de barrancos, y si fuere verano, esté bien regada, porque el polvo es muy mala cosa y muy peligroso, porque no viéndose unos a otros, se suelen encontrar y caer, y demás desto, con polvo, ni los cavalleros pueden ver lo que hazen ni menos pueden ser vistos. Y es muy gran çoçobra el polvo, assí para las damas que están en las ventanas como para todo lo demás, y por esto se deve regar muy bien la plaça si fuere verano, que en invierno no ay necessidad dello.

Assí juntos los cavalleros de dos en dos, entrarán en la plaça, mandando poner las

Chapter XII
How cane games should be played

Since we have talked about riding techniques, we shall talk here about how cane games should be played, in accordance with what I have witnessed. And I have been involved in many cane games, organising them, as much at the command of His Majesty as at the request of some knights and lords at court who thought it appropriate that I tell them how it should be done. And I shall state here as concisely as I can what I learned as a lad in the city of Úbeda, where I was born and where people pride themselves on the jennet riding style.

When knights wish to play cane games they should assemble and organise their teams with five on each side, or thereabouts, depending on how many knights there are, and each team should wear its own colour. And on the day of the tournament, they should all assemble in a square before going to the place where the game shall be played. And when they get there each team shall separate according to colour, and then they shall ride in pairs until they reach the entrance to the square where they are going to play.

The square should be cleared of stones and obstacles, and if it is summertime, it should be well watered, for dust is a very bad thing and very dangerous, because if some cannot see others, they tend to collide and fall, and besides this, with dust, the knights cannot see what they are doing and they can be seen even less. And dust is a very big concern, as much for the ladies who are standing at the windows as for everyone else, and for this reason the square should be well watered if it is summertime, for in the winter there is no need to do this.

So the knights, assembled in pairs, shall enter the square, with the order that

trompetas o atabales a la boca de la plaça, que toquen quando los cavalleros entren. Y han de mirar que, como fueren saliendo de dos en dos, los dexen yr un poco delante, por que las piedras o guijas que los cavallos de los delanteros van despidiendo con los pies no den en la cara a los que vienen detrás. Assimismo se ha de mirar que cada dos cavalleros que salieren juntos han de llevar las lanças de una manera yguales en la postura, porque de otra manera parecen mal. Y ansí entrados todos de dos en dos, tornarán [a]* arremeter todos juntos por la plaça a manera de batalla; darán dos o tres arremetidas y, hecho esto, darán una buelta todos juntos, passo a passo, a mirar las damas y cavalleros que están en las ventanas. Hecho esto, tomarán las adargas, e si quisieren bolver a entrar de dos en dos con las cañas y adáragas de carrera, poderlo han hazer, e si no, partirse han y jugarán a las cañas.

La manera cómo han de salir del puesto es esta. El cavallero se ha de em[b]raçar† su adáraga por ambas manijas hasta el cobdo, y tomará la rienda en la mano yzquierda, y en la otra su caña bien adereçada. Y partirán quatro o cinco, inertos sobre la rienda, y al salir del puesto sacarán los braços baxos y luego los alçarán para arriba todo lo que pudieren, y en llegando cerca del otro puesto tirarán sus cañas a las adáragas de los contrarios, y rebolverán sobre la mano derecha, cubriéndose con sus adáragas todo el cuerpo y parte de las ancas del cavallo. Y que el rostro lleve assí descubierto sobre el adáraga, que ha de yr muy pegada al cuerpo y no desviada como broquel, que paresce mal. Ni se ha de cubrir sin ver por qué. Y quando se cubriere, no ha de subir el adáraga sobre la cabeça, sino baxar un poco la cabeça al un lado del adáraga. Y desta manera bolverá a su puesto, teniendo mucho cuydado por do va

---

* *a*: Omitted in the original.

† Text: *emoraçar*.

---

trumpeters and drummers be placed at the entrance of the square, who should play when the knights make their entrance. And they should be careful that, since they are coming in two-by-two, they let them ride slightly ahead of each other, so that the stones or pebbles that the horses of those in front are kicking up with their feet do not strike those who are following behind in the face. Likewise care should be taken that each pair of knights who ride out together should hold their spears in exactly the same position, for otherwise they look bad. And once they have all entered two at a time, they shall all turn at the same time to charge through the square after the fashion of a battle; they shall do two or three sudden starts and, having done this, they shall ride a lap around the square together, slowly, so as to look at the ladies and knights who are at the windows. Having done this, they shall take the adargas, and if they wish to enter the square one more time in pairs with the canes and adargas, they may do so, and if not, they shall sally forth and play cane games.

The way in which they should fall into position is this. The knight should clutch his adarga through both straps up to his elbow, and he shall take the rein in his left hand, and in the other his well-prepared cane. And four or five shall sally forth, holding the rein motionless, and on falling into position they shall drop their arms low and then they shall raise them up as high as they can, and as they reach the other side they shall throw their canes at the adargas of the opponents, and they shall turn about on the right-hand side, covering the entire body and part of the horse's rump with their adargas. And let him hold his head exposed above the adarga, which should be held very close to the body and not turned away from it like a buckler, which looks bad. Nor should he be covered without being able to see. And when he covers himself, he should not lift the adarga above his head, but lower his head a bit to one side of the adarga. And in this way he shall return to his position, taking great care when he goes running

corriendo a la yda y a la venida de encontrar con otro cavallero. Ha de tener grande aviso sobre esto. Assimismo ha de mirar el cavallero de no salir de su puesto hasta que los contrarios ayan desembaraçado sus cañas y buelvan huyendo un poco de espacio, porque si antes salen a ellos, inertarse han todos y no parescerá bien, ni se pueden assí tirar. Y el que tira su caña al contrario llevándolo muy cerca y a la par, no paresce bien ni es bien hecho, ni menos se ha de tirar de través, ni rostro a rostro, sino a cavallero buelto o al puesto. Assimismo ha de mirar el cavallero de no salir solo, si no fuere muy buen cavallero y tuviere muy señalado cavallo, porque si lo haze mal, es más mirado, y da que reýr a la gente que lo mira.

También se ha de mirar que después de aver entrado a desparzir el juego no salga ninguno a tirar más caña a los contrarios. Y desto me paresce que basta lo dicho.

in and comes running back out not to collide with another knight. He should pay much heed to this. Likewise the knight should take care not to leave his position until the opponents have unleashed their canes and they are rather slowly beating it back, for if they charge first, they will all be crowded and it will not look good, nor will they be able to throw in this situation. And he who throws his cane at his opponent when he is too close alongside, it does not look good nor is it played well, nor yet should one throw sideways, nor head on, but at a knight who has turned or is in position. Likewise the knight should be careful not to ride out alone, unless he were a very good rider and had a very exceptional horse, because if he performs poorly, he will be noticed more, and he will give the people who are watching him something to laugh at.

One should also be careful that once he has begun engaging in the game no-one else rides out to throw more canes at the opposing team. And I believe that I have said enough about this.

Capítulo XIII
Cómo se han de esperar los toros a cavallo

Agora diremos cómo se han de esperar los toros a cavallo.

Antiguamente, los cavalleros toreavan desta manera, que a las ancas bueltas con la lança se preciavan de llevar los toros tras sí, poniéndole la lança en el rostro. Y agora* se usa esperarlos rostro a rostro. Y a quien hasta agora yo lo he visto hazer mejor es a don Pero Ponce de León, que le vi esperar muchos delante del Emperador Nuestro Señor y no errar lançada, y le vi matar muchos toros en la corte y no herirle ningún cavallo.

Diré aquí cómo lo hazía, para [que]† el que lo quisiere hazer y aventurar su cavallo lo sepa. El lo hazía desta manera: poníase en la plaça en su cavallo, al qual le ponía unos antojos de terciopelo, de manera que el cavallo no veya nada para adelante más de donde ponía las manos en el suelo; y se ponía en la parte por donde el toro avía de venir, y allí le esperava muy quedo el cavallo sin ver él al toro. Y como el toro se venía para él, como el cavallo no le veya, estava muy quedo, y entonces don Pero Ponce le ponía la lança para el pescueço o para la aguja del toro, y metiendo la lança, desviando el cavallo para la mano yzquierda; y el toro que llegava al cavallo tenía ya metida la lança en el cuerpo, y con el dolor desarmava la lança, y quando llegava al cavallo ya estava desatinado, y aun muchas vezes caya muerto. Desta manera se lo vi yo hazer muchas vezes. El que lo quisiere provar, yo le doy licencia para ello.

Chapter XIII
How bulls should be awaited on horseback

Now we shall speak of how bulls should be awaited on horseback.

In olden days, knights fought bulls in this way: turning back over the horse's rump with the lance, they prided themselves on having the bulls follow behind them, thrusting the lance in the face. And nowadays it is customary to await them face to face. And the person who up till now I have seen do this the best is Don Pero Ponce de León, for I saw him await many in front of our lord the Emperor and not miss one spear-thrust, and I saw him kill many bulls at court without injuring a single horse.[1]

I shall explain here how he used to do it, so that anyone who wants to do it and risk his horse will know how. He would do it like this: he would place himself in the bullring[2] on his horse, on which he would put some velvet blinkers, so that the horse could not see anything in front except where to place its feet on the ground; and he would place himself at the spot where the bull had to enter, and his horse would wait there very still without seeing the bull. And as the bull was coming towards him, since his horse could not see it, it would stand very still, and then Don Pero Ponce would thrust the spear at the bull's neck or its shoulder blades, and sticking in the spear, turning away his horse to the left-hand side; and by the time the bull reached the horse it would already have the spear stuck in its body, and in its agony it would shake loose the spear, and when it reached the horse it would already be weakened, and it would often even fall down dead. I saw him do it this way on many occasions. Should anyone wish to try it, I give him permission to do so.

---

* *Y agora*: The original has *Y porque agora*, which is clearly a mistake.

† *que*: Omitted in the original text.

Esto se ha de hazer con lança de pino y no de frexno, porque la de pino quebrará luego y el cavallero ganará honrra, y la de frexno por ventura lo sacará de la silla. Y ha de mirar que el hierro ha de entrar en el toro atravessados los filos, porque vaya cortando los niervos y goviernos, y sea el hierro ancho y de buenos filos, por que con el dolor de la herida el toro no llegue al cavallo.

This should be done with a pine spear and not one made of ash, because the pine one will soon break and the knight shall win honour, and one made of ash will quite possibly knock him out of the saddle. And he should make sure that the spearhead enters the bull with the blades crosswise, so that it cuts through the tendons and ligaments, and let the spearhead be wide and with good blades, so that the wound inflicts such agony that the bull does not reach the horse.

NOTES TO THE TRANSLATION

1 Pero Ponce de León was the most renowned bullfighter of the period. Similar anecdotes about his brilliant bullfighting technique are repeated in the second edition of Aguilar's *Tractado de la cavallería de la gineta* (1600), fol. 55r (but curiously Aguilar does not mention Ponce de León in the first edition of this treatise) and in the *Libro de la jineta y descendencia de los caballos Guzmanes* (1605), by Luis de Bañuelos y de la Cerda (Balenchana, ed. *Libros de jineta*, p. 48). For further contemporary references to Ponce de León's peerless technique in the bullring, see: Fernández de Oviedo, *Las memorias de Gonzalo Fernández de Oviedo*, ed. Avalle-Arce, vol. II, pp. 531–2; Zapata, *Miscelánea*, ed. Carrasco González, ch. 151, pp. 203–5; and Zapata, *Carlo Famoso*, ed. Terrón Albarrán, Canto 28, fol. 156rb.

2 *bullring*: Cp. Spanish *plaça*. At this time the bullring was also known in Spanish as *el coso*. Luis Zapata states that the best bullring in Spain at this time was in Medellín in Extremadura. It goes without saying, however, that Zapata himself was from Extremadura, so his opinion is biased. See Zapata, *Miscelánea*, ed. Carrasco González, ch. 40, p. 50.

Glossaries

Text-specific glossaries of technical terms in chronological order

El Passo Honroso de Suero de Quiñones

ALMETE (also ELMETE): helmet (armet or sallet)

ARANDELA: rondel; vamplate

ARÇÓN: arçon

ARNÉS DE PIERNAS: legharness

ASTA: shaft of the spear; often used to refer to the broken spear

BARASCURO DEL GUARDABRAÇO: besagew of the spaulder

BARRASCURO DE LA MANOPLA: rondel of the gauntlet

BASTO: saddle pad

BAVERA: bevor

BAVERA DEL ELMETE: wrapper of the armet

BORDE DEL GUARDABRAÇO: stop-rib on the pauldron

BORDE DE LAS PLATAS: stop-rib on the breastplate

BRAÇAL: vambrace

BUELTA DEL GUARDABRAÇO: haute-piece

CALVA DEL ALMETE: brow reinforce of the helmet

CAÑÓN DEL BRAÇAL: cannon of the vambrace

CARA DEL ALMETE: visor of the helmet

CARRERA: course

CHAPA: saddle steel

DEZIDOR: judge

DOBLADURA: double-piece; reinforcing piece

FALDA DEL GUARDABRAÇO: edge of the pauldron

FALDAJE DE LAS PLATAS: skirt of the cuirass

FALSO PETO: arming-doublet

FIERRO: spearhead

GALARO: surcoat

GUARDA DEL BRAÇAL: couter

GUARDA DEL GUARDABRAÇO: gardbrace; pauldron reinforcing plate

GUARDA DE LA MANOPLA: gauntlet reinforce

GUARDABRAÇO: pauldron

JUBÓN: jupon

LAMA: lame

LIÇA: lists

MANOPLA: gauntlet

PARAMENTOS: caparison; fabric horse trappings

PETO DE LAS PLATAS: upper breastplate

PETO DEL PIASTRÓN: breastplate reinforce

PIASTRÓN DE LAS PLATAS: plackart; lower breastplate

PONTECILLAS: vervelles; staples for securing the lance-rest (the 'arrêt à vervelles') to the breastplate

PUNTA: point of the spearhead

RISTRE: rest

SANGRADERA: mail voider

UÇA: tabard

VISTA DEL ELMETE: sight, eye-slit

VOLANTE DE LAS PLATAS: reinforcing piece

Lo Cavaller

ARÇON: arçon

ARMES D'ULTRANÇA: jousts of war

ARMES RETRETES: combats with rebated arms

BOSSA: pouch

BRAÇALET: vambrace

CARAGOL: flaon bolt

CARRERA: course

CIMERA: crest

COLP: blow with the lance

CORREJA: guige

ELM: frog-mouthed jousting helm

EMBARRERADA: full hit

ENCONTRAR: to attaint; to collide; to encounter; to make the encounter; to strike

ENCONTRE: attaint; encounter; stroke

ESPERONS: spurs

FUST: lance stave

GOCET DE LA LANÇA: grapper of the lance

GUANT: gauntlet

GUARDA: couter; gardbrace

GUARNICIÓ: garniture

MOSSA: bouche of the shield

PASSOS DE CÓRRER PUNTES: jousts with sharp lances

LANÇA: lance

PLAÇA: enclosure

PRIS: prize

PUNTA DE BILLETA: four-prong coronel

REGNA: reins

RENCH: lists; tilt; tilting competition

REST: lance-rest

RODA: vamplate

SCARCELLA: tasset

SCUT: shield

SELLA CLOSA: close saddle

SELLA DE LA GUISA: jousting saddle

STREP: stirrup

Doctrina del arte de la cavallería

ACIONES: stirrup leathers

AHIJADO: apprentice

ALMAGRE: red ochre

ALMETE: armet

ALPARTAZ DE MALLA: mail aventail; mail skirt

ARANDELA: vamplate

ARNÉS ENCAMPRONADO: reinforced harness

ARZÓN: arçon

BARASCUDO: rondel

BARBADA: curb chain

BAVERÓN: reinforcing bevor

BOCADO: mouthpiece

BOLANTE: plackart

BORNE: mourne, coronel

BRAÇAL: vambrace

CABEÇADA: head stall

CALVA: brow

CAMA: shank of the curb bit

CARRERA: lists, course

CAVALLERÍA: chivalry; metal frame of the saddle

CINCHA: cinch

CINCHA GRANDE: breast strap

CINCHA ORCADA: crupper

CINCHUELA: tab

CONTERA: butt of the lance; saddle steel

CONTRATELA: counter-tilt

COSCOJO: roller

COZ: arm of the lance-rest

CUELLO: closed crinet

CUJA (also CUXA): pouch

DAGA: dagger

EBILLA: single-pointed lance-head; buckle

ENCONTRAR: to encounter, to strike

ENCUENTRO: encounter, stroke

ENGOCETAR: to affix a grapper

ENRRISTRAR: to hold in rest, to place in the lance-rest

ESCARCELA: tasset

ESCARCELÓN: over-tasset

ESCARPE: sabaton

ESPADA DE ARMAS: arming sword

ESPEJUELO: rounded port of the bit

ESPUELA: spur

ESTOQUE: estoc

ESTRIBO: stirrup

FALDAJE: fauld

FRENO: bit

FRENO A TENAZAS: pincer-bit

GAMARRA: tie-down
GOCETE DE MALLA: mail voider
GRAN PIEÇA: grandguard
GREVA: greave
GUARDA: couter
GUARDABARRIGA: waist lame
GUARDABRAÇO: pauldron
HASTERO: lance-maker
HAZER CALADA: to swoop
HAZER SANTIGUADA: to make the sign
    of the Cross
JUEZ: judge
LANÇA: lance
LÁTIGO: latigo
MANOPLA: gauntlet
MARTILLO: hammer
MEDIA GREVA: half-greave
MEDIO BARBOTE: half-wrapper
MEDIO QUIXOTE: demi-cuisse
MELONES LISOS: smooth melon-rollers
MELONES RAJADOS: grooved melon-
    rollers
MOLINETE: molinet

MUGEROLA: muzzle
PADRINO: aider
PIEÇAS DOBLES: double pieces, exchange
    pieces
PLATAS: cuirass, breastplate and backplate
PRESA: belt-hook
QUIXERA: cheek piece
QUIXOTE: cuisse
REQUERIR: to couch
RISTRE: lance-rest
RODETE: rowel arm
SCACHA: scatch-roller
SILLA: saddle
SOBREGUARDA: pasguard
SOBREMANOPLA: manifer
SUELTA: tether
TAJUELA DE LA SILLA: saddle tree
TELA: tilt
TESTERA: shaffron
TIRO: pull
VAYNA: scabbard
VENTANICA: spur slit
VISTA: visor

Del Justador

ALAZANO TOSTADO: dark brown sorrel
ARANDELA: vamplate
ARÇÓN: arçon
ARMAS: armour
ARNÉS DE PIERNAS: legharness
BARREAR: to barricade
BRAÇAL: vambrace
CARRERA: course
CASTAÑO ESCURO: dark chestnut
CAVO DE LANZA: lance stub
CELADA: close-helmet
CONTRATELA: counter-tilt
CORAZA: cuirass
CUXA: pouch
ENPUÑADORA: grip
ENQÜENTRO: encounter; stroke
ESCARPE: sabaton
ESPUELA: spur
ESTRIVO: stirrup
FOLLA: mêlée
GREVA: greave
HACER CALADAS: to swoop
JUEGO DE CAÑAS: cane game

JUSTA DE GUERRA: joust of war
JUSTA DE ROE: joust of peace
LACAYO: footman
LANZA: lance
LLAVE: joint
MEDIO QUIXOTE: demi-cuisse
PENACHO: panache
PESCAR: to fish
PETO: breastplate
QUIXOTE ENTERO: entire cuisse
RISTRE: lance-rest
RODAJA: wing
ROPA: saddle cloth
RUCIO RODADO: silver grey
SAYETE: surcoat
SILLA: saddle
TARGETA: targetta, manteau d'armes
TELA: tilt
TORDILLO: dappled grey
VARA: jousting lance
VAYO: bay
VISTA: visor

Bibliography

Manuscript sources

Lanfranco of Milan, Guido, *Compendio de cirugía*, Madrid, Biblioteca Nacional, MS 2147

Libro de los linajes dirigido a Don Beltrán de la Cueva, Duque de Alburquerque, Madrid, Monasterio de las Descalzas Reales, MS F/30. Microfilm copy in Madrid, Biblioteca de Palacio, MC/MD/3193

Monte, Pietro, *Libro del exercicio de las armas*, Escorial, Real Biblioteca del Monasterio, MS a-IV-23, fols. 1r–52v

Rodríguez de Lena, Pero, *El Passo Honroso de Suero de Quiñones*, Escorial, Biblioteca del Monasterio de San Lorenzo de El Escorial, MS f.II.19

—— *El Passo Honroso de Suero de Quiñones*, Madrid, Real Academia de la Historia, MS 9-2-4/213

—— *El Passo Honroso de Suero de Quiñones*, Santander, Biblioteca Menéndez y Pelayo, MS M-104

Torre, Alfonso de la, *Compendio breve de los X libros de la Éthica de Aristótil*, Madrid, Biblioteca Nacional, MS 4514

Zapata de Chaves, Luis, 'Del Justador', in *Miscellánea de Zapata*, Madrid, Biblioteca Nacional, MS 2790, fols. 182r–188v

Printed primary sources

Aesop, *Fables of Aesop*, trans. S. A. Handford (Harmondsworth: Penguin, 1979)

Aguilar, Pedro de, *Tractado de la cavallería de la gineta* (Seville: Hernando Díaz, 1572)

—— *Tractado de la cavallería de la gineta*, 2nd edn (Málaga: Juan René, 1600)

—— *Tractado de la cavallería de la gineta* [Seville: Hernando Díaz, 1572], facsimile, ed. Ángel Caffarena Such (Málaga: El Guadalhorce, 1960)

—— *Tractado de la cavallería de la gineta* [Seville: Hernando Díaz, 1572], facsimile (Seville: Extramuros Edición, 2006)

Alava y Viamont, Diego de, *El Perfecto Capitán instruido en la Disciplina Militar y nueva ciencia de la Artillería* (Madrid: Ministerio de Defensa, 1994)

Alfonso X, *Las Siete Partidas*, ed. José Sánchez-Arcilla Bernal (Madrid: Reus, 2004)

—— *Las Siete Partidas*, trans. Samuel Parsons Scott and Robert I. Burns, S.J., 7 vols. (Philadelphia: University of Pennsylvania Press, 2001)

Ardemagni, Enrica J., ed., *Text and Concordance of Biblioteca Nacional MS 2147: 'Compendio de cirugia' by Guido Lanfranc of Milan* (Madison, WI: HSMS, 1988)

—— and Cynthia M. Wasick, eds., *Text and Concordance of Biblioteca Nacional MS 2165: 'Arte complida de cirugia'* (Madison, WI: HSMS, 1988)

Aristotle, *The Nicomachean Ethics*, ed. and trans. Horace Rackham (Cambridge, MA: Harvard University Press, 1990)

Ávila y Zúñiga, Luis de, *Comentario de la guerra de Alemania hecha por Carlos V, Máximo Emperador Romano, Rey de España, en el año de 1546 y 1547*, in *Historiadores de sucesos particulares*, ed. Cayetano Rosell, Biblioteca de Autores Españoles, vol. XXI (Madrid: Rivadeneira, 1946), 409–49

Balenchana, José Antonio de, ed. *Libros de jineta*, Sociedad de Bibliófilos Españoles, vol. XVII (Madrid: Aribau y compañía, 1877)

Barret, Robert, *The Theorike and Practike of Moderne Warres, Discoursed in Dialogue Wise* (London: William Ponsonby, 1598)

Barrientos, Don Lope, *Refundición de la crónica del halconero*, ed. Juan de Mata Carriazo (Madrid: Espasa-Calpe, 1946)

Bernaldez, Andrés, *Memorias del reinado de los Reyes Católicos*, ed. Manuel Gómez-Moreno and Juan de Mata Carriazo (Madrid: Real Academia de la Historia, 1962)

Bèze, Théodore de, *A View from the Palatine: The 'Iuvenalia' of Théodore de Bèze*, ed. and trans. Kirk M. Summers (Tempe, AZ: Arizona Center for Medieval and Renaissance Studies, 2001)

Bohigas, Pere, ed., *Tractats de cavalleria* (Barcelona: Barcino, 1947)

Bourdeille, Pierre de, Seigneur de Brantôme, *Œuvres complètes de Pierre de Bourdeilles, abbé et seigneur de Branthôme*, ed. Prosper Mérimée, 13 vols. (Paris: P. Jannet, 1858)

Bouvet, Honoré (also known as Bonet), *L'Arbre des Batailles*, ed. Ernest Nys (Brussels and Leipzig: C. Muquardt, 1883)

—— *The Tree of Battles of Honoré Bonet*, trans. G. W. Coopland (Liverpool: Liverpool University Press, 1949)

Cabanillas, Jerónimo, *Relación verdadera de las grandes fiestas que la serenísima Reina doña María ha hecho al Príncipe nuestro señor en Flandes, en un lugar que se dice Vince, desde XXII de agosto hasta el postrero día del mes*, in *Relaciones de los reinados de Carlos V y Felipe II*, ed. Amalio Huarte, 2 vols. (Madrid: Sociedad de Bibliófilos Españoles, 1941–50), vol. II, 199–221

Calvete de Estrella, Juan Cristóbal, *El felicíssimo viaje del muy alto y muy poderoso Príncipe don Phelippe*, ed. Paloma Cuenca (Madrid: Sociedad Estatal para la Conmemoración de los Centenarios de Felipe II y Carlos V, 2001)

Cancionero de Juan Alfonso de Baena, ed. Brian Dutton and Joaquín González Cuenca (Madrid: Visor Libros, 1993)

Carrillo de Huete, Pedro, *Crónica del halconero de Juan II*, ed. Juan de Mata Carriazo and Rafael Beltrán Llavador (Granada: Editorial Universidad de Granada, 2006)

Carroll, Lewis, *Alice's Adventures in Wonderland and Through the Looking-Glass*, ed. Roger Lancelyn Green (Oxford: Oxford University Press, 1982)

Cartagena, Alonso de, *Discurso sobre la precedencia del Rey Católico sobre el de Inglaterra en el Concilio de Basilea*, in *Prosistas castellanos del siglo XV*, ed. Mario Penna, Biblioteca de Autores Españoles, vol. CXVI (Madrid: Rivadeneira, 1959), 203–33

—— *Tratados Militares*, ed. Noel Fallows (Madrid: Ministerio de Defensa, 2006)

Castiglione, Baldesar, *Il Libro del Cortegiano con una scelta delle Opere minori*, ed. Bruno Maier (Turin: Unione Tipografico-Editrice Torinese, 1981)

—— *The Book of the Courtier*, trans. Leonard Eckstein Opdycke (New York: Barnes & Noble Books, 2005)

Cátedra, Pedro-Manuel, ed., *Poemas castellanos de cancioneros bilingües y otros manuscritos barceloneses* (Exeter: University of Exeter Press, 1983)

Ceballos-Escalera y Gila, Alfonso, *La orden y divisa de la Banda Real de Castilla* (Madrid: Prensa y Ediciones Iberoamericanas, 1993)

Cervantes, Miguel de, *Don Quixote*, trans. J. M. Cohen (Harmondsworth: Penguin, 1978)

—— *El ingenioso hidalgo Don Quijote de la Mancha*, ed. Luis Andrés Murillo, 3 vols. (Madrid: Castalia, 1982)

Chacón, Gonzalo, *Crónica de Don Álvaro de Luna*, ed. Juan de Mata Carriazo (Madrid: Espasa-Calpe, 1940)

Chacón, Hernán, *Tratado de la cauallería de la gineta* [Seville: Cristóbal Álvarez, 1551], facsimile, ed. Eugenio Asensio (Madrid: Bibliófilos Madrileños, 1950)

—— *Tractado de la cauallería de la gineta*, ed. Noel Fallows (Exeter: University of Exeter Press, 1999)

—— *Tratado de la caballería de la jineta*, ed. José Andrés Anguita Peragón (Torredonjimeno, Jaén: Jabalcuz, 2003)

Chaucer, Geoffrey, 'The Knight's Tale', in *The Riverside Chaucer*, ed. Larry D. Benson (Boston: Houghton Mifflin Company, 1987), 37–66

—— *The Canterbury Tales*, trans. Nevill Coghill (Harmondsworth: Penguin, 1982)

Chrétien de Troyes, *Arthurian Romances*, trans. D. D. R. Owen (London: Everyman, 1993)

—— *Cligès*, ed. Laurence Harf-Lancner (Paris: H. Champion, 2006)

—— *Le Chevalier de la Charrette (Lancelot)*, ed. A. Foulet and Karl D. Uitti (Paris: Bordas, 1989)

—— *Yvain ou Le Chevalier au Lion*, ed. Jan Nelson, Carleton W. Carroll and Douglas Kelly (New York: Appleton-Century-Crofts, 1968)

Corpus Iuris Canonici, ed. Aemilius Friedberg, 2 vols. (Leipzig: Graz, 1959)

Cortes de los antiguos reinos de León y de Castilla, 5 vols. (Madrid: Real Academia de la Historia, 1861)

Cortés, Hernán, *Cartas y Documentos*, ed. Mario Hernández Sánchez-Barba (Mexico City: Porrúa, 1963)

—— *Letters of Cortes: The Five Letters of Relation from Fernando Cortes to the Emperor Charles V*, trans. Francis Augustus MacNutt, 2 vols. (New York: Putnam, 1908)

Cossío, José María de, ed., *Advertencias y reglas para torear a caballo (siglos XVII y XVIII)*, Sociedad de Bibliófilos Españoles, Segunda Época, vol. XVIII (Madrid: Aldus, 1947)

Covarrubias Horozco, Sebastián de, *Tesoro de la Lengua Castellana o Española*, ed. Felipe C. R. Maldonado and Manuel Camarero (Madrid: Castalia, 1995)

Crónica del Rey Don Alfonso el Onceno, in *Crónicas de los Reyes de Castilla, I*, ed. Cayetano Rosell, Biblioteca de Autores Españoles, vol. LXVI (Madrid: Rivadeneira, 1953), 171–392

Crónica del Rey Don Juan, primero de Castilla e de León, in *Crónicas de los Reyes de Castilla, II*, ed. Cayetano Rosell, Biblioteca de Autores Españoles, vol. LXVIII (Madrid: Atlas, 1953), 65–144

Crónica del Rey Don Sancho el Bravo, in *Crónicas de los Reyes de Castilla, I*, ed. Cayetano Rosell, Biblioteca de Autores Españoles, vol. LXVI (Madrid: Rivadeneira, 1953), 67–90

Curial e Güelfa, ed. R. Aramon i Serra, 3 vols. (Barcelona: Barcino, 1930)

Dall'Agocchie, Giovanni, *On the Art of Fencing*, trans. William Jherek Swanger http://www.drizzle.com/~celyn/jherek/ ENGDALLAG.pdf (2008)

Davis, Norman, ed., *Paston Letters and Papers of the Fifteenth Century: Part I* (Oxford: Clarendon Press, 1971)

Decrees of the Ecumenical Councils, ed. and trans. G. Alberigo *et al.* and Norman P. Tanner, 2 vols. (London and Washington, DC: Sheed and Ward-Georgetown University Press, 1990)

Díaz, Bernal, *The Conquest of New Spain*, trans. J. M. Cohen (Harmondsworth: Penguin, 1981)

Díaz de Games, Gutierre, *El victorial*, ed. Rafael Beltrán Llavador (Salamanca: Ediciones Universidad de Salamanca, 1997)

—— *The Unconquered Knight: A Chronicle of the Deeds of Don Pero Niño, Count of Buelna*, trans. Joan Evans (Woodbridge: Boydell Press, 2004; 1st edn 1928)

Díaz Tanco, Vasco, *Triumpho béllico notable sobre la gloriosa victoria de España contra Francia quando su Rey fue en prisión*, facsimile, ed. José León Sancho Rayón (Madrid: J. Sancho Rayón, c. 1870)

Duarte I, King of Portugal, *Livro da ensinança de bem cavalgar toda sela que fez El-Rey Dom Eduarte de Portogal e do Algarve e Senhor de Ceuta*, ed. Joseph M. Piel (Lisbon: Livraria Bertrand, 1944)

—— *The Royal Book of Horsemanship, Jousting and Knightly Combat*, trans. Antonio Franco Preto and Luis Preto (Highland Village, TX: Chivalry Bookshelf, 2005)

Dutton, Brian, ed., *El Cancionero del siglo XV, c. 1360–1520*, 2 vols. (Salamanca: Biblioteca Española del Siglo XV, 1990)

Enríquez de Guzmán, Alonso, *Libro de la vida y costumbres de don Alonso Enríquez de Guzmán*, ed. Hayward Keniston, Biblioteca de Autores Españoles, vol. CXXVI (Madrid: Atlas, 1960)

Ercilla y Zúñiga, Alonso de, *La Araucana*, ed. Marcos A. Morínigo and Isaías Lerner, 2 vols. (Madrid: Castalia, 1983)

—— *The Araucaniad*, trans. Charles Maxwell Lancaster and Paul Thomas Manchester (Nashville, TN: Vanderbilt University Press, 1945)

Eschenbach, Wolfram von, *Parzival*, ed. Karl Lachmann, revised ed. Eberhard Nellmann, 2 vols. (Frankfurt am Main: Deutscher Klassiker Verlag, 1994)

—— *Parzival*, trans. A. T. Hatto (Harmondsworth: Penguin, 1980)

Fallows, Noel, *The Chivalric Vision of Alfonso de Cartagena: Study and Edition of the 'Doctrinal de los caualleros'* (Newark, DE: Juan de la Cuesta, 1995)

—— *Un texto inédito sobre la caballería del Renacimiento español: 'Doctrina del arte de la caualleria', de Juan Quijada de Reayo* (Liverpool: Liverpool University Press, 1996)

Fernández de Oviedo, Gonzalo, *Las memorias de Gonzalo Fernández de Oviedo*, ed. Juan Bautista Avalle-Arce, 2 vols. (Chapel Hill: University of North Carolina Press, 1974)

France, Marie de, *Les Lais de Marie de France*, ed. Jean Rychner (Paris: Champion, 1983)

—— *The Lais of Marie de France*, trans. Glyn S. Burgess and Keith Busby (Harmondsworth: Penguin, 1986)

Francolin, Hans von, *Thurnier Buch* (Frankfurt am Main: Georg Raben, 1566)

Froissart, Jean, *Chroniques: Livre III (du Voyage en Béarn à la campagne de Gascogne) et Livre IV (années 1389–1400)*, ed. Peter Ainsworth and Alberto Varvaro (Paris: Livre de Poche, 2004)

—— *The Chronicle of Froissart*, trans. Sir John Bourchier, Lord Berners, The Tudor Translations, vols. XXVII–XXXII, 6 vols. (London: David Nutt, 1901–3; 1st edn 1523–5)

García Cerezeda, Martín, *Tratado de las campañas y otros acontecimientos de los ejércitos del Emperador Carlos V en Italia, Francia, Austria, Berbería y Grecia, desde 1521 hasta 1545*, ed. G. Cruzada Villaamil, Sociedad de Bibliófilos Españoles, vol. XII, 3 vols. (Madrid: Aribau y compañía, 1873)

García de Palacio, Diego, *Diálogos militares* [Mexico: Pedro de Ocharte, 1583], facsimile (Madrid: Ediciones Cultura Hispánica, 1944)

García de Paredes, Diego, *Chrónica del Gran Capitán, Gonzalo Hernández de Córdoba y Aguilar*, in *Crónicas del Gran Capitán, Nueva Biblioteca de Autores Españoles*, ed. Antonio Rodríguez Villa, vol. X (Madrid: Bailly-Baillière, 1908), 1–259

García de Santa María, Álvar, *Crónica de Juan II de Castilla*, ed. Juan de Mata Carriazo (Madrid: Real Academia de la Historia, 1982)

Garrard, William, *The Arte of Warre*, corrected and finished by Captaine Hichcock (London: Roger Warde, 1591)

Girón, Pedro, *Crónica del Emperador Carlos V*, ed. Juan Sánchez Montes (Madrid: CSIC, Escuela de Historia Moderna, 1964)

Grisón, Federico, *Reglas de la Cavallería de la Brida*, trans. Antonio Flórez de Benavides (Baeza: Juan Baptista de Montoya, 1568)

Gutiérrez de la Vega, Luis, *Nuevo tratado y compendio de re militari* (Medina del Campo: Francisco del Canto, 1569)

Hechos del Condestable Don Miguel Lucas de Iranzo (Crónica del siglo XV), ed. Juan de Mata Carriazo (Madrid: Espasa-Calpe, 1940)

Heusch, Carlos, and Jesús D. Rodríguez
Velasco, eds., *La caballería castellana de
la baja edad media: Textos y Contexos*
(Montpellier: ETILAL, 2000)

Hierro, Baltasar del, *Libro y primera parte
de los victoriosos hechos del muy valeroso
cavallero don Álvaro de Baçán, señor de las
villas del Viso y Sancta Cruz, capitán general
del mar Océano. Dirigido al muy illustre
señor don Luys Çapata, señor de las villas
de Albuñol y Torbiscón, con sus partidas,*
facsimile (New York: De Vinne Press, 1903;
1st edn Granada, 1561)

Ketham, Johannes de, *Compendio de la
humana salud*, ed. María Teresa Herrera
(Madrid: Arco Libros, 1990)

*La espantosa y maravillosa vida de Roberto el
Diablo*, in *Libros de Caballería*, ed. Alberto
Blecua (Madrid: Editorial Juventud, 1969),
193–239

Laschitzer, Simon, ed., *Der Theuerdank*, in
*Jahrbuch der Kunsthistorischen Sammlungen
in Wien* 8 (1888)

Leidinger, Georg, *Miniaturen aus
Handschriften der Kgl. Hof- und
Staatsbibliothek in München*, Heft 3:
*Turnierbuch Herzog Wilhelms IV von
Bayern* (Munich: Riehn & Tietze, 1912)

Leseur, Guillaume, *Histoire de Gaston
IV, comte de Foix*, ed. Henri Courteault,
Société de l'Histoire de France,
vols. CCLXIII and CCLXXVII, 2 vols.
(Paris: Librairie Renouard, 1893–6)

Llull, Ramón, *Llibre de l'Orde de Cavalleria*,
ed. Marina Gustà (Barcelona: Edicions 62,
1981)

Londoño, Sancho de, *Discurso sobre la forma
de reducir la disciplina militar a mejor y
antiguo estado* (Madrid: Blass, 1943)

Lopes, Fernão, *Crónica de D. João I*, ed.
António Sérgio, 2 vols. (Oporto: Livraria
Civilização, 1945–9)

López de Gómara, Francisco, *Annales del
Emperador Carlos Quinto*, ed. Roger
Bigelow Merriman (Oxford: Clarendon
Press, 1912)

Macpherson, Ian, *The 'Invenciones y Letras'
of the 'Cancionero general'*, Papers of the
Medieval Hispanic Research Seminar,
vol. IX (London: Department of Hispanic
Studies Queen Mary and Westfield
College, 1998)

Maldonado, Alonso de, *Hechos de Don
Alonso de Monroy, Clavero y Maestre
de la Orden de Alcántara*, in *Memorial
Histórico Español: Colección de Documentos,
Opúsculos y Antigüedades*, vol. VI (Madrid:
Real Academia de la Historia, 1853), 73–110

Mançanas, Eugenio, *Libro de enfrenamientos
de la gineta* [Toledo: Francisco de Guzmán,
1570], facsimile, ed. Cesáreo Sanz Egaña
(Valencia: Talleres de Tipografía Moderna,
1956)

Manuel, Don Juan, *Crónica abreviada*, in
Obras completas, ed. José Manuel Blecua,
2 vols. (Madrid: Gredos, 1982), vol. II,
505–815

—— *Libro de las armas*, in *Obras completas*,
ed. José Manuel Blecua, 2 vols. (Madrid:
Gredos, 1982), vol. I, 117–40

—— *Libro del cauallero et del escudero*, in
Obras completas, ed. José Manuel Blecua,
2 vols. (Madrid: Gredos, 1982), vol. I, 35–116

March, Pere, 'L'arnès del cavaller', in *Obra
Completa*, ed. Lluís Cabré (Barcelona:
Barcino, 1993), 200–60

Martínez de Toledo, Alfonso, *Arcipreste de
Talavera o Corbacho*, ed. Joaquín González
Muela (Madrid: Castalia, 1984)

—— *Little Sermons on Sin: The Archpriest
of Talavera*, trans. Lesley Byrd Simpson
(Berkeley: University of California Press,
1959)

Martorell, Joanot, *Tirant lo Blanch*, ed. Albert
Hauf (Valencia: Guada Litografía, 2004)

—— *Tirant lo Blanc: The Complete Translation*,
trans. Ray LaFontaine (New York: Peter
Lang, 1993)

Menaguerra, Ponç de, *Lo Cavaller*, ed.
Ignacio Janer, Ernesto Moliné y Brases,
Luis Faraudo, Recull de Textes Catalans
Antichs, vol. III (Barcelona: La Acadèmica,
1906)

Mendoza, Bernardino de, *Teórica y práctica de guerra*, ed. Juan C. Saavedra Zapater and Juan A. Sánchez Belén (Madrid: Ministerio de Defensa, 1998)

—— *Theorique and Practise of Warre*, trans. Sir Edwarde Hoby (Middelburg: Richard Schilders, 1597)

Mexía, Pedro, *Historia del Emperador Carlos V*, ed. Juan de Mata Carriazo, Colección de Crónicas Españolas, vol. VII (Madrid: Espasa-Calpe, 1945)

Michalski, André, *La 'Razón' de Lupus de Moros: Un poema hermético* (Madison, WI: HSMS, 1993)

Monte, Pietro, *Exercitiorum Atque Artis Militaris Collectanea in Tris Libros Distincta* (Milan: Giovan'Angelo Scinzenzeler, 1509)

Montes, Diego, *Instrución y regimiento de guerra* (Saragossa: Georg Koch, 1537)

Padilla, Lorenzo de, *Crónica de Felipe I llamado el hermoso*, ed. Miguel Salvá and Pedro Sainz de Baranda, Colección de Documentos Inéditos para la Historia de España, vol. VIII (Madrid: Imprenta de la Viuda de Calero, 1846), 5–267

Palencia, Alfonso de, *Gesta Hispaniensia ex annalibus suorum dierum collecta*, ed. and trans. Brian Tate and Jeremy Lawrance (Madrid: Real Academia de la Historia, 1998)

Pérez de Guzmán, Fernán, *Crónica del Serenísimo Príncipe Don Juan, segundo rey deste Nombre en Castilla y León*, Biblioteca de Autores Españoles, ed. Cayetano Rosell, vol. LXVIII (Madrid: Atlas, 1953), 273–695

—— *Generaciones y semblanzas*, ed. Robert Brian Tate (London: Tamesis, 1965)

Pineda, Fray Juan de, *Libro del Passo Honroso*, ed. Martín de Riquer (Madrid: Espasa-Calpe, 1970)

Pizan, Christine de, *The Book of Deeds of Arms and of Chivalry*, trans. Sumner Willard and Charity Cannon Willard (University Park: Pennsylvania State University Press, 1999)

Pulgar, Hernando de, *Claros varones de Castilla*, ed. Robert Brian Tate (Oxford: Clarendon Press, 1971)

—— *Crónica de los señores reyes católicos don Fernando y doña Isabel de Castilla y de Aragón*, ed. Cayetano Rosell, Biblioteca de Autores Españoles, vol. LXX (Madrid: Atlas, 1953), 223–511

Pyke, Richard, *Three to One: Being an English-Spanish Combat, Performed by a Westerne Gentleman of Tavistoke in Devonshire, with an English Quarter-Staffe, against Three Spanish Rapiers and Poniards, at Sherries in Spaine, the Fifteene Day of November 1625. In the Presence of Dukes, Condes, Marquesses, and Other Great Dons of Spaine, being the Counsell of Warre* (London: Printed by Augustine Mathewes for John Trundle, 1626)

Quaderno de Leyes, Ordenanças, y Provisiones, hechas a suplicación de los tres Estados del Reyno de Navarra, por su Magestad o en su nombre, ed. Guillermo Sánchez Martínez, 2 vols. (Pamplona: Universidad Pública de Navarra, 2002)

Quintus Curtius Rufus, *Historiae Alexandri Magni*, ed. and trans. John C. Rolfe, 2 vols. (Cambridge, MA: Harvard University Press, 1962)

Rabelais, François, *Gargantua and Pantagruel*, trans. J. M. Cohen (Harmondsworth: Penguin, 1979)

—— *Les Cinq Livres*, ed., Jean Céard, Gérard Defaux and Michel Simonin (Paris: Livre de Poche, 1994)

Renart, Jean, *The Romance of the Rose or of Guillaume de Dole (Roman de la Rose ou de Guillaume de Dole)*, ed. and trans. Regina Psaki (New York: Garland, 1995)

René of Anjou, King, *A Treatise on the Form and Organization of a Tournament*, ed. and trans. Elizabeth Bennett http://www.princeton.edu/~ezb/rene/renebook.html (2008)

Rhetorica ad Herennium, ed. and trans. Harry Caplan (Cambridge, MA: Harvard University Press, 1964)

Riquer, Martín de, ed., *Lletres de batalla: Cartells de deseiximents i capítols de passos d'armes*, 3 vols. (Barcelona: Barcino, 1963–8)

Rodríguez de Lena, Pero, *El Passo Honroso de Suero de Quiñones*, ed. Amancio Labandeira Fernández (Madrid: Fundación Universitaria Española, 1977)

Rodríguez de Montalvo, Garci, *Amadís de Gaula*, ed. Edwin B. Place, 4 vols. (Madrid: CSIC, Instituto 'Miguel de Cervantes', 1959–69)

—— *Amadis of Gaul*, trans. Edwin B. Place and Herbert C. Behm, 2 vols. (Lexington: University Press of Kentucky, 1974)

—— *Las sergas del muy esforzado caballero Esplandián*, in *Libros de caballerías*, ed. Pascual de Gayangos, Biblioteca de Autores Españoles, vol. XL (Madrid: Atlas, 1950), 403–561

—— *The Labors of the Very Brave Knight Esplandián*, trans. William Thomas Little (Binghamton, NY: Center for Medieval and Early Renaissance Studies, State University of New York at Binghamton, 1992)

Rojas, Fernando de, *Comedia o Tragicomedia de Calisto y Melibea*, ed. Peter E. Russell (Madrid: Castalia, 1991)

—— *The Celestina: A Fifteenth-Century Spanish Novel in Dialogue*, ed. and trans. Lesley Byrd Simpson (Berkeley: University of California Press, 1955)

Rozmital, Leo of, *The Travels of Leo of Rozmital through Germany, Flanders, England, France, Spain, Portugal and Italy*, trans. Malcolm Letts (Cambridge: Hakluyt Society, 1957)

Rühl, Joachim K., 'Regulations for the Joust in Fifteenth-Century Europe: Francesco Sforza Visconti (1465) and John Tiptoft (1466)', *International Journal of the History of Sport* 18.2 (2001), 193–208

Ryder, Hugh, *Practical Chirurgery. Being a Methodical Account of divers Eminent Observations, Cases and Cures Very Necessary and Useful for Surgeons, both Military and Naval* (London: John Taylor, 1689)

Salazar, Diego de, *Tratado de Re Militari*, ed. Eva Botella Ordinas (Madrid: Ministerio de Defensa, 2000)

Sandoval, Fray Prudencio de, *Historia de la vida y hechos del Emperador Carlos V*, ed. Carlos Seco Serrano, Biblioteca de Autores Españoles, vols. LXXX–LXXXII, 2 vols. (Madrid: Rivadeneira, 1955)

Santa Cruz, Alonso de, *Crónica del Emperador Carlos V*, ed. Antonio Blázquez y Delgado-Aguilera and Ricardo Beltrán y Rózpide, 5 vols. (Madrid: Imprenta del Patronato de Huérfanos de Intendencia e Intervención Militares, 1920–5)

Sanz Egaña, Cesáreo, ed., *Tres libros de jineta de los siglos XVI y XVII*, Sociedad de Bibliófilos Españoles, Segunda Época, vol. XXVI (Madrid: Aldus, 1951)

Sinclair, Alexandra, *The Beauchamp Pageant* (Donington: Richard III and Yorkist History Trust and Paul Watkins, 2003)

Smith, C. Colin, ed., *Spanish Ballads* (London: Bristol Classical Press, 1996)

Strassburg, Gottfried von, *Tristan und Isold*, ed. Friedrich Ranke (Dublin and Zurich: Weidmann, 1968)

—— *Tristan: With the surviving fragments of the 'Tristran' of Thomas*, trans. A. T. Hatto (Harmondsworth: Penguin, 1967)

Suárez Peralta, Juan, *Tractado de la cavallería de la Gineta y Brida* (Seville: Fernando Díaz, 1580)

—— *Tratado de la jineta y de la brida*, ed. José Álvarez del Villar (Mexico, DF: José Álvarez del Villar, 1950)

Tafur, Pero, *Andanças e viajes de un hidalgo español*, ed. Marcos Jiménez de la Espada (Madrid: Ediciones Polifemo, 1995)

—— *Travels and Adventures, 1435–1439*, trans. Malcolm Letts (New York and London: Harper & Brothers, 1926)

Tapia y Salzedo, Gregorio de, *Exercicios de la gineta* [Madrid: Diego Díaz, 1643], facsimile (Madrid: Turner, 1980)

Theodoric of Lucca, *The Surgery of Theodoric ca. A.D. 1267*, trans. Eldridge Campbell and James Colton, 2 vols. (New York: Appleton-Century-Crofts, 1955–60)

The Adventures of the Knight Theuerdank, facsimile, ed. Stephan Füssel (Cologne: Taschen, 2003)

Thournier Kampff und Ritterspiel (Frankfurt am Main: Christian Egenolff, 1550)

Trexo, Luis de, *Advertencias y obligaciones para torear con el rejón* [Madrid: Pedro Tazo, 1639], facsimile (Valencia: Librerías París-Valencia, 1996)

—— *Advertencias y obligaciones para torear con el rejón*, ed. Augusto Butler, Colección Abenamar, vol. I (Bilbao: Indauchu Editorial, 1952)

Turell, Gabriel, *Arbre d'Honor*, ed. Cecília Burgaya (Barcelona: Barcino, 1992)

Valdés, Francisco de, *The Sergeant Major: A Dialogue of the Office of a Sergeant Major*, trans. John Thorius (London: John Wolfe, 1590)

Valera, Diego de, *Tratado de las armas*, in *Prosistas castellanos del siglo XV*, ed. Mario Penna, Biblioteca de Autores Españoles, vol. CXVI (Madrid: Rivadeneira, 1959), 117–39

—— *Tratado en defenssa de virtuossas mugeres*, in *Prosistas castellanos del siglo XV*, ed. Mario Penna, Biblioteca de Autores Españoles, vol. CXVI (Madrid: Rivadeneira, 1959), 55–76

Vegetius Renatus, Publius Flavius, *Epitoma Rei Militaris*, ed. M. D. Reeve (Oxford: Clarendon Press, 2004)

—— *Epitome of Military Science*, trans. N. P. Milner (Liverpool: Liverpool University Press, 1996)

Viña Liste, José María, ed., *Textos medievales de caballerías* (Madrid: Cátedra, 1993)

Wright, Roger, ed. and trans., *Spanish Ballads* (Warminster: Aris & Phillips, 1992)

Zapata, Luis, *Carlo Famoso*, facsimile, ed. Manuel Terrón Albarrán (Badajoz: Institución 'Pedro de Valencia' de la Excma. Diputación Provincial, 1981)

—— *El arte poética de Horacio*, facsimile, ed. Agustín G. de Amezúa (Madrid: Real Academia Española, 1954)

—— *Libro de cetrería: Facsímil del manuscrito inédito 4.219 de la Biblioteca Nacional de Madrid*, facsimile, ed. Manuel Terrón Albarrán, 2 vols. (Badajoz: Institución 'Pedro de Valencia' de la Excma. Diputación Provincial, 1979)

—— *Miscelánea*, ed. Antonio Carrasco González (Llerena: Editores extremeños, 1999)

—— *Miscelánea*, ed. Pascual de Gayangos, Memorial Histórico Español: Colección de Documentos, Opúsculos y Antigüedades, vol. XI (Madrid: Real Academia Española, 1859)

—— *Miscelánea*, facsimile, ed. Manuel Terrón Albarrán (Badajoz: Institución Pedro de Valencia, CSIC, 1983)

—— *Varia historia (Miscelánea)*, ed. Isidoro Montiel, 2 vols. (Madrid: Ediciones Castilla, 1949)

Secondary sources

Abad, Julián Martín, *Los primeros tiempos de la imprenta en España (c. 1471–1520)* (Madrid: Ediciones del Laberinto, 2003)

Alcover, Antoni Maria, *Diccionari català-valencià-balear*, 2nd edn, 10 vols. (Palma de Mallorca: Editorial Moll, 1969)

Alonso Luengo, Luis, *Don Suero de Quiñones, el del Passo Honroso* (Madrid: Biblioteca Nueva, 1943)

Álvarez Álvarez, César, *El condado de Luna en la Baja Edad Media* (León: Colegio Universitario de León-Institución 'Fray Bernardino de Sahagún' CECEL, 1982)

Andrés Díaz, Rosana de, 'Las fiestas de caballería en la Castilla de los Trastámara', in *En la España Medieval V: Estudios en memoria del profesor D. Claudio Sánchez-Albornoz*, ed. Miguel Ángel Ladero Quesada, 2 vols. (Madrid: Universidad Complutense, 1986), vol. I, 81–107

Angelucci, Angelo, *Armilustre e Torneo con Armi da Battaglia tenuti a Venezia addi XXVIII e XXX Maggio MCCCCLVIII: Documento inedito* (Turin: G. Cassone e Comp., 1866)

Anglo, Sydney, 'Archives of the English Tournament: Score Cheques and Lists', *Journal of the Society of Archivists* 2 (1961), 153–62

—— 'How to Win at Tournaments: The Technique of Chivalric Combat', *Antiquaries Journal* 68.2 (1988), 248–64

—— 'Jousting – the earliest treatises', *Livrustkammaren: Journal of the Royal Armoury* (1991–2), 3–23

—— *Spectacle, Pageantry, and Early Tudor Policy* (Oxford: Clarendon Press, 1997)

—— *The Great Tournament Roll of Westminster*, 2 vols. (Oxford: Clarendon Press, 1968)

—— *The Martial Arts of Renaissance Europe* (New Haven: Yale University Press, 2000)

Avalle-Arce, Juan Bautista, 'Tres poetas del *Cancionero General* (I): Cartagena', in *Temas hispánicos medievales: Literatura e Historia* (Madrid: Gredos, 1974), 280–315

Ayton, Andrew, *Knights and Warhorses: Military Service and the English Aristocracy under Edward III* (Bury St Edmunds: Boydell Press, 1994)

Bachrach, Bernard S., 'Caballus et Caballarius in Medieval Warfare', in *The Study of Chivalry: Resources and Approaches*, ed. Howell Chickering and Thomas B. Seiler (Kalamazoo, MI: Medieval Institute Publications, 1988), 173–211

—— *Early Carolingian Warfare: Prelude to Empire* (Philadelphia: University of Pennsylvania Press, 2001)

Badía Margarit, Antonio, *Gramática Histórica Catalana* (Barcelona: Noguer, 1951)

Barber, Richard, *The Knight and Chivalry* (New York: Harper & Row, 1982)

—— and Juliet Barker, *Tournaments: Jousts, Chivalry and Pageants in the Middle Ages* (New York: Weidenfeld & Nicolson, 1989)

Barker, Juliet, *The Tournament in England, 1100–1400* (Woodbridge: Boydell Press, 1986)

—— and Maurice Keen, 'The Medieval English Kings and the Tournament', in *Das ritterliche Turnier im Mittelalter: Beiträge zu einer vergleichenden Formen- und Verhaltensgeschichte des Rittertums*, ed. Josef Fleckenstein (Göttingen: Vandenhoeck & Ruprecht, 1985), 212–28

Barón de las Cuatro-Torres, Conde del Asalto, *El casco del Rey D. Jaime el Conquistador: Monografía Crítico-Histórica*, facsimile (Valencia: Librerías París-Valencia, 1980; 1st edn Madrid, 1894)

Becher, Charlotte, Ortwin Gamber and Walter Irtenkauf, *Das Stuttgarter Harnisch-Musterbuch, 1548–1563* (Vienna: Anton Schroll & Co., 1980)

Beltrán, Rafael, *Tirant lo Blanc, de Joanot Martorell* (Madrid: Síntesis, 2006)

Benito Ruano, Eloy, 'Lope de Stúñiga: Vida y cancionero', *Revista de Filología Española* 51 (1968), 17–109

BETA: Bibliografía Española de Textos Antiguos http://sunsite.berkeley.edu/ PhiloBiblon/phhmbe.html (2008)

BITAGAP: Bibliografia de Textos Antigos Galegos e Portugueses http://sunsite. berkeley.edu/Philobiblon/phhmbp.html (2008)

BITECA: Bibliografia de Textos Catalans Antics http://sunsite.berkeley.edu/ Philobiblon/phhmbi.html (2008)

Black, Antony, *Monarchy and Community: Political Ideas in the Later Conciliar Controversy, 1430–1450* (Cambridge: Cambridge University Press, 1970)

Blair, Claude, *European Armour circa 1066 to circa 1700* (London: B. T. Batsford, 1958)

—— 'Foreword', in *The Churburg Armoury*, ed. Carlo Paggiarino, Claude Blair and Ian Eaves (Milan: Hans Prunner Editore, 2006), 17–19

Blaylock, Curtis, 'The Study of Spanish in Tudor and Stuart England', in *Selected Proceedings: The Seventh Louisiana Conference on Hispanic Languages and Literatures: 'La Chispa' '86*, ed. Alfredo Lozada (Baton Rouge: Louisiana State University, 1987), pp. 61–72

Boardman, Andrew W., *The Medieval Soldier in The Wars of the Roses* (Stroud: Sutton, 1998)

Boccia, Lionello G., 'Le armature di Paolo Uccello', *L'Arte* 73.11–12 (1970), 55–91

—— *Le Armature di S. Maria delle Grazie di Curtatone di Mantova e l'Armatura Lombarda del '400* (Milan: Bramante Editrice, 1982)

—— and E. T. Coelho, *L'Arte dell'Armatura in Italia* (Milan: Bramante Editrice, 1967)

—— Francesco Rossi and Marco Morin, *Armi e Armature Lombarde* (Milan: Electa Editrice, 1980)

Bofarull y de Sartorio, Manuel de, ed., 'Inventario de los bienes del Príncipe de Viana', in *Colección de Documentos Inéditos del Archivo General de la Corona de Aragón*, 42 vols. (Barcelona: n.p., 1847–1910), vol. XXVI, 123–78

Borsi, Franco, and Stefano, *Paolo Uccello*, trans. Elfreda Powell (New York: Harry N. Abrams, 1994)

Bouza, Fernando, *Communication, Knowledge, and Memory in Early Modern Spain*, trans. Sonia López and Michael Agnew (Philadelphia: University of Pennsylvania Press, 2004)

Buttin, François, 'La lance et l'arrêt de cuirasse', *Archaeologia* 99 (1965), 77–178

—— 'Les adargues de Fès', *Hesperis-Tamuda* 1 (1960), 409–55

Calvert, Albert F., *Spanish Arms and Armour, being a Historical and Descriptive Account of the Royal Armoury in Madrid* (London and New York: J. Lane Company, 1907)

Camín, Alfonso, *Don Suero de Quiñones: O el Caballero Leonés (De cómo encontró Cervantes la figura de Don Quijote)* (Mexico: La Impresora Azteca, 1967)

Capwell, Tobias, 'A Depiction of an Italian Arming Doublet, c. 1435–45', *Waffen- und Kostümkunde* 44.2 (2002), 177–96

—— 'Introduction', in *A Celebration of Arms and Armour at Hertford House*, ed. Carlo Paggiarino, Jeremy Warren and Tobias Capwell (Milan: Hans Prunner Editore, 2008), 21–9

—— *The Royal Armouries: Armour and Equipment for the Joust* (forthcoming)

—— *The Real Fighting Stuff: Arms and Armour at Glasgow Museums* (Glasgow: Glasgow City Council, 2007)

Carrasco, A., 'Documentos de 1584 a 1595, relativos a Don Luis Zapata de Chaves, existentes en el Archivo municipal de Llerena', *Revista de Estudios Extremeños* 25 (1969), 333–71

Carlson, David, 'Religious Writers and Church Councils on Chivalry', in *The Study of Chivalry: Resources and Approaches*, ed. Howell Chickering and Thomas H. Seiler (Kalamazoo, MI: Medieval Institute Publications, 1988), 141–71

Carmena y Millán, Luis, *Bibliografía de la tauromaquia*, facsimile (Madrid: Julio Ollero, 1992; 1st edn 1883)

Casey, James, *Early Modern Spain: A Social History* (London: Routledge, 1999)

Catalogue de Livres, dessins et estampes de la Bibliothèque de feu M. J.-B. Huzard, troisième partie: médecine humaine et vétérinaire, équitation, sociétés littéraires, bibliographie, biographie (Paris: Imprimerie et Librairie de Mme Ve Bouchard-Huzard, 1842)

Cátedra, Pedro M., *El sueño caballeresco: De la caballería de papel al sueño real de don Quijote* (Madrid: Abada Editores, 2007)

—— 'Fiestas caballerescas en tiempos de Carlos V', in *La fiesta en la Europa de Carlos V*, ed. Pilar del Castillo and Juan Carlos Elorza Guinea (Madrid: Sociedad Estatal para la Conmemoración de los Centenarios de Felipe II y Carlos V, 2000), 93–117

—— 'Fiestas caballerescas: ideología y literatura en tiempos de Carlos V', in *Carlos V: Europeísmo y universalidad: La figura de Carlos V*, ed. Juan Luis Castellano Castellano and Francisco Sánchez-Montes González, 5 vols (Madrid: Sociedad Estatal para la Conmemoración de los Centenarios de Felipe II y Carlos V, 2001), vol. I, 81–104

Chefs-d'œuvre de la tapisserie: Grand Palais 26 octobre 1973–7 janvier 1974, ed. Francis Salet, Geneviève Souchal, Raynold Arnould (Paris: Éditions des Musées Nationaux, 1973)

Chodynski, Antoni Romuald, 'Horse Muzzles', *Waffen- und Kostümkunde* 1 (1987), 4–20

Cirlot, Victoria, 'El armamento catalán de los siglos XI al XIV' (doctoral dissertation, Universidad Autónoma de Barcelona, 1980)

—— 'El juego de la muerte: La elección de las armas en las fiestas caballerescas de la España del siglo XV', in *La civiltà del torneo (sec. XII–XVII): Giostre e tornei tra medioevo ed età moderna: Atti del VII convegno di studio, Narni, 14–15–16 ottobre, 1988* (Narni: Centro Studi Storici, 1990), 55–78

—— 'Techniques guerrières en Catalogne féodale: le maniement de la lance', *Cahiers de Civilisation Médiévale* 28 (1985), 35–42

Clare, Lucien, 'Fêtes, jeux et divertissements à la cour du Connétable de Castile Miguel Lucas de Iranzo (1460–1470). Les exercises physiques', in *La Fête et l'écriture: Théâtre de cour, cour-théâtre en Espagne et en Italie, 1450–1530: Colloque International France-Espagne-Italie: Aix-en-Provence, 6.7.8. Décembre 1985*, ed. Jeanne Battesti Pelegrin and Georges Ulysse (Aix-en-Provence: Université de Provence, 1987), 5–32

—— *La Quintaine, la course de bague et le jeu des têtes: Étude historique et ethno-linguistique d'une famille de jeux équestres* (Paris: Éditions du Centre National de la Recherche Scientifique, 1983)

—— 'Les deux façons de monter à cheval en Espagne et au Portugal pendant le siècle d'or', in *Des chevaux et des hommes: Equitation et société: Actes du premier colloque 'Sciences sociales de l'equitation' (Avignon 21–22 janvier 1988)*, ed. Jean-Pierre Digard (Lausanne/Paris: Favre, Caracole, 1988), 73–82

—— 'Un jeu équestre de l'Espagne classique: le jeu des "cannes"', in *Le Cheval et la Guerre du XVe au XXe siècle*, ed. Daniel Roche and Daniel Reytier (Paris: Association pour l'académie d'art équestre de Versailles, 2002), 317–31

Clephan, R. Coltman, *The Medieval Tournament* (New York: Dover Publications, 1995; 1st edn 1919)

Contamine, Philippe, 'Les tournois en France à la fin du moyen âge', in *Das ritterliche Turnier im Mittelalter: Beiträge zu einer vergleichenden Formen- und Verhaltensgeschichte des Rittertums*, ed. Josef Fleckenstein (Göttingen: Vandenhoeck & Ruprecht, 1985), 425–49

Contreras Martín, Antonio M., 'Comida y cortesía: los rituales alimenticios en la sociedad caballeresca de los siglos XIV y XV', in *Actes: 1r Col·loqui d'Història de l'alimentació a la Corona d'Aragó: Edat Mitjana*, 2 vols. (Lleida: Institut d'Estudis Ilerdencs, 1995), vol. II, 711–27

Cook, Weston F., Jr., 'The Cannon Conquest of Nasrid Spain and the End of the Reconquista', *Journal of Military History* 57 (1993), 43–70

Corominas, Joan, *Diccionari etimològic i complementari de la llengua catalana*, 10 vols. (Barcelona: Curial, 1980–2001)

—— and J. A. Pascual, *Diccionario crítico etimológico castellano e hispánico*, 6 vols. (Madrid: Gredos, 1980)

Cortés Echanove, Javier, 'Armas y armeros en la época de Felipe II', in *El Escorial 1563–1963: IV Centenario de la Fundación del Monasterio de San Lorenzo el Real*, 2 vols. (Madrid: Ediciones Patrimonio Nacional, 1963), vol. I, 257–92

—— *Museo Provincial de Alava: Armería (Vitoria)* (Vitoria: Diputación Foral de Alava, 1967)

Cripps-Day, Francis Henry, *Fragmenta Armamentaria*, vol. II: *Miscellanea*, part V: *An Inventory of the Armour of Charles V* (Cambridge: Ken Trotman, 2004; 1st edn 1951)

—— *The History of the Tournament in England and in France* (New York: AMS Press, 1982; 1st edn 1918)

Crouch, David, *Tournament* (London: Hambledon Press, 2005)

Curtius, Ernst Robert, *European Literature and the Latin Middle Ages*, trans. Willard R. Trask (London: Routledge & Kegan Paul, 1953)

Daichman, Graciela S., *Wayward Nuns in Medieval Literature* (Syracuse, NY: Syracuse University Press, 1986)

Davis, R. H. C., *The Medieval Warhorse* (London: Thames & Hudson, 1989)

De Cosson, Baron, and W. Burges, *Ancient Helmets and Examples of Mail: A Catalogue of the Objects Exhibited in the Rooms of The Royal Archaeological Institute of Great Britain and Ireland, June 3rd–16th, 1880* (London: Office of The Institute, 1881)

DeVries, Kelly, *Infantry Warfare in the Early Fourteenth Century: Discipline, Tactics and Technology* (Bury St Edmunds: Boydell Press, 1996)

—— *Medieval Military Technology* (Peterborough, Ont.: Broadview Press, 1992)

Del Río Nogueras, Alberto, 'Libros de caballerías y poesía de cancionero: Invenciones y letras de justadores', in *Actas del III Congreso de la Asociación Hispánica de Literatura Medieval (Salamanca, 3 al 6 de octubre de 1989)*, ed. María Isabel Toro Pascua, 2 vols. (Salamanca: Universidad, Departamento de Literatura Española e Hispanoamericana, 1994), vol I, 303–18

Dennistoun, James, *Memoirs of the Dukes of Urbino, Illustrating the Arms, Arts and Literature of Italy, from 1440–1630*, 2 vols. (London: Longman, 1851)

Díaz Arquer, Graciano, *Libros y folletos de toros: Bibliografía taurina* (Madrid: Pedro Vindel, 1931)

Dillon, Viscount, 'Tilting in Tudor Times', *Archaeological Journal* 55 (1898), 296–321, 329–39

Domínguez Ortiz, Antonio, Concha Herrero Carretero and José A. Godoy, *Resplendence of the Spanish Monarchy: Renaissance Tapestries and Armor from the Patrimonio Nacional* (New York: Metropolitan Museum of Art, 1991)

Duby, Georges, *Guillaume le Maréshal, ou le meilleur chevalier du monde* (Paris: Fayard, 1984)

Dufty, Arthur Richard, and William Reid, *European Armour in the Tower of London* (London: Her Majesty's Stationery Office, 1968)

Edge, David, and John Miles Paddock, *Arms and Armor of the Medieval Knight: An Illustrated History of Weaponry in the Middle Ages* (New York: Crescent Books, 1993)

Edgington, Susan, 'Medical Knowledge in the Crusading Armies: the Evidence of Albert of Aachen and Others', in *The Military Orders: Fighting for the Faith and Caring for the Sick*, ed. Malcolm Barber (Cambridge: Variorum, 1994), 320–6

Eisler, Colin, *The Genius of Jacopo Bellini: The Complete Paintings and Drawings* (New York: Harry N. Abrams, 1989)

Evans, P. G., 'A Spanish Knight in Flesh and Blood: A Study of the Chivalric Spirit of Suero de Quinones', *Hispania* 15 (1932), 141–52

Falk, Oren, 'Bystanders and Hearsayers First: Reassessing the Role of the Audience in Duelling', in *'A Great Effusion of Blood'? Interpreting Medieval Violence*, ed. Mark D. Meyerson, Daniel Thiery and Oren Falk (Toronto: University of toronto Press, 2004), 98–130

Fallows, Noel, 'Aproximaciones a la medicina militar en la Edad Media', in *Literatura y conocimiento medieval: Actas de las VIII Jornadas Medievales*, ed. Lillian von der Walde, Concepción Company and Aurelio González (Mexico: Universidad Nacional Autónoma de México, Universidad Autónoma Metropolitana, El Colegio de México, 2003), 475–93

—— 'Just Say No? Alfonso de Cartagena, the *Doctrinal de los caballeros*, and Spain's Most Noble Pastime', in *Studies on Medieval Spanish Literature in Honor of Charles F. Fraker*, ed. Mercedes Vaquero and Alan Deyermond (Madison, WI: HSMS, 1995), 129–41

—— 'Un debate caballeresco del Renacimiento español: "caballeros estradiotes" y "caballeros jinetes"', *Ínsula* 584–585 (Aug–Sep 1995), 15–17

Faulk, Odie B., *The Leather Jacket Soldier: Spanish Military Equipment and Institutions of the late 18th Century* (Pasadena, CA: Socio-Technical Publications, 1971)

Fernández Gallardo, Luis, *Alonso de Cartagena: Una biografía política en la Castilla del siglo XV* (Madrid: Junta de Castilla y León, 2002)

ffoulkes, Charles J., *Armour and Weapons* (Oxford: Clarendon Press, 1909)

—— *Inventory and Survey of The Armouries of the Tower of London*, 2 vols. (London: His Majesty's Stationery Office, 1916)

—— 'Jousting Cheques of the Sixteenth Century', *Archaeologia* 63 (1912), 31–50

—— *The Armourer and his Craft: From the XIth to the XVIth Century* (New York: Dover Publications, 1988; 1st edn 1912)

Flores Arroyuelo, Francisco J., 'El torneo caballeresco: De la preparación militar a la fiesta y representación teatral', in *Medioevo y Literatura: Actas del V Congreso de la AHLM (Granada, 27 septiembre–1 octubre 1993)*, ed. Juan Paredes Núñez, 4 vols. (Granada: Universidad de Granada, 1995), vol. II, 257–78

Florit y Arizcún, José María, and Francisco Javier Sánchez Cantón, *Catálogo de las armas del Instituto de Valencia de Don Juan* (Madrid: Reus, 1927)

Franzoi, Umberto, *L'Armeria del Palazzo Ducale a Venezia* (Dosson di Casier, Treviso: Edizioni Canova, 1990)

Frattale, Loretta, 'Trattati di cavalleria e norme sul torneo nella Catalogna medievale', in *La civiltà del torneo (sec. XII–XVII): Giostre e tornei tra medioevo ed età moderna: Atti del VII convegno di studio, Narni, 14–15–16 ottobre, 1988* (Narni: Centro Studi Storici, 1990), 221–9

Fraxno, Claudio del, and Joaquín de Bouligny, *Memoria sobre la teoría y fabricación del acero en general y de su aplicación a las armas blancas* (Segovia: Imprenta de D. Eduardo Baeza, 1850)

Frieder, Braden, *Chivalry and The Perfect Prince: Tournaments, Art, and Armor at the Spanish Habsburg Court* (Kirksville, MO: Truman State University Press, 2008)

Fuchs, Barbara, *Exotic Nation: Maurophilia and the Construction of Early Modern Spain* (Philadelphia: University of Pennsylvania Press, 2009)

Fustér, Justo Pastor, *Biblioteca Valenciana de los Escritores que florecieron hasta nuestros días*, facsimile, 2 vols. (Valencia: Librerías París-Valencia, 1980; 1st edn Valencia, 1827–30)

Gago-Jover, Francisco, 'Las voces militares en los diccionarios de español: el caso de yelmo', *Revista de Lexicografía* 4 (1997–8), 81–90

—— *Vocabulario Militar Castellano (siglos XIII–XV)* (Granada: Universidad de Granada, 2002)

Gaier, Claude, 'Technique des combats singuliers d'après les auteurs "bourguignons" du XVe siècle', *Moyen Âge* 91 (1985), 415–57, and 92 (1986), 5–40

Gallardo y Blanco, Bartolomé José, *Ensayo de una biblioteca española de libros raros y curiosos*, 3 vols. (Madrid: Rivadeneyra, 1863–89)

Gamber, Ortwin, 'Der Italienische Harnisch im 16. Jahrhundert', *Jahrbuch der Kunsthistorischen Sammlungen in Wien* 54 (1958), 73–120

—— 'Der Turnierharnisch zur Zeit Koenig Maximilians I. und das Thunsche Skizzenbuch', *Jahrbuch der Kunsthistorischen Sammlungen in Wien* 53 (1957), 33–70

—— 'Die Harnischgarnitur', *Livrustkammaren: Journal of the Royal Armoury* 7 (1955–7), 45–114

—— 'Kolman Helmschmid, Ferdinand I, und das Thun'sche Skizzenbuch', *Jahrbuch der Kunsthistorischen Sammlungen in Wien* 71 (1975), 9–38

—— and Christian Beaufort, *Kunsthistorisches Museum, Wien: Hofjagd- und Rüstkammer (edem. Waffensammlung): Katalog der Leibrüstkammer, II. Der Zeitraum von 1530–1560* (Busto Arsizio: Kunsthistorisches Museum and Bramante Editrice, 1990)

García Fitz, Francisco, *Castilla y León frente al Islam: Estrategias de expansión y tácticas militares (siglos XI–XIII)* (Seville: Universidad de Sevilla, 1998)

García-Valdecasas, Amelia, and Rafael Beltrán Llavador, 'La maurofilia como ideal caballeresco en la literatura cronística del XIV y XV', *Epos* 5 (1989), 115–40

Gil-Sotres, Pedro, 'Derivation and revulsion: the theory and practice of medieval phlebotomy', in *Practical Medicine from Salerno to the Black Death*, ed. Luis García-Ballester, Roger French, Jon Arrizabalaga and Andrew Cunningham (Cambridge: Cambridge University Press, 1994), 110–55

Gillmor, Carroll, 'Practical Chivalry: The Training of Horses for Tournaments and Warfare', *Studies in Medieval and Renaissance History*, new series 13 (1992), 5–29

Giner, Encarna Villafranca, *Constantí Llombart i el seu tempo* (Valencia: Publicacions de l'Acadèmia Valenciana de la Llengua, 2005)

Gladitz, Charles, *Horse Breeding in the Medieval World* (Dublin: Four Courts Press, 1997)

Glossarium Armorum, 7 vols., ed. Ortwin Gamber (Graz: Akademische Druck- u. Verlagsanstalt, 1972)

Goff, Frederick R., *Incunabula in American Libraries: A Third Census of Fifteenth-Century Books Recorded in North American Collections* (New York: Bibliographical Society of America, 1964)

Gómez Moreno, Ángel, 'La caballería como tema en la literatura medieval española: tratados teóricos', in *Homenaje a Pedro Sainz Rodríguez* (Madrid: Fundación Universitaria Española, 1986), vol. II, 311–23

Gonzalo Sánchez-Molero, José Luis, *El aprendizaje cortesano de Felipe II (1527–1546): La formación de un príncipe del Renacimiento* (Madrid: Sociedad Estatal para la Conmemoración de los Centenarios de Felipe II y Carlos V, 1999)

Goodman, Jennifer R., *Chivalry and Exploration, 1298–1630* (Woodbridge: Boydell Press, 1998)

Gordon, Benjamin Lee, *Medieval and Renaissance Medicine* (London: Peter Owen, 1960)

Grancsay, Stephen V., *Catalogue of Armour: The John Woodman Higgins Armory* (Worcester, MA: Davis Press, 1961)

Gravett, Christopher, 'Tournament Courses', in *Riddarlek och Tornerspel: Tournaments and the Dream of Chivalry*, ed. Lena Rangström (Stockholm: Livrustkammaren, 1992), 334–45

Haebler, Konrad, *Bibliografía ibérica del siglo XV*, 2 vols. (New York: B. Franklin, 1963; 1st edn The Hague, 1903–17)

Hale, J. R., 'Gunpowder and the Renaissance: an Essay in the History of Ideas', in *Renaissance War Studies* (London: Hambledon Press, 1983), 389–420

Hall, Bert S., *Weapons and Warfare in Renaissance Europe* (Baltimore: Johns Hopkins University Press, 1997)

Heers, Jacques, *Fêtes, jeux et joutes dans les sociétés d'Occident à la fin du Moyen Âge* (Montreal: Institut d'études médiévales, 1982)

Hénault, Maurice, 'La Tapisserie du "Tournoi" au Musée de Valenciennes', *Revue de l'Art Ancien et Moderne* 28 (1910), 145–56

Hoffmeyer, Ada Bruhn de, *Arms and Armour in Spain: A Short Survey*, 2 vols. (Madrid: Instituto de Estudios Sobre Armas Antiguas-CSIC, 1972 and 1982) [special issues of the journal *Gladius*]

Huizinga, Johan, *Homo Ludens: A Study of the Play-Element in Culture* (Boston: Beacon Press, 1960)

—— *The Autumn of the Middle Ages*, trans. Rodney J. Payton and Ulrich Mammitzsch (Chicago: University of Chicago Press, 2004)

Huth, F. H., *Works on Horses and Equitation: A Bibliographical Record of Hippology* (London: Bernard Quaritch, 1887)

Índice de la colección de Don Luis de Salazar y Castro, 49 vols. (Madrid: Real Academia de la Historia, 1949–79)

Infantes, Víctor, *Una colección de burlas bibliográficas: Las reproducciones fotolitográficas de Sancho Rayón* (Valencia: Albatros, 1982)

Inventario general de manuscritos de la Biblioteca Nacional de Madrid, 17 vols. (Madrid: Ministerio de Educación Nacional, 1953-)

Jackson, William Henry, 'The Tournament and Chivalry in German Tournament Books of the Sixteenth Century and in the Literary Works of Emperor Maximilian I', in *The Ideals and Practice of Medieval Knighthood: Papers from the first and second Strawberry Hill conferences*, ed. Christopher Harper-Bill and Ruth Harvey (Woodbridge: Boydell Press, 1986), 49–73

Jiménez Benítez, Manuel, *El caballo en Andalucía: Orígenes e Historia, Cría y Doma* (Madrid: Ediciones Agrotécnicas, 1994)

Jones, Peter N., 'The Metallography and Relative Effectiveness of Arrowheads and Armor during the Middle Ages', *Materials Characterization* 29 (1992), 111–17

Joubert, Felix, *Catalogue of the Collection of European Arms and Armour Formed at Greenock by R. L. Scott*, ed. Robert C. Woosnam-Savage and Tobias Capwell (Huntingdon: Ken Trotman Publishing, 2006)

Jourdan, Jean-Pierre, 'Le thème du Pas et de l'Emprise: Espaces symboliques et rituels d'alliance au Moyen Âge', *Ethnologie française* 22 (1992), 172–84

Kaeuper, Richard W., *Chivalry and Violence in Medieval Europe* (Oxford: Oxford University Press, 1999)

—— 'Literature as Essential Evidence for Understanding Chivalry', *Journal of Medieval Military History* 5 (2007), 1–15

Kamen, Henry, *Philip of Spain* (New Haven: Yale University Press, 1997)

Karcheski, Walter J., Jr., 'The Nuremburg *Stechzeuge* Armours', *Journal of The Arms and Armour Society* 14.4 (1993), 181–217

—— and Thom Richardson, *The Medieval Armour from Rhodes* (Leeds and Worcester, MA: Trustees of the Armouries and the Higgins Armory Museum, 2002)

Karlsson, Mattias, 'Iron and Steel Technology in Hispano-Arabic and Early Castilian Written Sources', *Gladius* 20 (2000), 239–50

Kasten, Lloyd A., and John J. Nitti, *Diccionario de la prosa castellana del Rey Alfonso X*, 3 vols. (New York: HSMS, 2002)

Keen, Maurice, *Chivalry* (New Haven: Yale University Press, 1984)

Keller, Evelyn Fox, *A Feeling for the Organism: The Life and Work of Barbara McClintock* (New York: W. H. Freeman & Company, 1983)

Klapsia, Heinrich, and Bruno Thomas, 'Harnischstudien', *Jahrbuch der Kunsthistorischen Sammlungen in Wien*, neue folge 11 (1937), 139–64

Krása, Josef, *The Travels of Sir John Mandeville: A Manuscript in the British Library*, trans. Peter Kussi (New York: George Braziller, 1983)

Krenn, Peter, 'Test-firing Selected 16th–18th Century Weapons', *Military Illustrated* 33 (1991), 34–8

Ladero Quesada, Miguel Ángel, *Castilla y la conquista del Reino de Granada* (Granada: Diputación Provincial, 1988)

—— *Las fiestas en la cultura medieval* (Barcelona: Areté, 2004)

Lanzardo, Dario, 'Il Convitato di ferro', in *Il Convitato di ferro: Torino, Palazzo Reale, 6 novembre–20 dicembre 1987*, ed. Dario Lanzardo (Turin: Il Quadrante Edizioni, 1987), 25–168

Lawrance, Jeremy, 'Las lecturas científicas de los castellanos en la Baja Edad Media', *Atalaya* 2 (1991), 135–55

—— 'The spread of lay literacy in late medieval Castile', *Bulletin of Hispanic Studies* 62 (1985), 79–94

Leguina, Enrique de, *Glosario de voces de Armería* (Madrid: Luis Faure, 1912)

Lerer, Seth, '"Represented now in yewer syght': The Culture of Spectatorship in Late Fifteenth-Century England', in *Bodies and Disciplines: Intersections of Literature and History in Fifteenth-Century England*, ed. Barbara A. Hanawalt and David Wallace (Minneapolis: University of Minnesota Press, 1996), 29–62

López de Haro, Alonso, *Nobiliario Genealógico de los Reyes y Títulos de España*, facsimile, 2 vols. (Ollobarren: Wilsen, 1996; 1st edn Madrid, 1622)

López Martín, Javier, 'La evolución de la Artillería en la segunda mitad del siglo XV: El reinado de los Reyes Católicos y el contexto europeo', in *Artillería y Fortificaciones en la Corona de Castilla durante el reinado de Isabel la Católica, 1474–1504*, ed. Aurelio Valdés Sánchez (Madrid, 2004), 180–223

Lucía Megías, José Manuel, *Imprenta y Libros de caballerías* (Madrid: Ollero & Ramos, 2000)

Macpherson, Ian, and Angus MacKay, 'Textiles and Tournaments', in *Love, Religion and Politics in Fifteenth-Century Spain* (Leiden: Brill, 1998), 196–204

—— 'The Game of Courtly Love', in *Love, Religion and Politics in Fifteenth-Century Spain* (Leiden: Brill, 1998), 236–53

MacKay, Angus, 'Signs Deciphered – The Language of Court Displays in Late Medieval Spain', in *Kings and Kingship in Medieval Europe*, ed. Anne J. Duggan (London: King's College London-Centre for Late Antique and Medieval Studies, 1993), 287–304

Maíllo Salgado, Felipe, 'Jinete, jineta y sus derivados: Contribución al estudio del medievo español y al de su léxico', *Studia Philologica Salmanticensia* 6 (1982), 105–17

Making History: Antiquaries in Britain, 1707–2007: A joint exhibition organised by the Royal Academy of Arts and the Society of Antiquaries of London (London: Royal Academy of Arts, 2007)

Maldonado Fernández, Manuel, 'Don Luis Zapata de Chaves, III Señor del Estado de Çehel de las Alpujarras y de las Villas de Jubrecelada (Llerena), Ulela y Ulula', *Revista de Estudios Extremeños* 58 (2002), 991–1030

Mann, Sir James, 'Notes on the Armour worn in Spain from the tenth to the fifteenth century', *Archaeologia* 83 (1933), 285–305

—— 'Notes on the Evolution of Plate Armour in Germany in the Fourteenth and Fifteenth Century', *Archaeologia* 84 (1935), 69–97

—— 'Six Armours of the Fifteenth Century', *Burlington Magazine* 72 (1938), 121–32

——*European Arms and Armour: Text with Historical Notes and Illustrations*, Wallace Collection Catalogues, 2 vols. (London: William Clowes & Sons, 1962)

Marín, María Carmen, 'Fiestas caballerescas aragonesas en la Edad Moderna', in *Fiestas públicas en Aragón en la Edad Moderna: VIII muestra de documentación histórica aragonesa* (Saragossa: Diputación General de Aragón, 1995), 109–18

Marqués de Alcedo y de San Carlos, *Un olvidado pleito del siglo XV: La herencia de Suero de Quiñones* (Madrid: Blass, 1926)

Marqués de la Torrecilla, *Libros, escritos o tratados de equitación, jineta, brida, albeitería, etc.: Índice de Bibliografía Hípica española y portuguesa* (Madrid: Rivadeneyra, 1916–21)

Márquez Villanueva, Francisco, *Fuentes literarias cervantinas* (Madrid: Gredos, 1973)

Martin, Graham, 'The Death of Henry II of France: A Sporting Death and Post-Mortem', *ANZ Journal of Surgery* 71.5 (2001), 318–20

Martín, José Luis, and Luis Serrano-Piedecasas, 'Tratados de Caballería: Desafíos, justas y torneos', in *Espacio, Tiempo y Forma, Serie 3: Historia Medieval: Revista de la Facultad de Geografía e Historia* (Madrid: UNED, 1991), 161–242

Martínez Laínez, Fernando, and José María Sánchez de Toca, *Tercios de España: La infantería legendaria* (Madrid: EDAF, 2006)

Menéndez Pidal, Don Juan, 'Discurso de Don Juan Menéndez Pidal', in *Discursos leídos ante la Real Academia Española* (Madrid: Tip. de la Revista de Archivos, Bibliotecas y Museos, 1915), 1–78

Menessier de la Lance, Général, *Essai de bibliographie hippique*, 2 vols. (Paris: Lucien Dorbon, 1915–17)

Mercier, Louis, 'Les Écoles espagnoles dites de la Brida et de la Gineta (ou Jineta)', *Revue de Cavalerie* 37 (1927), 301–15

Meyerson, Mark D., Daniel Thiery and Oren Falk, 'Introduction', in *'A Great Effusion of Blood'? Interpreting Medieval Violence*, ed. Mark D. Meyerson, Daniel Thiery and Oren Falk (Toronto: University of Toronto Press, 2004), 3–16

Mingote y Tarazona, Policarpo, *Varones ilustres de la Provincia de León* (León: Editorial Nebrija, 1978; 1st edn 1880)

Mitchell, Piers D., *Medicine in the Crusades: Warfare, Wounds and the Medieval Surgeon* (Cambridge: Cambridge University Press, 2004)

Moll, Francisco de B., *Gramática histórica catalana* (Madrid: Gredos, 1952)

Morera, Luis X., 'An Inherent Rivalry Between *Letrados* and *Caballeros*? Alonso de Cartagena, the Knightly Estate, and an Historical Problem', *Mediterranean Studies* 16 (2007), 67–93

Muhlberger, Steven, *Deeds of Arms: Formal Combats in the Late Fourteenth Century* (Highland Village, TX: Chivalry Bookshelf, 2005)

—— *Jousts and Tournaments: Charny and the Rules for Chivalric Sport in Fourteenth-Century France* (Union City, CA: Chivalry Bookshelf, 2002)

Mulertt, Werner, 'La fecha del manuscrito Escurialense del *Paso Honroso*', in *Homenaje a Don Miguel Artigas en conmemoración de su nombramiento de Director de la Biblioteca Nacional*, 2 vols. (Santander: Sociedad Menéndez Pelayo, 1932), vol. II, 242–5

Neste, Évelyne van den, *Tournois, joutes, pas d'armes dans les villes de Flandre à la fin du Moyen Âge (1300–1486)* (Paris: École des Chartes, 1996)

Nickel, Helmut, 'The Tournament: An Historical Sketch', in *The Study of Chivalry: Resources and Approaches*, ed. Howell Chickering and Thomas H. Seiler (Kalamazoo, MI: Medieval Institute Publications, 1988), 213–62

—— Stuart W. Pyhrr and Leonid Tarassuk, *The Art of Chivalry: European Arms and Armor from The Metropolitan Museum of Art* (New York: Metropolitan Museum of Art, 1982)

Nicolle, David C., *Arms and Armour of the Crusading Era, 1050–1350*, 2 vols. (White Plains, NY: Kraus International Publications, 1988)

Norman, A. V. B., 'The Effigy of Alexander Stewart Earl of Buchan and Lord of Badenoch (1343?-1405?)', *Proceedings of the Society of Antiquaries of Scotland* 92 (1958–9), 104–13

—— *The Rapier and Small-Sword, 1460–1820* (London: Arms and Armour Press, 1980)

—— 'The Tournament', in *Riddarlek och Tornerspel: Tournaments and the Dream of Chivalry*, ed. Lena Rangström (Stockholm: Livrustkammaren, 1992), 304–10

——*European Arms and Armour: Supplement*, Wallace Collection Catalogues (London: Balding & Mansell, 1986)

North, Anthony, *An Introduction to European Swords* (Owings Mills, MD: Stemmer House, 1982)

Oakeshott, Ewart, *European Weapons and Armour: From the Renaissance to the Industrial Revolution* (Woodbridge: Boydell Press, 2000)

Oatts, Lt. Col. L. B., *Proud Heritage: The Story of the Highland Light Infantry.* vol. 1: *The 71st Highland Light Infantry, 1777–1881* (London: Nelson, 1952)

O'Kane, Eleanor S., *Refranes y frases proverbiales españolas de la Edad Media*, Anejos del Boletín de la Real Academia Española, vol. II (Madrid: Real Academia Española, 1959)

Oman, Sir Charles, *A History of the Art of War in the Sixteenth Century* (London: Greenhill Books, 1991; 1st edn 1937)

The Oxford English Dictionary, 2nd edn, ed. J. A. Simpson and E. S. C. Weiner, 20 vols. (Oxford: Clarendon Press, 1991)

Pagden, A. R. D., 'The Diffusion of Aristotle's Moral Philosophy in Spain, ca. 1400– ca. 1600', *Traditio* 31 (1975), 287–313

Page, Geoffrey, *Tale of a Guinea Pig* (Canterbury: Wingham Press, 1981)

Palau Claveras, Agustín, *Bibliografía hispánica de veterinaria y equitación anterior a 1901* (Madrid: Imprenta Industrial, 1973)

Palau y Dulcet, Antonio, *Manual del librero hispano-americano*, 2nd edn, 28 vols. (Barcelona: A. Palau, 1948–77)

Parker, Geoffrey, *Philip II*, 4th edn (Chicago and La Salle, IL: Open Court, 2002)

—— *The Grand Strategy of Philip II* (New Haven: Yale University Press, 2000)

—— *The Military Revolution: Military Innovation and the Rise of the West, 1500– 1800* (Cambridge: Cambridge University Press, 1988)

Paterson, Linda M., 'Military Surgery: Knights, Sergeants and Raimon of Avignon's Version of the *Chirurgia* of Roger of Salerno (1180–1209)', in *The Ideals and Practice of Medieval Knighthood, 2: Papers from the Third Strawberry Hill Conference*, ed. Christopher Harper-Bill and Ruth Harvey (Bury St Edmunds: Boydell Press, 1986), 117–46

Peine, Hans-Werner, and Dirk H. Breiding, 'An Important Find of Late 14th and Early 15th Century Arms and Armour from Haus Herbede, Westphalia', *Journal of The Arms and Armour Society* 19.1 (2007), 1–28

Penney, Clara Louisa, *List of Books Printed Before 1601 in the Library of The Hispanic Society of America* (New York: Hispanic Society of America, 1929)

—— *Printed Books 1468–1700 in The Hispanic Society of America* (New York: Hispanic Society of America, 1965)

Pérez Pastor, Cristóbal, *La imprenta en Medina del Campo* (Madrid: Rivadeneyra, 1895)

Pfaffenbichler, Matthias, *Medieval Craftsmen: Armourers* (Toronto: University of Toronto Press, 1992)

Poucet, Jacques, *Recherches sur la légende sabine des origines de Rome* (Kinshasa: Éditions de l'Université Lovanium, 1967)

Prelle de la Nieppe, Edgar de, and Jean Van Malderghem, *Catalogue des armes et armures du Musée de la Porte de Hal* (Brussels: Emile Braylant, 1902)

Prestwich, Michael, *Armies and Warfare in the Middle Ages: The English Experience* (New Haven: Yale University Press, 1996)

Prévot, Brigitte, 'Le Cheval malade: l'hippiatrie au XIIIème siècle', in *Le Cheval dans le monde médiéval* (Aix-en-Provence: Centre Universitaire d'Études et de Recherches Médiévales d'Aix, 1992), 449–64

—— and Bernard Ribémont, *Le Cheval en France au Moyen Age: Sa place dans le monde médiéval; sa médecine: l'exemple d'un traité vétérinaire du XIVème siècle, la 'Cirurgie des chevaux'* (Orléans: Paradigme, 1994)

Price, Brian R., *Techniques of Medieval Armour Reproduction: The 14th Century* (Boulder, CO: Paladin Press, 2000)

Pyhrr, Stuart W., José A. Godoy and Silvio Leydi, *Heroic Armor of the Italian Renaissance: Filippo Negroli and his Contemporaries* (New York: Metropolitan Museum of Art, 1998)

—— Donald J. LaRocca and Dirk H. Breiding, *The Armored Horse in Europe, 1480–1620* (New Haven: Yale University Press and The Metropolitan Museum of Art, 2005)

Rayón, José Sancho, and Francisco de Zabalburu, eds., 'Armería del Duque del Infantado en Guadalajara', in *Colección de Documentos Inéditos para la Historia de España*, vol. LXXIX (Madrid: Imprenta de Miguel Ginesta, 1882), 477–541

Reitzenstein, Alexander von, 'Die Landshuter Plattner, ihre Ordnung und ihre Meister', *Waffen- und Kostümkunde* 11 (1969), 20–32

—— 'Die Ordnung der Augsberger Plattner', *Waffen- und Kostümkunde* 2 (1960), 96–100

Reverseau, Jean-Pierre, 'L'Habit de guerre des français en 1446: Le manuscrit anonyme fr. 1997 de la Bibliothèque Nationale', *Gazette des Beaux-Arts*, series VI, 93 (1979), 179–98

Ribelles Comín, José, *Bibliografía de la lengua valenciana*, 3 vols. (Nendeln / Liechtenstein: Kraus Reprint, 1969; 1st edn Madrid, 1915)

Rico, Francisco, '*Un penacho de penas*: Sobre tres invenciones del *Cancionero general*', *Romanistisches Jahrbuch* 17 (1966), 274–84

—— 'Una torre por cimera', in *Primera cuarentena y tratado general de literatura* (Barcelona: Quaderns Crema, 1982), 65–8

Ringrose, David R., *Transportation and Economic Stagnation in Spain, 1750–1850* (Durham, NC: Duke University Press, 1970)

Riquer, Martín de, *Caballeros andantes españoles* (Madrid: Espasa-Calpe, 1967)

—— *Caballeros catalanes y valencianos en el Passo Honroso* (Barcelona: CSIC, 1967)

—— *Caballeros medievales y sus armas* (Madrid: Instituto Universitario General Gutiérrez Mellado-UNED, 1999)

—— *Cavalleria fra Realtà e Letteratura nel Quattrocento* (Bari: Adriatica Editrice, 1970)

—— *Heràldica catalana des l'any 1150 al 1550*, 2 vols. (Barcelona: Quaderns Crema, 1983)

—— *L'Arnès del cavaller: Armes i armadures catalanes medievals* (Barcelona: Ariel, 1968)

—— 'La fecha del *Ronsasvals* y del *Rollan a Saragossa* según el armamento', in *Caballeros medievales y sus armas* (Madrid: Instituto Universitario General Gutiérrez Mellado-UNED, 1999), 163–95

—— 'Las armas en el *Victorial*', in *Caballeros medievales y sus armas* (Madrid: Instituto Universitario General Gutiérrez Mellado-UNED, 1999), 245–68

—— *Tirant lo Blanch, novela de historia y de ficción* (Barcelona: Sirmio, 1992)

Rodríguez Velasco, Jesús D., *Citizenship, Monarchical Sovereignty, and Chivalry* (Philadelphia: University of Pennsylvania Press, in press)

—— *El debate sobre la caballería en el siglo XV: La tratadística caballeresca castellana en su marco europeo* (Valladolid: Junta de Castilla y León, 1996)

—— 'Invención y consecuencias de la caballería', in Josef Fleckenstein, *La caballería y el mundo caballeresco* (Madrid: Siglo XXI, 2006), xi-lxiv

Rodríguez Villa, Antonio, 'El Emperador Carlos V y su corte (1522–1539): Cartas de D. Martín de Salinas', *Boletín de la Real Academia de la Historia* 43 (1903), 5–240, 393–511; 44 (1904), 5–36, 142–78, 197–246, 285–333, 365–414, 465–506; 45 (1904), 16–143, 315–52, 369–405, 465–95; 46 (1905), 5–44, 109–36, 177–225

—— *Inventario del moviliario, alhajas, ropas, armería y otros efectos del Excmo. Sr. D. Beltrán de la Cueva, tercer Duque de Alburquerque: Hecho en el año 1560* (Madrid: D. G. Hernando, 1883)

Roetzel, Bernhard, *Gentleman: A Timeless Fashion* (Cologne: Könemann, 1999)

Rogers, Clifford J., 'The Military Revolution of the Hundred Years War', in *The Military Revolution Debate: Readings on the Military Transformation of Early Modern Europe*, ed. Clifford J. Rogers (Boulder, CO: Westview Press, 1995), 55–93

Rossi, Francesco, and Nolfo di Carpegna, *Armi Antiche del Museo Civico L. Marzoli: Catalogo* (Milan: Bramante Editrice, 1969)

Rubin de la Borbolla, Daniel F., 'Origins of Mexican Horsemanship and Saddlery', in *Man Made Mobile: Early Saddles of Western North America*, ed. Richard E. Ahlborn, Smithsonian Studies in History and Technology, vol. XXXIX (Washington, DC: Smithsonian Institution Press, 1980), 21–38

Rühl, Joachim K., 'Behind the Scenes of Popular Spectacle and Courtly Tradition: The Ascertainment of the Best Jouster', *Stadion* 12–13 (1986–7), 39–48

—— 'German Tournament Regulations of the 15th Century', *Journal of Sport History* 17.2 (1990), 163–82

Ruiz, Teófilo F, *Crisis and Continuity: Land and Town in Late Medieval Castile* (Philadelphia: University of Pennsylvania Press, 1994)

—— 'Fiestas, Torneos y Símbolos de realeza en la Castilla del siglo XV: Las fiestas de Valladolid de 1428', in *Realidad e imágenes del poder: España a fines de la Edad Media*, ed. Adeline Rucquoi (Valladolid: Ámbito Ediciones, 1998), 249–65

Ruiz Alcón, María Teresa, 'Armaduras de caballos en la Real Armería de Madrid', *Reales Sitios* 9 (1972), 65–75

—— 'Real Armería: Sillas de montar de Diego de Arroyo', *Reales Sitios* 10 (1973), 49–54

Ruiz-Domènech, José Enrique, *El Gran Capitán: Retrato de una época* (Barcelona: Círculo de Lectores, 2002)

—— 'El torneo como espectáculo en la España de los siglos XV–XVI', in *La civiltà del torneo (sec. XII–XVII): Giostre e tornei tra medioevo ed età moderna: Atti del VII convegno di studio, Narni, 14–15–16 ottobre, 1988* (Narni: Centro Studi Storici, 1990), 159–93

Ruiz García, Elisa, and Pedro Valverde Ogallar, 'Relación de las fiestas caballerescas de Valladolid de 1527: un documento inédito', *Emblemata: Revista Aragonesa de Emblemática* 9 (2003), 127–94

Salicrú i Lluch, Roser, 'Caballeros cristianos en el Occidente europeo e islámico', in *'Das kommt mir spanisch vor': Eigenes und Fremdes in den deutsch-spanischen Beziehungen des späten Mittelalters*, ed. Klaus Herbers and Nikolas Jaspert (Münster: LIT, 2004), 217–89

Sánchez Jiménez, Antonio, *El Sansón de Extremadura: Diego García de Paredes en la literatura española del siglo XVI* (Newark, DE: Juan de la Cuesta, 2006)

Sanz Egaña, Cesáreo, 'El libro de enfrenamientos de Eugenio Manzanas', *Ciencia Veterinaria* 67 (1949), 520–30

—— *Historia de la veterinaria española: albeitería, mariscalería, veterinaria* (Madrid: Espasa-Calpe, 1941)

Scaglione, Aldo, *Knights at Court: Courtliness, Chivalry and Courtesy From Ottonian Germany to the Italian Renaissance* (Berkeley: University of California Press, 1991)

Scalini, Mario, 'The Weapons of Lorenzo de' Medici: An examination of the inventory of the Medici palace in Florence drawn up upon the death of Lorenzo the Magnificent in 1492', in *Art, Arms and Armour: An International Anthology*. vol. I: *1979–80*, ed. Robert Held (Chiasso, Switzerland: Acquafresca Editrice, 1979), 12–29

—— Rudolf H. Wackernagel and Ian Eaves, *L'Armeria Trapp di Castel Coira; Die Churburgen Rüstkamme; The Armoury of the Castle of Churburg* (Udine: Magnus Edizioni, 1996)

Segundo, Juan, *Nuevo método para embocar bien todos los caballos y tratado sucinto de equitación* (Madrid: Miguel González, 1855)

Segura Covarsí, Enrique, 'La *Miscelánea* de D. Luis Zapata', *Revista de Estudios Extremeños* 10 (1954), 413–66

Siraisi, Nancy G., *Medieval and Early Renaissance Medicine: An Introduction to Knowledge and Practice* (Chicago: University of Chicago Press, 1990)

Soler del Campo, Álvaro, 'Arreos y jaeces para caballería en al-Andalus', in *Al-Andalus y el caballo*, ed. Purificación de la Torre (Barcelona: Lunwerg Editores, 1995), 81–97

—— 'El armamento medieval hispano', in *Aproximación a la Historia Militar de España*, 3 vols. (Madrid: Ministerio de Defensa, 2006), vol. I, 125–41

—— 'La batalla y la armadura de Mühlberg en el retrato ecuestre de Carlos V', in *La restauración de 'El Emperador Carlos V a caballo en Mühlberg' de Tiziano* (Madrid: Museo Nacional del Prado, 2001), 87–102

—— *La evolución del armamento medieval en el reino castellano-leonés y al-Andalus (siglos XII–XIV)* (Madrid: Servicio de Publicaciones del EME, 1993)

—— 'La producción de armas personales: 1500–1700', in *Guerra y Sociedad en la Monarquía Hispánica: Política, Estrategia y Cultura en la Europa Moderna (1500–1700)*, ed. Enrique García Hernán and Davide Maffi, 2 vols. (Madrid: Ediciones del Laberinto, 2006), vol. II, 843–60

Sommer D'Andrade, Fernando Luis, *A Short History of the Spanish Horse and of the Iberian 'Gineta' Horsemanship for which this Horse is Adapted* (Lisbon: Oficinas de S. José, 1973)

Soria, Juan Martín, *El recado cordobés: Su origen, historia y estado actual* (Córdoba, Argentina: n.p., 2002)

Stanesco, Michel, *Jeux d'errance du chevalier médiéval: aspects ludiques de la fonction guerrière dans la littérature du Moyen Âge flamboyant* (Leiden: Brill, 1988)

Steinberg, S. H., *Five Hundred Years of Printing* (Harmondsworth: Penguin, 1974)

Stone, George Cameron, *A Glossary of the Construction, Decoration and Use of Arms and Armour in All Countries and in All Times, Together with Some Closely Related Subjects* (Mineola, NY: Dover Publications, 1999; 1st edn 1934)

Strohm, Paul, *Hochon's Arrow: The Social Imagination of Fourteenth-Century Texts* (Princeton: Princeton University Press, 1992)

Strong, Roy, *Art and Power: Renaissance Festivals, 1450–1650* (Berkeley: University of California Press, 1984)

Thomas, Bruno, and Ortwin Gamber, *Kunsthistorisches Museum, Wien: Waffensammlung: Katalog der Leibrüstkammer, I: Der Zeitraum von 500 bis 1530* (Vienna: Kunsthistorisches Museum and Verlag Anton Schroll & Co., 1976)

Toribio Medina, José, and Winston A. Reynolds, *El Primer Poema que trata del Descubrimiento y Conquista del Nuevo Mundo: Reimpresión de las partes correspondientes del Carlo Famoso de Luis Zapata* (Madrid: José Porrúa Turanzas, 1984)

Toro Buiza, Luis, *Noticias de los juegos de cañas reales tomadas de nuestros Libros de Gineta* (Seville: Imprenta Municipal, 1944)

Trapp, Oswald Graf, and James Gow Mann, *The Armoury of the Castle of Churburg* (London: Methuen, 1929)

Vale, Juliet, 'Violence and the Tournament', in *Violence in Medieval Society*, ed. Richard W. Kaeuper (Woodbridge: Boydell Press, 2000), 143–58

Vale, Malcolm, *War and Chivalry: Warfare and Aristocratic Culture in England, France, and Burgundy at the End of the Middle Ages* (Athens: University of Georgia Press, 1981)

Valencia de Don Juan, Conde viudo de [Juan Bautista Crooke y Navarrot], 'Bilderinventar der Waffen, Rüstungen, Gewänder und Standarten Karl V in der Armería Real zu Madrid', *Jahrbuch des kunsthistorischen Sammlungen in Wien des Allerhöchsten Kaiserhauses* 10 (1889), 353–4 (+ 23 plates)

—— 'Bilderinventar der Waffen, Rüstungen, Gewänder und Standarten Karl V in der Armería Real zu Madrid (Fortsetzung)', *Jahrbuch des kunsthistorischen Sammlungen in Wien des Allerhöchsten Kaiserhauses* 11 (1890), 242–58 (+ 56 plates)

—— *Catálogo histórico-descriptivo de la Real Armería de Madrid*, facsimile (Valencia: Librerías París-Valencia, 1996; 1st edn Madrid, 1898)

Villalon, L. J. Andrew, 'Putting Don Carlos Together Again: Treatment of a Head Injury in Sixteenth-Century Spain', *Sixteenth Century Journal* 26 (1995), 347–65

Vindel, Francisco, *Manual gráfico-descriptivo del bibliófilo hispano-americano (1475–1850)*, 12 vols. (Madrid: Imp. Góngora, 1931)

Viollet-le-Duc, Eugène-Emmanuel, *Dictionnaire raisonné du mobilier français de l'époque carlovingienne à la renaissance*, 6 vols. (Paris: A. Morel, 1872–5)

Wack, Mary F., *Lovesickness in the Middle Ages: The 'Viaticum' and its Commentaries* (Philadelphia: University of Pennsylvania Press, 1990)

Waldman, John, *Hafted Weapons in Medieval and Renaissance Europe: The Evolution of European Staff Weapons between 1200 and 1650* (Leiden: Brill, 2005)

Watanabe O'Kelly, Helen, 'Literature and the Court, 1450–1720', in *Early Modern German Literature, 1350–1700*, ed. Max Reinhart, Camden House History of German Literature, vol. IV (London: Camden House, 2007), 621–51

Watts, Karen, 'Une selle médiévale d'Europe centrale au Royal Armouries Museum', in *Armes et cultures de guerre en Europe centrale, fin XVe–fin XIXe siècle: Actes du colloque de février 2006*, ed. O. Chaline and P. Contamine (Paris: Cahiers du CERMA-Musée de l'Armée, 2008), 49–66

Webb, Henry J., *Elizabethan Military Science: The Books and the Practice* (Madison: University of Wisconsin Press, 1965)

Willetts, Pamela J., *Catalogue of the Manuscripts in the Society of Antiquaries of London* (Woodbridge: D. S. Brewer for the Society of Antiquaries of London, 2000)

Williams, Alan, 'The Grosschedel Family of Armourers of Landshut and their Metallurgy', *Journal of The Arms and Armour Society* 15 (1997), 253–77

—— *The Knight and the Blast Furnace: A History of the Metallurgy of Armour in the Middle Ages and the Early Modern Period* (Leiden: Brill, 2002)

Young, Alan, *Tudor and Jacobean Tournaments* (London: George Philip, 1987)

Zarco Cuevas, Julián, *Catálogo de los manuscritos castellanos de la Real Biblioteca de El Escorial*, 3 vols. (Madrid: Imp. Helénica, 1924–9)

Canallo alamoderna

Index

References in **bold type** indicate illustration numbers

Armour and Weapons

XII.

The Thun-Hohenstein Album: Cultures of Remembrance in a Paper Armory
Chassica Kirchhoff

XIII.

Medieval Arms and Armour: A Sourcebook. Volume II: 1400–1450
Ralph Moffat

Printed in the United States
by Baker & Taylor Publisher Services